Communications in Computer and Information Science 748

Commenced Publication in 2007
Founding and Former Series Editors:
Alfredo Cuzzocrea, Orhun Kara, Dominik Ślęzak, and Xiaokang Yang

Editorial Board

Simone Diniz Junqueira Barbosa
  *Pontifical Catholic University of Rio de Janeiro (PUC-Rio),
  Rio de Janeiro, Brazil*
Phoebe Chen
  La Trobe University, Melbourne, Australia
Xiaoyong Du
  Renmin University of China, Beijing, China
Joaquim Filipe
  Polytechnic Institute of Setúbal, Setúbal, Portugal
Igor Kotenko
  *St. Petersburg Institute for Informatics and Automation of the Russian
  Academy of Sciences, St. Petersburg, Russia*
Ting Liu
  Harbin Institute of Technology (HIT), Harbin, China
Krishna M. Sivalingam
  Indian Institute of Technology Madras, Chennai, India
Takashi Washio
  Osaka University, Osaka, Japan

More information about this series at http://www.springer.com/series/7899

Jakub Stolfa · Svatopluk Stolfa
Rory V. O'Connor · Richard Messnarz (Eds.)

Systems, Software and Services Process Improvement

24th European Conference, EuroSPI 2017
Ostrava, Czech Republic, September 6–8, 2017
Proceedings

Editors
Jakub Stolfa
Technical University of Ostrava
Ostrava
Czech Republic

Svatopluk Stolfa
Technical University of Ostrava
Ostrava
Czech Republic

Rory V. O'Connor
Dublin City University
Dublin
Ireland

Richard Messnarz
I.S.C.N. GesmbH
Graz
Austria

ISSN 1865-0929   ISSN 1865-0937 (electronic)
Communications in Computer and Information Science
ISBN 978-3-319-64217-8   ISBN 978-3-319-64218-5 (eBook)
DOI 10.1007/978-3-319-64218-5

Library of Congress Control Number: 2017948641

© Springer International Publishing AG 2017
This work is subject to copyright. All rights are reserved by the Publisher, whether the whole or part of the material is concerned, specifically the rights of translation, reprinting, reuse of illustrations, recitation, broadcasting, reproduction on microfilms or in any other physical way, and transmission or information storage and retrieval, electronic adaptation, computer software, or by similar or dissimilar methodology now known or hereafter developed.
The use of general descriptive names, registered names, trademarks, service marks, etc. in this publication does not imply, even in the absence of a specific statement, that such names are exempt from the relevant protective laws and regulations and therefore free for general use.
The publisher, the authors and the editors are safe to assume that the advice and information in this book are believed to be true and accurate at the date of publication. Neither the publisher nor the authors or the editors give a warranty, express or implied, with respect to the material contained herein or for any errors or omissions that may have been made. The publisher remains neutral with regard to jurisdictional claims in published maps and institutional affiliations.

Printed on acid-free paper

This Springer imprint is published by Springer Nature
The registered company is Springer International Publishing AG
The registered company address is: Gewerbestrasse 11, 6330 Cham, Switzerland

Preface

This textbook comprises the proceedings of the 24th Systems, Software and Services Process Improvement (EuroSPI) Conference, held during September 6–8, 2017, in Ostrava, Czech Republic.

Since EuroSPI 2010, we have extended the scope of the conference from software process improvement to systems, software, and service-based process improvement. EMIRAcle is the institution for research in manufacturing and innovation, which arose a result of the largest network of excellence for innovation in manufacturing in Europe. EMIRAcle key representatives joined the EuroSPI community, and papers as well as case studies for process improvement on systems and product level will be included in future.

Since 2008, EuroSPI partners have packaged SPI knowledge in job role training and established a European certification association (www.ecqa.org) to transport this knowledge Europe-wide using standardized certification and exam processes.

Conferences were held in Dublin (Ireland) in 1994, in Vienna (Austria) in 1995, in Budapest (Hungary) in 1997, in Gothenburg (Sweden) in 1998, in Pori (Finland) in 1999, in Copenhagen (Denmark) in 2000, in Limerick (Ireland) in 2001, in Nuremberg (Germany) in 2002, in Graz (Austria) in 2003, in Trondheim (Norway) in 2004, in Budapest (Hungary) in 2005, in Joensuu (Finland) in 2006, in Potsdam (Germany) in 2007, in Dublin (Ireland) in 2008, in Alcala (Spain) in 2009, in Grenoble (France) in 2010, in Roskilde (Denmark) in 2011, in Vienna (Austria) in 2012, Dundalk (Ireland) in 2013, in Luxembourg in 2014, in Ankara (Turkey) 2015, and in Graz (Austria) 2016.

EuroSPI is an initiative with the following major action lines http://www.eurospi.net:

- Establishing an annual EuroSPI conference supported by software process improvement networks from different EU countries.
- Establishing a social media strategy with groups in LinkedIn, Facebook, Twitter, and online statements, speeches, and keynotes on YouTube, and a set of proceedings and recommended books.
- Establishing an effective team of national representatives (from each EU- country) growing step by step into more countries of Europe.
- Establishing a European Qualification Framework for a pool of professions related to SPI and management. This is supported by European certificates and examination systems.

EuroSPI has established a joint newsletter with the European Certification and Qualification Association (www.eurospi.net, in the menu "About EuroAsiaSPI"), the SPI Manifesto (SPI = Systems, Software and Services Process Improvement), a set of social media groups including a selection of presentations and keynotes freely available on YouTube, and access to job-role-based qualification through the European Certification and Qualification Association (www.ecqa.org).

A typical characterization of EuroSPI is reflected in a statement made by a company: "... the biggest value of EuroSPI lies in its function as a European knowledge and experience exchange mechanism for SPI and innovation."

Since its beginning in 1994 in Dublin, the EuroSPI initiative has outlined that there is not a single silver bullet with which to solve SPI issues, but that you need to understand a combination of different SPI methods and approaches to achieve concrete benefits. Therefore, each proceedings volume covers a variety of different topics, and at the conference we discuss potential synergies and the combined use of such methods and approaches. These proceedings contain selected research papers under six headings:

- Section I: SPI and VSEs
- Section II: SPI and Process Models
- Section III: SPI and Safety
- Section IV: SPI and Project Management
- Section V: SPI and Implementation
- Section VI: SPI Issues
- Section VII: SPI and Automotive
- Section VIII: Selected Key Notes and Workshop Papers

Section I presents two papers related to the new standard ISO/IEC 29110 for very small entities. In the first paper, Sanchez-Gordón et al. investigate adding security practices in the software implementation process of the standard. The second paper presents research incorporating innovation management into ISO/IEC 29110.

Section II explores the theme of "SPI and Process Models," with Clarke et al. discussing variation in process due to situational context. In the second paper in this series, Barafort et al. examine risk management aspects of process reference models.

Section III presents three papers dealing with issues surrounding the topic of safety. In the first paper, Ito examines human and machine issues in safety-critical systems, while in the paper by Doss et al., safety assurance principles from a Scrum perspective are discussed. In the final paper of this set, Varkoi et al. explore compliance in a product line context.

Section IV discusses issues surrounding "SPI and Project Management" with the first paper reporting how to improve project portfolio management practices. In the second paper, Calderón et al. present a project management game perspective.

Section V explores the theme of "SPI Implementation" with the first paper discussing results from an experiment in improving model inspection processes. In the second, paper Krisper et al. propose a metric for evaluating residual complexity, while the third paper discusses the potential of self-adaptive software in an industrial control context. Finally, in the fourth paper, Ardila and Gallina explore ways to increased efficiency and confidence in process compliance.

Section VI looks at two related areas of SPI issues with a systematic review of software process improvement by Ali Khan et al. and a mechanism to overcome speaking anxiety by Yilmaz et al.

Section VII presents the last of the EuroSPI 2017 research papers and focuses on the topic of automotive aspect of SPI. In the first paper, Macher et al. explore issues of dependability engineering and in the second paper Oliveira et al. present a study involving the Automotive SPICE and ISO 26262 standard.

Section VIII presents selected keynotes from EuroSPI workshops concerning the future of SPI. From 2010 onward EuroSPI has invited recognized key researchers to publish work on new future directions of SPI. These key messages are discussed in interactive workshops and help create SPI communities based on new topics.

The first set of papers relates to the GamifySPI workshop and explores "Gamification and Persuasive Games for Software Process Improvement," "Information Technology," and "Innovation Management." The second collection of papers relate to the topic of SPI in Industry 4.0 – "The Digitalization of Design and Manufacturing" – and elaborates a set of best practices and success factors for the implementation of Industry 4.0. The third collection of papers surround the topic of "Best Practices in Implementing Traceability" and examines the issues from an automotive SPICE, functional safety, and medical device industry perspective. The fourth collection discusses the topic of "Good and Bad Practices in Improvement" with key contributions from European initiatives, which developed best practices for SPI. The fifth collection of papers relate to the topic of "Functional Safety" and addresses best practices from automotive industry to cope with cyber security and functional safety. The sixth collection addresses experiences with "Agile and Lean" and examines a series of success factors and examples of being lean and agile. The seventh collection of papers addresses the topic of "Standards and Assessment Models" and examines different ISO standards and assessment models that are introduced, explained, and discussed. The final collection of papers addresses "Team Skills and Diversity Strategies" and examines a variety of organizational and human factors as they relate to SPI.

September 2017

Jakub Stolfa
Svatopluk Stolfa
Rory V. O'Connor
Richard Messnarz

Recommended Further Reading

In [1], the proceedings of three EuroSPI conferences were integrated into one book, which was edited by 30 experts in Europe. The proceedings of EuroSPI 2005 to 2016 inclusive have been published by Springer in [2–12], respectively.

References

1. Messnarz, R., Tully, C. (eds.): Better Software Practice for Business Benefit – Principles and Experience, 409 pages. IEEE Computer Society Press, Los Alamitos (1999)
2. Richardson, I., Abrahamsson, P., Messnarz, R. (eds.): Software Process Improvement. LNCS, vol. 3792, p. 213. Springer, Heidelberg (2005)
3. Richardson, I., Runeson, P., Messnarz, R. (eds.): Software Process Improvement. LNCS, vol. 4257, pp. 11–13. Springer, Heidelberg (2006)
4. Abrahamsson, P., Baddoo, N., Margaria, T., Messnarz, R. (eds.): Software Process Improvement. LNCS, vol. 4764, pp. 1–6. Springer, Heidelberg (2007)
5. O'Connor, R.V., Baddoo, N., Smolander, K., Messnarz, R. (eds): Software Process Improvement.CCIS, vol. 16, Springer, Heidelberg (2008)
6. O'Connor, R.V., Baddoo, N., Gallego C., Rejas Muslera R., Smolander, K., Messnarz, R. (eds): Software Process Improvement. CCIS, vol. 42, Springer, Heidelberg (2009)
7. Riel A., O'Connor, R.V. Tichkiewitch S., Messnarz, R. (eds): Software, System, and Service Process Improvement. CCIS, vol. 99, Springer, Heidelberg (2010)
8. O'Connor, R., Pries-Heje, J. and Messnarz R., Systems, Software and Services Process Improvement, CCIS Vol. 172, Springer-Verlag, (2011)
9. Winkler, D., O'Connor, R.V. and Messnarz R. (Eds), Systems, Software and Services Process Improvement, CCIS 301, Springer-Verlag, (2012)
10. McCaffery, F., O'Connor, R.V. and Messnarz R. (Eds), Systems, Software and Services Process Improvement, CCIS 364, Springer-Verlag, (2013)
11. Barafort, B., O'Connor, R.V. and Messnarz R. (Eds), Systems, Software and Services Process Improvement, CCIS 425, Springer-Verlag, (2014)
12. O'Connor, R.V. Akkaya, M., Kemaneci K., Yilmaz, M., Poth, A. and Messnarz R. (Eds), Systems, Software and Services Process Improvement, CCIS 543, Springer-Verlag, (2015)
13. Kreiner, C., Poth., A., O'Connor, R.V., and Messnarz R. (Eds), Systems, Software and Services Process Improvement, CCIS 633, Springer-Verlag, (2016)

Organization

General Chair and Workshop Chair

Richard Messnarz — ISCN GesmbH, Graz, Austria

General Co-chair

Micheal Mac an Airchinnigh — ISCN, Ireland

Scientific Chair

Rory V. O'Connor — Dublin City University, Ireland

Organization Chair

Eva Christof — ISCN GesmbH, Graz, Austria

Local Organization Chairs

Jakub Stolfa — VSB - Technical University of Ostrava, Ostrava, Czech Republic
Svatopluk Stolfa — VSB - Technical University of Ostrava, Ostrava, Czech Republic

GamifySPI Workshop Co-chairs

Murat Yilmaz — Cankaya University, Turkey
Rory V. O'Connor — Dublin City University, Ireland

Industry 4.0 Workshop Co-chairs

Andreas Riel — Grenoble INP, France
Michael Reiner — University of Applied Sciences Krems, Austria

Best Practices in Implementing Traceability Workshop Co-chairs

Rainer Dreves — Continental automotive, Germany
Bernhard Sechser — Methodpark, Germany

Good and Bad Practices in Improvement Workshop Co-chairs

Eva Breske   Robert BOSCH Engineering, Germany
Tomas Schweigert   SQS, Germany

Functional Safety and Cybersecurity Workshop Co-chairs

Alexander Much   Elektrobit, Germany
Miklos Biro   SCCH, Austria
Jenny Gorner   KnowIT, Sweden
Richard Messnarz   ISCN GesmbH, Austria

Agile and Lean Workshop Co-chairs

Alexander Poth   Volkswagen AG, Germany
Susumu Sasabe   JUSE, Japan
Antonia Mas   University of the Balearic Islands, Spain

Standards and Assessment Models Workshop Co-chairs

Gerhard Griessnig   AVL, Austria
Timo Varkoi   FiSMA, Finland
Klaudia Dussa Zieger   IMBUS, Germany
Marion Lepmets   Softcomply, Ireland

Team Skills and Diversity Strategies Workshop Co-chairs

Gabriele Sauberer   Termnet, Austria
Mirna Munoz   CIMAT, Mexico

Board Members

EuroSPI Board Members represent centers or networks of SPI excellence having extensive experience with SPI. The board members collaborate with different European SPINS (Software Process Improvement Networks). The following have been members of the conference board for a significant period:

Rory V. O'Connor   Dublin City University, Ireland
Miklós Biró   Software Competence Center Hagenberg, Austria
Ricardo Colomo-Palacios   Ostfold University, Norway
Michael Reiner   IMC FH Krems, University of Applied Sciences,
                                        Austria
Gabriele Sauberer   TermNet, Austria
Christian Kreiner   Graz University of Technology, Austria

EuroSPI Scientific Program Committee

EuroSPI established an international committee of selected well-known experts in SPI who are willing to be mentioned in the program and to review a set of papers each year. The list below represents the Research Program Committee members. EuroSPI also has a separate Industrial Program Committee responsible for the industry/experience contributions.

Miklós Biró	Software Competence Center Hagenberg GmbH, Austria
Jose Antonio Calvo-Manzano	Universidad Politécnica de Madrid, Spain
Paul M. Clarke	Dublin City University, Ireland
Ricardo Colomo Palacios	Ostfold University College, Norway
Darren Dalcher	University of Hertfordshire, UK
Anca Draghici	Politechnic University of Timisoara, Romania
Elli Georgiadou	Middlesex University, UK
Christian Kreiner	Graz University of Technology, Austria
Pasi Kuvaja	University of Oulu, Finland
Dieter Landes	University of Coburg, Germany
Timo Mäkinen	Tampere University of Technology, Finland
Wolski Marcin	University of Poznan, Poland
Paula Ventura Martins	University of Algarve, Portugal
Antoina Mas	Universitat de les Illes Balears, Spain
Fergal Mc Caffery	Dundalk Institute of Technology, Ireland
Antoni Mesquida	Universitat de les Illes Balears, Spain
Mirna Muñoz	CIMAT-Zacatecas, Mexico
Rory V. O'Connor	Dublin City University, Ireland
Efi Papatheocharous	SICS Swedish ICT AB, Sweden
Michael Reiner	University of Applied Sciences Krems, Austria
Andreas Riel	Grenoble INP, France
Miran Rodic	University of Maribor, Slovenia
Tomas San Feliu	Universidad Politécnica de Madrid, Spain
Kerstin Siakas	Thessaloniki Institute of Technology, Greece
Jakub Stolfa	Technical University of Ostrava, Czech Republic
Svatopluk Stolfa	Technical University of Ostrava, Czech Republic
Dietmar Winkler	University of Technology Vienna, Austria
Murat Yilmaz	Cankaya University, Turkey

Acknowledgments

Some contributions published in this book have been funded with support from the European Commission. European projects (supporting ECQA and EuroSPI) contributed to this Springer book including AQU (Automotive Quality Universe), and InnoTEACH (LET'S BE INNOVATIVE! Development of Creativity, Innovation and Entrepreneurship), and EMVOI (ISO 17024 Certification for EU Project Managers).

In this case the publications reflect the views only of the author(s), and the Commission cannot be held responsible for any use that *may be made of the information contained therein.*

Contents

SPI and VSEs

Towards the Integration of Security Practices in the Software
Implementation Process of ISO/IEC 29110: A Mapping 3
   Mary-Luz Sánchez-Gordón, Ricardo Colomo-Palacios, Alex Sánchez,
   Antonio de Amescua Seco, and Xabier Larrucea

Incorporating Innovation Management Practices to ISO/IEC 29110 15
   Ricardo Eito-Brun

SPI and Process Models

Exploring Software Process Variation Arising from Differences
in Situational Context 29
   Paul M. Clarke, Rory V. O'Connor, David Solan, Peter Elger,
   Murat Yilmaz, Adam Ennis, Mark Gerrity, Sean McGrath,
   and Ryan Treanor

How to Elicit Processes for an ISO-Based Integrated Risk Management
Process Reference Model in IT Settings? 43
   Béatrix Barafort, Antoni-Lluís Mesquida, and Antònia Mas

SPI and Safety

HMI Requirements Creation, as the Collaboration Work of Human
and Machine in the Safety-Critical System 61
   Masao Ito

Integration of the 4+1 Software Safety Assurance Principles with Scrum 72
   Osama Doss, Tim Kelly, Tor Stålhane, Børge Haugset, and Mark Dixon

Towards Systematic Compliance Evaluation Using Safety-Oriented Process
Lines and Evidence Mapping 83
   Timo Varkoi, Timo Mäkinen, Barbara Gallina, Frank Cameron,
   and Risto Nevalainen

SPI and Project Management

Improving Project Portfolio Management (PPM)
for Improvement Projects 99
   Jan Pries-Heje, Peter Møller Jakobsen, Morten Korsaa,
   and Jørn Johansen

Coverage of ISO/IEC 29110 Project Management Process of Basic Profile
by a Serious Game 111
   Alejandro Calderón, Mercedes Ruiz, and Rory V. O'Connor

SPI and Implementation

Improving Model Inspection Processes with Crowdsourcing: Findings
from a Controlled Experiment....................................... 125
   *Dietmar Winkler, Marta Sabou, Sanja Petrovic, Gisele Carneiro,
Marcos Kalinowski, and Stefan Biffl*

A Metric for Evaluating Residual Complexity in Software 138
   *Michael Krisper, Johannes Iber, Christian Kreiner,
and Markus Quaritsch*

The Potential of Self-Adaptive Software Systems in Industrial
Control Systems 150
   Johannes Iber, Tobias Rauter, Michael Krisper, and Christian Kreiner

Towards Increased Efficiency and Confidence in Process Compliance 162
   Julieth Patricia Castellanos Ardila and Barbara Gallina

SPI Issues

Systematic Literature Reviews of Software Process Improvement:
A Tertiary Study.. 177
   *Arif Ali Khan, Jacky Keung, Mahmood Niazi, Shahid Hussain,
and He Zhang*

Overcoming Public Speaking Anxiety of Software Engineers
Using Virtual Reality Exposure Therapy 191
   *Merve Denizci Nazligul, Murat Yilmaz, Ulas Gulec, Mert Ali Gozcu,
Rory V. O'Connor, and Paul M. Clarke*

SPI and Automotive

Towards Dependability Engineering of Cooperative Automotive
Cyber-Physical Systems.. 205
   *Georg Macher, Eric Armengaud, Daniel Schneider, Eugen Brenner,
and Christian Kreiner*

An Analysis of the Commonality and Differences Between ASPICE
and ISO26262 in the Context of Software Development................. 216
   *Pedro Oliveira, André L. Ferreira, Daniel Dias, Tiago Pereira,
Paula Monteiro, and Ricardo J. Machado*

Selected Key Notes and Workshop Papers

GamifySPI

Deploying a Gamification Framework for Software Process Improvement:
Preliminary Results 231
   Eduardo Herranz, Ricardo Colomo-Palacios, and Abdullah Al-Barakati

ProDecAdmin: A Game Scenario Design Tool for Software Project
Management Training 241
   Alejandro Calderón, Mercedes Ruiz, and Rory V. O'Connor

State of the Use of Gamification Elements in Software
Development Teams 249
   Mirna Muñoz, Luis Hernández, Jezreel Mejia,
   Gloria Piedad Gasca-Hurtado, and María Clara Gómez-Alvarez

Examining Reward Mechanisms for Effective Usage of Application
Lifecycle Management Tools 259
   Çağdaş Üsfekes, Murat Yilmaz, Eray Tuzun, Paul M. Clarke,
   and Rory V. O'Connor

CHANGCE-Thinking – A Ludic Kick-Off to Chance Orientation 269
   Peter Witzgall, Peter Kapfhammer, Eva-Maria Trenz, Teresa Kiechle,
   Tobias Gebler, and Adrian Indefrey

Toward an Assessment Framework for Gamified Environments 281
   Gloria Piedad Gasca-Hurtado, María Clara Gómez-Alvarez,
   Mirna Muñoz, and Jezreel Mejia

InnoTEACH – Applying Principles of Innovation in School 294
   Richard Messnarz, Borut Likar, Jürgen Mack, Evelyn Schröttner,
   Damjan Ekert, Maria Hartyanyi, Urska Mrgole, and Janos Szabo

A Game Toolbox for Process Improvement in Agile Teams 302
   Antoni-Lluís Mesquida, Jovana Karać, Miloš Jovanović,
   and Antònia Mas

Gamification and Affordances: How Do New Affordances Lead
to Gamification in a Business Intelligence System? 310
   Tobias Christian Fischer

SPI in Industry 4.0

A Design Process Approach to Strategic Production Planning
for Industry 4.0 323
   Andreas Riel and Martina Flatscher

Industry 4.0 as Digitalization over the Entire Product Lifecycle:
Opportunities in the Automotive Domain.................................. 334
  Eric Armengaud, Christoph Sams, Georg von Falck, Georg List,
  Christian Kreiner, and Andreas Riel

Chances for Virtual and Augmented Reality Along the Value Chain........ 352
  Sonja Hammerschmid

Supporting the Integration of New Security Features in Embedded Control
Devices Through the Digitalization of Production....................... 360
  Tobias Rauter, Johannes Iber, Michael Krisper, and Christian Kreiner

A Conceptual Mixed Realities (AR/VR) Capability Maturity Model – With
Special Emphasis on Implementation..................................... 372
  Sonja Hammerschmid, Gerhard Kormann, Thomas Moser,
  and Michael Reiner

Best Practices in Implementing Traceability

Graceful Integration of Process Capability Improvement, Formal Modeling
and Web Technology for Traceability.................................... 381
  Miklós Biró, Felix Kossak, József Klespitz, and Levente Kovács

Good and Bad Practices in Improvement

The SPI Manifesto Revisited.. 401
  Eva Breske and Tomas Schweigert

Documentation of Improvement Competences............................... 411
  Jørn Johansen, Karsten Kristensen Back, Morten Korsaa,
  Jan Pries-Heje, and Tomas Schweigert

Experiences with SQIL – SW Quality Improvement Leadership Approach
from Volkswagen.. 421
  Richard Messnarz, Maik Sehr, Ingrid Wüstemann, Joachim Humpohl,
  and Damjan Ekert

Safety and Security

Need for the Continuous Evolution of Systems Engineering Practices
for Modern Vehicle Engineering... 439
  Richard Messnarz, Alexander Much, Christian Kreiner, Miklos Biro,
  and Jenny Gorner

Automotive Quality Universities – AQU – Integration of Modular Content
into the Higher Education Studies 453
  *Svatopluk Stolfa, Jakub Stolfa, Miran Rodic, Mitja Truntic,
  Christian Kreiner, and Richard Messnarz*

Experiences with Agile and Lean

Lean and Agile Software Process Improvement - An Overview
and Outlook 471
  Alexander Poth, Susumu Sasabe, and Antònia Mas

A New Approach: Not Agile vs. Traditional QM but Applying
the Best of Both 486
  Mirko Drobietz and Alexander Poth

Agile Development Offers the Chance to Establish Automated
Quality Procedures 495
  Marc Kösling and Alexander Poth

A Review on the Critical Success Factors of Agile Software Development... 504
  Abdullah Aldahmash, Andy M. Gravell, and Yvonne Howard

Agile Procedures of an Automotive OEM – Views from Different
Business Areas 513
  Alexander Poth and Fabian Wolf

Using a Statistical Method to Compare Agile and Waterfall
Processes Performance 523
  Alexssander A. Siqueira, Sheila Reinehr, and Andreia Malucelli

Standards and Assessment Models

Development of the 2nd Edition of the ISO 26262 535
  Gerhard Griessnig and Adam Schnellbach

Improvements in Functional Safety of Automotive IP Through ISO 26262:
2018 Part 11 547
  Alison Young and Alastair Walker

Using the ISO/IEC 27034 as Reference to Develop an Application Security
Control Library 557
  Alexssander A. Siqueira, Sheila Reinehr, and Andreia Malucelli

Analysis of the Practices for the CMMI-SVC in an ISO/IEC 20000-1
Certified Organization 567
  Ayşegül Ünal, Rabia Burcu Karaomer, and Onur Kaynak

A Lightweight Software Process Assessment Approach Based
on MDevSPICE® for Medical Device Development Domain 578
    Özden Özcan-Top and Fergal McCaffery

The Current Status of the TestSPICE® Project 589
    Klaudia Dussa-Zieger, Mohsen Ekssir-Monfared, Tomas Schweigert,
    Michael Philipp, and Monique Blaschke

Towards a Survival Analysis of Very Small Organisations 599
    Xabier Larrucea and Izaskun Santamaria

Team Skills and Diversity Strategies

A Model to Integrate Highly Effective Teams for Software Development. . . . 613
    Mirna Muñoz, Luis Hernández, Jezreel Mejia, Adriana Peña,
    Nora Rangel, Carlos Torres, and Gabriele Sauberer

Towards Developing a Software Process Improvement Strategy Through
the Application of Ethical Concepts. 627
    Harjinder Rahanu, Elli Georgiadou, Kerstin Siakas, and Margaret Ross

Diversity and PERMA-nent Positive Leadership to Benefit from
Industry 4.0 and Kondratieff 6.0 642
    Gabriele Sauberer, Andreas Riel, and Richard Messnarz

Do We Speak the Same Language? Terminology Strategies for (Software)
Engineering Environments Based on the Elcat Model - Innovative
Terminology e-Learning for the Automotive Industry 653
    Gabriele Sauberer, Blanca Nájera Villar, Jens R. Dreßler,
    Klaus-Dirk Schmitz, Paul M. Clarke, and Rory V. O'Connor

Accessible Information and Accessibility Through ICT: A Mega Trend
Creates the Need for Quality Certificates for Web Accessibility
Professionals in Europe and Beyond 667
    Ronald Bieber, Klaus Höckner, and Gabriele Sauberer

Team Members' Interactive Styles Involved in the Software
Development Process. 675
    Nora Rangel, Carlos Torres, Adriana Peña, Mirna Muñoz,
    Jezreel Mejia, and Luis Hernández

Author Index 687

SPI and VSEs

SPI and VSEs

Towards the Integration of Security Practices in the Software Implementation Process of ISO/IEC 29110: A Mapping

Mary-Luz Sánchez-Gordón[1(✉)], Ricardo Colomo-Palacios[2], Alex Sánchez[3], Antonio de Amescua Seco[1], and Xabier Larrucea[4]

[1] Computer Science Department, Universidad Carlos III de Madrid, Av. Universidad 30 Leganés, 28911 Madrid, Spain
mary_sanchezg@hotmail.com, amescua@inf.uc3m.es
[2] Faculty of Computer Sciences, Østfold University College, Postboks 700, 1757 Halden, Norway
ricardo.colomo-palacios@hiof.no
[3] LogicStudio, Ciudad del Saber, Building 235, Panama City, Panama
alex.sanchez@logicstudio.net
[4] Tecnalia, Bizkaia, Spain
xabier.larrucea@tecnalia.com

Abstract. Secure software practices are gradually gaining relevance among software practitioners and researchers. This is happening because today more than ever software is becoming part of our lives and cybercrimes are constantly appearing. Despite its importance, its current practice in the software industry is still scarce. Indeed, software security problems are divided 50/50 between bugs and flaws. In particular, it remains a significant challenge for software practitioners in small software companies. Therefore, there is a need to support small companies in changing their existing ways of work to integrate these new and unfamiliar practices. The aim of this study is twofold. First, to help building an awareness of the software security process among practitioners in small companies. Second, to help the integration of these practices with software implementation process of ISO/IEC 29110 which results in an extension of the latter with additional activities identified from the industry best practices. Nevertheless, the extension proposal is to be performed selectively, based on the value of the software as an asset to the stakeholders and on stakeholders needs.

Keywords: Software security · CSSLP · S-SDLC · Small companies · VSE · ISO/IEC 29110

1 Introduction

Today, more than ever, software has become part of our lives. It is integrated into systems that we use every day and we are increasingly dependent on those systems to work. Specially, developed nation´s economy and defense depend in large part on the reliable execution of software. In fact, software is ubiquitous —software is everywhere— affecting all aspects of our personal and professional lives [1]. Therefore, security becomes an important issue and a crucial requirement for software systems [2]. New security challenges arise when new —or old— technologies are put to new use. Opening the Internet to commercial use in the early 1990s raised the importance of security policies for remote transactions [3]. There is evidence that global interconnectedness combined with the proliferation of hacker tools means that today's computer systems are actually less secure than equivalent systems a decade ago [4]. Applications have been vulnerable for as long as they have existed. Over the past few years, aside from operating systems, they have been cited as the leading vector for attacks. In 2011, National Vulnerability Database maintained by US National Institute for Standards and Technology (NIST)[1] stated that 92% of the reported vulnerabilities are in applications and not due to insecure networks. That same year, top vulnerabilities included[2]: SQL injection, integer overflow, buffer overflow, uncontrolled format string, missing authentication, missing or incorrect authorization, and reliance on untrusted inputs in a security decision (aka tainted inputs). Already in 2003, the programming errors were 64% of the vulnerabilities in the NIST database, and 51 out of those were repeated basic mistakes such as buffer overflows, cross-site scripting, injection flaws [5].

According to the "2015 (ISC)^2 Global Information Security Workforce Study", 72% of the survey respondents (13,930 qualified information security professionals), indicated that application vulnerabilities are their top security concern [6]. Moreover, regarding cloud security threats, they pointed out that data breaches and data loss topped the list of concerns. In this sense, the "2016 Cost of Data Breach Study: Global Analysis" carried out by Ponemon Institute [7], stated that average total cost of a data breach for the 383 companies participating in this research increased from $3.79 to $4 million. The average cost paid for each lost or stolen record containing sensitive and confidential information increased from $154 in 2015 to $158 by 2016. Furthermore, Gartner [8] claims that worldwide spending on IT security products and services will reach $81.6 billion in 2016; an increase of 7.9% over 2015. Another issue is the loss of credibility, while intangible, has tangible repercussions. Paying the extra cost of developing software correctly from the start reduces the cost of fixing it after it is deployed —and produces a better, more robust, and more secure product [9]. This approach reduces the need to patch the software in order to fix security holes. Moreover, incorporating security in software is often misunderstood as an impediment to business agility and not necessarily as an enabler for the business to produce quality and secure software [10]. In certain situations, security in software is not even considered, it is overlooked [10, 11]. Moreover, the common approach towards the inclusion of security within a software system is to identify security requirements after the definition of a system [2]. Thus, incorporating security in later stages of software development will increase the risks of introducing security vulnerabilities into software. A vulnerability is a software defect that an attacker can exploit [9]. Software security problems are divided 50/50 between bugs and flaws [12]. A bug is an implementation-level software problem whereas a flaw is a design-level or architectural software defect.

---

[1] http://nvd.nist.gov/.
[2] http://cwe.mitre.org/top25/#Listing.

The most critical difference between secure software and insecure software lies in the nature of the processes and practices used to specify, design, and develop the software [9]. Traditionally, Software Engineering deals with security as a non-functional requirement and usually considers it after the definition of the systems [10]. Consequently, software that is developed with security in mind is typically more resistant to both intentional attack and unintentional failures [9, 13]. Security in the software development life cycle (SDLC) is necessary but not sufficient. In practice, there are a lot of aspects that are not part of the life cycle for any particular application such as building the security team, maintaining legacy code, gaining the organization's support (budget and respect), establishing an education and training program, establishing standards and metrics, handling breaches and incidents, tooling and building feedback loops for continuous improvement [13].

In the context of this research, a vast majority of small software companies are very small entities (VSEs) —enterprise, government, or not-for-profit organizations; departments; or projects with up to 25 people who develop systems with hardware and software components and/or software products [14]. They face unique challenges [15], their products are sold to their customers directly or are integrated into those developed by larger organizations, possibly distributed to thousands of users worldwide [14]. In addition to the time constraints placed on software development projects, scarce human resources are also noted as a limitation [15, 16]. Without enough resources in order to achieve all the essential tasks within the required timeline, considering the uptake of increased work effort (including security during software development) is noted as being difficult if not improbable. Therefore, the aim of this study is twofold. First, to create an awareness of the software security process among practitioners in small companies. Second, to provide the first approach towards narrowing the gap between security and ISO/IEC 29110 standard, which fix well in this type of companies. The integration of these practices with software implementation (SI) process of ISO/IEC 29110 results in an extension of the latter with additional activities identified from the industry best practices in security software —Certified Secure Software Lifecycle Professional (CSSLP) common body of knowledge (CBK). This body of knowledge was chosen because it is an approach agnostic and focuses on SDLC. Nevertheless, the extension proposal is to be performed selectively on the basis of the value of the software as an asset to the stakeholders and on stakeholders needs. The remainder of this paper is structured as follows: Sect. 2 outlines the CSSLP CBK and SI process ISO/IEC 29110. In Sect. 3 the research approach and results are presented. Finally, Sect. 4 summarizes a conclusion as well as outlines future work.

2 Background

2.1 Models and Software Security Certifications

There are a variety of models such as CERT Resilience Management Model "RMM", Building Security in Maturity Model "BSIMM", Capability Maturity Model Integration for Acquisitions "CMMI", SwA Forum Processes and Practices Group Process Reference Model "PRM", and OWASP Software Assurance Maturity Model "SAMM".

Similarly, Microsoft has a method for software development and on how to develop secure software which is called Security Development Lifecycle (SDL). Each one has their advantages and disadvantages. It seems overwhelming to non-security experts like software practitioners in small companies. As a consequence of the need for training and certification on software security, the industry has developed certifications based on specific languages and/or platforms. In what follows, there are some of the relevant certifications [17].

- Global Information Assurance Certification (GIAC) offers three software security certifications[3]. The certifications in Java and .NET —GIAC Secure Software Programmer-.NET/.JAVA (GSSP-.NET/.JAVA). And the GIAC Certified Web Application Defender (GWEB).
- The EC-Council offers a program known as EC-Council certified secure programmer (ECSP) that has certifications in Java and .NET[4] —Certified Secure Programmer in .NET (ECSP.Net) and Certified Secure Programmer in .Java (ECSP-Java).
- The CERT Secure Coding Professional Certificates is part of Carnegie Mellon University's Software Engineering Institute. This certificate program is designed for developers who are programming in C and C++, or Java language
- The International Information System Security Certification Consortium, also known as ISC[2] offers a Certified Secure Software Lifecycle Professional (CSSLP) certification. CSSLP was designed to validate SDLC security competencies based on a common body of knowledge (CBK).

The CSSLP CBK approach was chosen as a reference for this study due to its agnostic approach, its independence of any specific language or vendor and its focus on SDLC.

2.2 The Certified Secure Software Lifecycle Professional Common Body of Knowledge

The Certified Secure Software Lifecycle Professional (CSSLP) common body of knowledge (CBK) provides a comprehensive approach to building secure systems by incorporating security into all phases of the software lifecycle. The International Information Systems Security Certification Consortium (ISC) sponsors the CSSLP certification[5]. The CSSLP certification is international in its scope and therefore, does not explicitly address US standards such as those from NIST. The CSSLP certification emphasizes best practices in secure software development and covers the following eight domains of the CSSLP CBK [10]:

- **Secure Software Concepts** include the core software security requirements and foundational design principles as they relate to issues of privacy, governance, risk and compliance. The aim is to understand the software methodologies needed in order to develop software that is secure and resilient to attacks.

---

[3] http://www.giac.org/certifications/software-security.
[4] https://www.eccouncil.org/programs/certified-secure-programmer-ecsp/.
[5] https://www.isc2.org/csslp/default.aspx.

- **Security Software Requirements** provide concepts related to understanding the importance of identifying and developing software with secure requirements which could be incorporated in order to produce software that is reliable, resilient and recoverable.
- **Secure Software Design** gives an understanding of how to ensure that software security requirements are included in the design of the software. That means secure design principles and process.
- **Secure Software Implementation/Coding** allows understanding the importance of programming concepts that can effectively protect software from vulnerabilities. That means software coding vulnerabilities, defensive coding techniques and processes, code analysis and protection, and environmental security considerations that should be factored into software.
- **Secure Software Testing** includes the overall strategies and plans of functional and security testing that should be performed, the criteria for testing, concepts related to impact assessment and corrective actions, and the test data lifecycle.
- **Software Acceptance** provides an understanding of the requirements for software acceptance, paying specific attention to compliance, quality, functionality, and assurance before software is released or deployed into production.
- **Software Deployment, Operations, Maintenance and Disposal** is focused on the identification of processes during installation and deployment, operations and maintenance. Finally, disposal that can affect the ability of the software to remain reliable, resilient, and recoverable in its prescribed manner.
- **Supply Chain and Software Acquisition** give an understanding of the importance of supplier sourcing and being able to validate vendor integrity, from third-party vendors to complete outsourcing. That means how to manage risk through the adoption of standards and best practices for proper development and testing across the entire lifecycle of products.

2.3 ISO/IEC 29110 Standard

Although ISO/IEC 29110 is an emerging standard, a series of pilot projects have been completed in several countries utilizing some of the deployment packages (DPs) developed [18]. This ISO/IEC 29110 standard is applicable to Very Small Entities (VSEs). VSEs are enterprises, organizations, departments or projects of up to 25 people. This standard has a generic profile group that provides a four-stage roadmap for VSEs that do not develop critical systems or critical software: Entry, Basic, Intermediate and Advanced profiles [19]. This study is based on the Basic profile which describes the development practices of a single application by a single project team. Basic profile has two interconnected processes: Project Management (PM) and Software Implementation (SI). This study focuses on the SI process because its goal is to achieve a software product that satisfies the needs and expectations of all potential users, including security issues.

Software Implementation Process. The aim of the SI process is to achieve systematic performance of the analysis, design, construction, integration, and test activities for new or modified software products according to the specified requirements. The activities of the SI process are:

- **Software Implementation Initiation** ensures that the Project Plan established in Project Planning activity is committed to by the Work Team.
- **Software Requirements Analysis** analyzes the agreed Customer's requirements and establishes the validated project requirements.
- **Software Architectural and Detailed Design** transforms the software requirements to the system software architecture and software detailed design.
- **Software Construction** develops the software code and data from the Software Design.
- **Software Integration and Tests** ensures that the integrated Software Components satisfy the software requirements.
- **Product Delivery** provides the integrated software product to the Customer.

3 Research Approach

Due to increasing recognition of the importance of security throughout the entire life cycle, new initiatives strengthening ties for security within the SDLC have been conducted. However there is a need to assist organization in processes that minimize and ideally prevent security vulnerabilities [1]. This is especially true for small companies because they find hard to deal with their software process [15]. Consequently, it is important to harmonize software processes and security issues. The authors carried out mapping, as it is one of the most widely used strategies in harmonizing software processes. They follow the guidelines provided at [20] including these steps: (1) Analyze the models; (2) Design the mapping; (3) Carry out the mapping; (4) Present the outcomes and (5) Analyze the results. In what follows, the mapping performed is described using the method provided.

3.1 Models Analysis

The ISO/IEC 29110 standard and CSSLP certification were chosen for this study based on their approach agnostic and growing relevance among small organizations and security professionals, respectively. The first activity is to analyze each reference model involved in a mapping process. ISO/IEC 29110 and CSSLP CBK were studied in detail.

3.2 Mapping Design

The design involves the following activities: (i) Identification of elements to be compared, they are the SI process of ISO/IEC 29110 standard and the practices (in each domain) of CSSLP CBK. (ii) Direction of the comparison, it is from ISO/IEC 29110 standard to CSSLP CBK. (iii) Comparison scale definition, authors use a "traffic light" scale for the one to one mapping. This scale is also used in our previous works [21]:

- E: explicit, the item has appeared in the framework's definition.
- I: implicit, the item has not appeared explicitly in the framework definition. Inferred by the authors or referred inside a previous work of the authors.
- U: unavailable, the item has not appeared anyway.

(iv) Comparison template definition, all these values are analyzed and checked from a holistic point of view and the authors determine to what extent activities (from a SI process of ISO/IEC 29110) that are related to practices/techniques of CSSLP CBK could be extended.

3.3 Mapping

This mapping is an iterative process because the comparison is performed completely on one ISO/IEC 29110 activity and then on the others in turn. At the same time, it is incremental due to the comparison outcome grows and evolves with each iteration until it becomes the final one. The authors analyze the ISO/IEC 29110 with CSSLP CBK. For the SI process of ISO/IEC 29110 all activities are studied. Moreover, the authors identified specific practices and/or techniques of CSSLP CBK. The objective is not to set a naïve approach which compares just names. Therefore, a relationship between reference models is defined first and then a drilling down process analyzing in detail these relationships helps us to identify fine grained relationships. All mappings are managed by using several spreadsheets where ISO/IEC 29110 activities are displayed as rows and practices/techniques of CSSLP CBK are displayed as columns. As a result, a set of practices and techniques to help practitioners understand how to secure their development processes and to apply those principles in practice is defined. It represents an extension to the ISO/IEC 29110 standard.

3.4 Outcomes

Figure 1 depicts the resulting mapping for domains of CSSLP CBK. Each one has a fulfillment result based on the intersection of activities of ISO/IEC 29110. At first glance the result is not surprising but it is interesting from a security perspective. At high level, two domains, *Secure Software Concepts* and *Supply Chain and Software Acquisition*, have not appeared anywhere. Moreover, *Software Deployment, Operations, Maintenance and Disposal* are partially related with *Product Delivery*. Although *Software Implementation Initiation* is not apparently related at this level, it is crucial because it ensures that the project plan, including security issues, is committed by the team. The other five domains receive more coverage —*Requirement, Design, Implementation, Testing, and Acceptance*— as can be seen below. Next, the activities of SI process ISO/IEC 29110 and the pertinent practices of CSSLP CBK.

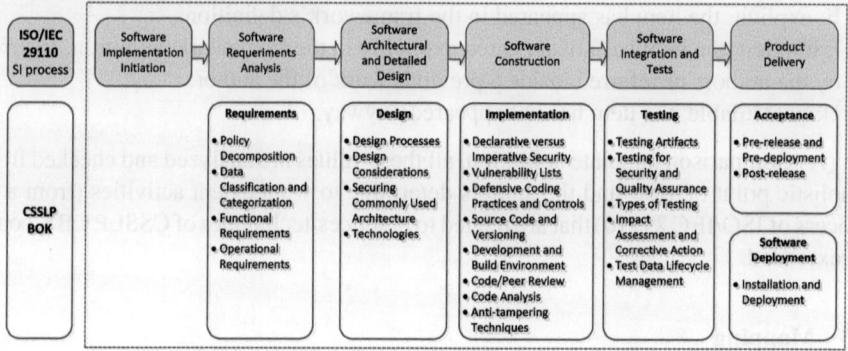

Fig. 1. Mapping between ISO/IEC 29110 to CSSLP CBK

Implementation Initiation. This activity prepares the team for the remainder of the activities and brings together all the necessary tools to accomplish the project. Small companies' constraint is limited budget for setting up the environment. At this point, it is important to be familiar with what each tool or technology can be used for and how it can impact the overall state of software security.

Software Requirement Analysis. This activity studies users' needs and expectations to define the project scope and identify key functionalities, including non-functional requirements —and security is often considered as such. Moreover, it is worth nothing that small companies cannot afford to have security experts and there are several types of security requirements that address the various principles of software security. Nevertheless, protection needs can be elicited using several methods including brainstorming, surveys, policy decomposition, data classification and use and misuse case modeling. The policy decomposition process is made up of breaking down high-level requirements into granular finer level software security requirements. Data classification can help with assuring that appropriate levels of security controls are assigned to data based on their sensitivity levels. Finally, use and misuse case modeling, sequence diagrams and subject–object models can be used to glean software security requirements.

Software Design. This activity is the keystone in the SDLC. Failure to describe a design architecture that will incorporate all the requirements is a common reason for project failure. Thus semantic or business logic flaws are related to design issues. Small companies' constraint is limited development team. When they design software, possible threats and security taken into account, and they should take into consideration secure design principles to assure confidentiality, integrity, and availability. In fact, the time that is necessary to fix identified issues is shorter when the software is still in the design phase. Below some considerations that could be useful to do that.

- Determine entry and exit points that an attacker could use to compromise the software asset or the data it processes. Take into account the following principles: least privilege, separation of duties, layered defense, fail secure, economy of mechanisms —

KISS (Keep It Simple Stupid) principle —, complete mediation, open design, least common mechanism, and leveraging existing components.
- Design considerations address the core security elements of confidentiality, integrity, availability, authentication, authorization, and auditing.
- Design process includes attack surface evaluation, threat modeling, control identification and prioritization, and documentation. Threat models are useful to identify and prioritize controls (safeguards) that can be designed, implemented (during the development phase), and deployed but it take time.
- Proven software architectures and technologies can be leveraged to enhance security in software. For instance, authentication, identity Management (IDM), Credential Management, Flow Control, Auditing/Logging, Data Loss Prevention (DLP), Virtualization and Digital Rights Management
- Review of the software's design and architecture from a security perspective.

Software Construction. This activity entails developers producing components using a systematic approach. Small companies' constraints are limited development team and short time to deliver. In fact, writing secure code is an important and critical factor in order to ensure the resiliency of software security controls. The mapping performed using the method provided is described in the following section.

- The security advantages or lack thereof of software development methodology must be taken in account.
- Build security protection controls based on common coding vulnerabilities and an understanding of how an attacker will try to exploit the software (because of limited space, details are not included but are available on [10]).
- Secure software development processes include versioning, code analysis and code review.
- Build Environment and Tools Security. The main kinds of build tools are compilers, packers and packagers —e.g. the Red Hat Package Manager (RPM) and the Microsoft Installer (MSI).

Software Integration and Tests. This activity comprises running a set of tests and identifying issues that must be. Small companies' constraints are limited development team. In this sense, security testing can be used to determine the means and opportunities by which software can be attacked. These tests are as follows:

- Both white box and black box security testing —e.g. fuzzing, scanning and penetration testing— are used to determine the threats to software. They are based on knowledge of how to test for common software vulnerabilities.
- Testing related to software security issues are testing for input validation, injection flaws testing, testing for nonrepudiation, testing for spoofing, failure testing, cryptographic validation testing, testing for buffer overflow defenses, testing for privilege escalations defenses, and anti-reversing protection testing.
- The use of tools which are applicable to the specific situation. Some of the common security tools include: reconnaissance (information gathering) tools, vulnerability scanners, fingerprinting tools, sniffers/protocol analyzers, password crackers, web

security tools —e.g., scanners, proxies, vulnerability management—, wireless security tools, reverse engineering tools —assembler and disassemblers, debuggers, and decompilers—, source code analyzers, vulnerability exploitation tools, security-oriented operating systems, and privacy testing tools.
- Fixing defects must never be performed directly in the production environment, and proper change management principles must be used to promote fixes from development and test environments into the user acceptance testing (UAT) and production environment.

Software product delivery. This activity ensures there would be no delays in order to gain product acceptance so the customer completes the payment to the company. Small companies' constraint is short time to deliver and ensure that software is not only operationally hack-resilient, but also compliant with applicable regulations —i.e. there is a formal software acceptance process which comprises the validation of security requirements and the verification of security controls. In what follows crucial considerations about the pre- and post-installation software security.

- Security requirements need to be validated and security controls verified by internal and/or independent third party security testing. Software must not be deployed/released until it has been certified and accredited that the residual risk is at the appropriate level.
- Hardening of software implicates:
  - Remove maintenance hooks before deployment.
  - Remove debugging code and flags in code.
  - Change the way to write code not to contain any sensitive information —i.e. unneeded comments, dangling code, or sensitive information from comments in code.
- Enforcement of security principles means:
  - Use pre-installation checklists in order to ensure that the needed parameters required for the software to run are appropriately configured.
  - Grant appropriate administrative rights (least privilege) to the software during the installation process.
  - Not allow developers access to production systems to install software.
- Development and test environment must be the same as the production environment in which the software will be deployed post-acceptance.
- Bootstrapping and secure startup could be achieved using hardware's trusted platform module (TPM) chip.

4 Conclusions

Despite of the growing understanding of the importance of including of security throughout the SDLC, it is usually treated superficially and the typical security process is to add a standard set of security mechanism, such as authentication, into the system [22]. While the current business environment is fast-paced and increasingly exposed to threats, software practitioners must go beyond when developing software. Although security throughout the SDLC requires allocation of resources such as time and has an impact on the project life cycle, it is worthy and valuable. In this paper, authors shed light on this fact. Its aim is to raise awareness on its importance and to provide the argument for better enforcement of security and its practices.

Furthermore, this paper presents the integration of these practices with software implementation (SI) process of ISO/IEC 29110. As a result of this, an extension of the latter with additional activities identified from the best practices of CSSPL CBK is presented. Since clearly an organization cannot protect and prevent every risk and threat, the extension proposal is to be performed selectively on the basis of the value of the software as an asset to the stakeholders and on stakeholders needs. It is worth noting that some of these practices appear to have common sense validity but there are others not so obvious deserving more attention. This study is a first step in exposing and addressing the challenging landscape of security in small companies. As future work, a sub-set of the extension will be adapted in a small company because the security should be properly considered as part of its software development process.

References

1. O'Connor, R.V., Colomo-Palacios, R.: Security awareness in the software arena. In: Engemann, K. (ed.) Routledge Companion to Risk, Crisis and Security in Business. Routledge (2017)
2. Salini, P., Kanmani, S.: Survey and analysis on security requirements engineering. Comput. Electr. Eng. **38**, 1785–1797 (2012)
3. Gollmann, D.: Computer security. Wiley Interdiscip. Rev. Comput. Stat. **2**, 544–554 (2010)
4. Garfinkel, S.L.: The cybersecurity risk. Commun. ACM **55**, 29–32 (2012)
5. Heffley, J., Meunier, P.: Can source code auditing software identify common vulnerabilities and be used to evaluate software security? In: 37th Annual Hawaii International Conference on System Sciences, pp. 1–10 (2004)
6. Suby, M., Dickson, F.: Global Information Security Workforce Study. Frost & Sullivan (2015)
7. Ponemon Institute LLC: 2016 Cost of Data Breach Study: Global Analysis (2016)
8. Gartner Says Worldwide Information Security Spending Will Grow 7.9 Percent to Reach $81.6 Billion in 2016. http://www.gartner.com/newsroom/id/3404817
9. Allen, J.H., Barnum, S., Ellison, R.J., McGraw, G., Mead, N.R.: Software Security Engineering: A Guide for Project Managers. Addison-Wesley Professional, Boston (2008)
10. Mano, P.: Official (ISC)2 Guide to the CSSLP. CRC Press, Boca Raton (2015)
11. Daud, M.I.: Secure Software Development Model: A Guide for Secure Software Life Cycle. Presented at the Proceedings of the International MutiConference on Engineers and Computer Scientists (IMECS), Hong Kong (2010)
12. McGraw, G.: Software Security: Building Security. Addison-Wesley Professional, Boston (2006)
13. Chess, B., Arkin, B.: Software security in practice. IEEE Secur. Priv. **9**, 89–92 (2011)
14. Laporte, C.Y., O'Connor, R.V.: Systems and software engineering standards for very small entities: accomplishments and overview. Computer **49**, 84–87 (2016)
15. Sánchez-Gordón, M.-L., O'Connor, R.V.: Understanding the gap between software process practices and actual practice in very small companies. Softw. Qual. J. **24**, 549–570 (2015)

16. Sanchez-Gordon, M.-L., O'Connor, R.V., Colomo-Palacios, R.: Evaluating VSEs viewpoint and sentiment towards the ISO/IEC 29110 standard: a two country grounded theory study. In: Rout, T., O'Connor, Rory V., Dorling, A. (eds.) SPICE 2015. CCIS, vol. 526, pp. 114–127. Springer, Cham (2015). doi:10.1007/978-3-319-19860-6_10
17. Grover, M., Durham, N.C., Cummings, J., Janicki, T.: Moving beyond coding: why secure coding should be implemented. J. Inf. Syst. Appl. Res. **9**(1), 38–46 (2016)
18. O'Connor, R.V., Laporte, C.Y.: The evolution of the ISO/IEC 29110 set of standards and guides. Int. J. Inf. Technol. Syst. Approach IJITSA **10**, 1–21 (2017)
19. ISO: Software engineering – Lifecycle profiles for Very Small Entities (VSEs) Part 5-1-2: Management and engineering guide: Generic profile group: Basic Profile, Geneva (2011)
20. Baldassarre, M.T., Caivano, D., Pino, F.J., Piattini, M., Visaggio, G.: Harmonization of ISO/IEC 9001:2000 and CMMI-DEV: from a theoretical comparison to a real case application. Softw. Qual. J. **20**, 309–335 (2011)
21. Sanchez-Gordón, M.-L., Colomo-Palacios, R., Herranz, E.: Gamification and human factors in quality management systems: mapping from octalysis framework to ISO 10018. In: Kreiner, C., O'Connor, Rory V., Poth, A., Messnarz, R. (eds.) EuroSPI 2016. CCIS, vol. 633, pp. 234–241. Springer, Cham (2016). doi:10.1007/978-3-319-44817-6_19
22. Haralambos, M., Giorgini, P.: Integrating Security and Software Engineering: Advances and Future Visions: Advances and Future Visions. Idea Group Inc (IGI) (2006)

Incorporating Innovation Management Practices to ISO/IEC 29110

Ricardo Eito-Brun(✉)

Universidad Carlos III de Madrid, c/Madrid 124, 28903 Getafe, Madrid, Spain
`reito@bib.uc3m.es`

Abstract. Studies on Innovation management are often focused on large companies and organizations. On the other side, small companies or VSE (Very Small Entities), constitute a significant part of the entrepreneurial landscape, and contribute – in a great extent – to the economic outputs of society and to the creation of employment. This is also valid for the system and software engineering business areas. Larger systems being built and deployed across Europe are usually built with the participation of small enterprises or research centers whose contributions have a key role in the resulting systems. Although these companies are sensitive to the importance of systematic innovation, most of the innovation models are targeted to large or medium enterprises and do not consider the specific characteristics of the system and software engineering industries. In this particular business area, innovation must consider two separate dimensions: (a) the opportunities to innovate that system and software development companies may offer to their customers and prospects, and (b) the application of techniques to innovate in the software development processes, to achieve better performance and leverage process capabilities and company productivity. Both dimensions require a systematic integration of the innovation management processes with the managerial and engineering processes of the organizations.

This paper proposes an extension of the process model described in the ISO/IEC 29110 standard to enable innovation management processes and activities addressed to VSE. The innovation activities and tools incorporated into the resulting model are based on existing innovation models, and on the feedback collected through interviews and surveys with different software development companies. SPEM (System and Software Process Engineering Metamodel) has been used as a process design framework to encode the resulting model and formally integrate innovation, managerial and engineering processes for VSE.

Keywords: ISO/IEC 29110 · Innovation management R&D projects · SPEM

1 Introduction

The capability to innovate and improve existing products, services and business models is recognized as a key factor for competitiveness. A great percentage of innovations in the current economic landscape is supported by software applications and computer-based systems. In knowledge intensive domains like automotive, aerospace or biomedicine, the identification, prototyping, building and delivery of innovation heavily depend on the capability of translating new ideas into working software applications. Software and computer technologies affect innovation from a double perspective: they are the tools that enable the prototyping, building and deploying innovative ideas, and they also provide engineers with new approaches to solve problems and optimize existing solutions.

Companies involved in software development should be aware of this tight relationship between software and innovation, and acknowledge their role as agents of innovation. A new approach is needed: an approach that may sound unfamiliar to most of the companies involved in software development, whose activities have traditionally been focused on the construction of business solutions that fulfil a set of requirements specified by their customers. In these cases, software development processes are understood as a set of sequential or iterative activities that generate a running solution through a set of transformations that start with the client requirements. This model offers software development companies little opportunities to participate in the ideas' generation process. Software engineering is similar to a black box, and innovation is implicit in the requirements proposed by the customer. Teams working on these projects dedicate their efforts on pure engineering activities aimed to ensure functionality, performance and robustness: this is far from the collaboration models proposed by Open Innovation strategies, which promote the participation of different agents to figure out potential solutions to business challenges.

To overcome the constraints implicit in these strategies, software development teams should consider the need of incorporating into their processes systematic innovation management practices. This paper proposes a framework to incorporate these practices into their process portfolio. The systematic planning, execution and control of innovation activities fully integrated with engineering and managerial processes shall improve the companies' capability to generate innovations and new business opportunities. Software development should no longer be viewed as the implementation of requirements stated by a third party, but as a dynamic, iterative process that interacts with stakeholders to figure out how software and computer technologies may re-define products, processes and business models. Software and computer technologies may help business recombine existing models and technologies into innovative value-added proposals.

This research focuses on innovation at SMEs (Small- Medium Enterprises). Although SMEs do not have at their disposal all the resources and the financial capability needed to complete complex R&D, production and marketing activities, they can be much more innovative than larger firms [8]. In the case of SMEs involved in software development, just a few studies have been completed. Capaldo [6] proposed a methodology to assess their innovation capabilities based on the available resources (resource-based competition approach), including financial and human resources and the involvement of the entrepreneurs and their personal know-how on both technical and managerial aspects. His study included – among the pull of available resources -, the deployment of software engineering methodologies as a means to increase technical know-how.

The paper is organized as follows: Sect. 2 discusses innovation management needs for SMEs; Sect. 3 discusses the use of the ISO/IEC 29110 standard as a referential for engineering and project management activities; Sect. 4 presents the UNE 166001 standard [1], which proposes a model for innovation management; Sect. 4 explains the proposed integration between ISO 29110 and UNE 166001; Sect. 6 explains the use of SPEM for modeling the resulting process and Sect. 7 summarizes the conclusions.

2 Reference Framework

System and software development companies need to incorporate innovation management practices as part of their process map and corporate procedures. Procedures and organizational routines are in fact the result of the knowledge accumulated after years of self-experience and captured from accepted industrial practices throughout a continuous improvement cycle. The strategic management of innovation (planning, deployment and monitoring), requires a similar approach to improve the probability of success in the design of new products and their delivery to the market.

The need of combining innovation management practices within corporate procedures has been discussed by Laperche and Liu [14] and Hage [9], among others. Laperche and Liu analyzed the opportunities that Open innovation strategies offer to SMEs to increase their knowledge capital. Hage's idea innovation network theory proposes a framework for assessing innovation capabilities of companies in knowledge-intensive sectors - that remarked the need of keeping a tight connection between the different activities involved in R&D: basic and applied research, product development and production, commercialization, marketing and quality control. According to this author, the lack of interaction between these areas is one of the factors that slow down innovation. Idea innovation network theory does not restrict quality control to the identification and correction of defects: this activity is seen as a means to reduce operating costs and "negative properties" of the products, an understanding that is aligned with the product assurance approach that is found on several system and software engineering standards.

This research proposes the combined use of innovation management activities and engineering and managerial practices for VSEs. The resulting approach integrates two models: the first one for guiding software development activities, and the second one for innovation management practices. Their combined deployment offers a global framework that puts together: (a) activities needed to build robust, reliable software following recognized software engineering practices, and (b) activities aimed to identify innovation opportunities, promote them and disseminate their results. To achieve this objective, the ISO/IEC 29110 - a software process model designed to meet the needs of VSEs involved in software development– has been extended with additional activities and work products identified in a set of innovation and R&D standards: UNE 16600X, Spanish national standard closely related to CEN/TS 16555-1 [3].

3 The Engineering and Managerial Referential: ISO/IEC 29110

The recently published ISO/IEC 29110 "Software engineering – Lifecycle profiles for Very Small Entities (VSEs)" is expected to become one of the most relevant standards for guiding system and software development activities. Software process models provide practitioners with descriptions of activities or groups of activities and product flows, that is to say, inputs and outputs for the activities, the control flow between processes and the relationships between activities, techniques, methods, tools and roles. Software process models are oriented toward the resolution of recurrent problems when building software, and they reflect the accumulated know-how regarding software development practices. In the case of an international standard like ISO/IEC 29110, this know-how also represents the consensus reached between different national standardization bodies participated by a wide spectrum of organizations of different types.

ISO/IEC 29110 is a prescriptive process model, as it provides organizations with instructions on how to develop software to achieve business objectives and improvement goals. The standard defines software development processes tailored to VSE (Very Small Entities): organizations, departments or project teams with no more than twenty five workers. Even in the case of bigger companies, the teams in charge of developing particular software applications fail within those dimensions. ISO/IEC 29110 was elaborated to solve one of the classical problems in process improvement at small software companies: organizations within this group do not have at their disposal the time and resources needed to deploy complex improvement models like CMMI or SPICE [16, 17]. These software process improvement models were developed to monitor the performance of big contractors for governmental projects, and imply complex and costly requirements different to fulfil for SMEs. This is a problem for both small and large organizations:

(a) for small companies, it is difficult to demonstrate their capability to develop reliable software following standard life cycle processes and best practices (Rimbaud, 2010);
(b) For large organizations subcontracting software development activities to SMEs, the lack of process models tailored to the characteristics of SMEs hinders the assessment of their capabilities as subcontractors.

ISO/IEC 29110 explicitly states its value for both contractors and acquirers of software. Having this standard as a reference, small companies and groups may adopt a sound process model to complete engineering activities, demonstrate their processes' capability to third parties and guide improvement efforts [5].

The ISO/IEC 29110 standard focuses on the definition of standard profiles, defined as "pre-tailored packages of related software engineering standards" (ISO/IEC 29110-2 sec. 2.2.1). Profiles are created by combining relevant elements from existing standards referred to as base standards. These elements may be processes, processes outcomes and objectives, activities, tasks and work products. One standard profile may be the result of merging elements defined in different base standards: for example, the Basic standard profile – the only one defined at the moment of writing this paper -, is built with process elements taken from ISO 12207:2008 [10] and work products defined in ISO 15289:2008 [11]. The creation of profiles must follow a set of rules that are also defined in one of the normative parts of ISO/IEC 29110: ISO/IEC 29110-2:2011 "Framework and Taxonomy". Profiles are put together within groups. Up to this moment just one profile group has been released: the Generic Profile Group defined in the normative part

ISO/IEC 29110-4-1 [12]. It is aimed at VSEs that develop or maintain non-critical software, regardless the application domain. The definition of an additional profile group for system engineering activities is in progress with the collaboration of INCOSE [15].

The definition of profiles is completed with other non- normative parts known as management and engineering guides. Two guides have been published for the profiles in the Generic group corresponding to the Entry level (ISO/IEC TR 29110-5-1-1) and the Basic level (ISO/IEC TR 29110-5-1-2 [13]), being the latter the only one that is certifiable. The elaboration of a guide for an intermediate level containing additional processes is in course. These guides are aimed to organizations interested in implementing the standard, and they provide the specific activities, tasks and work products that should be enacted when developing a software project.

The selection of ISO/IEC 29110 for conducting this research is due to several reasons. Firstly, the rationale behind the standard supports a modular architecture that combines elements from existing standards. This feature is necessary to leverage software development processes with innovation management practices. Secondly, the adoption of innovation management by SMEs deals with a problem similar to the one they faced when adopting software process models: existing innovation management frameworks are too complex for this type of companies.

4 The Innovation Referential

The selection of a reference model for identifying innovation management activities suited to SMEs is more complex. In this case, there is no international standard similar to ISO/IEC 29110 for innovation practices. Existing innovation management models present some difficulties and limitations for this type of companies. Models like Innospace®, an excellent tool for assessing innovation capabilities, do not provide a detailed activity model to support SMEs in the identification and sequencing of activities and work products. Other models proposed in the literature are targeted to large companies or networks with the capability of deploying complex innovation programs with a strategic, long-term view [7, 18]. In the case of VSEs, a more restrictive view needs to be applied, due to their resource constraints and short-term strategies: innovation management needs to be tightly integrated and coupled with the work completed as part of projects' execution. As stated in ISO/IEC 29110, VSEs focus on the successful completion of projects to ensure their continuity in the market. Similarly, innovation efforts need to be incorporated as part of the work completed in the context of projects.

This rationale guided the selection of the second component of the referential model toward the national standard UNE 166001:2006 "R&D&I management: Requirements for R&D&I projects". This standard developed by the Spanish standardization body – AENOR -, establishes requirements for the management of R&D projects. It is part of a family of standards grouped under the name UNE 16600X. The 16600X family includes parts focused on different aspects of innovation, like the requirements for a corporate R&D system, market intelligence and technology monitoring activities, innovation capability assessments, etc. The objective of this set of standards include: (a) establishing a framework to demonstrate to third parties the managed execution of R&D,

(b) improve the visibility of the investments on R&D made by companies and (c) communicate the outcomes and results. These objectives respond to the need of providing guarantees to decision-making agencies that evaluate opportunities and manage funding. The standard provides agencies and innovation agents with a framework for assessing the actual capabilities of companies and research groups involved on innovation. This is another similarity between UNE 166001 and ISO/IEC 29110, as both models serve as tools to demonstrate capability to third parties. There is another similarity between UNE 166001 and ISO/IEC 29110: the adoption of UNE 166001 is considered as a first step toward the adoption of more complex requirements stated in other standards of the 16600X family (those related to the R&D system characteristics). In a similar way, the adoption of ISO/IEC 29110 is considered as an entry point to the latter adoption of more complex standards like ISO/IEC 12207.

5 Model Analysis and Merging

This section describes the mapping and merging between the elements defined in ISO/IEC 29110 Basic profile for SW development, and the innovation management activities defined in UNE 166001. The ISO/IEC 29110 Basic profile establishes two mandatory processes: (a) Project management (PM) and (b) Software implementation (SI). For each process, the standard establishes their definitions, objectives, outcomes, activities, tasks, roles and work products, all of them traced to those defined in the base standards. The importance given to the Project management process is due to the fact that most VSEs need to focus on the successful completion of projects on time and budget.

The focus on project management is also a major feature of UNE 166001. This standard establishes a set of requirements for the systematic management and execution of R&D and innovation projects whose main characteristic is the fact that the final results may differ substantially from those initially stated. Section 4 of the standard establishes the requirements for managing R&D projects. A detailed comparison – completed as part of this research - of these requirements with those established by the ISO/IEC 29110 PM process results in no significant gaps. Other management requirements stated in UNE 166001 for the control of documents and records generated during the project life cycle, their identification and archival for at least 3 years may be traced to ISO/IEC 29110 activities for the control of configuration items.

Although project management is at the core of UNE 166001, this standard incorporates additional requirements that need to be incorporated into the VSE working processes. These requirements are described in Sect. 4.3 of the standard, and they refer to the diffusion of the innovation results. In particular, Sect. 4.3 requests an additional work product, the "Project Memorandum" and prescribes their content and structure. Project Memorandum contents include: objectives of the R&D project and the plan to achieve them, impact and opportunities, state of the art regarding the knowledge, products, processes and technologies, proposed scientific and technical advances, planned activities for protecting the results, regulations that affect the project, authorizations, collaboration agreements and licensing model.

The exploitation of results is the core of Sect. 5 of UNE 166001. A second work product – the exploitation plan – is requested. It should contain the planned actions to exploit, protect and disseminate the results, and the elaboration of information explaining the characteristics, applications and expected use of the new product or process. This work product must identify the innovation's potential market and clients, an economic forecasting and the planned participation of the involved companies in the exploitation of results. An analysis of the contribution of the project results on the company mid-term competitiveness is also requested.

The elaboration of these two work products requested by UNE 166001 as part of the project planning and execution, implies the need of incorporating additional tasks as part of the team activities: identify and describe the state of the art, environmental constraints, value added by the proposed innovation, etc. These activities are incorporated into the resulting model based on the ISO/IEC 29110 Basic profile.

But UNE 166001 just offers a partial coverage to the range of base practices needed to ensure the successful deployment of an innovation management program. Strategic aspects like the generation of ideas through creative and innovative thinking, the management and participation on collaboration networks and task to monitor the external environment are not explicitly mentioned in the standard. These points are covered in UNE 166002:2006 [2] that establishes the requirements for a R&D and innovation management system. Similar to other certifiable standards like ISO 9000, ISO 9100 or ISO 14000, UNE 166002 requests the definition of a corporate policy with planned objectives that are regularly reviewed by Management, setting up of a separate R&D unit provisioned with the necessary resources to execute R&D projects, and a designated responsible in charge of managing the system. This approach clearly exceeds the capabilities of most SMEs interested in the systematic planning and management of innovation. But UNE 166002 defines innovation-oriented activities and tools that cover the hole identified in UNE 166001. These activities and tools include, among others:

- Systematic monitoring of the technological landscape to capture, analyze, disseminate and use scientific and technical information,
- Management of alerts on scientific and technical innovations that may result in opportunities or threats to the organization,
- Identification of innovation needs, searching and assessment of external information,
- Capture, analysis and selection of ideas on the evolution of products, services and processes,
- Promotion of creativity to solve problems,
- Internal and external analysis of competitors, skills and competences,
- Identification and assessment of alliances,
- Commercialization of the resulting project.

UNE 166002 includes other requirements that may be difficult to fulfil in the context of VSEs, like those related to procurement, the execution of internal audits or the measurement and assessment of the R&D system.

The combination of the basic set of requirements stated in UNE 166001 with some of the activities defined in UNE 166002 provides an adequate coverage to the innovation management needs of a VSE. It must be considered that VSEs innovation efforts may be supported by innovation management agencies. Candidate activities to be done with external support are the monitoring of the technical environment, the use of external information sources or the search of partners for establishing alliances. The role of these innovation support agencies and the success factors related to their use has been widely discussed in the literature [4, 19]. In this research, these activities have been incorporated into the resulting process model attending to their value to generate innovation, regardless the possibility of outsourcing or making them in cooperation with external agents.

6 Process Model Design and Integration Through SPEM

The synthesis of the software process model defined by ISO/IEC 29110 with the identified subset of innovation activities extracted from UNE 16600X requires a conceptual, sound basis. A metamodel for process definition is needed to ensure the consistency of the resulting model. The SPEM (Software & Systems Process Engineering Meta-Model) modelling framework has been selected to model the integration. SPEM is a MOF-based metamodel and conceptual framework published by the Object Management Group (OMG) that provides process architects with the concepts and notations to represent, exchange, publish and enact different processes. Although it is usually applied for modelling software development activities, SPEM has a general scope and can be applied in a variety of scenarios.

SPEM does not specify a specific set of activities, tasks, roles or work products. It just provides the concepts used for building process definitions and their reusable elements, referred to as "method content". The main sources of method content are companies' experience and industry best practices, standards, and professional and academic literature. SPEM is not linked to a particular life cycle or development methodology, and consist of "the minimal elements needed to define any process and accommodate a large range of development methods and processes of different styles, cultural backgrounds, and levels of formalism, life cycle models and communities." (SPEM, p. 2). SPEM's philosophy roots on the definition of reusable elements. This is also the basis of the Unified Process framework and its RUP (Rational Unified Process) and OpenUP variants. Methods content act as building blocks that may be combined to define the organizational processes. They correspond to tasks definitions, work product definitions, role definitions and categories. Tasks, work products and role definitions are related: roles participate in tasks that generate or consume work products. Categories are used to classify method content items according to different criteria. Sample categories include:

- disciplines, used to group tasks,
- domains and
- work product kinds, both used to group work products,
- role sets and
- tools, to group roles and tools respectively.

Process architects can add custom categories to classify method content following other criteria: maturity levels, criticality, etc.

One of the advantages of using for modelling the integration of ISO/IEC 29110 with the innovation model is the possibility of defining activities, tasks and work products independently. These items can be later combined in process definitions tailored to different life cycles or project needs. This SPEM feature leverages reuse opportunities and avoids the risks derived from early decisions. SPEM supports an additional level of tailoring by breaking down tasks into steps. Steps do not represent a requested sequence or order, but a set of subtasks that may also be combined when enacting a task in a particular context. The selection of the steps that are needed to execute a defined task is part of the SPEM customization capabilities. Additional elements provided by SPEM are guidance items, which provide additional details on how to execute tasks, play a role or create a work product. Checklists, list of concepts, estimates, examples, guidelines, tool mentors, etc., are examples of guidance items.

The rules to combine method content items to create activities and processes are other components of the SPEM metamodel (in SPEM, both activities and processes represent two different levels of aggregation of method content items). Activity diagrams or Gantt breakdown structures are used to do that. The terms "Task use", "Role use" and "Work Product use" refer to the occurrences of task, roles and work product definitions in the definition of activities and processes. Two types of processes are distinguished: delivery processes and capability patterns, being the first one end-to-end process templates, and the latter sub-processes or process fragments that may be assembled to build delivery processes. Capability patterns are useful to group activities that are enacted in different projects and may be reused as a consistent set. SPEM also introduces the concept of phases, iterations and milestones. One of the reasons for adopting SPEM for the modeling of the ISO/IEC 29110 and the UNE 166001 requirements refer to the capability of this language to create reusable components that can be tailored to the context of the different organizations using both commercial and open source tools. SPEM goes beyond a diagramming language and offers wide possibilities for reusing the model templates as Gantt charts and as customized models.

7 Conclusions

SMEs constitute a significant part of the entrepreneurial landscape, and contribute – in a great extent – to the economic outputs of society and to the creation of innovation. Innovation management studies have traditionally focused on large corporations and networks, and the systematic management of innovation has been considered as something unaffordable for VSEs.

The recent publication of ISO/IEC 29110 for system and software development process model is the answer to the needs of SMEs. This standard not only provides companies with clear guidelines to do their process and support improvement programs. It also ensures the capability of demonstrating to third parties the maturity of their engineering and managerial processes. This promising set of standards and guidelines is called to demonstrate the weakness of the perception that promulgates the difficulties of VSEs to follow sound, well-established engineering and project management practices to develop reliable software.

The analysis completed as part of this research discusses the feasibility of a similar approach for the systematic management of innovation. R&D practices and activities must be carefully selected to avoid unaffordable costs for SMEs. In the software development sector, SMEs focus on short term results and their main stream of revenue depends on the completion of projects on time and within budget. These constraints constitute obstacles to the systematic management of R&D efforts understood as long-term initiatives that require complex investment on financial resources or human capital. A model supporting the needs of SMEs must integrate innovation practices in the context of the project management practices. The tailoring or extension of ISO/IEC 29110 with the addition of innovation practices is a promising area, as SMEs can leverage the effort required by the adoption of ISO/IEC 29110 to deploy valuable innovation practices and demonstrate compliance with other R&D standards like UNE 166001 (it is remarked that both ISO/IEC 29110 and UNE 166001 share core requirements for project management).

The integration of these models has been implemented using SPEM as a configuration tailored to the needs of SMEs. Configurations are a SPEM tailoring mechanism that allows the reuse and customization of method content without modifying the definitions of the reused items. The elements of ISO/IEC 29110 have been modeled using SPEM and grouped together in a reusable plug-in, taking as a reference the process description in ISO/IEC 29110-5-1-2. A separate plug-in has been created for the activities, tasks and work products identified in UNE 16600X. Another customization mechanism provided by SPEM, variability, has been applied to extend existing items using different rules: contribute, extends or replace. Innovation management activities have been either integrated within the PM or SI engineering processes, or grouped into a reusable capability pattern that may be enacted in a recurrent way in innovation or R&D projects. Activities related to the generation and assessment of ideas and the preparation of work products like the project memorandum or the exploitation plan have been integrated by extension within the PM and SI processes. On the other hand, activities related to the monitoring and surveillance of technologies and the external environment have been modelled as capability patterns. The process model has been implemented with the support of the SPEM 2.0 Eclipse Process Framework (EPF) open source tool.

The resulting framework extends ISO/IEC 29110 Basic profile with new deliverables, tasks and activities taken from UNE 166001. Additional activities are added for innovation-related tasks and work products: (a) identification and assessment of innovation opportunities, environment monitoring and innovation exploitation. Companies adopting this configuration may easily demonstrate the compliance of their projects to the requirements established in these standards. The verification of the model is being conducted as part of an action research project conducted with a SMEs building medical software. This practical work is aimed to validate the feasibility of the proposed model, assess the practical value of the tasks and deliverables incorporated into the process model and identify gaps and activities that should be integrated into the final framework.

References

1. AENOR: UNE 166001:2006. R&D&i management: Requirements for R&D&i projects (2006)
2. AENOR: UNE 166002:2006. R&D&i management: R&D&i management system requirements (2006)
3. AENOR: UNE-CEN/TS 16555-1 EX. Innovation Management. Part 1: Innovation Management System (2013)
4. Arvanitis, S., Sydow, N., Woerter, M.: Is there any impact of university-industry knowledge transfer on innovation and productivity? an empirical analysis based on swiss firm data. Rev. Ind. Organ. **32**, 77–94 (2008)
5. Boucher, Q., Perrouin, G., Deprez, J.-C., Heymans, P.: Towards configurable ISO/IEC 29110-compliant software development processes for very small entities. Commun. Comput. Inform. Sci. **301**, 169–180 (2012)
6. Capaldo, G., Iandoli, L., Raffa, M., Zollo, G.: The evaluation of innovation capabilities in small software firms; a methodological approach. Small Bus. Econ. **21**, 343–354 (2003)
7. Eversheim, W. (ed.): Innovation Management for Technical Products: Systematic and Integrated Product Development and Production Planning, vol. xii, p. 444. Springer, Heidelberg (2009)
8. Gay, B.: Open innovation, networking, and business model dynamics: the two sides. J. Innov. Entrepreneurship **3**(2), 1–20 (2014)
9. Hage, J., Mote, J.E., Jordan, G.B.: Ideas, innovations, and networks: a new policy model based on the evolution of knowledge. Policy Sci. **46**, 199–216 (2013)
10. ISO/IEC 12207 – Systems and Software Engineering – Software Lifecycle Processes (2008)
11. ISO/IEC 15289 – Systems and Software Engineering – Software Life Cycle Process – guidelines for the content of software life cycle process information products (documentation) (2006)
12. Laporte, C.Y., Alexandre, S., O'Connor, R.V.: A software engineering lifecycle standard for very small enterprises. In: O'Connor, R.V., Baddoo, N., Smolander, K., Messnarz, R. (eds.) EuroSPI 2008. CCIS, vol. 16, pp. 129–141. Springer, Heidelberg (2008). doi:10.1007/978-3-540-85936-9_12
13. ISO/IEC TR 29110-5-1-2 Software Engineering – Lifecycle profiles for Very Small Entities (VSEs) – Part 5-1-2: Management and Engineering Guide – Basic VSE Profile
14. Laperche, B., Liu, Z.: SMEs and knowledge-capital formation in innovation networks: a review of literature. J. Innov. Entrepreneurship **2**(21), 1–16 (2013)
15. Laporte, C., O'Connor, R.: Systems and software engineering standards for very small entities: accomplishments and overview. Computer **49**(8), 84–87 (2016)
16. Laporte, C., O'Connor, R., Fanmuy, G.: International systems and software engineering standards for very small entities. CrossTalk **26**(3), 28–33 (2013)
17. O'Connor, R.V., Laporte, C.Y.: Software project management in very small entities with ISO/IEC 29110. In: Winkler, D., O'Connor, R.V., Messnarz, R. (eds.) EuroSPI 2012. CCIS, vol. 301, pp. 330–341. Springer, Heidelberg (2012). doi:10.1007/978-3-642-31199-4_29
18. Pikkarainen, M., et al. (eds.): The Art of Software Innovation, vol. xxi, p. 200. Springer, Heidelberg (2011)
19. Tödtling, F., Kaufmann, A.: SMEs in regional innovation systems and the role of innovation support: the case of upper Austria. J. Technol. Transf. **27**, 15–26 (2002). Author, F.: Article title. Journal **2**(5), 99–110 (2016)

SPI and Process Models

Exploring Software Process Variation Arising from Differences in Situational Context

Paul M. Clarke[1,2(✉)], Rory V. O'Connor[1,2], David Solan[3], Peter Elger[4], Murat Yilmaz[5], Adam Ennis[1], Mark Gerrity[1], Sean McGrath[1], and Ryan Treanor[2]

[1] School of Computing, Dublin City University, Dublin, Ireland
{paul.m.clarke,rory.oconnor}@dcu.ie,
{adam.ennis22,mark.gerrity2,sean.mcgrath43}@mail.dcu.ie
[2] Lero – the Irish Software Research Centre, Limerick, Ireland
ryan.treanor2@mail.dcu.ie
[3] FINEOS Corporation, Dublin, Ireland
David.Solan@fineos.com
[4] nearForm Limited, Tramore, Ireland
elger.peter@gmail.com
[5] Çankaya University, Ankara, Turkey
myilmaz@cankaya.edu.tr

Abstract. The software development process is continuously changing, there is huge pressure to condense release cycles into shorter and shorter timeframes, tools are changing dramatically and companies must continually examine the efficacy of their development process. Attempting to hit a moving target is difficult and it is a decision which can have a major effect in terms of both the end-product and the business. In this paper, we discuss the role of situational context in deciding upon the software development process through the analysis of two case studies. The case studies take a detailed look at the organisational profile and context of each company in turn before we compare and contrast each situational context for factors that may influence the development process. We then compare the processes each company has chosen before our discussion of the role context plays in choosing a 'correct' software development process. While both companies have enjoyed sustained business growth and while both are agile in mindset, we find that they are in fact quite distinct in their processes, this distinction being driven by their different situational contexts.

Keywords: Agile · SAFe · Situational context · Software development process · Software engineering

1 Introduction

An evidence-driven, universal set of guidelines on how to approach the software development process is lacking in the literature. This is, in part, due to the complex nature of software development, the many factors of which may constitute a *complex system* [1]. A software development process can be defined as "a set of activities, methods, practices, and transformations that people use to develop and maintain software and the associated products" [2]. The factors that influence the process can be thought of as the situational context, these factors include the nature of the end-product, volatility of requirements, personnel skill levels, organisational culture and many others. Various software development processes have come to the fore over the years including the Waterfall [3], CMMI [4], Agile methods [5], each with benefits and drawbacks depending on the situational context to which they are applied

In deciding which process to use and how to apply it, organisations must compare differing approaches without a full appreciation of how that approach fits their particular context. Worse still, companies may arbitrarily choose one, which can lead to a sub-optimal process that may be damaging to organisational performance and software quality [6]. We apply work done previously on producing an initial reference framework [7] and use this framework to analyse the many elements of the software development process in two distinct case studies. The first is on FINEOS - an enterprise software development company developing primarily for the insurance industry [8]. The second is nearForm Ltd. - the world's' largest Node.js consultancy firm [9]. We will look for insight into how situational factors affect the performance of their development process and whether lessons can be learned for other companies managing their software development process.

In structuring the case studies, we adopted the following methodology: Firstly, the companies were invited to present on their software development process and also to indicate how their situational context has informed their software process decisions. This presentation typically lasted around 100 min, including extensive opportunity for questions and answers. Secondly, further research was conducted on the participating companies, for example by evaluating their websites and press releases, to build up a well-rounded view of the companies' operating context and reported development process initiatives. Thirdly, the relationship between their respective development process and situational context was examined. In the fourth step, the total learning from both companies was documented and shared with both organisations offered an opportunity for feedback and clarification. The results of this fourth step are consolidated in this paper.

Among the primary findings we conclude that they software development process in the participating companies is a mishmash of the various generic software development approaches. We also find that situational context played a vital role in informing software development process selection and evolution in the participating companies. It is tempting to reach the conclusion that this is representative of the broader software development sphere but we have not collected the broader industrial data that would be required to enable an evaluation of that perspective.

This paper is structured as follows: Sect. 2 describes in some detail the situational context of the software development process in one company. Section 3 provides equivalent detail but for the second case study organisation. Section 4 will compare and contrast the two situational contexts with a view of finding similarities and points of divergence. Section 5 will compare both software development processes again looking for pertinent similarities and differences. Section 6 contains a discussion and conclusion.

2 Case Study 1 - FINEOS

The first company we will consider is FINEOS; a software development company that delivers enterprise solutions for the insurance industry. The company was founded in 1993 by Michael Kelly, the current CEO, and has since grown to 500 employees and approximately 26,000 software users across multiple countries. Their HQ is in Dublin, Ireland, and they have offices in the US, Poland and Australia. Although they are based in Dublin, they estimate that as much as 50% of their customers are based in the United States. All accident claims in New Zealand, four of the top five insurers in Australia and eight of the top twenty health insurers in America use FINEOS software when processing claims.

The primary specialism of FINEOS is in insurance claims and payment management. Recently, they have moved into offering a full administration suite of components that will cover all aspects of insurance; claims, policy and billing. From this, their software manages six million claim cases annually, involving up to $7 billion.

In the early days of FINEOS, they evolved a plan-driven culture, which was highly organised and structured (and consistent with best practice at that time). Changing customer demands have led FINEOS to implement an Agile culture and environment for their employees and to service their customers. They have incorporated Agile principles (people, process and engineering) for many years, with their first purposeful implementation of agile begin applied to a UX refresh of their system (and implemented in Scrum). FINEOS continues to incorporate the Scrum methodology as one of their core process initiatives. This involves setting up project teams, usually consisting of 7–9 people. They work in iterative sprints, developing elements of the overall system within each sprint cycle. These cycles generally consist of five two-week sprints, with a system release to the customer at the end of the ten weeks. They also include a parallel planning process as part of entering each cycle in line with the need to change requirements. Other elements of the methodology that FINEOS has assimilated into their process are; daily stand-ups, sprint burndowns, Product Owners and Scrum Masters [10]. FINEOS implement Inspect and Adapt sessions regularly to learn from their experiences and implement changes which improve the overall flow of work and deliverables.

In recent years, they have been using the Scaled Agile Framework (SAFe). The SAFe uses a combination of various Lean and Agile concepts, and deals with three levels of an organisation; team, program and portfolio [11]. FINEOS do not implement all elements of the SAFe framework, but only those they deem beneficial for their business. They tend to merge elements of the framework together, for example, integrating multiple roles and assigning them to one person. Their release cycle has shrunk from every four months to at most ten weeks since implementing an Agile approach and as a result a substantial increase of automation has also been seen in the company. They now include a full suite of code checks, with build, test, and delivery automation running several times a day. In terms of personnel skill FINEOS believe in having 'T-shaped' people. This identifies people with an in-depth knowledge of one discipline, and a broad knowledge of other related areas of expertise, which are generally technology orientated in the case of FINEOS [12].

A key factor of their situational context is insurance industry attitudes to data accuracy and security. FINEOS offers the possibility for clients to utilise their cloud-based service. However, this can be a point of contention for customers as traditionally, some in the insurance industry have stored their data in on-site data centres. This is because they may not always trust cloud providers to store their data securely even though there is evidence showing there is adequate security in the cloud [13]. Incidents such as data breaches can greatly damage an insurer's reputation and undermine the public's confidence in the industry [14]. Plus, the integrity of insurance data, including records and calculations, has perhaps inclined insurance software providers to continue in their adoption of traditional methods such as Waterfall [15] which invest heavily in requirements clarification up front. Providing certain conditions are met, such as outlining performance requirements and testing protocols early, Agile methods are proving that they too can offer the type of certainty that traditional methods have proven to delivery [16]. FINEOS focuses on developing a flexible and configurable, modern suite of applications. This contrasts with the fact that some insurance companies that FINEOS engage with are found to be working with legacy systems [17]. Legacy systems are prominent in the insurance industry for a number of reasons, such as the risk associated with replacing the systems, and more commonly the inability to justify the cost of replacing a core system rather than maintaining it [18]. With this in mind, FINEOS has solutions to both replace existing software and to support existing technology [19].

3   Case Study 2 – nearForm Ltd.

The second company we will consider is nearForm Ltd., the World's first Node.js consultancy company. They have grown rapidly from employing 4 people to over 100 people in the last 5 years with revenue growing exponentially. The company was established in 2011 with the vision to change how software is built. Their headquarters is in Tramore, Co. Waterford, Ireland, with staff in the United States, South Africa, France and Romania. nearForm has delivered over 50 large-scale production systems for clients in Ireland, UK and the United States, clients include Intel, The Sunday Business Post and SAP [20]. They offer large enterprises the opportunity to embrace recent disruptive technologies to refactor their monolithic system architecture into a microservices architecture. This allows an Enterprise to change their approach to certain processes and accelerate their development with new tools.

When working on projects with large enterprises, nearForm don't religiously follow certain software development methodologies like Scrum. For example, they don't have the standard role of a Scrum Master, they have an Executive Architect. The difference being - like every member of the workplace - an Executive Architect is directly contributing to code within nearForm, while also adopting roles that may be emulated by a Scrum Master. Rapid and continuous delivery has become a key factor in the modern software development process. nearForm avoid strict Scrum methodology adoption as it might restrict their approach to dealing with clients and, preferring to choose a set of practices depending on the situational context of the client [21].

Given several production releases per day; uncertainty or resource mismanagement must be mitigated as much as possible. They need to be adaptable and be able to apply a modified software development process to any client they work with, they do this by considering factors such as personnel, organisation, business, management, operational, technical, requirements and application. Beginning with Personnel, nearForm boasts an impressive staff turnover of low single digit numbers annually while keeping team sizes across all projects to about 5 or 6. This means there is less need for documented process descriptions or product architecture. The presence of an Executive Architect instead of a conventional project manager allows their workforce to be more adaptable to change, by increasing the level of communication within the team. Cohesion is helped having all employees write code and get experience on all aspects of a project. This gives their teams the ability to work well with undefined elements and objectives they encounter from their clients. Elger believes that the best developers may be up to 30 times more productive than the average developers [21]. Because of this, skill, experience and productivity are aspects which benefit nearForm throughout their development process.

When looking at changeability, it is important that their process is flexible and adaptable as projects are often subject to drastic changes. For this reason, nearForm tend to apply Lean/Agile characteristics to their development process. Product quality is a key focus in the company. As quick delivery is crucial to be successful Time to Market is a factor taken into account when deciding on a delivery process and the tools they use. Deployment infrastructure like Docker has facilitated nearForm in being as efficient as possible when it comes to deployment.

The degree of risk is a big factor, they categorise projects by the strength of risk of data being leaked and in turn, its impact, and while they are not averse to risk, they must be conservative when it comes to delivery for a client, which has led to a strange dichotomy in the firm. For this reason, they tend to use tools and frameworks with a proven track record. Another interesting method used by nearForm is that of breaking conventional sprint constraints; the team will abandon a sprint, fix an urgent issue or scrap a feature bundle so as to adapt to new changes in their understanding or requirements. This may be unusual among generic software development processes found across a lot of firms. nearForm also avoids big bang integration by continually integrating new software. This helps to increase the efficiency of the entire development process.

Typically, nearForm commence a project with a *concept* sprint involving the client and all team members. Then an ideation stage which consists of workshops and scope meetings where developers from nearForm and the Product Owner meet to identify the features required. During this stage nearForm maintain that the responsibility of the project is to be shared to ensure the client's interest in what is going to be deployed and to build knowledge of the product from the client-side. The team work from a technical backlog with regular assessments to ensure the schedule. Open-source tooling allows the organisation to rapidly deliver high quality deployments. This organisation's process has a strong focus on the implementation of disruptive technologies in using a dynamic language like Node.js and also the Docker container engine that enables continuous deployment of an individual microservice solitarily, without disturbing the architecture as a whole.

4 Compare and Contrast of Situational Contexts

Personnel: As mentioned, FINEOS puts an emphasis on the importance of having T-shaped employees in their company. With employees that are knowledgeable in a given discipline, they are easily able to assign appropriate roles from the Scaled Agile Framework. When organising teams, they implement the Scrum methodology with team size 7–9 members, which are multi-functional, and are mostly co-located with the array of offices they have worldwide. Each of the team members knows exactly what the goal of the team deliverable is and they balance work activities across team members to ensure delivery. nearForm, in contrast, do not use the Scrum approach [21]. This can be partially attributed to nearForm's commitment to their open-source software (OSS) community engagement model [22]. When employing new staff, nearForm use this OSS model to recruit rather than other conventional methods like a recruitment agency. This approach ensures they only hire staff with an active interest in the wider scene and who code at the level expected of nearForm employees.

Organisation: With 500 employees FINEOS is a medium-sized organisation, it is multi-national with offices spanning worldwide. Different offices are oriented around separate fields. As previously mentioned, the location of their offices has an effect on the teams, as some but not all are co-located. The organisational size of nearForm is much smaller at just 100 employees but this figure could be a reflection of the organisations age. Their HQ is located in Waterford, Ireland but like FINEOS, are international in scope. Low organisational size can lead to efficient communication in Agile methodology methods through frequent virtual stand-up meetings and a reduction in any communication breakdown between hierarchical personnel with a lessened organisational size [23].

Business: The time to market for the applications that FINEOS develops is important. They are mainly influenced by constraining factors; the expectation of their sales force to output a quality product as quickly as possible and the expectation from their clients to have a high quality and secure system when the project is finished. Their current procedure, which consists of a major system release at approximately ten-week intervals, is what they deem most appropriate with the given constraints (though they continue to aggressively reduce release timeframes). Timescales are even more constrained at nearForm. They use Node.js, their deployment infrastructure uses the Docker container platform and their microservices architecture all assist in the implementation of rapid delivery for an even shorter time to market. nearForm operate in weekly sprints where at the end of each sprint, the team consults with the customer to confirm that the project is moving in the correct direction. Frequent deliveries help gain customer satisfaction, brand loyalty and critically, sales revenue.

Management: Over the course of 20 years FINEOS has been able to work with large international customers and boast high customer satisfaction [19]. The global customer presence that FINEOS has built in an industry like insurance will progress their business continuity as new customers will demand reliability. nearForm on the other hand have built their reputation via the Node.js and OSS community, so there is an underlying philosophy among the personnel on emerging technologies. This helps the organisation progress in unison without conflict on strategic decisions. This deep involvement in the Node.js community is a large factor in their continuity as one of the leading organisations in their field.

Operational: FINEOS has implemented an Agile methodology due to customer and internal demand; customers began to request the ability to adapt requirements more frequently and receive more frequent deliveries of software, thus avoiding the extended time delays that are sometimes associated with traditional software process approaches. nearForm have gone further in that they have no formal process but rather a set of practices (team, distributed workforce, Key Performance Indicators [KPIs]) that are varied from project to project. However, they also operate in a fast-moving market where clients' demands can change throughout the project lifecycle. Flexible process design in nearForm allows rapid changes to be made on projects based on the changing project context.

Technical: FINEOS uses a modern technology stack consisting of leading languages such as Java, HTML5 and JQuery. The tools they use in development consist of the most popular tools used in the industry [19]. Many are open source, e.g. Selenium and Tomcat. FINEOS promote technology learning and adoption via innovation days as part of their culture where teams try out new technologies which can often be adopted into their mainstream. nearForm are also using a very modern technology stack. Every year near-Form host NodeConf EU - a key Node.js event in Europe - providing a forum for the Node.js community. Despite the embedded appreciation for this dynamic technology, there is no dogmatic reason for its use, alternative technologies may accomplish the client's needs depending on context.

Requirements: Since the implementation of Agile methodology, FINEOS has supported the ability to change requirements throughout the development process. This is a factor in why they provide a highly customisable solution for their customers. It is also a reason for the focus on shortening their iterations length as it gives clients a clear picture of the work in progress allowing them to identify any changes they might want to make [24]. nearForm take a slightly different approach; during the ideation stage, client-side Project Owners are incorporated in the workshops that take place to ensure that the client shares the project responsibility for requirements. Clients might seem to demand the 'moon on a stick' and as all the personnel of nearForm are actively involved in code, there is a consistent understanding scoping and cost implications.

Application: The applications developed by both companies are not safety critical applications, i.e. there will not be a loss of life directly attributed to their software. Both companies risk repercussions from reputational damage from data loss. This pressure is arguably higher for FINEOS as the expectations for data integrity and security are very high in the insurance industry, as is product performance, scalability and reliability. There is also pressure on software quality at nearForm, with a need to prove quality to risk averse clients. They use Continuous Delivery systems, drip-fed changes to production and the breakdown of Docker containers to help achieve this high product quality. A further key aspect of *application* relates to the nature of the software being product-based or project-based. In FINEOS, the same product (or variations on the same product) is delivered to most customers, with the necessary demand therefore for product-level consistency and the need for an upgrade path being very high. Building software products which are upgradeable and considers the cost of maintenance and total ownership is necessarily characterised differently to once off project based development. This requires that the process is reliable to the extent that the software product will work in a broad range of settings, across a number of different revisions and patch levels, and for a wide number of diverse users. Whereas in nearForm, much of the development is of a consulting, project-based nature which does not incur the same type of product-level reliability demand.

5 Software Development Process Comparisons and Contrasts

In FINEOS the software development process is heavily oriented around the Scaled Agile Framework. They only incorporate elements of the frameworks that they deem necessary. This process is in the form of five two-week iterations with a system release at the end of the ten weeks… Similar to FINEOS, nearForm don't follow any strict framework, but instead take elements of multiple approaches and adapt them to best suit their client's needs, mostly focusing on Agile and Lean principles. Their process tends to differ more from project to project, as they work across multiple industries whereas FINEOS work strictly with insurance.

Since FINEOS' move to Agile there has been a growing focus on the importance of automation using open source tools such as Selenium, Junit and Jenkins. With iterations becoming shorter, the level of automation has increased. As with FINEOS, nearForm believe in regular and automated testing, while aiming to reduce Big Bang testing. Regression testing is something FINEOS emphasise, as clients will not tolerate receiving software updates that have lost functionality in other areas. Regression testing is also carried out meticulously at nearForm - as they introduce a microservices architecture for a client, they must ensure that all previous functionalities are working.

In FINEOS, cycles generally consist of five two-week sprints with a system release after ten weeks. Iteration lengths are shorter in nearForm, generally being one week in length. The reason for this is it limits the amount the team can go off-track while working on a project. At the end of each week, nearForm consult with the clients and receive feedback. One major difference is - FINEOS typically never break an iteration due to arising issues but nearForm will break sprints, make changes and begin another sprint if something changes in the meantime. FINEOS are perhaps more likely to definitively and explicitly define requirements prior to coding for some aspects which require high degrees of accuracy e.g. payment calculations. The FINEOS requirements may simply be more *definable* up front, not benefiting so much from elevated levels of experimentations through successive rapid sprints.

FINEOS only use the elements of SAFe that they deem relevant, nearForm are even more flexible in terms of following frameworks; they loosely interpret Agile and Lean methodologies. Both companies will often change depending on the client. A key difference between the two companies is that FINEOS tend to assign industry standard roles to their employees that correspond to the roles outlined in the SAFe/SCRUM. They only implement roles they deem necessary, and may appoint multiple roles from the SAFe to a single employee. For instance, FINEOS makes use of Scrum Masters, whereas nearForm don't use Scrum Masters, but instead have Executive Architects.

In terms of teams, at FINEOS they generally consist of about 7-9 people. Team size remains approximately constant in nearForm, where teams consist of about 5 or 6 people. However, there are differences with team structures. In FINEOS, the roles within the teams are well-understood and the team members know what is expected of them. The members of the team often have very different roles and FINEOS is evolving towards T shaped people where individuals play different roles as required within the scrum. For example, there will be a Scrum Master and not every team member will be expected to write production code, some will write test code and aspire to production code. This differs from nearForm, where teams are not as structured, every member of the team contributes to the code written. Members' roles may change across a project as they contribute to different parts of the code. Teams in nearForm are separated by different projects as opposed to different roles like in FINEOS. This observation perhaps highlights the key role of product versus project development as a key situational context constraint. Both companies are affected by the triple constraint of time, budget and quality when it comes to their clients' requirements. Given FINEOS' team structure this constraint may be difficult to manage; for example, the sales team may want new features as quickly as possible, but having limited knowledge of coding, they may not understand the time or resources needed for these features to be created. This is less of a problem in nearForm as everyone is actively contributing to the code – a key innovation in nearForm but perhaps not commonplace across the industry as the skills involved in selling might be considered very different to those required for software development itself.

Both companies differ slightly in regards to the impact of risk on their processes. With FINEOS, they are dealing only with insurance companies, which means it is crucial that any processes are regimented and always held to the same standard. As nearForm work with clients in different industries, they must assess each project individually in terms of risk. The result of this assessment can drastically alter their process from one project to another. To do this, they categorise projects by colour and alter their process where necessary. For instance, if a project is categorised as 'purple' it is deemed to be a high-risk project and depending on the case, the team may completely change their usual process and opt for a Waterfall-like approach - even if it is at the expense of efficiency, time, or cost. FINEOS do not adopt this freedom in their process, perhaps owing to the product development nature of their business. FINEOS may also have more long term customers on their books, giving rise to a more flow of new feature demands.

Technology and tooling also have a profound impact on the processes used by both organisations. In FINEOS, the tools used are open source, modern and generally widely used within the industry meaning staff remain current and skills are available. They take advantage of the open source community but do not let it restrict their ability to work with clients. Heavy automation and top-end software results in quicker iterations and a faster overall process. However, they do not directly mandate contributions to open source as an element of their job description or hiring process. FINEOS use open source tooling and software, but nearForm are even more committed; through a combination of recruitment via open source platforms, encouraging and sponsoring staff to work on personal projects or actively contributing to various communities. As industries vary from client to client with nearForm, when taking on a new project, they need to make sure they have the right tools at their disposal before beginning. Any software or tools they use must be tried and tested beforehand. This is something they feel very strongly about. nearForm have, on occasion, turned down projects when they were not confident enough in the tooling required. This is how heavily tooling is factored into their process; it can be a deciding factor before looking at anything else.

6 Discussion and Conclusion

In this comparison, we have seen in detail the situational context and software development processes in two companies. Both organisations can be considered to be highly successful, each witnessing strong and sustained business growth in recent years. In our investigations, we have learned that there is a pressure on software release cycles in industry – even shorter cycles are becoming the norm, releases can now be as often as multiple times per day [25]; and while multiple daily releases is not always the practice in nearForm, the operating reality is that automation, tooling and practice have moved to the point where such pace of delivery is possible, though clearly this speed of delivery may come at some cost as the basic long-established principle of balancing time, cost and quality constraints remains very much in effect.

To consider the case of FINEOS, a long term successful development firm, a key aspect of their situational context is the need for reliability and high quality in their software product: yes they are proven long term innovators in their field, but their's is a field that would not suffer absences of quality, especially if long-term client data was to become corrupted or if financial transactions were to be miscalculated or under-/overpaid. And while nearForm also produce software of high quality, their reality is that they can often be developing bespoke solutions, under time-and-materials based contract arrangements, and where their clients expect very frequent deliveries of software as a means to explore their own needs. This critical perspective in a situational context may alone largely determine a *minimum deployment frequency*. Where clients have a fundamental operating need for large volumes of personal and financial data over a long term and where multiple clients work with a common evolving product code base, highly reliable software may be more important than highly frequent releases. Though clearly, FINEOS have demonstrated a firm commitment to lowering delivery cycles and radically so. Perhaps therefore, in the longer term future, businesses such as theirs will move ever closer to rapid delivery times.

This micronising of software projects would previously have been impossible without the latest advances in tooling and automation and has led to benefits, such as; improved performance testing and improved quality measurements [26]. Both companies have had great success but without adhering strictly to any single methodology, Agile or otherwise. In fact, a key factor to their success cited by both has been the ability to pick and choose aspects of various generic frameworks based on situational factors such as industry, customers' demands or even on a per-project basis as in the case of nearForm.

Certainly at this point in time the selection of a software development process seems to be more of an art-form than a science, we have shown in this short paper a large number of differing aspects in situational context between two companies with similar objectives. We believe the situational factors are more important than perhaps some companies give them credit for, some companies may focus on the process itself rather than explicitly on the many factors external to the process that can shape outcomes and ultimately the success of the project. With so many situational factors exercising varying degrees of influence on a richly varied generic software development process landscape, we conclude that the selection and evolution of a software development process must be a challenging and constantly evolving concern for software development companies. This finding is consistent with some of our earlier theoretical and empirical contributions [1, 27, 28]. Even within individual domains of interest, for example safety critical software development, we have found that a significant degree of situational context and process variation may arise [29].

We further suggest that there is an absence of meaningful assistance for companies at the present time – it is simply not possible for companies, especially those fighting for survival, to allocate large amounts of time to research the myriad of software development approaches that continue to present on the broader landscape. And this task of researching the available process alternatives must be frustrated by the fragmented process terminology, where in previous basic research we have found that individual concepts can be branded using many different terms [30, 31]. Yet ironically, an absence of attention to the various available techniques could be damaging to the success of any given firm. For example, those companies who have underappreciated the power of continuous integration might find themselves an in economically untenable position as their competitors raise quality and increase release iterations.

There was evidence in the two case studies that there is an appetite, indeed a basic business requirement, to adapt the software development process. Sometimes this is a wholesale process change as in the case of FINEOS moving from a traditional Waterfall approach to Scrum, and later to incorporate SAFe. Other times it is tweaking a process to suit the needs of individual projects, as was seen in the case of nearForm. This observation is evidence that software development firms are continually changing their development processes, some times in small incremental and highly specific ways, other times in larger steps. This finding is consistent with earlier industry-based studies conducted by the authors [32]. The type of process evolution we have found can be termed *process reflexivity*, and in earlier work we have examined the relationship between this reflexivity and business performance [33], finding a positive association between these two phenomena. Therefore, the findings from the two case studies reported on in this paper are consistent with earlier related findings.

In selecting a software process a company must arbitrarily judge which contextual factors are most important and given the great number of process frameworks and factors at play, trial and error may have been the unfortunate strategy for some companies up until this point. The task of choosing an optimal process is hugely challenging given the vast array of factors and sub-factors [7]. The company must work against a multi-dimensional problem, balancing key aspects like (changing) technology, business pressures, customer expectations and personnel. Adding to the complexity is that perhaps none of these situational factors remain constant, changing and morphing continuously with repercussions for projects and products. It is perhaps then no surprise that these companies have either only selectively followed aspects of SAFe – in the case of FINEOS or have largely constructed their own processes using sporadic elements of Agile – in the case of nearForm.

We would suggest this paper puts forward some strong evidence that there is not likely to be any one-size-fits-all software development process solution for a software company. Furthermore, that the way in which process is chosen and implemented should be done with careful consideration to the most pertinent aspects of the individual situational context, perhaps on a per-project basis. Furthermore, at the present time, it seems that software process enactment is highly individualised to individual settings and that despite the advice of software framework, model and process creators, companies simply chop and change off-the-shelf processes to bring them into closer harmony with their own perceived needs.

Acknowledgement. This work was supported, in part, by Science Foundation Ireland grant 13/RC/2094 to Lero – The Irish Software Research Centre.

References

1. Clarke, P., O'Connor, R.V., Leavy, B.: A complexity theory viewpoint on the software development process and situational context. In: Proceedings of the 2016 International Conference on Software and System Process (ICSSP 2016). IEEE, San Francisco (2016)
2. CMMI Product Team: CMMI for systems engineering/software engineering/integrated product and process development, version 1.02, CMMI-SE/SW/IPPD, v1.02. Carnegie Mellon University, Software Engineering Institute, Pittsburgh, PA (1993)
3. Royce, W.: Managing the development of large software systems: concepts and techniques. In: Western Electric Show and Convention Technical Papers, 25–28 August. IEEE Computer Society, Los Alamitos (1970)
4. CMMI Product Team: CMMI for Development, Version 1.2, Software Engineering Institute, CMU/SEI-2006-TR-008. Pittsburgh, PA (2006)
5. Fowler, M., Highsmith, J.: The Agile Manifesto. Software Development (2001)
6. How would I know how badly we are losing out through sub-optimal software development. David Consulting Group (2015)
7. Clarke, P., O'Connor, R.: The situational factors that affect the software development process: towards a comprehensive reference framework. Inf. Softw. Technol. **54**, 433–447 (2012)
8. Leader in Life: Accident & Health Insurance Software. https://www.fineos.com/
9. Node.js Consulting: Training, Co-Development & Micro Services. http://www.nearForm.com/
10. Blom, M.: Is scrum and XP suitable for CSE development? In: International Conference on Computational Science, ICCS 2010, May 31–June 2, Computational Science, University of Amsterdam, The Netherlands (2010)

11. Vaidya, A.: Does DAD know best, is it better to do LeSS or just be SAFe? Adapting scaling agile practices into the enterprise. In: Thirty-Second Annual Pacific Northwest Software Quality Conference 2014, October 20–22, World Trade Center Portland, Portland, Oregon (2014)
12. Oskam, I.: T-shaped engineers for interdisciplinary innovation: an attractive perspective for young people as well as a must for innovative organisations. In: SEFI 37th Annual Conference, 01 July 2004, Rotterdam, Netherlands (2009)
13. Zhang, X., Du, H., Chen, J., Lin, Y., Zeng, L.: Ensure data security in cloud storage. In: 2011 International Conference on Network Computing and Information Security, May 14–15, Guilin Park Hotel, Guilin, China (2011)
14. Financial Crime Task Force: Issues Paper on Cyber Risk to the Insurance Sector. International Association of Insurance Supervisors (IAIS) (2016)
15. Owen Williams: It's Time for Insurers to Shift from Waterfall to Agile, 21 October 2013. http://iireporter.com/its-time-for-insurers-to-shift-from-waterfall-to-agile/
16. Lindvall, M., Basili, V., et al.: Empirical findings in agile methods. In: Wells, D., Williams, L. (eds.) XP/Agile Universe 2002. LNCS, vol. 2418, pp. 197–207. Springer, Heidelberg (2002). doi:10.1007/3-540-45672-4_19
17. Kumar, R., Fareign, G.D., Cullen, M., Cadavez, J., Prasad, K.: Maximizing the business value from silos: service based transformation with service data models. In: 2011 Annual IEEE India Conference (INDICON), 16–18 December BITS Pilani, Hyderabad Campus, Hyderabad, India (2011)
18. Henry, K.: The modernization problem, part 1: government & management of enterprise IT. ISACA J. **1**, 49–51 (2013)
19. Solan, D.: FINEOS Software Development Presentation, DCU, 23 February 2017
20. O'Brian, C.: Eran Hammer joins Waterford firm nearForm. http://www.irishtimes.com/business/technology/eran-hammer-joins-waterford-firm-nearForm-1.2244425
21. Elger, P.: nearForm Software Development Presentation, DCU, 6 March 2017
22. Hertel, G., Niedner, S., Herrmann, S.: Motivation of software developers in Open Source projects: an Internet-based survey of contributors to the Linux kernel. Res. Pol. **32**(7), 1159–1177 (2003)
23. Colombo, M., Piva, E., Rossi-Lamastra, C.: Open innovation and within-industry diversification in small and medium enterprises: The case of open source software firms. Res. Policy **43**, 891–902 (2014)
24. Paasivaara, M., Lassenius, C.: Could global software development benefit from agile methods? In: IEEE International Conference on Global Software Engineering, p. 109. IEEE, Helsinki (2006)
25. Larman, C., Basili, V.: Iterative and incremental developments. a brief history. Computer **36**, 47–56 (2003)
26. Dustin, E., Rashka, J., Paul, J.: Automated Software Testing: Introduction, Management, and Performance. 1st edn., p. 37. Addison-Wesley Professional, Boston (1999)
27. Clarke, P., O'Connor, R.V.: Changing situational contexts present a constant challenge to software developers. In: O'Connor, R., Umay-Akkaya, M., Kemaneci, K., Yilmaz, M., Poth, A., Messnarz, R. (eds.) Systems, Software and Services Process Improvement (EuroSPI 2015). CCIS, vol. 543, pp. 100–111. Springer, Cham (2015). doi: 10.1007/978-3-319-24647-5_9
28. O'Connor, R.V., Elger, P., Clarke, P.: Exploring the impact of situational context: a case study of a software development process for a microservices architecture. In: Proceedings of the International Conference on Software and Systems Process (ICSSP), Co-Located with the International Conference on Software Engineering (ICSE), pp. 6–10 (2016). doi: 10.1145/2904354.2904368

29. Nevalainen, R., Clarke, P., McCaffery, F., O'Connor, R.V., Varkoi, T.: Situational factors in safety critical software development. In: Kreiner, C., O'Connor, Rory V., Poth, A., Messnarz, R. (eds.) EuroSPI 2016. CCIS, vol. 633, pp. 132–147. Springer, Cham (2016). doi: 10.1007/978-3-319-44817-6_11
30. Clarke, P., et al.: An investigation of software development process terminology. In: Clarke, Paul M., O'Connor, R.V., Rout, T., Dorling, A. (eds.) SPICE 2016. CCIS, vol. 609, pp. 351–361. Springer, Cham (2016). doi:10.1007/978-3-319-38980-6_25
31. Clarke, Paul M., et al.: Refactoring software development process terminology through the use of ontology. In: Kreiner, C., O'Connor, R.V., Poth, A., Messnarz, R. (eds.) EuroSPI 2016. CCIS, vol. 633, pp. 47–57. Springer, Cham (2016). doi:10.1007/978-3-319-44817-6_4
32. Clarke, P., O'Connor, R.V., Yilmaz, M.: A hierarchy of SPI activities for software SMEs: results from ISO/IEC 12207-based SPI assessments. In: Proceedings of the 12th International Conference on Software Process Improvement and Capability dEtermination (SPICE 2012), CCIS 290/2012, pp. 62–74 (2012)
33. O'Connor, R.V., Clarke, P.: Software process reflexivity and business performance: initial results from an empirical study. In: Proceedings of the International Conference on Software and Systems Process 2015 (ICSSP 2015), pp. 142–146. ACM SIG on Software Engineering, Tallinn (2015)

How to Elicit Processes for an ISO-Based Integrated Risk Management Process Reference Model in IT Settings?

Béatrix Barafort[1], Antoni-Lluís Mesquida[2(✉)], and Antònia Mas[2]

[1] Luxembourg Institute of Science and Technology, 5 Avenue des Hauts-Fourneaux, 4362 Esch-sur-Alzette, Luxembourg
beatrix.barafort@list.lu
[2] Department of Mathematics and Computer Science, University of the Balearic Islands, Cra. De Valldemossa, km 7.5, Palma de Mallorca, Spain
{antoni.mesquida,antonia.mas}@uib.es

Abstract. Process performance remains a key challenge in organizations. Improving processes can be guided by Capability Maturity Models resting on processes that can be assessed. Several ISO standards propose process models for Management System Standards, such as ISO 9001, ISO/IEC 20000-1 and ISO/IEC 27001, and project management proposes processes in ISO 21500. The ISO 31000 standard provides guidance for Risk management with a process approach and systemic perspective. This paper presents the approach for eliciting processes based on ISO 31000 as the main thread in a process reference model (PRM). This PRM integrates risk management dimensions with the selected ISO standards: ISO 9001, ISO 21500, ISO/IEC 20000-1 and ISO/IEC 27001.

Keywords: Integrated risk management · IT settings · ISO · Process reference model · Process reference model engineering · Transformation process

1 Introduction

Process performance remains a key challenge in organizations, particularly in the era of digital transformations. More than ever, companies need to rely on their processes, and to improve them. Process improvement can be guided by Capability Maturity Models supported by processes described on a way that enables process assessments. Many process models exist in various fields. The International Standardization Organization (ISO) and various initiatives based on the ISO Process assessment standard series [1] have published several Process Reference Models (PRM) and Process Assessment Models (PAM) in various domains [2–5], enabling a very structured and systematic approach for process assessment and guided process improvement.

Our research works [6] have already investigated risk management activities in IT settings (IT settings meaning any IT department or IT organisation needing to integrate risk management activities) by comparing how risk is tackled in various ISO standards targeting management systems (also named Management System Standards or MSSs) for: quality perspectives in ISO 9001 [7], information security management in ISO/IEC

27001 [8], IT Service management (ITSM) in ISO/IEC 20000-1 [9], and project management in ISO 21500 [10]. This comparison had shown how to pave the way for a centralized and integrated risk management. That provides the basis to improve, coordinate and interoperate risk management activities in IT settings. This integration is particularly enforced by ISO standards which propose approaches that are the results of international consensus and that are requested by the market (i.e. ISO 27001 certification). It is especially true for the ISO 31000 [11] standard for Risk Management which is our Ariadne's thread, completed by the ISO High Level Structure (HLS) [12] for management systems, and an established common vocabulary regarding the main tackled concepts in project management, quality management, ITSM, and information security management. According to the authors experience and gained feedback from various R&D projects with companies in several domains, these topics are the most commonly addressed by many IT organizations, whatever their size and domain.

The objective of this research is to propose means to improve Risk management processes in IT settings, with a structured, integrated, interoperable, assessable, effective and efficient way. Then we intend to propose a PRM and a PAM as artefacts enabling process assessment and improvement. Both artefacts consolidates ISO standards which are already process-oriented (i.e. ISO 31000), but not structured neither organised for rigorous process assessment. So this paper presents how we initiated the development of a PRM for Integrated Risk Management in IT settings, by eliciting processes from the various ISO standards previously mentioned or from other ones derived from them. The approach relies on previous works which enabled to deploy a Transformation Process [13] for designing PRMs and PAMs fulfilling the Process Assessment ISO standard requirements for developing PRMs and PAMs [14]. The ISO/IEC 27005 [15] for Information security risk management is also of great help for dedicated Risk management processes, as well as the ISO 21500 for project management, proposing several processes covering Risk management activities.

The paper firstly presents in Sect. 2 some related works and in Sect. 3, terminology concerning the main concepts of an Integrated Risk Management Process Model in IT settings. Section 4 describes the methodology followed for eliciting the processes, with the proposition of a process map. Section 5 presents discussions before conclusions given in Sect. 6.

2 Related Work

Integrated risk management is a critical cornerstone which has not been addressed specifically from the IT organizations point of view. Integrated risk management addresses risks across a variety of levels in the organisation, including strategy and tactics, and covering both opportunity and threat [16].

Different authors have developed various frameworks and approaches to support Integrated risk management in IT companies. Chittister and Haimes [17] proposed a framework for the assessment and management of risk associated with the software development process. Special attention is given to the role of human resource development and improvement in risk assessment. Lyytinen et al. [18] developed a framework that synthesizes, refines, and extends different approaches to managing software risks. Bandyopadhyay et al. [19] explored the environment of IT in organizations, identified the probable threats and proposed a framework with four major components: risk identification, risk analysis, risk-reducing measures, and risk monitoring. Kontio [20] developed a method, called Riskit that complements existing risk management approaches by supporting qualitative and structured analysis of risks through a graphical modeling formalism. Associated with the method, he also developed a risk management improvement framework that supports continuous, systematic improvement of the risk management process. The ProRisk Management Framework from Roy [21] is intended to account for a number of the key risk management principles required for managing the process of software development. This framework focuses attention on primary project components, i.e. the business domain in which the project is created, and the operational domain when the project is actually carried out. The Risk Management Framework from SEI [22] helps provide a foundation for a comprehensive risk management methodology basis for evaluating and improving a program's risk management practice. It can be used to guide the management of many different types of risk (e.g., acquisition program risk, software development risk, operational risk, information security risk). Moreover, some works [23] have studied the most useful elements from several maturity models in order to facilitate the achievement of higher organizational maturity and capability levels. This approach has been applied to Risk management maturity models with unification of their practices and integrated multiple views; improvements are proposed in the software domain on the Risk management process of the PAM ISO/IEC 15504-5 [24].

In the Capability Maturity Models landscape, engineering has been questioned many times in the literature as some studies had shown some shortcomings in the development of such models [25]. Becker et al. explored various Capability Maturity Models [26] and Pöppelbuß some design principles for useful maturity models [27]. As the Capability Maturity Model was first developed in the Software engineering community and as the Process Assessment have its own ISO standard [1] with requirements for developing PRMs and PAMs [14], several process models have been developed in this field. A Brazilian initiative have developed a Framework for engineering process models in the software domain [28]; an Austrian one has developed methodological support in the same vein [29]. In Luxembourg, several process models for IT and non-IT works have been developed in an R&D initiative encompassing the TIPA Framework [30] with PRMs and PAMs for ITIL and Operational risks [31] to quote two of them.

Many works have considered the integration of management systems in particular from the ISO 9001 perspectives. In IT settings, ISO/IEC 20000-1 and ISO/IEC 27001 remain the flagship standards, as shown in the last ISO survey [32]. From a performance assessment perspective, the help of Capability Maturity Models and assessment approaches have been demonstrated (with the CMMI and ISO/IEC 15504-33000 series of process models) and ISO development works have proposed PRMs and PAM based on MSSs. It is the case for Information security management (ISO/IEC 33072 [33]), for ITSM ISO/IEC 15504-8 [4]) and for quality management based on ISO 9001 (under development at ISO under the project name ISO/IEC 33073 [34]). These three domains are of particular interest as they propose a common set of processes addressing the management system mechanisms from a generic perspective, as stated in the HLS for management systems.

Harmonization plays an important role in organizations that are seeking to resolve manifold needs at their different hierarchical levels through multiple models. A great diversity of models involves a wide heterogeneity not only about structure of their process entities and quality systems, but also with regards to terminology [35]. We have recently had a proliferation of language and term usage in the software development process domain, a problem which has implications for assessors and assessment frameworks, and for the broader community. In order to clarify as much as possible the terms of this research, the next section is analyzing and settling the terms that have been used.

3 ISO Background: Targeted ISO Standards and Terminology

In previous works, the authors explored risk management in IT settings from the angle of selected relevant ISO standards with ISO 31000 as main theme. Table 1 provides the full list with identification numbers and titles of each selected standard.

Table 1. List of selected ISO standards for exploring Risk management

ISO standard number	ISO standard title
ISO 31000:2009	Principles and generic guidelines on risk management
ISO Annex SL: 2015	Proposals for management system standards (in ISO/IEC Directives, Part 1, Consolidated ISO supplement)
ISO 9001:2015	Quality management systems - Requirements
ISO 21500:2012	Guidance on project management
ISO/IEC 20000-1:2011	Information Technology - Service management - Part 1: Service management systems requirements
ISO/IEC 27001:2013	Information Technology - Security techniques - Information security management systems - Requirements

There are key concepts conveyed by these standards. We are paying a particular attention to the ones provided by the ISO 31000 as our main reference, and checking shared used concepts with other standards we target in our works. Therefore, terms and definitions provided by ISO standards are our basis.

To start with, the definition of **Risk** in ISO 31000 states it is the *"effect of uncertainty on objectives"* (an objective being a result to be achieved). In ISO Annex SL, Risk is defined as *"effect of uncertainty"*. ISO 9000 defines Risk as the *"effect of uncertainty on an expected result"*. ISO/IEC 20000-1 and ISO/IEC 27000 [36] have the same definition as ISO 31000. The only definition proposed by ISO 21500 regarding Risk is *"Risk register: record of identified risks"*, including results of analysis and planned responses. We consider the selected standards are aligned for the term Risk.

Related to the terms Risk management, most definitions of ISO 31000 come from ISO Guide 73:2009 [37]. **Risk management** is defined as *"coordinated activities to direct and control an organization with regard to risk"*. The overall Risk management process described in ISO 31000 is part of a **context** (whether internal or external) defined in ISO 31000 as the *"environment in which the organization seeks to achieve its objectives"*. This notion of context is present in management systems such as ISO 9001, ISO/IEC 20000-1 and ISO/IEC 27001, driven by the Annex SL dedicated clause on the *"context of the organization"*. ISO 9000 specifically defines the context of the organization. ISO 21500 proposes a clause on *"project environment"*. We consider the selected standards have a common meaning for the terms Context and Environment, but we favour the term Context which is shared between ISO 31000 and MSSs (Management System Standards).

ISO 31000 dedicates a definition for the terms **Communication and consultation**: *"continual and iterative processes that an organization conducts to provide, share or obtain information and to engage in dialogue with stakeholders regarding the management of risk"*. ISO/IEC 27001 inherited exactly the same definition.

Monitoring: *"continual checking, supervising, critically observing or determining the status in order to identify change from the performance level required or expected"* and **Review**: *"activity undertaken to determine the suitability, adequacy and effectiveness of the subject matter to achieve established objectives"* are both definitions in ISO 31000. Annex SL and ISO 9000 define Monitoring as *"determining the status of a system, a process or an activity"*. ISO 9000 defines Review closely to ISO 31000. ISO/IEC 27000 defines Review as in ISO 31000. We consider the selected standards have a common meaning for the terms Monitoring and Review.

Regarding the overall risk management process, we can also precise key concepts as follows in ISO 31000 and ISO 21500, which propose sub-processes of risk management:

- **Risk assessment:** in ISO 31000, it is defined as the *"overall process of risk identification, risk analysis and risk evaluation"*. It is not defined in ISO 21500.
- **Risk identification:** in ISO 31000, it is defined as the *"process of finding, recognizing and describing risks"*. ISO 21500 states the purpose of Identify risks process is *"to determine potential risk events and their characteristics..."*.
- **Risk analysis:** in ISO 31000, it is defined as the *"process to comprehend the nature of risk and to determine the level of risk"*. It is not defined in ISO 21500.
- **Risk evaluation:** in ISO 31000, it is defined as the *"process of comparing the results of risk analysis with risk criteria to determine whether the risk and/or its magnitude is acceptable or tolerable"*. ISO 21500 states the purpose of Assess risks process is *"to measure and prioritize the risks for further action"*.
- **Risk treatment:** in ISO 31000, it is defined as the *"process to modify risk"*. ISO 21500 states a similar purpose of Treat risks process.

We can see that the terminology is not completely aligned between ISO 31000 and ISO 21500 with differences related to the use of *"assess"*, *"analyse"* and *"evaluate"*, even if the global risk assessment from the ISO 31000 perspective is similar.

From a systemic perspective (as embraced in management systems in general), we can see that the Risk management overall process is part of a global framework.

Then there are general terms related to governance and management. We can quote Mandate and commitment in ISO 31000, Leadership and commitment in Annex SL and MSSs (such as ISO 9001, ISO/IEC 20000-1 and ISO/IEC 27001), and Project Governance and Organization in ISO 21500. These terms are not always defined in these standards, but we admit there are common aspects. We can quote **Stakeholder**, **Policy**, and **Top management**. **Documented information** is also a common concern, even if not defined specifically in ISO 31000, but used and applied for all selected standards. Finally, **Continual improvement** is a concept related to the risk management framework.

In addition to Risk management concepts, Management systems ones play an important part from an integrated risk management perspective. The terms we went through in this section will be used as reference points in the next section of the paper.

4 The IT Settings Integrated Risk Management (IRM) Process Reference Model Development: How to Identify Processes

In order to design and build PRMs and PAMs, the authors have met the requirements of ISO/IEC 33004 [14] for designing PRMs and PAMS, and have used a Transformation Process. This process is a systematic approach, based on goal-oriented requirements engineering techniques. It contains 9 steps described in detail in [13] these steps are the following: 1 - Identify elementary statements in a collection of statements (in [13] we have used "requirements" as a generic term. In the context of the various selected ISO standards, we talk about "statements" and use this term equally); 2 - Organize and structure the statements; 3 - Identify common purposes upon those statements and organize them; 4 - Identify and factorize outcomes from the common purposes and attach them to the related goals; 5 - Group activities together under a practice and attach it to the related outcomes; 6 - Allocate each practice to a specific capability level; 7 - Phrase outcomes and process purpose; 8 - Phrase the Base Practices attached to Outcomes; and 9 - Determine Work Products among the inputs and outputs of the practices.

This Transformation Process has been used several times in the context of the TIPA Framework [30]. We aim at satisfying a set of criteria for the produced PRM and PAM. They will have to satisfy the following characteristics: assessability, interoperability, integration, completeness, adoption and applicability.

In this paper, we focus on the elicitation of processes, meaning the three first steps of the Transformation Process.

Step 1 – Identify elementary statements in a collection of statements
This step consists in identifying all of the statements under the form of a collection of elementary items. The final list was composed of 289 elementary items made up of a subject, a verb and a complement, without coordination, conjunctions, or enumeration. Table 2 shows an example of decomposed elementary requirements.

Table 2. Example of decomposed elementary statements

4.3.2 Extract from ISO 31000	Example of decomposed elementary statements
The risk management policy should clearly state the organization's objectives for, and commitment to, risk management **and** typically addresses the following: - the organization's rationale for managing risk;	The risk management policy should clearly state the organization's objectives for, and commitment to, risk management; The risk management policy should typically addresses the organization's rationale for managing risk;

Then from this list, the "should statements" (main statements) contained in the text of the ISO 31000 standard were easily identified (168 "should statements"). They are the basis for the next steps.

Step 2 – Organize and structure the statements

In this step, the elementary "should statements" were organized and structured under the form of a "mind map" for statement trees. This "mind map" helped to have a graphical view of the elementary items having the same object (or component). The requirements were then gathered around the objects they were relating to in order to build statement trees. A decision was made to distribute in various statement trees the set of statements; this was guided by the affiliation of statements within Clauses. These trees considered the Clauses and Sub-clauses titles, as well as the subject of each elementary item. For instance, elementary items starting with "The risk management policy should…" were grouped under a "Risk Management policy" label. This statement tree structuring was inspired by previous works on the Annex SL for Management Systems Standards, where some groupings were similar, and by mappings performed on the Risk term in the various selected standards. Therefore, related to the statements establishing the overall framework of risk management with objectives and policy, we identified a Statement tree named *Leadership*, which has the following nodes (each node comprising leaves where each leave is an elementary statement): Mandate and commitment, Context, Risk management policy, Accountability, and Risk management integration. The other following statement trees were developed: *Communication and reporting*, *Resources*, *Implementing risk management*, *Risk assessment*, *Risk treatment*, and *Monitoring and review*. Finally, with the integration criteria, the Statement trees developed by the authors for the HLS of management systems were superimposed for relevant similar items, guided by terminology and common meanings. For instance in the Leadership tree, "Mandate and commitment" clause in ISO 31000, represented in a leaf was superimposed with "Leadership and commitment" clause of the HLS.

Step 3 – Identify common purposes upon those statements and organize them

This step is aiming at identifying common purposes and at organizing them in such a way that can result in a proposition for elicited processes of an integrated risk management PRM for IT settings.

A goal tree was built for each pre-identified process which appeared progressively according to some logical grouping of common purposes. Within each goal tree, each low-level objective is linked to an elementary statement of the ISO standard. Moreover, each low-level objective resulting from the HLS is also superimposed, in order to cover the common purposes of all the selected ISO MSSs for an integrated risk management PRM. The six key criteria listed at the beginning of this section were kept in mind, and particularly the integration and adoption ones analysed from the process selection perspective.

Figure 1 shows the goal tree for the *Leadership* process, containing six different objectives.

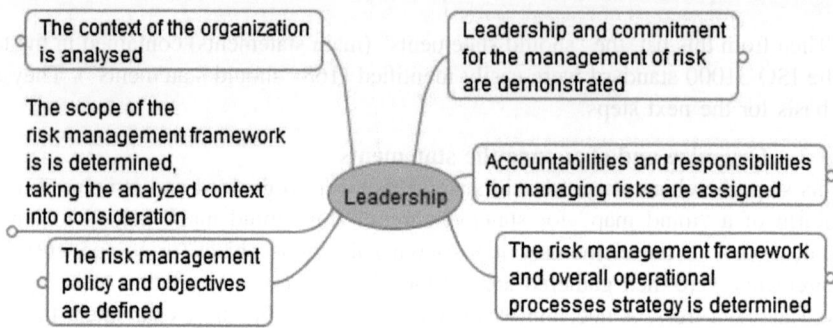

Fig. 1. Goal tree for the Leadership process.

In parallel and in order to help the identification of common purposes and processes, based on Statement trees performed in step 2, supported by the terminological work described in Sect. 3, and by previous works at the ISO for developing PRMs and PAMs based on ISO/IEC 20000-1, ISO/IEC 27001, and currently ISO 9001, a mapping was performed. It was between the sub-clauses of ISO 31000, and the process names of MSSs common processes related to the core processes of a management system. We are assuming here that the framework for risk management of the ISO 31000 shares the concepts of management systems (without seeking for a certification). This mapping also comprised the processes of ISO 21500. The mapping contributed to the identification of common purposes which are formulated into Goal trees (see Fig. 1) and to derive a first list of processes, to be refined (see Table 3 below).

Considering the Risk Management process viewed from ISO 31000 perspective, the *"Risk and opportunity management"* process proposed by PRM and PAM for Management Systems is not satisfactory. Indeed, it does not provide the necessary structure and details that we expect for a dedicated Risk Management PRM and PAM. As shown in our previous works [6], ISO 21500 proposes a subject group dedicated to Risk management, with four processes: Identify risks, Assess risks, Treat risks, and Control risks. These four processes support our idea for having the overall Risk management process split into more detailed ones. In order to strengthen the approach, we selected another ISO standard: the ISO/IEC 27005 Information Security risk management. This standard is fully aligned with ISO 31000 and provides a more detailed view for the Information security domain. A mapping was performed between

Table 3. Mapping between ISO 31000 sub-clauses and common processes of MSSs

ISO 31000 Sub-clauses	ISO/IEC 330xx PRM with common processes for MSS	Proposed processes for IRM PRM
4.2 Mandate and commitment	TOP.1 Leadership	Leadership
4.3.1 Understanding of the organization and its context		
4.3.2 Establishing risk management policy		
4.3.3 Accountability		
4.3.4 Integration into organizational processes	COM.08 Operational planning	Operational planning
4.3.6 Establishing internal communication and reporting mechanisms	COM.01 Communication management	Communication management
4.3.7 Establishing external communication and reporting mechanisms		
Notions of documents	COM.02 Documentation Management	Documentation management
4.3.5 Resources	COM.03 Human resource management	Resource management
4.6 Continual improvement of the framework	COM.04 Improvement	Improvement
No "audit" notion in 31000	COM.05 Internal audit	
5.6 Monitoring and review	COM.06 Management review COM.10 Performance evaluation	Review Monitoring
No "non-conformity" notion in 31000	COM.07 Non-conformity management	
4.4.1 Implementing the framework for managing risk	COM.09 Operational implementation and control	Operational implementation and control
5.4.2 Risk identification	COM.11 Risk and opportunity management	Risk identification
5.4.3 Risk analysis		Risk analysis
5.4.4 Risk evaluation		Risk evaluation
5.5.1 General - Risk Treatment		Risk Treatment
5.5.2 Selection of risk treatment options		
5.5.3 Preparing and implementing risk treatment plans		

the sub-clauses of ISO 31000 and ISO/IEC 27005. It confirmed our view for targeting Risk identification, Risk analysis, Risk evaluation and Risk treatment. Here is an extract of this mapping in Table 4:

Table 4. Mapping of sub-clauses of ISO 31000 and ISO/IEC 27005

ISO 31000	ISO/IEC 27005
5.1 General	
5.2 Communication and consultation	11. Information security risk communication and consultation
5.3.1 General	7. Context establishment
5.4.1 General	**8. Information security risk assessment**
	8.1 General description of information security risk assessment
5.4.2 Risk identification	8.2 Risk identification
	8.2.1 Introduction to risk identification
	8.2.2 Identification of assets
	Annex B Identification and valuation of assets and impact assessment
	8.2.3 Identification of threats
	Annex C Examples of typical threats
	8.2.4 Identification of existing controls
	8.2.5 Identification of vulnerabilities
	Annex D Vulnerabilities and methods for vulnerability assessment
	8.2.6 Identification of consequences
5.4.3 Risk analysis	8.3 Risk analysis
	Annex E Information security risk assessment approaches
	8.3.1 Risk analysis methodologies
	8.3.2 Assessment of consequences
	8.3.3 Assessment of incident likelihood
	8.3.4 Level of risk determination
5.4.4 Risk evaluation	8.4 Risk evaluation
5.5.1 General	**9 Information security risk treatment**
	9.1 General description of risk treatment
5.5.2 Selection of risk treatment options	9.2 Risk modification
	Annex F Constraints for risk modification
	9.3 Risk retention
	9.4 Risk avoidance
	9.5 Risk sharing
	10 Information security risk acceptance

(*continued*)

Table 4. (continued)

ISO 31000	ISO/IEC 27005
5.5.3 Preparing and implementing risk treatment plans	
5.6 Monitoring and review	**12 Information security risk monitoring and review**
	12.1 Monitoring and review of risk factors
	12.2 Risk management monitoring, review and improvement
5.7 Recording the risk management process	

Considering the approach of the Transformation Process for identifying elementary statements, grouping them in Statements trees, identifying common purposes and organizing them in Goal trees, completed by some mappings of clauses and sub-clauses of ISO 31000 with various ISO standards, the following list of processes is proposed in Fig. 2 for an IRM Process Model in IT settings.

TOP MANAGEMENT Process		
TOP.1 Leadership		

COMMON Processes		RISK MANAGEMENT Processes
COM.01 Communication management	COM.06 Review	RIS.01 Risk identification
COM.02 Documentation management	COM.07 Non-conformity management	RIS.02 Risk analysis
COM.03 Resource management	COM.08 Operational planning	RIS.03 Risk evaluation
COM.04 Improvement	COM.09 Operational implementation and control	RIS.04 Risk treatment
COM.05 Internal audit	COM.10 Monitoring	

Fig. 2. IRM PRM proposed list of processes

5 Discussions

In this paper, the integration aspect is paramount. This is the reason why the integration based on terminology and structuring is essential. As ISO standards are developed on the basis of international consensus, the terminology equipping these standards is proven and recognized. On top of that, ISO has performed a dedicated effort for harmonizing Management System Standards by imposing a common structure for all of them, with compulsory clauses and requirements. Even if our main line is driven by ISO 31000 which is not identified "directly" as a management system (defined in Annex SL as a "*set of interrelated or interacting elements of an organization to establish policies and objectives and processes to achieve those objectives*"), it is admitted that the risk management framework advocated by ISO 31000 ("*set of components that provide the foundations and organizational arrangements for designing, implementing, monitoring, reviewing and continually improving risk management throughout the organization*") is similar to a management system as defined in Annex SL (see above). The various mappings performed by the authors confirmed this. On the other hand, ISO 31000 being a guideline standard and not a requirements one, some identified processes labelled as "common processes" are not existing in ISO 31000 (no statements related to *Audit* neither *Non-conformity management*: their name is in italics in the process map). The authors chose to let them appear in the process map from an integration perspective with MSSs such as ISO 9001, ISO/IEC 27001 and ISO/IEC 20000-1.

From assessability and adoption perspectives, it is necessary to keep an adapted number of processes for a pragmatic and operational implementation in organizations. The process name has also to be clearly identified and understood by practitioners. The authors have made assumptions based on the current terminology of ISO 31000. For instance, the Review concept has been associated with Management; this is coming from MSSs; it is the same logic for Performance evaluation, close to Monitoring.

When developing a process reference model, as stated in ISO/IEC 33004: "*process descriptions shall not contain or imply aspects of the process quality characteristics beyond the basic level of any relevant process measurement framework conformant with ISO/IEC 33003*". The fact to deal with documentation and planning aspects could be linked to Capability Level 2. In order to simplify and clarify alignment with statements, a dedicated process for Documentation management and for Operational planning have been identified. Documentation management was not identified as such in ISO 31000. But the authors decided to propose a dedicated process and to adopt the same documentation management mechanisms as the ones of this process in MSS PRM and PAM.

The IT settings specificities are not particularly visible in the elicitation of processes at the PRM level. A particular attention will have to be paid on these aspects in PAM development criteria.

Finally, the risk management dedicated processes of the PRM are finding most of their inputs in ISO 31000, and ISO 21500, and ISO/IEC 27005 as complement. With the IT settings mindset, specific concerns related to risk management remain connected with service management and information security respectively for ISO/IEC 20000-1 and ISO/IEC 27001.

6 Conclusion and Next Steps

This paper describes the elicitation of processes for the construction of an IRM process model for IT settings. For doing so, a Transformation Process has been applied, complemented by some mappings with supporting ISO standards. The resulting process model is covering the processes identified from ISO 31000, with common ones in MSS and in ISO 21500 because management system mechanisms are present in all of them, even if all standards are not enabling certification. In addition, more specialised processes have been identified for the dedicated Risk management activities.

Because we consider that risk management organizational capabilities in companies with IT settings can be strengthened by IRM processes based on selected ISO standards, a PRM and a PAM are aiming at equipping organization for process assessment and improvement. The selected ISO standards were voluntarily empirically kept limited to the most significant ones in IT settings (i.e. ISO 31000, ISO 9001, ISO 21500, ISO/IEC 20000-1, and ISO/IEC 27001). This paper describes the first steps towards a full PRM and PAM with a first proposition of elicited processes. More iterations to refine this process list will have to be performed, as well as experts' validation. The continuation of the Transformation Process with steps 4 to 9 will also enable some refinements. Some field's experimentations will contribute to the artefacts validation. Situational factors may also be investigated in order to check the best way to apply this generic and integrated Risk management process reference model in IT settings.

Acknowledgements. This work has been supported by the Spanish Ministry of Science and Technology with ERDF funds under grants TIN2016-76956-C3-3-R and TIN2013-46928-C3-2-R.

References

1. ISO/IEC 33001: Information Technology - Process assessment – Concepts and terminology. International Organization for Standardization, Geneva (2015)
2. Automotive Spice. http://www.automotivespice.com/fileadmin/software-download/Automotive_SPICE_PAM_30.pdf
3. TIPA for ITIL. https://www.list.lu/fileadmin//files/projects/TIPA_T10_ITIL_PAM_r2_v4.1.pdf
4. ISO/IEC 15504-8: Information Technology – Process assessment – An exemplar process assessment model for IT service management. International Organization for Standardization, Geneva (2012)
5. MDevSPICE. http://www.mdevspice.com/
6. Barafort, B., Mesquida, A.L., Mas, A.: Integrating risk management in IT settings from ISO standards and management systems perspectives. Comput. Stand. Interfaces (2016)
7. ISO 9001: Quality management systems – Requirements. International Organization for Standardization, Geneva (2015)
8. ISO/IEC 27001: Information technology – Security techniques – Information security management systems – Requirements. International Organization for Standardization, Geneva (2013)
9. ISO/IEC 20000-1: Information Technology – Service management – Part 1: Service management system requirements. International Organization for Standardization, Geneva (2011)
10. ISO/IEC ISO 21500: Guidance on project management. International Organization for Standardization, Geneva (2012)
11. ISO 31000: Risk management – Principles and guidelines. International Organization for Standardization, Geneva (2009)
12. ISO/IEC Directives, Part1, Annex SL. International Organization for Standardization, Geneva (2014)

13. Barafort, B., Renault, A., Picard, M., Cortina, S.: A transformation process for building PRMs and PAMs based on a collection of requirements – example with ISO/IEC 20000. In: 8th International SPICE 2008 Conference, Nuremberg (2008)
14. ISO/IEC 33004: Information Technology – Process assessment – Requirements for process reference, process assessment and maturity models. International Organization for Standardization, Geneva (2015)
15. ISO/IEC 27005: Information technology – Security techniques – Information security risk management – Requirements. International Organization for Standardization, Geneva (2011)
16. Hillson, D.: Integrated risk management as a framework for organisational success. In: Proceedings of the PMI Global Congress 2006 North America, presented in Seattle WA, USA, 23 October 2006
17. Chittister, C., Haimes, Y.Y.: Risk associated with software development: a holistic framework for assessment and management. IEEE Trans. Syst. Man Cybern. **23**(3), 710–723 (1993)
18. Lyytinen, K., Mathiassen, L., Ropponen, J.: A framework for software risk management. J. Inf. Technol. **11**(4), 275–285 (1996)
19. Bandyopadhyay, K., Mykytyn, P.P., Mykytyn, K.: A framework for integrated risk management in information technology. Manag. Dec. **37**(5), 437–445 (1999)
20. Kontio, J.: Software Engineering Risk Management: A Method, Improvement Framework, and Empirical Evaluation. Doctoral dissertation (2001)
21. Roy, G.G.: A risk management framework for software engineering practice. In: Proceedings of the 2004 Australian Software Engineering Conference, pp. 60–67 (2004)
22. Alberts, C.J., Dorofee, A.J.: Risk Management Framework, SEI. Technical report. CMU/SEI-2010-TR-017. ESC-TR-2010-017, August 2010
23. Buglione, L., Abran, A., von Wangenheim, C.G., McCaffery, F., Hauck, J.C.R.: Risk management: achieving higher maturity & capability levels through the LEGO approach. In: 2016 Joint Conference of the International Workshop on Software Measurement and the International Conference on Software Process and Product Measurement (IWSM-MENSURA), pp. 131–138. IEEE, October 2016
24. ISO/IEC 15504-5. Information Technology – Process assessment – An exemplar software life cycle process assessment model. International Organization for Standardization, Geneva (2012)
25. de Bruin, T., Rosemann, M., Freeze, R., Kulkarni, U.: Understanding the main phases of developing a maturity assessment model. In: 16th Australasian Conference on Information Systems (ACIS), Sydney (2005)
26. Becker, J., Knackstedt, R., Pöppelbuß, J.: Developing maturity models for IT management. Bus. Inf. Syst. Eng. **1**(3), 213–222 (2009)
27. Pöppelbuß, J., Röglinger, M.: What makes a useful maturity model? A framework of general design principles for maturity models and its demonstration in business process management. In: ECIS 2011 (2011)
28. von Wangenheim, G., Hauck, J.C.R., Zoucas, A., Salviano, C.F., McCaffery, F., Shull, F.: Creating software process capability/maturity models. IEEE Softw. **27**(4), 92–94 (2010)
29. Stallinger, F., Plösch, R.: Towards methodological support for the engineering of process reference models for product software. In: Mitasiunas, A., Rout, T., O'Connor, R.V., Dorling, A. (eds.) SPICE 2014. CCIS, vol. 477, pp. 24–35. Springer, Cham (2014). doi:10.1007/978-3-319-13036-1_3
30. Renault, A., Barafort, B.: TIPA for ITIL – from genesis to maturity of SPICE applied to ITIL 2011. In: Proceedings of the 21th European System & Software Process Improvement and Innovation Conference 2014, Luxembourg (2014)

31. Di Renzo, B., et al.: Operational risk management in financial institutions: process assessment in concordance with Basel II. Softw. Process Improv. Pract. **12**(4), 321–330 (2007)
32. ISO Survey (2015). http://www.iso.org/iso/iso-survey
33. ISO/IEC 33072: TS Information Technology – Process Assessment – Process capability assessment model for information security management. International Organization for Standardization, Geneva (2016)
34. ISO/IEC 33073: PDTS Information Technology – Process Assessment – Process capability assessment model for quality management. International Organization for Standardization, Geneva (under development)
35. Pardo, C., Pino, F.J., García, F., Piattini, M., Baldassarre, M.T.: An ontology for the harmonization of multiple standards and models. Comput. Stand. Interfaces **34**(1), 48–59 (2012)
36. ISO/IEC 27000: TS Information Technology – Security techniques – Information security management systems – Overview and vocabulary. International Organization for Standardization, Geneva (2016)
37. ISO Guide 73, Risk management – Vocabulary. International Organization for Standardization, Geneva (2009)

SPI and Safety

HMI Requirements Creation, as the Collaboration Work of Human and Machine in the Safety-Critical System

Masao Ito[✉]

NIL Software Corp., Tokyo, Japan
nil@nil.co.jp

Abstract. In the safety-critical system, the Human-Machine Interface (HMI) is tightly coupled with system requirements; the functional requirements and the non-functional requirements. As the human has some limitations in his cognitive work, we cannot generate the HMI from the requirements of the complex system in the simplistic way. In this paper, we propose the HMI abstract model from the provisional system requirements, maintaining the simplicity of HMI. We do not intend to create HMI model from the final system requirements but rather traverse the both sides with keeping the safety property. In order to show our idea clearly, we use several examples in the automobile field.

Keywords: HMI · Requirements · Safety · DESH-G · ISO 26262 · Driver model

1 Introduction

The Human-Machine Interface (HMI) has the important role when we design the embedded system of the automobile. It provides environmental information, and we can know the status of my car and neighbouring objects such as other vehicles, the pedestrian and so on. As is well known, we cannot achieve the safety of the car just improving the reliability of the system's elements. When the fault occurs, the HMI plays important role. For example, it provides the information to avoid the accident or transition to the safe state.

The automobile functional safety standard, ISO 26262 [1] requires the functional safety requirements, and it says, "The warning and degradation concept shall be specified as functional safety requirements." (8.4.2.5). Generally, in HMI design the usability is important to focusing on driving, and the usability is a part of the charm of the car. But in this paper, we concentrate on the safety facet of HMI.

In this paper, we first explain the abstract analysis schema, DESH-G [2] for the vehicle. This model covers essential elements comprising driver, environment, system and goal of her or him. Then we will explain how to construct the abstract model of HMI regarding safety.

The motivation of this research comes from two major features in the recent system in the automobile.

The role of software is becoming more important: The software of automobile becomes vast and complicated. It uses the many sensor information and to making the complex decision to control actuators. So, we'd like to consolidate the interface of software at an abstract level.

Moving boundary: The system substitutes for the task of the user. For example, the cruise control system does the acceleration and deceleration instead of the driver. Here we can see the movement of the boundary between the system and the driver. And we know the internal state of the system through the HMI display. This boundary must be simple and easily understandable for the driver. If it is complicated, the driver might make a mistake and meet the accident.

We think that our idea fits better for the new system. The term "new" means the current Advanced Driving Assistant System (ADAS) system and beyond. In this area, the threats to the safety do not always come from the failure of the element. The various types of device and user-interface will be available. For example, we will think the remote parking assist system [15]. The driver is not in the car and uses the simple small device for parking. Such a device is easily lost or broken when he "drives" the car. This is a new type of driving experience, and we might pass over some crucial hazard or the hazardous situation.

2 Desh-G

We already proposed DESH-G [2] schema (Fig. 1) to calculate the controllability for identifying the ASIL (Automotive Safety Integrity Level). In this paper, we use this schema to create the conceptual model of HMI for the automobile. DESH-G has the five elements;

- Driver (D)
- Environment (E)
- Software (S)
- Hardware (H)
- Goal (G) of the driver

The driver is the operator of the car, and we also include the people who control the car outside of it. The environment is not only nature, but it includes elements like the other vehicles, pedestrians, signals, traffic rules and so on. The embedded system of the car consists of the software and hardware. The goal is the driver's aim, it is relating to the scenario of the driving, and we use it to count on the hazardous situations.

Next, we explain each element briefly.

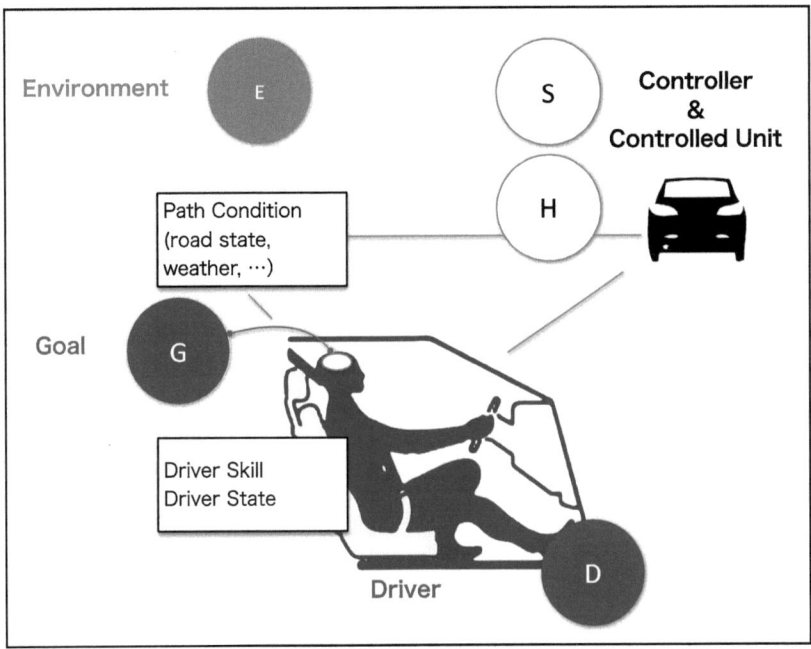

Fig. 1. DESH-G model

2.1 Environment

We use Situation-Scenario Matrix (SSM) [3] to express the environment around the car. This matrix has two axes. The one indicates the element of the environment, and the other is the time sequence. The former has the element's type showing below:

- Road type (rural, freeway, arterial, ...)
- Road surface (flat, dry asphalt, ...)
- Neighbouring cars (type of cars forward/backwards/side, ...)
- Traffic condition (congestion level)
- Non-vehicle actor (bike, pedestrian, ...)
- Weather condition (sunny/rainy/snowy, ...)
- Visibility
- Traffic rules (speed limits, traffic signs, ...)

What is to be the environmental element depends on the target system to be analysed. For example, if a system is the Cooperative Adaptive Cruise Control (CACC) [7], we have to add the communication state into the above element list of the environment. And if a system is the Parking Assist System (PAS), we might eliminate the road type and traffic condition and add the presence or absence of the lock plate.

A car is a moving object and the environment varies as it goes. The SSM has a time axis and one SSM means one scenario. Several scenarios exist to achieve a goal of the driver. We need to analyse this goal of the driver, but I will not describe its detail in this paper.

There are numerous drivers, and modelling of the driver is necessary when we consider the automobile safety. The important characteristic is that the driver is different from the operator of train or aeroplane (i.e. the motorman or pilot). Most of the motorman and pilot are the trained professionals. Vice versa, a large number of drivers are non-professionals and they don't regularly train driving after get the license.

2.2 Driver Model

In this paper, the main purpose of the driver model is to analyse the hazardous situation. So, we simply adopt the task capability interface model [4]. If the capability of the driver is under the task demand required, the driver cannot drive the car anymore.

We divide the ability of the driver into the driver skill and the driver state. The driver skill is the ability to perform a given task, and this skill doesn't change in the short term. But the driver state easily changes by the various factors. For example, the lack of sleep decreases the level of his state, and it affects the controllability. This doesn't come from the only health problem. If an urgent situation (for example, the driver has to go to school to pick up his/her child, but he doesn't have enough time to make it) occurs, the state of the driver also varies. If the driver's ability is low and the task demand is high, the situation might be dangerous. And the environment affects the task demand. For example, if we have to drive in the rainy night on the non-asphalt road, the task demand is high compared with running in a fine daytime on a highway.

In our approach, to calculate this task demand, we use the SSM, which shows the driver's situation in a particular time. So, we can calculate the change of task demand value in a scenario. We already proposed the several formulas to compute this task demand and the driver's ability [2].

Of course, there are various drivers, and more the car driven by her or him affect the task demand. But it helps us consider about hazardous situations relatively.

3 HMI Abstract Model

In this chapter, we think about the HMI abstract model based on the previous arguments about DESH-G model. That is, we will identify two types of interfaces: One is the interface between the system and the driver; another is the interface between the system and the environment.

3.1 Interfaces with the Driver and the Environment

Figure 2 shows the correspondence between the deformed DESH-G model and the interface classes.

We identified the four interface classes. There are two between the driver and the system (controller) and also the two between the system and the environment. We explain them respectively.

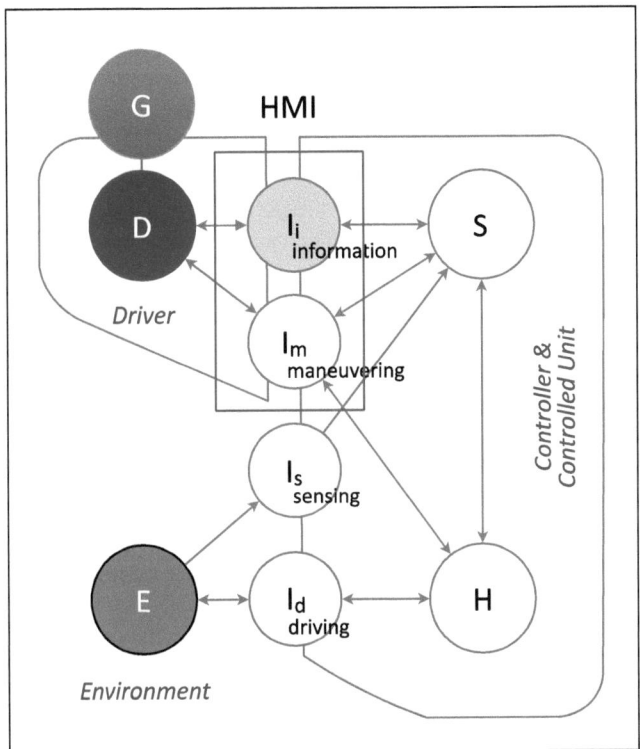

Fig. 2. DESH-G with interface classes [model: S0]

1. Driver Information interface class (I_i)
   By this interface, the system provides information to the driver. For example, traditionally we have the various instruments like speedometer and the several warnings and alerts. If the car has the new functionality, it will give us other type of information. For example, the car that has the adaptive cruise control (ACC) system has information of the distance between forwarding car and the self-car. The system knows information through the I_s interface, and this provided information is useful one for the driver.
   Recently in this class, we have another type of information flow from the driver to the system, not from the system to him. In the cockpit, there are sensors that observe the driver, and the system changes the behaviour. For example, in the driver monitoring system, the system has the camera to check the driver status and warns him by light or sound if it estimates that the driver status shows the low performance.
2. Maneuvering information class (I_m)
   This interface is relating to the driver's intention for the longitudinal and lateral movement of the car by the handle, the accelerator, the brake pedal and so on. We had only the mechanical interface, but nowadays those are partially supported by electric/electronic parts and software.

3. Environment information interface class (I_s)
   This class and next one is the interface between the system and environment. Mainly we can get the data of the environment around the car with the visual or radar sensors. Recently we can get the information via other cars (V2V) or the infrastructure (V2I).
4. Drive interface class (I_d)
   This interface relates the environment directory. For example, the tires transmit the driving and side force to the ground. The car light illuminates the front area.

3.2 HMI Abstract Model

The HMI abstract model is the model that is described by the previous interface class and it doesn't include the other properties like usability, the device type and so on. This is the basic model, and we think this is useful. When we have to think the new types of HMI, especially, in the ADAS area, it is not simply covered by the existing HMI techniques and we need another approach.

Example1: CACC

To explain how to use those interface classes. We use an example: CACC system. In the CACC system, the system is not closed in the single car. It communicates with other cars. The information from the other car is useful: in the conventional auto-cruise control (ACC) system, the system has to calculate the distance between the following car and self-car by using the camera or the millimetre-wave radar. It might not be accurate because of bad weather condition. And it has sometimes delay for the calculation of distance. But the CACC system can get the information of the actions of the driver of the following car almost simultaneously. So, the self-car can follow the forward car accurately and timely.

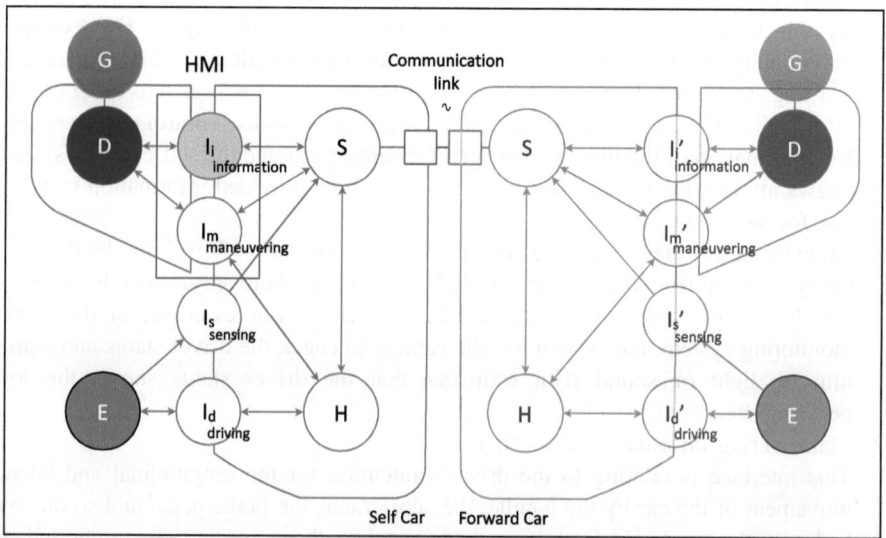

Fig. 3. CACC and DESH-G [model: S1 ∿ S2]

We convert the original model [S0] in order to express the CACC system. Figure 3 shows the CACC model. The new model name "S1 ~ S2" includes the symbol '~', and this denotes the communication between the self-car (S1) and the forward car (S2).

In Fig. 3, the left side shows the self-car, and the right side is the forward car. After establishing the communication link, the self-car can get the information of the forward car (and vice versa). Those are status (I_i') and operation (I_m') of the other driver, and sensory information (I_s') and driving information (I_d') of the forward car.

We show the sample display of this case in Fig. 4. In this figure we also indicate the relation with each interface classes. I_m' is the useful information for the driver to know about the operation of the forward car. And I_s' provides the environment information that the sensor of the self car cannot detect from his position. I_i and I_i' is the information of the driver if our car has the mechanism of driver observation. Of course, the interface information of the forward car, I_d' or I_m', is also the input of the controller of self-car and the behaviour of the self-car might change; for example, the self-car can know the

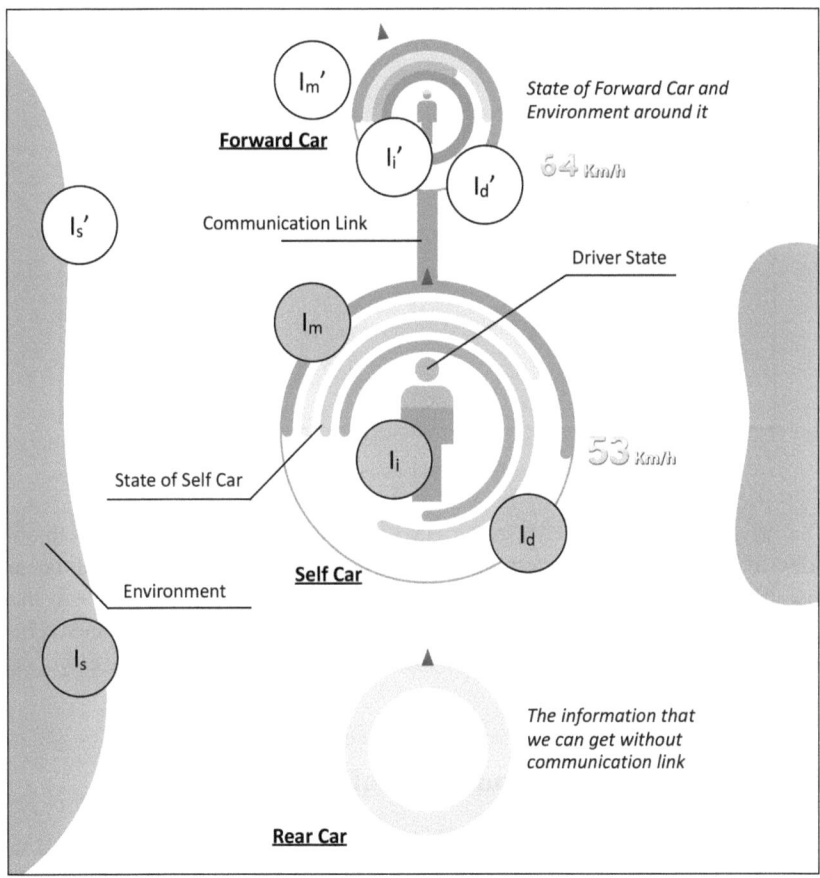

Fig. 4. Sample CACC HMI abstract model and interface classes

forward car will slow down from the information that the driver of the forward car pressed down the brake pedal, so the controller of the self-car can prepare for braking to keep the distance.

Those relations between the display information and the interface classes are useful in the preliminary design of HMI and the item, also from the viewpoint of safety. In chapter four, we take up the safety issue.

Example 2: Remote Parking Assist

Next we think about the remote parking assist system. In this system, "(a)ll drivers need to do is press and hold a button on their ignition key or smartphone. This tells the vehicle to automatically maneuver itself into the parking space" [15]. Figure 5 shows this situation.

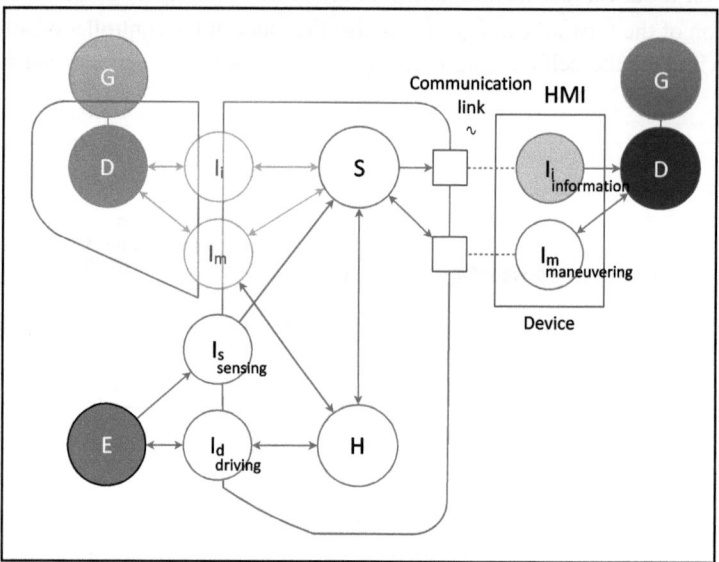

Fig. 5. Remote parking assist [model: S ∼ d]

The driver is outside the car, so the HMI is only on the small device in his hand. This device connects to the system of the car. The information displayed can be small, because the movement of a car is simple and the driver outside the car easily makes sure that the car position and the relation with the obstacles. Also, the maneuvering is restricted, that is, low speed and simple move, because we only can give the simple indication by the small device.

4 Using HMI Abstract Model for Safety Analysis

In this chapter, we consider the relationship between the HMI abstract model and safety analysis. We've already proposed the method, CARDION [3], to analyse the concept phase of system development. In this approach, we first analyse an item, which is the abstract system in the term of ISO 26262. The item has functional and non-functional requirements. We elaborate this item by using *the item sketch* and *the goal tree*. The item sketch is the rough description on an item from the static or dynamic view. The goal tree is the tree that is obtained by the dividing a top goal of an item iteratively: a top goal is divided into the sub-goals, and the sub-goal also is divided into the sub-sub-goal. In this process, we can find the *obstacle* to achieve a goal, (or it might be the divided goal). The failure of a part of the item can be the candidate of obstacle. To do this, we use the item sketch and guideword. After calculating the effect of obstacle, we design the counter-measure to treat the obstacle. This process corresponds the hazard analysis and risk assessments (HARA) and defining the safety goals.

Figure 6 show the goal model for the CACC system.

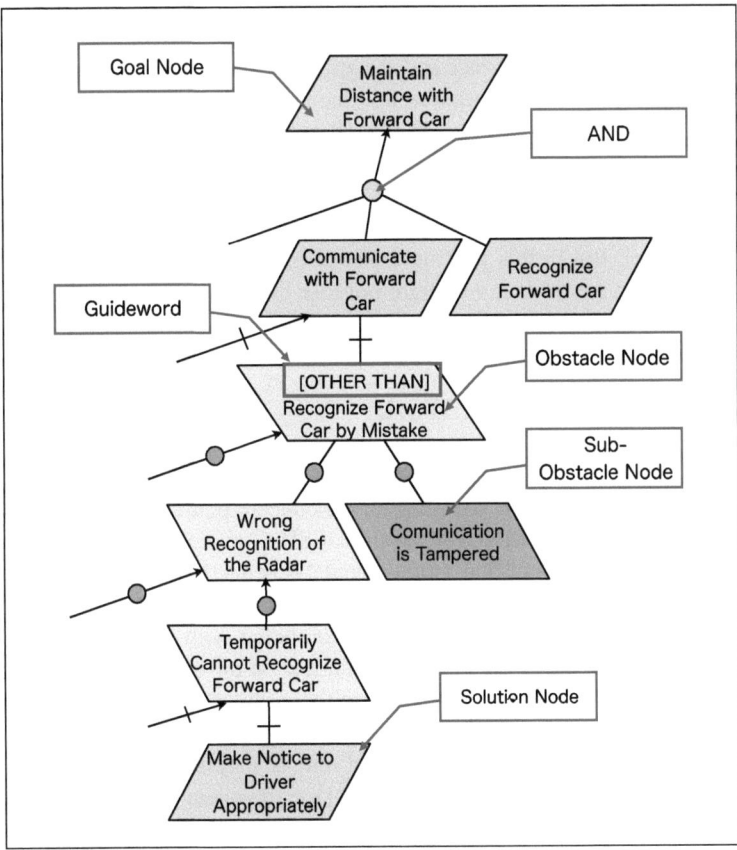

Fig. 6. CARDION goal tree

The HMI abstract model has a major role in this process. Usually, the hazard situation must be informed to the driver appropriately. If the system detects the malfunction of the item, for example, if the CACC system lost their connection link with the forward car, it doesn't work anymore. The driver has to know that the car cannot keep the speed or distance with the forward car correctly and might be controlled by him. In the Fig. 5, the driver lost the information of the forward car (I'_i, I'_m, I'_s and I'_d) abruptly. To know this is very important because when we calculate the automotive safety integrity level (ASIL) in the HARA process, the controllability of the driver is the key factor for calculation. The controllability is the ability to control the car in occurring the hazardous situation, and we can use the HMI abstract model with our CARDION [3] method to evaluate the controllability. We can know the place lacking information in the hazardous situation by the interface class and item sketch information.

Our approach has another valuable point about safety. In the ISO 26262, the cause of safety-threatening is the failure of a part of the system. But, there is another case. If the design or implementation has an error, we cannot make the car safe. The ADAS and its successors have a complicated structure, and those developments are the new experience for the system designer and the usage of them is challenge for the driver. So, in the early phase, it is important to find the hazard that isn't relating to the system failure, with evaluating the usability. The HMI abstract model is useful for this purpose. We think the remote parking assists system again. It is the new experience for us to drive the car outside a car. And we have neither steering wheel nor the accelerator/brake pedal. What if we drop the small device? Usually, we don't think that we drop the steering wheel. But in this parking assist case. We have to consider this situation (e.g. after dropping the device, we might not lose the measure to stop the car). This is relating to safety, but that doesn't come from system failure.

5 Conclusion and Future Work

This paper is preliminary research for the human-machine interface in the safety-critical system. Especially we are now focusing on the concept phase of the advanced system [11], such as ADAS. First, we introduce the DESH-G model. Traditionally one might use the control-plant model [12] as a fundamental schema, but we think that we have to include the driver and the environment around the car in it. Because there are numerous types of the driver, the operator of the car, compared with the other safety relating system like the power plant, the airplane, train and so on. In the DESH-G model, we distinguished four interface classes. If we use these classes with CARDION approach in order to functional safety analysis in the concept phase, we can clarify the HMI as the abstract model. We show the CACC and remote parking assist cases.

The HMI of the car is essential. If we would use the inappropriate user interface, we encounter the dangerous situation even if there is no system failure. We believe that this type of analysis becomes so important, as the system becomes more complicated and we also have to consider the collaboration with other system, that is, other cars (V2V) and infrastructure (V2I).

Without system failure, we would encounter the hazardous situation. If we misunderstand the alarm or the information displayed on the dashboard, we might do the wrong action. We think it is similar to an issue of the human computer interaction. The 'communicative breakdown' is the failure to exchange the information between the human and machine [14]. The work of Suchman is typical. She identified two types breakdowns: the false alarm and the garden path. "In the first case, a misconception on the user's part produces evidence of an error in her actions where none exists; in the second, a misconception on the user's part produces an error in her action, the presence of which is masked." [13] If we don't understand system behaviour correctly, we cannot communicate with the machine appropriately, even when the system work rightly. To avoid these breakdowns, we have to analyse dynamically the relation between the driver and system, but this is out of scope of this paper. But, we already have the SSM (Situation-Scenario Matrix) [3] to analyse the hazardous situation, so we believe that we will report the dynamic behaviour of the relationship between HMI and the driver in future.

References

1. ISO, ISO 26262. Road vehicles - Functional safety -, ISO (2011)
2. Ito, M.: Controllability in ISO 26262 and driver model. In: O'Connor, R.V., Akkaya, M.U., Kemaneci, K., Yilmaz, M., Poth, A., Messnarz, R. (eds.) EuroSPI 2015. CCIS, vol. 543, pp. 313–321. Springer, Cham (2015). doi:10.1007/978-3-319-24647-5_26
3. Ito, M.: Finding threats with hazards in the concept phase of product development. In: Barafort, B., O'Connor, R.V., Poth, A., Messnarz, R. (eds.) EuroSPI 2014. CCIS, vol. 425, pp. 277–284. Springer, Heidelberg (2014). doi:10.1007/978-3-662-43896-1_25
4. Fuller, R., Santos, J.A.: Psychology and the highway engineer. In: Human Factors for Highway Engineers, pp. 1–10 (2002)
5. van Lamsweerde, A.: Requirements Engineering: From System Goals to UML Models to Software Specifications. Wiley, Chichester (2009)
6. Redmill, F., Chudleigh, M., Catmur, J.: System Safety: HAZOP and Software HAZOP. Wiley, Chichester (1999)
7. Naus, G., et al.: Cooperative adaptive cruise control. In: IEEE Automotive Engineering Symposium, Eindhoven, The Netherlands (2009)
8. Weitkamp, C. (ed.): LIDAR: Range-Resolved Optical Remote Sensing of the Atmosphere, vol. 102. Springer, New York (2006)
9. (2015). https://eengenious.com/2016-bmw-7-series-adds-remote-control-parking-gesture-control/
10. Dijkstra, E.W., Buxton, J.N., Randell, B. (eds.) Software Engineering Techniques, Report on a Conference Sponsored by the NATO Science Committee, Rome, Italy, 27–31 October 1969, p. 16 (1970)
11. Ito, M.: How can we deal with the concept phase in the functional safety standard for automobiles? In: Proceedings of Safety-Critical Systems Symposium 2016 (SSS 2016) (2016)
12. Irwin, D.J.: The Industrial Electronics Handbook. CRC Press (1997)
13. Suchman, L.: Human-Machine Reconfigurations: Plans and Situated Actions, pp. 161–162. Cambridge University Press (2007)
14. Philip, J., Hayes, D.: Raj Reddy, Steps toward graceful interaction in spoken and written man–machine communication. Int. J. Man-Mach. Stud. **19**(3), 231–284 (1983)
15. http://www.bosch-presse.de/pressportal/de/en/bosch-technology-makes-parking-a-piece-of-cake-44809.html. Accessed 24 April 2017

Integration of the 4+1 Software Safety Assurance Principles with Scrum

Osama Doss[1(✉)], Tim Kelly[2], Tor Stålhane[3], Børge Haugset[4], and Mark Dixon[1]

[1] School of Computing, Creative Technologies, Leeds Beckett University, Leeds, UK
o.doss7788@student.leedsbeckett.ac.uk,
m.dixon@leedsbeckett.ac.uk
[2] Department of Computer Science, University of York, York, UK
tim.kelly@york.ac.uk
[3] Norwegian University of Science and Technology, Trondheim, Norway
tor.stalhane@idi.ntnu.no
[4] SINTEF ICT, Trondheim, Norway
borge.haugset@sintef.no

Abstract. Some researchers have attempted to tailor agile methods to comply with specific standards (e.g. SafeScrum and IEC61508). However, this risks over-configuring the agile method in such a way as to make it difficult to apply it to another safety standard. Our approach sought to look at the problems of addressing the more fundamental principles of safety assurance by adopting the 4+1 safety principles and investigating how a Scrum process challenges, and can be adapted to give strong indication that the practitioners felt that there is a significant potential for successful integration of the 4+1 principles within Scrum. There were some issues where practitioners were concerned to focus only on one safety standard, and neither the agile practitioners nor the safety practitioners had a clear understanding of the outlook and work of the other group. However, we used these issues to inform a further set of questions. We conducted semi-structured interviews with participants to explore the general feasibility of the approach, and to provide an assessment as to whether the 4+1 principles can be addressed without compromising agility.

Keywords: Safety-critical systems · Agile methods · Assurance case · Scrum

1 Introduction

Evidence and experience concerning the integration of Agile development in the field of safety-critical software development is limited. However, there are some published case studies and research on successes or failures in that field, [1, 2]). Agile methods are known for being fast, efficient and adaptive, as well as fostering discipline and good practices in engineers. The use of agile methods can support both quality and team productivity [3]. We need to investigate whether it is possible to use agile methods that are flexible with respect to planning, documentation and specification while still being acceptable by standards [9]. In particular, we need to consider how a structured argument providing assurance of the safety of the system can be incorporated with a typical agile development method.

2 Research Problem and Questions

We are concerned with the research problem of how assurance case development (including the incremental development of structured arguments) can best be integrated with a typical agile development method.

We propose the following two research questions (RQ) concerning the relationship between Agile Methods and Safety-Critical systems:

- *RQ1 What are the current concerns and opportunities voiced by safety-critical systems professionals regarding the use of agile development methods for safety-critical systems development?*
- *RQ2 What changes are necessary to the Scrum Process in order to address the 4+1 Software Safety Assurance Principles?*

Our research will focus on investigating best practice evolution of GSN arguments as a means for safety case development as part of a Scrum process. We expect to develop guidance that will support the development of a goal structure as an integral part of this process.

3 The 4+1 - Fundamental Principles of Software Safety Assurance

There are many standards that either directly or indirectly addresses software safety assurance (e.g. IEC 61508, ISO 26262, EN 50128, parts of UK Defense Standard 00-56, and DO-178B). Although there are differences between these standards, there are a number of common principles that can be observed [4]

- Principle 1: Software safety requirements shall be defined to address the software contribution to system hazards
- Principle 2: The intent of the software safety requirements shall be maintained throughout requirements decomposition
- Principle 3: Software safety requirements shall be satisfied
- Principle 4: Hazardous behavior of the software shall be identified and mitigated
- Principle 4+1: The confidence established in addressing the software safety principles shall be commensurate to the contribution of the software to system risk [5].

The focus of our work is to identify and address challenges associated with the integration of Agile methodologies into safety-critical systems development. In order to gain a deeper insight into the challenges identified for the integration of safety assurance into Scrum, and into the practicality of the recommendations [16], we conducted semi-structured interviews with safety engineers and Agile developers.

4 Related Work

Previous work discussed about how to integrate agile methods into a regulator environment [6]. Jonsson [7] describes a mapping between requirements in a regulated environment (EN 50128) and agile practices. They define a modular approach for building safety arguments incrementally using the Goal Structuring Notation (GSN) [8]. The process they propose "...precisely captures the notion of sufficient up-front design..." They also illustrate how to use safety patterns and introduce the notion of a modular safety argument to enable the iterative development of a safety argument. However, their conclusion is that agile practices may not change the nature of the entire safety-critical development procedure model, but might improve the agility of the development. Furthermore, it is important to note that this paper is intended as a conceptual proposal, and is far from industrial practice. Fitzgerald et al. [6] presented a case study to demonstrate that agile methods could be scaled to regulated environments. Their paper described a number of issues - quality assurance, safety and security, effectiveness, traceability, and verification and validation - and illustrated how they react with the model. The work also focused on how to implement an integrated model to achieve compatibility in terms of agility, safety/security, certification, and Quality Assurance. Stålhane et al. [9] proposed the "SafeScrum" approach. This was motivated by the need to make it possible to use methods that are flexible with respect to planning, documentation and specification while still adhering to the safety standard IEC 61508. Stålhane illustrates two kinds of Product Backlog within SafeScrum: the Functional Product Backlog and Safety Product Backlog. Other researchers have examined how conventional methods and techniques used for security assurance suit agile methodologies. Beznosov and Kruchten [10] evaluated how well security assurance practices match the typical practices of agile methods. For example, they identify that the informal review practices of agile methods match well, but that many agile approaches lack the external review and formal validation required for security. In addition, they identify that many security practices are independent of the adoption of agile practices – e.g. the use of security design principles. Similarly, Lotfi [11] found that some security assurance practices can be easily integrated.

However, our work focuses on the satisfaction of 4+1 principles within an agile framework "Scrum". Specially, the focus of the work is on assurance rather than being seen to comply with a specific safety standard.

5 Data Collection and Methods

The study was conducted as a qualitative survey using "semi-structured interviews" for data collection [12]. Shull et al. [13] illustrate the advantage and disadvantage of conducting a semi-structured interview. The interview will include some simple (e.g. Likert scale-based) question, as well as more open-ended questions that allow for greater depth of response. The purpose of these interviews was to investigate the proposed integration of the 4+1 principles and assurance safety case development with Scrum. The interviews lasted for at least 40 min, and explored perceptions around the 4+1

Principles of Software Safety Assurance and their implications for Scrum. Interviews were voice recorded with consent from the participants.

The interviews started by introducing the research goals and the topics to be discussed. Then the 4+1 principles were explained, together with an outline of the proposed integration of these principles in a Scrum development setting. Questions were then asked relating to the proposal – selecting specific features one-by-one (e.g. our recommendations for team composition). The questions touched both aspects of (a) whether the proposed approach challenges agility and (b) whether the proposed approach challenges safety assurance [14].

Transcripts were analyzed using thematic analysis. A researcher examined all of the interview transcripts, and coded the transcripts using first-cycle coding (Open Coding or Initial Coding), supported by the NVivo 11 software package. Main categories (or topics) were identified through clustering of codes. Codes and categories were constantly compared with the data and revised or refined as appropriate [14].

5.1 Participants and Interviews

We interviewed 12 participants at the XP 2016 Conference in Edinburgh, from the academic and industrial domains in order to use their experience and insight to gain feedback on our proposed approach. The participants had experience with safety critical-systems, agile methods, or both. The majority of our participants were based in the UK, Sweden, Germany, the USA, and Norway. The table below shows participant qualifications (Table 1):

Table 1. Participant description

Participant #	Interviewee job titles
1	Development Engineer
2	Professor of Software Engineering
3	Owner, Evolution and Information Technology and Services Consultant
4	Director and Consultant
5	Professor Vice-Director, Chair at…
6	Professor of Software Engineering
7	Independent Programmer and Consultant
8	Emeritus Professor of Computing Science
9	Founder and Director
10	Distinguished Consultant
11	VP Engineering
12	Professor, Vice-Director

5.2 Interview Findings

This section discusses the responses from the feedback sessions that have been conducted during the XP2016 conference and Agile Development of Safety-critical Software Workshop. We used the following categories in the final coding:

1. Safety requirements and functional requirements must be considered together
2. It is important to keep safety requirements and functional requirements separated
3. Safety expert needed to keep safety in focus and to make the right decisions
4. Needs to build a safety culture, not to rely on safety experts
5. QA-experts are needed
6. Difficult to get customer feedback
7. Safety-expert may be a bottleneck
8. Involve all competent stakeholders
9. Involve assessor
10. Tools needed
11. Daily stand-ups are not (should not be treated as just) status meetings
12. Analysis of architecture and safety up front
13. All requirements need a criticality score
14. Status/review meetings take too much time

Not all interviewees touched upon all categories. We have summed up who brought up which category in the following graph (Fig. 1).

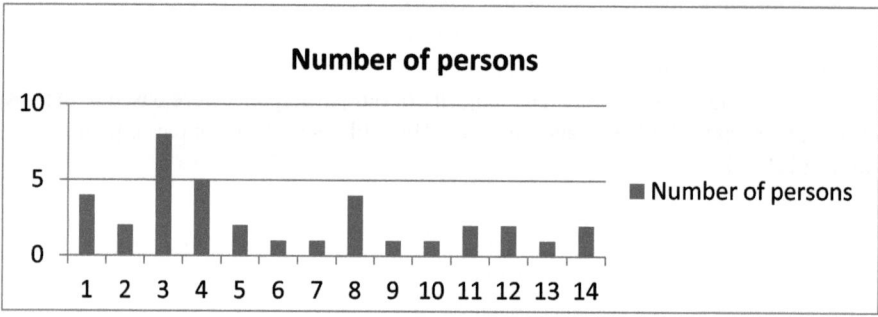

Fig. 1. Topics discussed by which interviewee

A. Second Product Backlog – A Safety Backlog

There are major differences of opinion among our respondents concerning the proposal in SafeScrum to introduce a second Product Backlog, the Safety Backlog, to track safety-critical concerns through the Scrum-based process. As will be seen from the extracts quoted below, the practitioners were split on this issue – four interviewees held the opinion that safety requirements and functional requirements should be handled together while two said that they should be separated. Note that "handled together" does not necessarily mean "in the same backlog". Nor does having separate backlogs mean a strict split – they may be kept in the same backlog but separated by tagging. However, some of the literature promotes the importance of a Security Backlog [15], to help to deal with the security "safety" issues in Scrum. The following extracts from our interviews indicate the practitioners' differing views:

The first feature to discuss is this need or otherwise to have an explicit safety backlog, the concept of safety backlog was agreed by the **[Interviewee2]** through experience and knowledge of 2 product backlogs

"The safety requirements separate from the others because they are... the first few requirements and the safety requirements and the fact that requirements somehow give rise to safety requirements and the other way around. It is nice to have them separated because they have to be treated differently. A lot of the thing also is that the safety requirements are usually at least more stable. The functional requirements would change much more often due to changed needs or so on. The problem is, of course, that the functional requirements will sometimes change and introduce new risks. But it opens up a new safety concern, then they would go back and they'll update the safety requirements and make sure it's linked to the original functional requirements." **[Interviewee1]** points out a different way of dealing with safety issues:

"We do not have 2 backlogs, we use only one backlog, so we mark every issue with criticality, complexity and risk, as well we have three levels low medium and high, we discussed if we could mark issues to safety issues and non-safety issues, we need to distinguish between issues and requirements. **[Interviewee8]** suggested to build safety features into the evaluation of everything, validating that every change still fulfills the safety need, through automating those checks: *"If you want another way, it's closer to a checklist that you do all the time. Yes. Basically, this checklist applies to any feature you implement. Whatever it is, you go through the activities to decide. Keep in mind; these are the safety implications for this feature because when you discuss the functionality, you may flush them out. We have to go against the checklist just to make sure that all the important things are done and none is forgotten. Some of them apply always. Some of them maybe apply only in some circumstances"* **[Interviewee6]** supported the need for safety backlog, *"It seems to me quite reasonable but of course it's starting to be very much like some requirements, documents, safety requirements, so I'm all for it".*

The general view is that addition of the Safety Backlog may be a good idea, but that we need to conduct more investigation to see if this is true. The interviews show that there is a question about the granularity of what should go into the backlog. One of the challenges is to keep track of the safety requirements explicitly since they require a different process that might not fit in with agility. This needs to be addressed by tailoring the agile process.

B. Safety Team Member

Almost all of the interviewees felt that our proposed addition of a team member with specific responsibility for safety issues was a sensible idea. We present extracts from the interviews below:

[Interviewee8] *"Yes, could be. Somebody in the team that is an expert about safety and so while the things are discussed and designed, he's there to ask the questions, so to make sure safety is taken into consideration because being the expert, he's the one that can ask the right questions to bring the problems to the surface".* **[Interviewee1]** mentioned to a new quality assurance (QA) role. We would, however, never instantly put QA and safety together because it's two different things, but we're saying there should be somebody who is the keeper of the flame of the safety issues that understands what's in the backlog. *"We have been trying to do quality assurance role in Scrum, the product owner is problem in Scrum, because he or she does not exist as a person, in our situation the product owner is a set of persons, we have a product owner but he is the marketing person, he does not know the system. We will start to define QA, the problem if you have too many, and I think the QA can be like a safety team member."*

The implementation of the safety team member can help to spread the safety culture into development team. **[Interviewee2]** *"There should be somebody who say, have you, well, they should be doing safety analysis because you have taken this user story, broken* it down into 3 functions and somebody has to say, "Has he really done some safety analysis there?" Mostly, I think if you have a real safety culture the little person will mostly be able to do that, but somebody has to think, "Has it been done?"

The idea behind the safety team member is to spread the safety culture across team to ensure safety. The safety team member will also improve communication between the development team and the independent assessor. This ensures that the safety requirements, safety criticality, and safety case will meet the customer requirements. In addition, it will help to ensure that the development team has a good understanding of the safety requirements, and helps spreading the safety culture.

C. Independent Stakeholders Are Required as Part of Sprint Review

The idea is having an identifiable, focal person within the team that is quote, "*The safety person*". The reason for that being having somebody who can be keeper of the flame. **[Interviewee11]** complained that independent stakeholders do not know enough about the features, as well, he mentioned to some concerns:

> "We tried it in each sprint review. But they never argue about what we are doing, what I think is to find someone who disagrees with you and has experience. So, you need to find a person whose only job is to disagree with you. And it is difficult to get a company to hire someone."

Contrariwise **[Interviewee6]** had good experience on dealing with independent stakeholders: "*I think it is a good point, if you have an independent stakeholder, like in our case was TÜV regulatory and standards services compliance*", so I probably ask that person, not in each sprint but when you realize something." **[Interviewee3]** explained his interest with some concerns: "*I would fear that such a person would become a bottleneck, in the sense that I need something, but I'm fifth in line. What I would probably hope for, would be that person, or people would be over-resourced, in the sense that it would be desirable if they were a developer, that did work with the other developers, but also had this special role, rather than they only had this special role.*" **[Interviewee5]** introduced an important link between the independent stakeholders and the daily Scrum meetings: "*Having someone responsible on the customer side almost directly implies there's also going to be someone on the development side as well, these Scrum meetings, we're saying that we think it's possible, even if only in a very light touch way that safety can be reviewed or highlighted as part of daily Scrum meetings.*"

However, the response to the questions related to stakeholders varies quite a lot. There seems to be two important messages: (1) it is difficult to get good feedback and (2) it is important to involve all stakeholders – e.g. safety experts and assessors. In addition, there are some worries, e.g. safety experts might be a bottleneck in the process.

D. Daily Scrum Meetings

The daily scrum meetings are important both to give informal feedback on problems and solutions. In addition, it enables the safety expert to influence solutions that directly or indirectly influence safety. This will, in the long term, help to create a safety culture in the team. There are two concerns with a negative impact: (1) the daily stand-ups must not degenerate to a status meeting and (2) a strong focus on safety can make the availability of the safety expert a bottleneck in the process.

Almost all the interviewees found that the daily scrum meeting useful, was also agreed by interviewees 1, 5 and 12 that the Daily scrum meetings can help the safety issues, especially safety be on the top of daily scrum meeting agenda:

"This is a good idea, as a Scrum-master I like the idea of asking [a] question every day: Have you checked safety-related issues?"

"I mean, that's important because you have what they're going to do, what you have done, you having problems. You should also get a question, "Have you done anything unrelated, that aren't on the safety requirements down here?" That's important just to keep safety on top of the agenda all the time."

"I completely agree, it is very important to have the safety requirements in the daily Scrum meeting and the safety person should always be at the daily Scrum meeting because of the early feedback. [This] can be used to provide an early opportunity to identify unintended side-effects emerging from a chosen implementation approach."

Daily scrum meetings can provide informal feedback of progress and satisfaction of safety requirements.

E. Sprint Planning

Before you start the Scrum development, the chosen modeling, implementation and development assessment approach and the tools to be used should be documented and assessed against the systems' criticality. The split between those who want to keep safety requirements and functional requirements together versus those who want to keep them apart is visible also here. We also register the need for an architectural analysis in the sprint planning process.

[Interviewee10] has a deeper view of planning safety requirements and it is sensible idea. *"Yes, but there's always the question. ...When [do] you start the sprint planning? You'll take functions out of functional backlog, but they're only used as stories and you have to detail them, turn them into functions. Doing that, you might introduce new safety problems, meaning that you'll have to maybe look at, "OK, this requirement, this link to this safety requirement, maybe that should be changed also." This is somewhat traceability issue."* In Scrum, every iteration begins with a sprint-planning meeting. Another view was introduced on organising the sprint planning **[Interviewee 7]** *"safety requirements need to be checked, at least, they have addressed all the safety questions. What will happen if ...]"* **[Interviewee11]** *"The criticality of chosen requirements for the sprint (or requirements related to those chosen) should be highlighted at the beginning of the sprint planning. Because the team should know how critical that particular requirement is for the sprint. Yes, hazard analysis should be conducted to on the chosen languages, processes and tools to identify the potential for the introduction of implementation errors."*

F. Sprint Review

How much we can get done in sprint reviews? Ideally, we should check whether somebody has fully satisfied a safety requirement and review the verification evidence. The main concern for a sprint review is that it is time-consuming, therefore we are recommending that hazard analysis should be an activity that takes place within a sprint.

[Interviewee7] *"I agree with you, but: If you should go through everything, which is dumb, people lose interest. For example a person, like QA person's look at the general work of the team, see how long has this been done, has everything been done properly? Have you looked at all the failing models, for instance? Sometimes you need somebody to do that."* **[Interviewee5]** has a different approach on dealing with sprint reviews:

"We don't use Sprint reviews as in "Scrum", In our project we use retrospective to improve safety, it takes half a day, so that is the time were you really look at the whole process, so we invite all the stakeholders, development team, safety person, product owner and the manager that is the big retrospective. As well we do small retrospective each week from one to two hours, and hazard analysis should be during the sprint not only in the review.

Important issues to consider are participation of a safety team member and that the team has a safety culture. The presence of a safety-culture will, in the long term, remove the need for a separate safety expert, which might be a bottleneck in the review process.

5.3 Conclusion and Issues Arising

We have reported on the results of 12 semi-structured interviews which were conducted in order to gain actual practitioners' reactions to our approach to integrating the 4+1 safety assurance principles within Scrum, and our initial assessment of the challenges associated with the approach. Although the research sample is limited, the study has benefitted from the introduction of a more pragmatic perspective, which complements our rather theoretical viewpoint.

We summarise the results in forms of answers to the two research questions we posed at the beginning of the study:

RQ1 *What are the current concerns and opportunities voiced by safety-critical systems professionals regarding the use of agile development methods for safety-critical systems development?*

We encountered some difficulties during the interviews. For example, on aspect that we briefly touched on was misunderstanding and lack of knowledge or awareness from both the Agile and the safety practitioners concerning each other's outlooks and work. Nonetheless, the semi-structured interviews have motivated us to propose further work involving interviews on a much larger scale in order to achieve better results. We need to move from the basic questions that we asked during the current research – i.e. "is it feasible to integrate safety into Agile methods?" – towards more specific questions, such as the following:

- Is it permitted to break a safety requirement which has been satisfied in one Sprint?
- Safety backlog - Yes or No?
- Safety team member - Yes or No?
- Hybrid agile approach - Yes or No?
- Sprint duration: 1 to 2 weeks? Or longer?
- Independence is particularly important for the developers of the verification procedures (testing, formal methods, etc.) Surely they should participate in the review as well?
- How will the software safety requirements be verified?
- Would it be desirable/possible to implement a "feature" in a particular Sprint, but NOT to implement its related safety requirements in the same Sprint?
- Is Scrum a good way to produce a prototype (as recommended in 26262, 61508)?

RQ2 *What changes are necessary to the Scrum Process in order to address the 4+1 Software Safety Assurance Principles?*

The findings indicate clear support for the recommendations that we propose to integrate the 4+1 safety assurance principles into the Scrum process [16] in order to help demonstrate compliance with safety standards, and with our initial survey of the challenges presented by such an approach. Our recommendations stem from the use of the 4+1 principles to build on the strengths of the Scrum process to improve management of safety issues in system development.

Ultimately, this research will develop and evaluate a process model of an adapted version of Scrum that clearly integrates the activities of software safety requirements evolution, software hazard analysis and software safety (assurance) case development. To support the assurance case development aspect of this process, the results from the survey and semi-structured interview have provided a clear direction in terms of the importance of incremental hazard analysis, safety requirements development, and assurance case development (i.e. they indicate clearly that these activities must be performed within an incremental, rather than simply being up-front or end-of-development activities).

5.4 Limitations

Our study suffered from some limitations which should be addressed in future work: (a) We had considerable difficulty finding practitioners who were sufficiently expert in both Agile and safety, especially Safety Manager who have experience and a deep technical understanding of product safety – in the end, we were able only to interview those with an interest in the integration of agile and safety; (b) The limited research sample meant that not enough data was collected from the practitioners; (c) We needed to establish specific criteria in order to avoid deviation from the interview script.

5.5 Future Work

It would be desirable for future researchers to conduct a pilot project. This should be formulated in such a way as to address the particular themes that emerge from our survey: for example, the pilot project could evaluate how difficult it was to establish safety requirements at the outset, and how much they change during the project.

Our initial survey in this area highlighted some areas of interest in the role of the safety case. Further work is required to explore how GSN safety cases could be linked to a notion of safety Product backlog within Scrum. The research indicates that existing assurance case activities need to be adjusted. Software safety argument patterns provide a way of capturing good practice in software safety arguments. Future research could develop a pattern-based approach to integrating software safety cases, Scrum's Safety Product Backlog, risk-based planning, and requirements-based evaluation. Software safety argument patterns describe the nature of the argument and safety claims that would be expected for any software safety case.

It would be useful for future researchers to engage in a larger-scale interview-based evaluation of an approach for safety case development within Scrum. In particular, research should address the development of pragmatic techniques to ensure that evidence to validate the safety case is developed and collected in all incremental (Sprint) processes. A realistic case study should be developed, to investigate where there are opportunities to build up a safety case as a part of an Agile development, to determine the risks and conflicts associated with this approach and how these risks could be mitigated.

References

1. Bowers, J., May, J., Melander, E., Baarman, M., Ayoob, A.: Tailoring XP for large system mission critical software development. In: Wells, D., Williams, L. (eds.) XP/Agile Universe 2002. LNCS, vol. 2418, pp. 100–111. Springer, Heidelberg (2002). doi:10.1007/3-540-45672-4_10
2. Bedoll, R.: A tail of two projects: how 'Agile' methods succeeded after 'Traditional' methods had failed in a critical system-development project. In: Maurer, F., Wells, D. (eds.) XP/Agile Universe 2003. LNCS, vol. 2753, pp. 25–34. Springer, Heidelberg (2003). doi:10.1007/978-3-540-45122-8_4
3. Bruce, D.: Agile analysis practices for safety-critical, 19 February 2013 http://www.ibm.com/developerworks/rational/library/agile-analysis-practicessafety-critical-development/
4. Kelly, T.: Software certification: where is confidence won and lost? In: Anderson, T., Dale, C. (eds.) Addressing Systems Safety Challenges, Safety Critical Systems Club (2014)
5. Doss, O., Kelly, T.P.: Challenges and opportunities in agile development in safety critical systems: a survey. SIGSOFT Software Eng. Notes **41**(2), 30–31 (2016)
6. Fitzgerald, B., Stol, K.J., Sullivan, R.O., Brien, D.O.: Scaling agile methods to regulated environments: an industry case study. In: 2013 35th International Conference on Software Engineering (ICSE), San Francisco, CA, pp. 863–872 (2013)
7. Jonsson, H., Larsson, S., Punnekkat, S.: Agile practices in regulated railway software development. In: 2012 IEEE 23rd International Symposium on Software Reliability Engineering Workshops (ISSREW), Dallas, TX, pp. 355–360 (2012)
8. Ge, X., Paige, R.F., McDermid, J.A.: An iterative approach for development of safety-critical software and safety arguments. In: Agile Conference, Florida, pp. 35–43 (2010)
9. Stålhane, T., Myklebust, T., Hanssen, G.: The application of Scrum IEC-61508 certifiable software (2011, Unpublished)
10. Beznosov, K., Kruchten, P.: Towards agile security assurance. In: Proceedings of the 2004 Workshop on New Security Paradigms (NSPW 2004), pp. 47–54. ACM, New York (2004)
11. Othmane, L.B., Angin, P., Bhargava, B.: Using assurance cases to develop iteratively security features using Scrum. In: 2014 Ninth International Conference on Availability, Reliability and Security (ARES), Fribourg, pp. 490–497 (2014)
12. Flink, A.: The Survey Handbook, 2nd edn. Sage Publications, Thousand Oaks (2003)
13. Shull, F., Singer, J., Sjøberg, D.I.K.: Guide to Advanced Empirical Software Engineering, 1st edn. Springer, London (2010)
14. Doss, O., Kelly, T.: The 4+1 principles of software safety assurance and their implications for Scrum. In: Sharp, H., Hall, T. (eds.) XP 2016. LNBIP, vol. 251, pp. 286–290. Springer, Cham (2016). doi:10.1007/978-3-319-33515-5_27
15. Azham, Z., Ghani, I., Ithnin, N.: Security backlog in Scrum security practices'. In: 5th Malaysian Conference in Software Engineering (MySEC), Johor Bahru, pp. 414–417 (2011)
16. Doss, O., Kelly, T.: Addressing the 4+1 software safety assurance principles within Scrum. In: Proceedings of the Scientific Workshop Proceedings of XP2016 (XP 2016 Workshops). ACM, New York (2016)

Towards Systematic Compliance Evaluation Using Safety-Oriented Process Lines and Evidence Mapping

Timo Varkoi[1(✉)], Timo Mäkinen[2], Barbara Gallina[3], Frank Cameron[2], and Risto Nevalainen[1]

[1] Finnish Software Measurement Association – FiSMA ry, Espoo, Finland
{timo.varkoi,risto.nevalainen}@fisma.fi
[2] Pori Department, Tampere University of Technology, Pori, Finland
{timo.makinen,frank.cameron}@tut.fi
[3] Mälardalen University, Västerås, Sweden
barbara.gallina@mdh.se

Abstract. The role of software is growing in safety related systems. This underlines the need for software process assessment in many safety-critical domains. For example, the nuclear power industry has strict safety requirements for control systems and many methods are applied to evaluate compliance to domain specific standards and requirements. This paper discusses the needs of the nuclear domain and presents alternatives to develop a process assessment method that takes into account domain specific requirements. The aim is to provide an approach that facilitates the use of assessment findings in evaluating compliance with the domain requirements and supports other assurance needs. Safety-oriented Process Line Engineering (SoPLE) is studied as a method for mapping assessment criteria to domain specific requirements. A binary distance metric is used to evaluate, how far a process mapping based method would solve problems found in compliance evaluation. Based on the results, SoPLE is applicable in this case, but process mapping is not adequate to facilitate compliance evaluation.

Keywords: Safety · Systems engineering · Process assessment · Process lines

1 Introduction

The growing use of digital instrumentation and control systems has amplified safety as a design constraint in many safety-critical domains. Domain specific safety requirements may also imply significant requirements for systems development processes. Process assessments are used to address the quality of the development processes. However, generic process assessment models (PAMs) may not adequately cover the domain specific requirements (DSRs) and additional effort is required to evaluate e.g. compliance to domain standards.

Most safety-critical domains have similar concerns with respect to domain specific and generic industry requirements. We have profound expertise in the nuclear power industry and therefore we limit the scope of this paper to that domain. Also, we use as examples of domain specific requirements the guidance given by the Finnish nuclear safety authority and some international standards that address software in nuclear power plants.

The nuclear power industry is an example of a domain in which numerous national and international regulations involve safety requirements. As safety is a vital, many methods are used to ensure that instrumentation and control systems meet strict safety requirements. The increasing dependence on software in these systems emphasizes the need for software process assessments. To be effective, process assessment methods need to take into account DSRs.

Process assessments produce large amounts of evidence data that can be used to evaluate compliance to DSRs. This, however, is not a trivial task. First, the approach and level of details in different requirements sets impose some mapping between process models and safety standards. Second, the evidence (information used to demonstrate that safety requirements are met) may imply findings that are relevant to multiple requirements. For example, an inappropriate test report may be used as a negative evidence for verification, project management and/or documentation process. Similarly, an assessment finding may be relevant in evaluating multiple safety requirements.

We studied two approaches to address the issues related to compliance evaluation: one for mapping the models and one for analyzing the ability of a mapping based method to accelerate compliance evaluation. The aim is to find approaches that facilitate the use of assessment findings in evaluating compliance with the DSRs and can also support other assurance needs. First, we compared requirements found in domain standards with the more generic requirements of a PAM to identify the relationships. The study in this paper provides a satisfactory solution for mapping the PAM elements to DSRs. Second, we analyzed the use of actual assessment findings in compliance evaluation to identify any regularities. Also, the analysis of assessment findings and their relationship to DSRs was successfully performed, but the actual result is not adequate to solve issues in compliance evaluation.

We are not aware of existing work aimed at enabling systematic compliance evaluation via usage of safety-oriented process line engineering practices or investigating the applicability of process mapping using binary distance metrics. In this respect, our work is new.

The rest of the paper is organized as follows. In Sect. 2, we present a domain specific process assessment method and the issues found in evaluating compliance to DSRs. Section 3 describes safety-oriented process line engineering as a possible solution to mapping model elements. In Sect. 4 we use binary distance metrics to study the relevance of process mapping as means to get evidence for DSRs from assessment findings. Section 5 contains a discussion and presents ideas for future work.

2 Process Assessment in Nuclear Power Domain

2.1 Nuclear SPICE

Nuclear SPICE [1] is a method to evaluate the development processes when delivering software systems in the nuclear power domain. Its main purpose is to reduce risks in deliveries and to systematically collect evidence for safety qualification. The Nuclear SPICE method consists of a process assessment model and an assessment process. The process assessment model contains the reference processes and a scale to evaluate the quality of each process. The assessment process is a documented guide for performing assessments and to ensure repeatability of assessment results.

Nuclear SPICE is based on the latest ISO/IEC process assessment standards and process models (also known as the SPICE models) [2, 3], domain specific safety standards and regulatory requirements. Nuclear SPICE is applicable to systems and software engineering processes. The process reference model in the latest edition is based on the recently revised ISO/IEC 15288 standard [4] for System life cycle processes. Base practices, tasks and information products are used as assessment indicators.

There are three main roles in the assessment: (1) the *assessors* who perform the assessment (one assessor is the lead assessor); (2) the *assessee* who represents the organization to be assessed; (3) the *sponsor* who acquires the assessment. Depending on the nature of the assessment, there are rules governing the independence of the assessors. There may be other stakeholders, e.g. national/international authorities who receive the assessment results.

The Nuclear SPICE assessment process [5] is presented in Fig. 1. The main phases of the assessment process are: Planning, Data collection, and Reporting. In the *planning phase* the lead assessor prepares the assessees' organization and ensures adequate resources for the assessment. This phase is important in creating trust between the assessor and the other involved parties. The assessors' aim in the *data collection phase* is to collect adequate evidence for a consistent assessment result. In the *reporting phase* the assessors produce one or more reports and provides all parties with the results in an understandable format including face-to-face feedback. The assessment process describes the activities within the phases. Detailed tasks within the activities are defined and templates are provided for the assessment output.

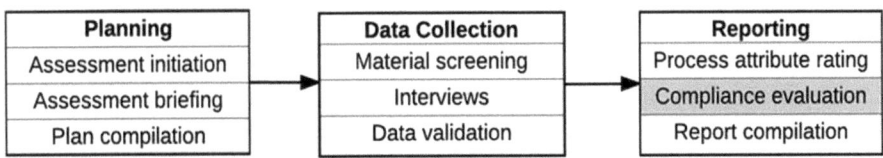

Fig. 1. Nuclear SPICE assessment process

Compared with ordinary SPICE assessments, Nuclear SPICE defines an additional activity for *Compliance evaluation*. This activity is an important part of the assessment in nuclear power industry, since complying with the domain standards is a key issue in qualification of the systems relevant to safety. For the nuclear power domain, the relevant standards are IEC 60880 [6] and IEC 62138 [7]. Since Nuclear SPICE was developed in Finland, requirements by the national nuclear safety authority are also important for us. These requirements are described in the YVL guidance [8, 9], which defines safety requirements concerning the use of nuclear energy in Finland. These may also be considered in the evaluation. Compliance evaluation is not intended to be used to claim compliance to one or more relevant standards, however, it may provide information or evidence on the achievement of individual requirements [5].

The collected assessment findings and ratings are analyzed and mapped to selected standards and requirements. The selection of standards and requirements for compliance evaluation is documented in the assessment plan. Possible issues with the assessed processes are identified and reported based on the lead assessor's expert judgment of these processes. Compliance evaluation does not imply any compliance of the actual software product and is optional depending on the assessment goal.

2.2 Nuclear Power Domain Specific Safety Requirements

The engineering of software based instrumentation and control systems to be used for safety purposes in nuclear power plants (NPPs) is a challenge due to the safety requirements to be fulfilled. The safety software used in NPPs, which is often required only in emergencies, has to be fully validated and qualified before being used in operation. To achieve the high dependability required, special care has to be taken throughout the entire life cycle, from the basic requirements, the various design phases and verification and validation procedures for operation and maintenance. The main aim of the IEC 60880 standard is to address the related safety aspects and to provide requirements for achieving the high software quality necessary [6].

IEC 60880 is one of the strictest standards for software development. It includes requirements and recommendations for the development of software to be used in the highest safety class. Requirements for software to be used in lower safety classes at NPPs are described in IEC 62138. To some extent, the requirements in both standards follow the same approach and address similar issues. Both IEC 60880 and IEC 62138 address the development process and the software to be produced. We have analyzed the IEC 60880 standard and found that most of the requirements are process-related and suitable for indicators in process assessment. Table 1 presents one group of the requirements related to the specification of software requirements. These requirements are used later in Sect. 3.2 to demonstrate mapping of PAM elements to DSRs.

2.3 Issues in Compliance Evaluation

Even though, the value of process assessment as such is recognized in many safety-critical domains, there is also a practical need to collect evidence for system qualification needs. The domain specific standards define what evidence is needed and a significant amount of it is related to process assessment data and results. Efficient management of that data requires first, a systematic approach for mapping the PAM and DSRs; second, a flexible technical solution to manage the assessment findings and their use in compliance evaluation.

The mapping between a PAM and DSRs is based on a systematic analysis of the existing process assessment indicators (base practices, tasks and information products) and the relevant domain related requirements and recommendations. Frequently changing models and requirements are challenging when keeping the mapping up-to-date.

Table 1. Some specific requirements from IEC 60880 and their corresponding types.

IEC 60880 6.1 Specification of software requirements	Type of requirement
6.1.1 The software requirements shall be derived from requirements of the safety systems and are part of the computer-based system specification	Process
6.1.2 The software requirements shall describe what the software has to do and not how the software shall do it	Process
6.1.3 The software requirements shall specify: – The application functions to be provided by the software; – The different modes of behavior of the software, and the corresponding conditions of transition; – The interfaces and interactions of the software with its environment; – The parameters of the software which can be modified manually during operation, if any; – The required software performance, in particular response time requirements; – What the software must not do or must avoid, when appropriate; – The requirements of, or the assumptions made by, the software regarding its environment, when applicable; – The requirements if any, of standard software packages	Process (categories of requirements) Software (content of specification)
6.1.4 Due to the significance of this phase of software development, the process of laying down software requirements shall be rigorous	Process (quality; vague requirement)
6.1.5 The software requirements specification shall be such that compliance of the I&C system to the requirements of IEC 61513 can be demonstrated	Process
6.1.6 The constraints between hardware and software shall be described	Process (performance) Software (content)
6.1.7 A reference to the hardware requirements specification shall be made within the software requirements specification for any hardware design impacts	Process (performance) Software (content)
6.1.8 Special operating conditions such as plant commissioning and refueling shall be described down to the software level for the functions that are impacted	Software (content)

The context of issues in compliance evaluation is displayed in Fig. 2. The assessors compile a set of observations, called assessment findings, based on the interviews and material screening of the data collection. Data collection is based on a PAM. These assessment findings can be used as supporting evidence that certain DSRs are being met. However, in general the assessors do not know in advance, which DSRs will be covered by the findings and which DSRs will require further investigation. Currently, compliance evaluation can be up to 25% of the assessment effort and requires scrupulous manual work to complete.

In the next two sections, we discuss two possible approaches to address the issues in compliance evaluation. First, safety-oriented process line engineering is applied in

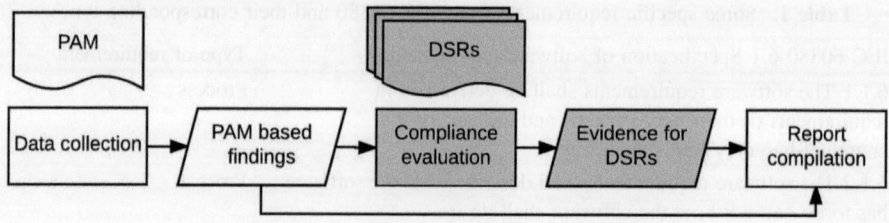

Fig. 2. Context of compliance evaluation

mapping the PAM and domain specific safety standards. Second, a binary distance metric is used to analyze existing assessment data to map findings to requirements. Our aim is to reduce the effort needed in qualification and enable the reuse of the evidence data for multiple purposes after a process assessment.

3 Model Element Mapping

3.1 Safety-Oriented Process Line Engineering

Safety-oriented process line engineering (SoPLE) [10, 11] consists of the concurrent engineering of a set of safety-oriented processes. A Safety-oriented process line (SoPL) represents a set of safety-oriented processes, which may exhibit: full commonalities, partial commonalities (structured process elements that are partially equal), and variabilities. A full commonality can be identified when a process element is present in all processes belonging to the set. A partial commonality can be identified when a structured process element, which contains a common substructure, is present in all processes belonging to the set. Finally, variability can be identified when a process element may vary (e.g., optionality, alternative).

To engineer according to SoPLE, a process engineer should first delimit the scope of the line, then engineer the domain (i.e., model the SoPL), finally, derive (safety-oriented) processes from the SoPL. The fundamental process elements to be interconnected to model processes are the following: tasks (which represent independent units of work), work products (e.g., deliverables), roles, guidance, and tools. Additional information on SoPLs as well as SoPLs Engineering (SoPLE) and its application can be found in [10–12].

3.2 Application of SoPLE: Focus on Commonalities & Variability Identification

We next give a brief application of SoPLE to identify commonalities between PAM indicators (base practices, tasks, and information products) and domain specific requirements. First, we delimit the scope of the line by considering IEC 60880 and Nuclear SPICE. Then, we perform a manual comparative study aimed at revealing commonalities and variabilities between PAM indicators and DSRs.

Table 2. Example of mapping PAM indicators to domain specific requirements

PAM indicators of system requirements definition process	IEC 60880 (Table 1)	Process element and type
TEC.3.BP1: Prepare for system requirements definition	6.1.1	Task/commonality
TEC.3.BP2: Define system requirements	See steps below	Task/commonality
(1) Define each function that the system is required to perform	6.1.1, 6.1.2	Step
(2) Define necessary implementation constraints	6.1.2	Step
(3) Identify system requirements that relate to risks, criticality of the system, or critical quality characteristics	6.1.3, 6.1.2, 6.1.8	Step
(4) Define system requirements and rationale.	6.1.2	Step
TEC.3.BP3: Analyze system requirements	See steps below	Task/commonality
(1) Analyze the complete set of requirements	6.1.4, 6.1.5	Step
(2) Define critical performance measures that enable the assessment of technical achievement	6.1.4, 6.1.3	Step
(3) Feedback the analyzed requirements to applicable stakeholders for review	(Annex A.2.3.4)	Step
(4) Resolve system requirements issues	6.1.8	Step
TEC.3.BP4: Manage system requirements	See steps below	Task/partial commonality
(1) Obtain explicit agreement on the system requirements	–	Step
(2) Provide key information items that have been selected for baselines	(In configuration management)	Step
(3) Maintain traceability of the requirements	6.1.7, (7.1.4.5)	Step
System description	System specification	Work product/commonality
System requirements	Software requirements; hardware requirements	Work product/commonality
System requirements report	–	Work product/variability
Critical performance measures	–	Work product/variability
Traceability mapping	–	Work product/variability

PAM elements can, to some extent, be mapped to DSRs. As an example, IEC 60880 *Configuration management requirements* correspond largely to Nuclear SPICE *Configuration management process*. Similarly, IEC 60880 *Specification of software requirements* (see Table 1) can be mapped to *System requirements definition process* in the Nuclear SPICE PAM. This mapping, presented in Table 2, is an example of the PAM/DSR mapping that is required as the basis for analyzing the adequacy of the PAM indicators in meeting the DSRs. In this case, also the evidence related to the process is mainly evidence for the DSRs.

4 Evidence Mapping

4.1 Evidence Base Approach

Nuclear SPICE has a special activity for compliance evaluation. It is used to evaluate the DSRs that originate from the domain safety standards or regulatory instructions. The evidence is based on assessment findings and results. Often, findings of one indicator might imply findings for entirely other areas. For example, suppose when assessing verification, it is found that tests exist that are not directly traceable to requirements. This could indicate weaknesses in test planning or requirements definition.

The compliance evaluation activity is quite a laborious task. It is difficult to analyze manually a large amount of evidence. Therefore, a systematic handling of the evidence is needed to fully make use of the collected information. To ease the assessor's burden, it would be convenient if a software tool existed which could help in mapping the assessment indicators to DSRs. Such a tool to manage the evidence base does not currently exist. In what follows we take the first steps in studying the feasibility of such a tool. For data we use three completed assessments as cases. The data contains assessment findings and ratings of three real-life assessments performed recently with Nuclear SPICE. The data is cleaned to ensure anonymity and cleared for research purposes by assessees and assessment sponsors. In all three cases, three DSR sets were present in the compliance evaluation: IEC 62138 [7], YVL B.1 [8], and YVL E.7 [9]. We focus on YVL E.7, which contains requirements of Finland's Radiation and Nuclear Safety Authority. Our aim here is to see if an assessment indicator maps to the same, or nearly the same, DSRs of YVL E.7. If so, a tool to manage the evidence base, which is based on the mapping of the indicators of the assessment model and the DSRs, would probably support the compliance evaluation activity. However, if the similarity is low, the tool might have to consider more the assessment findings which are the basis for the evidence.

4.2 Using a Binary Distance Metric

The study concentrated on the base practices of the assessment model and the YVL E.7 requirements. The binary distance metric proposed by Lance & Williams [13] was used to measure the difference of mapped elements in the three assessment cases.

Given sets R and S, let $common(R,S)$ and $noncommon(R,S)$ be the number of common and noncommon elements of R and S. Lance & Williams' distance measure is computed as follows:

$$d(R,S) = \frac{noncommon(R,S)}{2 \times common(R,S) + noncommon(R,S)}$$

The value of $d(R,S)$ is always between 0 and 1. If $d(R,S) = 0$, sets R and S are the same. If $d(R,S) = 1$, sets R and S have no common elements. For example, if $R = \{\alpha, \beta\}$ and $S = \{\alpha, \delta, \theta\}$, then $common(R,S) = 1$ and $noncommon(R,S) = 3$ and $d(R,S) = 2/5$. The measure $d(R,S)$ is undefined, if sets R and S are both empty.

Table 3 presents samples of the result representing different kinds of distances found in the study.

Table 3. Distances of element mappings in different assessments

Indicators (base practices)	YVL E.7 related findings			Distance metric			
	A	B	C	d(A,B)	d(A,C)	d(B,C)	Avg.
Ensure consistency	322 525 612	322 525 612	322 525 612	0,00	0,00	0,00	0,00
Construct software	623	563 623 627	331 623 648	0,50	0,50	0,67	0,56
Test integrated software against requirements	644		627 644 648	1,00	0,50	1,00	0,83
Prepare software for release	646	633 643 644		1,00	1,00	1,00	1,00
Plan the safety qualification of external resources	339 563 616	339 616	312 334 339 563 616	0,20	0,25	0,43	0,29

In the first column of Table 3 there are some base practices from the assessment model. The next three columns correspond to the three case assessments (labelled A, B and C). For each assessment and each base practice there is a set of YVL E.7 requirements that were mapped to the base practice in question. For example, for assessment A, only requirement 623 was mapped to the base practice 'Construct software'. The number 623 and all other numbers in the A, B and C columns are simply labels for different YVL E.7 requirements. The columns labelled d(A,B), d(A,C) and

$d(B,C)$ are distance measures for the three different pairs of assessments. The last column contains the average of $d(A,B)$, $d(A,C)$ and $d(B,C)$.

Table 3 contains only a small portion of the entire mapping between bases practices and YVL E.7 requirements for assessments A, B and C. In total, there are 87 base practices and 48 YVL E.7 requirements. For 33 of the base practices, at least two of the three assessments had non-empty sets of YVL E.7 requirements. For the remaining 54 base practices, at least one of the distance measures $d(A,B)$, $d(A,C)$ and $d(B,C)$ was undefined. If we only consider the 33 base practices where $d(A,B)$, $d(A,C)$ and $d(B,C)$ were all defined, then the mean of all 33×3 distances is 0,68 while the median of the means for these 33 base practices is 0,78. These are quite high distance measures and they indicate that the mappings between the assessment model and YVL E.7 requirements depend very much on the assessment instance. The reason for the result might be context dependency, which supports the idea of some kind of evidence based tool.

In any event, the lack of consistent mappings between base practices and YVL E.7 requirements indicates that any software tool to help an assessor would require some sophistication. For example, simply offering the assessor a complete set of all possible YVL E.7 requirements related to a given base practice and asking for approval or rejection would probably be more irritating than helpful.

5 Discussion and Future Work

In this paper, we have analyzed process assessment models, domain specific requirements and assessment findings. The aim was to find solutions that can help in compliance evaluation that, by experience, is very tedious. Some progress can be seen, but a major breakthrough is still missing. Considering the rigor required because of the strict requirements of the nuclear domain, any dubious methods or tools cannot be recommended.

One obvious constraint is the process assessment approach itself. Systems development is assessed using a process assessment model that cannot address all safety requirements of the domain. Many requirements are product-oriented or address other stakeholders than the systems developer.

Safety-oriented process line engineering can easily be applied to mapping process assessment models and domain specific requirements. This helps in the development of the process assessment model when trying to adopt the assessment model in using different sets of requirements. The requirement sets vary because of the safety class of the system, or national requirements, for instance. There is also some support for compliance evaluation: the mapping documents the obvious requirements that need to be checked.

The complicated part of compliance evaluation is the management of the evidence data. There are lots of findings that may imply exact finding for an assessment indicator, but they may give random findings to other indicators. The same applies for domain specific safety requirements. We tested a binary distance metric to see how consistent is the mapping between assessment indicators and one particular domain specific requirement set. With this distance metric, we obtain numerical results. What we observed was that some mappings are consistent, while the majority are more random. This confirms the supposition that proceeding directly from assessment indicators to domain requirements is difficult. A noticeable constraint is the availability of the assessment data. Assessments are always confidential and any information related to them needs to be specifically cleared. Another issue is the comparability of the data: different models and requirement sets are used, and they also tend to change over time.

Figure 3 summarizes the associations between PAM and DSRs. The associations represent links between the elements of the hypothetical 'Evidence Base' that help an assessor to conduct the compliance evaluation activity in Nuclear SPICE. The SoPLE approach can be used to identify beforehand common features between PAM and DSRs. When such commonalities exist, the assessor can produce supporting evidence for DSRs directly from the assessment ratings. Compliance evaluations in earlier assessments produce links when an assessment finding is selected as an evidence for a DSR. These links are based on an expert's judgements. Distance measures between the elements of PAM and DSRs collate the previous links. Using the measures, we could get answers to questions such as what PAM elements are typically associated with findings which are relevant to use as evidence for a DSR.

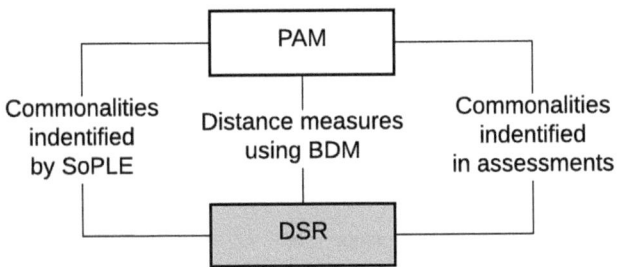

Fig. 3. Associations between PAM and DSRs

We are aware and we share the concerns regarding current standardization schemes including their inefficiency and in some cases their imprecision, see Bender et al. [14], Knight and Rowanhill [15], and others. However, in this paper we do not contribute to investigating how to improve such schemes by proposing new formulations or rational explanations within the standard but on how to make the compliance evaluation more systematic, since we believe that standards will always exist. We, however, believe that our findings will have a beneficial impact when planning new schemes or simplification of existing ones.

The compliance evaluation activity in Nuclear SPICE is considered very important by the assessment sponsors and the assessors. Further studies with larger amounts of data can be justified, even though our work indicates that a complete, tool-based solution might not be achievable. On the other hand, even a partial solution to support analysis and use of assessment evidence would be useful in assessment reporting.

Further work is needed on both PAM/DSR and evidence mappings. Also, consideration of the needs of different stakeholders, like authorities, assessors, NPPs and suppliers, is required. Even though, process assessment has proven to be an efficient method in evaluating systems development, including safety requirements, compliance evaluation remains one of the more tedious activities in it.

Acknowledgements. This work has been jointly funded by the Finnish national nuclear safety program SAFIR2018 (http://safir2018.vtt.fi/) and Finnish Software Measurement Association, FiSMA (www.fisma.fi), and the EU and VINNOVA via the ECSEL JU project AMASS (No. 692474) (http://www.amass-ecsel.eu).

References

1. Varkoi, T., Nevalainen, R., Mäkinen, T.: Toward Nuclear SPICE – integrating IEC 61508, IEC 60880 and SPICE. J. Softw. Evol. Process **26**, 357–365 (2013). Wiley
2. ISO/IEC 33001: Information technology – Process assessment – Concepts and terminology (2015)
3. ISO/IEC 33020: Information technology – Process assessment – Process measurement framework for assessment of process capability (2015)
4. ISO/IEC/IEEE 15288: Systems and software engineering—System life cycle processes (2015)
5. Varkoi, T., Nevalainen, R., Mäkinen, T.: Process assessment in a safety domain - assessment method and results as evidence in an assurance case. In: Proceedings of QUATIC 2016, Lisbon, Portugal, pp. 52–58. IEEE Computer Society, 6–9 September 2016
6. IEC 60880:2006 Nuclear power plants – Instrumentation and control systems important to safety – Software aspects for computer-based systems performing category A functions (2006)
7. IEC 62138:2004 Nuclear power plants – I&C Systems Important to Safety – Software aspects for computer-based systems performing category B or C functions (2004)
8. STUK: YVL B.1, Safety design of a nuclear power plant. Finnish Radiation and Nuclear Safety Authority (2013a)
9. STUK: YVL E.7, Electrical and I&C equipment of a nuclear facility. Finnish Radiation and Nuclear Safety Authority (2013b)
10. Gallina, B., Sljivo, I., Jaradat, O.: Towards a safety-oriented process line for enabling reuse in safety critical systems development and certification. In: Post-proceedings of the 35th IEEE Software Engineering Workshop (SEW-35), Heraclion, Crete, Greece. IEEE Computer Society (2012). ISBN:978-1-4673-5574-2
11. Gallina, B., Kashiyarandi, S., Martin, H., Bramberger, R.: Modeling a safety-and automotive-oriented process line to enable reuse and flexible process derivation. In: Proceedings of the 8th IEEE International Workshop on Quality-Oriented Reuse of Software (QUORS), Västerås, Sweden. IEEE Computer Society (2014)
12. Gallina, B., Kashiyarandi, S., Zugsbratl, K., Geven, A.: Enabling cross-domain reuse of tool qualification certification artefacts. In: Bondavalli, A., Ceccarelli, A., Ortmeier, F. (eds.) SAFECOMP 2014. LNCS, vol. 8696, pp. 255–266. Springer, Cham (2014). doi:10.1007/978-3-319-10557-4_28
13. Choi, S.-S., Cha, S.-H., Tappert, C.C.: A survey of binary similarity and distance measures. Systemics Cybern. Inform. **8**(1), 43–48 (2010)

14. Bender, M., Maibaum, T., Lawford, M., Wassyng, A.: Positioning verification in the context of software/system certification. In: Proceedings of the 11th International Workshop on Automated Verification of Critical Systems (AVoCS 2011), Electronic Communications of the EASST, vol. 46 (2011)
15. Knight, J.C., Rowanhill, J.: The indispensable role of rationale in safety standards. In: Skavhaug, A., Guiochet, J., Bitsch, F. (eds.) SAFECOMP 2016. LNCS, vol. 9922, pp. 39–50. Springer, Cham (2016). doi:10.1007/978-3-319-45477-1_4

SPI and Project Management

Improving Project Portfolio Management (PPM) for Improvement Projects

Jan Pries-Heje[1(✉)], Peter Møller Jakobsen[2(✉)], Morten Korsaa[3(✉)], and Jørn Johansen[3(✉)]

[1] Roskilde University, Roskilde, Denmark
janph@ruc.dk
[2] PMO Department, Vestas Windsystems, Aarhus, Denmark
pmj@vestas.com
[3] Whitebox, Hørsholm, Denmark
{mk,jj}@whitebox.dk

Abstract. Project Portfolio Management (PPM) focus on the integration and alignment of projects with the business operation in order to achieve most value and cost-efficiency for the investment in projects. PPM is often a challenge and especially so for improvement projects where PPM is considerably underdeveloped. In this paper, we present an approach that combines the ImprovAbility model and assessment with a version of a CMMI assessment developed by the Danish company Whitebox. This approach was developed in the world-leading Wind Turbine Company Vestas. The paper presents and discusses this new way of evaluating a portfolio of improvement projects and combine this evaluation with the effect they have on the CMMI maturity level. Further, the paper demonstrates how the combination of a strong senior management requirement for improved maturity and the focus on getting the most value out of PPM made it possible for Vestas to become "better at getting better".

Keywords: Improvement · Maturity · Process improvement · Success with improvement · CMMI · ImprovAbility

1 Introduction

Project Portfolio Management (PPM) focus on how project ideas and ongoing projects can be integrated and aligned with the business operation. "It brings projects into harmony with the strategies, resources, and executive oversight of the enterprise and provides the structure and processes for project portfolio governance" [1]. PPM is an important dynamic capability that has demonstrated its value in empirical studies [2]. It also has demonstrated its value in relation to innovation [3]. The 'portfolio' in PPM is the set of projects either being considered or going on. All the major organizations defining project management have defined what is meant by and included in PPM; see for example [4]. And a book on PPM coins it "… the biggest leap in project management technology since the … late 1950s" [1].

PPM is however a challenge for many organizations even if you subscribe to the best practice and theory on PPM. E.g. an empirical study of found that "Although companies manage project portfolios concordantly with project portfolio theory, they may experience problems in the form of delayed projects, resource struggles, stress, and a lack of overview" [5]. Another more recent study found that companies struggle with the sub-optimization and changes among their projects, even if various normative instructions and good practices have been introduced for PPM [6]. It is key to any PPM effort that one should align the strategy of the company with the business. What is relatively new is that you need "structural alignment", that is aligning your organisational structure as well [7].

Another challenge for PPM is the behaviour of internal stakeholders [8]. Not so much the portfolio manager – that was found to insignificant – but more the behaviour of management especially top- and senior-management. In any organization, there may be projects of many kinds. Product development projects aimed at a market and having an attractive business model will typically receive more attention than more internally-oriented Improvement projects aimed at improving internal processes in an organization. Hence, with an outset in the existing literature there is a research question begging to be answered namely: How can we improve PPM for improvement projects?

The way companies often organise and manage improvement efforts is by using a process improvement model. A few years back a new standard for process improvement called the ISO 33014 standard [9] for use in IT organizations was published. The standard operates at three levels called strategic, tactical and operational. At the strategic level an organization are to start with identifying business goals, identifying the scope of organizational change, selecting models and methods and identifying roles, and then identify the overall change strategy. This then leads on to the tactical level where the more specific planning of the organizational change and process improvement projects takes place.

One way of applying the standard is by using one of the maturity models such as ISO/IEC 330xx [12] or the Capability Maturity Model Integrated [10], and use the newly developed ImprovAbility model [11] (that specifically implements the ISO 33014 standard) to strengthen the success rate for the improvement initiatives identified in the maturity assessment. The ImprovAbility model includes a list of 20 critical monitoring parameters and an analysis method to assess an organisation.

However, even if the use of maturity models and the ISO standard is relatively widespread to identify improvement projects they do not specifically address the project portfolio management for improvement projects. Thus, a good follow to our research question above is whether one can use these improvement models to improve PPM for improvement projects? To answer that as well as the overall question we have undertaken a case study at Vestas, a global energy company dedicated exclusively to wind energy.

In the remainder of the paper we will, in Sect. 2, first give a more specific account with details of the ISO 33014 standard [9], the ImprovAbility model [11], and the CMMI [10]. Next, in Sect. 3, we discuss the second research question, namely in what way these improvement models can be used to improve PPM? In Sect. 4 we present the Vestas case and how the improvement models were used in Vestas. In Sects. 5 and 6 the PPM evaluations from the first and a second round is presented. Then in Sect. 7 follows a discussion. And, finally, a Conclusion answering both the overall and the more detailed research question.

2 The Improvement Models

Some years ago, the ImprovAbility model was developed in a very large Danish research project with two of the authors of this paper as project manager and responsible for research. The ImprovAbility model soon became part of ISO/IEC 33014 [9] standard for process improvement. As can be seen from Fig. 1 process improvement operates at three levels; strategic, tactical and operational.

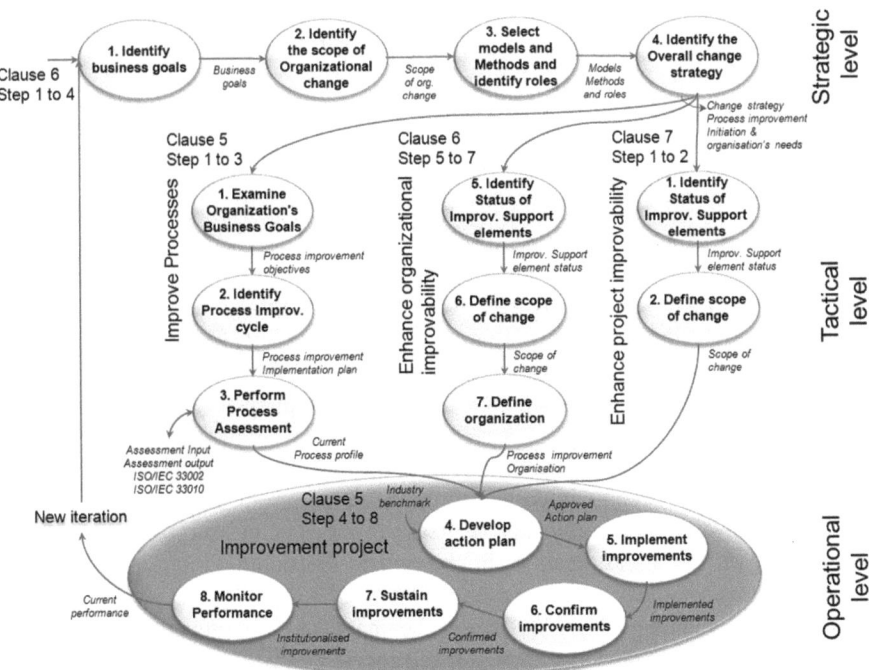

Fig. 1. Overview of the ISO/IEC 33014 [9]

At the strategic level an organization must start with identifying business goals, identifying the scope of organizational change, selecting models and methods and identifying roles, and then identify the overall change strategy. Then follows the tactical level where the more specific planning of the improvements takes place.

Many organizations perform process assessments (Step 3, Tactical level, Improve Processes) and get an insight in the maturity level for the organization, capability levels for the processes and several recommendations and ideas for improvement projects. Some of these recommendations and ideas lead to improvements programs and projects realized as projects at the operational level. Often it is a PMO, quality or method department, who manage and control these projects.

But as mentioned earlier in this paper, success with these programs, projects or initiative are unfortunate rare. So, if one would like to know how good the organization is to get success with the improvements – the ImprovAbility model can provide the answer. This is modelled in ISO/IEC 33014 (Clause 7, Step 1, Tactical level, Enhance project improvability). With this it is possible to evaluate a set of improvement projects against the enhancement parameters in the ImprovAbility model, and get a figure for the ability to improve.

If we perform this analysis over time it is also possible to see if the organization gets better at improvement in general.

Add to this what impact of the improvement projects has on the process capability. With this knowledge, you will know which projects have the best influence on the improvement of the organizational maturity and how likely it is they will succeed.

3 Using Improvement Models for PPM

While communication is always a challenge it is even worse when it comes to improvement projects. It is difficult to write a clear and objective business case including effort and expected benefit, which can be measured. If you increase sale 10% for a product it has an intuitively understandable and specific impact on the bottom line. If you improve the capability of a given process with 10%, it is not intuitively understandable in the same way, and the impact on the bottom line is not as specific. However, it remains the responsibility of senior management to prioritize between those two very different types of investments. The challenge is to provide them with high quality insights as basis for this prioritization.

At the next level of abstraction, we find the effectiveness of implementing the improvements. This become important for the leadership soon after the focus is established, but is even more complicated to measure. We need measures that can communicate how well the investments in improvements are building up competences that support the business goals and company vision.

Typically, a higher maturity level not is the final goal for improvement projects. But the maturity level is a powerful indicator of process performance – and what is more important – it is a measure that senior management can relate to and use for target settings.

In this case, the maturity measure is based on CMMI [10] that elicits the status of the development process on one page. In the case of Vestas, the assessments were carried out by the Danish company Whitebox to which two of the authors of this paper belong. The result of the assessment is presented as capability levels in quartiles per process and a single figure, e.g. 2.25. Along with the analysis follows a set of recommendations for improvement projects on specific processes. A maturity assessment delivers a clear and simple measure, which can be used by Senior management to identify improvement projects, focus the improvement effort and clearly communicate goals for improvement.

But it is often seen, that the result of a maturity assessment is neglected and not used for anything. Our best guess is around 50%. Success with improvement projects needs a Senior management, which can see the benefit of more professionalism in development and believe the investments in improvement projects will be beneficial in relation to less rework, less product errors, more reuse, less subculture or silos in the development organization – or other benefits related to visions or goals.

In reality, all companies have a lot of improvement projects going on. In the literature, there has been reported large companies with several hundreds of ongoing improvement projects; some of which have been well-known to management and some "flying under the radar" or carried out as skunk work. The reality is that most organizations doesn't know have many projects they have, and what effect they eventually will have. Therefore, the challenge is how we can focus and be more efficient in improving the development organization?

The first step in answering may be to establish a list of initiatives, simply by asking the employees what they are doing to improve the way they are working. With this list and the knowledge on what is ongoing it is possible for management to prioritize those who seem most appealing.

The second step is to evaluate all the projects; how "healthy" are they? For this evaluation, the ImprovAbility model can be used. The model includes 17 success enhancement parameters, which characterizes the "healthiness" of an improvement project (for an organizations ability to improve 20 enhancement parameters are used). By interview of the project manager and eventually other key persons, the assessors can score the parameters and give a score for the project. The parameters are shown in the Fig. 2 below in the 4 categories: Initiation, Projects, In Use and Foundation. The parameters are described in ISO/IEC 33014 [9].

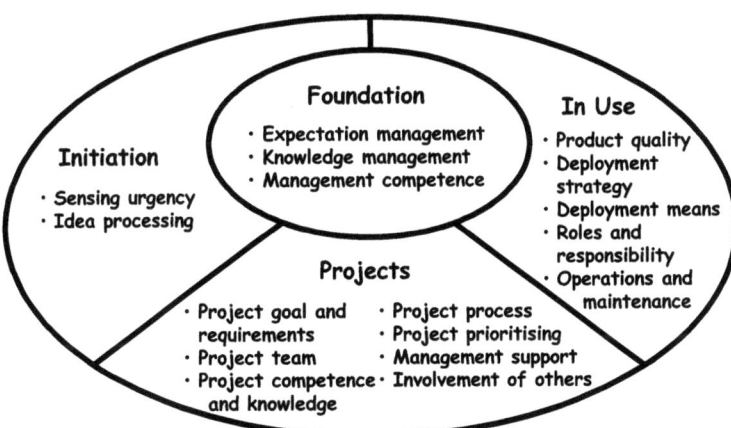

Fig. 2. The ImprovAbility enhancement parameters for success with improvement projects

During the interview with representatives from the improvement project, each enhancement parameter is scored through a set of questions. In Fig. 3 below is presented a set of questions related to one of the enhancement parameters – here Deployment means. The questions behind the enhancement parameters is at the highest level described in the book [11] describing the details of the ImprovAbility model.

Deployment means		1	2	3	4	N A	Score	Notes
1.	To what extent are sufficient information and communication about deployment ensured?			X				
2.	To what extent is an adequate training program included in the deployment?	X						
3.	To what extent is support availability established (e.g. Help-desk)?		X					
	Deployment means total						P	

Fig. 3. Excerpt from questions used to measure "Deployment means". Scale: 1 = not at all (N), 2 = partly (P), 3 = largely (L), and 4 = fully (F), with NA = not applicable. Same scale as used in ISO/IEC 330xx.

Across all parameters you also get a figure per improvement project on a scale from 1 to 4 (1 is lowest and 4 is highest).

When you conduct an ImprovAbility assessment, you aim at providing an overall 'helicopter' view of the improvement project. Given that most of the parameters are very non-technical, you will be forced to focus on the stakeholders and the context of the project—the culture, the management, the team-work, the interfaces to other stakeholders—and put the product itself in the background for a little while.

The entire project team benefits from the assessment process, as everyone can discuss issues and matters that many usually don't have time for. After the assessment, communication and negotiation between the project team and Senior Management become easier.

And - important for the overview on all the improvement projects – every project gets a score, which is an average of the enhancement parameters. This is also a measurement, which is easy to present and important to establish an overview of all ongoing improvement projects across the organization.

This paper will demonstrate how it is possible in one figure to show the "health" of a set of improvement projects and how the organizations ability to improve - improve over time.

We believe such an insight to be very valuable for an organization for navigating in the landscape of improvement projects – especially for Senior management. Which projects need more support, which projects need to be reconsidered in relation to scope, which projects must be reconsidered in general, and which projects seems to be successful and have the right scope?

Third step is to evaluate what effect each initiative will have on the organizations maturity/process performance. This is done by the maturity assessors who based on the models evaluate how the improvement projects will affect the set of specific and generic process practices on a scale from 1 to 10 (1 equal nothing; 10 equal complete).

So, the problem we by this research will demonstrate and validate is for a set of improvement projects in an organization to be able to sort and show their "health" combined with the impact on a higher maturity – as a one pager – and how it develops over time.

4 Vestas Case and How It Was Done

Vestas, for which this analysis took place, is a very large Danish company – the largest wind turbine company in the world, which operate globally and together with a lot of suppliers. The company develops very large and complex products, which include delivery at the operation place (a project itself) and includes ongoing support for many years afterwards. At Vestas there was established an improvement program to focus on the recommendations from the assessment.

Nr	Initiation			Project							In Use						Foundation			
1	F	P	L	N	P	P	N	L	P	P	P	P	N	N	N	N	N	N	P	P	P
2	P	P	P	N	N	N	N	P	N	P	N	P	L	P	L	N	P	N	N	N	N
3	F	L	L	L	F	F	L	F	L	F	F	L	F	F	F	L	F	F	L	F	F
5	N	P	P	L	P	F	N	N	N	L	P	P	L	L	F	N	L	N	N	N	N
6	N	P	P	P	L	L	N	P	N	P	P	P	L	P	P	P	P	P	N	P	P
7	P	P	P	L	L	P	N	L	L	L	P	L	F	L	F	F	L	P	P	L	P
8	L	L	L	L	L	P	P	P	N	N	P	P	N	N	P	N	N	N	P	P	P
10	L	P	L	P	F	F	P	L	L	P	L	L	L	P	L	N	P	P	L	P	P
11	L	P	L	P	F	F	P	L	L	P	L	L	L	P	L	N	P	P	L	P	P
12	L	P	P	N	P	L	P	L	L	P	P	F	N	P	N	P	P	P	P	P	P
13	L	L	L	L	F	L	P	N	P	P	P	L	N	N	P	N	P	L	N	P	P
14	L	L	L	L	F	L	P	N	P	P	P	L	N	N	P	N	P	L	N	P	P
16	F	P	L	F	F	P	P	P	P	P	P	L	N	N	P	L	P	P	N	L	P
17	F	P	L	F	F	P	P	P	P	P	P	L	N	N	P	L	P	P	N	L	P
18	P	P	P	L	F	F	L	F	L	L	L	L	P	F	L	L	L	P	P	N	P
19	P	L	L	L	L	L	L	F	L	F	L	L	L	F	L	L	L	P	P	N	P
20	L	L	L	N	F	L	L	F	L	L	L	L	P	L	L	L	L	P	P	P	P
21	L	F	L	F	L	F	F	F	F	F	F	P	L	F	L	F	L	L	L	P	L
22	L	L	L	L	L	F	L	L	P	P	L	P	P	L	P	L	P	P	N	P	P
23	P	P	L	L	F	F	P	F	L	L	L	L	P	F	P	L	L	P	N	P	P
24	P	P	P	L	L	P	L	P	P	P	P	P	P	L	P	P	P	L	N	P	P
25	F	L	L	P	F	F	P	L	F	P	L	P	N	N	L	N	N	L	L	P	L
26	F	L	L	P	F	F	P	L	F	P	L	P	N	N	L	N	N	L	L	P	L
27	F	L	L	P	F	F	P	L	F	P	L	P	N	N	L	N	N	L	L	P	L
28	L	L	L	L	L	L	P	F	F	L	L	F	L	F	F	F	F	L	F	F	F
29	P	P	P	L	P	F	L	N	N	P	P	L	L	L	P	P	L	P	N	P	P
30	N	P	N	P	F	F	N	L	N	N	P	P	N	P	N	N	N	N	N	P	N
31	L	P	L	P	L	P	P	P	P	P	P	P	F	L	P	L	L	P	P	P	P
32	L	L	L	F	F	L	F	F	L	P	L	P	L	L	F	L	P	L	P	P	P
34	F	P	L	L	P	F	N	N	N	P	P	L	X	X	P	P	P	P	N	P	P
36	P	L	P	P	L	L	L	P	L	X	L	L	F	F	F	L	L	F	L	F	F
37	P	L	P	P	L	F	N	F	F	L	L	L	L	L	F	L	L	P	L	L	L

Fig. 4. ImprovAbility score for the improvement initiatives

4.1 Identification of the Improvement Projects

After the Whitebox assessment, which came up with several recommendations for improvement projects, the organization decided to ask the many development departments to create a list of their ongoing improvement projects. It was the PMO department, which took that task and handled the process of this improvement project investigation.

It came as a surprise that more than 140 improvement projects were active – and a deeper investigation would have revealed even more. All these improvement projects were local projects driven by the departments by enthusiastic employees who had the specific need for the improvement.

Given the very different nature of all the improvement initiatives, it was decided to focus on those that were expected to have the greatest impact on the company maturity.

The Danish company Whitebox helped with evaluation of the 140 improvement projects and identified the 40 most relevant improvement projects to be evaluated. These 40 projects were then supported and managed by the PMO departments as focused CMMI improvement projects.

4.2 Evaluation of the Improvement Projects

The PMO department and Whitebox scheduled an ImprovAbility based interview-based evaluation with each of the 40 projects over a two-week period. One or two persons from each improvement project took part in an interview performed by two assessors from Whitebox.

Before the interviews took place, each improvement project was asked to provide information on their improvement project, such as: Project name: Business goal, Deliverables, Resources, Stakeholders, Budget, Schedule, Hours used, Activities planned, Activities finished, Deployment activities, Risks and mitigations.

The Whitebox assessors carried out the interviews with a division of work so that one assessor performed the interview and scored the parameters during the interview, and the other assessor took detailed notes. After the interview the two assessors aligned their opinions and eventually adjusted the score. In reality it ended with interviews in 37 out of 40 improvement projects.

4.3 Analysis

To establish an overview for the PMO two separate steps were required for each improvement initiative. The first step was to score the ImprovAbility enhancement parameters using the NPLF – scale from ISO/IEC 330xx [12]. This was done during and just after each interview. An average score for each category in the ImprovAbility model was calculated as well as the overall score for the project. This is done from a scale from 1 to 5, and represent the improvement projects "chance of success".

5 First PPM Evaluation at Vestas

In Fig. 5, the "Bless and follow up" quadrant was the initiatives that did not need a lot of attention, but was expected to have a high impact. Suggested PMO activities: Reporting and steering group.

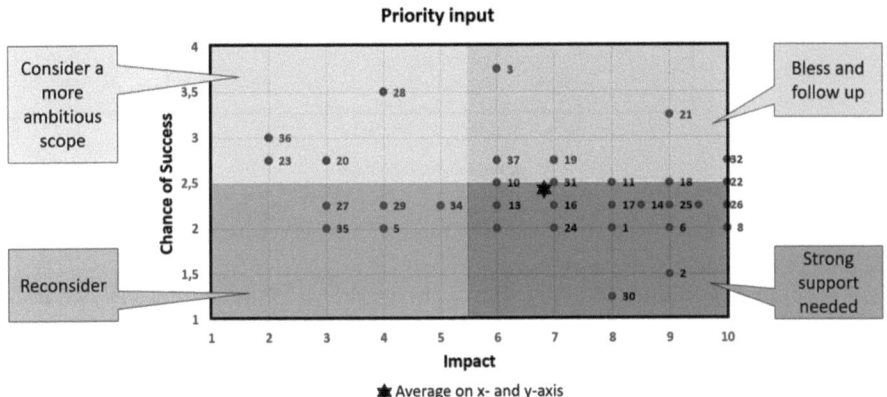

Fig. 5. First evaluation - Chance of success versus impact

Below in the "Strong support needed" quadrant were those improvement projects that needed support from the PMO department if they should deliver the expected high impact. Suggested PMO department activities: Training, support, resources, prioritization, conflict solving, mentoring, etceteras.

In the top left "Consider a more ambitious scope" quadrant was the improvement projects that was in a good shape, but had less impact. Maybe good enough, but maybe the PMO department could use the inertia and boost the scope.

In the "Reconsider" quadrant was those that maybe was not worse the effort, but in this case, they were all ok.

6 First PPM Evaluation at Vestas

8 month later, a new group of improvement projects was initiated and ready to be included in the PMO departments overview of ongoing improvement initiatives. 8 improvement projects were re-scoped or re-started from projects from the first evaluation and were now part of 6 of the projects in the second analysis due to more focus and support – and are therefore part of both analysis. In total we ended with interview of 26 improvement projects.

Same analysis was applied, and the effect of the increased focus was visible. The selected projects had a higher impact and a greater chance of success, which is illustrated by the change from Figs. 5 to 6 where you can see the "average star" has moved to a higher degree of change for success and higher degree of impact on the maturity.

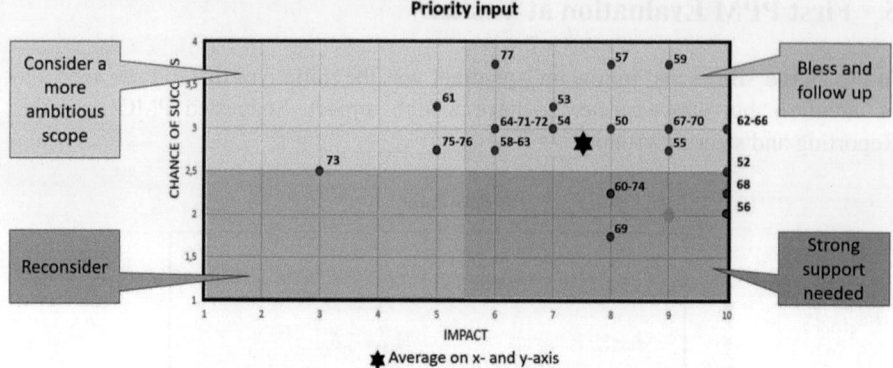

Fig. 6. Second evaluation - Chance of success versus impact

A set of data (as illustrated in Fig. 4) was also generated for the second analysis. If the two set of data are compared it is clear, that all enhance parameters have improved – with the largest positive difference for the parameters: Sensing urgency, Idea processing, Involving others and Management Competences.

6.1 Development of the Ability to Improve over Time

The second analysis revealed that both the impact and the chance of success has increased over the 8 month. This is of course due to more factors, but the end result is that the overall organizational maturity will increase – faster. Which by the end of the day is the sole purpose of this exercise? The increased impact was likely and partly due to:

1. Improvement projects initiated by management as opposed to initiated by engineers
2. Better prioritizing of improvement projects for the evaluation.

The increased chance of success was likely and partly due to:

1. Increased focus on the importance of treating the projects the same way as product development projects
2. Allocating hours and budgets and hour registration
3. Looking for successes
4. Organizational changes
5. Promotion of leaders with a strong improvement agenda.

The breakthrough with this analysis is that it has proven the effect, and provided the leadership with insight to speed up the process even more.

The Whitebox analysis has also enabled or supported Senior management and PMO department in the following activities as part of leading process improvements:

- Organizing improvements to ensure success
- Change of scope for optimal benefit
- Knowledge exchange between different – but related – improvement projects

- Collaboration between projects
- Mergers of improvement projects when they share the same goal and must be global oriented
- Performance expectation management in the organization. Is the roadmap realistic?
- Initiation of new projects in weak processes that is not covered by the actual projects
- Include relevant, but not yet identified, stakeholders in the projects
- Demonstrating progress on specific enhancement parameters.

7 Discussion and Next Steps

The accuracy of both the "chance of success" and the "impact" is obvious depending on the level of analysis performed. In this specific case a light version of both the ImprovAbility analysis and the CMMI impact analysis was performed and seemed sufficiently accurate, since the use of the results was internal, and it was not used as the final answer. The responsible managers have in all cases applied their final judgement to all decisions. What is unknown is what benefit a deeper analysis would have brought.

The analysis was performed by assessors who have performed hundreds of maturity assessments and were responsible for the project that developed the ImprovAbility model. What is unknown is what level of experience is required to perform the analysis.

A deeper analysis of the "chance of success" could almost auto-generate a specific risk profile for each improvement project from the ImprovAbility model. When would this be valuable? We have no doubt that this approach speed up the organizations ability to improve. Can it be measured how much is however up for further discussion. Or would a senior management consider "being ahead of competition" as a strong enough driver to pursue this approach.

8 Conclusion

In this paper, we set out to answer the overall research question, *How can we improve PPM for improvement projects?*

The overall answer to that is that you can combine the use of a CMMI model [10] and assessment and an ImprovAbility model [11] and assessment thereby establishing an overview of the organizations improvement projects. This overview can then be used to prioritize, lead and manage the portfolio of improvement projects in a way that optimize the improvement effect on business goals.

In the concrete case of Vestas, we also demonstrated the answer to the second research question we phrased, *whether one can use these improvement models to improve PPM for improvement projects?* The answer given in Sects. 4, 5, 6 and 7 of this paper documents how Vestas established a strong focus on process improvement, managed by the PMO department, based on CMMI maturity assessments to establish the baseline and using the ImprovAbility model to evaluate, prioritize and focus improvement projects.

The effort that went into the PPM undertaking for Vestas included approximately 2.5 consultancy month and 1 Vestas month covering approx. 60 improvement projects.

For the Vice President at the Vestas PMO department it is obvious, that the benefit from using the combined ImprovAbility and CMMI approach at Vestas was the ability to prioritize between the improvement projects to be able to optimize the budget for improvement projects to get the best impact on the maturity improvement. It was also beneficial as communication mean – the visualization of the improvements of the ability to improve.

References

1. Levine, H.A.: Project Portfolio Management. San Francisco (2005)
2. Daniel, E.M., Ward, J.M., Franken, A.: A dynamic capabilities perspective of IS project portfolio management. J. Strateg. Inf. Syst. **23**(2), 95–111 (2014)
3. Hunt, R., et al.: Project portfolio management for product innovation. Int. J. Qual. Reliab. Manage. **25**(1), 24–38 (2008)
4. PMI: The Standard for Portfolio Management, 3rd edn. Project Management Institute (2013)
5. Blichfeldt, B.S., Eskerod, P.: Project portfolio management–there's more to it than what management enacts. Int. J. Project Manage. **26**(4), 357–365 (2008)
6. Martinsuo, M.: Project portfolio management in practice and in context. Int. J. Project Manage. **31**(6), 794–803 (2013)
7. Kaiser, M.G., El Arbi, F., Ahlemann, F.: Successful project portfolio management beyond project selection techniques: Understanding the role of structural alignment. Int. J. Project Manage. **33**(1), 126–139 (2015)
8. Beringer, C., Jonas, D., Kock, A.: Behavior of internal stakeholders in project portfolio management and its impact on success. Int. J. Project Manage. **31**(6), 830–846 (2013)
9. ISO: ISO/IEC/TR 33014, in Information technology – Process assessment – Guide for process improvement, Geneva, Switzerland (2013)
10. CMMI: CMMI® for Development, Version 1.3, Improving processes for developing better products and services. No. CMU/SEI-2010-TR-033. Software Engineering Institute (2010)
11. Pries-Heje, J., Johansen, J. (eds.) ImprovAbility: Success with process improvement. DELTA, Hørsholm, (2013)
12. ISO/IEC_33001: Information technology – Process assessment – Concepts and terminology. Geneva, Switzerland. (the first of the ISO/IEC 330xx serie of standards) (2015)

Coverage of ISO/IEC 29110 Project Management Process of Basic Profile by a Serious Game

Alejandro Calderón[1(✉)], Mercedes Ruiz[1], and Rory V. O'Connor[2]

[1] University of Cádiz, Cádiz, Spain
{alejandro.calderon,mercedes.ruiz}@uca.es
[2] Dublin City University, Dublin, Ireland
rory.oconnor@dcu.ie

Abstract. The ISO/IEC 29110 standard aims to assist and encourage Very Small Entities (VSEs) in understanding, adopting, assessing and improving their software processes to their specific needs. Although the integration of international software standards in VSEs is a relevant topic, the learning/teaching process is a considerable challenge for industrial trainers, practitioners and VSEs. In this paper, we analyze the Project Management process of the Basic Profile of the ISO/IEC 29110 and propose a simulation-based serious game for supporting the learning/teaching process of the standard. The paper provides a mapping between the different stages of the game lifecycle and the Project Management process of the standard. Moreover, we present the results of a preliminary study to assess the idea of using the proposed serious game for supporting software process education, which allows getting initial positive evidence about the potential of the game for helping to understand the Project Management process of the standard.

Keywords: ISO/IEC 29110 · Serious games · Teaching standards · Software project management · VSE

1 Introduction

Very Small Entities (VSEs) refer to "an enterprise, organization, department or project having up to 25 people" which have special characteristics that making their business styles different to SMEs [1]. Due to their small number of employees, VSEs often perform their management processes in an informal and less documented way, than larger organizations. For that reason, the ISO/IEC 29110 standard has been developed in order to assist and encourage VSEs in evaluating and improving their software processes [2], but the understanding and integration of the standard's processes could be a difficult task for practitioners who are inexperienced in applying or adapting the processes, activities, tasks and outcomes of the international standards to their specific needs.

Teaching international software standards is a challenge that moves industry trainers to use new methods and techniques in order to reduce the time and effort invested for both practitioners and VSEs in the learning process of the standards [3].

Serious games, designed with a different purpose than only entertainment, are powerful tools that allow participants to experiment, learn from their own mistakes and acquire experience and helps trainers to teach practical knowledge within a risk-free environment [4].

Taking into account the important of teaching international software standards to VSEs and the advantages of using serious games in the learning/teaching process, the main contributions of this paper are: (i) analyzing the use of serious games for software process, concretely for ISO/IEC 29110, (ii) providing a mapping between the different stages of a proposed serious game and the Project Management process of Basic profile of ISO/IEC 29110, and (iii) evaluating the idea of using the proposed simulation-based serious game to support VSEs for teaching practitioners in the standard.

The structure of the paper is as follows: Sect. 2 shows the background of this study. Section 3 describes the simulation-based serious game and assesses the coverage of the Project Management process of ISO/IEC 29110 of our serious game. Section 4 discusses the idea of using the proposed serious game to support VSEs for teaching practitioners in the standard. Finally, Sect. 5 summarizes the paper and presents our conclusions and future work.

2 Background

2.1 ISO/IEC 29110

ISO/IEC 29110 [5, 6] is an international systems and software engineering standard that establishes lifecycle profiles for VSEs. The standard provides frameworks and guides for VSEs that do not have experience in applying or adapting the processes, activities, tasks and outcomes of ISO/IEC 12207 or ISO/IEC 15288 standards to their specific needs.

The standard defines processes according to different profiles, which have been designed to implement specific process for VSEs at different stages of development The "Generic Profile Group" of the standard is a collection of four profiles (Entry, Basic, Intermediate and Advanced) which are related either by composition of processes (i.e. activities, tasks, etc.) and is applicable to a vast majority of VSEs that do not develop critical systems or software products and have typical situations factors. Currently, only the Basic and Entry profiles have been published. The Basic profile contains the Entry profile and its purpose is to define software and systems development and project management guide for describing a single application by a single project team of a VSE.

The ISO/IEC 29110 Basic Profile Management and Engineering Guide [7] provides Project Management and Software Implementation processes in order to be used by VSEs to establish processes to implement any development approach or methodology including, e.g., agile, evolutionary, incremental, test driven development, etc. based on the VSE organization or project needs.

The Project Management process of Basic profile aims to establish and perform in a systematic way the tasks of the software implementation project that allows fulfilling the project's goals in the expected quality, time and cost [8]. As we can observe in

Fig. 1, the Project Management process establishes four main activities: Project Planning, Project Plan Execution, Project Assessment and Control and Project Closure. These activities start with the development of the project plan using the customer's Statement of Work and end with the closure activity that provides the project's documentation and products in accordance with contract requirements.

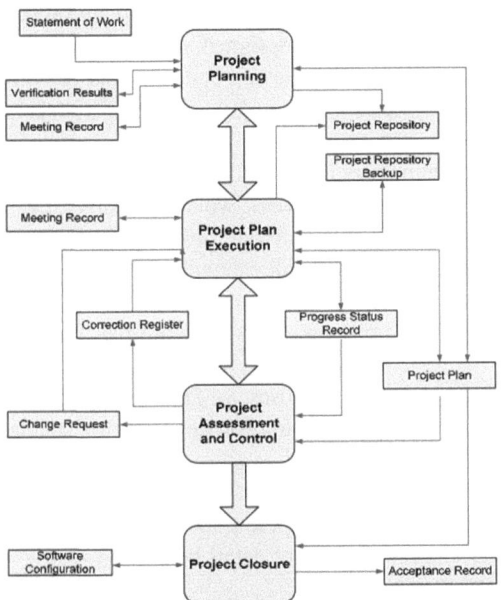

Fig. 1. Project management process diagram [7].

2.2 Serious Games in Software Process

Software development is a critical activity that is supported by standards such as ISO/IEC 21500, ISO/IEC 12207 or ISO/IEC 29110, with the goal to help on the road of creating software systems, products or services with quality. These standards define a set of processes and activities needed to model and address a broader range of issues that take place during the software development. Regarding the relevance of software process in the software development success, equal attention should be given to the training that practitioners and future software engineers receive in this scope.

As a consequence, in recent years an increased interest has been observed in the development and use of new methods and techniques to teach in a highly practical way, promote active and interactive learning, increase the motivation and engagement of learners and design new training strategies to train software process practitioners as skilled and qualified professionals. Among these new approaches, we can found the use of serious games [4]. Serious games are designed for purposes other than mere fun or entertainment [9]. They are powerful learning resources that allow participants to experiment, learn from their own mistakes and acquire experience, in a safe way within risk environments.

We can find several serious games in the field of software engineering education [10], but if we focus on software process education, we can observe few initiatives in the literature. The following serious games for software process education are some examples:

- SimSE is a serious game completely developed as a software tool that is based on software project simulation. The game supports several development methodologies and focuses on the development of abilities for software process management [11].
- DesignMPS is a computer game designed to support the teaching of software process modelling by reinforcing relevant concepts and providing software process modelling exercises, in where learners play the role of a process engineer who must model a process [12].
- Problems and Programmers is an educational serious card game to teach learners about the software engineering process, which is designed as a competitive game where participants try to finish a software project [13].
- Go for it! is a non-technological educational card game for the ISO/IEC 29110 standard elements teaching. Using the game, players are encouraged to understand the project management process and to reinforce their project management knowledge [14].
- Floors is a serious game that proposes a 3D interactive learning environment to introduce ISO/IEC 12207 where various processes of the standard are discussed and implemented [3].
- ProDec is a simulation-based serious game to teach and motivate software developers in learning and practicing the principles of software project management [15]. (This will be discussed in more detail below).

Although there are some initiatives that promote the use of serious games for software process education, only the non-technological proposal of Go for it! is focused on understanding the ISO/IEC 29110 standard, but there is not any digital proposal that allows to acquire a basis understanding and put into practices the software project management processes of this standard. For that reason, in this work we analyze the capability of ProDec, a simulation-based serious game, to cover the project management process of the ISO/IEC 29110 standard and we assess the idea of using the proposed serious game as a potential learning resource to support learners and practitioners in the learning the ISO/IEC 29110 standard.

3 Coverage of ISO/IEC 29110

In this section, we introduce the main features of ProDec, comment on the different activities and tasks of the Project Management process of the Basic profile of the ISO/IEC 29110 standard and map these activities and tasks with the different stages and functionalities of ProDec.

3.1 Game Description

ProDec [16] is a simulation-based serious game to teach and motivate software developers in learning and practicing the principles of software project management, as well as supporting the comprehension and knowledge acquisition of project management lifecycle processes and activities, in a risk-free environment.

As a simulation-based serious game, ProDec automatically generates a source code file with the equations of a discrete-event simulation model that simulates the execution of a project plan. During the simulation of the project plan execution, the serious game allows learners to practice their decision-making skills by controlling and monitoring the progress of the project execution in order to correct the potential deviations of the progress of the project.

As we can see in Fig. 2, ProDec gameplay follows a three-stage lifecycle (Onset, Execution, and End stages) that allow learners to take contact with the main project management processes involved from the creation of a project plan until the closure of a project. The aim of the gameplay of ProDec is to successfully manage a software project, this means that players win when they are able to complete the project within the time and cost constraints. On the other hand, the game is over when the project significantly overruns either the approved budget or the allocated time.

In the following subsections, we describe the different elements and functionalities associated with each stage of the gameplay's lifecycle and discuss their mapping with the project management processes and their activities of the Basic profile of the ISO/IEC 29110.

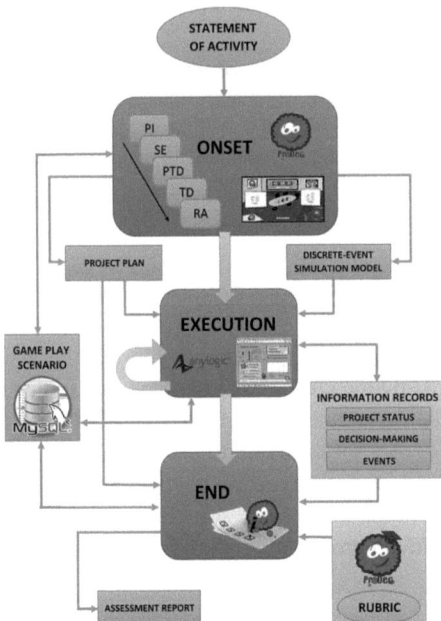

Fig. 2. ProDec gameplay's lifecycle.

3.2 Project Planning Activity

The first activity in the project management process of the ISO/IEC 29110 is the Project Planning (PM.1). In this activity takes place the definition of all the planning details needed to manage a project. During this activity, taking into account the Statement of Work provided by the customer, the Project Plan is defined and accepted. With the goal to perform the Project Planning activity, the standard defines 15 tasks as we can see in Table 1[1].

Table 1. List of tasks of the Project Management Activity of the ISO/IEC 29110 [7].

Task ID	Task Description
PM.1.1	Review the Statement of Work.
PM.1.2	Define with the Customer the Delivery Instructions of each one of the Deliverables specified in the Statement of Work. This task produces the planning details of the Delivery Instructions within the Project Plan.
PM.1.3	Identify the specific Tasks to be performed in order to produce the Deliverables and their Software Components identified in the Statement of Work. In this task all Projects' Tasks are defined and documented.
PM.1.4	Establish the Estimated Duration to perform each task.
PM.1.5	Identify and document the Resources of the Project: human, material, toots, etc. In this task all the needed Resources of the project are identified.
PM.1.6	Establish the Composition of Work Team assigning roles and responsibilities according to the Resources. The Work Team is defined in this task.
PM.1.7	Assign estimated start and completion dates to each one of the Tasks in order to create the Schedule of the Project Tasks taking into account the assigned Resources, sequence and dependency of the Tasks.
PM.1.8	Calculate and document the project Estimated Effort and Cost.
PM.1.9	Identify and document the risks which may affect the project.
PM.1.10	Document the Version Control Strategy in the Project Plan.
PM.1.11	Generate the Project Plan integrating the elements previously identified and documented.
PM.1.12	Include Product Description, Scope, Objectives and Deliverables in the Project Plan.
PM.1.13	Verify and obtain approval of the Project Plan.
PM.1.14	Review and accept the Project Plan.
PM.1.15	Establish the Project Repository using the Version Control Strategy.

Regarding ProDec gameplay's lifecycle (see Fig. 2), the Project Planning Activity of the standard is covered by the Onset stage of the game. In this stage, players follow a process that guides them to create from scratch a software Project Plan taking into account the Statement of Activity provided by trainers.

At the beginning of the stage, players review and analyze the Statement of Activity in order to know the specifications of the software project to be developed (PM.1.1is covered). Then, they follow a process that allows them to define all the planning details

---

[1] Note: in the tables we show the tasks of the ISO/IEC 29110 standard that ProDec is able to cover by highlighting the cell in grey shadow.

to generate the new software Project Plan. This process is composed of five stages, which are the following:

- Project Information (PI). In this stage, players define and provide the general information of the project such as its scope, objective, specifications, etc. and the specific information of the project that is needed to start the size estimation stage such as the salary of the workers, the delivery date, the number of use cases, etc. This stage allows ProDec covering the tasks PM.1.2 and PM.1.12 of the ISO/IEC 29110 standard.
- Size Estimation (SE). In this stage, players perform the size estimation of the project using a method of function points-based estimation and calculate and document the estimated effort and cost of the project. This stage allows ProDec to cover the task PM.1.8 of the ISO/IEC 29110 standard.
- Project Team Definition (PTD). In this stage, players design and define the human resources of the project and establish the composition of the work team. This stage allows ProDec to cover the tasks PM.1.5 and PM.1.6 of the ISO/IEC 29110 standard.
- Tasks Definition (TD). In this stage, players define the project Tasks, estimate the duration of each of them, allocated the human resources for each Task and create the schedule of the project Tasks taking into account the estimated start and completion dates, the assigned human resources and the dependency of the Tasks. Taking into account the list of tasks of the Project Management Activity of the ISO/IEC 29110 standard through this stage ProDec is able to cover the tasks PM.1.3, PM.1.4 and PM.1.7.
- Risks Analysis (RA). In this stage, players identify and make a quantitative risk analysis. Hence, through this stage, ProDec is able to cover the task PM.1.9 of the standard.

Once this process is finished, players need to review all the provided data and accept the Project Plan in order to generate the Project Plan and allow ProDec the creation of a source code file with the equations of a discrete-event simulation model that simulates the project created. Then, the tasks PM.1.11, PM.1.13 and PM.1.14 are covered at the end of this process.

3.3 Project Plan Execution Activity

The Project Plan Execution Activity (PM.2) is the second activity in the Project Management process of the ISO/IEC 29110 standard. This activity executes the Project Plan documented in the previous activity. To perform this activity the standard defines 6 tasks related to the Project Plan monitoring, the Change Request and the Project versions management (see Table 2).

The Project Plan Execution Activity (PM.2) is covered by the Execution stage of ProDec gameplay's lifecycle. This stage of the gameplay process consists of executing the Project Plan created during the Onset stage. In this stage of the gameplay, the Discrete-Event Simulation Model is launched and players start the monitoring of the project. For that reason, the game provides several screens where the progress of the project is presented and shows the value of the Earned Value Analysis indicators in

Table 2. List of tasks of the Project Plan Execution Activity of the ISO/IEC 29110 [2].

Task ID	Task Description
PM.2.1	Monitor the Project Plan execution and record actual data in Progress Status Record.
PM.2.2	Analyze and evaluate the Change Request for cost, schedule and technical impact.
PM.2.3	Conduct revision meetings with the Work Team, identify problems, review risk status, record agreements and track them to closure.
PM.2.4	Conduct revision meetings with the Customer, record agreements and track them to closure.
PM.2.5	Perform backup according to the Version Control Strategy.
PM.2.6	Perform Project Repository recovery using the Project Repository Backup, if necessary.

every moment. Hence, players need to put into practice their knowledge for understanding all the information provided and discussing within their team (if the game is playing by teams) for monitoring the progress of the project. Through these activities of the Execution stage, ProDec is able to cover the tasks PM.2.1 and PM.2.3 of the ISO/IEC 29110 standard.

3.4 Project Assessment and Control Activity

The third activity of the Project Management process of the ISO/IEC 29110 standard is the Project Assessment and Control Activity (PM.3). In this activity, the progress of the project is assessed against the commitments of the documented project and it establishes actions to correct the problems, deviations or identified risks related to the accomplishment of the Project Plan. The standard defines 3 tasks within this activity, which are listed in Table 3.

Table 3. List of tasks of the Project Assessment and Control Activity of the ISO/IEC 29110 [2].

Task ID	Task Description
PM.3.1	Evaluate project progress with respect to the Project Plan.
PM.3.2	Establish actions to correct deviations or problems and identified risks concerning the accomplishment of the plan, as needed, document them in Correction Register and track them to closure.
PM.3.3	Identify changes to requirements and/or Project Plan to address major deviations, potential risks or problems concerning the accomplishment of the plan, document them in Change Request and track them to closure.

The Project Assessment and Control Activity (PM.3) is also covered by the Execution stage of ProDec gameplay's lifecycle. During this stage, players not only perform the monitoring the project but also control its progress by correcting the potential deviations against the Project Plan with the goal of ending the project within the time, cost and quality established. Players need to evaluate the different screens presented by the game in order to get the needed information to identify the problems, deviations or risks that could be affecting the adequate progression of the Project Plan. Then, ProDec covers the tasks PM.3.1 and PM.3.3 of the standard. If a corrective action is needed, the game provides a set of actions that allows players to make decisions to control the progress of the project such as manage the Schedule of the Tasks of the project or the Work Team. Through this decision-making, the game is able to cover the task PM.3.1 of the ISO/IEC 29110 standard.

On the other hand, during the whole of the Execution stage, the game records information about the status of the project, the decision-makings and the events occurred. Hence, the game stores automatically all the needed information to monitor, track and control the execution of the Project Plan.

3.5 Project Closure Activity

Finally, the last activity of the Project Management process of the Basic profile of the ISO/IEC 29110 standard is the Project Closure Activity (PM.4). This activity is composed of 2 tasks that consist of providing the project's documentation and products according to the contract requirements (see Table 4).

Table 4. List of tasks of the Project Closure Activity of the ISO/IEC 29110 [2].

Task ID	Task Description
PM.4.1	Formalize the completion of the project according to the Delivery Instructions established in the Project Plan, providing acceptance support and getting the Acceptance Record signed.
PM.4.2	Update Project Repository.

Regarding the ProDec gameplay's lifecycle, this activity is covered by the Execution and End stages. At the end of the Execution stage, the game shows the results of the simulation of the execution of the project. In this step of the gameplay players can accept the results of the game scenario or can run the simulation again as many times as they want until they agree with the achieved outcomes, this is until they win the game or get a solution close to the winner solution. Therefore the task PM.4.1 can be covered in this stage of ProDec gameplay's lifecycle.

Once players agree with their solution and accepts the outcome of the gameplay, ProDec begins the End stage. In this stage, ProDec using the information records generated during the Execution stage and the assessment rubric provided by the trainers through the administration tool it concludes with the generation of a detailed report. This Assessment Report allows players to get the lessons learned from their performance during the game. These lessons help players analyze the events occurred along the game to learn from their own mistakes, acquire decision-making skills, make new ideas for future plays or even get the enough knowledge for improving the life cycle process of the project.

4 Discussion

Regarding the Project Management process diagram (Fig. 1) and the ProDec gameplay's lifecycle diagram (Fig. 2), we can observe the similarities and do a visual mapping between both processes. In fact, as we have analyzed during the previous section ProDec is able to cover 19 tasks of the 26 tasks that the ISO/IEC 29110 standard defines for the Project Management process of the Basic profile. That means ProDec support players to take into contact with at least 70% of the whole Project Management process.

On the other hand, the tasks, ProDec cannot currently cover, are related to the Change Request, Version Control Strategy and Project Repository management and the interactivity with the Customer (meetings, revisions, etc.). Nevertheless, during a gameplay, all the information related to the gameplay scenario and players' progression inside it is stored in the Gameplay Scenario database. Then, we can conclude that ProDec could indirectly provide supporting for tasks related to Project Repository and Version Control Strategy. In addition, the trainers could perform the role of Customers during the gameplay scenario in order to cover the tasks that need the Customers' presence. Hence, ProDec could cover almost the whole of the Project Management process of the Basic profile of the ISO/IEC 29110 standard.

The idea of using ProDec for supporting software process education have been assessed by a group of undergraduate and graduate students as part of a Computer Engineering Degree and Master degree from the University of Cadiz and some practitioners of the software engineering scope that work in VSEs. A total of 21 participants performed a practical session with ProDec in order to assess its educational potential as a learning resource. Participants were invited to complete a post-game questionnaire to obtain their feedback on their player experience and perceived learning with the use of ProDec. The post-game questionnaire is composed of 59 items rating in a Likert-like scale (–2, –1, 0, 1, 2), where 2 means strongly agree and –2 strongly disagree. Table 5 shows a summary of the achieved outcomes related to the perceived learning of different areas of knowledge that players put into practice during the game plays.

Table 5. Results of the perceived learning ProDec's assessment.

Knowledge areas	Median	Mean	Knowledge areas	Median	Mean
Plan project	1	1.30	Project tasks	1	1.22
Size estimation	1	1.13	Risks analysis	1	0.9
Work team	2	1.37	Controlling and monitoring the project	1	1.30

As we can observe the assessed areas of knowledge rate a median value equal or greater than 1 and an average value among 0.9 and 1.37. These values mean that participants agree on ProDec helps to understand and put into practice the concepts and practices related to these knowledge areas of the software project management. Moreover the score related to the player experience reaches a median value of 1 and an average of 0.82 allowing us to know that participants consider that ProDec can be a potential learning resource not only in terms of learning goals but also in terms of usability, relevance, confidence, challenge, satisfaction, focused attention, social interaction and fun that it is able to provide.

5 Conclusions and Further Works

Although the use of international software standards is an important topic in software systems, products or services with quality and improves the software process, the learning/teaching process of them is not easy and it turns into a challenge if we focus in VSEs and practitioners that have never taken contact with them.

The ISO/IEC 29110 standard is intended to be used by VSEs that do not have experience in applying or adapting ISO/IEC 12207 or ISO/IEC 15288 standards to their specific needs. Taking into account this standard, in this work, we have analyzed the capability of ProDec, a simulation-based serious game, for covering the Project Management process of the Basic profile of the ISO/IEC 29110 standard and we have evaluated the idea of using the serious game to support and carry out the learning/teaching process of the standard.

ProDec has a gameplay's lifecycle that shares a high level of similarity with the Project Management process of the standard, being able to cover directly more than 70% of the tasks defined by the standard and indirectly almost 100% of the Project Management process, if we perform some adaptations. This coverage of the standard and the preliminary outcomes of the effectiveness evaluation of ProDec in terms of player experience and perceived learning give us positive evidence about the potential idea of using ProDec as a learning resource for supporting software process education and help practitioners of VSEs understanding and practicing the Project Management process of the Basic profile of the ISO/IEC 29110 standard.

Our aim is to create a learning tool to support the learning/teaching process of software process education and help practitioners to understand and adopt the international software standards such as ISO/IEC 29110 and ISO/IEC 12207. For this reason, our future works are related to perform evaluations of the game with VSEs in order to get the necessary feedback for improving and adapting it in order to provide a complete coverage of the software project management processes of the main international software standards.

Acknowledgements. This work has been partially supported by the Spanish Ministry of Science and Technology with AEI/FEDER/UE funds (grants TIN2013-46928-C3-2-R and TIN2016-76956-C3-3-R) and the Andalusian Plan for Research, Development and Innovation (grant TIC-195).

References

1. Sanchez-Gordón, M.-L., O'Connor, R.V., Colomo-Palacios, R., Herranz, E.: Bridging the gap between SPI and SMEs in educational settings: a learning tool supporting ISO/IEC 29110. In: Kreiner, C., O'Connor, R.V., Poth, A., Messnarz, R. (eds.) EuroSPI 2016. CCIS, vol. 633, pp. 3–14. Springer, Cham (2016). doi:10.1007/978-3-319-44817-6_1
2. Laporte, C.Y., Alexandre, S., O'Connor, R.V.: A software engineering lifecycle standard for very small enterprises. In: O'Connor, R.V., Baddoo, N., Smolander, K., Messnarz, R. (eds.) EuroSPI 2008. CCIS, vol. 16, pp. 129–141. Springer, Heidelberg (2008). doi:10.1007/978-3-540-85936-9_12
3. Aydan, U., Yilmaz, M., Clarke, P.M., O'Connor, R.V.: Teaching ISO/IEC 12207 software lifecycle processes: a serious game approach. Comput. Stand. Interfaces (2016). doi:10.1016/j.csi.2016.11.014
4. Kosa, M., Yilmaz, M., O'Connor, R.V., Clarke, P.M.: Software engineering education and games: a systematic literature review. J. Univ. Comput. Sci. **22**(12), 1558–1574 (2016)
5. ISO/IEC: ISO/IEC TR 29110-1:2016 - Systems and software engineering – Lifecycle profiles for Very Small Entities (VSEs) – Part 1: Overview (2016)
6. O'Connor, R., Laporte, C.: The evolution of the ISO/IEC 29110 set of standards and guides. Int. J. Inf. Technol. Syst. Approach **10**(1), 1–21 (2017)
7. ISO/IEC: ISO/IEC TR 29110-5-1-2:2011 - Software engineering – Lifecycle profiles for Very Small Entities (VSEs) – Part 5-1-2: Management and engineering guide: Generic profile group: Basic profile (2011)
8. O'Connor, R.V., Laporte, C.Y.: Software project management in very small entities with ISO/IEC 29110. In: Winkler, D., O'Connor, R.V., Messnarz, R. (eds.) EuroSPI 2012. CCIS, vol. 301, pp. 330–341. Springer, Heidelberg (2012). doi:10.1007/978-3-642-31199-4_29
9. Abt, C.: Serious Games. University Press of America, Lanhan (2002)
10. Caulfield, C., Xia, J., Veal, D., Maj, S.: A systematic survey of games used for software engineering education. Modern Appl. Sci. **5**(6), 28–43 (2011)
11. Navarro, E.O., van der Hoek, A.: SimSE: an interactive simulation game for software engineering education. In: Proceedings of the 7th IASTED International Conference on Computers and Advanced Technology in Education, Kauai, Hawaii (2004)
12. Oliveira Chaves, R., Gresse von Wangenheim, C., Costa Furtado, J.C., Ronaldo Bezerra Oliveira, S., Santos, A., Favero, E.L.: Experimental evaluation of a serious game for teaching software process modeling. IEEE Trans. Educ. **58**(4), 289–296 (2015)
13. Baker, A., Oh Navarro, E., Van Der Hoek, A.: An experimental card game for teaching software engineering processes. J. Syst. Softw. Eng. Educ. Training **75**, 3–16 (2005)
14. Sánchez-Gordón, M.-L., O'Connor, R.V., Colomo-Palacios, R., Sanchez-Gordon, S.: A learning tool for the ISO/IEC 29110 standard: understanding the project management of basic profile. In: Clarke, P.M., O'Connor, R.V., Rout, T., Dorling, A. (eds.) SPICE 2016. CCIS, vol. 609, pp. 270–283. Springer, Cham (2016). doi:10.1007/978-3-319-38980-6_20
15. Calderón, A., Ruiz, M.: Coverage of ISO/IEC 12207 software lifecycle process by a simulation-based serious game. In: Clarke, P.M., O'Connor, R.V., Rout, T., Dorling, A. (eds.) SPICE 2016. CCIS, vol. 609, pp. 59–70. Springer, Cham (2016). doi:10.1007/978-3-319-38980-6_5
16. Calderón, A., Ruiz, M.: ProDec: a serious game for software project management training. In: Proceedings of the 8th ICSEA, Venice, Italy (2013)

SPI and Implementation

Improving Model Inspection Processes with Crowdsourcing: Findings from a Controlled Experiment

Dietmar Winkler[1(✉)], Marta Sabou[1], Sanja Petrovic[1], Gisele Carneiro[2], Marcos Kalinowski[2], and Stefan Biffl[1]

[1] Institute of Software Technology, Vienna University of Technology,
Favoritenstrasse 9-11, 1040 Vienna, Austria
{dietmar.winkler,reka.sabou,sanja.petrovic,
stefan.biffl}@tuwien.ac.at
[2] Graduate Program in Computing, Fluminense Federal University, Niterói, RJ, Brazil
{gcarneiro,kalinowski}@ic.uff.br

Abstract. The application of best-practice software inspection processes for early defect detection requires considerable human effort. Crowdsourcing approaches can support inspection activities (a) by distributing inspection effort among a group of human experts and (b) by increasing inspection control. Thus, the application of crowdsourcing techniques aims at making inspection processes more effective and efficient. In this paper, we present a crowdsourcing-supported model inspection (CSI) process and investigate its defect detection effectiveness and efficiency when inspecting an Extended Entity Relationship (EER) model. The CSI process uses so-called Expected Model Elements (EMEs) to guide CSI inspectors during defect detection. We conducted a controlled experiment on defect detection effectiveness, efficiency, and false positives. While CSI effectiveness and efficiency is lower for CSI inspectors, the number of false positives decreases. However, CSI was found promising for increasing the control of defect detection and supports the inspection of large-scale engineering models.

Keywords: Software inspection · Software models · Crowdsourcing · Empirical study · Process improvement

1 Introduction

Verifying software engineering models prior to the creation of software is of particular relevance for database design, creating software architectures, and agreeing on mission critical test cases [1]. In model-based software engineering, the quality of increasingly large models has become a critical issue for deriving mission-critical system parts as software artifacts are directly derived from models [2]. A major challenge is to verify the correct representation of reference documents in corresponding models that were derived from these reference documents.

Software inspection [3] is an important human-based approach to detect defects in software artifacts that are hard to detect automatically. Software model inspection typically focuses on checking whether a conceptual model correctly and completely represents the content of suitable reference documents, such as systems specifications [4]. Although the verification of software models is key to ensure high quality for mission-critical software, this verification faces several challenges [5]. First, large software models and large associated reference documents are challenging to inspect with the limited resources in one inspection session. Second, there are only limited means for the cost-effective coordination of inspector teams to achieve systematic coverage of large inspection materials. Third, best-practice reading techniques for inspection can systematically guide the inspectors in an inspection team, but there is only limited tool support available for the coordinated inspection of models [5].

Based on these challenges, we explore how software model verification can be improved with *Human Computation and Crowdsourcing (HC&C)* methods. HC&C techniques rely on splitting large and complex problems into multiple, small tasks that can be solved quickly by an average contributor in a suitable population and then coordinating the collection and aggregation of individual micro-contributions into a larger result [6]. However, the application of HC&C techniques in traditional inspection processes needs some adaptations on process and method level.

In this paper we present the *Crowdsourced Software Inspection (CSI)* process based on traditional best-practice inspection and HC&C techniques and evaluated the CSI process in a controlled experiment with focus on defect detection performance, i.e., defect detection effectiveness, efficiency, and false positives. The remainder of this paper is structured as follows: Sect. 2 presents related work and Sect. 3 presents our study goals and research issues. We present the CSI process in Sect. 4, the study design in Sect. 5, and the results in Sect. 6. Section 7 discusses the results and presents threats to validity. Finally, Sect. 8 concludes and presents future work.

2 Background and Related Work

This section summarizes background and related work on software inspection and crowdsourcing in Software Engineering.

2.1 Software Inspection

Software inspections enable defect detection in different types of artifacts, such as text documents, models, or software code before delivering them to next software life cycle activities [3]. Figure 1 presents the traditional process [3] consisting of five

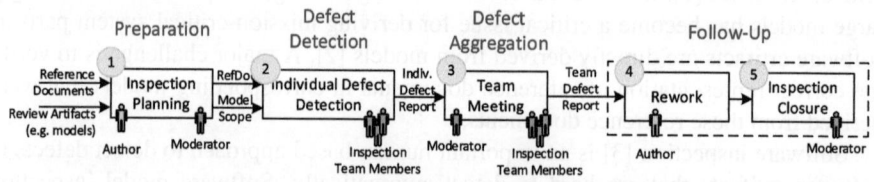

Fig. 1. Traditional software inspection process.

steps: (1) *Inspection Planning* for preparation, scheduling, and team composition; (2) *Individual Defect Detection* by inspection team members to identify defects in related artifacts; (3) *Team meetings* to collect, discuss, and aggregate individual defect reports; (4) *Rework* by the authors based on the team defect list; and (5) *Inspection Closure*. Reading techniques can be used to guide inspectors through the defect detection process [7].

However, traditional inspection is time-consuming and involves expensive experts as inspectors. The typical two-hour limit recommended for defect detection and team meeting activities [4] limits the scope of the inspection artifact and requires appropriate scoping during inspection preparation. Appropriate scoping is particularly challenging for large software models and reference documents. To address high effort for inspection, tool support can help to reduce effort and improve coordination of activities and results. Some tool support has been proposed to support overall inspection process coordination. For instance, the web-based tools presented in [8, 9] allowed reducing inspection meeting effort by supporting a slightly modified inspection process that replaces the face to face meetings with asynchronous discussions. However, those tools do not support scoping during inspection preparation.

Analyzing traditional inspection processes [10] there is a need for (a) appropriate scoping to enable efficient and effective defect detection for large-scale software artifacts; (b) systematic method support for defect detection, validation of defects, and coordination of inspection activities as these tasks are typically executed manually; and (c) guidelines for defect detection, such as reading techniques for model inspection as traditional reading techniques provide limited support for model inspection.

2.2 Crowdsourcing in Software Engineering

HC&C methods have recently enjoyed a significant uptake to solve a diversity of Software Engineering (SE) tasks [6] and lead to the emerging research area of *Crowdsourced Software Engineering (CSE)* defined as *"the act of undertaking any external software engineering tasks by an undefined, potentially large group of online workers in an open call format"* [6, 11]. A plausible reason for the intensified interest in the application of crowdsourcing techniques in SE is the appearance of mechanized labor *(micro-tasking)* platforms such as *Amazon Mechanical Turk*[1] or *CrowdFlower (CF)*[2]. Micro-tasking differs from traditional models of distributed work in SE, such as collaboration and peer-production, by being more scalable due to parallel execution of small task units by non-necessarily expert contributors. Therefore, micro-tasking is promising to address challenges in software inspection, e.g., improved coordination and control (of inspection team members, tasks, and results), increased coverage (as some parts of large artifacts might not be covered with traditional, weakly-coordinated approaches), more diversity (support for dealing with various inspection artifacts), and accelerated inspection processes (by parallelization of small tasks).

---

[1] Amazon Mechanical Turk: www.mturk.com.
[2] CrowdFlower: www.crowdflower.com.

In context of SE, Mao *et al.* [11] have recently performed a survey on the application of CSE approaches within the software development life cycle with focus on micro-tasking, collaboration, and peer-production. While the authors identified contributions of CSE to most of the software life cycle phases (i.e., planning and analysis (17 papers), design (4 papers), implementation (26 papers), testing (22 papers), and maintenance (26 papers)) software model inspection tasks have not been addressed by CSE approaches yet. Our work addresses on this gap and explores how HC&C micro-tasking principles can be used to improve software inspection processes through expert-based crowdsourcing, typically available within a community or organization.

3 Research Issues

Main goal of this paper is to improve model inspection with HC&C technologies with focus on improving defect detection capabilities. Main questions are (a) how to adapt/extend a best-practice inspection approach with crowdsourcing and (b) what are the effects of this CSI process approach. We describe the CSI process approach and evaluate this process in a controlled experiment by following the guidelines described by Wohlin *et al.* [12]. For evaluation purposes we applied the traditional Pen&Paper (P&P) approach as control group and derived two research hypotheses.

H1.0. Defect detection effectiveness of the CSI process is similar to traditional software inspection. The alternative Hypothesis H1.1 is that the CSI process is less effective compared to P&P inspection. We define effectiveness as the share of identified true defects and seeded defects.

H2.0 Defect detection efficiency of the CSI process is similar to traditional inspection. The alternative hypothesis H2.1 is that CSI performs better compared to the P&P approach, because CSI inspectors focus on small entities with clear tasks for defect detection. We define efficiency as the number of identified true defects per unit of resources spent, i.e., in the context of this paper defect found per hour.

4 Crowdsourced Inspection (CSI)-Process

To address these challenges, we adapted the traditional Software Inspection process to exploit HC&C capabilities with *Crowdsourcing-based Software Inspection (CSI)*.

4.1 Expected Model Elements (EMEs)

To manage small tasks for crowdsourcing application in context of model inspection, related model elements for the inspection process are required. We introduced the concept of *Expected Model Elements (EMEs)*, i.e., key concepts that can be expected in the model under inspection based on inputs from reference documents, i.e., software requirements and specifications [13]. The elicitation of these EMEs from reference documents can be done with a text analysis, executed by human experts or based on natural language processing (NLP) approaches [14]. In context the CSI process, human experts provide a set of EMEs that build an *Extended Entity Relationship* (EER) model

[15], i.e., from the requirements specification they derive entities, entity attributes, relationships, and relationship attributes. These EMEs are further applied to analyze the model and to identify deviations, i.e., defects.

4.2 CSI Process Approach

Based on the traditional inspection approach, we focus on the *Preparation* and *Software Inspection phases* (i.e., individual defect detection and team meeting) as core part of the inspection process. Figure 2 presents the adapted CSI process that consists of four phases: (1) *Preparation*; (2) *Text Analysis* to identify Expected Model Elements (EMEs); (3) *Model Analysis* to find defects based on EMEs; and (4) *Defect Analysis and Aggregation*: Note that the *Follow-Up Phase* (compared to the traditional inspection process, Fig. 1) has been excluded from Fig. 2 because of readability issues.

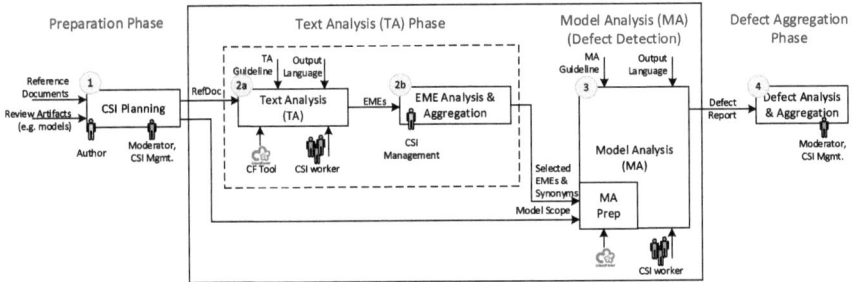

Fig. 2. Crowdsourced Inspection (CSI) process approach.

In the *Preparation Phase*, the moderator performs inspection planning and takes, in addition, the CSI management role. The author supports the moderator. Main tasks include (a) scoping of inspection artifacts, (b) preparing the crowdsourcing environment, and (c) uploading reference documents and inspection artifacts into the crowdsourcing platform. The *Text Analysis Phase* includes the analysis of the reference document with focus on identifying EMEs, executed by the CSI workers and reported via the crowdsourcing application (2a) and the analysis and aggregation of delivered EMEs, executed by the CSI management (2b). This process step also includes removing duplicate EMEs and the mapping of synonyms.

In the *Model Analysis Phase*, the CSI management prepares a selected set of EMEs, derived from manual text analysis and EME aggregation (output of step 2b) for model inspection. Furthermore, the CSI management prepares the model or a sub-model to be inspected. Sub-models are of specific interest if large models have to be inspected. In context of our study, there is no need for scoping the model because of an acceptable model size. For defect detection (i.e., model analysis), CSI workers receive an EME, e.g., an entity attribute, locate it in the model, and report either that the EME was modeled correctly or report at least one defect. In the *Defect Aggregation Phase*, the CSI management aggregates reported defects. Note that the author is not included in the crowdsourced defect detection tasks. He receives the aggregated defect detection reports for the follow-up phase, i.e., rework.

5 Experimental Study

In a controlled experiment we evaluated the effects of the CSI process with focus on defect detection effectiveness, efficiency, and false positives. The study has been initially described in [13, 16]. The goal of this paper is to extend the evaluation parts with focus on improving the software inspection process.

Following guidelines for conducting controlled experiments [12], the experimental study includes three key phases: *study preparation*, *study execution*, and *data collection and analysis*. The *study preparation phase* focuses on setting up the controlled experimental in terms of material preparation, tool setup for CSI and traditional inspection, study group definition, formal language for reporting EMEs and defects (i.e., "output language" in Fig. 2), and experiment schedule. Material includes reference documents and scenarios, guidelines, list of reference defects (seeded defects), and questionnaires (to capture participant experience and feedback). To test the study setup, we piloted the study in two iterations with domain experts to ensure the basic feasibility of the method and tool support in context of the study material. The *study execution phase* includes tutorials for CSI and P&P inspectors and the experiment. *Data collection and analysis* focused on preliminary data screening, assignment of reported defects to reference defects, and the evaluation of research questions. We analyzed the defect reports according to a list of reference defects, which was extended if a new true defect was found. This paper reports on preliminary findings of the study after the first data screening and data analysis run.

In the following we describe the main aspects of the controlled experiment, i.e., the *study process, participants, study material, tool configuration, study variables,* and applied concepts for *data collection & analysis*.

Study Process. Figure 3 presents an overview of the study process. The experiment was conducted in a classroom setting with 75 participants, who had to solve similar defect detection tasks in two main groups: CSI and P&P inspection. The majority of participants (63 participants, 84%) used the CSI approach while the rest of participants (12

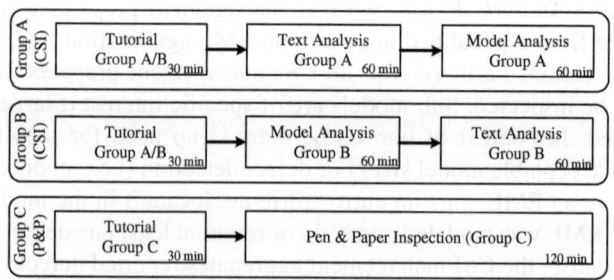

Fig. 3. Experimental process.

participants, 16%) were invited to use the traditional P&P approach. CSI inspectors were further divided in two sub-groups (A and B), who executed text and model analysis in a different sequence. P&P inspectors were assigned to group C (i.e., the control group). Group assignment was conducted randomly by using a sort card mechanism. Note that CSI and P&P participants were assigned to different rooms to avoid communication and interaction between individual groups.

In the first 30 min of the experiment, all inspectors received a tutorial on the processes, assigned to their group, to ensure that they were able to conduct the process steps and could discuss open issues before the experiment. For training purposes we used a different reference document and EER model in the tutorial, i.e., selected scenarios from a parking garage use case with a few defects and EMEs. The results of this tutorial can also give a first indication on the inspector capability for detecting defects in the target setting. The following 120 min were dedicated to the experiment with focus on a different application domain, i.e., restaurant scenarios. While group C applied a traditional (P&P) best-practice software inspection approach, groups A and B spent 60 min on the Text Analysis and 60 min on the Model Analysis task. We applied a cross-over design for the CSI part of the study, i.e., text analysis (60 min) followed by the model analysis (60 min) for group A and similar tasks in an inverse order for group B. For model analysis, we used a pre-defined set of EMEs to avoid dependencies between different tasks within the groups. These EMEs were provided by the experiment team, i.e., the authors, to focus on model analysis. Note that individual groups focused on a different part of the model.

Participants. A total of 75 study participants were recruited from undergraduate students attending the course on "Software Quality Assurance" at the TU Wien. Assignment to groups A, B and C relied on a random distribution of the participants. Since group C was a control group, less participants were assigned (12 inspectors) than to groups A& B (63 inspectors). Given the high number of participants the experiment was run during four different workshops each attended by maximum 20 participants. To assess the qualification of participants we used an experience questionnaire to capture their background skills related to their software engineering experiences and the number of projects they were involved in the past. The initial results showed that only 6 participants (8%) had limited experiences, while 51 (68%) had medium, and 18 (24%) had high experience in software engineering. Thus, the participants can be classified as junior professionals in industry context.

Study Material. Common material for both experiment parts (i.e., P&P inspection and CSI) consists of an experience questionnaire to capture background skills of the participants at the beginning of the study and feedback questionnaires after each step of the experiment process. The experience questionnaire includes demographics, working experiences in software development and quality assurance. The feedback questionnaire captures feedback on the method applied for improvement purposes. Questionnaires were realized using *Google.forms*. We also provided guidelines (as hardcopies) to guide the participants during their specific inspection tasks. We used an *Experiment Management System (EMS)* that holds relevant information for all groups, i.e., electronic documents (if applicable), web links to questionnaires, and links to CSI tasks (CSI inspectors only) in sequence of the task to be solved. To avoid domain-specific knowledge limitations, we applied a well-known application domain, i.e., typical scenarios of a restaurant process. Study material was a textual reference document, i.e., a system requirements specification including 3 pages in English language, consisting of 7 scenarios and approximately 110 EMEs. During study preparation, the scenarios were split into 33 sentences and numbered as vehicle for defect reporting and referring purposes. System requirements specification was considered to be correct. We used a medium-scale EER Diagram (9 entities, 13 relationships, and 32 attributes) including 33 seeded defects. These seeded defects were introduced by the experiment team (i.e., the authors) based on defects typically occurring during the typical software engineering processes. Furthermore, the participants received selected printed material, i.e., guidelines. For participants, these guidelines were used as supporting material complementary to guidelines provided by the EMS. For the experiment management, we used this guidelines for group assignment and to track the participants. Group C (P&P inspectors) participants also received printed version of the scenario description (i.e., the requirements specification) and the EER model. Participant had to hand-over all hardcopies to the experiment management team when finishing the workshop.

Tool Configuration. For *text analysis (TA)*, each CSI inspector received sentences drawn from half of the reference document, had to identify EMEs and report them via the *CrowdFlower* application. The P&P inspectors did not apply any explicit text analysis. For *model analysis (MA)*, each CSI inspector received up to three batches of EMEs linked to three scenarios, which were different than the scenarios inspected during text analysis to avoid bias. These batches of tasks have been assigned to the CSI participants via links to *CrowdFlower* jobs and the EMS. The CSI inspectors used the *CrowdFlower* platform to report defects. In more detail, for MA, a CSI inspector received (a) a scenario from the reference document to provide a reference context for defect detection and (b) an EME that is related to this scenario. In the study setting, CSI inspectors were encouraged to report all relevant defects related to a given EME (or a synonym) they found in the MA process. Group C inspectors used a spreadsheet solution to report defects and uploaded the final defect reports to EMS.

Variables. We define independent and dependent variables: Independent variables include the seeded defects of the EER model, defect types, tool configuration, and the study treatments. Dependent variables are effort for task execution, reported and true defects, effectiveness (share of reference defects found by a participant), false positives (candidate defects that do not match to seeded defects), and efficiency (reference defects found per hour).

Data Collection and Analysis. Organized by the EMS, we collected data electronically. For P&P inspection we collected all reported defects in the spreadsheet solution via the EMS. For text and model analysis we organized all data in the *CrowdFlower* application, i.e., EMEs and reported detects. To avoid a heterogeneous data input by individuals, we introduced an "output language", i.e., a data schema and formal language elements to make the analysis of reported EMEs and defects more efficient. Defects were reported as: (a) expected correct model conditions, e.g., a key should be valid; (b) the deviation in the model from the expectation; and (c) a severity level on a three-level severity scale (i.e., critical, normal, low severity). Questionnaire results were captured with *Google.forms*. All data were exported from the individual application and imported in a MySQL database for further evaluation, including consistency checks and data cleanup. We used a unique identifier to link different data sources. For data analysis, we applied descriptive statistics and the Mann-Whitney Test at a significance level of 95% (two-sided) for hypothesis testing.

6 Study Results

This section summarizes defect detection effort, effectiveness, efficiency, and false positives of the CSI process and P&P.

6.1 Effort

In the context of this study, we extracted the defect detection effort based on the reported starting and end time for P&P inspection and CSI inspectors. The defect detection task of CSI inspectors focuses on model analysis (MA) with a maximum duration of 60 min (CSI-MA). We did not consider the effort for the text analysis in this paper because it is not dedicated explicitly to defect detection (but to some kind of preparation effort). The P&P inspectors spent a maximum duration of 120 min for defect detection. Table 1 presents the descriptive statistics of individual defect detection tasks. The results showed that P&P requires on average less time for defect detection but included a higher standard deviation (SD). We also observed individual outliers for CSI and P&P because (a) some participants had to leave earlier and (b) others required more time to complete ongoing tasks after time has finished.

Table 1. Duration of P&P and CSI tasks [in min].

Group	#participants	Mean	SD	Min	Max
CSI-MA	63	53 min	11.9 min	28 min	80 min
P&P	12	107 min	27.5 min	28 min	135 min

6.2 Defect Detection Effectiveness

Effectiveness is the share of true defects and seeded defects in [%]. On average, all participants reported 16 defects (SD: 6.8) and 7 true defects (SD: 4.9) resulting in an effectiveness of 21.5% (SD: 14.82%). True defects that were identified more than once were calculated once at the first time of detection. Table 2 presents the results of reported defects, true defects, and effectiveness per study group (we did not separate CSI groups A and B in the evaluation context of this paper).

Table 2. Reported defects/True defects/Effectiveness.

Group	#participants	Reported defects		True defects		Effectiveness	
		Mean	SD	Mean	SD	Mean	SD
CSI-MA	63	15	6.5	7	4.9	30%	12.8%
P&P	12	21	5.7	10	4.6	20%	14.4%

The observations showed a higher number of reported defects and true defects for the P&P group compared to the CSI group. A main reason could be that the CSI group spent maximum 60 min for defect detection. Applying the Mann-Whitney-Test at a significance level of 95% (two-sided) showed significant differences for reported defects (p-value: 0.003(S)), reported true defects, i.e., seeded defects (p-value: 0.015(S)), and effectiveness (p-value: 0.015(S)). Thus, this evaluation showed benefits for P&P inspectors compared to CSI participants. However, the CSI group spent at most 60 min for defect detection (i.e., for model analysis) while P&P inspectors used at most 120 min for defect detection.

6.3 False Positives

An important question is whether or not the EMEs (i.e., pre-requisites for model analysis) can support defect detection by providing a clearer focus on individual model elements and, therefore, reduce false positives (because of that specific focus). In context of this study, we define False Positives (FP) as reported defects that cannot be mapped to a true defect. This mapping process has been executed by the experiment team (i.e., the authors).

Note that multiple reported defect that map to one true defect were counted once. Table 3 summarizes the absolute number of FP per study group. The results showed a lower number of FP for CSI, i.e., 8 FP on average (SD: 5.0) CSI participants and 11 FP (SD: 4.7) for P&P participants. These results indicate that EMEs can support defect detection processes by driving the inspection process. However, statistical significance was not observed (p-value: 0.055(–)).

Table 3. Absolute number of false positives.

Group	#participants	Mean	SD	Min	Max
CSI-MA	63	8	5.0	1	18
P&P	12	11	4.7	5	22

6.4 Defect Detection Efficiency

Defect Detection Efficiency refers to true defects found per resource unit spent, i.e., defects per hour. We calculated defect detection efficiency per hour, even if the defect detection effort was less than 60 min. Table 4 contains the descriptive statistics of defect detection efficiency for P&P and CSI with focus on defect detection duration (i.e., max. 120 min for P&P and max. 60 min for CSI).

Table 4. Defect Detection Efficiency with focus on real effort [Defects per hour].

Group	#participants	Mean	SD	Min	Max
CSI-MA	63	7.5	5.29	0	23
P&P	12	5.7	2.17	2	9

The initial results showed a higher defect detection efficiency for CSI participants compared to P&P inspectors. However, the standard deviations for CSI participants is higher. We also observed outliers in the CSI group, i.e., three CSI inspectors did not report any of the seeded defects and three CSI participants achieved an efficiency value of 20 defects per hour (or more). This is a calculated value as some CSI participants did not spend one hour for model analysis. However, applying the Mann-Whitney Test we did not observe any significant differences (p value: 0.379(–)). Based on the results we see a high potential for the CSI process to enable addressing large and complex models and to reduce false positives based on introduced EMEs. CSI is a promising and complementary approach for defect detection.

7 Discussion and Limitations

This section presents the discussion of the main findings related to the research issues and hypotheses. The main goal was to adapt/extend a best-practice inspection approach with crowdsourcing. Figure 2 presented the CSI process approach with two main activities, a text analysis to capture *Expected Model Elements (EMEs)* and a model analysis task for defect detection. For analysis purposes we executed a controlled experiment to investigate the effect on defect detection performance, i.e., effectiveness, false positives, and efficiency. Defect *detection effectiveness* is the share of true defects found related to the number of seeded defects. The analysis results showed significant benefits for P&P inspectors (p-value: 0.015(S)). Thus, H1.0 that CSI and P&P groups perform similar must be rejected. Main reasons include a smaller defect detection effort for CSI inspectors (60 min for CSI inspectors and 120 min for P&P inspectors). *False positives (FP)*, i.e., reported defects that do not match to a true defect, is important to keep analysis effort low after inspection. As EMEs guide model inspection processes, the results showed benefits for CSI. CSI inspectors report on average less FPs compared to P&P inspectors (p-value: 0.055(–)). *Defect detection efficiency* refers to the number of identified true defects per resource unit spent (i.e., per hour). CSI inspectors achieved on average higher (but not significantly higher) defect detection efficiency levels compared to P&P inspectors (p-value: 0.379(–)). Following this observations, we had to reject H2.0.

We identify and discuss important potential threats to validity of our study and describe how we addressed them [12]. *Internal validity* concerns a causal relationship between the experiment treatment and the observed results, without the influence of potential confounding factors that are not controlled or measured [12]. The authors introduced 33 reference defects in the EER diagram based on typical defects collected during typical software engineering processes. Further analysis steps might raise additional defects which might have been overseen in the preliminary analysis. Domain specific issues have been addressed by selecting a well-known application domain. The experiment package was intensively reviewed by experts to avoid errors. Furthermore, we executed a set of pilot runs to ensure the feasibility of the study design. We applied a random distribution of the group assignment using a sort card algorithm. The overall duration was limited to 120 min. Individual breaks were allowed; break periods had to be reported. *External Validity* refers to the generalization of the results to a larger population or to environments that differ from the one studied [12]. Interaction of selection and treatment. Participants were 75 undergraduate students at TU Wien. The authors are aware of limitations of student experiments [17].

8 Conclusion and Future Work

To support advancement towards the goal of effective and efficient quality assurance for large software models and associated reference documents, we described in this paper a crowdsourcing-supported inspection (CSI) process. We focused on investigating the effects of CSI model analysis for an Extended Entity Relationship (EER) model with an associated scenario-based requirements document. We reported on a controlled experiment with 75 participants to explore the CSI process. The empirical study provided foundational evidence that the core task of the CSI process, the model analysis task for defect detection guided by EMEs is both, feasible and useful. Thus, the presented process approach can gain benefits for model quality assurance for different types of models (based on the concept of the CSI process) and is promising for large-scale models (based on the crowdsourcing mechanisms, i.e., splitting up large tasks in smaller tasks and increase inspection control for introducing additional CSI workers if needed).

Future work will include (a) more detailed investigation of defect detection capabilities of CSI as preliminary results show promising but no significant results; (b) replication of the controlled experiment in different settings, e.g., large scale models, different model types, and different populations (e.g., in industry setting); (c) investigating the effects of nominal inspection teams and inspector qualification levels; and (d) possible automation that supported inspection processes with tool support to improve the overall inspection process in a distributed setting.

References

1. Parnas, D.L., Lawford, M.: The role of inspection in software quality assurance. IEEE Trans. Softw. Eng. **29**(8), 674–676 (2003)
2. Brambilla, M., Cabot, J., Wimmer, M.: Model-Driven Software Engineering in Practice. Morgan & Claypool Publishers, San Rafael (2012)
3. Fagan, M.E.: Design and code inspections to reduce errors in program development. IBM Syst. J. **15**(7), 182–211 (1976)
4. Aurum, A., Petersson, H., Wohlin, C.: State-of-the-art: Software Inspections after 25 Years. Softw. Test. Verificat. Reliab. **12**(3), 133–154 (2002)
5. Travassos, G.H., Shull, F., Carver, J., Basili, V.: Reading techniques for OO design inspections. Technical report, Fraunhofer Center-Maryland, U. Maryland (2002)

6. LaToza, T.D., van der Hoek, A.: Crowdsourcing in Software Engineering: Models. IEEE Softw. Motiv. Challenges **33**(1), 74–80 (2016)
7. Shull, F., Rus, I., Basili, V.: How perspective-based reading can improve requirements inspections. IEEE Softw. **3**(7), 73–79 (2000)
8. Kalinowski, M., Travassos, G.H.: A computational framework for supporting software inspections. In: Proceedings of ASE, Linz, Austria, pp. 46–55 (2004)
9. Lanubile, F., Mallardo, T.: Tool support for distributed inspection. In: Proceedings of COMPSAC. IEEE (2002)
10. Hernandes, E.M., Belgamo, A., Fabbri, S.: Experimental studies in software inspection process - a systematic mapping. In: Proceedings of ICEIS, pp. 66–76 (2013)
11. Mao, K., Capra, L., Harman, M., Jia, Y.: A survey of the use of crowdsourcing in software engineering. J. Syst. Softw., 28 p. (2016)
12. Wohlin C., Runeson P., Höst, M., Ohlsson, M., Regnell, B., Wessl, A.: Experimentation in Software Engineering. Springer, Heidelberg (2012)
13. Winkler, D., Sabou, M., Petrovic, S., Caneiro, G., Kalinowski, M., Biffl, S.: Improving model inspection with crowdsourcing. In: Proceedings of the International Workshop on Crowdsourcing in SE, ICSE, Buenos Aires (2017, to appear)
14. Manning, C.D., Raghavan, P., Schütze, H.: Introduction to Information Retrieval. Cambridge University Press, Cambridge (2008)
15. Thalheim, V.: Extended entity-relationship model. In: Liu, L., Özsu, M.T. (eds.) Encyclopedia of Database Systems, pp. 1083–1091. Springer, New York (2009)
16. Winkler D., Sabou, M., Petrovic, S., Caneiro, G., Kalinowski, M., Biffl, S.: Investigating model quality assurance with a distributed and scalable review process. In: Proceedings of CIbSE, Buenos Aires, Argentina (2017, to appear)
17. Runeson, P.: Using students as experiment subjects–an analysis on graduate and freshmen student data. In: Proceedings of the 7th EASE Conference (2003)

A Metric for Evaluating Residual Complexity in Software

Michael Krisper[✉], Johannes Iber, Christian Kreiner, and Markus Quaritsch

Graz University of Technology, Graz, Austria
{michael.krisper,johannes.iber,christian.kreiner,
markus.quaritsch}@tugraz.at

Abstract. A new metric for evaluating the complexity of software is proposed: The residual complexity. This is the combination of a complexity metric with a code coverage metric. It indicates how well the complexity of a software is handled by software tests, and how much complexity still remains untested. In this paper we give an overview over existing source code metrics and code coverage metrics. Afterwards the residual complexity is described and the consequences are discussed. In the end a use case is shown on a real life example of a software application implemented in .NET.

Keywords: Software quality · Software metric · Residual complexity · Complexity metric · Cyclomatic complexity · Branch coverage

1 Introduction

Why Do We Need Software Metrics? Software metrics are useful to measure quality properties of software e.g. the size, the complexity, or the test coverage. These properties show how readable, understandable and generally maintainable source code is, and therefore can be used to prove the quality of a software to a customer, or a stakeholder in a project, or an assessor during a quality standard assessment (e.g. the software quality standard series ISO25000 [7,8]). This helps to build trust in the implemented solution. In this paper we use two kinds of software metrics: Firstly, *size and complexity metrics* (e.g. lines of code, class count, method count, cyclomatic complexity), and secondly *code coverage metrics* (line coverage, branch coverage). An overview over the metrics is given in Sect. 2.1.

Source code metrics are already proven and used in industry. Many companies already work with them and use them to support and evaluate their development efforts. While complexity metrics point out the methods which are complicated and difficult to understand, they do not show which of them are already tested and behave like they should. In contrast to that, code coverage metrics show how well the source code is tested, but not if the tests actually cover the complicated parts of a software. This is why we propose a combination of complexity metrics and coverage metrics in order to get the still hidden residual complexity of the source code. This metric hints to the methods which are complicated AND not well tested - which are the methods which have to be taken core of.

1.1 A New Metric: Residual Complexity

We propose a new metric to measure the complexity in a software product: the Residual Complexity. It depicts the remaining complexity of the methods, which is not covered by any software test. It can be calculated for a method by taking a complexity metric and reducing it by the percentage of test coverage. After that, it can be summed up for classes and modules to get an aggregated value. The exact method is described in Sect. 3.

Although the complexity of a software can not be decreased by writing software tests, these tests help to understand and handle complexity. When the functionality and behavior of a method get tested, it can be shown that it works like intended. By writing software tests, a contract for the functionality and behavior is established, which limits the complexity a method can exhibit to the outside. This behavioral contract makes a method manageable from the outside, and therefore makes the inner complexity manageable. By handling the complexity via software tests, the perceived complexity for the outside decreases, and the respective method can be seen as a black box with reduced *residual complexity*.

By combining the complexity with test coverage one can calculate the residual complexity for a whole software product. The goal is then to decrease the residual complexity remaining in the software. There are 3 ways to reduce it: (1) the complexity of the methods themselves must be reduced, (2) comprehensive software tests have to be written, and as last resort (3) the method has to be removed completely. As described in more detail in Sect. 3.2, all different ways lead to an increased software quality.

1.2 Use-Case: VECTO

We show the usefulness of the proposed residual complexity by applying it to a real life project called VECTO [11]. VECTO is simulation software for calculating the fuel-consumption and CO_2 emissions of heavy duty vehicles and was developed at the Graz University of Technology [5,10]. It will be used for CO_2 certification and legislation in Europe to certify the CO_2 emissions of all new administered heavy duty vehicles [3]. It consists of approximately 20.000 lines of code and has gone through several evolutionary development steps over the last few years. VECTO is a good medium sized example of a real life software product, which makes it ideal as a demonstrative use case for the residual complexity metric. In Sect. 5 we describe it in more detail, and apply the complexity metrics on that project.

2 Related Work

2.1 Metrics

In order to calculate the residual complexity, a complexity metric and a reasonable code coverage metric is needed as a basis. Some of the best known and useful metrics are listed here, but there exist many more. The metrics listed here will be used in Sect. 3, where the calculation of the residual complexity is described and the meaningful combinations of metrics are discussed.

Complexity Metrics. Complexity metrics calculate how simple or difficult a source code is to understand and maintain. It is assumed that complex code is hard to understand, while simple code is easy. Many formulas and techniques are used to calculate the complexity, which also implies different meanings.

Lines of Code (LOC) [1,15]. Simply counts the lines of code which are contained in the source code, or individual blocks (like files, classes, methods). While this is a controversial and sometimes ambiguous metric, it depicts the approximate size of a software. It is assumed that bigger software (=high LOC) is more complex. But since different languages and programming styles have different amount of growth in lines of code this metric has to be used carefully [9]. The LOC may often also be depicted as average lines per class, average lines per method and so on.

Halstead Metrics [4] are a collection of metrics which take the operators and operands into account. The more different operators and operands a specific code has, the more difficult it gets to understand. Based on the count of operators and operands the Halstead Volume, Difficulty and Effort can be defined as follows:

- N_o: total count of operators, η_o: count of unique operators
- N_n: total count of operands, η_n: count of unique operands
- Halstead Volume: Measures the size of a code. $V = (N_o + N_n)\log_2(\eta_o + \eta_n)$
- Halstead Difficulty: Measures the understandability. $D = \frac{\eta_o N_n}{2\eta_n}$
- Halstead Effort: Metric for the writing effort. $E = D \times V$

Cyclomatic Complexity (CC) [12,18] is the total count of branches (decisions) in a method. This is one of the most useful metrics for calculating the complexity of source code, because with every decision the source gets more difficult to understand. It was proposed by McCabe. For a single method cyclomatic complexity is useful in measuring the decision complexity, but extending it to a class, namespace or even module this usefulness gets lost when just summing up or averaging it. Summing up the values results in a number which just has the semantic meaning of size. A class with 2 very complicated methods could have the same summed up complexity as a class with 20 simple methods. Therefore the sum is just an indicator for the size, just like the lines of code. Averaging over the methods would be a better indicator for complexity, but is still deceiving: many simple methods (e.g. getter and setter) could average out complicated methods. At least a class with 2 complicated methods has an much higher average than a class with 20 simple methods, which is a desired property. Both kinds of aggregation were not useful for our projects.

The Software Assurance Technology Center (SATC) [17] at NASA proposes the evaluation of cyclomatic complexity together with LOC to reason about the reliability and maintainability of a software module: The complexity and the size should correlate to each other. Methods which are too big for their complexity tend to have the lowest reliability, while methods which are to small for their complexity hint to terse code which is hard to maintain and understand [17]. Following that idea, one could calculate an average cyclomatic complexity over the lines of code for every method. Such a weighted average reflects the complexity over the size of a method, and the extreme values would hint to code stenches. This still has some problems: when methods are complicated but long enough, they would be completely unsuspicious. Although the good correlation of complexity to size is a desired property, it has its limits and other metrics have to be used to find such overcomplicated and long methods. Also aggregating this to a class or module has the same faults like in the unweighted case: the extreme cases lose their meaning. To high and to low values could average out, and a sum would merely indicate the size.

The flaws in aggregating the cyclomatic complexity are the reason why we propose *Residual Complexity* as a new metric for evaluating the complexity of a software on higher than method levels (class, namespace, modules, whole product). See Sect. 3 for a detailed description.

Maintainability Index (MI) [13,16] is an index which combines the Halstead Volume, the Cyclomatic Complexity and the Lines of Code into a complexity metric in order to determine the maintainability of a source code. While the Maintainability Index incorporates several other metrics by combining decisions, understandability and size metrics, the result are more than vague. The numeric weighting factors have been drafted more than a decade ago and may not be suitable in modern languages or programming styles. Also, the interpretation of the result is very subjective: Microsoft proposes that values between 100 and 20 are good, 19 to 10 are moderately maintainable, and values below 9 indicate low maintainability [14]. But this, as well as the used factors in the formula are subjective values which may or may not be useful for all kind of programming languages and styles.

$$MI = max(0, 171 - 5.2ln(avg(HV)) - 0.23avg(CC) - 16.2ln(avg(LOC)) * \frac{100}{171}$$

MI: Maintainability Index
HV: Halstead Volume
LOC: Lines of Code
CC: Cyclomatic Complexity

Code Coverage Metrics. Code coverage is the percentage of code which is covered by software tests (e.g. unit test, integration tests, system tests). Code counts as covered (or tested) if it was executed during a test and the test was successful. The different coverage metrics differ by the basic element they count as covered e.g. lines, statements, branches, etc.

Line Coverage (LC) is the most used kind of code coverage and shows the share of source code lines which are covered by tests. This is one of the most common coverage metrics, but it is dangerous. Line coverage does not cover the whole semantics of the programming language. Writing as many lines as possible would result in a high line coverage, which is not meaningful in such a case. Conditions and Loops are not correctly counted, because the conditions could be short-circuited but count as covered, and loop bodies are counted as covered already after the first loop. Despite these shortcomings the line coverage is often used as a first indicator how well source code is tested.

Block Coverage (BLC) is the share of linear code blocks which are covered by tests. This has to consider the semantics of the programming language, and is therefore a more meaningful metric than line coverage. Still loops yield some kind of uncertainty because blocks are covered by single-hitting them, therefore loops are counted after the first loop, regardless of how often the loop-body should have been executed.

Branch Coverage (BC)/Predicate Coverage (PC). Depicts the share of covered branches in the source code. Branches are the possible paths an execution could take after a decision. This decision could be evoked in an if-condition, loop conditions, or switch statements. On every decision new branches are opened, and branches count as covered if the decision is at least once evaluated in that favor (e.g. once true and once false in if-conditions). Predicate Coverage goes even a step further and demands that for all boolean expressions in the condition. Branch coverage has the flaw of not being able to consider exception handling in .NET (e.g. try-catch blocks). Another flaw would be a fluid interface composite model, where small methods are daisy-chained on composites via the "." operator. Here the branch coverage would count the call as simple control flow even if the called methods contain decision logic.

3 Residual Complexity

The *residual complexity* is a complexity metric which describes the remaining unmanaged and untested complexity for a software product. It is an aggregated value for the complexity which is not covered by software tests.

3.1 Calculation

To calculate the residual complexity the complexity for the individual methods has to be calculated and reduced by their respective code coverage. The result can then be summed up for classes or even namespaces and modules in order to get the residual complexity for the whole software product. Equation 1 shows how it can be calculated for a class. In this case summation is reasonable, because the complexity has already been adjusted for every individual method. The remaining residual complexity can therefore be summed up for classes, namespaces and modules and still has the same semantics of how much untackled complexity is hidden inside.

$$\text{Residual Complexity}_{Class} = \sum_{m \in Methods} \text{Complexity}_m \times (1 - \text{Coverage}_m) \quad (1)$$

Equation 1 does not define the exact metrics used for the complexity and the coverage because multiple different combinations are possible. Theoretically any complexity metric can be combined with every code coverage metric, but there are some reasonable choices, which are directly related to each other:

- Cyclomatic Complexity with Branch Coverage: This is the most reasonable choice for the residual complexity, and that is why the authors also propose this method as the standard for the term "Residual Complexity". The cyclomatic complexity counts all theoretical branches in a method, while the branch coverage counts the tested branches. Covering more branches by tests, reduces the residual complexity by the same amount, which is a deterministic and desired behavior. The two metrics combined depict the remaining untested branches and decision complexity in a software.
- Lines of Code with Line Coverage: This depicts the remaining untested lines of code in the source. While also being useful, it shows just the amount and size of the untested parts, and not necessarily the complexity contained within.

3.2 Consequences

The residual complexity gives hints to directions where to look first when looking for complicated and untested methods. In order to use it, software tests are needed - otherwise it would be the same as the ordinary cyclomatic complexity. As soon as the source code gets tested (code coverage gets increased) the residual complexity of the whole projects gets lower, which is desired. There are three possible ways to reduce the residual complexity:

1. **Remove the code.** This results in smaller methods and cleaner classes, which just have the methods and functionality they actually need. But more often than not, it is not possible to simply remove code. Nevertheless, it should be the first consideration before doing anything else.
2. **Decrease the complexity of methods.** This can be achieved by refactoring, simplifying statements or using different (maybe easier) algorithms if possible. This also could involve much work and thinking and refactoring effort, but is the second best method to reduce complexity.
3. **Write test cases to cover the complexity.** This results in more test cases to increase the code coverage and also increases the documentation via testcases and establishment of behavioral contract for the method. Writing test cases is at least a way of documenting and describing the intended behavior, which is also a way of handling complexity and therefore reduces the residual complexity.

In all three cases, decreasing the residual complexity leads to better code quality, easier understanding, or at least better definition of the behavior, which all are desired and useful properties of source code.

4 Method

To evaluate the proposed metric we used existing tools (Visual Studio, SharpDevelop, OpenCover) to calculate the base metrics (cyclomatic complexity, branch coverage) for existing source code. Based on the single metrics we calculated the residual complexity. We evaluated this for the source code in the VECTO project, which is described in more detail as Use-Case in Sect. 5.

Following tools where used for the calculations:

- Visual Studio [13]: **Cyclomatic Complexity**, Maintainability Index, Lines of Code
- SharpDevelop (with OpenCover and NUnit) [2,19]: **Branch Coverage**
- Microsoft Excel: To combine the metrics and calculate the **Residual Complexity** for every method, class, and namespace.

The process of finding the metrics was:

1. Calculating the cyclomatic complexity for every method.
2. Executing the test cases and evaluate the branch coverage.
3. Exporting/transforming the data to Excel and (4) calculating the residual complexity.
4. Manually examining some samples of methods with highest/lowest/intermediate values to check if the values are justified.

5 Use-Case: VECTO

We discuss the quality properties on a real software product, which was developed over several years in a project funded by the EU. This software is the basis for software-based legislation and certification of CO_2 emissions for heavy duty vehicles in Europe. It is called "VECTO" (Vehicle Energy Consumption Calculation Tool) and is developed at the Graz University of Technology [6].

5.1 Environment

VECTO was written in C# 5.0 and VB.NET 11.0 with the .NET Framework 4.5. To calculate the code coverage, the cyclomatic complexity and the maintainability index, Visual Studio 2017 was used [13]. The statement coverage was obtained with JetBrain's dotCover. Due to the lack of branch coverage in Visual Studio we used the software OpenCover in combination with SharpDevelop to run the test cases and evaluate the branch coverage metric.

5.2 Evaluation

In the following sections the quality properties of VECTO will be evaluated and discussed. VECTO consists of several libraries from which the two main libraries will be evaluated: VectoCore and VectoCommon. VectoCore is the library which implements the physical models for the calculations. VectoCommon is a library providing the interfaces and common functionality which is also used by many other libraries in the project. Table 1 shows the results of the complexity measurement on the two libraries. It lists the metrics for those two libraries: Lines of Code (LOC), Line Coverage, Cyclomatic Coverage, Branch Coverage, and the resulting Residual Complexity. The LOC just show the size of the libraries and their Line Coverage shows how well these lines are tested. The Cyclomatic Complexity shows the complexity of the code and the Branch Coverage, how much of this complexity was tested. The Residual Complexity is the decreased complexity after decreasing it by the percentage of all tested branches for every individual method.

Code Coverage. As can be seen in Table 1 the code coverage is relatively high in VectoCore with 86% for 13233 lines of code, and 77% for VectoCommon with its 1370 lines of code. These values are good for a software of this size.

Table 1. VECTO complexity metrics results

Library	LOC	Line coverage	Cyclomatic complexity	Branch coverage	Residual complexity
VectoCore	13233	86.56%	4639	66.2%	2260.8
VectoCommon	1370	77.01%	968	67.64%	333.7

Looking at the Branch Coverage it can be seen that branch coverage is still good, but already falls behind. Still, VectoCore has 66.2% branch coverage and VectoCommon 67.64%.

Complexity Metrics. Regarding the complexity metrics VectoCore has 4639, and VectoCommon has 968. This is the summed up cyclomatic complexity. Here already it can be seen that the complexity metric for modules does not say much, except for the size of the module. Figure 1 shows the complexity values of the top 300 most complex methods sorted from highest to lowest value. It also shows that the simple arithmetic average complexity of the methods is about 7.6, which does not make much sense because of all the getters and setters dragging down the average.

Residual Complexity. In the last column in Table 1 the residual complexity for the main libraries in VECTO can be seen. VectoCore has a residual complexity of 2260.8 and VectoCommon has a value of 333.7. By comparing these values to the original complexity one can already see that the software tests

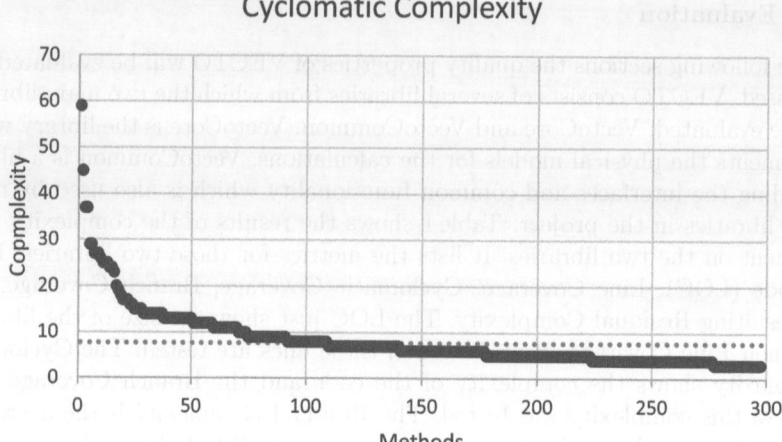

Fig. 1. CYCLOMATIC COMPLEXITY IN VECTO: The first 300 methods with the highest cyclomatic complexity are shown in this figure. The orange dotted line shows the arithmetic average over all files, which is about 7.6. (Color figure online)

lowered the complexity by a huge amount (−51% for VectoCore, and −65% for VectoCommon), but still much of the complexity resides in the software which has been untested. Also, it can be seen that a simple reduction of the summed up cyclomatic complexity by the branch coverage would not suffice, because the values are different. This was an interesting discovery for the developers when they first stumbled upon such high residual complexity.

This shows that even though the line coverage is high, there could still exist a high residual complexity and this should be an alarm sign to create more test cases for the missing branches, or simplify the code. Maybe many of the branches aren't even needed and can be removed. This has to be investigated more deeply by looking at the methods which actually still have the highest residual complexity.

In Fig. 2 we looked at the methods with the highest complexity and how their complexity was reduced with the branch coverage resulting to a residual complexity. The reduction was significant as can be seen in the figure. This also shows that the methods with the highest cyclomatic complexity are not the methods which should be taken care of. But the methods with the highest residual complexity are the ones which should be revised.

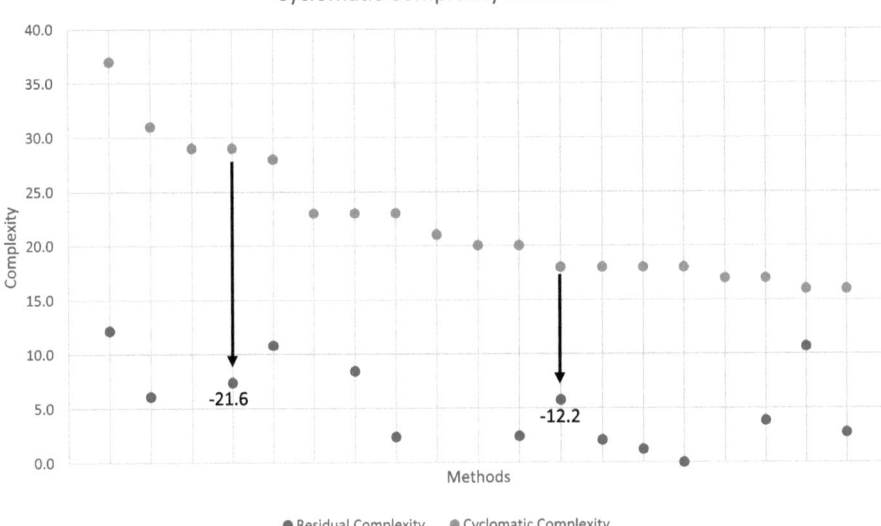

Fig. 2. CYCLOMATIC COMPLEXITY REDUCTION: This figure shows that the residual complexity is for many methods significantly lower than the cyclomatic complexity due to testing.

6 Discussion

The proposed metric of residual complexity gives new insight how complex a software product is; or to be exact, how much remaining untested complexity a software has. This can be used to find the methods inducing the most residual complexity and taking care of them by either removing them, making them simpler or writing test cases which cover the missing branches. All this helps to increase software quality and maintainability. The methods which induce the most residual complexity would not have been found otherwise and the development time and resources may have been wasted on simplifying already tested and behaviorally well defined methods.

With all metrics the usefulness depends upon the context. The Residual Complexity measures the Complexity of a code, which is also a metric for the quality of a code. However, there are other desirable properties as well, like reliability, confidence, or security which are not covered by this metric, and even work against it. Reliable and secure code is almost always more complex than source code without these properties. But even in such cases rigorous testing helps to tame the complexity beast and reduce the residual complexity.

7 Conclusion

We proposed a new complexity metric for software products: the residual complexity. This metric measures the untested and unmanaged complexity which still resides in the software application even after using software tests. It is the combination of the cyclomatic complexity metric together with branch coverage. This is useful for finding the remaining complexity still hidden in the software. We showed the practicality of the residual complexity on the use-case of a real software application. While the line coverage of the applied software tests was relative high (>80%), the residual complexity revealed that still much of the complexity contained in the source was untested and unmanaged. This showed, that the residual complexity is a useful metric for evaluating the maintainability and understandability of software.

References

1. Boehm, B., Abts, C., Chulani, S.: Software development cost estimation approaches - a survey. Ann. Softw. Eng. **10**(1), 177–205 (2000). http://dx.doi.org/10.1023/A:1018991717352
2. C#Code: Sharpdevelop (2012). http://www.icsharpcode.net
3. Dünnebeil, F., Reinhard, C., Lambrecht, U., Kies, A., Hausberger, S., Rexeis, M.: Zukünftige Maßnahmen zur Kraftstoffeinsparung und Treibhausgasminderung bei schweren Nutzfahrzeugen. Umweltbundesamt Texte **2015**(32) (2015). https://www.umweltbundesamt.de/publikationen/zukuenftige-massnahmen-zur-kraftstoffeinsparung
4. Halstead, M.H.: Elements of Software Science. Operating and Programming Systems Series. Elsevier Science Inc., New York (1977)
5. Hausberger, S., Rexeis, M., Luz, R.: Transmission and gear shift calculation in VECTO, pp. 1–10, March 2013
6. Hausberger, S., Rexeis, M., Luz, R., Kreiner, C., Krisper, M., Quaritsch, M., Gretzl, P., Eichlseder, H.: VECTO tool development (2016)
7. ISO, IEC: ISO/IEC 25010:2011 system and software quality models. Technical report (2011). http://www.iso.org/iso/cataloguedetail.htm?csnumber=35733
8. ISO, IEC: ISO/IEC 25000 systems and software quality requirements and evaluation (square). Technical report, ISO/IEC (2014). https://www.iso.org/obp/ui/#iso:std:iso-iec:25000:ed-2:v1:en
9. Jones, T.C.: Measuring programming quality and productivity. IBM Syst. J. **17**(1), 39–63 (1978)
10. Kies, A., Rexeis, M., Silberholz, G., Luz, R., Hausberger, S.: Options to consider future advanced fuel- saving technologies in the CO2 test procedure for HDV. Technical report, Forschungsgesellschaft für Verbrennungskraftmaschinen und Thermodynamik mbH (2013)
11. Luz, R.: Simulationsbasierte Methode zur Zertifizierung der CO2 Emissionen von schweren Nutzfahrzeugen. Ph.D. thesis, Graz University of Technology (2015)
12. McCabe, T., Watson, A.: Software complexity. J. Def. Softw. Eng. **7**(12), 5–9 (1994)
13. Microsoft: Visual studio code metrics values. https://msdn.microsoft.com/en-us/library/bb385914.aspx

14. Naboulsi, Z.: Code metrics - maintainability index (2011). https://blogs.msdn.microsoft.com/zainnab/2011/05/26/code-metrics-maintainability-index/
15. Nguyen, V., Deeds-Rubin, S., Tan, T., Boehm, B.: A SLOC counting standard (2008)
16. Oman, P., Hagemeister, J.: Metrics for assessing a software system's maintainability. In: Proceedings of the Conference on Software Maintenance, pp. 337–344 (1992)
17. Rosenberg, L., Hammer, T., Shaw, J.: Software metrics and reliability. In: IEEE International Symposium on Software Reliability Engineering (1998)
18. Watson, A., McCabe, T.: Structured testing: a testing methodology using the cyclomatic complexity metric. NIST Special Publication 500–235 (1996)
19. Wilde, S.: Sharpdevelop (2014). https://github.com/OpenCover/opencover/wiki

The Potential of Self-Adaptive Software Systems in Industrial Control Systems

Johannes Iber[✉], Tobias Rauter, Michael Krisper, and Christian Kreiner

Institute of Technical Informatics, Graz University of Technology,
Inffeldgasse 16, Graz, Austria
{johannes.iber,tobias.rauter,michael.krisper,christian.kreiner}@tugraz.at

Abstract. New generations of industrial control systems offer higher performance, are networked and can be controlled remotely. Following this progress, the complexity of such systems increases through heterogeneous systems, hardware and more capable software. This may lead to an increase of unreliability and insecurity. Self-adaptive software systems offer a mean of dealing with complexity by monitoring a control system, detecting anomalies and adapting the control system to problems. Regarding such methods, industrial control systems have the advantage of being less dynamic. The network topology is fixed, devices rarely change, and the functionality of all the resources is known in principle. In this work, we examine this advantage and present the potential of self-adaptive software systems. The context of the presented work is control systems for hydropower units.

1 Introduction

Industrial control systems are computer systems that monitor and control physical processes. Essentially, they are used in critical infrastructures, such as electricity generation and industrial plants. New generations offer higher performance, are networked and can be controlled remotely. Such systems are considered to be part of the broad range of cyber-physical systems.

According to a National Institute of Standards and Technology workshop report [10] the key challenges of cyber-physical systems development include what is needed to cost-effectively and rapidly build in and assure the safety, reliability, availability, security and performance of next-generation systems. Industry is using more and more commercial off-the-shelf hardware platforms, which are inexpensive and offer a high performance. The downside of these platforms is that typically they only offer sparse safety and fault tolerance features [1,6]. Furthermore, industrial control systems are increasingly becoming targets of security attacks [2,8].

Industrial control systems have a big advantage compared to other kinds of systems. The devices used, including hardware and software, network topology, and communication patterns etc. are known and rarely change during operation [2,3]. In our opinion this broad knowledge enables automatic mechanisms that can react e.g. to permanent hardware faults and security attacks. The goal of such mechanisms would be to increase the reliability of a control system and to defend it against hackers. Self-adaptive software systems offer a means of orchestrating such automatic mechanisms. The underlying idea of self-adaptive software systems is to monitor a managed system and to adapt it in dependence on defined goals. Such a system would not change the architecture of the control systems themselves, but a self-adaptive system would run on top of it instead.

The contribution of this work is an attempt at enumerating this potential of self-adaptive software systems in industrial control systems. We outline the application possibilities in the context of hydropower plants; a domain with which we are familiar. The highlighted application areas of self-adaptive software are hardware faults, security attacks and hacks, software bugs, misconfiguration of the control logic, and faults in the physical environment. We list different anomalies originating from these areas. We present various detection and adaption mechanisms corresponding to the anomalies. It is important to note that we do not wish to change the control logic itself. What we aim to do instead is to strengthen the underlying hardware and software stacks.

The remainder of this paper is structured as follows: the next Section provides a brief introduction to self-adaptive software systems. In Sect. 3 the industrial setting of our work is presented. Subsequently, the different application areas are presented in Sect. 4. In Sect. 5 we discuss the commonalities between the different areas. Finally, concluding remarks are given in Sect. 6.

2 Self-adaptive Software Systems

Self-adaptive software modifies its own behavior in response to changes in its operating environment. By operating environment, we mean anything observable by the software system, such as end-user input, external hardware devices and sensors, or program instrumentation [11].

Typically, self-adaptive software systems follow an external (architecture) approach [13]. An internal approach interweaves application and adaption logic based e.g. on programming language features such as exceptions, conditions, and parametrization. The issue with an internal approach is that sensors, actuators, parallel adaption processes and purpose of an application are complicated to engineer within one software design. This leads to notable drawbacks, e.g. with respect to scalability, testability and maintainability.

In an external approach, as illustrated in Fig. 1, the domain-specific application logic termed *Managed Subsystem* is monitored by a *Managing Subsystem*. The *Managing Subsystem* is where the actual adaption logic resides. It additionally monitors the *Environment* that may consist of other software, hardware, network, or of the physical context including humans. In the presented setting, a *Managing Subsystem* observes anomalies of a control system (*Managed Subsystem*). By applying different detection mechanisms a *Managing Subsystem* is supposed to analyze the root cause of the observed anomalies. In the final step it chooses an appropriate adaption mechanism for circumventing the problem.

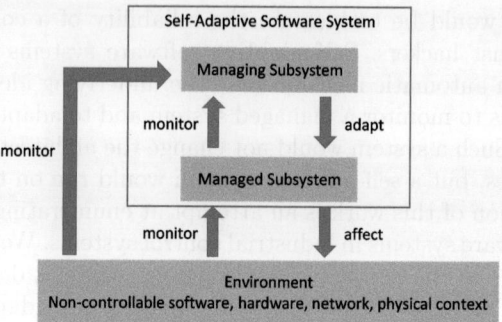

Fig. 1. Parts of a self-adaptive software system (adapted from [14])

Typically, the *Managing Subsystem* itself comprises an adaptive loop that coordinates different detection mechanisms and adapts accordingly. Muccini et al. [9] reveal in a systematic literature review that in the context of a cyber-physical system, the so-called MAPE-K loop (**M**onitor, **A**nalyze, **P**lan, **E**xecute - **K**nowledge) is by far the dominant adaptive loop in science with a share of 60%.

3 Industrial Setting

The industrial setting of the following application areas are networked control devices that operate hydropower plant units. We choose this setting because it is also our project context and we are familiar with it. Figure 2 illustrates a simplified overview of such an industrial control system.

On network level, control devices are connected via Ethernet and operated by supervisory computers. These supervisory computers are responsible for observing the state of physical processes and adjusting parameters of control devices in order to control the energy conversions. The observation and adjustment actions are done by using so-called datapoints which are variables with a specific basic data type such as integer or boolean.

The control devices are connected to hydropower plant units. Their functional responsibility is to operate these units through one of the four different functions namely excitation, synchronization, protection and turbine control.

Technically, these devices have a programmable logic controller (PLC) architecture. In the context of the hardware design, a control device is built out of central modules and interface modules. A central module consists of a communication CPU (CCPU) and an application CPU (ACPU). The CCPU is responsible for network connections and controlling/monitoring the ACPU. It runs a customized Linux distribution and can be accessed by various protocols such as SSH and Modbus. From the security perspective this protects the ACPU and verifies incoming commands. The ACPU is a multi-core processor and executes the actual control logic. It runs a real-time operating system in order to ensure guaranteed cycle times. The interface modules connecting the control device with

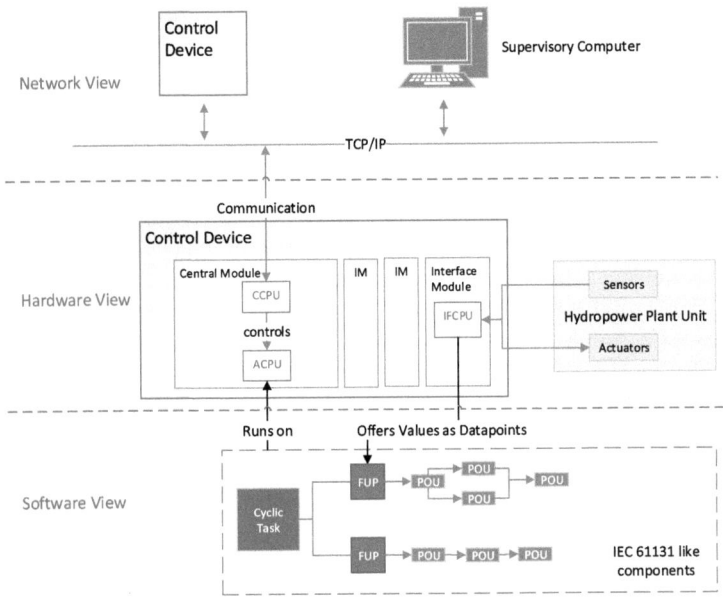

Fig. 2. Overview of the industrial control system

the sensors and actuators of the hydropower plant unit. Central modules and interface modules are connected via Ethernet.

The control logic executed by the ACPU of a central module is component-based and heavily influenced by the IEC 61131 standard for programmable logic controllers [7]. It is hierarchically built out of components, compositions and tasks. Components are termed Program Organization Units (POU) and compositions are named Function Plans (FUP). POUs are coded with the C-programming language and stored as binaries on the devices. Such POUs implement basic functions, e.g. simple logic gates, or complex algorithms. Based on these POUs, reusable FUPs are designed by plant engineers that implement the specific control logic for a hydropower plant unit. Finally, such FUPs are executed by cyclic tasks in real-time.

FUPs operate on datapoints that are set and read by the interface modules. At the start of a cyclic task the necessary datapoints are collected, then the FUPs are executed, and subsequently the calculated datapoints are written back. The interface modules receive these datapoints and actuate accordingly. Further, datapoints can be shared with other control devices or supervisory computers.

The supervisory computers are themselves part of a control hierarchy. Higher hierarchy levels control for instance different hydropower plants along a river.

4 Application Areas

Figure 3 illustrates a network of control devices, a supervisory computer and a hydropower plant unit containing sensors and actuators. The arrows from the left and right side represent areas we are proposing to tackle with detection and adaption mechanisms. In the issue of hardware faults, we are targeting those faults located inside a control device. The hydropower unit is out of scope. In the context of security attacks, our interest is to detect hacks of sensors, actuators and control devices. Unknown software bugs can be added through updating the software or occur if an untested state arises. The area misconfiguration relates to the case of a human operator making a mistake in the design of the control logic. *Faults in the physical environment* relates to the sensors and actuators that form a part of the hydropower unit. We discuss such anomalies from the point of view of a control device. In the following, we examine these five areas on the control device and network level. We present the observable anomalies together with corresponding detection and adaption mechanisms. Note that the presented anomalies, detection and adaption mechanisms are not complete and are imaginable concerning hydropower units. They may not be appropriate for all kinds of domains.

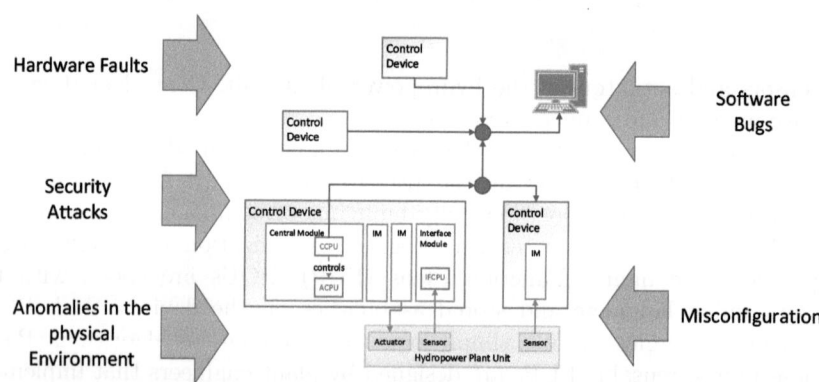

Fig. 3. Overview of the presented application areas of self-adaptive software in hydropower control systems

4.1 Hardware Faults

In this area we focus on hardware faults located in central and interface modules part of a control device. Table 1 illustrates an overview of where a fault can be located, what anomalies can occur originating from a hardware fault, how hardware faults can be detected based on the anomalies, and what can be done concerning adaption. The left hand side of Table 1 shows the location. *ACPU* is part of the central module and the place where the actual control logic resides. The *CCPU* is responsible for the communication with the network and controls

Table 1. Different locations where a permanent hardware fault can reside with corresponding anomalies, and possible detection and adaption mechanisms.

	Dead	System performance	Faulty datapoint	Parameter change has no effect	Task misses deadline	Frequency of datapoint	Missing traffic	Hardware redundancy	Software diversity	Outlier detection (eg. machine learning)	Datapoints from other control devices	Data from other hydropower plants	Cyclic memory test	System monitor	Migrate to different CPU	Migrate to different central module	Migrate to different device	Use other interface module	Use datapoint from other device	Circumvent network resource	Alarm	Tell OS to mask memory cells
ACPU																						
Memory cell	●	●	●					●	●	●	●		●	●	●	●					●	●
CPU	●	●	●	●	●			●	●	●	●			●	●	●	●					●
CCPU																						
Memory cell	●	●						●	●				●		●	●					●	●
CPU	●	●						●	●					●	●	●	●					●
Control device																						
Interface module	●	●	●	●				●	●	●	●		●	●			●	●	●		●	
Network																						
Connected device	●		●	●		●	●	●		●	●	●					●			●	●	
Network resource	●		●	●		●	●	●		●	●	●					●			●	●	●
	Anomaly							**Detection**							**Adaption**							

the *ACPU*. Further, the interface modules are connected with the sensors and actuators of a hydropower unit. They transmit their measured values as datapoints to the *ACPU* and receive parameters as datapoints. The network part is presented from a control device perspective. *Connected device* represents a control device that sends or receives datapoints. *Network resource* can be any other kind of devices in a network such as a switch or a supervisory computer.

The anomalies in the first set of columns may occur because of a fault residing in the locations on the left hand side. *Dead* means that it is not responding on interaction attempts. *System performance* describes the capability of a system in how it executes a task. It consists of CPU load, memory consumption and latency. The anomaly *Faulty datapoint* refers to a datapoint that is wrong. *Parameter change has no effect* describes the situation that a task or supervisory computer wants to change an actuator through a datapoint, but the sensed datapoints do not indicate that anything is behaving differently. *Task misses deadline* refers to the situation that a task needs to finish its work before the cycle starts again. *Frequency of datapoint* describes the distribution of datapoints within a network. *Missing traffic* is an anomaly concerning the absence of distributed datapoints and communication.

The second set of columns refers to detection mechanisms that use such anomalies as evidence for a hardware fault. *Hardware redundancy* is about duplication of components or devices in order to increase the reliability. A voter can then detect discrepancies. *Software diversity* refers to the idea of realizing a software functionality in two or more distinct ways. Diversity can be achieved by developing the functionality of a software several times in different ways by using independent development teams and technologies. Another approach is to compile software with different settings [5]. Since diverse software is working in other ways, there is a chance that permanent hardware faults can be detected in a manner similar to *Hardware redundancy*. *Outlier Detection* refers to mechanisms that detect patterns that do not correspond to an expected behavior. One such a technique is machine learning. A simpler one would be utilizing certain thresholds of datapoint values. *Datapoints from other control devices* can be used for redundancy and plausibility checks. *Data from other hydropower plants* can be used for a plausibility check of the sensed data concerning the river and how the hydropower units are behaving. *Cyclic memory test* is about checking the memory regularly and detecting permanent faults manifesting in memory cells. A *System monitor* keeps watch on a system regarding CPU usage, temperature, available memory or network traffic. A change of one of the watched parameters can indicate a hardware fault.

The third set of columns shows possible adaption mechanisms. These mechanisms can be applied after a hardware fault with the corresponding location is detected. In general these mechanisms assume the existence of some redundant hardware, otherwise it would be difficult to circumvent permanent hardware faults.

Migrate to different CPU means to use an alternative ACPU or CCPU. This adaption mechanism assumes that either a CPU is available on a module, or that a standby central module is plugged into the control device. *Migrate to different central module* is similar to the adaption mechanism described above. It assumes that another central module is available for migrating the ACPU and CCPU. *Migrate to different device* is a costlier process where a redundant device is selected for taking over the control activities. *Use other interface module* assumes that an interface module offering the same datapoints is available. This is not restricted to one device. In general, it is possible to transmit datapoints, e.g. a datapoint for voltage, from one device to another. *Circumvent network resource* depends on the affected network device. A switch can be circumvented if other paths exist. A supervisory computer can be replaced with a redundant one. *Alarm* is a general mechanism that notifies a human operator who can change parts of the control system. *Tell OS to mask memory cells* leverages the capabilities of operating systems to blacklist faulty memory areas.

4.2 Security Attacks and Hacks

Industrial control systems usually behave in a foreseeable and deterministic manner. In principal, each control device knows from and to whom it receives or sends data. Furthermore, the used software running on top of a devices is known. An attacker would have to introduce a different behavior or software in order to harm a control system.

Table 2. Different locations that can be hacked and the corresponding anomalies, detection and adaption mechanisms. The hydropower unit is also considered.

	Anomaly								Detection									Adaption					
	Dead	System performance	Faulty datapoint	Parameter change has no effect	Frequency of datapoint	Missing traffic	Connection from unknown	Unknown software	Behavior of software	Hardware redundancy	Higher CPU load	Outlier detection (eg. machine learning)	Datapoints from other control devices	Data from other hydropower plants	Firewall	Network traffic patterns	Remote attestation	Honeypot	Secure Boot	Sandboxing	Migrate to different central module	Migrate to different device	Use other interface module	Use datapoint from other device	Alarm	Isolate
Hydropower unit																										
Sensor	•		•	•						•		•	•	•								•			•	•
Actuator	•		•	•						•		•	•	•								•			•	•
Control device																										
Interface module	•		•	•	•			•		•		•	•	•				•			•	•		•		
Central module	•	•	•	•				•	•	•	•						•		•	•	•	•		•		
Network																										
Connected device	•	•	•	•	•	•	•			•	•	•			•	•	•	•							•	•
Network resource	•	•	•	•	•	•	•			•	•				•	•	•	•							•	•

Table 2 shows different parts that could be hacked. An attacker could manipulate sensors and actuators which may lead to faulty datapoints or parameters with no effect. Such a situation can be detected with mechanisms such as those pointed out in Subsect. 4.1. At control device level, an interface or central module could be hacked. The anomalies *Unknown software* and *Behavior of software* are related to the detection mechanisms *Secure Boot* and *Sandboxing*. *Secure Boot* ensures that only trusted software is started. *Sandboxing* restricts the environment of a software and mitigates the impact of e.g. a buffer overflow. On network level, the traffic between devices plays a key role of identifying security breaches in addition to the states and effects of datapoints. The detection mechanism *Network traffic patterns* leverages the fact that the traffic in an industrial control system follows cycles and deterministic behavior [4]. *Remote Attestation* can be used to prove the integrity of one control device to another [12]. Using this method a hacked control device would fail to prove that its integrity has not been violated. A *Honeypot* is a bait for attackers that behaves like a control device in the network. Any connection attempt to a honeypot would indicate a security problem. The illustrated adaption mechanisms are known from above. The adaption mechanism *Isolate* stands for circumventing and blocking an infected device.

Table 3. Locations where anomalies of software bugs can be detected and adapted.

	Anomaly								Detection								Adaption						
	Dead	System performance	Faulty datapoint	Parameter change has no effect	Task misses deadline	Frequency of datapoint	Missing traffic	Behavior of software	Hardware redundancy	Software diversity	Higher memory consumption	Higher CPU load	Outlier detection (eg. machine learning)	Datapoints from other control devices	Data from other hydropower plants	Runtime verification	Migrate to different central module	Migrate to different device	Use other interface module	Use datapoint from other device	Circumvent network resource	Alarm	Replace software with former version
Control device																							
Interface module	•	•	•	•				•	•	•	•	•	•			•		•	•	•		•	•
ACPU	•	•	•	•	•			•	•	•	•	•	•			•	•	•				•	•
CCPU	•	•		•				•	•	•	•					•	•	•				•	•
Network																							
Connected device	•		•	•		•	•		•					•	•					•	•		
Network resource	•			•		•	•		•						•					•	•	•	•

4.3 Software Bugs

In this area, our target is to detect and adapt to software bugs (Table 3). There are two kinds of bugs that we consider. One kind are bugs that are introduced after an update. The other kind is already present in the software but lurks around until an untested case or state occurs.

The detection method *Hardware redundancy* on network level assumes that not all software is updated at once or that the hardware uses different means of obtaining data. *Runtime Verification* corresponds directly to the anomaly *Behavior of software*. It is about analyzing logs and interactions of software in order to detect new behavior. The adaption mechanism *Replace software with former version* is a rollback and assumes that a former version does not contain the detected software bug.

4.4 Misconfiguration of the Control Logic

Industrial control systems are configured by human operators. This opens the possibility of logical mistakes. Control devices and other devices are usually observed for a period of time in order to ensure that they behave as expected. Here, detection mechanism can accelerate test times. Furthermore, it may happen that single control devices are replaced and parts of a plant configuration change. Table 4 shows anomalies originating from misconfiguration. The last three anomalies are solely traceable to configuration mistakes. *Specific mechanisms for logical mistakes* stands for detection mechanisms that are domain specific for common misconfigurations. Concerning adaption mechanisms there

The Potential of Self-Adaptive Software Systems

Table 4. Locations where anomalies of misconfiguration can be detected and adapted.

	Parameter change has no effect	Task misses deadline	Frequency of datapoint	Missing traffic	Calculated datapoint is not used	Datapoints are received from different unit	Datapoints are sent to a different unit	Outlier detection (e.g. machine learning)	Datapoints from other control devices	Specific mechanisms for logical mistakes	Use datapoint from other device	Alarm
Control device												
ACPU	•	•			•			•	•			•
CCPU						•	•		•			•
Network												
Connected device			•	•		•		•	•		•	•
	Anomaly							**Detect.**			**Adap.**	

are not many strategies for resolving misconfigurations. Configuring a control device is a creative task. Automatically creating control logic in a safe manner requires a deep understanding of all kinds of devices.

4.5 Faults in the Physical Environment

Control devices in our setting are not directly connected with a water turbine. The link is mediated by sensors and actuators and these can break or drift over

Table 5. Faults in the physical environment reside in sensors and actuators between a control device and the turbine.

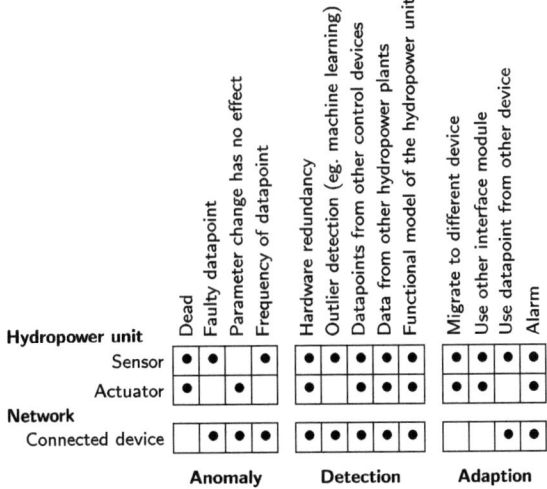

	Dead	Faulty datapoint	Parameter change has no effect	Frequency of datapoint	Hardware redundancy	Outlier detection (eg. machine learning)	Datapoints from other control devices	Data from other hydropower plants	Functional model of the hydropower unit	Migrate to different device	Use other interface module	Use datapoint from other device	Alarm
Hydropower unit													
Sensor	•	•		•	•	•	•	•		•	•	•	•
Actuator	•		•			•		•	•	•	•		•
Network													
Connected device		•	•	•	•	•	•	•	•			•	•
	Anomaly				**Detection**					**Adaption**			

time. Detecting and adapting to such problems can again make a control system more reliable.

Table 5 shows anomalies that can originate from sensors and actuators. Furthermore, such anomalies can be observed through a connected device if it merely forwards them. The detection mechanisms presented are similar to the ones above. What we added is to leverage a *Functional model of the hydropower unit*. The idea behind such a model is to verify the change of parameters with the expected outcome. The proposed adaption mechanisms are similar to the ones above.

5 Discussion

As we can see from the different tables, there are several shared anomalies, detection and adaption mechanisms. Some of these presented detection and adaption mechanism rely on having redundant or stand-by hardware. One could argue that the different mechanisms can be implemented separately and focused on only one problem area. The downside of keeping them strictly separate is that they could interfere with each other or reach wrong conclusions about the real cause of a problem. A self-adaptive software system offers means to deal with cross-cutting anomalies by orchestrating different mechanisms. It would have to reason about the combined outcome of several detection mechanisms in order to find the affected area containing the real cause. Based on the cause, a suitable adaption mechanism would have to be selected. It is important to note that adaption mechanisms do need some execution time. This may introduce delays into control processes. The problem of how bad a small delay really is depends on the domain. E.g. in the hydropower plant context one could argue that the benefit of fixing a permanent hardware fault, but at the cost of introducing a small delay, is preferable to a broken or faulty control activity. Furthermore, testing an adaption before it is carried out is a complicated procedure. This means a self-adaptive system must have a precise representation of the real system in order to ensure that an adaption works as intended. All in all, it is our considered opinion that the presented detection and adaption possibilities would add a valuable improvement to industrial control systems by making them meta-adaptive. A system incorporating some or all of these features has the potential of being more reliable and secure than state of the art control systems.

6 Conclusion

In this work, we presented five areas where a self-adaptive system could improve current and future generations of industrial control systems. The highlighted application areas are hardware faults, security attacks and hacks, software bugs, misconfiguration of the control logic and faults in the physical environment. Self-adaptive software systems are part of our ongoing research towards increasing the reliability and security of control system for hydropower units. The presented anomalies, detection and adaption mechanisms are real possibilities to be faced in our industrial setting, but may differ or appear to be different in other domains. Despite this we believe that most of our observations are readily transferable to other industrial domains.

References

1. Alhakeem, M.S., Munk, P., Lisicki, R., Parzyjegla, H., Parzyjegla, H., Muehl, G.: A framework for adaptive software-based reliability in COTS many-core processors. In: ARCS 2015 (2015)
2. Cárdenas, A.A., Amin, S., Lin, Z.S., Huang, Y.L., Huang, C.Y., Sastry, S.: Attacks against process control systems. In: ASIACCS 2011. ACM Press (2011)
3. Cheung, S., Dutertre, B., Fong, M., Lindqvist, U., Skinner, K., Valdes, A.: Using model-based intrusion detection for SCADA networks. In: Proceedings of the SCADA Security Scientific Symposium (2007)
4. Hadeli, H., Schierholz, R., Braendle, M., Tuduce, C.: Leveraging determinism in industrial control systems for advanced anomaly detection and reliable security configuration. In: Conference on Emerging Technologies & Factory Automation. IEEE (2009)
5. Höller, A., Rauter, T., Iber, J., Kreiner, C.: Patterns for automated software diversity to support security and reliability. In: EuroPLoP 2015. ACM (2015)
6. Höller, A., Spitzer, B., Rauter, T., Iber, J., Kreiner, C.: Diverse compiling for software-based recovery of permanent faults in COTS processors. In: DSN-W 2016. IEEE (2016)
7. John, K.H., Tiegelkamp, M.: IEC 61131-3: Programming Industrial Automation Systems. Springer, Heidelberg (2010)
8. Miller, B., Rowe, D.: A survey SCADA of and critical infrastructure incidents. In: RIIT 2012. ACM Press (2012)
9. Muccini, H., Sharaf, M., Weyns, D.: Self-adaptation for cyber-physical systems: a systematic literature review. In: SEAMS. ACM Press (2016)
10. NIST: Foundations for Innovation in Cyber-Physical Systems. Technical report (2013)
11. Oreizy, P., Gorlick, M., Taylor, R., Heimhigner, D., Johnson, G., Medvidovic, N., Quilici, A., Rosenblum, D., Wolf, A.: An architecture-based approach to self-adaptive software. IEEE Intell. Syst. **14**(3), 54–62 (1999)
12. Rauter, T., Höller, A., Iber, J., Kreiner, C.: Thingtegrity: a scalable trusted computing architecture for the internet of things. In: EWSN 2016. Junction Publishing (2016)
13. Salehie, M., Tahvildari, L.: Self-adaptive software: landscape and research challenges. ACM Trans. Auton. Adapt. Syst. **4**(2), 14 (2009)
14. Weyns, D., Schmerl, B., Grassi, V., Malek, S., Mirandola, R., Prehofer, C., Wuttke, J., Andersson, J., Giese, H., Göschka, K.M.: On patterns for decentralized control in self-adaptive systems. In: Lemos, R., Giese, H., Müller, H.A., Shaw, M. (eds.) Software Engineering for Self-Adaptive Systems II. LNCS, vol. 7475, pp. 76–107. Springer, Heidelberg (2013). doi:10.1007/978-3-642-35813-5_4

Towards Increased Efficiency and Confidence in Process Compliance

Julieth Patricia Castellanos Ardila[✉] and Barbara Gallina

IDT, Mälardalen University, Box 883, 721 23 Västerås, Sweden
{julieth.castellanos,barbara.gallina}@mdh.se

Abstract. Nowadays, the engineering of (software) systems has to comply with different standards, which often exhibit common requirements or at least a significant potential for synergy. Compliance management is a delicate, time-consuming, and costly activity, which would benefit from increased confidence, automation, and systematic reuse. In this paper, we introduce a new approach, called SoPLE&Logic-basedCM. SoPLE&Logic-basedCM combines (safety-oriented) process line engineering with defeasible logic-based approaches for formal compliance checking. As a result of this combination, SoPLE&Logic-basedCM enables automation of compliance checking and systematic reuse of process elements as well as compliance proofs. To illustrate SoPLE&Logic-basedCM, we apply it to the automotive domain and we draw our lessons learnt.

Keywords: ISO 26262 · Automotive SPICE · Compliance by design · Reuse · Defeasible logic · Process assessment · Software process improvement

1 Introduction

In the context of safety critical systems engineering, quality (and more specifically safety) standards act as a baseline aimed at contributing to "assuring society at large that deployment of a given system does not pose an unacceptable risk of harm" [1]. Standards impose requirements on the processes to be adopted to engineer the systems as well as on the expected behaviour of the systems. To adhere to the requirements regarding the processes, companies adapt their practices, and provide evidence (e.g., arguments or even proofs of compliance), which to some extent supports the fulfilment of the requirements. Providing such evidence is a time-consuming and costly activity, which risks to steal time and focus from other activities related to e.g., verification of system's behaviour. Since the ultimate goal of our work is to free time for such verification activities, we believe that process compliance would be highly benefit from automation and systematic reuse. Moreover, confidence in the evidence could be increased via logic-based approaches. Safety-oriented Process Line Engineering (SoPLE) [2,3] permits process engineers to systematise the reuse of process-related information. To argue about or prove compliance, SoPLE is not enough. In a previous work [4,5], SoPLE was combined with argumentation patterns and model-driven engineering principles to automate the creation of reusable process-based argument fragments aimed at showing compliance. In this paper, we intend to provide an additional layer of confidence by offering a logic-based framework that enables formal proofs of compliance. To do that, we build on top of results stemming from the business process-related community and legal compliance. Specifically, we use defeasible logic, a rule-based approach for efficient reasoning with incomplete and inconsistent information, a typical scenario in normative systems [6]. Our approach represents a novelty which contributes to (1) increasing efficiency (via automation and systematic reuse) and confidence (via formal checking) in process compliance, and (2) cross-fertilising previously isolated communities. In this paper, we do not only present our new approach but we also apply it to the automotive domain. In particular, we consider ASPICE (Automotive Software Process Improvement and Capability Determination) [7], which provides a software process assessment model, and ISO 26262 [8], a safety standard that regulates the development process of safety-critical automotive systems. The motivation for this choice is that it is well-known that process reference models of these two standards overlap and exhibit several similarities [3,9], specially in process elements related to software and system engineering [10].

The rest of the paper is organised as follows. In Sect. 2, we provide background information related to our work. In Sect. 3, we introduce SoPLE&Logic-basedCM for efficient and confidence process compliance. In Sect. 4, we apply SoPLE&Logic-basedCM to the automotive domain, and based on the application of our approach, we derive our lessons learned. In Sect. 5, we discuss related work. Finally, in Sect. 6, we present conclusions and future work.

2 Background

This section provides basic information on which we base our work. In Sects. 2.1 and 2.2, we present two automotive standards. In Sect. 2.3, we recall SoPLE. In Sect. 2.4, we present defeasible logic, and in Sect. 2.5, we recall an abstract formal framework for regulatory compliance.

2.1 Automotive SPICE

ASPICE [7] is a standard that addresses the software process capability maturity in automotive. To determine maturity, the process assessment model selects the process reference model and augments it with indicators. These indicators are used to identify if the process outcomes (PO), the result of the achievement of the process, and the process attribute outcomes (PA), the result of the achievement of a specific process attribute, are present. Base practices (BP) (activity-oriented PAs), must be evaluated to establish the capability of the process to be achieved. BPs for the process Software Detailed Design and Unit Construction (SWE.3) are: *BP1-Develop software detailed design, BP2-Define interfaces of software units, BP3-Describe dynamic behavior, BP4-Evaluate software detailed*

Table 1. POs for ASPICE SWE.3.

ID	Process outcome description
PO1	A detailed design is developed that describes software units
PO2	Interfaces of each software unit are defined
PO3	The dynamic behavior of the software units is defined. NOTE: Not all software units have dynamic behavior to be described
PO4	Evaluate the software detailed design in terms of interoperability, interaction, criticality, technical complexity, risks and testability
PO5	Consistency and bidirectional traceability are established between e.g., software requirements and software units. NOTE: Consistency is supported by bidirectional traceability
PO6	The software detailed design and the relationship to the software architectural design is agreed and communicated to all affected parties
PO7	Software units defined by the software detailed design are produced

design, BP5-Establish bidirectional traceability, BP6-Ensure consistency, BP7-Communicate agreed software detailed design, and *BP8-Develop software units*. These BPs are related to one or more of the POs presented in Table 1.

2.2 ISO 26262

ISO 26262 [8] is a standard that focuses on the functional safety of electrical/-electronical systems in vehicles (gross mass up to 3500 kg). In ISO 26262, ASIL (Automotive Safety Integrity levels) are used to specify applicable safety requirements, but both safety and non-safety requirements are implemented within one development process. Specifically, in the sub-phase Software Unit Design and Implementation (SUDI), described in part 6, clause 8 of the standard, single software units are addressed, and the following activities are included: *A1-Specify the software units, A2-Verify the software unit design, A3-Implement the software units*, and *A4-Verify the software unit implementation*. These activities are related to one or more of the requirements presented in Table 2.

2.3 SoPLE

As recalled in the introduction, SoPLE is a methodological framework to systematically model commonalities and variabilities between highly-related processes to facilitate reuse and flexible process derivation. To identify commonalities and variabilities, common terminology that allows the comparisons between the standards is required. In [3], a mapping of common terms between ASPICE and ISO 26262 is provided (see Table 3). These terms are used as follows: if an *activity* in ISO 26262 is equivalent to a *base practice* in ASPICE, the elements are mapped to the common identifier *activity*, and are modeled in SPEM2.0/EPF (Eclipse Process Framework)-Composer with a *TaskUse*. SPEM2.0/EPF-Composer is

Table 2. Requirements for ISO 26262 SUDI.

ID	Requirements description
R1	The requirements of this subclause shall be complied with if the software unit is safety-related ("Safety-related" means that the unit implements safety requirements)
R2	Software units are designed by using a notation that depends on the ASIL and the recommendation level
R3	The specification of the software units shall describe the functional behaviour and the internal design to the level of detail necessary for their implementation
R4	Design principles for software unit design and implementation shall be applied depending on the ASIL and the recommendation levels to reach properties like consistency of the interfaces, correct order of execution of subprograms and functions, etc.
R5	Software unit design and implementation are verified by applying verification methods according to the ASIL and the recommendation levels to demonstrate, e.g., traceability
R6	When ASIL and recommendation levels are not followed, a rationale that explains the reasons for this behavior must be provided (Interpretation of tables, ISO 26262-Section 4.2)

Table 3. Mapping of terms in ISO 26262, ASPICE and SPEM2.0/EPF [3].

Common identifier	ISO 26262	ASPICE	SPEM2.0/EPF
Activity	Activity	Base practice	TaskUse/

suggested in the application of SoPLE. SPEM2.0 (Software and Systems Process Engineering Metamodel) [11] is a standard that provides the elements required to define software and systems development process. SPEM2.0 is implemented in EPF Composer [12], a tool able to store reusable core methods separated from its application in processes. One basic method content is the *Task*, which symbolizes an assignable unit of work. *Method content variability* allows adaptation of created content without affecting the original content. We recall one variability type called *contributes*, which provides a way for process elements instances to contribute with their properties into the base variability element. Process structures can be built incorporating method content elements (for example, a task realized as a TaskUse) in a *breakdown structure*. *Commonalities* in processes are usually *partial*, i.e., a process element contains a subset of common aspects. Common aspects constitute the *commonality points (CP)* while *variability points (VP)* are the process elements that are replaced with particular instances of process elements (called variants). It should be noted that in SPEM2.0 there is no notion of variability point, thus, we introduce an empty task, which is made vary via contributes.

2.4 Defeasible Logic

Defeasible logic [13] is a rule-based logic that provides reasoning with incomplete/inconsistent information. A defeasible theory is a knowledge base in defeasible logic, which contains: (a) *facts:* indisputable statements; (b) *strict rules:* rules in the classical sense, whenever the premises are indisputable, so is the conclusion; (c) *defeasible rules:* rules that can be defeated by contrary evidence; (d) *defeaters:* rules used only to prevent conclusions; (e) *superiority relation:* a relation among rules used to define priorities. Formally, r: A(r) $\hookrightarrow$ C(r), a rule r consists of an antecedent A, the consequence of the rule C, and the rule $\hookrightarrow = \{\rightarrow (strict), \Rightarrow (defeasible), or \rightsquigarrow (defeater)\}$. A defeasible proof requires that we: (a) Put forward a supported rule for the conclusion we want to prove; (b) consider all possible reasons against the desired conclusion; and (c) rebut all counterarguments, by either showing that some premises of the counterargument do not hold, or the argument is defeated by another argument.

2.5 Compliance Checking Approach

In this subsection, we recall the abstract formal framework for modeling *compliance by design* defined in [6], an approach in which compliance of a process with a set of rules is verified before deploying. This approach is based on deontic logic of violations [14], in which deontic notions are modelled using defeasible logics. Deontic notions are present in normative systems e.g., an *obligation* is a deontic effect that arises when a norm bounds the bearer to a specific situation. When a violation occurs, a reparational obligation is in force. For compliance checking, we should: (1) determine the obligations of the rules, (2) determine the state of each task in a process, (3) determine the obligations in force for each task, and (4) check if the obligations in force have been fulfilled or violated. The approach requires that the *traces* of the process (sequence of tasks, in which a process can be executed, respecting the order given by the connectors), and semantic annotations (functions that describe the environment in which a process operates) are defined. The function $Ann(n,t,i)$ returns the state of a *trace (n)* obtained after a *task (t)*, in the *step (i)*. The function $Force(n,t,i) = \{p\}$ associates to each *task (t)* in a *trace (n)*, in the *step (i)* a set of *obligations (p)*.

3 SoPLE&Logic-BasedCM

This section provides an overview of SoPLE&Logic-basedCM (see Fig. 1), our approach for increasing confidence and efficiency in process compliance, by combining safety-oriented process line engineering, the definition of defeasible theories as presented in Sect. 2.4, and the use of the framework for modelling compliance, presented in Sect. 2.5. As Fig. 1 depicts, a process engineer is expected to: (1) model a SoPL (which includes manually modelling the skeleton of the process sequence); (2) formalise the standards rules, select the set of rules that overlap, and analyse the compliance of the SoPL commonalities with the overlapping rules; (3) analyze the effects of the tasks that contributes to the variabilities in the in the standard-specific process.

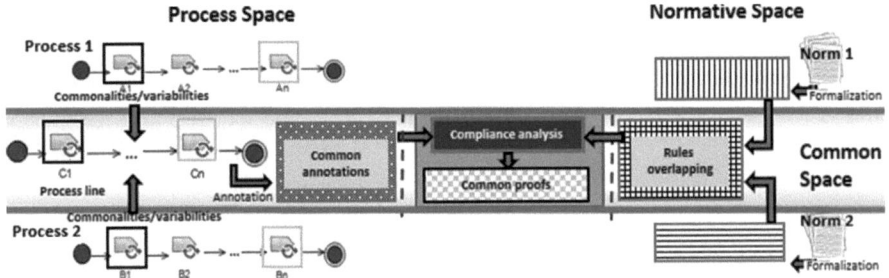

Fig. 1. SoPLE&Logic-basedCM overview.

4 Applying SoPLE and Logic-BasedCM

In this section, for illustration purposes, we apply SoPLE&Logic-basedCM to the software unit development process part provided by ASPICE and ISO 26262. The remaining part of this section is structured as follows: in Sect. 4.1, we model a SoPL. In Sect. 4.2, we define the proofs of compliance. In Sect. 4.3, we present the lessons learnt.

4.1 SoPL Modeling

In this subsection, we apply SoPLE, recalled in Sect. 2.3. The scope is ASPICE SWE.3, and ISO 26262 SUDI recalled in Sects. 2.1 and 2.2 respectively. In the domain engineering phase, we find the equivalent process activities by applying the terminology mapping presented in Table 3, and by analysing the scope of each activity. Terminological similarity is found between BP1 and A1. However, the scope of A1 (see Table 2 - R4) is broader than the scope of BP1, including also BP2 and BP3. Hence, the commonality point (CP1) is defined as a task called *Define software unit design*, which contains three successive steps, namely *develop software detailed design, define interfaces of software units*, and *describe dynamic behavior*. A similar analysis is done for CP2, where there is a correspondence between A2 (scope determined in Table 2 - R4/R5) with BP4/BP5/BP6. CP3 is a straightforward comparison between A3 and BP8. Our comparison also includes standard-specific variants, for example, ISO 26262 variants are activities that deal with ASIL. Variants of this type are *A1a-Define software unit design concerning safety* derived from A1, and *A2a-Verify the software unit design concerning safety* derived from A2. These and other activities that are standard-specific are represented as variability points (VP) (see Table 4). The result of the domain engineering phase is a SoPL, depicted in Fig. 2.

Table 4. SPICE SWE.3/ISO 26262 SUDI activities mapping.

ID	Step in the trace	ISO 26262	ASPICE	Common name
CP1	1	A1	BP1, BP2, BP3	Define software unit design
VP1	2	A1a		Define software unit design concerning safety
CP2	3	A2	BP4, BP5, BP6	Verify the software unit design
VP2	4	A2a		Verify the software design concerning safety
			BP7	Communicate agreed software detailed design
CP3	5	A3	BP8	Implement the software units
VP3	6	A4		Verify the software developed units

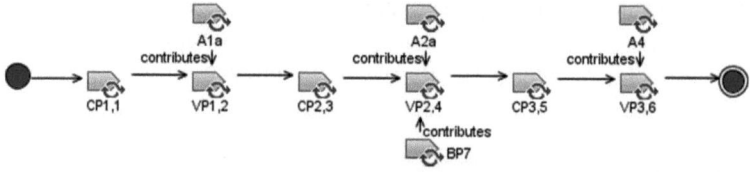

Fig. 2. SoPL model embracing ASPICE SWE.3 and ISO 26262 SUDI.

4.2 Definition of the Proofs of Compliance

In this subsection, we formalize the standards requirements and discover the overlapping set of formal rules. These rules are used to annotate the commonality points of the SoPL model to define common proofs of compliance. Then we define the effects of the rules that apply to the variability points of the SoPL model and analyse their effects in the common proofs. The formalization of the rules includes the definition of defeasible theories, as recalled in Sect. 2.4. For ASPICE SWE.3 (see Table 5) the rules PO2, PO4, PO5 and PO6 (see Table 1) can be translated into the strict rules RA3, RA5, RA6 and RA7 respectively, since these requirements are indisputable statements that are necessary to achieve for compliance. PO1 and PO7 are also indisputable, but each one can be expressed in a more granular way, RA1, RA2 and RA8, RA9, respectively. PO3, instead, is a defeasible rule (RA4), since the note, *"not all software units have dynamic behaviour to be described"*, presented in the requirement, defeats the rule. This defeasible rule does not have a defeater, so its conclusion is considered provable, as well as the conclusions of the strict rules.

For ISO 26262 SUDI, a similar analysis is done (see Table 6). Hence, nine strict rules and three defeasible rules have resulted. The defeasible rules have a defeated rule, namely RI12, which is in favor of the conclusions. For example, if RI7 is not achieved ($sud \Rightarrow \neg dp$) then a rationale is provided ($\neg dp \to r$).

Table 5. Defeasible theories for ASPICE SWE.3.

PO	ID	Rule	Rule description
PO1	RA1	sud → d	Software unit design (sud) is developed (d)
	RA2	sud → su	sud describes software units (su)
PO2	RA3	su → i	su has defined interfaces
PO3	RA4	su ⇒ db	su has usually described dynamic behavior (db)
PO4	RA5	sud → v	sud is verified (v)
PO5	RA6	su → tc	su has established traceability and consistency (bt)
PO6	RA7	sud → ac	sud is agreed and communicated (ac)
PO7	RA8	sui → sud	Software unit implementation (sui) is based on sud
	RA9	sui → i	sui is implemented (i)

Rules of this type are provable, because their counterargument is a strict rule. The mapping of the defeasible theories is presented in Table 7. Direct mapping is done for the strict rules CR1 (RA1/RI2), CR2 (RA2/RI4), CR5 (RA8/RI8) and CR6 (RA9/RI9), since these rules affect the processes in a similar way. CR3 is the mapping between RA3 (definition of the interfaces) and RA4 (description of dynamic behavior) to RI6 (description of the internal design). This mapping is base on the premise that ISO 26262 is not specific on what the software unit should show as internal design. However, definition of interfaces and dynamic behavior are defined as properties that shall be reached by the software unit design (see Table 2 - R4). For CR4 a similar situation occurs, since traceability is considered one of the aspects that have to be demonstrated in ISO 26262 when verification is carried out (see Table 2 - R5). Hence, the mapping for CR4 is RA5 (software unit is verified) and RA6 (software unit has established traceability) to RI10 (software unit design is verified).

The SoPL model (see Fig. 2) is constituted by one trace *tSoPL*. The effects of its tasks (*tSoPL:<CP1, VP1, CP2, VP2, CP3, VP3>*) are determined with the function *Ann* (defined in Sect. 2.5) and presented in Listing 1.1.

```
Ann(tSoPL,CP1,1)={CP1}
Ann(tSoPL,VP1,2)=Ann(tSoPL,CP1,1) U {VP1}
Ann(tSoPL,CP2,3)=Ann(tSoPL,VP1,2) U {CP2}
Ann(tSoPL,VP2,4)=Ann(tSoPL,CP2,3) U {VP2}
Ann(tSoPL,CP3,5)=Ann(tSoPL,VP2,4) U {CP3}
Ann(tSoPL,VP3,6)=Ann(tSoPL,CP3,5) U {VP3}
```

Listing 1.1. Annotations for the trace *tSoPL*.

A task determines its state taking its effect and inheriting the previous effects. Once the states are determined, the obligations in force (rules that apply to the tasks) are assigned, using the function *Force* (recalled in Sect. 2.5). In Table 8, common defeasible theories (Table 7) are assigned to the commonality points (CPs) of the SoPL trace *tSoPL*. In *tSoPL*, rules CR1, CR2, CR3 are effective at CP1, meaning that for the software unit design task (CP1), software unit is designed (CR1), units are described (CR2), and the internal design, including interfaces and dynamic behaviour is described (CR3) (Proof 1). Rule

Table 6. Defeasible theories for ISO 26262 SUDI.

Req.	ID	Rule	Rule description
R1	RI1	sud → sr	Software unit design (sud) is safety related (sr)
R2	RI2	sud → d	sud is design (d)
	RI3	d ⇒ n	d is usually implemented by using a notation that depends on the ASIL and the recommendation level (n)
	RI4	sud → su	sud describes software units (su)
R3	RI5	sud → fb	sud has described functional behavior (fb)
	RI6	sud → id	sud has described internal design (id)
R4	RI7	sud ⇒ dp	sud is implemented by using design principles (dp) that depends on the ASIL and the recommendation level
	RI8	sui → sud	software unit implementation (sui) is based on sud
	RI9	sui → i	sui is implemented (i)
R5	RI10	sud, sui → v	sud, sui are verified
	RI11	v ⇒ m	v is usually done by using a method that depends on the ASIL and the recommendation level (m)
R6	RI12	¬n, ¬dp, ¬vm → r	If n, dp or m are not applied depending on the ASIL and the recommendation levels, then rationale (r) is required

Table 7. Rules comparison and commonality identification.

SPICE SWE.3		ISO 26262 SUDI		Common Rule	Description
ID	Rule	ID	Rule		
RA1	sud → d	RI2	sud → d	CR1	Software unit design (sud) is developed (d)
RA2	sud → su	RI4	sud → su	CR2	sud describe software units (su)
RA3	su → i	RI6	sud → id	CR3	Internal design is described, including interfaces and dynamic behavior
RA4	su ⇒ db				
RA5	sud → v	RI10	sud → v	CR4	su is verified and traceability demonstrated
RA6	su → tc				
RA8	sui → sud	RI8	sui → sud	CR5	su implementation (sui) is based on sud
RA9	sui → i	RI9	sui → i	CR6	sui is implemented (i)

CR4 is effective at CP2, meaning that in the verification of the software design task, the software is verified and traceability is demonstrated (CR4) (Proof 2). Finally, CR5 and CR6 are effective at CP3, meaning that in the develop of the software units activity, implementation is based on design (GR5) and unit implementation is carried out (GR6) (Proof 3). The obligations triggered by the rules are fulfilled in the corresponding step, meaning that the obligation cannot be postponed for other steps. As presented in Sect. 2.5, this means that the commonality points of the trace *tSoPL* are compliant with the set of rules presented in Table 7.

Table 8. Applicable rules and obligations in force for tSoPL.

Task, Step	Rule	Obligations in force
CP1,1	CR1, CR2, CR3	Force(tSoPL,CP1,1) = {CR1} U {CR2} U {CR3}
VP1,2	(standard-specific)	Force(tSoPL,VP1,2) = Force(tSoPL,CP1,1) U {standard-specific}
CP2,3	CR4	Force(tSoPL,CP2,3) = Force(tSoPL,VP2,2) U {CR4}
VP2,4	(standard-specific)	Force(tSoPL,VP2,4) = Force(tSoPL,CP2,3) U {standard-specific}
CP3,5	CR5, CR6	Force(tSoPL,CP3,5) = Force(tSoPL,VP2,4) U {CR5} U {CR6}
VP3,6	(standard-specific)	Force(tSoPL,VP3,6) = Force(tSoPL,CP3,5) U {standard-specific}

Standard-specific processes are generated when variability points are deployed with specific tasks. ASPICE SWE.3 process is t_A:<*CP1, CP2, BP7, CP3*>, where VP2 is contributed with BP7. ISO 26262 SUDI process is t_I:<*CP1, A1a, CP2, A2a, CP3, A4*>, where VP1 is contributed with A1a, VP2 with A2a and VP3 with A4. Table 9 shows the influence of the obligations in force for these tasks.

In ASPICE SWE.3, the proof obtained for CP1 (Proof 1), and the one obtained in CP2 (Proof 2) are not altered, since the variability point (VP1) do not have any corresponding task in the trace. The rule applied in VP2 (replaced by BP7) is triggered and fulfilled in BP7, so the proof obtained for CP3 is not altered. In ISO 26262 SUDI, the proofs obtained in CP1 (Proof 1), CP2 (Proof 2) and CP3 (Proof 3) corresponds to non-safety related rules, while the rules that apply to the variability points corresponds to safety-related rules. Hence, the proofs obtained in VP1 and VP2 adds information to the trace, and influence the proofs obtained in CP2 (Proof 2) and CP3 (Proof 3) respectively. In this case, we can conclude that the proof can be partially used.

4.3 Lessons Learnt

Our automotive SoPL describes commonality and variability points presented in ASPICE and ISO 26262, as a sequence of ordered tasks distributed in a trace. Tasks have assigned states and obligations in force (normative rules) that produce tasks effects. These effects can influence the tasks' behaviors in the trace, and define whether the designed trace is compliant or not with a given set of rules. Our analysis started with the annotation of the commonality points

Table 9. Applicable rules for the variability points.

tSoPL	tA	tI	Rules	Influence of the obligations in force
VP1		A1a	RI1, RI3, RI5, RI7	For the design of the software units concerning safety (A1a), the software is safety-related (RI1), the design is usually implemented by using a notation that depends on the ASIL and the recommendation level (RI3), the design has described functional behavior (RI5), and the design is usually implemented by using design principles that depend on the ASIL and the recommendation level (RI7)
VP2	BP7		RA7	The software unit design communication (BP7) is done (RA7)
		A2a	RI11	The verification of the software unit design concerning safety (A2a) is done according to methods that depends on the ASIL and the recommendation level (RI11)
VP3		A4	RI10, RI11	The verification of the software unit implementation (A4) is done (RI10) according to methods that depends on the ASIL and the recommendation level (RI11)

of the SoPL with the overlapping set of rules, obtained from the comparison of the requirements provided by the two standards. These annotations provide the possibility to derive a common set of proofs of compliance. However, the states and obligations in force for the tasks that contribute to the variability points, once the standard-specific processes are deployed, can affect the proof obtained for the commonality points. Hence, proofs of compliance can be fully reused or may be partially reused, depending on the effects produced by the variability points. Fully reused proofs can be applied to commonality points that are not preceded by a variability point, or that are preceded by a variability point that either remains empty after deployment, or its state after deployment does not produce effects that can be spread out in the trace. Partially reused proofs can be applied to variability points that are contributed with standard-specific tasks which states and obligations in force influence the process proofs obtained. Therefore, a classification of the standard-specific tasks that contribute to the standard-specific processes is required to understand whether the common proofs can be fully/partially reused.

5 Related Work

Related work regarding increased efficiency via automation and reuse was already discussed in [4,5]. Thus, in this paper, we limit our attention to automated compliance checking, the novel layer added to SoPLE. Automated compliance checking is not a new research area, specially in business management. An example of a framework that define proofs of compliance by design is presented in [15], where rules are formalized using logics. However, these frameworks do not contemplate the reuse of proofs of compliance. A more closely related work is presented in [20] where business process are augmented with reusable fragments to ensure process compliance by design. In this approach, rules are formalized with temporal logics. In our approach, we seek to establish compliance proofs for safety compliance, using defeasible logic and deontic logic of violations, instead of temporal logics. Approaches for reusing proofs are also found in other areas. For example, in [16,17], software verification tasks are benefited by the reuse of chunks of proofs. Our reusable chunks of proofs are instead derived from the comparison between the set of rules and the process reference model provided by a normative system.

6 Conclusions and Future Work

In this paper, we introduced SoPLE&Logic-basedCM, a novel approach for confident and efficient process compliance based on the combination of safety-oriented process line engineering, defeasible logic, and an approach for compliance by design. We have applied SoPLE&Logic-basedCM to the automotive domain to illustrate its potential in terms of reuse of proofs. More specifically, we have limited our illustration to a specific portion of automotive standards (ASPICE and ISO 26262) and we have shown that sets of compliance-related proofs can be fully/partially reused.

The formalization of the approach presented in this paper is limited to process-related activities, and a general view of the deontic notion *obligation*. For future work, other process elements, e.g., work products will be addressed, as well as a broader range or deontic notions classification (permissions and prohibitions). Further validation of the approach on more complex processes is also required, as well as the exploration of tools that can potentially support the automation of our work, like Regorous [18], a compliance checker, and logic reasoners like SPINdle[1] and Deimos[2], programs that are used to compute the consequence of defeasible logic theories.

Acknowledgments. This work is supported by the EU and VINNOVA via the ECSEL JU project AMASS (No. 692474) [19]. We thank Mustafa Hashmi for his valuable comments on an earlier version of this paper.

---

[1] http://spindle.data61.csiro.au/spindle/.
[2] http://www.ict.griffith.edu.au/arock/defeasible/Defeasible.cgi.

References

1. Rushby, J.: New challenges in certification for aircraft software. In: 9th ACM International Conference on Embedded Software (EMSOFT), pp. 211–218 (2011)
2. Gallina, B., Sljivo, I., Jaradat, O.: Towards a safety-oriented process line for enabling reuse in safety critical systems development and certification. In: 35th Annual IEEE Software Engineering Workshop (SEW), pp. 148–157 (2012)
3. Gallina, B., Kashiyarandi, S., Martin, H., Bramberger, R.: Modeling a safety- and automotive-oriented process line to enable reuse and flexible process derivation. In: IEEE 38th International Computer Software and Applications Conference Workshops (COMPSACW), pp. 504–509 (2014)
4. Gallina, B., Lundqvist, K., Forsberg, K.: THRUST: a method for speeding up the creation of process-related deliverables. In: IEEE/AIAA 33rd Digital Avionics Systems Conference (DASC), p. 5D4-11 (2014)
5. Gallina, B.: A Model-driven safety certification method for process compliance. In: 2nd International Workshop on Assurance Cases for Software-Intensive Systems (ISSREW), pp. 204–209 (2014)
6. Hashmi, M., Governatori, G., Wynn, M.T.: Normative requirements for regulatory compliance: an abstract formal framework. Inf. Syst. Front. **18**(3), 429–455 (2016)
7. Automotive SPICE: Process Assessment/Reference Model (2015)
8. ISO 26262: Road Vehicles-Functional Safety. International Standard (2011)
9. Lami, G., Falcini, F.: Automotive SPICE assessments in safety-critical contexts: an experience report. In: IEEE International Symposium on Software Reliability Engineering Workshops (ISSREW), 497–502 (2014)
10. Bleakley, G.: How rational can help with compliance to ISO 26262 & ASPICE. Technical report, IBM Software Group (2014)
11. SPEM 2.0: Software & Systems Process Engineering Meta-Model (2008)
12. Eclipse Composer Framework. https://eclipse.org/epf/
13. Antoniou, G., Billington, D., Governatori, G., Maher, M.J.: Representation results for defeasible logic. ACM Trans. Comput. Logic **2**, 255–287 (2000)
14. Governatori, G., Rotolo, A., Sartor, G.: Temporalised normative positions in defeasible logic. In: 10th International Conference on Artificial Intelligence and Law (ICAIL), pp. 25–34 (2005)
15. Awad, A., Decker, G., Weske, M.: Efficient compliance checking using BPMN-Q and temporal logic. In: Dumas, M., Reichert, M., Shan, M.-C. (eds.) BPM 2008. LNCS, vol. 5240, pp. 326–341. Springer, Heidelberg (2008). doi:10.1007/978-3-540-85758-7_24
16. Reif, W., Stenzel, K.: Reuse of proofs in software verification. In: Shyamasundar, R.K. (ed.) FSTTCS 1993. LNCS, vol. 761, pp. 284–293. Springer, Heidelberg (1993). doi:10.1007/3-540-57529-4_61
17. Beckert, B., Bormer, T., Klebanov, V.: Reusing Proofs when Program Verification Systems are Modified. Long Beach, California (2005)
18. Governatori, G.: The regorous approach to process compliance. In: IEEE 19th International Enterprise Distributed Object Computing Workshop (EDOCW), pp. 33–40. IEEE (2015)
19. AMASS: Architecture-driven, multi-concern and seamless assurance and certification of cyber-physical systems. http://www.amass-ecsel.eu/
20. Schumm, D., Turetken, O., Kokash, N., Elgammal, A., Leymann, F., van den Heuvel, W.-J.: Business process compliance through reusable inits of compliant processes. In: International Conference on Web Engineering (ICWE), pp. 325–337 (2010)

SPI Issues

SPI Issues

Systematic Literature Reviews of Software Process Improvement: A Tertiary Study

Arif Ali Khan[1(✉)], Jacky Keung[1], Mahmood Niazi[2], Shahid Hussain[1], and He Zhang[3]

[1] Department of Computer Science, City University of Hong Kong,
Kowloon Tong, Hong Kong
{aliakhan2-c,shussain7-c}@my.cityu.edu.hk,
jacky.keung@cityu.edu.hk
[2] Information and Computer Science Department,
King Fahd University of Petroleum and Minerals, Dhahran, Saudi Arabia
mkniazi@kfupm.edu.sa
[3] Software Institute, Nanjing University, Nanjing, China
hezhang@nju.edu.cn

Abstract. Systematic Literature Review (SLR) is becoming a vital part of present day research in software process improvement (SPI). Nevertheless, there is no available study that provides detail review of the published software process improvement SLRs. **Objective**: The aim of this article is to classify the SLRs of SPI in order to identify the main research areas covered and evaluate the quality of the published SLRs. **Methodology**: A tertiary study was conducted to review the SLRs published by other researchers on the topic of SPI. **Results**: Twenty-four SLR articles were identified in the field of SPI. Results show that the quality of the selected SLRs on SPI is decreasing over the recent years. The most popular research topics are factors affecting SPI and process models. **Conclusions**: This study provides the review and state of the art in the context of SPI research. The results of this article would be of great interest for future SPI researchers by providing in depth understanding of various research areas in SPI. The number of process improvement SLRs is increasing and the overall quality is decreasing, which could lessen their potential impact on SPI practice. Currently, SPI literature is weak in the knowledge areas such as quality and software testing process improvement.

Keywords: Software process improvement · Systematic literature review · Tertiary study · Systematic mapping

1 Introduction

Zahran [1] define SPI as "the discipline of defining, characterizing, improving and measuring software management, better product innovation, faster cycle time, greater product quality and reduced development costs simultaneously". According to O'Connor et al. [2], various process improvement models and techniques have been developed in order to help software organizations to achieve effective management of software development processes. However, regardless of the availability of different process improvement models and standards, the success rate of SPI programs is very low [3], i.e. about 30% [4]. Khan and Keung [5] justify it by reporting that little attention has been given to the process improvement activities. Software development organizations have recognized that the failure to effectively direct the software process is one of the main causes of unsuccessful projects [5].

Research to mitigate the issues related to SPI is expanding and SLR approach is increasingly used to explore the available literature. SLR has a long tradition in SPI research and various review studies are conducted using the SLR technique [5–13, 15, 17, 18]. SLR assists the SPI researchers to highlight state of the art in a specific domain. According to Kitchenham [6], SLR is an approach for investigating, classifying, and assessing the existing literature related to a specific research area and questions of interest [7].

Systematic mapping study is a type of SLR that focus on particular research area in order to categorize the resulting literature to present a 'map' of that specific area [6].

Tertiary study approach is used to extract the data and information from available SLRs of a specific research topic. Tertiary studies present information about the number of SLRs published in a particular research field, their quality and main research focus. Several tertiary studies are published in the domain of software engineering [3, 8–13, 17], but none of the published tertiary studies emphasized on SLRs in the context of SPI.

The aim of this research study is to present a tertiary study of published SLRs on SPI between 2004 and October 2015. The time range is based on the deployment of systematic review approach in the field of software engineering in 2004 [7]. This tertiary study will provide a thorough understanding of the available SPI research and assist the researchers by enriching their background knowledge on SPI.

The next section of the paper presents the adopted research methodology. Section 3 highlights the extracted results of the review. In Sect. 4, we discuss threats to validity and our conclusions are presented in Sect. 5.

2 Research Methodology

Systematic literature review is a type of the secondary study that assess all the primary studies "studies which are used for exploring a specific research area" in order to identify, analyze and explore all evidences related to research questions in an unbiased and iterative way [6, 7]. According to Kitchenham [6], SLR has three main phases i.e. "planning the review, conducting the review and reporting the review". The three SLR phases are reported in the following sections.

2.1 Phase 1: Planning the Review

Research Questions. We have followed the previously published tertiary studies [3, 8–13, 17] in order to structure the following research questions.

(RQ1) What SLR studies have been published in the field of software process improvement from 2004 to October 2015?

(RQ2) What software process improvement topics have been discussed?
(RQ3) What is the quality of the available SLR articles on SPI?

Search Process. A comprehensive search process was conducted in order to classify all the available research articles relevant to our questions of interest. We have break down the research questions and extracted the major terms. We have also reported the list of synonyms, abbreviations, and alternative words of the major terms. The keywords and their synonyms were based on the existing literature in the domain of process improvement [1, 2, 4, 5, 14]. The major keywords and their synonyms were concatenated with the help of "OR" and "AND" operators to construct the search strings that were used for the identification of relevant primary studies.

We have developed the following search strings: ((("software process improvement" OR "SPI" OR "software process models" OR "software process standards" OR "software process frameworks" OR "software maturity models") AND ("systematic literature review" OR "SLR" OR "systematic mapping" OR "literature review" OR "meta-analysis" OR "in-depth survey" OR "previous studies" OR "existing literature" OR "review of literature" OR "survey of available literature" OR "in-depth overview" OR "mapping study")).

The search strings were deployed in several digital repositories in order to identify the relevant articles. The selection of repositories was based on previous research experience and suggestions provided by other researchers [13]. A total of five databases were selected, i.e., IEEE, Scopus, Google Scholar, Science Direct and ISI Web of Science. The given combinations of search terms have been used to extract the required results from the selected digital repositories.

Inclusion and Exclusion Criteria. All published studies that focused on SLRs or systematic mapping studies in journals, conferences or books in the domain of SPI were included in the study to the best knowledge. Relevance to the earlier mentioned research questions were the basic consideration.

Research studies that did not explicitly discuss SLRs in the context of SPI were excluded. We have also excluded the Master and PhD dissertations that are not published in journals or conferences. Furthermore, all informal literature surveys were ignored. The duplicated articles were not considered. Additionally, those articles were also excluded that were reported in other languages except English.

Quality Criteria for the studies selection. Quality is the degree to which a specific study minimizes the bias and maximizes the internal and external validity [19]. Quality assessment assists to interpret the results and determine the strength of the elaborated inferences [9]. The most commonly used approaches for quality assessment are checklist [15]. Each primary study was assessed for quality using a checklist (i.e. Database of Abstracts of Reviews of Effects (DARE)) defined by the Centre for Reviews and Dissemination (CDR), York University [16]. The DARE checklist is based on four questions illustrated in Table 1. The same quality assessment approach has been adopted by other researchers [8, 17].

Table 1. Checklist for quality assessment of selected studies.

QA Questions	Score	Description
QA1: "Are the review's inclusion and exclusion criteria described and appropriate?"	1	Explicit inclusion criteria
	0.5	Implicit inclusion criteria
	0	No inclusion criteria
QA2: "Is the literature search likely to have covered all relevant studies?"	1	Extract data from four or more digital libraries with additional search strategies
	0.5	Limited searched of three or four digital libraries with no additional search strategies
	0	Limited search of two digital libraries or restricted search
QA3: "Did the reviewers assess the quality/validity of the included studies?"	1	Applied explicit quality criteria
	0.5	Research question involves quality issues that are addressed by the study
	0	No study quality assessment strategy
QA4: "Were the basic data/studies adequately described?"	1	Clear description of the information for each selected primary study
	0.5	Abstract level information about selected primary studies
	0	The outcomes of the specific studies are not quantified

2.2 Conducting the Review

Primary Studies Selection. A comprehensive search was conducted and a total of 7684 articles were extracted from all the selected databases. The tollgate technique developed by Afzal et al. [18] was applied to the articles selection process, which comprise of five phases as described in Fig. 1. After applying the inclusion and exclusion criteria, a total of 24 primary studies that focused on SLRs of SPI were selected using the tollgate approach [18].

- Phase 1: Search through search terms (7684 articles were selected)
- Phase 2: Title and abstract based inclusion/exclusion (4112 articles were selected)
- Phase 3: Introduction and conclusions based inclusion/exclusion (323 articles were sorted out)
- Phase 4: Full text based inclusion/exclusion (135 articles were filtered)
- Phase 5: Final selection of articles to be included in the primary studies selection (24 articles were selected as a primary studies)

Complete details of the 24 selected primary studies are given in Appendix 1.

Data Extraction. The first author of this study has executed the search strings and selected the 24 SLRs by applying the inclusion and exclusion criteria. The third author has reviewed and reported the references, number of citations (CI), research focus (RF) and number of primary studies (PS) cited by the selected 24 SLR studies. The quality assessment process has been carried out by the first and third authors. The

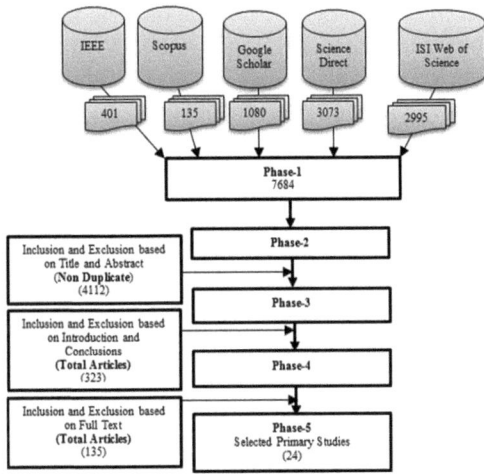

Fig. 1. Tollgate approach for articles selection.

second and fourth authors have reviewed and updated the quality assessment score for each selected SLR. The results and analysis phases have been mainly done by the first and third author. A complete list of all the 24 selected primary studies with the extracted information is provided in Appendix 1.

Data Synthesis. We have performed the data synthesis by aggregating the extracted data using a simple frequency analysis technique. We have not rejected the papers of the same authors discussed the results on the same topic in multiple papers. We are sure that conference papers have limited space, which do not allow the authors to discuss all the results.

The results extracted from all the selected articles were reported together and all the research questions were explicitly evaluated against these results.

3 Reporting the Results

In this section, all the extracted results in relation to each of the research questions are addressed.

(RQ1) What SLR studies have been published in the field of software process improvement from 2004 to October 2015?

Appendix 1 presents the results of the 24 selected SLRs on SPI. Eleven (45%) articles were published in conferences and 13 (54%) articles were published in journals. Among the 24 selected SLRs, [SL6] has cited the minimum number of primary studies (i.e. 4) and [SL24] has quoted a maximum number of 404. Citation of the SLRs ranged from 0 [SL1, SL5, SL11, SL12, SL21, SL23] to 193 [SL3] including self-citation. The articles having no citation are recently published SLR studies (2012-2015). As this tertiary study was conducted in 2015, therefore we have not found any citation for the given six articles. Three articles [SL1, SL5, SL12] have low quality assessment scores and it might be the reason that they have no citation. The reaming three SLRs [SL11, SL21, SL23] are published in 2014-2015 and we believe that they will have multiple citations in the coming years.

Figure 2 demonstrates the year wise distribution of the selected primary studies. The first SLR on SPI was published in 2007 and the number recorded a gradual increase after 2009 until there was a distinct decrease in 2013. Since 2013, there has been an incessant increase of SLRs on SPI and 5 SLRs were published in 2015.

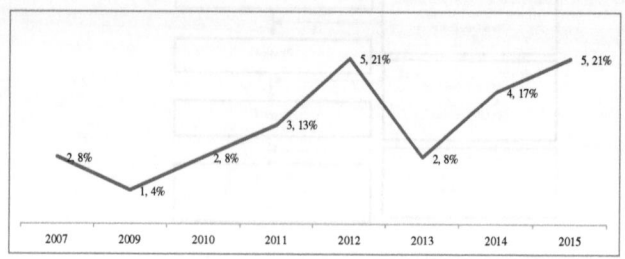

Fig. 2. Tollgate approach for articles selection.

(RQ2) What software process improvement topics have been discussed?

Results provided in Table 2 show that SLRs on SPI focus on five key areas, i.e. (1) factors (2) small and medium-sized enterprises (SMEs) (3) process models (4) software quality and (5) testing. Among all the topics, *factors and process models* were highlighted as the most common SPI topics as 8 SLRs were classified under each category. Articles discussed under the *factors* category have reported different success factors and barriers that might influence the design and execution of the SPI activities in the software industry. They also proposed various practices to address the identified success factors and barriers.

Eight SLRs discussed various aspects of SPI process models. For example, [SL13] reviewed the existing SPI problems and developed criteria for multimodal SPI solutions. The capability maturity model (CMM) and capability maturity model integration (CMMI) process models were the main research focus of articles [SL16, SL22]. One study [SL12] looked into the state of the art on SPI models and identified the strength of evidence from empirical work reported within SPI literature. Article, [SL15] provided in depth knowledge about the implementation of SPI models in a distributed environment and [SL19] gave a brief view of process improvement models for developing service based applications. One SLR, [SL24] has reported the implementation of process improvement models in a game development environment.

Research in SMEs was found to be the third most important research area. Six SLRs have discussed the concept of SPI in SMEs and covered various aspects of SPI in the domain of SMEs. Two SLRs [SL6, SL8] presented the current state of research in SPI models and techniques used by web development in SMEs. Two studies [SL11, SL14] highlighted the existing literature for SPI initiatives in establishing new companies. Existing SPI approaches used in SMEs were reported in [SL3] and the need for SPI implementation in the domain of SMEs was examined in [SL4].

Table 2. SPI research topics covered in selected SLRs

ID	Type	Citation	No. of primary studies	Research focus
SL1	Conference	0	10	Factors
SL2	Conference	4	28	
SL5	Conference	0	100	
SL7	Conference	17	26	
SL10	Journal	94	148	
SL18	Journal	28	60	
SL20	Journal	1	29	
SL23	Journal	0	38	
SL3	Journal	193	45	SMEs
SL4	Conference	6	Not mentioned	
SL8	Conference	13	8	
SL11	Conference	0	11	
SL14	Journal	24	43	
SL6	Conference	19	4	
SL9	Conference	8	7	Process models
SL12	Conference	0	400	
SL13	Journal	11	78	
SL15	Journal	54	26	
SL16	Journal	6	81	
SL19	Journal	29	57	
SL22	Journal	98	49	
SL24	Conference	1	404	
SL17	Journal	1	74	Software quality
SL21	Journal	0	18	Software testing

One study, [SL17] focused on up to date state of the art regarding the contribution of SPI implementation towards the improvement of product quality. In [SL21], the authors underlined available software testing process improvement approaches and their characteristics.

(RQ3) What is the quality of the available SLR articles on SPI?

Quality assessment (QA) criteria discussed in Table 1 were used to assess all the selected SLRs. Figure 3 shows the list of the scores for each SLR against the four quality assessment questions (Table 1). A total of 24 SLRs were selected and their QA scores were calculated by adding the assessment score against the four QA questions.

Table 3 reported the percentage and numbers of the selected SLRs against each QA question.

QA1 emphasized on the clear description of inclusion and exclusion criteria. Eleven articles (45.8%) have explicitly indicated the inclusion and exclusion criteria while ten articles (41.6%) discussed it partially. Total three studies (12.5%) did not consider the inclusion or exclusion criteria for their SLRs.

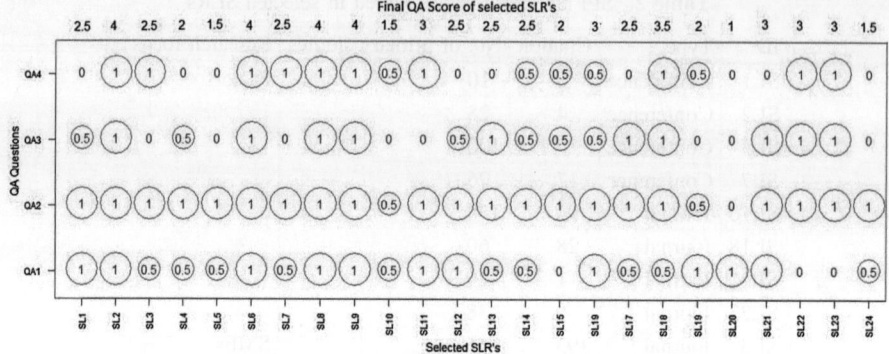

Fig. 3. Tollgate approach for articles selection.

Table 3. SPI research topics covered in selected SLRs

ID	Quality assessment criteria	Yes/1	Partially/ 0.5	No/0
QA1	"Are the review's inclusion and exclusion criteria described and appropriate?"	11 (45.8%)	10 (41.6%)	3 (12.5%)
QA2	"Is the literature search likely to have covered all relevant studies?"	21 (84.5%)	2 (8.3%)	1 (4.1%)
QA3	"Did the reviewers assess the quality/validity of the included studies?"	10 (41.6%)	6 (25.0%)	8 (33.3%)
QA4	"Were the basic data/studies adequately described?"	10 (41.6%)	5 (20.8%)	9 (37.5%)

QA2 inquires whether the SLRs have covered all the relevant studies or not. Most of the SLRs succeeded (84.5%), while (8.3%) of them gave partial details about the relevant studies. One study (4.1%) didn't consider QA2 for their SLR.

QA3 tackles the quality assessment of the selected primary studies. Results demonstrate that (41.6%) of the SLRs have clearly assessed their selected primary studies and (25%) of the articles have embarked on partial assessment. The result for QA3 shows that (33.3%) of the SLRs did not define quality assessment criteria for primary studies.

Results for QA4 demonstrate that (41.6%) of the SLRs have adequately described the primary studies and (20.8%) gives partial details. The results illustrate that in total (37.5%) of the selected SLRs did not provide any information about their selected primary studies.

Based on the above discussion, we could argue that majority of the selected primary studies (84.5%) have explicitly fulfilled the assessment criteria of QA2 (Table 3). The QA2 focused on the search strategy to extract the most relevant studies. It means that most of the SLR studies have selected the appropriate search criteria and they have mined the most relevant studies.

We have also concluded that, (41.6%) of the selected SLRs have partial inclusion and exclusion criteria (QA1) and (33.3%) have failed to evaluate the quality of the included primary studies (QA3). As shown in Table 3, (41.6%) SLRs did not provide complete overview of the included primary studies (QA4).

It illustrates that most of the 24 SLRs have not completely satisfied the quality assessment criteria (Table 3). It is known that the main difference between SLR and the traditional literature review is the rigor process [10], where the ignorance of this factor will likely not yield reliable and useful results. This issue needs further consideration in the domain of SPI SLRs. It is because if the selected primary studies could not fulfill the QA criteria, then there might be serious threats to the validity of the results presented by the SLRs [10].

4 Threats to Validity

Most of the SLR data were collected by the first and third authors and there exists a high risk that two researchers could be biased and frequently extracting wrong data. In view of such threat, the remaining authors were involved to randomly check the different steps involved in this tertiary study. Nevertheless, the random checks of the authors have not been reported in the sense of review manner, time, effort and impacts of the checks.

Additionally, we might have missed some of the related keywords and their synonyms to develop a complete set of search strings. It may cause to miss numerous numbers of related articles of process improvement. However, we corroborated our search strategy against previous tertiary studies [3, 8–13, 17] and track our tertiary study considering all SLRs in SPI.

We have addressed RQ2 by classifying the identified articles based on the reported research topics. A possible threat to the validity of this study is that, we have not found a specific framework that could be used to map the identified articles into the five categories of research topics (Table 2). We were not able to formally validate the classification. However, all of the authors were involved in the informal mapping process.

Finally, this SLR study might suffer from over-constraints in the search terms. Due to this limitation, the study may have missed additional aspects of SPI that were not previously examined using SLR approach.

5 Conclusions

Twenty four SLRs that were conducted between 2004 and October 2015 in the domain of SPI have been successfully selected. It is a first attempt to conduct a tertiary study for SPI related studies. The collected data and the results presented in this paper could be of great value for future SPI researchers, in particular for doctoral students who may need an effective starting point for an overview of all the research areas so far in SPI. Furthermore, limitations of the existing SPI related SLRs were discussed. It is beneficial for those who are keen to select interested research areas of process improvement.

The most common concerns of the SLRs are research areas of factors and SPI process models. Most of the selected SLR studies have discussed success factors and their impacts on SPI implementation, as well as various process models. It suggests that, currently researchers might have great interest in these two research areas and these are the most active research topics in the domain of SPI.

The quality of the selected SLRs decreased over time because most of the SLRs neglected to thoroughly assess the quality of their selected primary studies. The absence of this quality assessment factor will likely not bring reliable and useful results. Therefore, researchers should put strong emphasis on the implementation of quality assessment criteria.

With these considerations, we hope to increase the knowledge of available literature regarding SPI and the actual state of the research based on systematic reviews. The analysis of the results suggests that a few knowledge areas of SPI like quality and software testing process have not yet become the focus of researchers. With this study, it is hoped that researchers would investigate the SPI research areas that until now still receive limited attention or have not yet been explored.

In the future, we will update this tertiary study by considering the SLRs published after October 2015. This research work will also be extended by conducting secondary search from reviewing the primary studies of the 24 selected SLR studies. Detailed analysis upon the data extraction completion from the secondary search can be performed. The remaining steps of thematic synthesis will be applied to come up with a model for the themes.

Acknowledgment. This work is supported in part by the General Research Fund of the Research Grants Council of Hong Kong (No. 9042328), and the research funds of City University of Hong Kong (No. 7004683 and 7004474).

Appendix 1

See Table 4.

Table 4. Selected Primary Studies

ID	Reference	CI	RF	PS
SL1	Bayona, S., Calvo-Manzano, A.J., Feliu. S.T.: Review of critical success factors related to people in software process improvement. European Conference on Software Process Improvement. Springer Berlin Heidelberg (2013)	0	Factors	10
SL2	Bayona, S., Calvo-Manzano, A.J., Feliu. S.T.: Critical success factors in software process improvement: A systematic review. International Conference on Software Process Improvement and Capability Determination. Springer Berlin Heidelberg (2012)	4	Factors	28

(*continued*)

Table 4. (*continued*)

ID	Reference	CI	RF	PS
SL3	Pino, J.F., García, F., Piattini, M.: Software process improvement in small and medium software enterprises: a systematic review. Software Quality Journal. 16(2), 237–261 (2007)	193	SMEs	45
SL4	Claudia, V., Mirna, M., Jezreel, M.: Characterization of software processes improvement needs in SMEs." IEEE International Conference on Mechatronics, Electronics and Automotive Engineering (ICMEAE) (2013)	6	SMEs	Nil
SL5	Mirna, M., Jezreel, M., Brenda, D., Claudia, V.: Software Process Improvement from a Human Perspective. New Perspectives in Information Systems and Technologies, Springer International Publishing, 287–298 (2014)	0	Factors	100
SL6	Sulayman, M., Mendes, E.: A systematic literature review of software process improvement in small and medium web companies. International Conference on Advanced Software Engineering and Its Applications. Springer Berlin Heidelberg (2009)	19	SMEs	4
SL7	Lavallée, M., Robillard, N.P.: The impacts of software process improvement on developers: A systematic review. Proceedings of the 34th international conference on software engineering (2012)	17	Factors	26
SL8	Sulayman, M., Mendes, M.: An extended systematic review of software process improvement in small and medium web companies. 15th Annual Conference on Evaluation & Assessment in Software Engineering (EASE) (2011)	13	SMEs	8
SL9	García-Mireles, A.G., Moraga, A.M., García, F.: Development of maturity models: a systematic literature review. 16th Annual Conference on Evaluation & Assessment in Software Engineering (EASE), 279–283 (2012)	8	Process Models	7
SL10	Unterkalmsteiner, M., Gorschek, T., Moinul Islam, A.K.M., Cheng, K.C., Permadi, B.R., Feldt, R.: Evaluation and Measurement of Software Process Improvement— "A Systematic Literature Review" IEEE Transaction on Software Engineering, 38(2), 398–424 (2012)	94	Factors	148
SL11	Almomani, T.A.M., Basri, S., Mahamad, S., Bajeh, O.A.: Software Process Improvement Initiatives in Small and Medium Firms: A Systematic Review. IEEE 3rd International Conference on Advanced Computer Science Applications and Technologies (ACSAT), (2014)	0	SMEs	11

(*continued*)

Table 4. (*continued*)

ID	Reference	CI	RF	PS
SL12	Bano, M., Ikram, N.: Software process improvement: a systematic literature review. 15th IEE International Multitopic Conference (INMIC) (2012)	0	Process Models	400
SL13	Kelemen, D.Z., Kusters, R., Trienekens, J.: Identifying criteria for multimodel software process improvement solutions based on a review of current problems and initiatives. Journal of software: Evolution and Process 24 (8), 895–909 (2011)	11	Process Models	78
SL14	Paternostera, N., Giardinoa, C., Unterkalmsteinera, M., Gorscheka, T., Abrahamssonb, P.: Software development in startup companies: A systematic mapping study. Information and Software Technology 56(10), 1200–1218 (2014)	24	SMEs	43
SL15	Prikladnicki, R., Audy, N.L.J.: Process models in the practice of distributed software development: A systematic review of the literature. Information and Software Technology 52(8), 779–791 (2010)	54	Process Models	26
SL16	Silva, S.F., Santana, F., Peres, L.A., Azevedo, Mde. I., Ana Vasconcelos, Paula, L.F.A, Kamei, K.F., Meira, Lde, R.S.: Using CMMI together with agile software development: A systematic review. Information and Software Technology, 20–43 (2015)	6	Process Models	81
SL17	García-Mireles, A.G., Moraga, A.M., Garcia, F., Piattini, M.: Approaches to promote product quality within software process improvement initiatives: A mapping study. Journal of Systems and Software, 150–166 (2015)	1	Software Quality	74
SL18	Müller, D.S., Mathiassen, L., Balshøj, H.H.: Software Process Improvement as organizational change: A metaphorical analysis of the literature. Journal of Systems and Software 83(11), 2128–2146 (2010)	28	Factors	60
SL19	Lane, S., Richardso, I.: Process models for service-based applications: A systematic literature review. Information and Software Technology 53 (5), 424–439 (2011)	29	Process Models	57
SL20	Zarour, M., Abran, A., Desharnais, M.-J., Alarifi, A.: An investigation into the best practices for the successful design and implementation of lightweight software process assessment methods: A systematic literature review. Journal of Systems and Software. 180–192 (2015)	1	Factors (Best practices)	29

(*continued*)

Table 4. (*continued*)

ID	Reference	CI	RF	PS
SL21	Afzal, W., Alonec, S., Glocksienc, K., Torkar, R.: Software test process improvement approaches: A systematic literature review and an industrial case study. Journal of Systems and Software. 1–33 (2015)	0	Testing	18
SL22	Staples, M., Niazi, M.: Systematic review of organizational motivations for adopting CMM-based SPI. Information and software technology 50(7), 605–620 (2007)	98	Process Models	49
SL23	Niazi, M.: A comparative study of software process improvement implementation success factors. Journal of Software: Evolution and Process 27(9), 700–722 (2015)	0	Factors	38
SL24	O'Hagan, O.A., Coleman, G., O'Connor, V.R.: Software development processes for games: a systematic literature review. European Conference on Software Process Improvement. Springer Berlin Heidelberg (2014)	1	Processes	404

Article title (TL), Total number of citations (CI), Main research focus (RF), Number of primary studies (PS)

References

1. Zahran, S.: Software process improvement: practical guidelines for business success. J. Softw. Mainten. Res. Pract. **11**, 285–291 (1999)
2. O'Connor, R.V., Basri, S., Coleman, G.: Exploring managerial commitment towards SPI in small and very small enterprises. In: Riel, A., O'Connor, R.V., Tichkiewitch, S., Messnarz, R. (eds.) EuroSPI 2010. CCIS, vol. 99, pp. 268–279. Springer, Heidelberg (2010). doi:10.1007/978-3-642-15666-3_24
3. Marques, A.B., Rodrigues, R., Conte, T.: Systematic literature reviews in distributed software development: a tertiary study. In: IEEE Seventh International Conference on Global Software Engineering (ICGSE), pp. 134–143 (2012)
4. Ngwenyama, O., Nielsen, P.A.: Competing values in software process improvement: an assumption analysis of CMM from an organizational culture perspective. IEEE Trans. Eng. Manag. **50**(1), 106–144 (2003)
5. Khan, A.A., Keung, J.: Systematic review of success factors and barriers for software process improvement in global software development. IET Softw. (2016)
6. Kitchenham, B., Brereton, P.O., Budgen, D., Turner, M., Bailey, J., Linkman, S.: Systematic literature reviews in software engineering a systematic literature review. Inf. Softw. Technol. **51**(1), 7–15 (2009)
7. Kitchenham, B.: Procedures for performing systematic reviews. NICTA Technical Report 0400011T.1, Keele University (2004)
8. Da Silva, F.Q.B., Santos, A.L.M., Soares, S., França, A.C.C., Monteiro, C.V.F., Maciel, F.F.: Six years of systematic literature reviews in software engineering: an updated tertiary study. Inf. Softw. Technol. **53**(9), 899–913 (2011)

9. Kitchenham, B., Pretorius, R., Budgen, D., Brereton, O.P., Turner, M., Niazi, M., Linkman, S.: Systematic literature reviews in software engineering - a tertiary study. Inf. Softw. Technol. **52**(8), 792–805 (2010)
10. Bano, M., Didar, Z., Naveed, I.: Systematic reviews in requirements engineering: a tertiary study. In: IEEE Fourth International Workshop on Empirical Requirements Engineering, pp. 9–16 (2014)
11. Imtiaz, S., Bano, M., Naveed, I., Niazi, M.: A tertiary study: experiences of conducting systematic literature reviews in software engineering. In: Proceedings of the 17th International Conference on Evaluation and Assessment in Software Engineering (EASE), pp. 177–182 (2013)
12. Verner, J.M., Brereton, O.P., Kitchenham, B.A., Turner, M., Niazi, M.: Systematic literature reviews in global software development: a tertiary study. In: Proceedings of the 16th International Conference on Evaluation and Assessment in Software Engineering (EASE), pp. 2–11 (2012)
13. Kitchenham, B., Pretorius, R., Budgen, D., Brereton, O.P., Turner, M., Niazi, M., Linkman, S.: Systematic literature reviews in software engineering - a tertiary study. Inf. Softw. Technol. **52**(8), 792–805 (2010)
14. Niazi, M.: Software process improvement: a road to success. In: Münch, J., Vierimaa, M. (eds.) PROFES 2006. LNCS, vol. 4034, pp. 395–401. Springer, Heidelberg (2006). doi:10.1007/11767718_34
15. Wohlin, C., Per, R., Martin, H., Mangus, O.C., Bjorn, R., Anders, W.: Experimentation in Software Engineering. Springer, Heidelberg (2012)
16. Centre for Reviews and Dissemination, About DARE (2015). http://www.york.ac.uk/inst/crd/darefaq.htm. Accessed 12 Nov 2016
17. Cruzes, D.S., Dybå, T.: Research synthesis in software engineering: A tertiary study. Inf. Softw. Technol. **53**(5), 440–455 (2011)
18. Afzal, W., Torkar, R., Feldt, R.: A systematic review of search-based testing for non-functional system properties. Inf. Softw. Technol. **51**(6), 957–976 (2009)
19. Cochrane Collaboration: Cochrane Reviewers' Handbook. Version 4.2.1 (2003)

Overcoming Public Speaking Anxiety of Software Engineers Using Virtual Reality Exposure Therapy

Merve Denizci Nazligul[1,3], Murat Yilmaz[2,3(✉)], Ulas Gulec[2,3], Mert Ali Gozcu[2,3], Rory V. O'Connor[4,5], and Paul M. Clarke[4,5]

[1] Department of Psychology, Çankaya University, Ankara, Turkey
[2] Department of Computer Engineering, Çankaya University, Ankara, Turkey
{mervenazligul,myilmaz,ulasgulec}@cankaya.edu.tr, mertaligozcu@gmail.com
[3] Virtual Reality Research and Development Laboratory,
Çankaya University, Ankara, Turkey
[4] School of Computing, Dublin City University, Dublin, Ireland
[5] Lero, The Irish Software Engineering Research Center, Limerick, Ireland
{rory.oconnor,paul.m.clarke}@dcu.ie

Abstract. Public speaking anxiety is a type of social phobia, which might be commonly seen in novice software engineers. It is usually triggered by a fear of social performance especially when the performer is unfamiliar with the audience. Today, many software engineering activities (e.g. code inspection, peer review, daily meetings, etc.) require social gatherings where individuals need to present their work. However, novice software engineers may not be able to reduce their performance anxiety during their course of education. In this study, we propose a virtual reality approach to construct a practice environment for improving novice software engineers' pubic speaking experiences. Consequently, we examine the effects of virtual reality intervention on the public speaking experience of six novice software engineers from a computer engineering department. We designed a virtual auditorium to simulate the presentation delivery environment and findings suggest that using this infrastructure for training purposes can reduce presenter anxiety levels – which is consistent with related published studies. We believe that this virtual auditorium environment can deliver benefits for students and practitioners alike in terms of addressing the anxiety that is often associated with early stage career presenters.

Keywords: Virtual reality · Public speaking anxiety · Personal process improvement

1 Introduction

Software development is a social activity that requires a variety of social gatherings such as daily stand-up meetings, project presentations, and public speaking. These activities are usually essential to improve a software practitioner's career and therefore important to practice at early stages of a software engineering (SE) career. Although such social skills are very important in the career of a software engineer, it has been observed that novice software engineers (i.e. individuals who have less than one year of industrial experience) are worried when making presentation or meeting with others [1]. To date, a number of studies have attempted to evaluate the impact of social skills in SE careers. Hazzan and Har-Shai [2] conducted a study to figure out the thoughts of the novice software engineers about their skills. According to the results of this study, novice software engineers see themselves as inadequate to make presentations, and they want to fill this gap with the help of experts in SE area. Additionally, Peters and Moreno [3] organized a study to learn the opinions of novice software engineers about what skills will be more important for them when they will be project managers in the future. The results point out that public speaking and presentation skills are listed as one of the factors that affects their success or failure. As it can be seen, when the demands of both education and business are considered, public speaking is one of the essential skills for novice software engineers [4]. In fact, most of the anxious individuals suffer from feeling nervous and helpless before a presentation or an assignment, panicking, or losing concentration during a test [5]. Consequently, they may fail to fulfill their potential both at school and at their work-life.

Developing a pre-speech before the presentation or testing yourself in the presentation environment is some of the suggested solutions to overcome public speaking and presentation anxiety of the individuals [6]. However, people cannot find a way to test themselves in a real-life environment similar to the presentation environment before the presentation. It is difficult to prepare a real environment that provides the same conditions as the presentation environment. Virtual reality (VR) solves this problem by providing a useful and immersive training environment that includes real-life conditions for individuals [7]. Therefore, people can develop themselves and gain experience by training in the virtual environment designed similar to a real experience [8]. Due to this feature of the virtual environment, VR is one of the most effective tools that is used for training of individuals in recent years. There are many studies in different working areas such as increasing firemen's spatial navigation skills [9] and developing the skills of the medical residents [10,11] that benefit from the applications of VR. Finally, it has been demonstrated that a serious game is beneficial to train novice software engineers about ISO/IEC 12207:1995 [12] which has also confirmed the effectiveness of a virtual simulation environment.

The goal of this study is to design a virtual auditorium in order to increase the novice software engineers' ability to make presentations to a group of individuals and to reduce their worries about public speaking. The aim of designing virtual auditorium is to test whether virtual reality exposure therapy (VRET), a kind of systematic exposure to feared real life situations by using virtual worlds, produces significant improvements on the symptoms of public speaking anxiety (PSA) for novice software developers. It was hypothesized that a significant difference would be found on self-report measures of public speaking anxiety before and after the intervention.

The remainder of this paper is divided as follows: In Sect. 2, a review of literature is introduced. The following section explains the research process. The Sect. 4 presents the findings of the research. Finally, the last section gives a brief summary and critique of the results. It further suggests future directions.

2 Background and Related Works

Anxiety is a natural emotion conceptualized by Spielberger [13] as a sense of tension, nervousness, and worry related with arousal of the nervous system [14]. From the evolutionary perspective, some forms of anxiety have functional value to adapt potential threats and risks. It means that an appropriate level of anxiety is crucial to stimulate person for fight or flight in response to a danger. However, when anxiety is perceived as uncontrollable and uncertain, it has many disruptive effects on individuals in various contexts such as social or academic [15]. For instance, Vitasari et al. [14] conducted a study to illustrate the relation between excessive anxiety and academic performance. Based on the results of this study, the higher levels of anxiety individuals show the poorer academic performance.

PSA is a specific form of social anxiety occurring in real or anticipated an oral performance situation. Individuals with PSA usually tend to avoid anxiety-eliciting situations [16]. They demonstrate a loss of physiological, cognitive and behavioral control where social or academic performance has become inevitable for the speakers. Accordingly, when autonomic nervous system is activated, individuals with PSA experience increased heart rate, blood pressure, sweating, gastrointestinal discomfort, diarrhea and muscle tension [17,18]. In addition to these physical symptoms, the cognitive system represents self-monitoring and negative cognitions when preparing and presenting speeches [19]. In the cognitive model of PSA, irrational beliefs (e.g., "It is awful that I am in this situation") leads to response expectancies (e.g.,"I expect to be anxious in this situation") and automatic thoughts (e.g.,"They will laugh at me") respectively, which results in speech-related anxiety [20]. Besides, behavioral aspects of PSA include a list of anxious behaviors such as stiff, restless, or trembling displayed while speaking [19]. Research evidence suggested that anxiety level during a public speaking performance is likely to occur with the highest volume at the open. In other words, anticipatory anxiety starts out at the peak level just before speaking and over time anxiety descend to a lower level through the speaking and post-speaking periods [21].

Since PSA is more and more recognized as a serious problem leading to distress and dysfunction in those suffering from it, increasing efforts to develop and document various treatment strategies have emerged. Namely, exposure-based treatments have been found to be effective for the treatment of PSA. The basic premise of exposure-based treatment is that individuals realize that the expected catastrophic situation does not happen through repeated approach toward fear provoking stimuli; thus, they have a chance to modify their maladaptive cognitions and reprocess their emotions in more functional manner [22]. Recently, VRET has increasingly been utilized to treat PSA [16,23–25]. In most cases, no differences have been found between VRET and exposure therapy; however, additional work is needed to address the equivalency of effect sizes. Moreover, it was supported that VRET is superior to wait list in treating social anxiety disorder. Accordingly, the participants receiving VRET significantly improved on standardized measures of public speaking fears and a behavioral avoidance task as compared to wait list. In the following 3- and 12-month, it was shown that they maintained treatment gains [26].

VRET, characterized by utilizing sophisticated hardware and software techniques to immerse individuals in virtual environments, has gained an increasing amount of attention in scientific research in recent years [27]. It consists of real-time computer graphics, body tracking devices as well as other sensory inputs to create a virtual environment for patients [28]. One of the major strengths of this technique is that VR environment provides emerging opportunities to individuals with an active participation in a three-dimensional world. Moreover, participants are able to manipulate their environment via a second position sensor for some environments [29]. In terms of validity as another strength, various research findings suggested that VR environment based performance is predictive of real-world performance. In other words, individuals suffering from anxiety demonstrate behavioral, affective, and cognitive reactions in a VR environment similar to those experienced with a live audience [30]. The underlying mechanism of VRET is based on systematically exposure individuals to feared stimuli that are relevant to context while avoidance is prevented [28,31].

In particular, head mounted display (HMD) or computer automatic virtual environment (CAVE) to enable immersion. Through these techniques, it allows individuals to get involved in the virtual world through experiencing a subjective sense of *"really being in one place or environment"* [32]. In exposure-based therapy such as in vivo or imaginal, graded exposure is used to work on a hierarchy of anxiety-producing situations in a gradual manner. The therapist arranges therapy sessions to desensitize the patient for those situations and they continue until habituation to occur. All exposure-based treatments including repeated contact to threat-related cues have the information that disconfirms anxiety beliefs; however; the distinctive feature of VRET is that the illusion of being in a different place which can be described as *"presence"*. For the effectiveness of VRET, the essential point is the level of immersion. Moreover, the more intense and vivid emotions the VRET elicits, the better results individuals get. In addition, generalization to daily life situations without any avoidance is important [32].

It is evident that VRET has several clinical and methodological advantages, though for some individuals there may also be a downside associated with VR related sweating, stomach awareness, dizziness, headache, and drowsiness [33]. First of all, it is a cost-effective program compared to other exposure-based methods. Although in vivo and imaginal exposure has similar therapeutic goals with VRET, it provides well-controlled and idiosyncratic context in terms of the quality, duration and frequency of exposure. Furthermore, several actual trauma-related scenarios (e.g. war or accidents) can be difficult to repeat; however, by means of VRET it is possible to recreate them in virtual environment without confronted with real anxiety provoking stimuli. Besides, therapists have more control over exposure process to modify and manipulate the stimuli eliciting anxiety. This approach allows the therapist to simultaneous measure physiological and cognitive variables. Notably, some patients do not respond to traditional exposure therapies due to overt avoidance behaviors or failure to imagine situations. However, VRET uses immersion to confront patients with their anxiety in safe and gradual manner. Hence, the patients to more easily realize the difference between non-threatening and threat-related stimuli [34,35].

3 Methodology

3.1 Participants

The current study was conducted with 6 novice software engineers who suffer from public speaking anxiety at Çankaya University. The sample (N = 6) was predominantly female (83.3%) and the mean age for participants was 21 years (SD = 1.41 years, Range = 21–23). All participants fulfilled criteria for social phobia as determined by the Liebowitz Social Anxiety Scale (cut-off > 25 in the sub-scale of *"fear or anxiety"*; cut-off > 25 in the sub-scale of *"avoidance behaviour"*) [36]. Moreover, participants who have high level of anxiety about social interaction were accepted as second inclusion criteria. Exclusion criteria were, (a) history of neurological or physical impairment; (b) cognitive impairment; (c) comorbid psychotic disorder; (d) using any medication; (e) current psychological or psychiatric treatment.

3.2 Measures

– **Demographic Information Form:** The questions of the demographic information form will consist of an e-mail address, gender, age, education status, socioeconomic status, occupational status, duration of social phobia symptoms, and history of psychiatric and chronic illness diagnosis.
– **Liebowitz Social Anxiety Scale:** Liebowitz Social Anxiety Scale (LSAS) [36] will be used to examine the anxiety level of social phobic people in a wide range of social situations. Each item is rated separately for *"fear or anxiety"* (anchors of 0: none to 3: severe) and for *"avoidance behaviour"* (anchors of 0: never and 3: usually). The internal consistency of the scale ranges from .81 to .92. The Turkish adaptation of LSAS scale was studied by [37].
– **Subjective Units of Distress Scale (SUDs):** Subjective Units of Distress Scale (SUDs) is used to examine an individual's baseline level of anxiety. Participants rate their anxiety level using a scale of 0 to 100, where 0 = totally relaxed and 100 = highest distress/fear/anxiety/discomfort that you have ever felt [38].
– **Interaction Anxiousness Scale:** Interaction Anxiousness Scale (IAS) [39] is a self-report measure on a 5-point Likert scale with anchors ranging from

not at all characteristic of me (1) to very characteristic of me (5). It measures the subjective experience of anxiety associated with social interactions. The internal consistency of the scale was .88. The Turkish adaptation of scale was studied by [40].
- **Speech Task:** A speech task was administered to study on cognitive, behavioral, and physiological components of anxiety to a social stressor (i.e. public speaking) at baseline, during intervention and post-intervention. Subjects were invited in the virtual reality laboratory and said that they would be participating in a task to examine their public speaking anxiety. The task involved an impromptu speech which required the subject to speak to a number of audiences in a virtual class setting. Just before the speech, the therapist asked participants to rate their level of situational anxiety from 0 (not anxious) to 100 (extremely anxious) by using SUDs.

3.3 Procedure

First of all, ethical approval was obtained from the Çankaya University Human Subjects Ethics Ethical Committee. Eligibility for the current study was assessed via self-measurement instruments mentioned above to a group of novice software engineers if participants met inclusion criteria. Then, candidates were invited to participate in the treatment program. All were volunteered for the study and an informed consent was given to each participant.

The study consisted of two intervention sessions. Firstly, participants received an individual therapy session lasting about an hour according to a treatment manual [41]. This therapy session covers the material such as components of anxiety, possible causes of anxiety and dysfunctional thinking patterns. At the end of the session, an anxiety hierarchy about performing a speech in front of a class that unique for each participant was built and participant's anxiety rate was assessed by using the SUDs (A1). In addition, the effect of avoidance on the maintenance of anxiety was discussed. An individual therapy session was followed by virtual reality exposure intervention (VREI).

During VREI, the participant wore a head-mounted display (Oculus RIFT) that presented a computer-generated environment including a virtual class. The session lasted about 35–40 min. In this session, the speech task adapted from a standardized speech assessment protocol [42] was implemented. Participants were told that they would talk on one or more of the 3 controversial topics (e.g., gay marriage, religion in school, illegal immigration) which were blindly selected one of five note cards. After that, three minutes were given to prepare their speech. Before exposure, a trial simulation was shown participants to adapt virtual reality exposure. Anxiety was assessed using the SUDs at four points during the exposure: prior to giving instructions for the exposure (T1), immediately after introduction to the audience but before the speech began (T2), a retrospective rating of peak anxiety during the speech (T3) and immediately after the exposure (T4). During VREI, the therapist could manipulate audience reactions (e.g., looking bored, yawning, asking question, talking or playing with phone).

Virtual audience members could also ask to speak in a loud voice or predetermined questions (e.g., *"Could you explain last words again?"*). Meanwhile, the therapist elaborated the participant's anxiety and encouraged therapeutic exposure to feared situations according to the personal anxiety hierarchy. Participants were exposed to the items on their hierarchy until their anxiety decreased.

3.4 System Functions and Implementation

In this study, a virtual environment was designed so that the participants could make presentations in an environment similar to the real life auditorium environment. At this point, they have an opportunity to reduce their worries and anxiety levels by facing the events that increase their level of anxiety during presentations in real life. In addition to this property of designed environment, the therapist was given the authority to control the virtual environment. Hence, the therapist can measure the anxiety levels of the individuals during the presentation by using the events or situations that increase the anxiety levels of those detected during the first intervention. These events and situations are listed as: number of people in the class, clothing style (e.g.; formal, informal) and gender of the people, and activities of the audiences (e.g.; messaging, ringing phone, asking question, yawning, laughing, talking, leaving from the auditorium).

There are 2 types of users in the virtual environment, one being a therapist and the other being a presenter. The therapist has the authority to set up the virtual environment at the desired characteristics. At the same time, the therapist has the authority to control the environment simultaneously while the presenter makes a live presentation in the environment created by the therapist.

When the users in both user types connect to the environment, the main screen appears as shown in Fig. 1. In this screen, *"LAN Host"* button is designed and enabled for the therapist and *"LAN Client"* button is designed and enabled for the presenter. After the therapist clicks *"LAN Host"*, she is directed to the screen (Fig. 2) to enter the properties of the virtual auditorium that she will design for the presenter. In this screen, text-boxes were placed to allow the therapist to enter formal and informal male and female numbers. The auditorium has a maximum of 32 people, and people are automatically created as much as the values entered in the text-boxes. A total of 8 different models, two different formal and informal male and female models, are placed randomly in order to increase the reality in the auditorium. After the therapist creates the class, the presenter can enter the designed auditorium (Fig. 4) by inputting the IP address of the host computer.

After the presenter is connected to the class environment, she may start to present in the class environment especially designed for him/her. During the presentations, the therapist has the ability to control audiences by navigating the auditorium with w, a, s and d keys on keyboard, as seen in Fig. 3. The therapist chooses one of the audience by clicking the left button of the mouse. Then, a list of actions appears on the screen. By choosing one of the action buttons on this screen that comes against the therapist, the participant gets the action she chooses.

 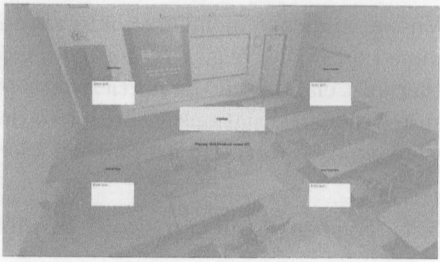

Fig. 1. Home screen of the auditorium

Fig. 2. Feature input screen for the environment to be created

Fig. 3. Event selections screen

Fig. 4. View of auditorium from the view of presenter

4 Results

The data was analyzed with SPSS 20 using the Wilcoxon signed-rank test which is suitable analysis for small subject numbers and repeated measures [43]. The results are seen in Fig. 5.

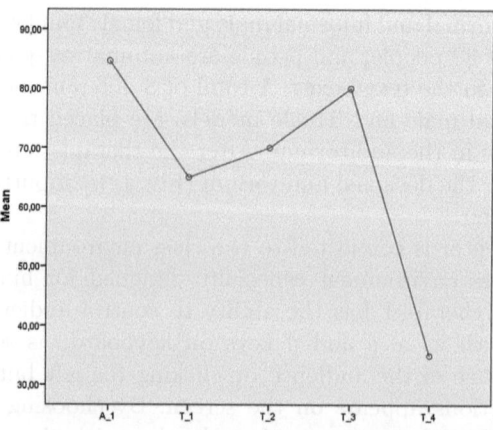

Fig. 5. Scores of individuals in each time point of VREI

In the study, the average anxiety level of participants is 84.67 ($SD = 13.66$) at the assessment, 65.00 ($SD = 12.25$) prior to giving instructions for the exposure, 70.00 ($SD = 20.00$) before the speech began and 80.00 ($SD = 10.96$) at peak during the speech; however, the mean anxiety level is 35.00 ($SD = 25.69$) immediately after the exposure. In addition to these numerical values, Fig. 5 shows that participants' SUDs levels were significantly lower at T4 than at A1, $z = -2.20$, $p < .05$, $r = -.90$; lower at T4 than at T1, $z = -2.21$, $p < .05$, $r = -.90$; lower at T4 than at T2, $z = -2.21$, $p < .05$, $r = -.90$; lower at T4 than at T3, $z = -2.20$, $p < .05$, $r = -.90$.

5 Discussion and Conclusion

A software development organization can be considered as a social ecosystem that connects a variety of stakeholders by using a software process which is certainly affected from interpersonal relationships. These relationships usually based on presentation of a software artifact (e.g. source code, documentation). In particular, some parts of this work should be presented in front of a group of audience. PSA, a subtype of social phobia, which can be a destructive disorder among novice software engineers. Such individuals might have excessive concerns about being embarrassed and judged by other people [44]. Some research indicated that subjects exposed to the feared social situations and learnt to modify their thoughts and behaviors show decreased anxious symptoms [45]. In virtual reality exposure therapy, this kind of anxiety is elicited by a predesigned virtual environment, and here in this study, it is used to observe a small set of novice computer engineers. Indeed, virtual reality has increasingly been used as a therapeutic tool to explore human behaviors and emotions as well as cognition. It provides a well-controlled environment so that therapist can manipulate the stimuli determined beforehand. Since VRET can be adapted to individual's needs, it opens door to creativity and flexibility for therapeutic usage [46]. The purpose in the present study was to test the effects of VREI on public speaking anxiety of novice software engineers.

In the current research, it was hypothesized that novice software engineers with PSA would report not only the highest level of anxiety during intervention but also lower level of anxiety after the VREI. The findings supported possible effects of VREI and showed significant decrease in anxiety rates. This result suggested that the virtual public speaking environment did successfully provoke high anxiety in the participants and that can be used to manage this anxiety in an appropriate way.

Methodological limitations of the study must be considered when interpreting the results. First of all, this study involved small sample size; therefore, these data should be considered preliminary. Most obviously, it will be important to replicate these data with large samples. Secondly, the data is based on self-reported measures. However, future work should use additional measures of PSA such as a structural clinical diagnostic interview. The third one is that causal inferences cannot be made due to the cross-sectional nature of the study design.

Longitudinal research is needed to demonstrate the lasting impact of repeated exposure.

The main advantage of using virtual reality is that it allows participants a safety environment to test their fears and thoughts in a social context. However, further studies need to be conducted to test whether our results can also be generalized to real social situations by using behavioral task which is implemented before and after the VREI. Moreover, future research should implement a study with a control group so that the differences between intervention group and control group can clearly be identified. Although our primary results are encouraging, a set of exposure sessions is also needed to improve the protocol used in this pilot study. In our study, subjects could be exposed (in the VR environment) to various types of audiences, with anxiety levels being self-reported. However, further experimental investigations are needed to expand the findings of this study such as how anxiety levels fluctuate for different audience groups where psychophysiological measures (i.e. heart rate or skin temperature) may also be added the protocol to understand stress response in an extended way.

References

1. Bernárdez, B., Durán, A., Parejo, J.A., et al.: A controlled experiment to evaluate the effects of mindfulness in software engineering. In: Proceedings of the 8th ACM/IEEE International Symposium on Empirical Software Engineering and Measurement, p. 17. ACM (2014)
2. Hazzan, O., Har-Shai, G.: Teaching and learning computer science soft skills using soft skills: the students' perspective. In: Proceedings of the 45th ACM Technical Symposium on Computer Science Education, pp. 567–572. ACM (2014)
3. Peters, L., Moreno, A.M.: Educating software engineering managers-revisited what software project managers need to know today. In: 2015 IEEE/ACM 37th IEEE International Conference on Software Engineering (ICSE), vol. 2, pp. 353–359. IEEE (2015)
4. Darmuki, A., Andayani, A., Nurkamto, J., Saddhono, K.: Evaluating information-processing-based learning cooperative model on speaking skill course. J. Lang. Teach. Res. **8**, 44–51 (2017)
5. Vitasari, P., Wahab, M.N.A., Herawan, T., Othman, A., Sinnadurai, S.K.: A pilot study of pre-post anxiety treatment to improve academic performance for engineering students. Procedia Soc. Behav. Sci. **15**, 3826–3830 (2011)
6. Huff, W.K.: Public Speaking: A Concise Overview for the Twenty-First Century. Peter Lang, New York (2008)
7. Sampaio, A.Z., Martins, O.P.: The application of virtual reality technology in the construction of bridge: the cantilever and incremental launching methods. Autom. Constr. **37**, 58–67 (2014)
8. Jang, S., Vitale, J.M., Jyung, R.W., Black, J.B.: Direct manipulation is better than passive viewing for learning anatomy in a three-dimensional virtual reality environment. Comput. Educ. **106**, 150–165 (2017)
9. Bliss, J.P., Tidwell, P.D., Guest, M.A.: The effectiveness of virtual reality for administering spatial navigation training to firefighters. Presence Teleop. Virtual Environ. **6**, 73–86 (1997)

10. Seymour, N.E., Gallagher, A.G., Roman, S.A., O'brien, M.K., Bansal, V.K., Andersen, D.K., Satava, R.M.: Virtual reality training improves operating room performance: results of a randomized, double-blinded study. Ann. Surg. **236**, 458–464 (2002)
11. Grantcharov, T.P., Kristiansen, V., Bendix, J., Bardram, L., Rosenberg, J., Funch-Jensen, P.: Randomized clinical trial of virtual reality simulation for laparoscopic skills training. Br. J. Surg. **91**, 146–150 (2004)
12. Aydan, U., Yilmaz, M., Clarke, P.M., O'Connor, R.V.: Teaching ISO/IEC 12207 software lifecycle processes: a serious game approach. Comput. Stand. Interfaces **54**, 129–138 (2016)
13. Spielberger, C.D.: Manual for the state-trait anxiety inventory STAI (form Y) ("self-evaluation questionnaire") (1983)
14. Vitasari, P., Wahab, M.N.A., Othman, A., Herawan, T., Sinnadurai, S.K.: The relationship between study anxiety and academic performance among engineering students. Procedia Soc. Behav. Sci. **8**, 490–497 (2010)
15. Maner, J.K., Kenrick, D.T.: When adaptations go awry: functional and dysfunctional aspects of social anxiety. Soc. Issues Policy Rev. **4**, 111–142 (2010)
16. Harris, S.R., Kemmerling, R.L., North, M.M.: Brief virtual reality therapy for public speaking anxiety. Cyberpsychol. Behav. **5**, 543–550 (2002)
17. Bernátová, I., Balis, P., Goga, R., Behuliak, M., Zicha, J., Sekaj, I.: Lack of reactive oxygen species deteriorates blood pressure regulation in acute stress. Physiol. Res. **65**, S381 (2016)
18. Granigg, G.M.: Essential oils and single fragrance compounds in health care. Ph.D. thesis, UniWien (2013)
19. Bodie, G.D.: A racing heart, rattling knees, and ruminative thoughts: defining, explaining, and treating public speaking anxiety. Commun. Educ. **59**, 70–105 (2010)
20. Vîslă, A., Cristea, I.A., Tătar, A.S., David, D.: Core beliefs, automatic thoughts and response expectancies in predicting public speaking anxiety. Pers. Individ. Differ. **55**, 856–859 (2013)
21. Behnke, R.R., Sawyer, C.R.: Milestones of anticipatory public speaking anxiety. Commun. Educ. **48**, 165–172 (1999)
22. Hindo, C.S., González-Prendes, A.A.: One-session exposure treatment for social anxiety with specific fear of public speaking. Res. Soc. Work Pract. **21**, 528–538 (2011)
23. Anderson, P.L., Zimand, E., Hodges, L.F., Rothbaum, B.O.: Cognitive behavioral therapy for public-speaking anxiety using virtual reality for exposure. Depress. Anxiety **22**, 156–158 (2005)
24. Safir, M.P., Wallach, H.S., Bar-Zvi, M.: Virtual reality cognitive-behavior therapy for public speaking anxiety: one-year follow-up. Behav. Modif. **36**, 235–246 (2012)
25. Wallach, H.S., Safir, M.P., Bar-Zvi, M.: Virtual reality cognitive behavior therapy for public speaking anxiety: a randomized clinical trial. Behav. Modif. **33**, 314–338 (2009)
26. Anderson, P.L., Price, M., Edwards, S.M., Obasaju, M.A., Schmertz, S.K., Zimand, E., Calamaras, M.R.: Virtual reality exposure therapy for social anxiety disorder: a randomized controlled trial. J. Consult. Clin. Psychol. **81**, 751 (2013)
27. Diemer, J., Lohkamp, N., Mühlberger, A., Zwanzger, P.: Fear and physiological arousal during a virtual height challenge - effects in patients with acrophobia and healthy controls. J. Anxiety Disord. **37**, 30–39 (2016)

28. Opriş, D., Pintea, S., García-Palacios, A., Botella, C., Szamosközi, Ş., David, D.: Virtual reality exposure therapy in anxiety disorders: a quantitative meta-analysis. Depress. Anxiety **29**, 85–93 (2012)
29. Anderson, P., Jacobs, C., Rothbaum, B.O.: Computer-supported cognitive behavioral treatment of anxiety disorders. J. Clin. Psychol. **60**, 253–267 (2004)
30. Brundage, S.B., Hancock, A.B.: Real enough: Using virtual public speaking environments to evoke feelings and behaviors targeted in stuttering assessment and treatment. Am. J. Speech Lan. Pathol. **24**, 139–149 (2015)
31. Burstin, A., Brown, R.: Virtual environments for real treatments. Pol. Ann. Med. **17**, 101–111 (2010)
32. Krijn, M., Emmelkamp, P.M., Olafsson, R.P., Biemond, R.: Virtual reality exposure therapy of anxiety disorders: a review. Clin. Psychol. Rev. **24**, 259–281 (2004)
33. Bush, J.: Viability of virtual reality exposure therapy as a treatment alternative. Comput. Hum. Behav. **24**, 1032–1040 (2008)
34. Morina, N., Ijntema, H., Meyerbröker, K., Emmelkamp, P.M.: Can virtual reality exposure therapy gains be generalized to real-life? A meta-analysis of studies applying behavioral assessments. Behav. Res. Ther. **74**, 18–24 (2015)
35. Tichon, J., Banks, J.: Virtual reality exposure therapy: 150-degree screen to desktop PC. CyberPsychol. Behav. **9**, 480–489 (2006)
36. Liebowitz, M.R.: Social Phobia. Karger Publishers, Basel (1987)
37. Soykan, Ç., Özgüven, H.D., Gençöz, T.: Liebowitz social anxiety scale: the Turkish version. Psychol. Rep. **93**, 1059–1069 (2003)
38. Wolpe, J.: Psychotherapy by reciprocal inhibition. Integr. Physiol. Behav. Sci. **3**, 234–240 (1958)
39. Leary, M.R., Kowalski, R.M.: The interaction anxiousness scale: construct and criterion-related validity. J. Pers. Assess. **61**, 136–146 (1993)
40. Coşkun, H.: Etkileşim kaygısı ölçeği: Geçerlik ve güvenirlik çalışması. Türk Psikoloji Yazıları **12**, 41–49 (2009)
41. Hope, D.A., Heimberg, R.G., Turk, C.L.: Managing Social Anxiety: A Cognitive-Behavioral Therapy Approach. Oxford University Press, Oxford (2010)
42. Beidel, D.C., Turner, S.M., Jacob, R.G., Cooley, M.R.: Assessment of social phobia: reliability of an impromptu speech task. J. Anxiety Disord. **3**, 149–158 (1989)
43. Field, A.: Regression. In: Discovering Statistics Using SPSS, vol. 2, pp. 143–217 (2005)
44. Ling, Y., Brinkman, W.P., Nefs, H.T., Qu, C., Heynderickx, I.: Effects of stereoscopic viewing on presence, anxiety, and cybersickness in a virtual reality environment for public speaking. Presence Teleop. Virtual Environ. **21**, 254–267 (2012)
45. Klinger, E., Bouchard, S., Légeron, P., Roy, S., Lauer, F., Chemin, I., Nugues, P.: Virtual reality therapy versus cognitive behavior therapy for social phobia: a preliminary controlled study. Cyberpsychol. Behav. **8**, 76–88 (2005)
46. Wiederhold, B.K., Wiederhold, M.D.: A review of virtual reality as a psychotherapeutic tool. CyberPsychol. Behav. **1**, 45–52 (1998)

SPI and Automotive

Towards Dependability Engineering of Cooperative Automotive Cyber-Physical Systems

Georg Macher[1(✉)], Eric Armengaud[1], Daniel Schneider[2], Eugen Brenner[3], and Christian Kreiner[3]

[1] AVL List GmbH, Graz, Austria
{georg.macher,eric.armengaud}@avl.com
[2] Fraunhofer IESE, Kaiserslautern, Germany
daniel.schneider@iese.fraunhofer.de
[3] Graz University of Technology, Graz, Austria
{brenner,christian.kreiner}@tugraz.at

Abstract. Numerous industrial sectors are investing in Cyber-Physical-Systems (CPS). CPS provide their functionality by the interaction of various subsystems which are usually developed by different suppliers and are expected to cooperate safely. The open and cooperative nature of CPS poses a significant challenge for industrial sectors with stringent dependability constraints, such as, autonomous automobile systems, medical monitoring, process control systems, or automatic pilot avionics. As CPS may reconfigure itself during run-time, for instance in order to handle failures or to adapt on changing conditions (such as connected car features relying on availability of environmental information), the dependability of this adaptation must still be ensured. To tackle this assurance issue, several recommendations rely on a set of contracts to describe components attributes and evaluate the robustness of the configuration at run-time. In our research project, DEIS, we address these important and unsolved challenges by developing technologies for dependable system integration at run-time. At the core of these technologies lies the concept of a Digital Dependability Identity (DDI) of a component or system. DDIs are composable and executable in-the-field, facilitating (a) efficient synthesis of component and system dependability information over the supply chain and (b) effective evaluation of this information in-the-field for safe and secure composition of highly distributed and autonomous CPS. In contrast to other approaches mainly focusing on software specifics (such as SOME/IP or other SoA approaches), DDI focuses on system development level (also taking into account HW specifics and system decomposition). The paper is describing the approach focusing on the support for functional safety and validation of automated and connected vehicles, by providing an initial framework to manage dependability aspects.

Keywords: ISO 26262 · SAE J3061 · Automotive systems · Dependability · Cyber-security · Functional safety · Cyber-Physical Systems

1 Introduction

Prior to the introduction of wireless connections and automated driving functionalities, vehicles were physically isolated machines with mechanical controls. Extra-functional properties of concern were mainly timing, reliability and functional safety. The emergence of cyber-physical automotive systems over the last decades has affected the development of vehicles, promising to support new applications and altering the customer added value of the passenger car. This is enabled through the availability of information (e.g. powertrain control strategy, traffic information, as well as infotainment and connectivity features) and further opens new markets.

In this context, the rising vehicle-to-vehicle and vehicle-to-infrastructure connectivity causes multiple inter-vehicle connections as well as capabilities for (wireless) networking with other vehicles and non-vehicle entities. Automotive systems are developing from stand-alone systems towards systems of systems, interacting and coordinating with each other and influencing vehicle actions. Connections are not restricted to internal systems (e.g. steering, sensor, actuator, and communications) but also include other road users and the infrastructure. Future vehicles will be able to utilize connectivity features for over-the-air updates, integration of cloud-services and remote automation.

The systems are integrated - more often dynamically at run-time - into so-called Systems of Systems (SoS), which consist of different collaborating systems (i.e. entities encompassing both hardware and software) that host several applications. Moreover, dynamic application updates, reconfigurations or adaptations are most probably key features of all future systems. Although CPS offer tremendous potential for new applications, they also impose significant challenges regarding the assurance of dependability. In most critical domains, assurance activities are guided by functional safety standards. Such standards typically provide means for risk identification and classification and give guidance on how to reduce the involved risk to an acceptable level at development time. These practices require the entire system and all system contexts to be defined and known at design time. This prerequisite is barely satisfactorily fulfilled by adaptive CPS and their dynamic compositions and reconfigurations. Thus, for future CPS contexts, novel safety engineering approaches are required. Promising approaches to tackle these issues rely on a set of contracts to describe components attributes and evaluate the robustness of the configuration at run-time.

In the DEIS project we address these important and unsolved challenges by developing technologies for dependable system integration at run-time. The core technology for this concept is a Digital Dependability Identity (DDI) of a component or system. DDIs are composable and in-the-field executable contracts, which enable (a) efficient synthesis of component and system dependability information and (b) evaluate these contract information in-the-field for safe and secure composition of highly distributed and autonomous CPS. In contrast to other approaches mainly focusing on software specifics (such as SOME/IP or other SoA approaches), DDI focuses on system development level and is also taking HW specifics and system decomposition into account.

In the course of this paper, we propose a way for dependable system integration at run-time. To that aim, we analyze the automotive process landscape to support such an approach and provide a framework to manage dependability aspects on system development level (also taking into account HW specifics and system decomposition).

The paper is organized as follows: Sect. 2 presents an overview of related work. In Sect. 3 a description of a recently proposed addon for service infrastructures for Automotive SPICE 3.0 is provided. In this context, Sect. 4 provides a description of the proposed DDI approach. Finally, Sect. 5 concludes with an overview of the approach presented.

2 Related Work

A key concept for product development of a safety-critical system in many domains is the provision of a safety case. Safety standards such as ISO 26262 [1] for road vehicles have been established to provide guidance during the development of safety-critical systems. They provide a well-defined safety lifecycle based on hazard identification and mitigation, and they define a long list of work-products to be generated. One of these explicitly mentioned work-products is the safety case.

The role of a safety case is to communicate and explicitly show implicit domain knowledge, to summarize safety arguments, and the referencing reports capturing the supporting evidence. It is intended to provide evidence that a system meets its safety requirements and clarify reasons for why each decision has been made or not in a coherent, reproducible, and compact way. In ISO 26262 Part 10 [1] section 5.3.1 states the purpose of a safety case as

> '... to provide a clear, comprehensive and defensible argument, supported by evidence, that an item is free from unreasonable risk when operated in an intended context.' [1]

The **A**utomotive **S**oftware **P**rocess **I**mprovement and **C**apability Determination reference model [2] is based on the international standard ISO 33000 [3] and is primarily used in Europe and in some parts of East Asia. The reference model is intended to provide a basis for comparison and alignment of development processes for embedded automotive systems. It does not specify how processes have to be implemented. Instead, desired process outcomes are defined and described in more detail by base practice (BP) characterization. This approach further supports the provision of a clear, comprehensive and defensible safety case argumentation. But neither the functional safety standard ISO 26262 [1] nor Automotive SPICE [2] have been designed for dynamic applications and reconfigurable or adaptive systems. These approaches provide means for risk identification and classification and give guidance on how to reduce the involved risk to an acceptable level at development time. These practices require the entire system and all system contexts to be defined and known at design time.

Novel Systems of Systems (SoS) approaches [4] are integrations of heterogeneous systems delivering capabilities and services without exact knowledge of the internals of an involved subsystem. A promising method for definition of SoS architectures lies in interface specification and a quasi contract-based development. Bryans et al. [4] establish a semi-formal notation to model SoS architectures with SysML. These contract-based approaches foster model-based development and traceability of development decisions. Although these approaches are not yet very common in the automotive domain, more recent publications highlight the benefits of such approaches also in this area.

The AUTOSAR Adaptive Platform [5] implements a run-time environment for Adaptive Applications (ARA). The platform follows a Service-oriented Architecture (SOA) approach for future use for automated driving functionalities (ADF) and advanced driver assistance systems (ADAS). The initial version of AP R17-03 has been released as planned on March 31st 2017. It describes behavior of the software platform from application and network perspective but does not constrain the SW architecture of a platform implementation. In comparison the AUTOSAR run-time environment (RTE) for the Adaptive Platform [6] dynamically links services and clients during run-time. Nevertheless, the focus of this approach is set on the software development level. The approach does not take into account HW specifics and decomposition rules at system development level.

Service-oriented Architecture (SOA) is known as one popular method for creating dynamically changing, distributed applications. Essentially, it consists of encapsulating all functionalities into so-called services that can be reached via a well-defined interface from anywhere in the network. Each service holds a contract that describes the ways of accessing this functionality, and the different services are composed by an orchestration algorithm.

The work of Amorim et al. [7] focuses on a safety certification solution for safety-critical, open, and adaptive multi-core systems. ConSerts M are modular and composable contracts created at development time as part of a sound and mostly traditional safety argumentation. The focus is set on ensuring safety through the system lifecycle, even if parts of the system are replaced or updated as part of maintenance or upgrades. In [8] a combination of this composable contract approach with an ontology-based run-time reconfiguration (ORR) is proposed for the use in automotive applications.

VerSaI (Vertical Safety Interfaces) [9] is a contract-based modeling approach created to assist the integrator of an integrated architecture in checking whether the application software components are able to run safely on the execution platforms of the system. VerSaI checks the safety compatibility between the application and the platform through demands and guarantees (contract-based approach). Demands are used to express all the properties an application needs for safe execution. Guarantees represent the safety-related properties the platform possesses. They are modeled using a language that consists of a number of elements, each representing a certain type of demand or guarantee exchanged between application and the platform.

The work of Iber et al. [10] presents a concept for modeling contracts and a vision of a generic modeling language for specifying contracts for extra-functional properties. Furthermore the authors introduce a contract state machine for environmental changes and different timing behaviors.

Finally, in the work of Schneider et al. [11] the focus is set on system safety as one integral part of dependability. Additionally, an initial concept of DDIs is provided and explained based on an illustrative example.

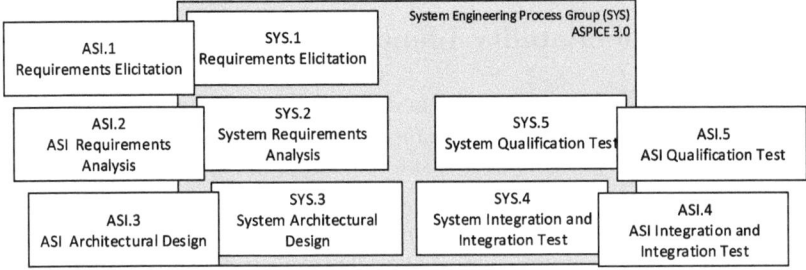

Fig. 1. Extension of Automotive SPICE 3.0 with Automotive Service Infrastructure processes [12]

3 Service Infrastructure Integration

As mentioned earlier in this document neither the functional safety standard ISO 26262 [1] nor Automotive SPICE [2] have been designed for dynamic applications, and reconfigurable or adaptive systems. Novel applications relying on the availability of information (e.g. advanced powertrain control strategy, traffic information, as well as infotainment and connectivity features) shift the customer added value of the passenger car to novel functionalities. Nevertheless, such functionalities, relying on external (probably not certifiable) information, are currently not considered by the most automotive development environment. Automotive systems are developing from stand-alone systems towards such interconnected systems of systems, which interact and coordinate with each other and influence safety-critical vehicle actions. The connected car features will contribute to major driving and safety functionalities in the near future. Since such connections are not restricted to internal systems (e.g. steering, sensor, actuator, and communications) but also include other road users, the infrastructure, and cloud-services standardized approaches and reference models are required for homologation and assessment of such systems.

Therefore, an additional service life cycle model for these connected car services will be required in the future. In [12] such an Automotive SPICE 3.0 process extension, referred to as automotive service infrastructure (ASI) processes, is briefly proposed and motivated based on ADAS functions integrating connectivity features (depicted in Fig. 1). Following the spirit of ISO 26262, the monitoring of the infrastructure services and Quality-of-Service (QoS) measures to assure correct operation and dependability is required. In this case, the DDI approach can overcome demands for deterministic systems at development time and enable dependability guarantee evaluation at run-time. With the DDI approach in combination with the proposed ASI processes it will be possible to state requirements for the cloud-based services and also assess the provided information from the infrastructure.

4 Digital Dependability Identity (DDI) Concept

DDIs are defined as 'data that uniquely describes a thing and contains information about the subjects relation' [11]. Due to the dynamically interconnected and largely unpredictable nature of CPS the dependability cannot be fully assured prior to deployment time. In order to assure the dependability of such in-field integration of services, DDIs must become executable specifications (as depicted in Fig. 2). These meta-information of the DDI are produced during design and continually maintained over the complete lifetime of a component. In this example DDI the infrastructure provides services for the connected car (such as cornering speed recommendations for the specific vehicle type) plus an additional service DDI. Based on the information provided by the service DDI, the vehicle can generate and evaluate the dependability of the specific configuration with the additional service provided by the infrastructure. This way it can decide whether or not to make use of the (temporally) available service and adapt to the current situation.

Essential for the realization of the DDI concept are: (a) an open meta-model for specification of DDIs and exchange of dependability information. Which is a subject of the refinement and evolution within the time span of the DEIS project, and (b) a concept for the dynamic integration and evaluation of DDIs. In a way that the systems may determine whether they can collaborate dependably with other systems or not.

The DDI approach uses a language subset which was created to describe the contracts based on an extension of XML. The language ties together basic meta-information about demands and guarantees and facilitates the automated evaluation process. The demands and guarantees are currently focusing on safety requirements. Safety requirementx are either requested to be fulfilled by somebody (demand) or are guaranteed to be fulfilled (guarantee). They always consist of a statement (i.e., what is guaranteed or demanded) together with a level of confidence with respect to the actual fulfillment of that statement. They are currently used for binary decisions on whether or not to accept the specific service.

The DDI approach is also being applied to a traffic light assistant (TLA) system, which allows ego-vehicles to follow an optimally calculated (on-board vehicle) velocity trajectory that enables following efficiently a Green Wave, see Fig. 3. The TLA relies on V2I communication, via Wi-Fi and also considers

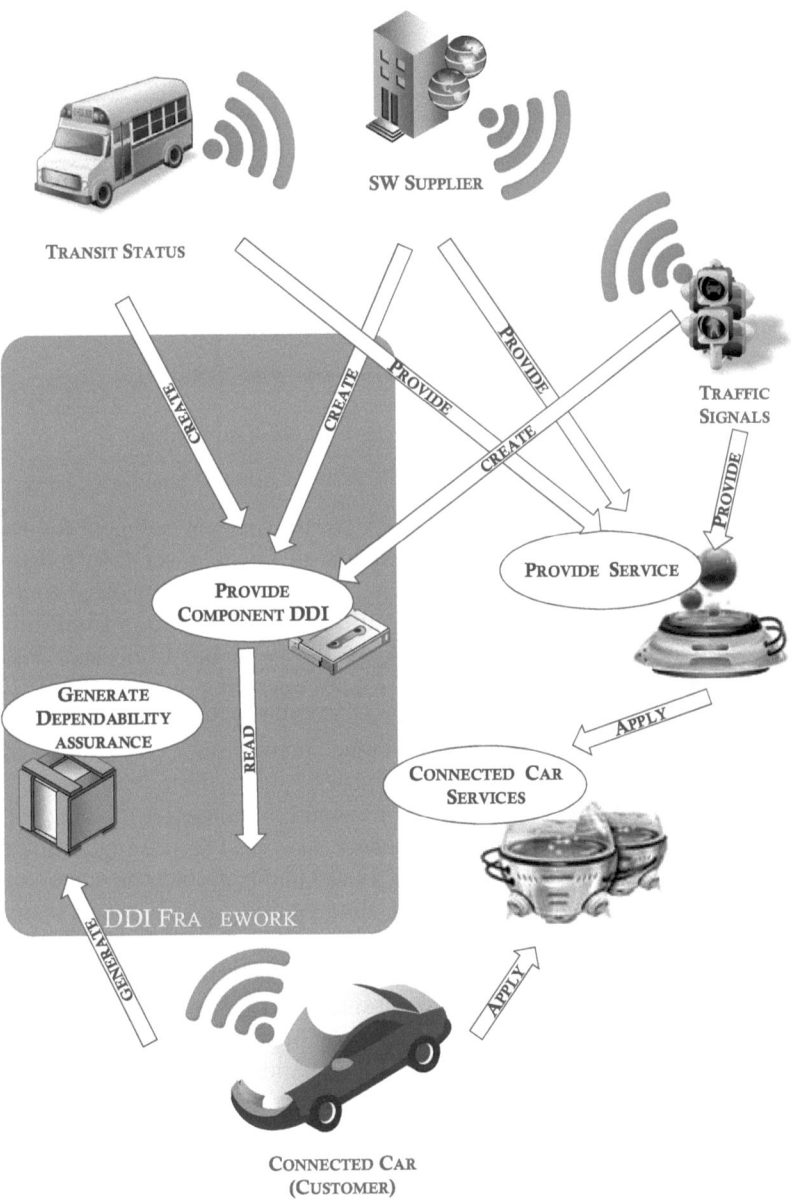

Fig. 2. Depiction of the DDI concept

powertrain dynamic states. This V2I communication makes use of the DDI to decide whether or not to accept the specific service information, namely TL green and red phase and TL position information, from the traffic light or make use only of on-board systems.

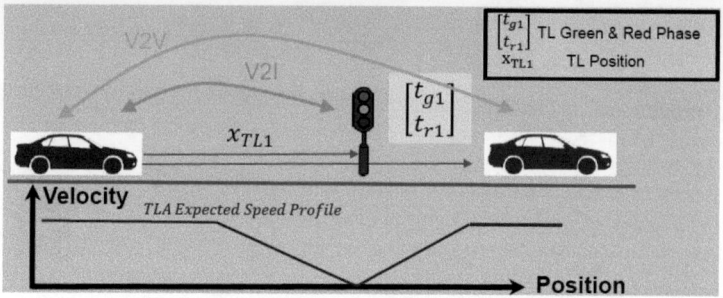

Fig. 3. V2x based TLA concept (Color figure online)

The second development scenario features a run-time environment for electric powertrains which combines the functionality of an E-Motor Controller Unit (EMCU) with the Vehicle Controller Unit (VCU) in one automotive controller unit (VEMCU). In this demonstrator setup software integration from different software suppliers on an AURIX multi-core device is being focused. Figure 4 depicts the demonstrator setup. Here a robot- operating system (ROS) based gateway receives software updates and related DDIs, evaluates and validates the safety contracts for the new software and thus enables safety contracts - online validation at run-time.

Listing 1.1 shows an exemplary DDI of a cloud-based corner steering service. The service provided is an automated corner steering based on environmental information (such as weather conditions, road condition and previously driven corner speeds) with an *ASIL D* quality (line 5) and security level 3 (line 6). This guarantee is only valid if the required 'DemandSet' (line 7–38) is provided. Demands to be satisfied range here from signals (acceleration signal, line 8–11), required functionalities (Lane Keep Assistant, line 12–15), to platform services (line 16–19) and monitoring functions (line 28–37). This DDI, is evaluated at run-time and the service is only started if all demands are provided and thus the safety of the new software can be made evident.

```
1  <DDI>
2  <ComponentName> Cloud-based Corner Steering Service </ComponentName>
3  <Guarantee>
4  <ConfigurationName> CornerSteering </ConfigurationName>
5  <IntegrityLevel> D </IntegrityLevel>
6  <SecurityProperty> 3 </SecurityProperty>
7  <DemandSet>
8     <Demand>
9     <ConfigurationName> acceleration </ConfigurationName>
10    <IntegrityLevel> D </IntegrityLevel>
11    </Demand>
```

```
12      <Demand>
13      <ConfigurationName> Lane Keep Assistant </ConfigurationName>
14          <IntegrityLevel> D </IntegrityLevel>
15      </Demand>
16      <Demand>
17      <ConfigurationName> emSpeed </ConfigurationName>
18          <IntegrityLevel> B </IntegrityLevel>
19      </Demand>
20      <Demand>
21          <Platform_Service>
22          <Failure> Lane Keep Assistant Failure </Failure>
23          <Reaction> detected </Reaction>
24          <IntegrityLevel> D </IntegrityLevel>
25          <Error> 3 % </Error>
26          </Platform_Service>
27      </Demand>
28      <Demand>
29          <HealthMonitoring>
30          <Failure>
31          <Application> Application Runtime Failure </Application>
32          <ApplicationResourceName> Lane Keep Assistant
                </ApplicationResourceName>
33          <Latency> more than 10 ms </Latency>
34          </Failure>
35          <IntegrityLevel> D </IntegrityLevel>
36          </HealthMonitoring>
37      </Demand>
38  </DemandSet>
39  </Guarantee>
40  </DDI>
```

Listing 1.1. DDI for Cloud-based Corner Steering Service

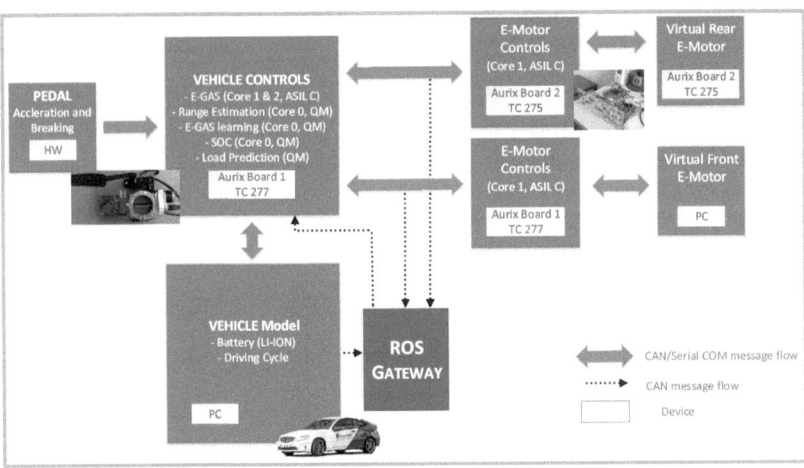

Fig. 4. Depiction of the electric powertrain demonstration setup

5 Conclusion

Vehicle manufacturers are currently gearing up for the newly arising complexity and dependability evaluation challenges coming from more advanced connected car features and Cyber-Physical-Systems (CPS) integration. These systems provide their functionality via interaction of various subsystems or cennected systems and may reconfigure themselves during run-time, which poses a significant challenge for established dependability approaches.

To tackle these issues, novel approaches focus on a set of contracts to describe components attributes and evaluate the robustness of the configuration at run-time. In our research we address these important and unsolved challenges by developing technologies for the dependable system integration at run-time. The presented approach relies on the concept of a Digital Dependability Identity (DDI) of a component or system, which, in contrast to other approaches, does not only focus on software specifics, but also takes system development level considerations into account. The paper provides an initial step for a framework to manage dependability aspects at run-time with respect to recently presented service infrastructure integration addons for ASPICE 3.0.

Acknowledgments. This work is supported by the *DEIS* project - Dependability Engineering Innovation for automotive CPS. This project has received funding from the European Unions Horizon 2020 research and innovation programme under grant agreement No. 732242.

References

1. ISO - International Organization for Standardization, ISO 26262 Road vehicles Functional Safety Part 1–10 (2011)
2. The SPICE User Group, Automotive SPICE Process Assessment/Reference Model V3.0, July 2015
3. ISO - International Organization for Standardization, ISO/IEC 33000 Series on Process Assessment (2014)
4. Bryans, J., Payne, R., Holt, J., Perry, S.: Semi-formal and formal interface specification for system of systems architecture. In: 2013 IEEE International Systems Conference (SysCon), pp. 612–619, April 2013
5. AUTOSAR Development Cooperation, Adaptive Platform Release Overview (2017)
6. AUTOSAR development cooperation, AUTOSAR AUTomotive Open System ARchitecture (2009)
7. Amorim, T., Ruiz, A., Dropmann, C., Schneider, D.: Multidirectional modular conditional safety certificates. In: Koornneef, F., Gulijk, C. (eds.) SAFECOMP 2015. LNCS, vol. 9338, pp. 357–368. Springer, Cham (2015). doi:10.1007/978-3-319-24249-1_31
8. Amorim, T., Schneider, D., Ratasich, D., Grosu, R., Macher, G., Ruiz, A., Driussi, M.: Runtime safety assurance for adaptive cyber-physical systems - conserts M and ontology-based runtime reconfiguration applied to an automotive case study. In: Druml, N., Genser, A., Krieg, A., Menghin, M., Hoeller, A. (eds.) Handbook of Research on Solutions for Cyber-Physical Systems Ubiquity. IGI Global (2017)
9. Zimmer, B., Bürklen, S., Knoop, M., Höfflinger, J., Trapp, M.: Vertical safety interfaces – improving the efficiency of modular certification. In: Flammini, F., Bologna, S., Vittorini, V. (eds.) SAFECOMP 2011. LNCS, vol. 6894, pp. 29–42. Springer, Heidelberg (2011). doi:10.1007/978-3-642-24270-0_3

10. Iber, J., Hoeller, A., Rauter, T., Kreiner, C.: Towards a generic modeling language for contract-based design. In: 2nd International Workshop on Model-Driven Engineering for Component-Based Software Systems (ModComp), 2015 Workshop Proceedings, p. 24 (2015)
11. Schneider, D., Trapp, M., Papadopoulos, Y., Armengaud, E., Zeller, M., Hoefig, K.: Digital dependability identities. In: Proceedings of the IEEE 26th International Symposium on Software Reliability Engineering, ISSRE 2015, pp. 324–329 (2015)
12. Messnarz, R., Kreiner, C., Macher, G., Walker, A.: Extending automotive SPICE 3.0 for the use in ADAS service architectures. In Review - IEEE Softw. J. (2017)

An Analysis of the Commonality and Differences Between ASPICE and ISO26262 in the Context of Software Development

Pedro Oliveira[1,2], André L. Ferreira[3], Daniel Dias[1,2], Tiago Pereira[1,2], Paula Monteiro[1(✉)], and Ricardo J. Machado[1,2]

[1] CCG-Centro de Computação Gráfica, Guimarães, Portugal
Paula.monteiro@ccg.pt
[2] Centro ALGORITMI, Escola de Engenharia,
Universidade do Minho, Guimarães, Portugal
{b7262,b7260,b7481}@algoritmi.uminho.pt,
rmac@dsi.uminho.pt
[3] Bosch Car Multimedia Portugal S.A., Braga, Portugal
andre.ferreira2@pt.bosch.com

Abstract. The automotive industry is facing new challenges resulting from recent technological evolutions. Software is having a major impact on the level of functionality being delivered by systems present in vehicles and the role of software is believed to be more relevant in the future. This stresses organizations in the automotive domain to improve their software development capability to deal with the increasing levels of systems complexity. In this paper, a harmonization exercise is performed considering the Automotive SPICE and ISO 26262 which are two of the most relevant quality standards for organizations developing systems in the automotive domain. The goals are to have a deeper understanding of the scenario where organizations have a sub-scope of ASPICE adopted (HIS scope) and wish to adopt jointly the ISO26262 standard as a strategic approach to improving development capability. The results show that an organization with HIS implemented still has a considerable scope of ISO26262 to implement.

Keywords: ASPICE v3 · ISO 26262 · Gap analysis · Multi-model · Process quality · Product safety · Compliance · Harmonization · Automotive industry

1 Introduction

Technological evolution is pushing several industries to deliver additional levels of functionalities. One of the industries that witnessed, in recent years, the highest growing of technological innovation for software-intensive components, was the automotive industry [1]. Software is becoming a critical component for Automotive since it is part of Electronic Control Units (ECU) that now deliver 85% of the automobile's functionalities [2].

Software engineering capability is therefore stressed for existing and new companies delivering software for the automotive domain. This new automotive reality, pushes organizations to improve their software engineering capability in order to cope with increasing levels of system complexity driven by software.

Automotive quality models aim to help automotive companies to improve their engineering capability. If they are suppliers, it pushes them to improve their development capability by allowing them to identify improvement areas and achieving higher levels of product quality by implementing engineering best practices. For contractors, to assess supplier capability in delivering quality products, improved supplier monitoring and better relationship with suppliers. Quality models and standards provide an approach to assessing and institutionalizing new or improved processes to become more competitive and produce high-quality products [3]. Adopting quality models or standards requires experience and knowledge as each model has its own particularities, which can be reflected in concepts, terminology, and structure, among others.

State of practice on software development in the automotive industry cannot be characterized without considering Automotive Software Process Improvement and Capability Determination (ASPICE) [4]. ASPICE is the reference model that European car manufacturers have promoted to measure the capability of their software suppliers and define a qualification mechanism for supplier selection. The Hersteller Initiative Software (HIS) was created by is a group of automakers that defined a sub-scope of ASPICE with a selection of base practices for the automotive industry to promote an easier adoption of the standard.

ISO26262 [5] is an emergent standard for automotive defined by International Organization for Standardization (ISO). It was published in November 2011 and addresses the area of functional safety for road vehicles. Safety is now one of the key issues for automotive and ISO26262 focus is on functional safety of Electric/Electronic (E/E) systems, defining a set of requirements for establishing a safety lifecycle. This involves determining Automotive Safety Integrity Levels (ASIL), validation and confirmation measures for acceptable levels. With the publication of ISO26262, manufacturers, suppliers, and automotive organizations share a common schema for the classification of automotive software regarding safety.

The work described in this paper aims to support automotive organizations in understanding how ASPICE and ISO26262 share their scope, in the use case where an organization with established compliance with ASPICE desires to have an understanding of fulfillment of ISO26262 expected practices. The goal is to provide a detailed analysis of similarities and differences in process requirements set by both standards to identify a roadmap to establish compliance with ISO26262.

Several studies in the literature addressed this topic, as automotive organizations are considering the adoption of these two standards into the same organizational environment. A harmonization exercise is performed considering the bilateral mapping method, where is it assumed that an implementation of ASPICE exists and an adoption of ISO26262 is desired.

The paper is structured as follows, an overview of related work in given in Sect. 2. The steps for the harmonization exercise are presented in Sect. 3. Section 4 elaborates on the results from the harmonization exercise and Sect. 5 summarizes the exercise and identifies future work.

2 Related Work

When establishing improvement strategies based on multiple quality models or standards, harmonization provides a strategy towards understanding how multiple models relate to each other and how a simultaneous adoption can be tackled. A multi-model environment in software process improvement exists when an organization decides to integrate new practices that are described or promoted by different standards [6].

The number of reports on harmonization of multiple quality standards and models in the literature is relatively small but the number of studies increased in recent years. Examples are the integration of several improvement models to evaluate software process by maturity levels. This approach has proved to be a major benefit for Spain software companies when pursuing standard certification [7]. More general studies propose meta-models for harmonizing multiple models into a single environment [8–10] that provide an approach for homogenization, comparison, and integration of quality standards. Relevant initiatives in multi-model are available in [11–13].

An example of a harmonization of ASPICE and ISO26262 is presented by Morayo Adedjouma et al. [14], where ISO26262 practices are considered implemented and an assessment of coverage of ASPICE v2.5 (HIS scope) base practices is performed. The results describe the full coverage of HIS scope in an ISO26262 organization when is performed an assessment. A similar exercise is presented in [15], where a detailed analysis of how ISO26262 clauses are covered by CMMI+SAFE goals. The results demonstrate that +SAFE provides a 70% coverage of ISO26262 requirements. Another example is the harmonization of ISO 25010 with CMMI-DEV and ISO/IEC 12207, showing that adoption of early product quality characteristics (sustainability metrics) can be a driver to deploy sustainable objectives using a goal-oriented approach.

A relevant exercise of combining automotive standards is presented by Messnarz et al. [14, 16] considering the draft of ISO26262 and ASPICE 2.5 to support assessments of automotive projects with both standards combined which is detailed in [17]. Another work in extending ASPICE with safety consideration is presented in [18] where process groups of ASPICE are identified and adapted to have distinguishable processes and practices extended with functional safety concerns.

3 Harmonization Process

Siviy et al. [19] introduced the concept of harmonization as a possible solution to deal with the need to have multi-model environments. Harmonization is introduced as a general framework to align different improvement models into a single environment. In summary, the following steps are defined: (1) Alignment of organizational and improvement objectives and identification of improvement technologies: (2) Categorization of improvement technologies, strategically: (3) Design the improvement solution and: (4) Implement the multi-model solution and measure results.

A technique applied in multi-model scenarios is the model mapping technique. It is used to compare quality standards with the purpose of finding associations/relations between standards by using a mapping function. Model mappings can be used in the harmonization context to support selection and composition of improvement models.

The semantic associated with the mapping function determines the type of model comparison and composition. A type of model mapping is bilateral comparison, which can be created having two standards and taking a point of view of a standard and describe the second standard in terms of the first. Typically, this is created considering textual descriptions from both standards. This technique is suitable for the goals of our exercise because a detailed analysis of the models is expected. The goals are to use ASPICE as the reference model and assess which requirements in the form of shall statement from ISO26262 could be fulfilled by implemented ASPICE practices.

3.1 Standards Selection and Mapping Function

The ASPICE is a process assessment model and process reference model based on the ISO/IEC 15504 standard [4], (now superseded by ISO330xx standard series) is conformant with the ISO/IEC 33004 and can be used as the basis for conducting an assessment of process capability. The update from version 2.5 to Version 3.0 comprises some structural changes: the engineering processes were divided into the two groups System (SYS) and Software (SWE) with some changes in their structures; Unit construction and unit verification have been separated into two processes. A "Plug-in Concept" allows integration of mechanical and hardware processes (but not provided); Small changes and improvements for capability levels 1–3 (base practices reworked and modifications on work products characteristics) and few changes which may increase project efforts, e.g., evaluation of alternative solutions is required for system and software architectures.

ASPICE is used by car manufacturers (OEMs) and first tier suppliers as the core process reference model to push software process improvement internally and to assess and monitor software suppliers [17]. For the harmonization exercise, it was considered the HIS scope, which is the reference scope used by automotive OEMs for the qualification of suppliers of software-intensive car components. This narrow scope allows the mapping exercise to focus on the initial core areas expected by OEMs. Table 1 lists the process areas part of the HIS scope v2.5 assessment in the context of ASPICE v3.0.

In recent year the focus on quality shifted to safety due to the increasing levels of functionally resulting from software technological evolutions [18]. Even if ASPICE assessments are valuable for the development of safety-related software, there are some conceptual gaps in ASPICE that are desirable for automotive product development.

ISO 26262 provides the specifics related to ensuring product safety and ASPICE focus on process capability. The safety standard states *"an organization's process definitions must address multiple standards at the same time. If a SPICE assessment is performed, then this SPICE assessment and a functional safety audit can be simultaneously performed. There is sufficient commonality in content that can help to avoid duplication of work or process between both standards and to allow synchronization of the planning"*.

Table 1. HIS scope considered for the mapping

ASPICE V3.0 (HIS scope v2.5)	
ACQ.4 Supplier monitoring	MAN.3 Project management
SUP.1 Quality assurance	SUP.8 Configuration management
SUP.9 Problem resolution management	SWE.1 Software requirements analysis
SUP.10 Change management	SWE.2 Software architectural design
SYS.2 System requirements analysis	SWE.3 Software detailed design and unit construction
SYS.3 System architectural design	SWE.4 Software unit verification
SYS.4 System integration and integration test	SWE.5 Software integration and integration test
SYS.5 System qualification test	SWE.6 Software qualification test

ISO26262 is a fairly recent standard, the latest version was published in 2011 and is structured in 10 parts. Each part focus on different concerns relevant to the engineering of E/E systems. Table 2 identifies the parts of the ISO26262 standard concerning software development (excluding Part 1 - Vocabulary, Part 5 - Hardware level, Part 9 - ASIL-oriented and safety-oriented analyses and Part 10 - Guideline on ISO 26262). Each of this parts (except Part 1 and 10) define requirements to be implemented by organizations adopting the standard.

Table 2. ISO 26262:2011 parts considered for the mapping and total of requirements

ISO 26262:2011		
Part 2	Management of functional safety	53
Part 3	Concept phase	49
Part 4	System level	96
Part 6	Software level	56
Part 7	Production and operation	27
Part 8	Supporting processes	131

3.2 Components Selection and Mapping Function

ASPICE is composed of Process Categories which include Process Groups where we find individual processes. A Process has a Purpose, Outcomes, Base Practices and Work products associated. Base Practices and Work product contribute to achieving one or several Outcomes. For the process evaluation, Base Practices are commonly used to determine Capability Level 1. For other Capability Levels, the evaluation is based on the Process Attributes. Process Attribute includes capability indicators such as Generic Practice and Generic Resources. Resources are either Tool, Infrastructure, Method, or Human Resources. Notes for additional information can be attached to Outcome, Base Practice, and Process Attribute.

In ASPICE, *"each process is described in terms of a purpose statement. These statements contain the unique functional objectives of the process when performed in a particular environment. A list of specific outcomes is associated with each of the process purpose statements, as a list of expected positive results of the process performance".*

ISO 26262 is composed of Parts and a *Part* is composed of Clauses. For each Clause an *Objective* is defined, a *General purpose*, *Work products* as described as input (external to the projects, mandatory or optional) and other as outputs. Output work products are the result of Requirements and Recommendations which are represented as one or more shall statements (SS). A requirement has a specific ASIL (QM, A, B, C, D) associated. Examples and Notes give additional information to better understand the requirements and also can have references in form of Annex or Table of Property or Method. The table's elements must be used alternatively or in parallel and are subject to different recommendation levels according to an ASIL classification and are explained when necessary in a Notes section.

To define a harmonization strategy the two models were compared in term of their structure, considering the harmonization technique presented by Pardo et al. [14], their structure was compared (see Table 3). Each component of both standards was compared to generate a joint classification.

Table 3. Semantic harmonization of ASPICE and ISO26262

ASPICE V3.0	ISO 26262:2011	Joint
Category	Safety lifecycle	Category
Group	Part	Part
Process group	Clause	Process group
Purpose	Objective	Purpose
Outcome	Requirement	Outcome
Work product	Work product	Work product
N/A	ASIL	ASIL
Base practice	Shall statement	Shall statement

The mapping allows to have a view of how each standard is organized and identify which elements can be used for the purpose of a harmonization exercise. As an example the *Process Group* of ASPICE V3.0 and *Clause* of ISO26262:2011 are used by both standards to represent a similar concept.

Based on the harmonization use case defined for this paper, where an implementation of ASPICE is assumed and an assessment of fulfillment of ISO26262 is desired, entities chosen for the mapping were outcomes from ASPICE and requirements in the form of SS from ISO26262. Therefore, every Outcome was mapped to every SS from ISO26262 to assess if the existence of the outcome could provide any evidence of implementation of an ISO26262 requirement. This perspective aims to have a view of shared scope between an existing ASPICE implementation and a desired ISO26262 implementation. The mapping function associated with the mapping aims to translate this rationale into a qualitative evaluation of how a SS from ISO26262 is fulfilled when an ASPICE outcome exists. Table 4 details the rating scale used by the mapping

Table 4. Rating scale used

Value	Acronym	Description
0%	O - Off any overlap	No information is found to be useful to support that a SS is partially or totally implemented
[1–25%]	L - Light overlap	Insufficient information exists to state that a SS is partially or totally implemented
[26–50%]	F - Fair overlap	Information is absent to fulfil the mapped SS
[51–75%]	M - Medium overlap	Information is present or judged to be adequate to fulfil the mapped SS but some information is missing
[76–100%]	H - High overlap	Information associated to outcomes can be judged to be fully applicable to fulfil a SS

function. As an example the mapping between an ASPICE outcome when compared to an ISO26262 SS can be classified as L-Light overlap, meaning that the outcome provides little evidence that could be used to ensure ISO26262 requirement implementation.

In this mapping exercise, an ISO 26262 SS may be fulfilled by multiple ASPICE outcomes, meaning that information present in ASPICE outcomes can be used to assess the fulfillment of an ISO 26262 SS. This, however, does not mean that the mapping is cumulative, e.g., a SS that was mapped with a Fair overlap [26%, 50%], by considering a specific ASPICE outcome and a second outcome mapping to the same SS, mapped with Medium overlap [50%, 74%], does not mean that the SS is fully covered by the set of outcomes. It provides, however, information that the ISO 26262 SS as several sources of information that could provide confidence for a full requirement fulfillment.

3.3 Harmonization Execution

The harmonization exercise considered the following steps:

1. HIS scope of ASPICE was considered as the implemented practices of the standard. All ISO26262 Parts that define requirement were considered except the Part 5: Product development at the hardware level, as the focus of this mapping, is centered in software development.
2. The mappings were performed between ASPICE outcomes and ISO26262 SS deriving a classification using the metric defined in Table 4. For each pair of outcome/requirement, a classification was given based on the textual description of ASPICE outcomes and shall statement from ISO26262 a spreadsheet was used to store the mappings.

As an example the mapping of outcomes from ASPICE Project Management process (MAN.3) is detailed.

The purpose of the Project Management Process *"is to identify, establish and control the activities and resources necessary for a project to produce a product, in the context of the project's requirements and constraints"*. The mapping exercised started by considering Outcome1 of MAN.3, defined as *"the scope of the work for the project is defined"*, represented by work product 08–12 Project plan and detailed by base practice MAN.3.BP1. The next action was to map the description with all shall statements of ISO 26262, considering specific keywords that define the outcome, e.g., scope, project, defined. When a match occurred it was taken into context. An example of an identified match is between Outcome 1 and Part 3 – Item definition, with SS 5.4.1 and 5.4.2 clauses.

- 5.4.1-*"The functional and non-functional requirements of the item as well as the dependencies between the item and its environment shall be made available. This information is more detailed by Note 1, Note 2 and the clauses: (a) (b) (c) d) (e) (f)"*
- 5.4.2-*"The boundary of the item, its interfaces, and the assumptions concerning its interaction with other items and elements, shall be defined considering: (a) (b) (c) (d) (e) (f) (g)"*

The interpretation is that scope of the item definition can only be briefly created with information from the project plan unless the project plan is very detailed in the functional description of the product to be developed. In this view, an item definition relates more with a requirements document than with a project plan. But a project plan may provide some information that can be used to elaborate an item definition, if available from external resources (Part 2 – Management of functional safety in 6.3.2). Even so, from the identified SSs, is considered that some information is absent or judged to be inadequate to fulfil the mapped requirement of Outcome 1 is used, thus received a rating of F – Fair overlap. A representation of the full mapping for MAN.3 is given in Fig. 1. Considering product outcome 1 (PO1) a mapping was identified with Part3 rated as Fair overlap. Figure 1 also highlights the number of SS identified – 2. The overall rating was computed by considering the most frequent value of the rating. As an example, the rating from the 2 SS for the PO1 gave origin to a Fair classification.

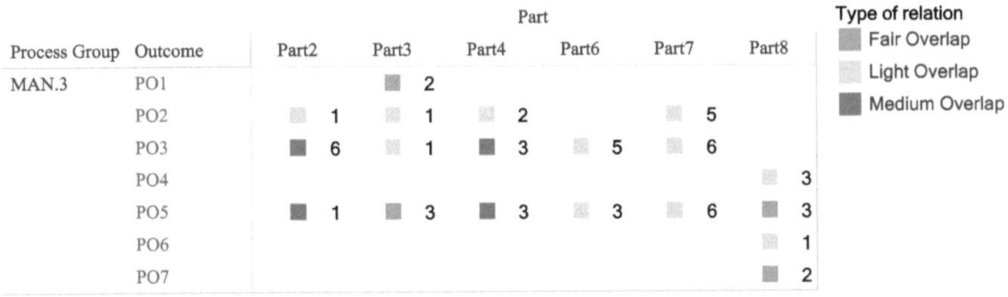

Process Group	Outcome	Part2	Part3	Part4	Part6	Part7	Part8	Type of relation
MAN.3	PO1		2					■ Fair Overlap
	PO2		1	1	2		5	▨ Light Overlap
	PO3	■ 6		1	3	5	6	■ Medium Overlap
	PO4						3	
	PO5		1	3	3	3	6	3
	PO6						1	
	PO7						2	

Fig. 1. Illustration of mappings between ASPICE MAN.3 and ISO 26262 Parts

Each outcome was then mapped to all parts of ISO considering their textual descriptions and computing an overlap rating. From Fig. 1 it is possible to identify the parts of ISO26262 and the amount of SS that were identified that have overlap and also the strength of that overlap. The mapping was completed for all process areas from HIS scope using the same approach as described for MAN.3.

4 Analysis of the Mapping Results

Having all the mappings performed, from a total of 412 SS identified in ISO26262 a total of 580 mappings resulted in a mapping where an overlap was identified. This happens as an outcome can provide information relevant for more than one SS, thus resulting in a higher number of references than SS.

A complete perspective of the results is given in Fig. 2. It illustrates the level of coverage that an organization may expect to achieve on ISO26262 when HIS from ASPICE is implemented. A percentage of total shall statement addressed is given for each ISO26262 part, e.g., for part 2, 6% of (total number of SS is presented in Table 2) SS are addressed. It also illustrates the percentage of statements considering the mapping classification, with 1%, 4%, 1% with Medium, Fair and Light overlap, respectively. Overall Fig. 2. depicts the ISO 26262 parts with a higher level of coverage by HIS from ASPICE. Part 4, part 6 and part 8 evidence higher number of SSs referenced and also are the ones with a higher percentage of SS with higher levels of overlapping classification.

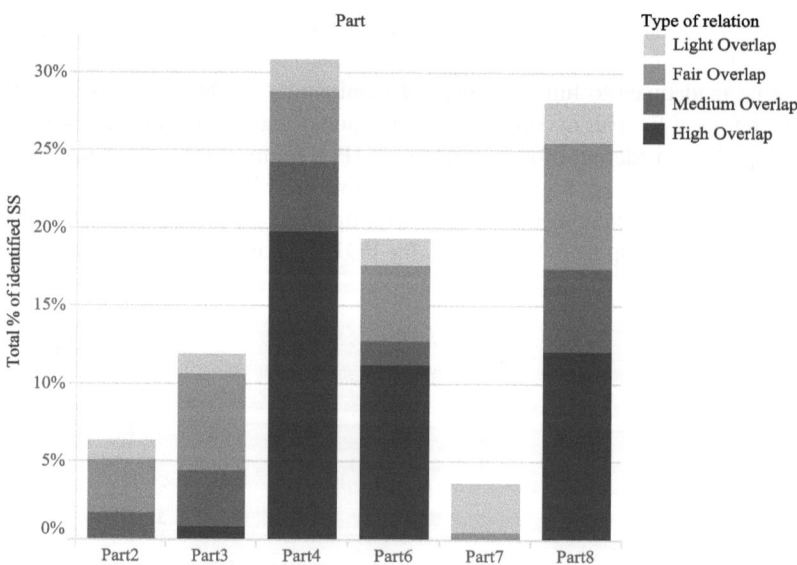

Fig. 2. Overall coverage of ISO26262 by HIS scope from ASPICE

Table 5 presents a detailed view of the mapping results. It lists all process areas from ASPICE HIS scope and the respective mapping count to ISO26262 parts. The first value in each column represents the percentage of all requirements with a mapping established and the associated value of the classification according to the rating defined in Table 4. As an example, 15% of the SS from Part 2 may benefit from information generated in ASPICE outcomes of MAN.3.

Table 5. Overview of the mapping results

ASPICE V3.0 (HIS 2.5 scope)	ISO 26262									
	Part 2		Part 3		Part 4		Part 6		Part 7		Part 8	
	Total SS identified part/Total SS part* and classification									
ACQ.4											12	H
MAN.3	**15**	**M**	14	F	8	M	14	L	63	F	7	F
SUP.1	45	F										
SUP.8											8	L
SUP.9	8	F/M							15	L/F	5	M
SUP.10											20	H
SYS.2			24	L/F	9	F	2	F			9	F
SYS.3			29	M	18	F					8	F
SWE.1			22	L/M			30	F/M/H			8	M
SWE.2			31	F			18	H			4	L/M
SWE.3			14	F			27	H			1	F
SWE.4		F	2	F	2	L	23	H			8	H
SWE.5			2	F			50	H			11	M
SWE.6			2	L			36	F			7	F
SYS.4					82	H					5	F
SYS.5					67	M/H					15	F/H

* means multiplied by 100, percentage %

As all mappings have a mapping classification associated the value represented in Table 5 represents the most frequent classification (given by the statistical mode) for the mappings established with SS from that part of ISO 26262. Again, for the example of the value in the table, the 15% of SS with mappings established the most frequent classification rating of Medium was considered.

In order to understand which SS from IS26262 has the higher number of mappings established, Table 6 present which clauses could benefit more from information present in HIS scope from ASPICE. It lists, for each part of ISO 26262 the top 3 SS that have more mappings established. Additionally, as result of the mapping, all outcomes from HIS scope add at least one mapping established to ISO 26262 SS, meaning all ASPICE outcomes generate information relevant to ISO 26262.

Table 6. Top 3 SS mappings established for each ISO26262 Part

Part / SS													
Part2			Part3			Part4			Part6		Part7			Part8		
6.4.2.3	6.4.9.6	6.4.9.3	5.4.2.	8.4.5.1	5.4.1	8.4.4...	8.4.3...	8.4.2...	10.4.2	9.4.2	10.4.1	5.4.1.1	5.4.1.4	5.4.1.5	9.4.2.2	10.4.1	5.4.4.1
3	3	3	12	11	9	7	7	7	8	6	5	3	3	3	10	10	9

Count of SS broken down by Part and SS. The data is filtered on count of Number of Records, which ranges from 2 to 12 and keeps Null values. The view is filtered on Exclusões (Part,SS) and SS. The Exclusões (Part,SS) filter keeps 104 members. The SS filter keeps 147 of 166 members.

5 Conclusions and Future Work

Organizations in the automotive domain are being challenged by technological evolution. Software is now responsible for an increase in new functions being delivered by systems present in vehicles. The increase in complexity of software systems stresses software development capability of these organizations. ASPICE and ISO 26262 are two standards that aim to support these organizations in improving software development practices and capability. Both standards have different purposes but are highly relevant for automotive organizations. The work presented in this paper aims to help organizations that aim to have both standards as a strategy to improve their capability. A harmonization exercise was performed to identify the portion of scope of ISO26262 is covered by having ASPICE HIS scope implemented. A mapping was performed considering ASPICE expected outcomes and process requirements from ISO26262. Their descriptions were analyzed to identify which outcomes could contribute to fulfilling ISO26262 requirements and an overlap rating was computed from the analysis.

In summary, there is a fair overlap of ISO 26262 by ASPICE with HIS scope from v2.5. Overall, 199 from 412 distinct requirements (48%) from ISO 26262 can benefit from outcomes from ASPICE HIS scope. Part 4 and Part 8 from ISO 26262 relate to engineering practices and thus achieve a higher coverage by HIS scope. Part 2, Part 3 and Part 7 are poorly covered by HIS scope from ASPICE. As a practical conclusion from this research work is that an organization with HIS scope implemented still has a considerable number of requirements and possible effort to have ISO26262 implemented.

The next step in understating deeper both standards will be to consider a full implementation of ASPICE and a scenario where the HIS scope is extended with +SAFE and +SECURE Process Groups of CMMI and analyze the coverage of ISO 26262 standard. Also, a roadmap for a joint adoption of both standards is to be developed according to requirements of different ASIL levels. This research is sponsored by the Portugal Incentive System for Research and Technological Development. Project in co-promotion n° 002797/2015 (INNOVCAR 2015–2018).

References

1. Ross, H.: Functional Safety for Road Vehicles. Springer, Cham (2016). doi:10.1007/978-3-319-33361-8
2. Loon, H.Van: Process Assessment and ISO/IEC 15504: A Reference Book. Springer, New York (2007)
3. Pardo-Calvache, C.J., García-Rubio, F.O., Piattini-Velthuis, M.G., Pino-Correa, F.J., Baldassarre, M.T.: A 360-degree process improvement approach based on multiple models (2015)
4. VDA QMC Working Group 13/Automotive SIG: Automotive SPICE Process Assessment/Reference Model (2015)
5. ISO: ISO 26262:2011 (2011)
6. Pardo, C., Pino, F.J., García, F., Piattini, M.: Homogenization of models to support multi-model processes in improvement environments. In: Proceedings of the 4th International Conference on Software and Data Technology - ICSOFT 2009, vol. 1, pp. 151–156 (2009)

7. Garzás, J., Pino, F.J., Piattini, M., Fernández, C.M.: A maturity model for the Spanish software industry based on ISO standards. Comput. Stand. Interfaces. **35**, 616–628 (2013)
8. Pardo, C., Pino, F.J., Garcia, F., Baldassarre, M.T., Piattini, M.: From chaos to the systematic harmonization of multiple reference models: a harmonization framework applied in two case studies. J. Syst. Softw. **86**, 125–143 (2013)
9. Pardo-Calvache, C.J., García-Rubio, F.O., Piattini-Velthuis, M.: A reference ontology for harmonizing process-reference models Una ontología de referencia para la armonización de modelos de referencia de procesos (2014)
10. Pardo, C., Pino, F.J., Garcia, F., Piattini, M., Baldassarre, M.T.: A process for driving the harmonization of models. In: 11th International Conference on Product Focused Software - PROFES 2010, pp. 51–54 (2010)
11. SEI: The PrIME project. http://www.sei.cmu.edu/process/research/prime-details.cfm
12. Alarcos: ARMONÍAS. http://alarcos.esi.uclm.es/armonias/
13. SPICE: Enterprise SPICE. http://www.enterprisespice.com/
14. Adedjouma, M., Dubois, H., Terrier, F., Kitouni, T.: Merging the quality assessment of processes and products in automotive domain. In: Dieste, O., Jedlitschka, A., Juristo, N. (eds.) PROFES 2012. LNCS, vol. 7343, pp. 275–289. Springer, Heidelberg (2012). doi:10.1007/978-3-642-31063-8_21
15. Winkler, D., O'Connor, R.V., Messnarz, R. (eds.): EuroSPI 2012. CCIS, vol. 301. Springer, Heidelberg (2012). doi:10.1007/978-3-642-31199-4
16. Messnarz, R., Ross, H.-L., Habel, S., König, F., Koundoussi, A., Unterrreitmayer, J., Ekert, D.: Integrated automotive SPICE and safety assessments. Softw. Process Improv. Pract. **14**, 279–288 (2009)
17. Messnarz, R., König, F., Bachmann, V.O.: Experiences with trial assessments combining automotive SPICE and functional safety standards. In: Winkler, D., O'Connor, R.V., Messnarz, R. (eds.) EuroSPI 2012. CCIS, vol. 301, pp. 266–275. Springer, Heidelberg (2012). doi:10.1007/978-3-642-31199-4_23
18. Johannessen, P., Halonen, Ö., Örsmark, O.: Functional safety extensions to automotive SPICE according to ISO 26262. In: O'Connor, R.V., Rout, T., McCaffery, F., Dorling, A. (eds.) SPICE 2011. CCIS, vol. 155, pp. 52–63. Springer, Heidelberg (2011). doi:10.1007/978-3-642-21233-8_5
19. Siviy, J., Kirwan, P., Morley, J., Marino, L.: Maximizing your process improvement ROI through harmonization. Software Engineering Institute (SEI), Carnegie Mellon University (2008). http://resources.sei.cmu.edu/library/asset-view.cfm?assetid=28907

GamifySPI

Gandhi SP1

Deploying a Gamification Framework for Software Process Improvement: Preliminary Results

Eduardo Herranz[1], Ricardo Colomo-Palacios[2(✉)], and Abdullah Al-Barakati[3]

[1] Computer Science Department, Universidad Carlos III de Madrid, Av. Universidad 30,
Leganés, 28911 Madrid, Spain
eduardo.herranz@uc3m.es
[2] Faculty of Computer Sciences, Østfold University College, Postboks 700,
1757 Halden, Norway
ricardo.colomo-palacios@hiof.no
[3] Department of Information Systems, Faculty of Computing and Information Technology,
King Abdulaziz University, Jeddah, Saudi Arabia
aaalbarakati@kau.edu.sa

Abstract. Gamification is intended to increase engagement and motivation among its users by means of a set of game design elements. This field of study has expanded in popularity in the recent years in several areas needed to improve engagement among their actors. One of this areas is software engineering. This discipline is a human-centric activity needed of motivated engineers performing a wide panoply of tasks. In this scenario, in this paper authors present an effort conducted to deploy a gamification framework devoted to increase engagement among software practitioners in software process improvement initiatives. Preliminary results show both encouraging outcomes and areas of improvement in the implementation approach and in the needed breadth of areas or processes involved in the gamification proposal.

Keywords: Software process improvement · Gamification · Deployment

1 Introduction

Gamification as a discipline is maturing in the last few years [1]. From their beginnings in which gamification was just a basic idea to more recent advances and researches, the field of study is evolving towards a more mature state. According to a recent study [2], Gamification started in marketing with mechanisms like loyalty cards, stamp books, competition and reward memberships, however the rise of gamification came with cheaper technology solutions and the generalization of game culture [3]. Not in vain, according to [4], Gamification has a greater impact in an online context. As a result of the importance of Gamification, researchers have focused on the phenomenon and are increasingly studying it, defining theories and documenting challenges and opportunities on its use.

Gamification presents many definitions. Maybe the simplest definition is as follows: gamification is the use of game elements in non-game contexts [3] in order to alter and inspiration the behavior of people [5]. The final intent is the injection of fun, play, and passion into tasks and processes [6]. However, in the context of this paper authors will adopt the definition provided by [7]: Gamification is a transformation process in which interaction patterns, game mechanisms, reusable game components are operationalized to solve problems in an intended environment that is situated within a real world context.

Literature reported the fact that the concept of game and games on the one hand, and gamification on the other hand are really close. According to [8], games are concentrated on entertainment and pleasure while gamification focuses on changing players' behavior, engagement with their environment and co-players towards achieving meaningful interaction and engagement and possibly achieve recompenses. There are also different names applied to the concept or similar endeavors, including pervasive games, game based learning or serious games.

Gamification is grounded on several well-grounded psychological theories, namely, the Fogg Behavior Model, the self-determination theory and the flow theory. Regarding its components, gamification is built on game elements: dynamics, mechanics and components of the game [5]. The first element, dynamics of the game, is about endowing the objectives and the potential effects on the people participating in the gamification proposal. Secondly, mechanics are the basic actions that motivate the user in order to accomplish the aims specified by the game [5]. Game mechanics aim to govern the behavior of people through incentive systems, feedback and competition, among others, with a reasonably predictable outcome [9]. The last element is game elements referring to specific instances of the dynamics and game mechanics [5]. A good explanation of game design elements can be found in the works of [3].

In this scenario, a gamification proposal can increase the engagement and motivation and by doing so, upsurge productivity and performance of the personnel [10]. However, gamification also entails some specific drawbacks. Thus, firstly, it is not easy to manage, secondly, there is a danger of misinterpretation the conceptualization and improper implementation of game elements [11] and lastly, gamification could go against the values of the organization by introducing unwarranted competitiveness, a factor that is highly demotivating [5].

Gamification has its impact in the broad field of software engineering. A recent paper [12] reviews current literature on the topic and concludes literature reports simple gamification mechanics and few provide empirical evidence of the impact of gamification. This paper aims at bridging the gap between gamification in software engineering and empirical evidence by presenting an effort to deploy a gamification framework devoted to software process improvement in real settings.

The remainder of this paper is structured as follows: Sect. 2 outlines the proposed gamification framework. In Sect. 3 the case study is presented including a description of the company, research approach and main deployment internals. Finally, in Sect. 4 authors present main preliminary results, wrap up the work and outline future developments.

2 The Framework

In this chapter, authors will present the framework by explaining its phases and outcomes and, Gamiware, the supporting tool developed to deploy the framework in real scenarios.

2.1 Framework Description

Previous works justified the need to develop a methodological framework for gamification efforts in SPI initiatives that takes into account specific features in terms of organization, processes and personnel. The last version of the framework was presented in a previous work [10] as an evolution of previous initiatives in the area [10, 13]. The latter version implemented the lean Startup (Build-Measure-Learn) method initiated by Ries [14]. The resulting framework (Fig. 1) presents the following phases:

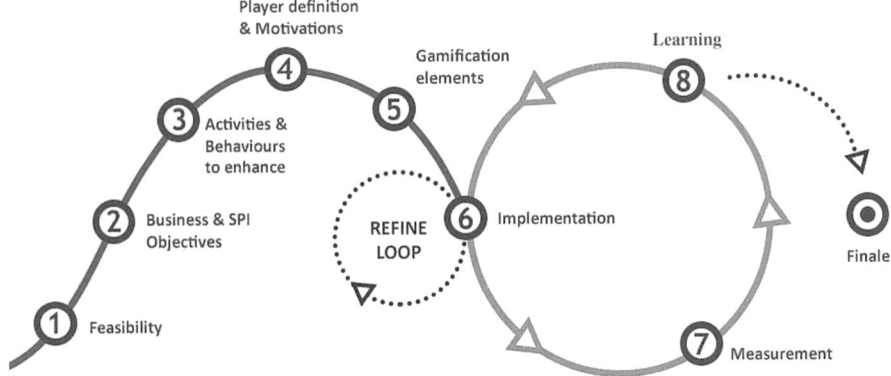

Fig. 1. Phases of the SPI-Gamification framework

PHASE 1: FEASIBILITY: There is a need to work out if the current organization and time is accurate for the deployment of the framework. Therefore, factors such as having the necessary resources, commitment of top managers and an SPI infrastructure to estimate the feasibility of implementing the SPI gamification initiative, need to be analyzed.

PHASE 2: BUSINESS and SPI GOALS: Once verified the applicability, the business objectives and their associated KPIs need to be established. These objectives are defined under the SMART criteria established by [15]. Lastly and aligned with the business goals, SPI objectives and their respective metrics need to be defined. If the software metrics are not very clear, GQM techniques [16] could be used in order to find those metrics.

PHASE 3: ACTIVITIES and BEHAVIOURS TO ENHANCE: SPI activities and the practitioners' behaviors are identified and analyzed. For SPI activities, the level of intrinsic motivation of the SPI activity is analyzed through the IMI test [17]. Next, the walk-through SPI activity is analyzed from the practitioner's perspective through the

Technical Customer Journey Map [18]. Finally, the practitioners' behaviors to be improved in the related activities are identified and analyzed.

PHASE 4: PLAYER DEFINITION and MOTIVATIONS: Consequently, it is necessary to analyse the motivational factors [19, 20] for each of the software practitioners groups or SPI roles. It is also desirable to identify each group of professionals or SPI roles with some type of players' classification [21] for the gamification proposal.

PHASE 5: GAMIFICATION ELEMENTS: For each SPI activity, it is necessary to outline:

1. Dynamic, mechanic and game elements, based on the approach of [5] and refined by means of the Octalysis framework [22] as explained in previous research [23].
2. Metrics for each of the game elements defined above.
3. The Feedback process through which the user receives information on practitioner's activity in real time.
4. Resistance to change and commitment must be considered.

PHASE 6: IMPLEMENTATION: Next, the gamification proposal from the previous phase is executed and implemented at the technological level. However, before implementing the proposal, it is necessary to communicate this to everyone in the organization in order to ensure all parties understand and adopt the process as a critical aspect in SPI initiatives [24]. For this implementation, Gamiware, the tool was developed. This tool is explained in the next section.

PHASE 7: MEASUREMENT: The different key performance indicators (KPIs) of the SPI, motivation metrics and the defined game elements are collected and measured.

PHASE 8: LEARNING: Results are evaluated and the main conclusions for future iterations are considered and documented.

REFINE LOOP: To conclude, taking into account the results of the previous phases, the necessary adjustments are made in stages 2–5.

2.2 Gamiware: The Tool

Gamiware is a SaaS open source tool to support the gamification process in an easy and affordable way. This tool is able to support the defined gamified iterative process making viable gamification implementation easier. The tool has been designed and implemented to be project and process independent. Gamiware is able to adapt to any context by means of a form-oriented parametric customization. Thus, it is possible to code business objectives, software objectives or SPI objectives. Taking into account the intrinsic nature of software process as human capital intensive activity [25], it is also important the identification of software practitioners participating in the gamification process, their tasks and their associated KPIs. Furthermore, with the purpose of improving the alignment of business objectives and activities, it is possible to define the specific contribution of each task to the given business objective and by this mean check the fulfilment of these objectives. The tool is depicted in [26].

3 The Case Study

Due to increasing recognition of the importance of security throughout the entire life cycle, new initiatives strengthening ties for security within the SDLC have been conducted. However there is a need to assist organization in processes that minimize and ideally prevent security.

3.1 The Company

ABC (fictional name) is a SME devoted to develop custom made software solutions placed in Madrid, Spain. This organization follows the ISO/IEC 29110 and some of its members hold the CSSLP (Certified Secure Software Lifecycle Professional) certification.

The aim of the company in the gamification is the improvement of its process of definition, execution and overall management of software testing, normally affected by a general lack of time and resources.

ABC decided to split the validation into two different phases. A first phase of 1 month, would make available 5 people involved in different types of projects. The second phase would extend to 2 departments in full, but its execution would be subject to the results of the first pilot phase.

3.2 Research Approach

The main objective of this research is to validate the framework presented and to study its feasibility and application in practice. Although empirical studies on punctual implementation of gamification techniques are beginning to emerge [27], they do not have enough consistency [2]. Concerning these objectives, the research question that guided the research is,

> **RQ:** does the motivation of the participants increase after carrying out SPI activities under the techniques of gamification established in the methodological framework presented?

To address this research question, participants will be given a questionnaire at the beginning and the end of the implementation. The aim of this instrument is to measure the variation of the motivation of participants in relation to the tasks. These questionnaires are based on task evaluation questionnaire from intrinsic motivation inventory [17]. These questionnaires were adapted to the organizational context and the tasks. Each of the questionnaires were composed of 23 items assessed by means of a 5-point Likert scale. In addition to this questionnaire, multiple data will be collected during the experiment. Data collection will be done in a manual basis.

3.3 The Deployment

The deployment of the gamification proposal involves the implementation of each of the phases of the methodological framework presented. In this way, the viability of the organization was analysed by validating one by one the different factors identified in the feasibility phase.

Once the viability of the initiative was confirmed, the business and SPI objectives were established, with their corresponding KPIs. In this line, established business objectives are related, on the one hand, to the requirement to improve customer satisfaction and, on the other hand, to the need to improve the accuracy in software testing estimation. Subsequently, SPI objectives were established to improve the specification, registration and execution of software tests, as well as the establishment of a data repository that allows to know the actual effort used in each type of project. Finally, it was verified that the objectives specified follow the SMART approach [15].

The next step was the definition of SPI activities, in this case, the definition, execution and registration of software tests. To do so, together with ABC, researchers developed a small Customer Journey Maps [18]. The aim of this instrument is the identification of the roles and the part of the process in which such software tests were executed.

Afterwards, the motivations and types of players of the participants were analysed. Using the models by Baddoo and Hall [19, 20], motivators and demotivators of the two roles involved in the deployment were analysed: project managers and software developers. In addition, the people involved in the gamification proposal were classified according to the player profiles specified by Bartle [21]. The results of this classification indicate a predominance of competitive profiles, at least as the first and second option among the participants.

Once all the information has been collected and analyzed, a fully adapted gamification proposal is proposed. In this line, a competitive dynamic 1 vs. 1 was presented, where the people involved compete with each other in the definition, execution and registration of software tests. The gamification experience is divided into phases according to the different types of tests defined by the organization, in this case, unit tests, integration tests, system tests, and acceptance tests. For the accomplishment of each one of the activities, the participants receive a series of points previously collected in a scheme of rewards. This scheme has been agreed with top managers and is known and accepted by all participants. As a result of the activity, a ranking is created where possible to check the overall ranking, according to each phase is carried out. This is intended to enhance the sense of progress in the activity [5, 28] and social recognition, identified as one of the main intrinsic motivators [29, 30].

Since participants are involved in different types of software projects, the points assigned to each activity are weighted based on the complexity of each project. This weighting was specified by the manager and reviewed by the researchers.

One of the most relevant aspects of the experimentation was the analysis carried out in identifying the ideal tool to implement this proposal within the organization. The final decision and the implementation process of the proposal are detailed in the following section.

Finally, after the definition of the gamification proposal, it is the start of the cycle of the methodological framework in which we are at present, formed by the phases of Implementation, Measurement and Learning.

3.4 The Gamification Tool in Practice

One of the most relevant aspects of the research was the analysis carried out at the time of implementing this gamification proposal within the organization. Taking into account the encouraging results of Gamiware in previous settings [26], it was initially considered as the tool to support the process. However, after analyzing the organization's work in relation to software testing, it was found that, at least in this case, the use of Gamiware could add additional complexity to the process. Therefore, in order to reduce resistance to change as much as possible, we opted for tools that were part of the company's current workflow and ecosystem. ABC is using Gitlab[1] to register software tests in software projects. In addition, the existence of a public API in Gitlab expands the possibilities of integration and automation of tasks in hypothetical later executions of a gamified workflow. Therefore, the following process was established:

1. Developers define software tests within Gitlab by doing an Open of one Issue for each type of test. The tests will be defined on the basis of a nomenclature and the 'Label' functionality will be used to identify the type of test.
2. Each test is self-assigned to each of the authors of the definition, and the researchers subscribe to the Issue in order to receive automatic notifications on updates.
3. In addition, in each test definition, the specific function of Gitlab '/ estimate' is used, which will reflect the estimated time to execute and register the test.
4. Manager gives a range of points according to the quality of the definition, based on the default rewards scheme.
5. For each type of test, the results are executed and recorded. The result is registered in the Issue and, in case of error, the error log is attached. In any case, it is marked with the function '/ spend' the time invested in its execution and registration. The use of these '/ estimate' and '/ spend' functions will allow us to analyze the efficiency in the estimation of the tests.
6. The manager reviews the execution and registration, checks that no cheating has been done, and assigns the corresponding points according to the rewards scheme. Once this is done, he or she marks the Issue as Closed.

4 Results and Conclusions

When analyzing the preliminary results, we must take into account a series of constraints that not only compromise the validity of the results but, based on academic literature, can reduce the effectiveness of gamification techniques. Thus, it should be noted first of all that the feedback provided to the participants has not been possible in real time, but every 12–24 h due to a lack of technological integration in the workflow of the company

---

[1] https://about.gitlab.com/.

and after a manual review. This fact is against literature on the topic [5, 28–31] and this fact regarding the reduction of the effectiveness due to a lack of integration in the workflow becomes has been underlined in previous works by authors [26]. Secondly, participants have not only done the definition of software tests, their execution and registration, but also carry out associated software development. Literature reported biases and under performance in error detection by developers [32, 33]. In the third and last place, it is important to note that the sample is small, which connotes the generalization of the results. However, in spite of these limitations, a number of noteworthy preliminary results can be anticipated:

1. Although Gamiware has been designed in an adaptable and flexible way [26], It appears that its use in practice will only work in very controlled environments and under very specific activities. This conclusion is based on the lack of integration of Gamiware in the work workflow of the company and confirms one of the assumptions that were made in previous studies [26] where preliminary implementations of Gamiware were carried out in controlled environments. In organizations this lack of integration implies that, in order to implement gamification techniques through Gamiware, it will be necessary, on the one hand, to devote time to learning how the tool works, although it is not complicated, implies different ways of doing things and this leads to the emergence of resistance to change. Therefore, it does not seem recommendable to add factors that can lead to resistance to change in the implementation of gamification techniques in organizations.
2. The feedback of the activities carried out should not be extended, as much as 12–14 h after completion. After that time, it is common for the participants to ask what their score is and deviations in the results of these tasks are perceived in advance. Feedback is one of the main motivators identified for developers, according to Baddoo and Hall [19, 20]. Due to the lack of real-time feedback, there is a risk of breaking the cycle of motivation: motivation-action-feedback [5, 31].
3. Achieving the commitment of the top managers is a very hard task. Even though they have been verbally committed, day-to-day orders and any urge tends to break that commitment and the gamification proposal execution. Probably one of the main reasons behind this fact is the lack of a perceived need for urgency in improving SPI activities. In fact, "Need sense of urgency" as feasibility factor has been one of the integrated modifications after the validation of experts reflected in a previous investigation [23].
4. As the sample is small, it becomes difficult to implement collaborative or social game mechanics, which are identified as the most effective gamification techniques in practical applications [27]. In addition, although it has not happened in this experiment, it is anticipated that with a small sample it is difficult to establish a uniform gamification proposal since there is a risk that the profile of the players involved will be very different from one another.
5. If the nonparticipants in the gamification proposal are aware that other partners are participating in an initiative in relation to performance in a given SPI activity that they also perform, there is an interesting effect: in the short term, non-participants raise their performance in such SPI activity artificially only by the perception that

they are being observed and under the hypothesis that their work will be evaluated/compared to that of the participants in the gamification proposal.
6. In the middle of the first pilot phase of the experiment, and in the absence of results of intrinsic motivation, it can be affirmed that the perceived performance increase in the definition, registration and execution of software tests has improved significantly.

Future work will focus on validating the framework presented in different types of organizations assuring a greater sample for the experimentation. In addition, the nature of SPI activities will be diverse. Other future developments include the evaluation of the framework through affective computing techniques with biometric signals during framework activities evaluation. Finally it is intended to deploy the framework in a setting covering all the ISO/IEC 29110 areas [34, 35].

References

1. Nacke, L.E., Deterding, S.: The maturing of gamification research. Comput. Hum. Behav. **71**, 450–454 (2017)
2. Seaborn, K., Fels, D.I.: Gamification in theory and action: a survey. Int. J. Hum. Comput. Stud. **74**, 14–31 (2015)
3. Deterding, S.: Gamification: designing for motivation. Interactions **19**, 14–17 (2012)
4. Hsu, C.-L., Chen, Y.-C., Yang, T.-N., Lin, W.-K.: Do website features matter in an online gamification context? Focusing on the mediating roles of user experience and attitude. Telemat. Inf. **34**, 196–205 (2017)
5. Werbach, K., Hunter, D.: For the Win: How Game Thinking Can Revolutionize Your Business. Wharton Digital Press, Philadelphia (2012)
6. Wood, L.C., Reiners, T.: Gamification. In: Khosrow-Pour, M. (ed.) Encyclopedia of Information Science and Technology, 3rd edn., pp. 3039–3047. IGI Global, Hershey (2015)
7. Yilmaz, M., O'Connor, R.: A scrumban integrated gamification approach to guide software process improvement: a Turkish case study. Teh. Vjesn. Tech. Gaz. **23**, 237–245 (2016)
8. Xu, F., Buhalis, D., Weber, J.: Serious games and the gamification of tourism. Tour. Manag. **60**, 244–256 (2017)
9. Dorling, A., McCaffery, F.: The gamification of SPICE. Softw. Process Improv. Capab. Determ. 295–301 (2012)
10. Herranz, E., Colomo-Palacios, R., de Amescua Seco, A., Yilmaz, M.: Gamification as a Disruptive factor in software process improvement initiatives. J-JUCS **20**, 885–906 (2014)
11. Mittelmark, A.: Enterprise gamification - buzzword or business tool? (2012). https://www.digitalpulse.pwc.com.au/enterprise-gamification-pwc-report/
12. Pedreira, O., García, F., Brisaboa, N., Piattini, M.: Gamification in software engineering – a systematic mapping. Inf. Softw. Technol. **57**, 157–168 (2015)
13. Herranz, E., Colomo-Palacios, R., Amescua-Seco, A.: Towards a new approach to supporting top managers in SPI organizational change management. Procedia Technol. **9**, 129–138 (2013)
14. Ries, E.: The Lean Startup: How Today's Entrepreneurs Use Continuous Innovation To Create Radically Successful Businesses. Crown Business, New York (2011)
15. Doran, G.T.: There's a SMART way to write management's goals and objectives. Manage. Rev. **70**, 35–36 (1981)
16. Basili, V.R.: Software modeling and measurement: the Goal/Question/Metric paradigm (1992)

17. Ryan, R.M., Koestner, R., Deci, E.L.: Ego-involved persistence: when free-choice behavior is not intrinsically motivated. Motiv. Emot. **15**, 185–205 (1991)
18. Richardson, A.: Using customer journey maps to improve customer experience. Harv. Bus. Rev. **15** (2010). https://hbr.org/2010/11/using-customer-journey-maps-to/
19. Baddoo, N., Hall, T.: Motivators of software process improvement: an analysis of practitioners' views. J. Syst. Softw. **62**, 85–96 (2002)
20. Baddoo, N., Hall, T.: De-motivators for software process improvement: an analysis of practitioners' views. J. Syst. Softw. **66**, 23–33 (2003)
21. Bartle, R.: Hearts, clubs, diamonds, spades: players who suit MUDs. J. MUD Res. **1**, 19 (1996)
22. Chou, Y.K., Fuqua, J., Yuan, W.: Actionable Gamification: Beyond Points, Badges, and Leaderboards. CreateSpace Independent Publishing Platform (2015)
23. Herranz, E., Colomo-Palacios, R., de Amescua Seco, A., Sánchez-Gordón, M.-L.: Towards a gamification framework for software process improvement initiatives: construction and validation. J. Univers. Comput. Sci. **22**, 1509–1532 (2016)
24. Korsaa, M., Biro, M., Messnarz, R., Johansen, J., Vohwinkel, D., Nevalainen, R., Schweigert, T.: The SPI Manifesto and the ECQA SPI manager certification scheme. J. Softw. Evol. Process **24**(5), 525–540 (2012)
25. Casado-Lumbreras, C., Colomo-Palacios, R., Gomez-Berbis, J.M., Garcia-Crespo, A.: Mentoring programmes: a study of the Spanish software industry. Int. J. Learn. Intellect. Cap. **6**, 293–302 (2009)
26. Herranz, E., Colomo-Palacios, R., de Amescua Seco, A.: Gamiware: a gamification platform for software process improvement. In: O'Connor, R.V., Akkaya, M.U., Kemaneci, K., Yilmaz, M., Poth, A., Messnarz, R. (eds.) EuroSPI 2015. CCIS, vol. 543, pp. 127–139. Springer, Cham (2015). doi:10.1007/978-3-319-24647-5_11
27. Hamari, J., Koivisto, J., Sarsa, H.: Does gamification work? – a literature review of empirical studies on gamification. In: 2014 47th Hawaii International Conference on System Sciences (HICSS), pp. 3025–3034 (2014)
28. Zichermann, G., Linder, J.: The Gamification Revolution: How Leaders Leverage Game Mechanics to Crush the Competition. McGraw Hill Professional, New York (2013)
29. Paharia, R.: Loyalty 3.0: How to Revolutionize Customer and Employee Engagement with Big Data and Gamification. McGraw-Hill Professional, New York (2013)
30. Burke, B.: Gamify: How Gamification Motivates People to Do Extraordinary Things. Bibliomotion Inc., Boston (2014)
31. Marczewski, A.: Even Ninja Monkeys Like to Play. Gamified UK, London (2015)
32. Stacy, W., MacMillan, J.: Cognitive bias in software engineering. Commun. ACM **38**, 57–63 (1995)
33. Çalıklı, G., Bener, A.B.: Influence of confirmation biases of developers on software quality: an empirical study. Softw. Qual. J. **21**, 377–416 (2013)
34. Sanchez-Gordon, M.-L., O'Connor, R.V., Colomo-Palacios, R.: Evaluating VSEs viewpoint and sentiment towards the ISO/IEC 29110 standard: a two country grounded theory study. In: Rout, T., O'Connor, R.V., Dorling, A. (eds.) SPICE 2015. CCIS, vol. 526, pp. 114–127. Springer, Cham (2015). doi:10.1007/978-3-319-19860-6_10
35. Larrucea, X., O'Connor, R.V., Colomo-Palacios, R., Laporte, C.Y.: Software process improvement in very small organizations. IEEE Softw. **33**, 85–89 (2016)

ProDecAdmin: A Game Scenario Design Tool for Software Project Management Training

Alejandro Calderón[1(✉)], Mercedes Ruiz[1], and Rory V. O'Connor[2]

[1] University of Cádiz, Cádiz, Spain
{alejandro.calderon,mercedes.ruiz}@uca.es
[2] Dublin City University, Dublin, Ireland
rory.oconnor@dcu.ie

Abstract. Teaching Software Project Management (SPM) for Information Technology (IT) learners is a relevance issue. The necessity of teaching SPM in a highly practical way moves trainers towards the use of new methods and techniques such as simulations, serious games or gamification strategies. The majority of the existing serious games for SPM do not offer flexibility, in terms of the ability to provide and dynamically change game scenarios during the life of the serious game, and not allow assessing learners' new skill automatically. In this paper, we introduce the administration tool of the serious game ProDec, that allow trainers to design the game scenarios of the game trying to overcome the lacks found in the scope of serious games for SPM.

Keywords: Gamification · Serious game · Game scenario design · Software Project Management · Education

1 Introduction

Teaching SPM for IT learners is a topical issue that has always been supported by organizations such as the Association for Computing Machinery (ACM) and IEEE-Computer Society [1]. These organizations have not only highlighted the importance of this topic, but they have also emphasized the need of teaching SPM in a highly practical way, where learners can put into practice their knowledge in real-life scenarios. This necessity moves trainers towards the use of new methods and techniques that allow teaching in a highly practical way, promoting active learning and increasing the motivation and the engagement of learners in the learning-teaching process of SPM [2, 3].

Gamification is "the use of game elements and game design techniques in non-game contexts" [4]. It has become "an increasingly popular approach to increasing end-user engagement in many contexts, including employee productivity, marketing, citizens awareness, and education" [5]. The design and use of gamification strategies are one of the new methods using to improve user's engagement, motivation, and performance within the learning-teaching process and to provide a more interesting education in software engineering [6]. Once of the common practice in the road to apply gamification in education is the use of games as a component of the gamification strategy [7]. The use of games and simulation-based experiences allows learners to experiment, learn from their own mistakes and acquire experience with real-life scenarios within a free-risk environment. These kinds of games, designed with a different purpose than only entertainment, are called serious games [8, 9].

Regarding the scope of serious games for training SPM, there are a limited number of games available [10–12], with well-known examples being: SimSoft [13], SimSE [14], X-MED [15], DELIVER! [16]. The analysis of the current proposals of serious games for teaching SPM allows shows their main weaknesses in this scope are that: (a) they focus on learning specific techniques of project management or specific stages of the project's lifecycle; (b) they do not usually reach all levels of Bloom's taxonomy; (c) they do not allow assessing learner's new skills automatically; and (d) their flexibility in terms of game scenarios is very limited [17].

Regarding the lack of the serious games for training SPM, in this paper, we introduce the administration tool of ProDec, a simulation-based serious game for SPM. This tool tries to overcome the main weaknesses found in this scope by allowing trainers to design the game scenarios of the serious game. The structure of the paper is as follows: Sect. 2 shows the background of this work. Section 3 introduces the administration tool of ProDec for game scenarios design. Finally, Sect. 4 summarizes the paper and presents our conclusions and future work.

2 Background

In previous works, we have introduced ProDec [18], a simulation-based serious game to teach, motivate and assess learners in the learning-teaching process of SPM concepts and practices, and we have analyzed different features about their capability to be integrated into the learning process [17] or their ability to cover some software processes of international standards [19].

Among these features we can find that ProDec's main goal is to place learners in a virtual environment where the can manage software projects and practice their knowledge with real-life scenarios in a risk-free environment. For this, the serious game provides two different modes of play, called "Full Play" and "Quick Play". In a "Full Play", learners create their own project plans from scratch and then, they execute the simulation of their own project scenario. On the other hand, in a "Quick Play", learners play with a project scenario created by trainers. In both modes of play, the main goal is to successful manage a project. This involves ending the project within the time and costs constraints established on the project plan of the scenario.

In order to allow these features, ProDec is part of a learning-teaching environment that follows a three-layer architecture and has been developed using Java, Anylogic and MySQL technologies. Two software tools developed using Java and the simulation model deal with the presentation and business layer and two databases managed by MySQL deal with the data layer of the architecture. As we can see in Fig. 1, the ProDec environment is composed of the following applications:

(a) ProDec is the software application (simulation-based serious game) used by the players. This application is composed of three main stages that allow players to

engage in the game and put in practices their knowledge about SPM. The three main stages are described as follow:
- An initial stage, called Onset, where players chose the mode of play and create or select the project scenario that they want to play it. At the end of this stage, the game automatically generates the source file of the discrete-event simulation model required to simulate the project plan of the scenario.
- A simulation stage, called Execution, where players execute the simulation of the project scenario and monitor it in order to cover the goal of the game.
- A final stage, called End, which finishes the game scenario and performs the players' assessment by applying the criteria set by the trainers for the scenario that has been played.

(b) ProDecAdmin is the software application that allows trainers to manage all the information required by ProDec. The trainers use this application to design the different game scenarios for the "Quick Play" mode and to set the rubrics for players' assessment.

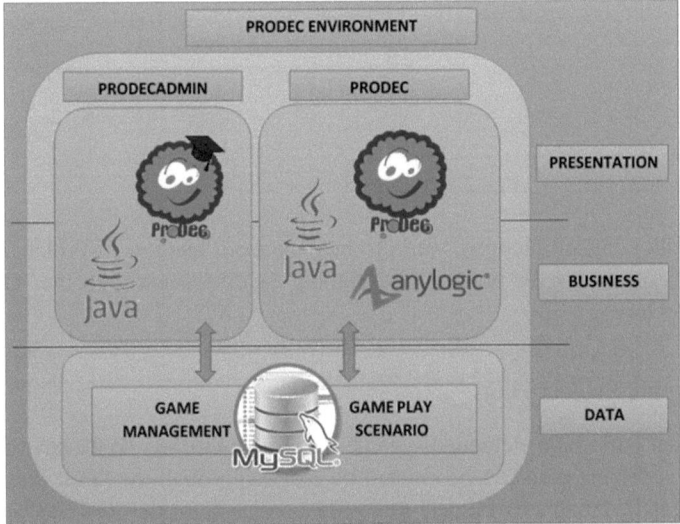

Fig. 1. ProDec's architecture.

Taking into account the architecture of ProDec environment, in the following sections, we introduce ProDecAdmin, the administration tool of ProDec for trainers that allows them to design game scenarios for teaching SPM according to their learning goals.

3 ProDecAdmin

ProDecAdmin is an application to be used by trainers within the ProDec environment with the goal that they can design all the needed elements for the correct operation of

ProDec and for assessing of the players' performance through the ProDec scenarios (see Fig. 2). In order to cover the functionalities mentioned above, the tool allows trainers to perform the following main activities: (a) creating all the needed elements to design project plans that will be used by ProDec; (b) establishing the criteria to assess players' performance during the use of ProDec; and (c) creating game scenarios for the "Quick Play" mode of ProDec.

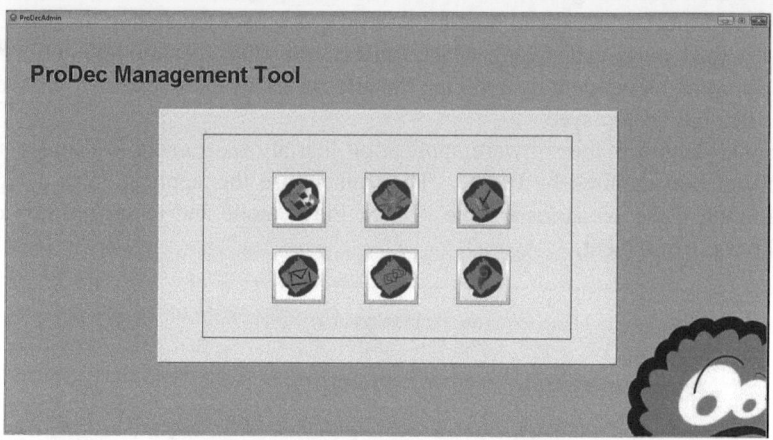

Fig. 2. ProDecAdmin's main screen.

In the following subsections, we introduce the main features of ProDecAdmin and the elements involve in the process of designing a game scenario for the "Quick Play" mode of ProDec.

3.1 Designing Project Plans

A project plan is the main element of a game scenario in ProDec. As we have commented previously, a project plan can be created by players through the "Full Play" mode of ProDec or can be created by trainers to design a scenario for the "Quick Play" mode of ProDec.

The administration tool, ProDecAdmin, allows trainers to create these project plans as a part of the process to design a game scenario. For this, the tool provides trainers three main functionalities: tasks, risks and project management. The functionalities of tasks and risk management allows trainers to design general project tasks and project risks that can be included in a project during its design.

Furthermore, the project management tool allows trainers to manage and design project plans. As we can see in Fig. 3, to design a project plan, trainers have to follow a five-stage process that guides them from the definition of the project context to the definition of the risks that can be occurred during the project execution. These five stages are defined as following:

- **Project Information (PI).** In this stage, trainers provide the general information of the project such as its scope, objective, specifications, etc. and the specific information of the project that is needed to start the size estimation stage. Through this stage, trainers define the context of the project scenario and the complexity of the project in terms of the project requirements and duration.
- **Size Estimation (SE).** In this stage, trainers perform the size estimation of the project. This stage allows trainers to estimate the effort in term of human resources and costs of the project.
- **Project Team Definition (PTD).** In this stage, trainers design and define the human resources of the project and establish the composition of the work team. This stage also allows trainers to design the features in terms of experience and personality traits of each human resource involves in the project work team.
- **Tasks Definition (TD).** In this stage, trainers define the project tasks, estimate the duration of each of them, allocate the human resources for each task and create a schedule of the project tasks taking into account the estimated start and completion dates, the assigned human resources and the dependency of the tasks. Through this stage, trainers can increase or reduce the complexity of the game scenario depending on the number of tasks, the human resources involve and the different combination of teams and tasks dependency.
- **Risks Analysis (RA).** In this stage, trainers define the risks that can occur during the project execution. This means that trainers define the risks that can produce changes in a game scenario during its execution.

At the end of this process, trainers have evolved a project plan that can be used in a game scenario, with complexity dependent upon the different features related to the tasks, risks and human resources features involve in the project. Moreover, the different elements involved in a project plan that trainers have to design, allows them to create project plans focusing on specific learning goals such as the influence of synergy, size or experience of the human resource in the productivity of a work team, the important of defining a good schedule of project tasks, etc.

3.2 Designing Players Assessment

The players' assessment process involve elements from several sources within ProDec environment such as the initial estimates, the project monitoring data and the kind of decisions that the players made during the play of a scenario. In this process, trainers need to define the rubrics that will be used to assess the players' performance during a game scenario. ProDecAdmin allows trainers to design these rubrics.

In the game, a rubric is composed of a set of sections. At the same time, each section is composed of a set of assessment criteria. An assessment criterion links the information recorded in the rubric with the information recorded during the game. By using a labelling system, the labels describing the skills of an assessment criterion are matched with the records of the game that contain the information needed to assess such criterion. Then, the design of a rubric involves the definition of each section and the selection of the labels that are going to be assessed by the criteria.

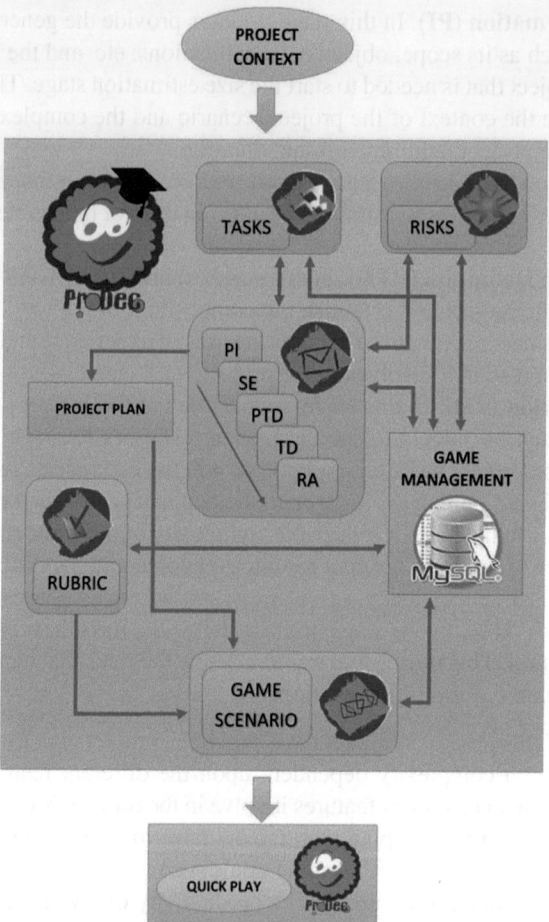

Fig. 3. Game scenario design process.

3.3 Designing Game Scenarios

Once trainers have designed a project plan and an assessment rubric, the last step in a game scenario design is to link the project scenario with the assessment rubric that trainers want to use in its evaluation process. Using ProDecAdmin, trainers are able to create new game scenarios for the "Quick Play" mode of ProDec by connecting a defined rubric with a designed project. As a result, players can select a new game scenario when they play a Quick Play with ProDec.

4 Discussion and Further Works

Regarding the relevance of teaching SPM in a highly practical way, there is no doubt that the use of gamification, simulation and serious games are good methods and techniques to bring real-life scenarios to the learning-teaching process and turn theoretical lectures in a more practical environment. In this paper, taking into account our previous works, we have identified the main lacks found in the scope of serious games for SPM and we have commented the main features of ProDec, with the goal to introduce ProDecAdmin, the administration tool of ProDec that provides trainers with an environment for designing game scenarios according to their learning goals.

Flexibility, defined as the ability of a serious game to provide game scenarios that can be changed dynamically during the game, is an important feature to take into account in a serious game for SPM. In a game for teaching SPM, if game scenarios are static, learners will always experience the same activities. This maybe uninteresting for learners and they may quickly lose interest. At the other side, if game scenarios change dynamically and on a real-time basis, learners can face different challenges and apply their knowledge in different situations. In addition, the lifecycle of the SG as a learning resource within a course can be longer, as trainers can set up the scenarios repetitively.

SPM is a subject where learners need to take into account an extensive amount of information during the whole project lifecycle and they need to analyze the information of the project and make decisions continuously. Thus, a serious game that allows automatic assessment helps (a) trainers to analyze and evaluate all the actions performed by learners during the game scenario and (b) learners to get instant feedback on their performance, helping them, at the same time, to improve their knowledge during the game scenario.

The features of ProDecAdmin provide a high degree of flexibility, thus trainers are able to design any game scenario for ProDec that they want in order to cover their learning goals. Moreover, it allows trainers to design the assessment criteria to evaluate the users' performance, knowledge acquisition and progression with the game, which will be used by the ProDec in order to provide an automatically assessment report of the game scenario played. Therefore, we can conclude that ProDecAdmin helps to overcome the lacks of flexibility and automatic assessment identified in the scope of serious games for SPM.

Finally, from our point of view, we believe that simulation tools, serious games and gamification strategies are needed to prepare new practitioners for their professional life. For that reason, we go on working in this scope in order to improve the features of ProDecAdmin and ProDec. Moreover, we are evaluating the benefits of integrating our game with social networks and designing a gamification strategy that integrates the use of ProDec, in order to enrich the learning-teaching process and allow learners to acquire the concepts and practices of SPM in a practical environment where they can experiment with real-life scenarios during their studies.

Acknowledgements. This work has been partially supported by the Spanish Ministry of Science and Technology with AEI/FEDER/UE funds (grants TIN2013-46928-C3-2-R and TIN2016-76956-C3-3-R) and the Andalusian Plan for Research, Development and Innovation (grant TIC-195).

References

1. ACM/IEEE-CS Joint Task Force on Computing Curricula: Computer Science Curricula 2013. ACM Press and IEEE Computer Society Press (2013)
2. Kosa, M., Yilmaz, M., O'Connor, R., Clarke, P.: Software engineering education and games: a systematic literature review. J. Univ. Comput. Sci. **22**(12), 1558–1574 (2016)
3. Martí-Parreño, J., Méndez-Ibáñez, E., Alonso-Arroyo, A.: The use of gamification in education: a bibliometric and text mining analysis. J. Comput. Assist. Learn. **32**(6), 663–676 (2016)
4. Werbach, K., Hunter, D.: For the Win: How Game Thinking can Revolutionize Your Business. Wharton Digital Press, Philadelphia (2012)
5. Sheth, S.K., Bell, J.S., Kaiser, G.E.: Increasing student engagement in software engineering with Gamification (2012)
6. Pedreira, O., García, F., Brisaboa, N., Piattini, M.: Gamification in software engineering - A systematic mapping. Inf. Softw. Technol. **57**, 157–168 (2015)
7. Yildirim, I.: The effects of gamification-based teaching practices on student achievement and students' attitudes toward lessons. Internet High. Edu. **33**, 86–92 (2017)
8. Abt, C.: Serious Games, Lanhan, MD: University Press of America (2002)
9. Zyda, M.: From visual simulation to virtual reality to games. Computer **38**, 25–32 (2005)
10. Caulfield, C., Xia, J., Veal, D., Maj, S.: A systematic survey of games used for software engineering education. Mod. Appl. Sci. **5**(6), 28–43 (2011)
11. Calderón, A., Ruiz, M.: A systematic literature review on serious games evaluation: An application to software project management. Comput. Edu. **87**, 396–422 (2015)
12. Petri, G., von Wangenheim, C.G.: How games for computing education are evaluated? A systematic literature review. Comput. Edu. (2017). http://dx.doi.org/10.1016/j.compedu.2017.01.004. (In Press, Accepted Manuscript)
13. Caulfield, C., Veal, D., Maj, S.: Teaching software engineering project management – a novel approach for software engineering programs. Mod. Appl. Sci. **5**(5), 87–104 (2011)
14. Navarro, E.O., Hoek, A.V.D.: SimSE: an interactive simulation game for software engineering education. In: Proceedings of the 7th IASTED International Conference on Computers and Advanced Technology in Education, Kauai, Hawaii (2004)
15. Von Wangenheim, C.G., Thiry, M., Kochanski, D.: Empirical evaluation of an educational game on software measurement. Empir. Softw. Eng. **14**(4), 418–452 (2009)
16. Von Wangenheim, C.G., Savi, R., Borgatto, A.F.: DELIVER! – an educational game for teaching earned value management in computing courses. Inf. Softw. Technol. **54**(3), 286–298 (2012)
17. Calderón, A., Ruiz, M.: Bringing real-life practice in software project management through a simulation-based serious game. In: Proceedings of the 6th International Conference on Computer Supported Education, Barcelona, Spain (2014)
18. Calderón, A., Ruiz, M.: ProDec: a serious game for software project management training. In: Proceedings of the 8th ICSEA, Venice, Italy (2013)
19. Calderón, A., Ruiz, M.: Coverage of ISO/IEC 12207 software lifecycle process by a simulation-based serious game. In: Proceedings of spice, Dublin, Ireland (2016)

State of the Use of Gamification Elements in Software Development Teams

Mirna Muñoz[1(✉)], Luis Hernández[1], Jezreel Mejia[1], Gloria Piedad Gasca-Hurtado[2], and María Clara Gómez-Alvarez[2]

[1] Centro de Investigación en Matemáticas, Av. Universidad no 222, 98068 Zacatecas, Mexico
{mirna.munoz,luis.hernandez,jmejia}@cimat.mx
[2] Facultad de Ingeniería, Maestría en Ingeniería de Software, Universidad de Medellín, Carrera 87 no. 30-65, Medellín, Colombia
{gpgasca,mcgomez}@udem.edu.co

Abstract. One of the fundamental skill that every professional should have, especially in the area of software engineering, is collaborative work, because teams' members are required to collaborate to develop software. In this environment, one of the techniques currently being used for achieving activities involving collaborative teamwork is gamification. However, there is a lack of techniques to create software development teams through gamification. This paper presents a study of the use of gamification elements in the software engineering environment for collaborative work, in order to identify those elements that can be applied to create highly effective teams for software development.

Keywords: Gamification elements · Software engineering · Teamwork · Collaborative work

1 Introduction

In software engineering, team members require to collaborate for the development of software. Therefore, working in a team is an essential soft-skill that a software engineer needs [1]. However, even when organizations benefit from higher people commitment and faster implementation of changes, as a result of employees working together in teams, not all teams provide the expected results due to the human factors.

Gamification techniques are methods that promote teamwork through motivation and improved communication skills, so that teams can achieve better work performances [2].

The term gamification applies to any use of an element of a game in a non game environment, in order to obtain better experiences and commitment of participants [3].

Gamification is extending the use of games in different environments with not just a ludic purpose [4, 5]. In environments such as education, health, marketing or software engineering it is being used increasingly.

Specifically in software engineering environment, gamification is used within educational and industrial environments as follows:

- In educational environments, gamification is a viable tool because it effectively promotes participant interaction in classroom projects [6, 7]. It motivates students [8] to learn more as learning becomes more enjoyable [9].
- In industrial environments, gamification initiatives are used to improve social interaction [10] and to improve communication skills [4] through the use of web applications, questions and answer platforms, or new centers.

The goal of this paper is to identify the use of the gamification elements currently being applied during teamwork within the software engineering environment, in order to identify those that can be applied to reinforce the creation of high effective teams for software development.

The rest of the paper is organized as follows: Sect. 2 describes the related works; Sect. 3 describes the gamification elements; Sect. 4 shows the results of performing the analysis to the gamification elements; and Sect. 5 presents the discussion, conclusions and future work.

2 Related Works

This section shows five papers that present relevant knowledge regarding the use of gamification in teamwork.

- *A serious game to develop and assess teamwork competency* [11]: this research work aims to demonstrate the consequences in decision-making to improve communication among team members. The research presents an assessment of a teamwork, supported by gamification elements, using a serious game. It is useful to know the impact of the gamification elements in a team.
- *Gamiware: A gamification platform for software process improvement* [12]: this research work aims to improve the motivation team members have to participate in software process improvement activities. The research presents a platform focused on supporting the implementation of software process improvement using gamification elements. It is useful to know the team performance with respect to the use of a web platform that uses gamification elements.
- *Structuring flipped classes with lightweight teams and gamification* [13]: this research work aims to integrate light teams to improve students learning in programming courses. The research focuses on teamwork in academic environment. It is useful to identify the benefits of teams based learning by taking off the stress associated with the projects development risks.
- *What do we know about high performance teams in software engineering? Results from a systematic review* [14]: this research work aims to understand the environments and conditions under which software engineering teams work. The research provides an overview of the factors that a software engineering team should take into account to become a high performance team. It is useful for analyzing the factors that have high and low impacts upon a software engineering team.
- *Increasing collaborative communications in programming course with gamification: a case study* [15]: this work aims to improve the communication of students using a

gamification model. The work analyzes the gamification elements that can increment the communication in teams in academic environment. It is useful to know which factors of communication to take into account in a team.

3 Gamification Elements Description

To identify the gamification elements presented in this paper, a systematic review was performed, published in [16]. As result, a sample of 31 primary studies were analyzed in which it was possible to identify a set of 11 gamification elements that are next briefly described. The description of the benefits of their use are analyzed in next sections.

- *Leaderboards:* are useful to show the user progress or success and to compare it with that of the other users.
- *Points systems:* are useful to measure the success in achieving an activity.
- *Badges:* are useful to represent the success or achievement of personal goals and, therefore to motivate an individual to achieve his/her goals.
- *Levels:* are useful to provide challenges, and to increase the challenge difficulty depending on the individual progress.
- *Progress Bars:* are useful to provide an overview of the achieved progress when performing an activity.
- *Rewards:* are useful to make a gift to an individual in recognition of his/her performed work.
- *Scores:* are useful to measure a user performance while executing an activity.
- *Challenges:* are useful to make users apply their knowledge and skills to achieve an activity.
- *Achievements:* are useful to represent the specific goals in a main activity.
- *Feedback:* is useful to provide information messages to identify how to perform the activities.
- *Unblocking content:* is useful to unblock activities when users achieve goals.

4 Results of the Gamification Elements Analysis

This section describes the results of performing an analysis of the actual state of the gamification elements in software development teams. As mentioned before, the results shown in this paper were obtained by performing a systematic review published in [16]. The systematic review was focused on the following three questions.

- *RQ1. What have been the main implementations or tools for applying gamification elements?* This question aims to identify the tools used to implement gamification techniques in teamwork.
- *RQ2. What are the goals set out to achieve with gamification elements?* This question aims to identify gamification elements, the goals in the implementation of the gamification elements and why they have been selected.

- *RQ3. What has been the result of the implementation of gamification elements?* This question aims to identify what are some of the key aspects or factors that need to be taken into account to achieve established goals.

4.1 Most Used Gamification Elements

As Fig. 1 shows, the most used gamification elements are: (1) leaderboards, (2) points systems, (3) badges, (4) levels and (5) progress bars. It is important to highlight that in a general way; the combination of 2 or more gamification elements seems to generate good results. However, the expected success is subject to the application environment.

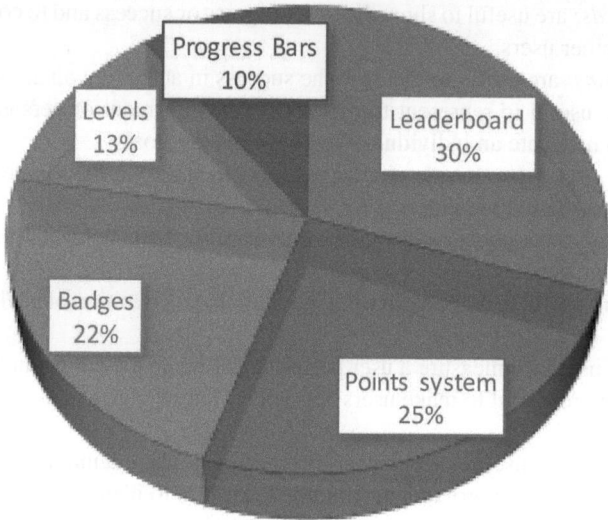

Fig. 1. Most used gamification elements

As figure shows leaderboards were the most applied gamification element. It is a useful gamification element to improve participation [17], as well as to produce a positive influence in students [18]. The second most used gamification element were points systems. They increase students' participation, commitment and motivation [4].

Other gamification elements such as rewards, scores, challenges, achievements, feedback and unblocking content are less used. Finally, it is important to mention that typically in health and marketing environments the gamification elements: points systems, badges and leaderboards are named as PBLs.

4.2 Support Tools

According to the results, four support tools were identified to implement gamification elements, described below:

1. *Web platforms*: The most common tool used to implement gamification elements; refers to the use of previous created or new web platforms to implement gamification elements. These platforms have been developed for: supporting process improvement [17], supporting knowledge management [19], improving the social interaction and learning in enterprise environments [14], and increasing collaborative communication [12].
   The use of web platforms has been shown to increase team members' motivation when participating and performing designated activities.
2. *Own methods*: Refers to the creation of new methods instead of relying on existing methods or tools to apply gamification elements. Own methods have been used and developed for: increasing user motivation and happiness perception [3, 19] and improving students' participation in a classroom [20].
3. *Learning Manage System-web platform*: This refers to the use of gamification elements in Learning Manage System (LMS) to reinforce academic learning. LMS has been developed for improving the abilities and knowledge of students [21] and integrating teams [13].
4. *Serious game*: This refers to the use of serious games for applying gamification elements to reinforce knowledge in enterprise environments. For example, serious game has been developed to explain the consequences decision making has, and how it can improve communication among team members [11].

4.3 Implementation Environment

The three environments, in which gamification elements have been implemented, are the:

1. *Classroom*: This refers to how gamification elements are used to improve education. The use of gamification elements in classrooms facilitates learning for students. Examples of what the use of gamification elements in classrooms have been developed for demonstrating the abilities of students in the software development [22], improving the education of students in software development [18] and improving the students learning [8, 10].
2. *Software Development*: This refers to the application of gamification elements in performing software development activities. Gamification elements in software development have been developed for including gamification in software development [7] and applying gamification in code review activities [23].
3. *Software process improvement*: This refers to the use of gamification elements to promote the participation of individuals in activities related to software process improvement. Gamification elements in software process improvement has been developed for achieving the participation of individuals in software process improvement using SPICE [24].

4.4 Barriers to Adopt Gamification

This section provides a list of barriers that make successful implementation of gamification elements difficult due to its negative impact. The barriers have been classified as: users' barriers and production barriers.

1. User Barriers:
    - *Not taking care of participants' feelings*: as a result, the participants can feel frustrated and unmotivated. Therefore, it is necessary to take into account the enjoyment of participants.
    - *Too much time to perform an activity*: as a result, the participants can feel bored. Therefore, it is necessary to consider the time activities take to be completed in a gamification proposal.
    - *Not balanced difficulty of the challenges*: as a result, the participants can feel frustrated. Therefore, challenges should be set to the level of the participants' knowledge, so that, they are motivated to achieve the presented challenge.
2. Production Barriers:
    - *Bad estimation of budget and time to develop the gamification proposal*: as a result, the costs of developing the gamification proposal can deviate significantly from expected time and cost values. Therefore, it is necessary that before developing the gamification proposal, the time and cost of it should be taken into account.
    - *Not taking care of population size*: as a result, the obtained performance of the gamification proposal can be affected so that it is not possible to generalize the results. Therefore, it is necessary to validate a gamification proposal to have a sample significant enough to be able to generalize the gamification proposal results.
    - *Developing the gamification proposal taking into account a specific group of individuals*: as a result, not all participants can be benefited with the gamification proposal. Therefore, it is necessary that the gamification proposal reflects the learning style of most of the users, so that, they can reinforce their abilities and knowledge.
    - *Defects injection rate developing a gamification proposal*: as a result, the amount of defects in the gamification proposal increases in the real environment without having the expected results. Therefore, during the gamification proposal development it is important to consider its validation and verification as well as the real environment in which it will be implemented.

4.5 Benefits of Using Gamification

This sections provides a list of benefits identified, related to the use of gamification. The benefits have been classified in: academic environment benefits and enterprise environment benefits.

1. Academic environment benefits:
    - *Supports the use of software development methodologies and tools:* the application of gamification in software engineering has achieved increased commitment, participation and motivation of students. Moreover, the students have showed interest in getting new knowledge.

- *Improves the participation in academic projects*: the application of gamification has achieved the motivation of students related to an effective interaction and participation in academic projects in subjects related to software development.
- *Facilitates learning in programming courses*: gamification has demonstrated to be a great support to motivate students to achieve 100% of their grade in programming subject. Besides, it allows for getting knowledge in new technologies and development of best practices.
- *Improves communication among students*: the use of gamification supports the collaboration of students working in teams to solve problems, achieve difficult task or additional activities, so that, it improves the communication among team members reducing the feedback time. Besides, students are motivated to share their experience.

2. Enterprise environment benefits:
   - *Promotes the participation in organizational specific activities*: the application of gamification improves the participation of individuals in the adoption of activities. Besides, it offers them the opportunity to get a faster feedback regarding the way they are preforming the assigned activities, so that, the activities can be performed in a correct way and in time.
   - *Improves the social interaction*: the application of gamification has encouraged the improvement of the individuals' participation in the development of assigned activities and the collaboration among them in an adequate way, so that, the teams get reinforced. Besides, it has allowed individuals to share their knowledge and experience with others, increasing their commitment and enthusiasm.

5 Discussion and Conclusions

The use of gamification elements has been applied in two environments, the academic and the enterprise. However, is in the enterprise environment that the use of gamification in software development teams is starting to be applied.

In the one way, in the education environment the use of gamification elements is focused on improving the abilities or knowledge of student. Then, to support the teamwork there have been implemented gamification elements that aim: (1) to increase collaboration; (2) to improve communication; (3) to increment effective participation and interaction; (4) to increment social activity in classrooms; (5) to achieve curse activities and (6) to increase teamwork. It has allowed improving the academic performance of students.

In the other way, in the enterprise environment the use of gamification is focused on improving social interaction due to activities that are performed by teams. Then, to support the teamwork there have been implemented gamification elements that aim: (1) to achieve the assigned activities; (2) to create, refine and share knowledge for learning; (3) to improve the participation, collaboration and contribution of workers in software development and (4) to increment the behavior of social interaction of workers.

In both environments, gamification aims to improve the motivation and commitment of team members. Moreover, it was identified the use of web platforms as the most used tool to implement gamification elements. However, the use of gamification elements and tools may vary depending on the goals to be achieved, in which it is possible to implement one or more gamification elements as necessary in order to achieve a specified goal.

Besides there were identified five gamification elements as the most used in both environments which are: (1) leaderboards, (2) points systems, (3) badges, (4) levels and, (5) progress bars.

As future work, we are developing a set of environments focused on the appropriate integration of teams taking into account the skills, knowledge and interactive styles. These environments aim to reduce the integration time among the team members, so that, they can achieve the integration of highly effective software development teams.

Acknowledgements. CIMAT- Unidad Zacatecas for the facilities to perform this research.

References

1. Chen, G.Q., Yuan, L., Zhang, L., Lu, G.: Assessing teamwork performance in software engineering education: a case in a software engineering undergraduate course. Presented at Asia-Pacific Software Engineering Conference (2011). http://dx.doi.org/10.1109/APSEC.2011.50
2. Knutas, A., Ikonen, J., Nikula, U., Porras, J.: Increasing collaborative communications in a programming course with gamification. Presented at 15th International Conference on Computer Systems and Technologies (2014). http://dx.doi.org/10.1145/2659532.2659620
3. Korn, O., Funk, M., Schmidt, A.: Towards a gamification of industrial production. a comparative study in sheltered work environments. Presented at 7th ACM SIGCHI Symposium on Engineering Interactive Computing Systems (2015). http://dx.doi.org/10.1145/2774225.2774834
4. Jurado, J.L., Fernández, A., Collazos, A.: Applying gamification in the context of knowledge management. Presented at 15th International Conference on Knowledge Technologies and Data-driven Business (2015). http://dx.doi.org/10.1145/2809563.2809606
5. Estacio, B., Prikladnicki, R., Mora, M., Notari, G., Caroli, P., Olchik, A.: Software kaizen: Using agile to form high-performance software development teams. Presented at Agile Conference (AGILE) (2014). http://dx.doi.org/10.1109/AGILE.2014.10
6. Berkling, K.: Gamification behind the scenes: designing a software engineering course. In: Zvacek, S., Restivo, M.T., Uhomoibhi, J., Helfert, M. (eds.) CSEDU 2015. CCIS, vol. 583, pp. 274–292. Springer, Cham (2016). doi:10.1007/978-3-319-29585-5_16
7. Akpolat, B.S., Slany, W.: Enhancing software engineering student team engagement in a high-intensity extreme programming course using gamification. Presented at Conference on Software Engineering Education and Training (CSEE&T) (2014). http://dx.doi.org/10.1109/CSEET.2014.6816792
8. Iosup, A., Epema, D.: An experience report on using gamification in technical higher education. Presented at 45th ACM Technical Symposium on Computer Science Education (2013). http://dx.doi.org/10.1145/2538862.2538899
9. Lynch T.D., Herold, M., Bolinger, J., Deshpande, S., Bihari, T., Ramanathan, J., Ramnath, R.: An agile boot camp: using a LEGO®-based active game to ground agile development principles. Presented at Frontiers in Education Conference (FIE) (2011). http://dx.doi.org/10.1109/FIE.2011.6142849

10. Bartel, A., Figas, P., Hagel, G.: Towards a competency-based education with gamification design elements. Presented at Annual Symposium on Computer-Human Interaction in Play (2015). http://dx.doi.org/10.1145/2793107.2810325
11. Guenaga, M., Eguiluz, A., Rayon, A., Nunez, A., Quevedo, E.: A serious game to develop and assess teamwork competency. In: 2014 International Symposium on Computers in Education, SIIE 2014, pp. 183–188 (2014). https://doi.org/10.1109/SIIE.2014.7017727
12. Herranz, E., Colomo-Palacios, R., de Amescua Seco, A.: Gamiware: a gamification platform for software process improvement. In: O'Connor, R., Umay Akkaya, M., Kemaneci, K., Yilmaz, M., Poth, A., Messnarz, R. (eds.) EuroSPI 2015. CCIS, vol. 543, pp. 127–139. Springer, Cham (2015). 10.1007/978-3-319-24647-5_11
13. Latulipe, C., Long, N.B., Seminario, C.E.: Structuring flipped classes with lightweight teams and gamification. In: Proceedings of the 46th ACM Technical Symposium on Computer Science Education, pp. 392–397 (2015). https://doi.org/10.1145/2676723.2677240
14. Dutra, A.C.S., Prikladnicki, R., Franca, C.: What do we know about high performance teams in software engineering? results from a systematic literature review. Presented at Euromicro Conference on Software Engineering and Advanced Applications (2015). http://dx.doi.org/10.1109/SEAA.2015.24
15. Knutas, A., Ikonen, J., Nikula, U., Porras, J.: Increasing collaborative communications in a programming course with gamification. In: Proceedings of the 15th International Conference on Computer Systems and Technologies, vol. 883, pp. 370–377 (2014). http://dx.doi.org/10.1145/2659532.2659620
16. Hernández, L., Muñoz, M., Mejia, J., Peña, A.: Gamification in software engineering teamworks: a systematic literature review. In: 2016 International Conference on Software Process Improvement (CIMPS), pp. 1–8. IEEE Conference Publications (2016)
17. Stanculescu, L.C., Bozzon, A., Sips, R.J., Houben, G.J.: Work and play: an experiment in enterprise gamification. Presented at 19th ACM Conference on Computer-Supported Cooperative Work & Social Computing (2016). http://dx.doi.org/10.1145/2818048.2820061
18. Buisman, A.L.D., van Eekelen, M.C.J.D.: Gamification in educational software development. Presented at South African Institute for Computer Scientists and Information Technologists Conference (2013)
19. Korn, O., Funk, M., Schmidt, A.: Design approaches for the gamification of production environments. In: Proceedings of the 8th ACM International Conference on PErvasive Technologies Related to Assistive Environments, pp. 1–7 (2015). http://dx.doi.org/10.1145/2774225.2774834
20. Knutas, A., Ikonen, J., Maggiorini, D., Ripamonti, L., Porras, J.: Creating software engineering student interaction profiles for discovering gamification approaches to improve collaboration. In: Proceedings of the 15th International Conference on Computer Systems and Technologies, pp. 378–385 (2014). http://dx.doi.org/10.1145/2659532.2659612
21. O'Donovan, S., Gain, J., Marais, P.: A case study in the gamification of a university-level games development course. In: Proceedings of the South African Institute for Computer Scientists and Information Technologists Conference, SAICSIT 2013, pp. 242–251 (2013). http://dx.doi.org/10.1145/2513456.2513469
22. Dubois, D.J., Tamburrelli, G.: Understanding gamification mechanisms for software development. In: Proceedings of the 2013 9th Joint Meeting on Foundations of Software Engineering, pp. 659–662 (2013). http://dx.doi.org/10.1145/2491411.2494589

23. Unkelos-Shpigel, N., Hadar, I.: Gamifying software engineering tasks based on cognitive principles: the case of code review. In: Proceedings of the 8th International Workshop on Cooperative and Human Aspects of Software Engineering CHASE 2015, pp. 119–120 (2015). http://dx.doi.org/10.1109/CHASE.2015.21
24. Dorling, A., McCaffery, F.: The gamification of SPICE. In: Mas, A., Mesquida, A., Rout, T., O'Connor, R.V., Dorling, A. (eds.) SPICE 2012. CCIS, vol. 290, pp. 295–301. Springer, Heidelberg (2012). doi:10.1007/978-3-642-30439-2_35

Examining Reward Mechanisms for Effective Usage of Application Lifecycle Management Tools

Çağdaş Üsfekes[1,2(✉)], Murat Yilmaz[1], Eray Tuzun[2], Paul M. Clarke[3,4], and Rory V. O'Connor[3,4]

[1] Computer Engineering, Çankaya University, Ankara, Turkey
cusfekes@havelsan.com.tr, myilmaz@cankaya.edu.tr
[2] HAVELSAN A.Ş, Ankara, Turkey
etuzun@havelsan.com.tr
[3] School of Computing, Dublin City University, Dublin, Ireland
{paul.m.clarke,rory.oconnor}@dcu.ie
[4] Lero – the Irish Software Research Centre, Dublin, Ireland

Abstract. Application lifecycle management (ALM) highlights the rules of the road for the entire software ecosystems' lifecycle. Successful ALM enables clarity around the entire delivery effort, from defining requirements to deploying the software product. One of the challenges in software engineering today is to orchestrate ALM tools to a set of software projects effectively. In particular, it is challenging for software practitioners to continuously fully engage with the tasks that are assigned to them. The goal of this study is to address such situations using a game theoretic approach by utilizing a reward mechanism, which we intent to test in a medium-sized software development organization. Based on a set of game elements, this study proposes an auction mechanism to address human resource allocation and task optimization issues, and consequently tackle the potential problem of software practitioners' engagement.

1 Introduction

The notion of games is relevant to studies of social aspects of software development, which have gained an increasing attention among researchers. Recently, a number of researchers have conducted research to explore the potential usage of games in software development activities in terms of collective behavior: altruism and selfishness that ultimately affect the health of a software project. Games are special kind of social activities, which can easily highlight the social interactions or engagements that could offer a variety of measurable societal outcomes. Over the last decade, games have reshaped the ways of communication by the help of the social media to promote cooperation and competition. Serious games are used for game-based social skill training that helps individuals to gain social responsibility through the creation of fun and engaging environments. Emerging trends improve the popularity of among researchers and practitioners who have redefined the notion of games in non-gaming contexts. Consequently, the term gamification (i.e. the use of game elements in non-gaming practices) becomes an emerging subject for improving the software development processes. It not only has a great potential to align individuals' motivations with software development task but also helpful to address a variety of information technology related issues.

Defining application lifecycle management (ALM) is not straightforward. ALM can be grouped in three distinct areas. These are governance, development, and operations. In governance step, we have to be sure the application always provides what the business needs [1]. Governance includes the all periods of ALM so this is the most important area of ALM. Development is a basic part of every software product's custom lifecycle. Operation step comes after development step. After deployment, every product needs to monitored and managed.

The whole spectrum of ALM process is addressed with various ALM tools. In particular, it is challenging for software practitioners to continuously fully engage with the tasks that are assigned to them in these ALM tools. In this study, we will address such situations using a game theoretic approach by utilizing a reward mechanism. Based on a set of game elements, this study proposes an auction mechanism to address human resource allocation and task optimization issues, and consequently tackle the potential problem of software practitioners' engagement.

The remaining part of the paper proceeds as follows: Sect. 2 gives a brief overview of theory of games in software engineering literature. In Sect. 3, we discuss the foundations of our proposed game based resource distribution framework, and finally in Sect. 4 provides a discussion and outlines future work.

2 Theory of Games in Software Engineering Literature

Research into games has a long history. The theory of games first appeared in the literature at 1930s. A game highlights strategic interactions among individuals, teams, units, or infrastructures. Historically, research investigating the individuals' interactions associated with games has focused on analytical methods and tools to aid the decision-making process [2]. Around the early 1960s, small-scale research and case studies began to emerge linking theory of games with social science successfully. Especially, in last fifteen years, games become popular. In last fifteen years, companies are using game elements to analysis their employee characteristics.

Game Theory is a set of analytical tools, which can be used to model the interactions between participants (e.g. individuals, companies, nations, etc.) in a game form. In addition, it can be used to explore the actual or essential decisions and behaviors, and ultimately their consequences that may include tradeoffs or conflicts among individuals. The most important fact about game theory is that it assumes all players as rational. In other words, all players follow the rules of a game and hence their goal is to win. In the last decade, game theory was not used only in economy. It was used in psychology, biology, and computer science [3]. Game theory has both cooperative and non-cooperative forms. However, it is mostly known with its "non-cooperative" form [3]. In this approach, the goal is to design a controlled competition where selections of participants are likely to affect every single player's benefits. These players are considered as successful when they mind their own benefits based on a choice architecture. Nash [4] coined "Nash Equilibrium", which describes the optimal outcomes of a game by predicting the outcome of strategic interactions. In recent years, we can see many examples about using game theory in software engineering [5, 6]. By the result of these examples, we can conclude that game theory can be used to address many challenges that are known in software development.

There are many examples about using the theory and practices of games and the use of game elements to address a set of problems in software development. For example, Lagesse [7] created a game theoretic model for assigning tasks to software practitioners. Cockburn [8] accepted that software development is a kind of game based on limited project resources, communication and coordination skills. Baskerville [9] analyzed high-speed internet development from a balancing game viewpoint that depends on high usage of resources. Sullivan [10] worked to evaluate software design decisions by economic approach. Sazawal and Sudan [11] combined the theory of games and decision modeling structure to improving software design. In this work, they designed a game called "software design evaluation". This game aims to address problems between developers and customers. Moreover, they suggested a lightweight game theoretical analysis technique to assess software development teams.

Gao [12] designed a game theoretic model to configure software products and decision errors. Gao-hui [13] worked about depending corporate software developments to game theory. Soska et al. [14] worked about students in academic life. In this work, they designed a card game to teach students about software testing. In addition, Pedreira et al. [15] created a systematic map about usage of gamification in software engineering. By this work, they aimed to find opportunities for future works. In recent years, gamification becomes more popular in software engineering research. Sweedyk [16] worked about the popularity of gamification in academic programs and conferences. In 2016, Kitagawa and others created a game on code review. Code review has a big effect on software quality in development process and it aims to decrease the number of bugs [17]. Szabo [18] applied "Game Dev Tycoon" game to students for teaching software engineering. This game is about business simulation. Amir [19] worked about getting systems more gamified and effective with using gamification. Ranganathan [20] used gamification in hardware engineering. He supported a low power timer on circuit by a game theoretic model which is based on the "Nash equilibrium".

A game is a useful tool to reveal interpersonal conflicts. This situation is known as a "social dilemma". "Prisoner's dilemma" is a basic framework that often used by researchers to observe such issues. Hazzan and Dubinsky [21] suggest that "prisoner's dilemma" is useful to highlight the problems in software development. Fejis [22] designed a game theoretic model for software developers and testers. He worked about the results of this game and said that these results may cause "prisoner's dilemma". Costa [23] combined the "Prisoner's dilemma" with gamification and designed war and peace game by using this combination. In another work, Mortensen used "prisoner's dilemma" in security and privacy of web technologies. In this work, he defined seven strategies and created a strategy to exceed "prisoner's dilemma" of web technologies by using a set of strategies [24].

The software process improvement methods should cover various activities so as to improve the quality of the software product [2, 25]. These activities should be reevaluated by taking into account factors affecting software development activities (e.g. human factors in software development, social interaction problems, etc.). In software development process, people are not working alone; they are working in teams so all of these working activities accepted as a social activity [26]. The practitioners working in these development teams are affected by several social factors including but not limited to their working conditions, personalities, rationality and interdependence [27]. An important goal of software process improvement is to increase the quality of software development projects and comply the project plan and budget [3]. To this end, a coordination mechanism among development, maintenance and management is essential. For example, the readability of not only source code but also technical documentation is decreasing when project is getting bigger. Therefore, a software unit that has to work in a coordination and number of employees is increasing. The coordination level of these units affects the quality of a software product. At this point, the problems, which occur in software development, can be addressed by assigning responsibilities to the right people as more competent they become.

Several lines of evidence suggest that building a mechanism for automating the software development activities by designing game-like activities is essential [28–30]. Yılmaz [31] designed a game-like approach to explore the effects of team personality characteristics in software development activities. Yılmaz et al. [30] created a gamification approach to improve the software development process. The idea of creating an economic mechanism for software development is introduced by [29], which was one of the first serious discussions about the subject matter. One study by Yilmaz et al. [32] proposed an economic mechanism for improving the software development process. Yılmaz and O'Connor [33] suggested a complementary approach to ScrumBan to improve the software development process using gamification. In another work, Yilmaz and O'Connor [34] considered software development as an economic activity and created a market-based approach to investigate task assignment problems. Collectively, these studies confirm that using game-like approaches in the software development activities have a significant impact for software productivity improvements.

2.1 Reward Mechanisms

A reward mechanism is a feedback device, which is an important aspect of game design. A considerable amount of literature has been published on computational features of these mechanisms. Houk et al. [35] investigated the models of intelligent behaviors and its relation to reward mechanisms. Singh [36] proposed a reward mechanism for online learning systems. Lua [37] worked on a reward mechanism which is designed for P2P systems. Wang and Sun [38] explored reward mechanisms which was designed for computer games.

Reward mechanisms have a crucial impact on human learning and cognition. In addition, they are related to game elements. If a reward system is constructed properly, it is likely to improve the motivation of the participants. Game elements potentially assist people to solve problem in an enjoyable way, e.g. while they are working on routine tasks. Walz [39] defined a game as a closed system that depends on social and cultural fundamentals of cultural values. Gonzales [40] described the advantages of games for teaching a process in computer engineering. Qu [41] worked about teaching software engineering. Largo [42] collected lots of feedbacks from students and he examined game elements in learning process.

Big corporations are using more complex systems. These can be engineering management tools, financial automation tools etc. To use these systems efficiently, employees must be experienced. At this point, employees make more effort to use these systems efficiently. In this process using gamification accelerates the employees learning process. For example, in software engineering, Pariza [43] designed a game about traceability in software tests and while conducting source code inspections. He designed a game about traceability in software tests and code artifacts [44].

Application lifecycle management (ALM) defines the rules of an outlet for the entire software development lifecycle, which provides clarity around the entire delivery effort, from defining requirements to building, packaging, and deploying the software product [1]. Therefore, it supports a powerful reporting ability and traceability in development process [45]. These tools provide engineers with a single framework for the many modules that the software development process requires [46]. These modules can be requirement management, test management, build management, project management and source code management. All these different processes are integrated with each other successfully and this ability is very important on software project delivery. In this work, our aim is to create a reward mechanism to use ALM tools more efficiently.

3 Game Based Resource Distribution Framework for Application Lifecycle Management

Application lifecycle management systems do not suggest the most efficient methods to software developers while they are assigning tasks. The goal of this model is using individual choices to improve software productivity while developers are assigning tasks. Users can join multiple auctions which is defined in this software model. Auctions can be related with requirement analysis, software testing or etc. Therefore, users can choose the tasks that motive them the most from a pool with resource distribution method. This model is proposed as a resource management framework to define the task choices based on priority of software developer's selection. This system aims to make the task assignment and time planning in an efficient way.

The main aim of this mechanism is to reform the software development activities in a resource economy model where software practitioners have initial credits, which enable them to select these tasks regarding their preferences. Based on the proposed model, we announce the tasks to the software developers in an auction like structure. Similar to story cards, these tasks are based on their effort and complexity points. A practitioner requests a set of specific tasks depending on the amount of credit they might be able to pay by using auction mechanism. From these requests, proposed mechanism selects the practitioner who desires to do this job the most. In this way, a gamification based value mapping occurs between tasks and resources. The system ensures that a user has to bid on their own budget and allows the price stay constant over time. The system uses a set of game elements to motivate its users such as giving reputation, badges and leaderboards (i.e. to create community leader with more privileges). Consequently, participants who finish their tasks in time are rewarded by the system based on the importance of their achievements. All this information is announced to system participant to foster their motivation (see Fig. 1).

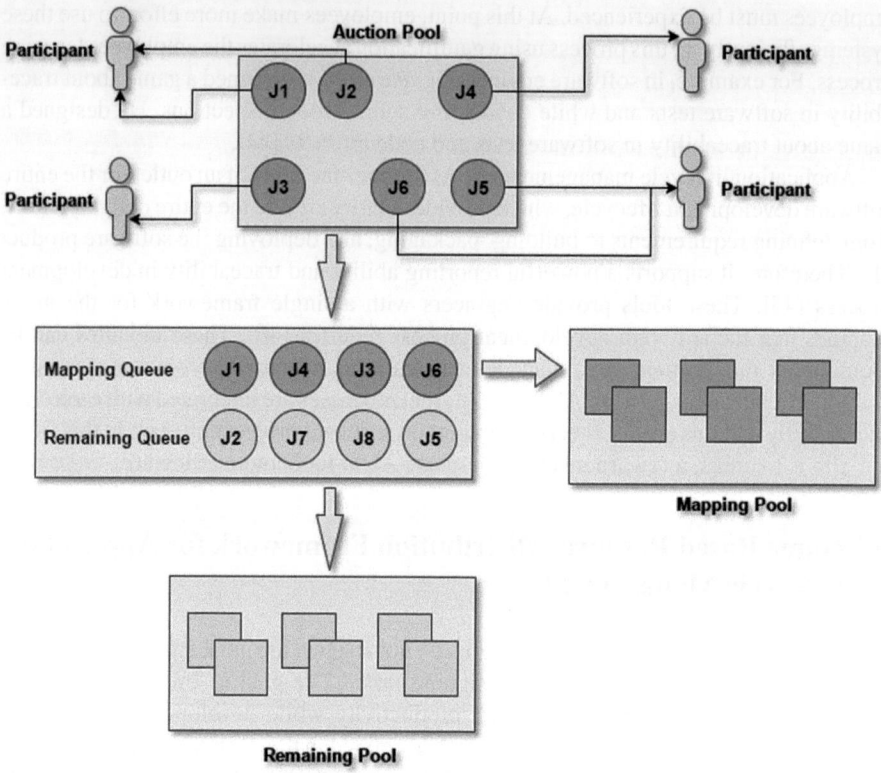

Fig. 1. Auction-based resource distribution model to software lifecycle management

Using this technique, individuals in a team can bid for the work they would like to perform and in the context of their available credits. We believe that this could have interesting ramifications for productivity and knowledge diversity among individuals in software development teams. Here, we suggest that this is a useful vehicle for risk reduction in software companies, since everyone has the right to bid for work in the context of their credit position. Let's look to a metaphor – a golfing handicap. In amateur golfing competitions, individuals participate in competitions but their score is modified on the basis of their handicap/ability with the result that the winner is not the player who shot the absolute score for the round of golf but rather the winner who shot the lowest score taking into account their own ability. This means that everyone competes with the ability to win the competition and everyone is trying to improve his or her own personal performance.

4 Discussion

This preliminary resource allocation model explains the possibility of using an auction based reward mechanism in the service of distributing the tasks of a software development process. The goal is to propose a reward mechanism based on game design concepts and explore potential methods for application game elements to software development activities and ultimately improve software development practices. Overall, this study strengthens the idea that software practitioners should be able to select which tasks they prefer in an auction style mechanism based on a series of decision criteria (e.g. credits, reputation, and defined skills). To benefit from the power of game elements these choices are represented in a game like structure. Games may foster motivational factors, which potentially create a positive impact on practitioners' performance with a marked effect on task awareness. This preliminary study claims that playing an auction style business game provides participants a "mental workout" and routine activity pattern becomes less boring. In addition, it would guide individuals to create a habit of working in a more structural way. An implication of this approach is the possibility to improve the social structure of a software organization. A further benefit of this practice is to improve overall project awareness (as is noted in the discussion section) and potentially improved tacit knowledge distribution.

Our initial proposal was submitted to the management board of HAVELSAN where we received positive feedback, and it is selected for an initial funding. HAVELSAN is the largest software development company in Turkey with around 800 engineers. There are four main divisions in HAVELSAN. These are education and simulation systems, cyber security systems, command control and combat systems and information technologies. All these areas focus different sectors so various technologies and software development methodologies (such as agile, waterfall) are using in projects. Project groups are using different ALM tools such as TFS (Team Foundation Server), Atlassian etc. in software development processes. We are designing a web based serious game application that can communicate with these tools using restful services. Firstly, we selected TFS as a pilot ALM tool. In the future, tools like Jira is also supported, so we can position this serious game application on top of the all software projects in HAVELSAN.

This study has surfaced many questions in need of further investigation. Future research should therefore concentrate on the implementation of the proposed model and more assessments is essential to determine its effectiveness.

Acknowledgement. This work was supported, in part, by Science Foundation Ireland grant 13/RC/2094.

References

1. Chappell, D.: What is Application Lifecycle Management?. Chappell & Associates, San Francisco (2008)
2. Yilmaz, M., O'Connor, R.: Oyun Kuramı Kullanarak Yazılım Takımlarının Üretkenliğini Artırmak İçin Geliştirilen Bir Yazılım Süreç Mühendisliği Yaklaşımı, Turkish National Software Engineering Symposium (2011)
3. Zahran, S.: Software Process Improvement: Practical Guidelines for Business Success. Addison Wesley, Reading (1998)
4. Maskin, E.: Nash equilibrium and mechanism design, Institute for Advanced Study, Princeton University, United States (2008)
5. Dingsøyr, T., Dybå, T., Moe, N.B.: Agile Software Development: Current Research and Future Directions, 1st edn. Springer, Heidelberg (2010)
6. Deek, F.P., McHugh, J.A., Eljabiri, O.M.: Strategic Software Engineering: An Interdisciplinary Approach. CRC Press, Boca Raton (2005)
7. Lagesse, B.: A game-theoretical model for task assignment in project management. In: 2006 IEEE International Conference on Management of Innovation and Technology, Singapore, pp. 678–680 (2006)
8. Cockburn, A.: Agile software development: the cooperative game. Addison-Wesley (2007). A Game-Theoretical model for task assignment in project management. In: 2006 IEEE International Conference on Management of Innovation and Technology, Singapore, pp. 678–680 (2006)
9. Baskerville, R.L., Levine, L., Ramesh, B., Pries-Heje, J.: The high speed balancing game: how software companies cope with internet speed. Scand. J. Inf. Syst. 16(1), 11–54 (2004)
10. Sullivan, K., Chalasani, P., Jha, S.: Software design decisions as real options. University of Virginia, Technical Report (1997)
11. Sazawal, V., Sudan, N.: Modeling software evolution with game theory. In: Wang, Q., Garousi, V., Madachy, R., Pfahl, D. (eds.) ICSP 2009. LNCS, vol. 5543, pp. 354–365. Springer, Heidelberg (2009). doi:10.1007/978-3-642-01680-6_32
12. Gao, X., Zhong, W., Mei, S.: A game-theory approach to configuration of detection software with decision errors (2013)
13. Gao-hui, N.: Analysis on Enterprise's Software Project Management Based on Game Theory, Management Science and Engineering (2006)
14. Soska, A., Mottok, J., Wolff, C.: An experimental card game for software testing: development, design and evaluation of a physical card game to deepen the knowledge of students in academic software testing education. In: 2016 IEEE Global Engineering Education Conference (EDUCON) (2016)
15. Pedreira, O., García, F., Brisaboa, N., Piattini, M.: Gamification in software engineering – a systematic mapping. Inf. Softw. Technol. 57, 157–168 (2015)
16. Sweedyk, E., Keller, R.M.: Fun and games: a new software engineering course. In: ITiCSE 2005 Proceedings of the 10th Annual SIGCSE Conference on Innovation and Technology in Computer Science Education, pp. 138–142 (2005)
17. Kitagawa,N., Nara, H.H., Ihara, A., Kogiso, K., Matsumoto, K.: Code review participation: game theoretical modeling of reviewers in gerrit datasets. In: CHASE 2016 Proceedings of the 9th International Workshop on Cooperative and Human Aspects of Software Engineering, pp. 64–67 (2016)
18. Szabo, C.: Evaluating GameDevTycoon for teaching software engineering. In: Proceeding SIGCSE 2014 Proceedings of the 45th ACM Technical Symposium on Computer Science Education, pp. 403–408 (2014)

19. Amir, B., Ralph, P.: Proposing a theory of gamification effectiveness. In: Proceeding ICSE Companion 2014 Companion Proceedings of the 36th International Conference on Software Engineering, pp. 626–627 (2014)
20. Ranganathan, N., Murugavel, A.K.: A low power scheduler using game theory. In: CODES + ISSS 2003 Proceedings of the 1st IEEE/ACM/IFIP International Conference on Hardware/Software Codesign and System Synthesis, pp. 126–131 (2003)
21. Hazzan, O., Dubinsky, Y.: Social perspective of software development methods: the case of the prisoner dilemma and extreme programming. In: Baumeister, H., Marchesi, M., Holcombe, M. (eds.) XP 2005. LNCS, vol. 3556, pp. 74–81. Springer, Heidelberg (2005). doi:10.1007/11499053_9
22. Feijs, L.: Prisoner dilemma in software testing. Comput. Sci. Rep. **1**, 65–80 (2001)
23. Costa, C.J., Costa, P.J.: A peace war game application, OSDOC 2011 Proceedings of the 2011 Workshop on Open Source and Design of Communication, pp. 71–74 (2011)
24. Mortensen, P., Wai, C.: Avoiding the prisoner's dilemma of the web. In: DUX 2007 Proceedings of the 2007 Conference on Designing for User eXperiences (2007)
25. Conradi, R., Fuggetta, A.: Improving software process improvement. IEEE Softw. **19**(4), 92–99 (2002)
26. Dittrich, Y., Floyd, C., Klischewski, R.: Social thinkingsoftware practice. The MIT Press, Cambridge (2002)
27. Grechanik, M., Perry, D.E.: Analyzing software development as a noncooperative game. In: IEE Seminar Digests, vol. 29 (2004)
28. Yilmaz, M.: A software process engineering approach to understanding software productivity and team personality characteristics: an empirical investigation. Ph.D. thesis, Dublin City University (2013)
29. Yilmaz, M., O'Connor, R.: Maximizing the value of the software development process by game theoretic analysis. In: 11th International Conference on Product Focused Software, 21–23 Jun 2010, Limerick, Ireland (2010). ISBN 978-1-4503-0281-4
30. Yilmaz, M., Yilmaz, M., O'Connor, R.V., Clarke, P.: A gamification approach to improve the software development process by exploring the personality of software practitioners. In: Clarke, Paul M., O'Connor, R.V., Rout, T., Dorling, A. (eds.) SPICE 2016. CCIS, vol. 609, pp. 71–83. Springer, Cham (2016). doi:10.1007/978-3-319-38980-6_6
31. Schwaber, C., et al.: The Changing Face of Application Lifecycle Management. Forrester Research, 18 August 2006
32. Yilmaz, M., O'Connor, R., Collins, J.: Improving software development process through economic mechanism design. In: 17th European Software Process Improvement Conference, 1–3 September 2010, Grenoble, France (2010). ISBN 978-3-642-15666-3
33. Yilmaz, M., O'Connor, R.: A Scrumban integrated gamification approach to guide software process improvement: a Turkish case study. Tehnicki Vjesnik (Technical Gazette) **23**(1), 237–245 (2016). ISSN 1330-3651
34. Yilmaz, M., O'Connor, R.V.: A market based approach for resolving resource constrained task allocation problems in a software development process. In: Winkler, D., O'Connor, R.V., Messnarz, R. (eds.) EuroSPI 2012. CCIS, vol. 301, pp. 25–36. Springer, Heidelberg (2012). doi:10.1007/978-3-642-31199-4_3
35. Houk, J.C., Davis, J.L., Beiser, D.G.: Models of Information Processing in the Basal Ganglia, p. 185. MIT Press, Cambridge (1994)
36. Singh, N., Chaudhari, N.S.: Differential reward mechanism based online learning algorithm for url-based topic classification. In: 2014 International Conference on Computational Intelligence and Communication Networks (CICN). IEEE (2014)

37. Lua, K., Wanga, S., Xiea, L., Wanga, Z., Li, M.: A dynamic reward-based incentive mechanism: reducing the cost of P2P systems. Knowl.-Based Syst. **112**, 105–113 (2016)
38. Wang, H., Sun, C.-T.: Game Reward Systems: Gaming Experiences and Social Meanings (2011)
39. Walz, S.P., Deterding, S.: Gamification and Learning, p. 688. MIT Press, Cambridge (2014)
40. González, C.S., Carreño, A.M.: Methodological proposal for gamification in the computer engineering teaching. In: 2014 International Symposium on Computers in Education (SIIE). IEEE (2014)
41. Qu, W.-Q., Zhao, Y.-F., Wang, M., Liu, B.-Q.: Research on teaching gamification of software engineering. In: 2014 9th International Conference on Computer Science & Education (ICCSE). IEEE (2014)
42. Largo, F., Durán, F., Arnedo, C., Rosique, P., Cuerda, R., Carmona, R.: Gamification of the learning process: lessons learned. In: IEEE Revista Iberoamericana de Tecnologias del Aprendizaje, p. 1. IEEE (2016)
43. Parizi, R.M.: On the gamification of human-centric traceability tasks in software testing and coding. In: 2016 IEEE 14th International Conference on Software Engineering Research, Management and Applications (SERA). IEEE (2016)
44. Parizi, R.M., Kasem, A., Abdullah, A.: Towards gamification in software traceability: between test and code artifacts. In: 2015 10th International Joint Conference on Software Technologies (ICSOFT) (2015)
45. Aytekin, A.İ., Tüzün, E., Macit, Y., Tekinerdoğan, B.: Uygulama Yaşam Döngüsü Yönetimi - Sistematik Eşleme Çalışması, UYMS (2015)
46. Shaw, K.: Application Lifecycle Management for the Enterprise, Serena Software, White Paper (2007). http://www.serena.com/Docs/Repository/company/Serena_ALM_2.0_For_t.pdf (available 24.04.2008)

CHANGCE-Thinking – A Ludic Kick-Off to Chance Orientation

Peter Witzgall[1(✉)], Peter Kapfhammer[1], Eva-Maria Trenz[2], Teresa Kiechle[2], Tobias Gebler[2], and Adrian Indefrey[1]

[1] PI.con – Pulse of Innovation Consulting, Lindberghstr. 11, 82178 Puchheim, Germany
peter.witzgall@picon.services
[2] Technical University of Munich (TUM), Arcisstraße 21, 80333 Munich, Germany

Abstract. In this paper, we introduce a novel framework called CHANGCE-thinking, which is first and foremost a mental model. The key idea is to foster a holistic view on change initiatives that inspires thinking in terms of chances and opportunities rather than of problems and risks. The CHANGCE-thinking framework provides tools and methods to guide the change process towards realization of chances. In doing so it draws from concepts in change process design, diversity and gaming simulation. The CHANGCE-Game is used to kick-off the change process and it is implemented as a board game with haptic playing elements, which correspond to eight chance-rooms as well as eight types of the CHANGCE-thinking framework. In total, CHANGCE-thinking embodies a structured approach to chance orientation, which is initiated in a game setting and followed by a change process which needs to be lead rather than managed.

Keywords: Chance orientation · Gaming simulation · Gamification · Serious games · Change process · Innovation

1 Introduction

The identification and realization of chances is an essential key for any organization. This is usually the core reason for starting a business in the first place and thus makes chance orientation an integral part of a start-up mentality. For some reasons, however, this initial mindset appears to diminish over time the more established an organization grows. Instead, many established companies tend to focus predominantly on problem solving and risk management, possibly to defend their market positions. Few are aware or unable to avoid that this change in mentality compromises their ability to innovate.

One approach could be to treat chances alike risks. For example, a risk management is responsible for identifying risks, probability of occurrence, severity and for defining preventive and/or corrective actions to take to decrease their negative effects. An according chance management could apply basically the same methods to increase the positive effects of chances. Taking risks can enhance chances and chances implicate risks.

However, risks and chances are not exact opposites. Risks are often recurrent and occur irrespective of people recognizing them. Chances on the other hand typically do not just happen by coincidence, their value depends on a specific window of opportunity and the possibilities and skills needed to realize them. These are not always given. Managing chances alike managing risk does not suffice. Thus, a different approach is needed.

Herein lies the problem most companies face. They tend to cling to static approaches and treat chances unsystematically, disregarding their possibilities. For example, software development companies are confronted with rapid changes [1]. Therefore, in this paper we suggest CHANGCE-thinking as a tool to internalize the proper attitude and behavior for an innovative organization.

CHANGCE-thinking provides a new approach combining the systematic identification and realization of chances, turning risk aversion into chance affinity. CHANGCE-thinking is a framework that provides guidance to the change process of an organization, for example through structuring chances into a holistic model with eight chance-rooms and through the notion of balance between these rooms.

The kick-off to a change process inspired by CHANGCE-thinking is implemented in a ludic manner, which creates intrinsic motivation for change and a lasting momentum. During the CHANGCE-Game the players are enabled to expand their views by exploring the eight chance-rooms while representing eight different roles. The game results determine which change directions are required to achieve a better balance and thus a promising future.

Based on these results, business strategies are drafted and the new mindset is established within the organization. Hereby, the company is enabled to actively shape its own future while drawing guidance from CHANGCE-thinking.

In this paper, we describe the underlying concepts used by CHANGCE-thinking such as business games' features like the theory of gaming, role playing, debriefing along with facets of innovation and change management such as the model of change by Kurt Lewin.

The paper is structured as follows: Sect. 2 refers to related work which reveals principles supporting the CHANGCE-thinking, which itself is introduced in Sect. 3. In Sect. 4 we will describe the components and structure of the CHANGCE-Game. Section 4 summarizes the results and benefits of CHANGCE-thinking and provides a prospect for future work.

2 Background

2.1 Change

Kurt Lewin defines the change process as composed of three distinct phases – the Unfreezing, the Change and the Refreeze. Recognizing and putting those three stages into practice enables organizations to manage change and chances in an efficient and effective way [2].

Further Lewin notes that to strengthen the driving forces of change it is vital to involve all people at stake, especially the employees [2]. Enhancing the engagement and commitment of employees is a significant factor of process improvement.

The process of change is also connected to continuous learning, giving rise to an empirical process control. While there are different approaches on learning, an active kind of experience is fundamental. By involving people with the material to be learned - like a new perception of specific chances - the knowledge, skills, and attitudes resulting are internalized [3].

Embedding a new mindset as an objective of a change initiative is a time-consuming process. Sustaining the permanent commitment of all people involved in the change initiative is not easy and closely related to its purpose [4]. Fortunately, chances are implicitly meaningful as they embed future orientation.

2.2 Diversity

It is largely accepted that a team with multifaceted characters can exhibit higher performance than one that is composed of like-minded people. This also applies to a team responsible for driving a change project.

There is a multitude of role models available for various purposes. Figure 1 depicts two examples, the Team Role model by Meredith Belbin [5, 6] and the 'Ten Faces of Innovation' by Tom Kelley respectively, which specifically relates to a team capable of innovating [7].

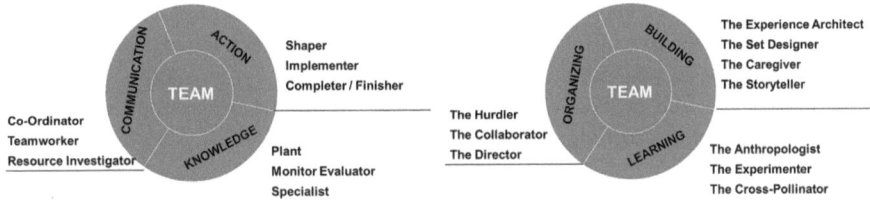

Fig. 1. Team Role models inspired by Meredith Belbin (left) and Tom Kelley (right)

One of the fundamental reasons for higher performance of a diverse team is that the variety of perspectives implied by differing characters both enables a more holistic view and unleashes creativity. The 'Six Thinking Hats' by Edward de Bono apply these insights to form a tool used at creativity workshops. His model pushes individuals to deliberately adopt a variety of perspectives on a subject which may not be conform with the one they would assume most naturally [8, 9].

2.3 Gaming Simulation

Playing an assigned role as suggested by de Bono is one possibility of a gaming element. The transfer of gaming elements into a non-gaming context is subject to current studies and applications and used as well for business games as for gamification [8, 9].

Various components can be part of simulation and gaming. Simulation gaming can be defined as 'a facsimile of reality' for 'simulations offer a more effective way to understand the future than the extrapolation of trend lines, forecasting and brainstorming' [10]. Provided that simulations are deduced from practical, significant examples of business practice, they are enabling the participants to elaborate potentials embedded in their industry.

By including simulations in games, didactic principles of constructivist learning are put into practice. Simulation models hold epistemological aspects for they are not solely constructs of reality but also of possibilities. The explorative learning during the simulation allows the players to create opportunities which do not exist yet [11]. Keys describes this explorative or experiential character of games as useful because the "learning and behavioral changes can be observed" [12].

Games can create a relaxed and open atmosphere. Thereby they enhance innovative thinking as creativity particularly arises from environments without fear [4, 13]. This desired atmosphere is supported when a game takes place at a location outside of the everyday workplace, in which case it helps to escape from the daily routine. Thus, the novel environment unrelated to the familiar surroundings provides the space, time and opportunity needed to think about new ideas [4].

When games are used in a business setting there is, however, a need to extend beyond entertainment and distraction. Reflection is a critical factor. To ensure learning effects a debriefing of the game is necessary. According to Thatcher's definition debriefing is "the part of the process in which the reflection takes place and from which the change in the persons will occur (..) Thus, the debriefing is the most important point of learning from the use of games and simulations" [3].

This approach is corresponding with Kolb's model of experiential learning whereas reflection or the reflective observation is the crucial link between the experience and the process of change and adaption in the mind. He stated that by promoting a discussion of the experience, the process of learning can be assisted because the thoughts and embryonic ideas of the participants are raised to the surface [14].

3   CHANGCE-Thinking

CHANGCE-thinking derives its name from blending chance with change and from starting with a mental model. The key idea is to foster a holistic view on change initiatives that inspires thinking in terms of chances and opportunities of change rather than of problems and risks.

This innovative concept also correlates with 'Lateral Thinking', described by Edward de Bono, which is about solving problems and finding alternatives distinct from the prevalent line of thought [9]. Lateral thinking aims at a change of perception and concepts through an indirect and creative approach, using reasoning that is not immediately obvious and therefore involving ideas that may not be obtainable by using only traditional linear thinking [15].

CHANGCE-thinking is based on a multi-dimensional structure of future chances, which are referred to as chance-rooms, listed in Table 1. There are eight in total, the first four of them stand for topic areas that are highly important for a company's success and development, the latter four represent the main stakeholder groups. This concept aims at providing a coherent and holistic view of the company and its environment.

Table 1. The CHANGCE-thinking rooms of chances

Chance-room	Description
Spirit	'Spirit' combines enthusiasm, imagination and creativity and therefore is the base for innovation and change. The main driver of Spirit is a company's collective willingness to manage and design change
Opportunities	This chance-room deals with vision, culture and resources of the company, making up the possibilities within the firm. We discuss if the company exploits its full potential and if not, how this can be achieved
Capabilities	The individual competences of the employees form the centerpiece of every company. The chance-room 'Capabilities' joins their social competences, methodical expertise and specialist skills
Collaboration	'Collaboration' follows up with the modern ways of communication, networks and exchange of information. We concentrate on comprehensive cooperation and want to establish flexible and transparent communication
Shareholders	Making worthwhile investments is the aim of the shareholders. Hence, within this chance-room, we need to find convincing arguments for aspired change-processes and the advantages they bring along for the company
Flow	'Flow' stands for a collaborative and co-creative teamwork within a company. It is characterized by composure, confidence and clearness and ensures the involvement of all employees
Customers	This chance-room implies marketing strategies, customer-relationships and provided services. We examine the reasons of the company's customers to buy its products, talk about the company's aim to act as a solution provider for its customers and discuss the future market positioning
Environment	Within the chance-room 'Environment' we combine everything surrounding the company that is not directly connected to our business: Company location, public opinion, politics, regional and national associations, private surroundings. The main issues being discussed within this chance-room refer to the company's culture, image, ethic and trust

At the early stage of a change project inspired by CHANGCE-thinking the opportunities residing within the chance-rooms are explored to identify which directions are most promising to shape the company's future in a most effective way. The core concept is the notion of balance. Priorities are assigned to achieve a balance between the chance-rooms.

Identifying chances and their relative importance is a creative challenge and does by far exceed linear thinking and intellectual analysis. This is where gaming elements come into play.

The kick-off to the CHANGCE-thinking process is implemented in a ludic manner, which creates intrinsic motivation for change and a lasting momentum. The initial application of the CHANGCE-Game, described in more detail in the following section, is aimed at setting an initial impulse. This corresponds to the Unfreezing phase of the change process as outlined above [2]. During this Unfreezing phase, the opportunity identification takes place. Furthermore, the ground for taking measures and a communication structure are entrenched.

The change-stage reverts to the company-portrayal developed during the game, drafting a guiding principle for a common vision of the future. The strategic planning is based on the chances unveiled by the game results. Because the employees of an organization are the crucial factor for success [2], CHANGCE-thinking includes the engagement of the whole firm as a prerequisite to identify internal and external potentials and for the implementation of the formulated strategy. The implementation of the definite planning proceeds within the enterprise in subtasks, projects and processes attended by the CHANGCE-Pilot. The CHANGCE-Pilot can either be represented by an individual or a team that is responsible for realizing the drafted strategies.

The Re-freeze Lewin mentions [2] is resembled in the CHANGCE-thinking framework as the supervision of the performance. Thereby the organization retains the innovative mindset, which arose during the CHANGCE-Game, remaining open for new chances and opportunities.

4 The CHANGCE-Game

The CHANGCE-Game is used as an instrument to trigger the change process and to establish a basis for drafting new approaches and strategies. During the game, the eight chance rooms are explored, discussed and processed equally and systematically to exploit all existing and hidden potentials of a company.

One key component of the CHANGCE-Game is the role playing with each role representing a diverse perspective. By playing their roles as actors, the players take part in an active and direct way, thereby shaping a world that is no longer solely a distant observation and investigation [16].

The CHANGCE-thinking typology is a role model consisting of eight types, which correspond to the eight chance-rooms (see Table 2 and compare to Table 1). This correlation ensures the equality of the chance-rooms.

Assigning the roles according to their functionalities increases the engagement of the players, because the roles are freed from strong subjectivity, which, in turn, drives creativity. This creative freedom is deepened even further by the short and open description of the roles in the CHANGCE-Game [11].

In addition, the adaption of a role releases the employees from any form of hierarchy since they solely represent a given definition. This enables the players to express different views without the fear of exposing themselves. This principle of overcoming barriers by neglecting hierarchy enhances creativity [8, 9].

Taking advantage of the opportunities offered by the CHANGCE-Game, eight company employees are invited to take part. The game is supervised and moderated by an experienced business consultant – the CHANGCE-Game Moderator.

There are three phases in the CHANGCE-Game: The preparation, the playing and the debriefing afterwards.

Table 2. The CHANGCE-thinking typology

Type	Functionality	Description
Spirit type	Creator, reformer initiative, intuitive, lively	Creativity will always be a success factor. This regards employees as well as the business model. Change and transformation need constant inspiration and activeness of the Spirit Type to be implemented
Space type	Leader, manager defining, aware, fact oriented, controlling	The intelligent leadership of complex processes is the Space Type's specialty. He/she ensures the realisation of visions and ideas. Pull replaces push – role model vs. superior
Skill type	Worker, structured, process and result oriented, constant	Skill Types are diligent workers. They are the necessary implementers to achieve important goals. They are reliable. Their experience tells them what to do and how to react in all kinds of situations
Collaboration type	Team player, connector, Motivating, open, communicative, cooperative	The quality of communication and interconnection triggers the quality of teamwork. Empathy and transparency are essential. Collaboration combines the functions of antenna, sender, receiver and amplifier
Shareholder type	Business man, director, goal oriented, motivating, visionary, dominant	He/she represents the owners', shareholders' and entrepreneurs' interests. Besides the payment of interest this can cover norms, visions, other ideals or individual conceptions
Flow type	Bridge builder, caring, calm, supportive, balanced, cautious	The Flow Type takes care of the comfort of all participants of the CHANGCE-thinking process. He/she detects negative disturbances in time and counteracts them
Customer type	Buyer, user confident, demanding, selective, critical	He/she represents the interests and expectations of the customers and lead-users. He/she considers how customers can be satisfied and positively surprised
Social minder type	Observer, protector, social, just, preserving, sensible	The Social Minder Type focuses on the surrounding environment, the public and the social compatibility of all actions. He/she observes the alignment of the enterprise's and the environment's interests

Preparation Phase. Prior to the game each player chooses a role which they like to represent during the game. The roles are embodied by game pieces (see Fig. 2) and belong to eight corresponding perspectives.

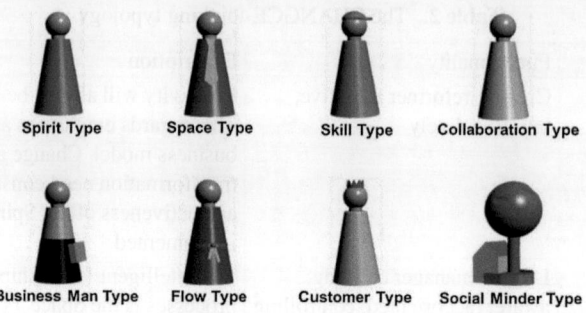

Fig. 2. The CHANGCE-thinking types as haptic game elements

Another element of the preparation is the development of an enterprise-portrayal for the present as well as for the future. For this the players are ought to rank a deck of cards by importance and relevance. Those cards are labeled with different adjectives describing their company's culture, possible problems or changes within and outside of the firm. The elected ones are then laid down onto a ranking pyramid as shown in Fig. 3.

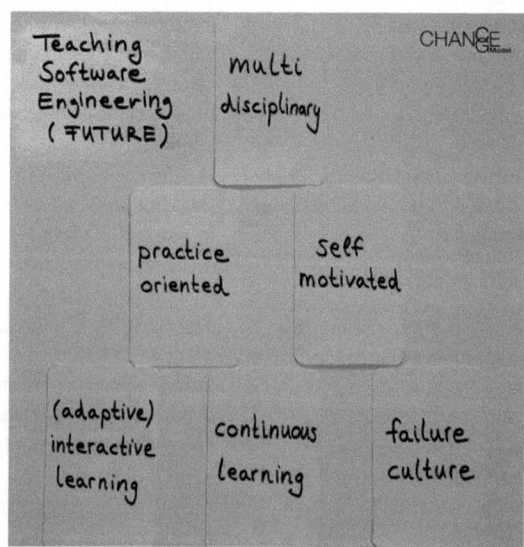

Fig. 3. Example of a ranking pyramid (result from the GamifySPI workshop at EuroSPI 2016)

Playing Phase. At the beginning of the game each game piece starts on its playing field. The playing fields encircle a platform with seesaw-effect on which "houses" containing the chance-rooms stand.

The playing pieces representing chance-rooms are spread over the playing field (see Fig. 4), each divided into three segments. The game target is to balance the central platform which can either be achieved when all the houses are empty – like at the starting point of the game – or when all of them are filled with their appropriate segments.

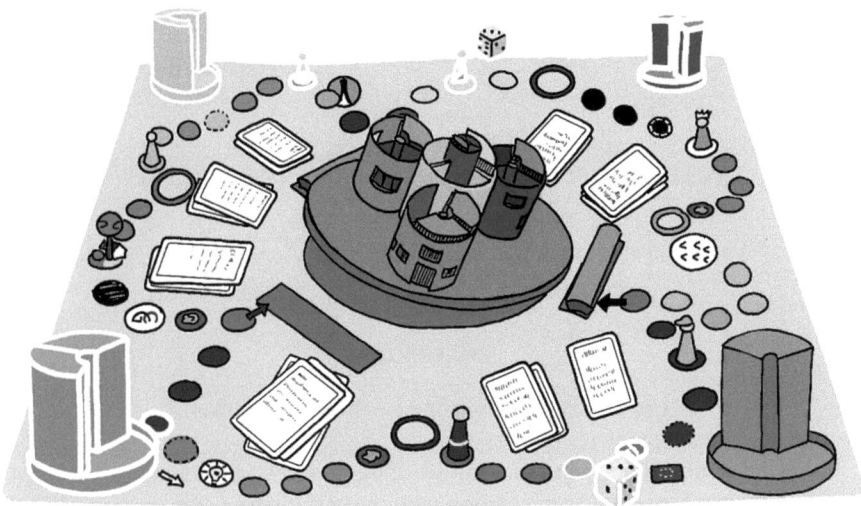

Fig. 4. The playing field of the CHANGCE-thinking Game

A typical turn begins with the rolling of the dice and the figures advancing clockwise around the board the corresponding number of fields. The fields are either assigned to one of the eight chance-rooms or event cards.

In case a player lands on the field of a chance-room, a card corresponding to the chance-room is drawn. These cards contain statements which are then discussed by the group. The statements are classified numerically, displaying how much they coincide with the company along with a justification and a suggestion for potential improvement.

During those dynamic discussions, new options, possibilities and ideas are written down on the back side of the cards. Once the playing cards of a chance-room-segment are answered, the players may put the respective segment into its designated space on top of the CHANGCE-Platform. Thereby, all the houses are filled during the playing process which also visualizes the progress achieved throughout the game.

In case a player lands on an event-field an event-card is drawn. The event-cards are independent of the chance-rooms and encourage unconventional ideas, picking up the basic idea of the "WIBNI" creativity technique, where questions starting with the phrase "Wouldn't it be nice if..." lead to interesting and innovative approaches [17, 18]. The game ends once all the cards of the eight chance-rooms have been discussed equally and the balance within the CHANGCE-Platform is restored.

Debriefing phase. After the game is finished each player is asked to fill in a prepared web-chart to estimate the actual potentials of the eight chance-rooms within the company according to one's own assessment. In the meantime, the CHANGCE-thinking Moderator analyzes the numerical ratings of the playing-cards and creates a web-chart with the common results (see Fig. 5).

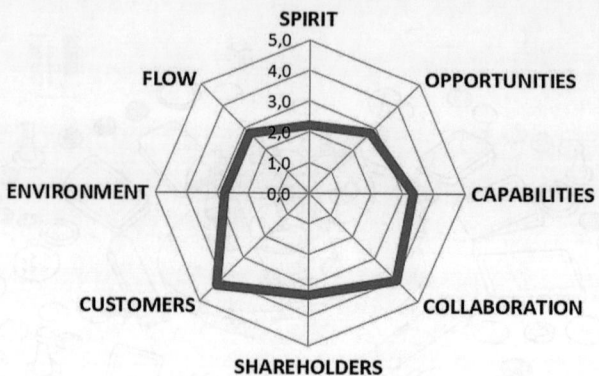

Fig. 5. Example result of the web-chart evaluation

Using the results of the game, an analysis of the chances and potentials is derived to serve as the basis for strategic orientation with the self-image as the guiding objective and the further CHANGCE-thinking process. Moreover, these results have been accomplished by involving a team of employees in a playful setting to remember and by using different dimensions and steps of reflection during the CHANGCE-Game.

The first reflections take place during the preparation phase, before the playing begins. Having to choose a role is an intra- and interpersonal reflection [11]. The participants are faced with different roles described by their functionalities, thus naturally assessments by themselves and the group come to pass. This does not imply that they are supposed to choose a role according to their character but one whose functionalities they can comply with.

A second stage of reflection is done by the players while reaching an agreement on the present and future portrayal of their company. As stated above this is a very dynamic process. Until they reach a consensus they are confronted with the different perceptions of the other players concerning the company and its objectives. This is an aspect of the adjusting reactions that occur during the simulation. The participants become very emotionally involved in the simulation and are surprised that they cannot easily reach consensus since there is not one right answer but instead many approaches [19]. This discussion enhances the learning potential for a novel mindset built upon diversity due to the distinct perspectives displayed.

Once the game starts more discussions arise as the cards are elaborated. Under non-gaming circumstances certain difficulties would occur such as the psychological safety to go along with the majority decision or the psychological amputation where someone is ostracized from the group because of an unpopular point of view [19]. This however, is prevented by the role-playing component of the CHANGCE-Game and thus a slow and growing involvement in the game is taking place cultivating a gainful interaction. The active involvement of the players correlates to Thatcher's findings that for debriefing the doing, the actual playing, is essential to guarantee a personal growth [3].

Lastly there is a post-experience learning after the game is finished. Each player is asked to estimate the outcomings of the game. Thereby, there is a stage of self-reflection focusing on one's own perception. The results are compared to the estimations of the other participants deepening the awareness of other mindsets. Finally, the estimations are examined in comparison to the analysis of the CHANGCE-Game Moderator adding an external and professional assessment.

Thus, the CHANGCE-Game itself is a very reflective process where the participants are guided by the CHANGCE-Game Moderator to a self-reliant learning experience obtained during playing [19]. The analysis of the experiences allows them to create new perceptions and knowledge of reality - new "cognitive maps" as Miller et al. describe it [19]. Then as a final phase of the CHANGCE-Game the experience is being linked to the participants day-to-day activities [19] leading into the CHANGCE-thinking process – the drafting of a future strategy with a new understanding of the company modeled by the activity.

5 Conclusion

As outlined above the CHANGCE-thinking framework is not merely a theoretical, but a practical approach for acquiring innovative behavior. It combines many scientific approaches and puts them into practice while overcoming personal and structural barriers. The CHANGCE-Game provides an opportunity to start the approach towards identification and realization of chances in a both structured and playful manner. This creates intrinsic motivation for change and a lasting momentum. This momentum, however, needs to be sustained over time, lead by the CHANGCE-Pilot. From the conception through to the implementation of new chances, the CHANGCE-Pilot supervises and supports the CHANGCE-thinking process within an organization. The application of further ludic elements during this process is a subject to further studies. As an underlying framework, CHANGCE-thinking facilitates innovation and encourages companies to not only recognize but realize chances appropriately.

References

1. Highsmith, J., Cockburn, A.: Agile software development. Bus. Innov. Comput. (2001). doi: 10.1109/2.947100
2. Lewin, K.: Frontiers in group dynamics. Hum. Relat. (1947). doi:10.1177/001872674700100103
3. Thatcher, D.C.: Promoting learning through games and simulations. Simul. Gaming **21**(3), 262–273 (1990)
4. Wahren, H.-K.: Erfolgsfaktor Innovation. In: Ideen systematisch generieren, bewerten und umsetzen; mit 4 Tabellen. Springer, Berlin (2004)
5. Belbin, R.M.: Team roles at work, 2nd edn. Butterworth-Heinemann, Amsterdam (2011)
6. Belbin, R.M.: Management Teams. Why They Succeed or Fail, 3rd edn. Elsevier/Butterworth-Heinemann, Amsterdam (2011)
7. Kelley, T., Littman, J.: The ten faces of innovation. IDEO's strategies for beating the devil's advocate & driving creativity throughout your organization. Profile, London (2008)
8. Bono, E.: Das Sechsfarben-Denken. Ein neues Trainingsmodell. Econ, Düsseldorf (1987)
9. Bono, E.: Serious creativity. Die Entwicklung neuer Ideen durch die Kraft lateralen Denkens. Schäffer-Poeschel, Stuttgart (1996)

10. Day, G.S., Reibstein, D.J., Gunther, R.E.: Wharton on Dynamic Competitive Strategy. Wiley, Hoboken (2004)
11. Geuting, M.: Planspiel und soziale Simulation im Bildungsbereich. Studien zur Pädagogik, Andragogik und Gerontagogik, vol. 10. Lang, Frankfurt am Main (1992)
12. Keys, B., Wolfe, J.: The role of management games and simulations in education and research. J. Manag. **16**(2), 307–336 (1990)
13. Hüther, G., Quarch, C.: Rettet das Spiel! Weil Leben mehr als Funktionieren ist. Carl Hanser Verlag, München (2016)
14. Kolb, D.A.: Experiential Learning. Experience as the Source of Learning and Development. Pearson Education Inc., Upper Saddle River (2014)
15. Cobuild English learner's dictionary. Collins, London (2003)
16. Herz, D. (ed.): Simulation und Planspiel in den Sozialwissenschaften. Eine Bestandsaufnahme der internationalen Diskussion. Grundlegung und Methoden der politischen Wissenschaft, vol. 1. Lit, Münster (2000)
17. Hicks, M.J.: Problem Solving and Decision Making. Hard, Soft and Creative Approaches, 2nd edn. Thompson Learning, London (2004)
18. Isaksen, S.G., Dorval, K.B., Treffinger, D.J.: Creative Approaches to Problem Solving. A Framework for Innovation and Change. SAGE, Los Angeles (2011)
19. Crookall, D., Arai, K.: Simulation and Gaming Across Disciplines and Cultures. ISAGA at a Watershed. Sage Publications, Thousand Oaks (1995)

Toward an Assessment Framework for Gamified Environments

Gloria Piedad Gasca-Hurtado[1], María Clara Gómez-Alvarez[1]([✉]),
Mirna Muñoz[2], and Jezreel Mejía[2]

[1] Facultad de Ingeniería, Ingeniería de Software,
Universidad de Medellín, Carrera 87 No. 30-65, Medellín, Colombia
{gpgasca,mcgomez}@udem.edu.co
[2] Centro de Investigación en Matemáticas,
Av. Universidad no 222, 98068 Zacatecas, Mexico
{mirna.munoz,jmejia}@cimat.mx

Abstract. Gamification is a recent strategy used in several contexts, in our case we implement gamification as a strategy to promote a dynamic environment in Software Process Improvement (SPI) initiatives. Gamification can be a mechanism to transform SPI approaches, since it has great potential to increase engagement and enjoyment in teams. In this paper, we present a proposal for the assessment of gamified environments in order to assure that gamified experiences meet the purposes, goals, principles and elements that are defined as gamification fundamental components. Our proposal is oriented towards the definition of an assessment framework for gamified environments that comprises the identification and adoption of gamification principles, as well as a design method for gamified activities.

Keywords: Software process improvement · Gamification · Gamification principles

1 Introduction

Gamification is a recent strategy used in several contexts where the human factor is a key for the success of the different initiatives. In particular, gamification is an alternative to increase the motivation and commitment levels in work teams. The propose of use gamification in software process improvement initiatives is achieving high levels of motivation to work with team members, integrate participants to increase technical knowledge and increase progress indicators of project teams [1]. However, not only is necessary procedures and methods that guide the gamification of a non-gamified context, because it is also important have mechanisms to verify if the principles and fundamental gamification elements are properly incorporated in a gamification environment for achieving the expected results.

In this paper, we present a proposal for the assessment of gamified environments to assure that gamified experiences meet the purposes, goals, principles and elements that are defined as gamification fundamental components. Our proposal is oriented towards the definition of an assessment framework for gamified environments that comprises the identification and adoption of gamification principles, as well as a design method for gamified activities.

Section 2 presents the main concepts that fundaments the proposal. In Sect. 3 the assessment framework proposal is described. This section presents each framework layer and its components in a detailed manner. In Sect. 4 an example of the use of the framework are described. Finally, in Sect. 5 the conclusions and future work are presented.

2 Background

2.1 Gamification

Gamification is a growing trend where the human factor is fundamental in terms of motivation and engagement of the work teams [2–4]. Such trend can promote in individuals' social interaction, quality and productivity of his actions [5]. Gamification can be defined as: (i) an approach that involves the same psychological experiences of the games [4]; (ii) the application of the same principles and environments of the games, regardless of expected results [2] and (iii) a process implementing motivational affordances for obtain psychological and behavioral outcomes in individuals [6, 7].

The growing interest in gamification as a strategy for process improvement in organization is evident because: (i) the growth of computer game industry over the last two motivating individuals to play; (ii) the pervasiveness of social media and mobile and web-based technologies is changing the way how individuals interact inside organizations [8]; and (iii) organizations are continually looking new ways for influence the behavior of employees and clients.

However, there are a few well-established theoretical guidelines for design gamified experiences. This problem is the main motivation of this work oriented to propose a framework like a set of tools for create gamification environments guaranteeing the application of gamification principals and the achievement of the specific goals.

2.2 The MDE Framework

MDE Framework is an approach to design games emphasizing the need to understand games mechanics, dynamics and emotions for obtain an improvement in commitment levels from team members, employees and customers [9]. Figure 1 shows the framework elements: mechanics, dynamics and emotions:

1. *Mechanics* are related with the designers' decisions for gamify a non-game context such as: goals, rules and the guidelines that stablish the boundaries of the gamified environment. Game mechanics are known before the gamified experience beginning and are the same for all game participants. However, mechanics are not enough to create a gamified environment allows to obtain behavior changes in participants. For this purpose, its necessary keep in mind the others two elements of MDE Framework described below.

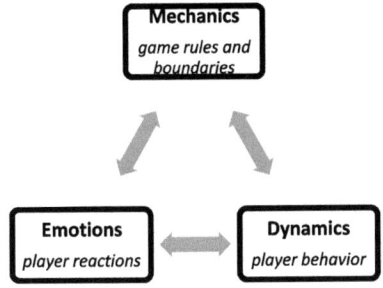

Fig. 1. MDE framework

2. *Dynamics* is a result of how the players follow the game mechanics. In other words, game dynamics emerge during play [10]. In the case of gamified environments, the interaction of team members can lead to dynamics like cooperation, competition or conspiracy.
3. *Emotions* refers to the mental affective state and reactions promoted in players when they participate in a gamified environment. In this sense, the main goal for gamification is create the player enjoyment for guaranteeing the continuity of the gamified experience. Some positive emotions promoted by games are excitement, surprise, wonder and amazement.

2.3 Gamification Principles

Oprescu *et al.* propose ten principles for implement gamification experiences [12]:

1. *Orientation:* the participant is the center of the experience for achieving engagement, sense of control and self-efficacy.
2. *Persuasive elements:* through game elements, we can obtain change initial behavior of participants.
3. *Learning orientation:* games can develop skills and motivational outcomes.
4. *Achievement based on rewards:* games could be oriented to a positive feedback related with goals achievement as a way to increase self-efficacy.
5. *Y Generation adaptable:* games allow Y generation individuals express their opinion in a fun, engaging and rewarding environment.
6. *Amusement factors:* games include humor, play and fun elements to increase participants' motivation and satisfaction.
7. *Transformative:* gamification combines competition and collaboration and could integrate moral decisions to enhance the desired skills in participants.
8. *Well-being oriented:* games could focus on personal well-being.
9. *Research generating:* games could allow participants to collaborate in order to identify future improvements in the application area.
10. *Knowledge-based:* gamification could be based on knowledge, either as an outcome or as feedback.

2.4 Assessment Proposals

Gamification is a trend that receives increasing attention from researchers as well as practitioners. For this reason, exists different approaches to faces gamification projects [13] including the phases business modeling, design, implementation and monitoring and adaptation [14]. However, the activity less mature is the monitoring of the gamification designs. For this reason, Heilburnn et al. [14] suggest the use of gamification analytics tools to measure the success of gamification designs allowing to quantify and understand user behavior improvements [15]. Moreover, they propose the use of semi-structured interviews as a mechanism for obtain a direct feedback of user satisfaction and additional requirements for the gamified experiences. In [16] the authors identify relevant software solutions for measure the fulfillment of user requirements in gamification projects.

In such proposals, the assessment is centered in collecting data for software applications about user behavior using gamification analytics. However, our proposal is oriented to a generic gamification environment, supported of not by software artefacts. For this reason, the data of participants' behavior will be collected directly for users through neuroscience equipment. This alternative will allow discover at first-hand how participants react to the different elements of the gamified environment.

3 Assessment Framework Proposal

Software process improvement is an approach used by software industries for increase the productivity and quality of their processes and products. One important issue is the social interaction among the team members is improve motivation and engagement levels in participants. This situation could be address-using gamification like a strategy to improve the social factors related to the software development process. In this sense is necessary to define methods, guidelines and frameworks to assurance the adequate implementing of the gamification strategy.

In general, the framework proposed in this work is a conceptual structure aims to serve as a support or guide for creating gamified environments focused on SPI.

Our framework is a layered structure indicating what kind of components can or should be built and how they would interrelate. The framework structure is the result of the analysis of different studies, cited in the previous section, that describes gamification elements, components and principles. Such framework is composed by layers containing basic components (fundamentals, methods, procedures) looking for obtain the expected results with the incorporation of gamified environments in SPI initiatives. Figure 2 shows the layers of proposed framework. The framework proposes the creation of gamification environments starting from the identification and adoption of gamification elements. The identification and adoption of the principles is related to the analysis and contextualization of useful fundamentals for software process improvement, although the framework is structured in a general way.

The framework begins with a principles identification layer as a conceptual support of the principles adoption layer. The first layer allows to reflect the elements necessary to guarantee that gamification is using adequately as a strategy to improve the participants'

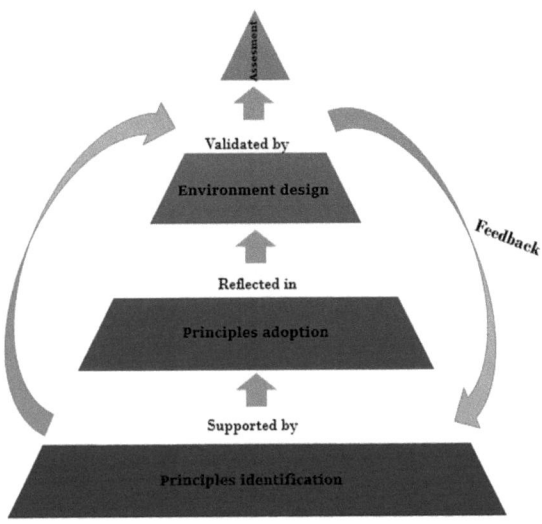

Fig. 2. Assessment framework for gamified environments

behavior. Starting with the gamified environment design, the validated assessment is carried out based on principles identified, adopted and reflected in the design.

Finally, the framework improves through constant feedback including the four-layer conforming it. In the next section, each framework layer is described indicating the level of progress reached in the project in the actual status of the research.

3.1 Framework Layers

The four-layer conforming the framework are: (1) *principles identification* that will contextualized the gamified environment; (2) *principles adoption* identified at the previous layer; (3) *gamified environment design* and (4) *assessment of gamified environment* validating its design from the principles adopted at previous layers.

The framework layered-structure is defined identified for each layer three key elements: (a) base component, (b) procedural component and (c) results component.

- *Base component* of a layer includes the fundamental aspects for the use of the framework. Each layer will have a basic starting point, so that the framework user can establish the application basis of each layer.
- *Procedural component* of a layer is equivalent to methods, procedures and guidelines allowing to obtain each layer goals and expected results.
- *Results component* of a layer includes templates and standards for indicating to framework user the structure of expected results in each layer.

First Layer: Identification
This layer establishes a procedure for identifying, defining and contextualizing the gamification. The components of this layer are:

- *Base component*: basic gamification principles for the framework. Such principles are described by Oprescu et al. [12] taking advance of their easy of adaptation in a gamification strategy.
- *Procedural component*: procedure for recent studies selection where the gamification and basic components are defined (See Fig. 3). In different studies, gamification definition is accompanied by basic principles as a fundamental pillar for the gamified environment construction. For this reason, in this layer is recommended the identification of additional principles, when the base principles established in the layer base component are not sufficient or a specific change is required.

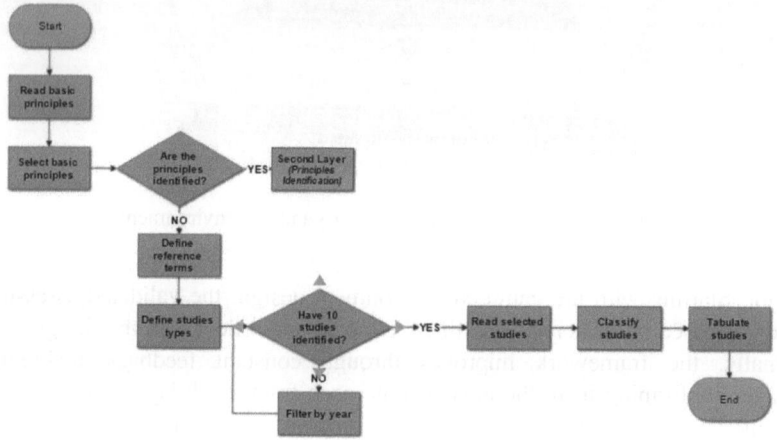

Fig. 3. Identification layer procedural component

- *Results component*: Table 1 shows the suggested template for this component construction starting from gamification principles definition established in the layer base component (Oprescu et al. [12] proposal).

Table 1. Template for result component of Identification layer

ID	Principle name	Description	Expected benefits

Second Layer: Adoption

Set of rules based on software engineering experimentation [17]. We used recommendation and methods generated from software engineering experimentation area because is considered a paradigm to helps establish a scientific and engineering basis for the software engineering field. This paradigm helps to build, analyze and evaluate models of the software process and products [17].

The selection of the appropriate research method to clarify the research question is one of the first activities proposed in this area. Table 2 shows the different types of research questions.

Table 2. Research questions types [18]

Research question type	Definition	Such as
Exploratory questions	In the early stages of a research program. As we attempt to understand the phenomena, and identify useful distinctions that clarify our understanding	• Existence questions • Description and classification questions • Descriptive-comparative questions.
Base-rate questions	The answers to these questions result in a clearer understanding of the phenomena	• Frequency and distribution questions • Descriptive-process questions
Relationship	We are interested in the relationship between two different phenomena, and specifically whether occurrence of one is related to occurrence of the other	• Relationship questions
Causality questions	Once we have established that a relationship exists between two phenomena, it is natural to try to explain why the relationship holds by attempting to identify a cause and effect	• Causality questions • Causality-comparative questions • Causality-comparative interaction

The components of this layer are described below:

- *Base component*: basic gamification principles identified in the identification layer. This component includes the principles described in the suggested templated for the principles identification layer (Table 1). Besides, we suggest the use of the MDE framework for the construction of this component as a guideline for games design.
- *Procedural component*: the adoption of gamification principles aims to complete gamification conceptual basics. This component is built from activities and procedure rules (Table 3), as a fundamental basics for the comparison of tabulated principles, implementing the set of rules for adoption layer construction.
- *Results component*: The graph shown in Fig. 4 is an example of result of the adoption layer. In this component, the construction of a similar structure as a comparison map is expected as a result component of this layer. The adoption of gamification principles related to MDE framework for games design is achieved when a structure like the graph of Fig. 5 is established.

An alternative representation of the result layer-component is by means of the template shown in Table 4.

Table 3. Activities and rules of procedural component of adoption layer

Activities	Rules
Frameworks identification	1. Identify a framework for gamified environment design 2. The base for this component is the MDE framework 3. A *base + 1* framework is selected when MDE is not adapted to the needs of the framework users or to the needs of the design gamification strategy
Resarch question formulation	1. Formulate an initial research question 2. The question is a base question if is formulated as a relationship question i.e. *"Does the identified gamification principle X correlate with the MDE framework?"* 3. The question is an essential research question if generates any change in the question type. It suggests considering the question types presented in Table 2
Comparison and relationship	1. Answer the research question for each gamification principle of Table 1, generated in Identification layer 2. Analyze the existence of relationships between each Table 1 gamification principle and the MDE framework or *base + 1* framework 3. A relation between the gamification principle and framework exists when some of design components coincide with the principles tabulated in the Identification layer

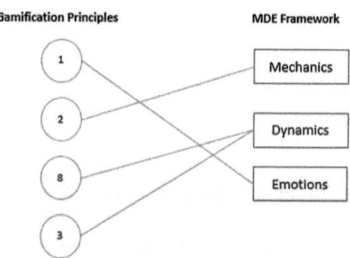

Fig. 4. Layer result component for adoption layer

Table 4. Result layer-component template for adoption layer

Gamification principle	MDE Framework
1	Emotions
2	Mechanics
8, 3	Dynamics

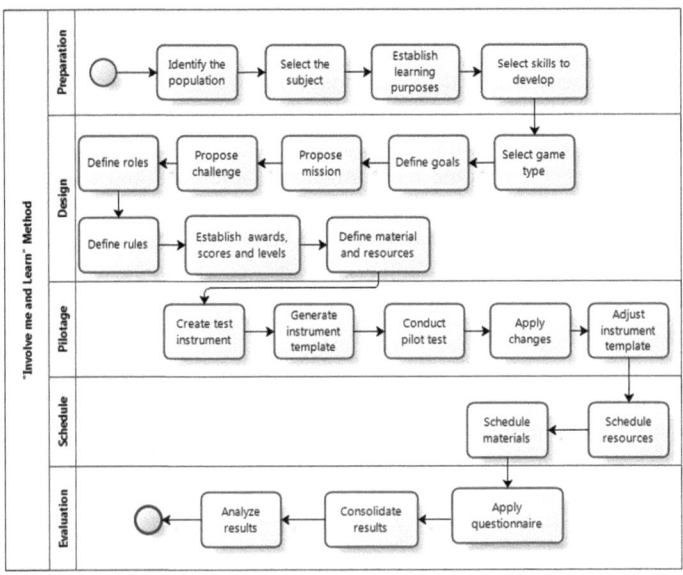

Fig. 5. Gamified activities design method [20]

Third Layer: Design

Sequential route for makes more dynamic the process of a gamified environment construction. This layer is built from sequential steps for generating gamified learning activities in a systematic way. Although the method [19] shown in this layer is focused on gamification as teaching strategy, it is expected that the evolution of the framework proposed in this work will lead us to generate a refinement of the method for design gamified activities that conforms a gamification environment for software process improvement. The components of this layer are:

- *Base component*: the template and the comparison map established in the adoption layer are the basics for the construction of the design layer.
- *Procedural component:* a method for gamified activities design. Such method aims to guide the creation of gamified activities based on: (a) experience as immediate resource for learning, (b) gamification as a teaching strategy for dynamizing the students classroom work and increase the motivation levels in participants [19]. The method is a sequential route that allows to gamified activities designer obtain a set of activities for the teaching of a specific topic. Figure 5 shows the sequential steps for the construction of the design layer.
- *Results component*: gamified activities. The results of the application of the procedural component must be a set of activities necessary to gamify an environment. The basic elements of a gamified environment are: goals, materials, roles, steps and rules [20].

Forth Layer: Assessment

Application and gamification data contain valuable information about users and their behavior. This data can be used to measure the success of gamification projects, to analyze user behavior, and to continuously improve gamification designs.

However, to support the process of gamification analysis, appropriate tool support is missing. Moreover, the specific requirements for methods and tools have not been studied yet and remain unclear [14]. Some proposals like Heilbrunn et al. work shows the results of semi-structured interviews for evaluate gamification tools facilitating the identification of relevant software solutions and assesses them with regards to their fulfillment of user requirements in the gamification analytics domain [16].

Such proposal of evaluation of gamification analytics tools considering that the design of a gamification project required the implementation of related activities, where the design is implemented as software artifacts and functionally tested [16].

Although the gamified environment assessment can be conceived from this principle and it is possible to use the tools evaluated in [14] and in [16], our proposal in this work will be focused on the capture and analysis of user data that allow to measure participants behavior in a gamified environment independent to the support of technology. In other words, the assessment to be propose will be independent to the generation of software artifacts as part of the gamification environment.

One of the first alternatives we intend to design as a part of the framework is the used of data captured with neuroscience equipment. The propose is incorporating in this assessment the concepts that neuroscientists are discovering about the ways in which humans react to interactive design elements.

As some initial components of this layer we propose the following alternatives:

- *Base component*: basic elements of a gamified environment. The basis for the construction of this layer includes the basic elements of a gamified environment defined in the design layer [20] and software artefacts and requirements identified, if they exist as part of the gamification activities defined in the design.
- *Procedural component*: methods of measurement and data collection. The procedure that will be designed as a procedural component of assessment layer will include methods for collect user data for assessing their behavior through neuroscience equipment and HCI design aspects and assessment methods in the case that the gamified environment elements include software artefacts of user requirements.
- *Results component*: Data analysis facilitating the improvement of the gamified environment. The expected results in this layer will be data analysis because these elements could show the effectivity of gamification in terms of user satisfaction faces of the gamified environment.

4 Framework in Action

In this section, we present a brief example of the framework application for creating a gamified activity related with the defect tracking in software development process. For the first layer (Identification), using the base component consists of gamification

Table 5. Results component for identification layer

ID	Principle name	Description	Expected benefits
2	Persuasive elements	Different game elements for promote actions in participants	Changes in participants' behavior
3	Learning orientation	Games promote skills related with knowledge transfer	Knowledge transfer
6	Amusement factors	Games elements for promote participation	Increase motivation and satisfaction in participants

principles, the results of this layer are presented in Table 5, where some principles and expected benefits are summarized.

For the second layer (Adoption), using the principles identification (Table 5) and the activities and rules defined in the procedural component, the result is a relation between gamification principles and MDE framework elements as shown in Table 6.

Table 6. Relation between gamification principles and MDE Framework

Gamification principle	MDE framework
1, 2, 3, 4	Mechanics
2, 7, 9, 10	Dynamics
5, 6, 8	Emotions

In relation with the Design Layer, in [20] the use of the method for design the gamified activity for defect tracking are described. This work includes generates the definition of basic elements of the gamified activity: goals, roles, steps, materials and rules. The next step consists on define the components of the Assessment layer and apply them to different gamified activities confirming a gamified environment. The purpose is verifying if such activities meet the goals and expected results of the gamification initiatives.

5 Conclusions and Future Work

This work proposes an assessment framework for gamified environments aims to facilitate the verification of principles and gamification elements identified and adopted as a part of the design of gamified activities includes in a gamified environment for software process improvement. The framework pretends to be a first guide to orientate from the contextualization of a gamification strategy for software process improvement initiatives to the assessment of the gamified environment.

The assessment goal is verifying that the gamification principles are fulfilled in the gamification environment. For the reason, the proposed framework pretends to include several assessment strategies related to data analysis for measure the participants behavior.

Although we are working on the construction and adaptation of the framework layers, there are some proposals for HCI methods and approaches with tools and technologies from neuroscience laboratories that can be part of the framework as an assessment strategy.

As a future work, we suggest: (1) analysis for mix HCI measures and approaches for assessing the users' behavior of a gamified environment under the framework and (2) adaptation or refinement of the method for design gamified activities oriented to industrial contexts.

References

1. Dorling, A., McCaffery, F.: The gamification of SPICE. In: Mas, A., Mesquida, A., Rout, T., O'Connor, R.V., Dorling, A. (eds.) SPICE 2012. CCIS, vol. 290, pp. 295–301. Springer, Heidelberg (2012). doi:10.1007/978-3-642-30439-2_35
2. Deterding, S., Dixon, D., Khaled, R., Nacke, L.: From game design elements to gamefulness: defining gamification. In: Proceedings of the 15th International Academic MindTrek Conference: Envisioning Future Media Environments. ACM (2011)
3. Hamari, J., Lehdonvirta, V.: Game design as marketing: how game mechanics create demand for virtual goods (2010)
4. Huotari, K., Hamari, J.: Defining gamification: a service marketing perspective. In: Proceeding of the 16th International Academic MindTrek Conference. ACM (2012)
5. Hamari, J.: Transforming homo economicus into homo ludens: a field experiment on gamification in a utilitarian peer-to-peer trading service. Electron. Commer. Res. Appl. **12**(4), 236–245 (2013)
6. Hamari, J., Koivisto, J., Sarsa, H.: Does gamification work?–A literature review of empirical studies on gamification. In: 2014 47th Hawaii International Conference on System Sciences (HICSS). IEEE (2014)
7. Robson, K., et al.: Is it all a game? Understanding the principles of gamification. Bus. Horiz. **58**(4), 411–420 (2015)
8. Kietzmann, J., et al.: Social media? Get serious! Understanding the functional building blocks of social media. Bus. Horiz. **54**(3), 241–251 (2011)
9. Hunicke, R., LeBlanc, M., Zubek, R.: MDA: a formal approach to game design and game research. In: Proceedings of the AAAI Workshop on Challenges in Game AI, vol. 4, no. 1 (2004)
10. Camerer, C.: Behavioral Game Theory: Experiments in Strategic Interaction. Princeton University Press, Princeton (2003)
11. Rednic, E., et al.: Organize distributed work environments in a game-like fashion. In: Recent Advances in Knowledge Engineering and Systems Science, pp. 213–218 (2013)
12. Oprescu, F., et al.: I PLAY AT WORK—ten principles for transforming work processes through gamification. Front. Psychol. **5** (2014)
13. Herzig, P., Ameling, M., Wolf, B., Schill, A.: Implementing gamification: requirements and gamification platforms. In: Reiners, T., Wood, L.C. (eds.) Gamification in Education and Business, pp. 431–450. Springer, Cham (2015). doi:10.1007/978-3-319-10208-5_22
14. Heilbrunn, B., Herzig, P., Schill, A.: Towards gamification analytics-requirements for monitoring and adapting gamification designs. In: GI-Jahrestagung (2014)
15. Kumar, J.: Gamification at work: designing engaging business software. In: Marcus, A. (ed.) DUXU 2013. LNCS, vol. 8013, pp. 528–537. Springer, Heidelberg (2013). doi:10.1007/978-3-642-39241-2_58

16. Heilbrunn, B., Herzig, P., Schill, A.: Tools for gamification analytics: a survey. In: 2014 IEEE/ACM 7th International Conference on Utility and Cloud Computing (UCC). IEEE (2014)
17. Basili, V.: The role of experimentation in software engineering: past, current, and future. In: Proceedings of the 18th International Conference on Software Engineering (ICSE 1996), pp. 442–449. IEEE Computer Society, Washington, DC (1996)
18. Easterbrook, S., Singer, J., Storey, M.A., Damian, D.: Selecting empirical methods for software engineering research. In: Shull, F., Singer, J., Sjøberg, D.I.K. (eds.) Guide to Advanced Empirical Software Engineering. Springer, London (2008). doi:10.1007/978-1-84800-044-5_11
19. Gómez-Alvarez, M.C., et al.: Method of pedagogic instruments design for software engineering. In: 2016 11th Iberian Conference on Information Systems and Technologies (CISTI), Gran Canaria, pp. 1–6 (2016)
20. Gasca-Hurtado, G.P., Gómez-Alvarez, M.C., Muñoz, M., Mejía, J.: Gamification proposal for defect tracking in software development process. In: Kreiner, C., O'Connor, R.V., Poth, A., Messnarz, R. (eds.) EuroSPI 2016. CCIS, vol. 633, pp. 212–224. Springer, Cham (2016). doi:10.1007/978-3-319-44817-6_17

InnoTEACH – Applying Principles of Innovation in School

Richard Messnarz[2(✉)], Borut Likar[3,5], Jürgen Mack[1],
Evelyn Schröttner[1], Damjan Ekert[2], Maria Hartyanyi[4],
Urska Mrgole[3], and Janos Szabo[4]

[1] ORG Schulschwestern, Graz, Austria
{juergen.mack,evelyn.schroettner}@schulschwestern.at
[2] ISCN GesmbH, Graz, Austria
{rmess,dekert}@iscn.com
[3] Korona plus d.o.o, Ljubljana, Slovenia
info@innovation.si
[4] IT STUDY, Gödöllö, Hungary
maria.hartyanyi@itstudy.hu
[5] Faculty of Management, University of Primorska, Koper, Slovenia

Abstract. The research and development of new and improved services, systems, and products is an important driver for the European market. Innovation requires people that can interact in innovation teams, innovative and new ideas, creative environments supporting the creation of innovation, and innovation processes that support the entire chain from idea creation to the implementation of an innovation project. Innovation is intimately linked with entrepreneurship. Ideas, Innovation and Entrepreneurship are considered the keys to a wealthy and sustainable economy [1, 3, 5, 6, 8]. The InnoTEACH project empowers the innovation mind-set in the European Union by establishing learning environments in schools which fertilize the grounds for young people to apply innovation principles in problem solving and learning about entrepreneurship concepts at the same time. This paper presents "InnoTEACH", a European project that transfers the innovation best practices from industry to the education and certification of school teachers.

Keywords: Innovation · Entrepreneurship · Teacher

1 Introduction

Nowadays innovations are of crucial importance for the development and economic results of the European Union [7, 3, 5, 6, 8] and its members. Slovenia, Austria and Hungary invest a lot in the field of innovation, yet there are still challenges to be faced involving innovation in all fields. One of them is related to the educational system [4] which has to be continuously adapted to the needs of the modern society. It should address the nowadays needs, e.g. creativity, innovation and entrepreneurship. Creativity, innovation and entrepreneurship (CI&E) are crucial competences that cannot be taught in a simple manner. The project's aim is to trigger different ways of thinking in primary and high schools and to show that creativity, innovation and entrepreneurship are crucial for success - anywhere; in all subjects, in daily situations in school, in real life challenges, and to teach participants how to implement that in practice.

The InnoTEACH project uses a pool of previous knowledge and project results which were developed for innovation processes management in industry, and transfers the principles of innovation from industry into schools [2,8]. E.g. In industry creative learning environments are used to open the minds and to continuously come up with new ideas and improvement suggestions. Teachers learn to apply similar project based tasks for student teams in problem solving situations. E.g. In industry specific team roles are defined for innovation teams and so teachers will learn how to apply such roles in student team work. E.g. In industry specific analysis methods are used to identify strengths, weaknesses, threats and potentials and to identify root causes of problems to be solved. Teachers will learn how to explain such methods and how to use them with student teams in problem solving scenarios. InnoTEACH develops the materials applying European skills definition standards and skills and learning portals [8, 9].

Skills set/skills card. The skills set is defined for a job role and a job role contains areas of knowledge (skills units), specific skill topics (learning elements), and tasks a student can perform after acquiring the knowledge per learning element (learning objectives, performance criteria). This structure is based on the NVQ (National Vocational Qualification Program) of UK and has been adapted and mapped to the EQF (European Qualification Framework). Every learning element has ECTS (European Credit Transfer System) and ECVET points (European Credits for Vocational Education Training). The skills set has been developed for teachers and mentors of teachers.

Job Role. A job role is a specific role which a person can play at the work place. It can be understood as an upgrade of skills to play a specific role and it is certified by the ECQA (European Certification and Qualification Association, www.ecqa.org). In case of InnoTEACH teachers, their additional job role will be related to CI&E training within school and support to innovative activities of students.

Certified Training Structure. To fulfil the ECQA guidelines the training material must be consistent with the skills set. This means that learning elements and performance criteria are mapped onto the training material.

Certified Test Questions Pool. To fulfil the ECQA guidelines the test questions are developed as a pool to be shared among the regions in Europe and are mapped onto the skills set and training material.

Job Role Committee. At the end of the project an ECQA job role committee is formed with training bodies, schools and innovators to maintain the skills card and the network between the educational institutions.

The objectives are to connect InnoTEACH with existing other European initiatives to form a comprehensive framework for innovation in European schools, universities, and industry.

Figure 1 illustrates that InnoTEACH is part of an overall innovation framework which has been set up in various EU initiatives in the past years.

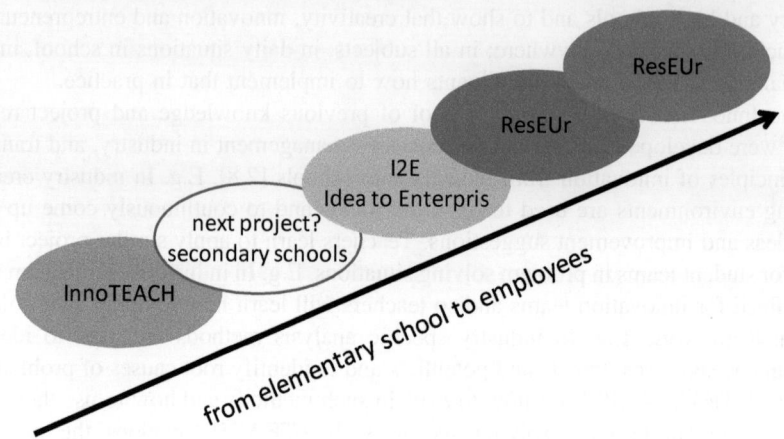

Fig. 1. Innovation layers: teachers – students – researchers - industry

InnoTEACH is an EU project in the Erasmus+ program (2010–2018) which trains and certifies teachers to apply innovation methods in their teaching classes. Teachers will receive an ECQA certificate. Idea to Enterprise was an EU LLP (Life Long Learning) project (2012–2014) which developed an ECQA certificate and training material for students to apply innovation methods [7].

ResEUr (Researcher Entrepreneur) was an EU LLP (Life Long Learning) project (2010–2011) which developed an ECQA certificate and training material for researchers and PhD students to apply innovation methods [8].

Innovation manager (2003–2005) was an EU Leonardo da Vinci project which developed training materials and an ECQA certificate for industrial innovation managers which manage innovation processes in leading industry [9].

InnoTEACH (Fig. 1) has a core role in this innovation framework because teachers are empowering the students that later become researchers and eventually become innovators in industry.

2 InnoTEACH Skills Set

The InnoTEACH skills set structure is outlined in Fig. 2 below. There are three main skills units: U1 Development of Innovation, U2 Innovative Teaching, and U3 Making Innovation Work. U stands for Skills Unit.

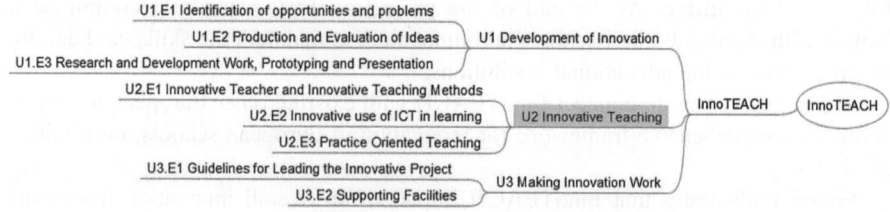

Fig. 2. InnoTEACH skills set architecture

The skills unit U1 Development of Innovation contains the following learning elements (specific skills areas):

- U1.E1 Identification of Opportunities and Problems
- U1.E2 Production and Evaluation of Ideas
- U1.E3 Research and Development Work, Prototyping, and Presentation

The skills unit U2 Innovative Teaching contains the following learning elements (specific skills areas):

- U2.E1 Innovative Teacher and Innovative Teaching Methods
- U2.E2 Innovative Use of ICT in Learning
- U2.E3 Practice Oriented Teaching

The skills unit U3 Making Innovation Work contains the following learning elements (specific skills areas):

- U3.E1 Guidelines for Leading the Innovative Project
- U3.E2 Supporting Facilities

For each learning element performance criteria are defined which relate to task based learning. For each performance criteria the teachers must be able to demonstrate skills to perform a task correctly applying the criteria. In InnoTeach 2 skills sets are developed, one for teachers and a second one for mentors of teachers.

Figure 3 below shows the sample performance criteria table for the skills element "U1.E1 Identification of Opportunities and Problems" for the teachers:

2.1 U1.E1 Identification of Opportunities and Problems (for Teachers)

Innovation starts with identifying an opportunity to change an existing process, product, service and in most cases it starts with identifying a problem to solve. Identified problems and opportunities often need to be analysed to identify root causes for the problems. This relates to methods such as:

- Sources of innovations
- Innovation Cube
- Ishikava diagram
- Quadim method

2.1.1 Related I2E Element: U1.E2

The performance criteria for this element are:

INNOTEACH.U1.E1.PC1	The teachers is able to use methods and tools to identify problems and opportunities.
INNOTEACH.U1.E1.PC2	The teacher knows the principles of decomposing the problem and identify real roots of the problem.

Fig. 3. InnoTEACH performance criteria for teachers for U1.E1

Figure 4 below shows the sample performance criteria table for the skills element "U1.E1 Identification of Opportunities and Problems" for the mentors: **U1.E1 Identification of Opportunities and Problems (for mentors).** Innovation starts with identifying an opportunity to change an existing process, product, service and in most cases it starts with identifying a problem to solve. Identified problems and opportunities often need to be analysed to identify root causes for the problems. This relates to methods such as:

- Sources of innovations
- Innovation Cube
- Ishikava diagram
- Quadim method

The role of the mentor is to coach teachers in applying this element of knowledge in the classroom.

2.1.2 Related I2E Element: U1.E2

The performance criteria for this element are:

INNOTEACH.U1.E1.PC1	The mentor is able to use & coach teachers in using methods and tools to identify problems and opportunities.
INNOTEACH.U1.E1.PC2	The mentor is able to use & coach teachers to know the principles of decomposing the problem and identify real roots of the problem

Fig. 4. InnoTEACH performance criteria for mentors for U1.E1

3 InnoTEACH Training Strategy

For each learning element there is a set of training materials. Each unit has an underlying teaching workflow and strategy. Figure 5 illustrates the teaching workflow for unit 1 "Development of Innovation" [2]. First teachers learn how to form student teams and to use creative methods to identify problems and opportunities (U1.E1). In U1.E2 teachers learn about creative methods to produce and evaluate ideas to solve the problems which they could apply with their student teams. And in U1.E3 teachers are trained about how research the selected ideas, come up with potential solutions and present them.

Figure 6 shows the teaching workflow for unit 2 "Innovative Teaching". First teachers learn how to use innovative teaching methods (U2.E1). Some of the innovative teaching methods are based on the use of ICT tools for teamwork and teaching (U2.E2). And U2.E3 trains teachers in task based and practice based teaching methods where students get tasks and upload results into the ICT infrastructure and their work gets rated and is the basis for the next tasks to be performed.

Figure 7 shows the teaching workflow for unit 3 "Making Innovation Work". In the learning workflow the unit 3 is after the units 1 and 2. Once the ideas and potential solutions have been analysed in unit 1 and once the teachers have applied the course of the training the innovative teaching environment and methods an innovation project is

Innovative Teaching – Student Teams are Coached to Apply Innovation (U1)

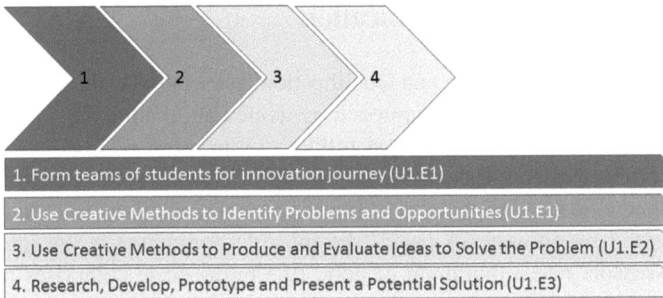

Fig. 5. InnoTEACH workflow for unit 1 development of innovation

Innovative Teaching – Teachers Use an Innovative Environment (U2)

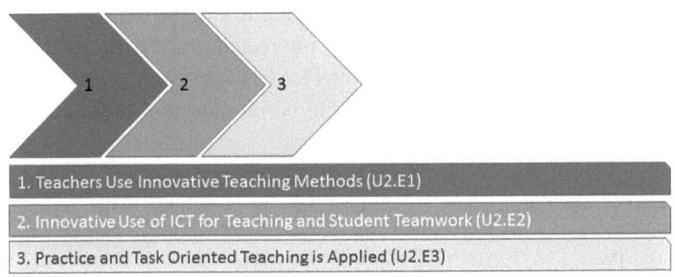

Fig. 6. InnoTEACH workflow for unit 2 innovative teaching

Innovative Teaching – Teachers Train Students in Realisation Steps (U3)

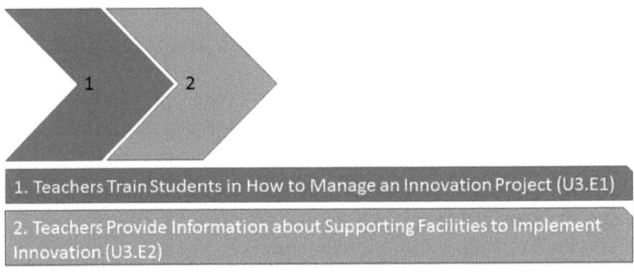

Fig. 7. InnoTEACH workflow for unit 3 making innovation work

set up to implement the innovation (U3.E1). Also the teachers get trained on how such innovation projects are supported in the EU (U3.E2).

4 InnoTEACH Teacher Certification

The ECQA (European Certification and Qualification Association) offers 2 types of test and certification: 1. The test based approach generates an exam from a pool of test questions and attendees of the exam must fulfil a minimum of 67% of each learning element area; 2. The evidence based skills assessment approach offers an interface for teachers to upload evidences of their work (in this case the exercises from units 1 to 3) which get assessed by an assessor panel (see job role committee in the introduction part). When assessors rate a minimum of good (the rating scale comprises poor, fair, good, excellent) in all skills elements the teacher passes the exam and a certificate is provided by the ECQA to the teacher.

The InnoTEACH project decided to implement the evidence based skills assessment approach. As an additional value for the InnoTEACH teachers, the InnoTEACH project will follow the Europass methodology and guidelines. InnoTEACH Teacher Mentors trained within the Joint International Trainings for Teachers from Participating Schools (C1) will be awarded with the Europass Mobility Certificate.

The InnoTEACH projects starts with EU funded training of teachers in July 2017. If teachers from different EU countries are interested they can be invited to the InnoTEACH classes and disseminate the InnoTEACH approach across Europe. In the exploitation it is planned to establish a job role committee to which different schools from different regions of Europe can join.

Acknowledgements. The "InnoTEACH" project has been funded with support from the European Commission under the Programme: Erasmus+, KA2, Strategic Partnerships for school education with the Project No. 2016-1-SI01-KA201-021641.

The European Commission support for the production of this publication does not constitute endorsement of the contents which reflects the views only of the authors, and the Commission cannot be held responsible for any use which may be made of the information contained therein.

References

1. Likar, B.: Innovation investment and economic performance in transition economies: evidence from Slovenia. Innovation Manage. Policy Pract. **16**(1), 53–66 (2014)
2. Likar B.: The Art of Managing Innovation Problems and Opportunities. Faculty of Management at the University of Primorska, ISBN: 978-961-266-180-9
3. Likar, B.: Factors of successful innovation in services and a performance comparison with manufacturing sector. Int. J. Innov. Learn. **12**(4), 379–401 (2012)
4. Likar, B.: Educational model for promoting creativity and innovation in primary schools. Behav. Sci. **32**(2), 205–213 (2014)
5. Gaynor, J., Mackiewicz, A., Ramaswami, R.: Entrepreneurship and innovation. In: The Keys to Global Economic Recovery. Ernst & Young (2009)

6. Final Report: Report on the results of public consultation on The Entrepreneurship 2020 Action Plan. http://eur-lex.europa.eu/legal-content/EN/TXT/?uri=celex%3A52012DC0795. Accessed 04 Jun 2017
7. Homolová, E., et al.: Empowering entrepreneurship in Europe: going from the idea to enterprise in 4 EU Countries. In: Barafort, B., O'Connor, R.V., Poth, A., Messnarz, R. (eds.) EuroSPI 2014. CCIS, vol. 425, pp. 262–270. Springer, Heidelberg (2014). doi:10.1007/978-3-662-43896-1_23
8. Messnarz, R., Riel, A., Sauberer, G., Reiner, M.: Forming a European innovation cluster as a think tank and knowledge pool. In: Kreiner, C., O'Connor, R.V., Poth, A., Messnarz, R. (eds.) EuroSPI 2016. CCIS, vol. 633, pp. 293–301. Springer, Cham (2016). doi:10.1007/978-3-319-44817-6_25
9. Riel, A.: Innovation managers 2.0: which competencies? In: O'Connor, Rory V., Pries-Heje, J., Messnarz, R. (eds.) EuroSPI 2011. CCIS, vol. 172, pp. 278–289. Springer, Heidelberg (2011). doi:10.1007/978-3-642-22206-1_25

A Game Toolbox for Process Improvement in Agile Teams

Antoni-Lluís Mesquida[1(✉)], Jovana Karać[2], Miloš Jovanović[1,3], and Antònia Mas[1]

[1] Department of Mathematics and Computer Science, University of the Balearic Islands,
Cra. de Valldemossa, km 7.5, 07122 Palma de Mallorca, Spain
{antoni.mesquida,milos.jovanovic,antonia.mas}@uib.es
[2] Institute of Digital Business, Johannes Kepler University Linz,
Altenberger Strasse 69, 4040 Linz, Austria
jovana.karac@jku.at
[3] Faculty of Technical Sciences, University of Novi Sad, Trg Dositeja Obradovica 6,
21000 Novi Sad, Serbia

Abstract. This paper demonstrates the use of game techniques for Software Process Improvement. InnoBox, a game toolbox for process improvement and innovation in agile teams is presented. Authors selected 12 collaborative games to be used in team meetings. Each game card in InnoBox has been created and classified based on a design thinking approach and team maturity level. InnoBox is a ready to use tool designed for agile teams to facilitate, innovate and improve communication, cohesion and their way of working.

Keywords: Process improvement · Retrospective games · Design thinking · Group development stages · InnoBox

1 Introduction

Commitment and engagement of the people is one of the most important factors for a successful deployment of agile methods in teams and process improvement in organizations. In order to implement a process model, companies should be aware of available tools and techniques that may be used in order to obtain the expected outcomes. Agile methods are increasingly used by software development organisations, and according to agile values and principles [1], development team should be proactive in defining, implementing and improving business processes affecting the organization as a whole or specific project. Engaging project stakeholders and providing a context where positive and innovation driven discussion would be conducted, while having fun at the same time, is crucial to continuously improve the established processes [2].

Significance of agile process tailoring is well recognized, but exact steps of the process tailoring highly depend on situational context in the company, and team and the process itself is described to a limited extent in the research literature [3]. Agile process tailoring involves as disciplined and well organized endeavour as any other plan driven method [4]. Agile practices and methods often have to be customized and tailored to accommodate specific situations in order to be integrated in the already established company processes [5, 6].

In this paper we demonstrate a toolbox named InnoBox, a set of ready to use game and behavioural techniques designed for project teams. The toolbox offers various solutions which can be used by team members for Software Process Improvement (SPI) and implementing innovations in their way of working. Collaborative games can be helpful in certain aspects of agile methods deployment in software development organizations. These games can be considered as a good example of tools to be used for facilitating the implementation of the techniques recommended by process reference models. Our research objective was to facilitate SPI in organizations and teams, and to create a ready to use tool that can be used quickly without time consuming preparation. Organizations are interested to adopt new techniques but often their time is limited to explore available tools in the market, or to analyse their current situation at the organizational or project level. Having this in mind we propose a toolbox that is mainly oriented for practical use in industry in project teams. Having a pre-planned set of collaborative games (toolbox) helps in bringing business value out of retrospective [7]. The research conducted in this paper presents a continuation of a previous research where game techniques for SPI in retrospectives were classified according to team development stages [8], and in this paper we propose additional classification based on game design method.

The paper is structured as follows. Section 2 presents the related work used for developing InnoBox - use of games in process improvement, group development stages and design thinking. Section 3 presents the research conducted to develop InnoBox and the results obtained - description and classification of the collaborative games in InnoBox. Section 4 concludes the paper and brings up the potential research initiatives to be undertaken.

2 Research Background

In this section, theoretical concepts important for development of InnoBox are demonstrated. Possibility and positive impact of using game elements in SPI is commented, followed by the group development stages proposed by Tuckman and the design thinking concept.

2.1 Game Elements in Software Process Improvement

Project leader together with project team members, should select the appropriate set of the games depending on their previous (individual and team) background and current phase or context of the project. Team maturity, size, distribution, time boxed meetings are important factors influencing proper game selection. Different aspects may be taken into account when selecting games for SPI like comprehensive framework of situational factors for software development process [9] or criteria affecting process tailoring [10].

Integrating gamification approach in software development process positively influences motivation of team members, and supports resources to be task and object oriented [11]. Various game thinking approaches in software development may be found in the research such as: theory of drama – used to define an SPI game [12], software development process can be perceived as a game where project resources act as a limitation

[13], or it may be observed as a balancing game depending on skill decision making in software [14]. Gamification approach in the company using Scrumban method can be used to guide SPI [11].

Retrospective meeting, agile practice for product and process improvement, provides endless insight and help teams to continuously improve [15]. Games used in agile retrospectives are made of basic game elements, but they help teams to improve and be motivated, have an important impact on social behaviour, team building and help organizations to become more lean and agile [7, 16].

2.2 Group Development Stages and Software Process Improvement

Agile software development is people centric, conducted through projects, and project members are organised in small groups-teams. Depending on situation in the company, one team might be working on several projects in parallel, or one bigger project may "consume" more teams with fully dedicated resources towards project objectives.

In the year 1965, Tuckman proposed four general sequential stages of group development: *Forming, Storming, Norming* and *Performing* [17]. Each sequential stage of group development consists of two types of activity: social or interpersonal and group/task related. Tuckman identified changes in group behaviour typical for each of the four stages [17]: (1) *Forming* is the phase of orientation, testing and dependence in the terms of social behaviour and group structure, (2) *Storming* represents the phase of intragroup conflicts and in terms of tasks emotional response of group members is expected, (3) *Norming* starts when group member's resistance is replaced with sense of group belonging and open discussion and increased communication among group members is expected, (4) *Performing* phase starts when group members care about efficiency, group roles become flexible and energy is focused on successful task completion.

Using games in agile retrospectives may help and improve adoption of team roles, problem solving approach or resolving group behaviour issues in each group development phase. Games to be used in SPI initiatives – agile retrospective meetings, and their classification depending on group development stage is demonstrated in a research study [8]. The results of research propose integrated table of retrospective games classified as a best fit, good fit and possible fit to 4 stages of group development proposed by Tuckman.

2.3 Design Thinking

Even though design thinking has its origins in training of designers, it can be practiced by everyone to every field of activity. Design thinking is not limited to designers only. More recently, this concept has been applied not just to physical products, but also to consumer experience, interaction processes and other disciplines and markets. Practicing design thinking involves a movement from "divergent thinking" which generates alternatives and gives more choices. Following by "convergent thinking", options are sorted so the best one among them could be chosen. "Analysis and synthesis" are applied for breaking patterns down and identifying a meaningful one [18]. Design thinking is associated with having a human-centred approach to problem solving and it is less technology or organization centred [19].

3 The Development of InnoBox

InnoBox contains a set of 12 collaborative games to be used by the team members during a meeting with the main objective of improving communication, cohesion and coordination. For each game, a description card describing different aspects of the game (purpose, rules, expected results, etc.) is given. Moreover, the needed assets and materials to run the game are also provided in the box.

The first decision to be made was the selection of the games to be implemented. From past research of the authors on the usage of games for SPI [20, 21], and taking as a basis the integrated list of games provided in [8], 12 collaborative games with different purpose, team dynamic and outcomes were selected.

One of our main objectives when developing the game box was to offer different classifications of the games. One of the groupings is related to the meeting time phase in which the game is most applicable. Derby and Larsen [16] proposed five different stages in a retrospective meeting: set the stage, gather data, generate insights, decide what to do and close the retrospective. Gray et al. [22] propose three different stages: open, explore and close. In our work, we have proposed three different time phases for a meeting: *Warming up*, *Playing* and *Wrapping up*.

As name suggests, the first meeting time phase is the *warming up* people's mind and possibilities. This phase is suitable for brainstorming, proposing new ideas and opportunities but not for critical thinking and scepticism. The following meeting time phase, *playing* is the experimental phase suitable for exploration and trying to see old things in a new way. Lastly, *wrapping up* should be critical and realistic overview, conclusion toward decisions and summarizing tasks to be done before next meeting. In the Table 1, two levels of games "fitting" to the meeting time phase is presented: the best fit games with symbol ●● and possible fit with symbol ●.

1. *Understanding the group knowledge* mostly appeals to the first phase. This activity has an aim to understand the group knowledge by giving statements on the following: "We know that we know", "We know that we don't know", "We didn't know that we know", and "We didn't know that we don't know".
2. *Roles we play* encourages a conversation about all roles played in life. It suits to the first phase but to the second phase also. Especially it is useful for a group that starts working together.
3. *Visual Phone* is an energizer for communication and interpretation improvement. Therefore, this game appeals to the first phase more than to the second phase, but it can be applied in both.
4. *The team is - is not - does - does not* is an activity that reveals positive and negative aspects about the team by explaining the team. Because it involves exploring and discovering this activity is the most appropriate for the second phase, but also for the last phase because it provides answers and explanations to asked questions.

5. *Role expectations matrix* aims to map out the expectations among team members. The goal of this activity is to find out how each member can benefit from each other. It is appropriate for the second phase.
6. *Defining the team principles* is an activity fostering conversation and discussion among participants. It suits better to the first phase, but it can be used in the last phase.
7. *Peaks and valleys timeline* is a visual activity especially useful for the last phase. It is effective way for uncovering interactions among team members as well as "ups and downs".
8. *Speed Car* is a simple way for helping the team identifying things that makes team moving faster and things that slow it down. It suits best to the second phase.
9. *Starfish* appeals best to the second phase, but also to the third phase. Involves data gathering and helping team members to understand each other's perceived value.
10. *Lessons learned - planned vs. success* falls in the third phase and refers on seeking learned lessons after a big event.
11. *Future Facebook posts* is best suitable for the second phase, but it can be used during the first phase as well. It motivates team members to be focused on future directions, where they want to go.
12. *Who-What-When steps to action* is helpful for defining commitments among team members by providing a clear action to whole group who is going to do what by when. It best fits to the third phase.

Table 1. Classification of games based on the meeting time phase.

Game	Meeting time phase		
	Warming up	Playing	Wrapping up
1. Understanding the group knowledge	••		
2. Roles we play	••	••	
3. Visual phone	••	•	
4. The team is - is not - does - does not		••	•
5. Role expectations matrix		••	
6. Defining the team principles	••		•
7. Peaks and valleys timeline			••
8. Speed car		••	
9. Starfish		••	•
10. Lessons learned - planned vs. success			••
11. Future Facebook posts	•	••	
12. Who-What-When steps to action			••

Another categorization of the games is related to the Tuckman's group development stages. In [8] we provided a classification of games based on the four-stage group development model proposed by Tuckman. The best applicable development stage has been assigned to each game card in InnoBox.

3.1 InnoBox Game Description Cards

With the aim demonstrating the structure and contents of each game description card in the InnoBox, this section shows the card of one specific game. The collaborative game selected (from the list of twelve) is *Role expectations matrix*. This is a team-forming game that aims to map out the expectations among team members. It helps the team to better define their roles and avoid future conflicts due to hidden or unknown expectations.

Figure 1 shows the appearance of the front and back sides of the card.

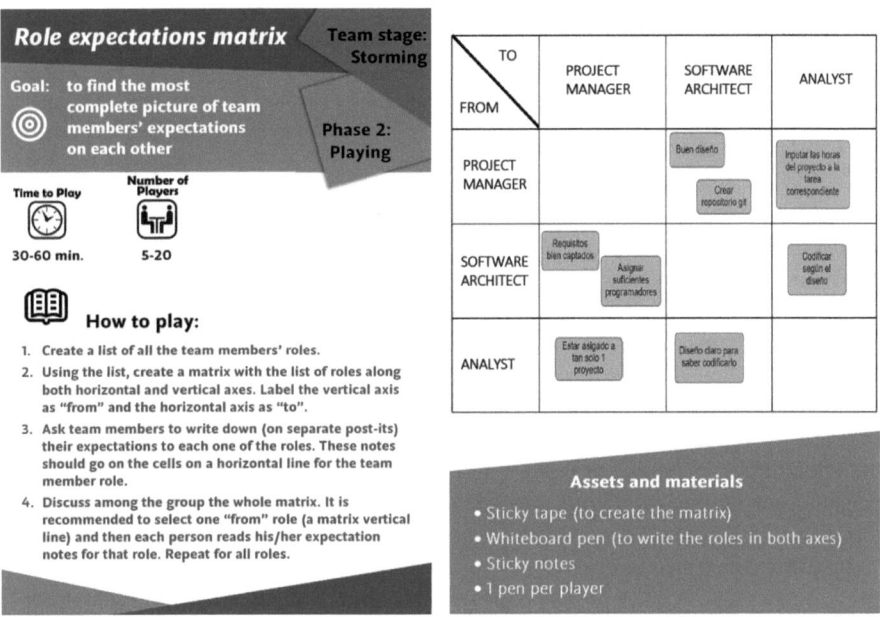

Fig. 1. Example of a card game in InnoBox (front and back).

Each card contains the following fields, which are described in continuation for the selected game.

- *Name of the game*: Role expectations matrix.
- *Goal of the game*: to find the most complete picture of team members' expectations on each other.
- *Classification of the game based on the meeting time phase in which it is most applicable*: Phase 2 - Playing.
- *Classification of the game based on the Tuckman's group development four-stage model*: Storming.
- *Number of players*: 5–20.
- *Time to run the game*: 30–60 min.
- *How to play*:
    1. Create a list of all the team members' roles.

2. Using the list, create a matrix with the list of roles along both horizontal and vertical axes. Label the vertical axis as "from" and the horizontal axis as "to".
3. Ask team members to write down (on separate post-its) their expectations to each of the roles. These notes should go on the cells on a horizontal line for the team member role.
4. Discuss among the group the whole matrix. It is recommended to select one "from" role (a matrix vertical line) and then each person reads his/her expectation notes for that role. Repeat for all roles.

- *Graphical presentation of the game being played.*
- *Needed assets and materials*: Sticky tape (to create the matrix), Whiteboard pen (to write the roles in both axes), Sticky notes and one pen per player.

4 Conclusion and Future Work

This paper presents the creation and contents of InnoBox, a game toolbox used for process improvement in agile teams. Positive feedback from practitioners demonstrates positive influence of game techniques in agile retrospectives – process and product improvement and innovation in agile teams. InnoBox creation was motivated by usual problems in organisations – limited time to investigate which techniques of many available to use in their retrospectives. Therefore, the proposed game toolbox is a fun and ready to use tool created for agile teams. Only 12 collaborative games were selected and designed for InnoBox, in order to keep it simple. Keeping it simple also presents a limitation of the research, but in the future, more games will be added. All the rules of the games are demonstrated on cards so no previous education or training is needed to start using the toolbox.

InnoBox was tested in one IT service organization, where it was used on five retrospective meetings. Also, a group of 30 students simulated an agile Sprint and a retrospective meeting in which they used all the games. Proposed improvements from the gathered feedback are embedded in the current version of InnoBox. Unclear games were removed and design was improved. As future work we will continue testing the game box in both academic and industrial setup. Also, it is planned to add some more games, but in a balanced manner, to saturate each group development stage or meeting phase.

Acknowledgments. This work has been supported by the Spanish Ministry of Science and Technology with ERDF funds under grants TIN2016-76956-C3-3-R and TIN2013-46928-C3-2-R and by the Erasmus Mundus Euroweb+ project.

References

1. Fowler, M., Highsmith, J.: The agile manifesto. Softw. Dev. **9**, 28–35 (2001)
2. Jovanovic, M., Mesquida, A.-L., Mas, A.: Process improvement with retrospectives gaming in agile software development. Commun. Comput. Inf. Sci. **543**, 287–294 (2015)
3. Cao, L., Mohan, K., Xu, P., Ramesh, B.: A framework for adapting agile development methodologies. Eur. J. Inf. Syst. **18**, 332–343 (2009)

4. Fitzgerald, B., Hartnett, G., Conboy, K.: Customising agile methods to software practices at Intel Shannon. Eur. J. Inf. Syst. **15**, 197–210 (2006)
5. Campanelli, A.S., Parreiras, F.S.: Agile methods tailoring - a systematic literature review. J. Syst. Softw. **110**, 85–100 (2015)
6. Moe, N.B., Dingsøyr, T., Dybå, T.: Overcoming barriers to self-management in software teams. IEEE Softw. **26**, 20–26 (2009)
7. Gonçalves, L., Linders, B.: Getting Value Out of Agile Retrospectives. A Toolbox of Retrospective Exercises (2013)
8. Jovanovi, M., Mesquida, A.-L., Radakovi, N., Mas, A.: Agile retrospective games for different team development phases. J. Univers. Comput. Sci. **22**, 1489–1508 (2016)
9. Clarke, P., O'Connor, R.V.: The situational factors that affect the software development process: Towards a comprehensive reference framework. Inf. Softw. Technol. **54**, 433–447 (2012)
10. Kalus, G., Kuhrmann, M.: Criteria for software process tailoring: a systematic review. In: Proceedings of the 2013 International Conference on Software and System Process - ICSSP 2013, p. 171 (2013)
11. Yilmaz, M., O'Connor, R.V.: A scrumban integrated gamification approach to guide software process improvement: a turkish case study. Tehnicki vjesnik **23**, 237–245 (2016)
12. Ogland, P.: The game of software process improvement: some reflections on players, strategies and payoff. In: Norsk konferanse for organisasjoners bruk av informasjonsteknologi (NOKOBIT-16), Trodenheim, Norway, pp. 23–25 (2009)
13. Cockburn, A.: The end of software engineering and the start of economic-cooperative gaming. Comput. Sci. Inf. Syst. **1**, 1–32 (2004)
14. Pries-Heje, J., Baskerville, R., Levine, L., Ramesh, B.: The high speed balancing game. Scand. J. Inf. Syst. **16**, 11–54 (2004)
15. Kua, P.: The Retrospective Handbook. Leanpub (2013)
16. Derby, E., Larsen, D.: Agile retrospectives - Making Good Teams Great. The pragmatic bookshelf, Dallas (2007)
17. Tuckman, B.W.: Developmental sequence in small groups. Psychol. Bull. **1**(63), 384–399 (1965)
18. Brown, T.: Change by Design. HarperCollins e-books (2009)
19. Kimbell, L.: Rethinking Design Thinking: Part I. Des. Cult. **3**, 285–306 (2011)
20. Jovanovic, M., Mesquida, A.-L., Mas, A.: Process improvement with retrospectives gaming in agile software development. Commun. Comput. Inf. Sci. **543**, 287–294 (2015)
21. Mesquida, A.-L., Jovanovic, M., Mas, A.: Process improving by playing: implementing best practices through business games. In: Kreiner, C., O'Connor, R.V., Poth, A., Messnarz, R. (eds.) EuroSPI 2016. CCIS, vol. 633, pp. 225–233. Springer, Cham (2016). doi:10.1007/978-3-319-44817-6_18
22. Gray, D., Brown, S., Macanufo, J.: Game Storming - A Playbook for Innovators, Rulebreakers, and Changemakers. O'Reilly Media (2010)

Gamification and Affordances: How Do New Affordances Lead to Gamification in a Business Intelligence System?

Tobias Christian Fischer(✉)

Uppsala University, Kyrkogårdsgatan 10, 753 13 Uppsala, Sweden
christian.fischer@fek.uu.se

Abstract. Gamification provides new affordances when integrated into BI systems. The paper highlights visibility, editability, persistence and association as organisational affordances that motivate people to use a BI system through gamification functionalities. The study is conducted at a car manufacturer where, for example, rewards and leaderboards are integrated into a BI system that responds to game interface design patterns. The result suggests an affordance model that could be used to develop and implement BI systems better and increase the use in a company.

Keywords: Affordance · Association · BI · Business intelligence · BI system · Car manufacturer · Case study · Game design elements · Game thinking elements · Gamification · Rewards · Sales process · VEPA affordance model

1 Introduction

Gamification lead to new affordances [1–4]. In a recent call, Te'eni [5] sees a need to study gamification in an organisational setting to understand its relation to affordances. Huotari [1:20] relates gamification and affordances by defining gamification as "process of enhancing a service with affordances for gameful experiences in order to support users' overall value creation". This leads to the following research question: *How do new affordances lead to gamification in a Business intelligence system?*

The question is related to business intelligence (BI) as gamification is an emerging topic in that literature. Huotari [1] argues that "more than 50% of organizations that manage innovation processes will gamify those processes." Gamify processes are found in different industries like banking [6], healthcare [7], higher education [8], marketing [9], service [10], and tourism [11]. BI systems use gamification to support work in new ways and guide people in processes. A gap presents the limitations of studies, which explore how gamification is actually applied to BI [12–14].

The paper fills the gap by presenting a study about a recently implemented BI system, which salespeople use in their sales process to satisfy customers. The single case study plays in the car manufacturing industry, in which the BI system measures customer satisfaction, evaluates the performance of salespeople, and guides readers through the sales process. Furthermore, the BI system affords salespeople the freedom to take action in the process. The affordances for the salespeople consist of the four affordances of visualisation, editability, persistence, and association in the studied sales process.

© Springer International Publishing AG 2017
J. Stolfa et al. (Eds.): EuroSPI 2017, CCIS 748, pp. 310–320, 2017.
DOI: 10.1007/978-3-319-64218-5_26

The paper highlights that affordances are connected to game design elements of a BI system. In conclusion, gamification is, according to Te'eni [5:474], connected to "certain fun elements of games and plug[s] them into a work context in which the worker must complete some task". The objectives of the paper are fivefold. First, the theoretical framework presents the terms *BI, gamification*, and *affordances* with its concepts, definitions, and elements. Second, the method introduces the single case study with its background, research design, data collection and analysis. Third, the findings illustrated gamification in the BI system based on the case studied. Fourth, the discussion introduces a developed affordance model with an illustration of the case. Last, the conclusion summarises the paper, shows its managerial implications, and future research.

2 Theoretical Framework

2.1 Business Intelligence

BI is a multisided tool for a knowledge worker to support decisions through analysis, databases and techniques [15–17]. Techniques consist beside others of cloud computing, data mining, reporting, text mining, and visualisation with the aim to get new insights and present data in different ways [18]. A way of compiling the data available are platforms, which support multiple knowledge workers through dashboards, and scorecards are usable by multiple knowledge workers [19, 20]. According to Quagini and Tonchia [21], the improvement and motivation of knowledge workers is strengthened through BI dashboards, which focus on evaluation and the value of customers.

2.2 Gamification

Gamification is, according to Harman et al. [22:1448] "worthy of serious study," and calls for more studies that conceptualise and problematise gamification and affordances in an organisational context [5].

The bridge between gamification and affordances is built by its definition. Huotari [1:20] defines gamification as the process of enhancing a service with affordances for gaming experiences in order to support users' overall value creation". One value factor is highlighted by Tynan [23], who claims that gamification shapes the future of work. The result is shown in businesses like education, e-learning [24], health, recruiting and training of people, all of which use gamification [4, 25, 26].

Gamification uses game thinking elements, which impact components, dynamics, and mechanics [27]. *Components* are gamified applications, which include achievements, badges or points and present a specific form of dynamics and mechanics as they belong to game design patterns [27–29]. *Dynamics* give a bigger picture of a gamified system by describing the effects of mechanics, which involve, apart from other factors like competition, experience over time, and the motives of the user [7, 10, 30]. *Mechanics* involve processes which drive actions and generate a certain engagement like achievements, badges, scoring systems or time pressure [7, 28, 30]. Mechanics and dynamics describe the umbrella term of mechanics-dynamics-aesthetics (MDA), which are conceptual game models using experiences, which belong to game design elements [29].

Game design elements are characteristics of games which come from game thinking elements [31] and results based on the human-computer interaction (HCI) in five components of game design elements [29, 31]: interface design patterns; design patterns and mechanics; design principles and heuristics; game models; and design methods [31].

First, *interface design pattern* combines design components and solutions for known problems to increase the human-computer interaction through visual feedback like badges, leaderboards, levels, process bars, and scores [27, 29, 32]. Second, *design patterns and mechanics* are reoccurring game parts which influence the game and the interaction [31]. Examples are turn-based playing, time constraints and real-time play, which aims to increase HCI [29]. Third, *design principles and heuristics* provide guidelines and rules, which provides a design solution to a recurring problem through clear goals, enduring play, and different styles of playing the game [27, 29]. The aim is to increase the participation, and connect the process of playing with fun and positivity [33, 34]. Fourth, *game models* consist of components and experiences which challenge people and create curiosity, fantasy, and MDA [29, 31]. Last, *design methods* describe practices and processes analysing the game environment through play testing, play-centric design [29, 31], and "afford game-play-characteristic motivation, enjoyable experiences". [3:294]

According to Saran [24:20], gameplay's experiences are "hardwired into our DNA", which can be applied in business contexts by implementing game design patterns in IT systems [35]. Game design patterns change how people adapt, use, and work, which gives the power to gamification for "real-world change". [36:3] Gamifications potential and value lays in its motivational characteristics like optimism [10], habit breaking [37], and satisfaction of users [38], which solve problems [38], and increase learning [39]. An example presented Huotari [1], who looked into Nike's running application, which compares and motivates runners through sharable activities and leaderboards through the process of running. The value of gamification lies in the process, which enhances "a service with affordances for gameful experiences". [1:20]. A literature review by Hamari et al. [2] revealed that certain services require an implementation of affordances to invoke gameful experiences and behavioural outcomes [1].

2.3 Affordance

The concept of affordances originated from animals and their perception of their environment. Animals use objects like rocks in distinct ways depending on their activity and usefulness [40]. Affordances are actions, which the environment and objects within it permit and deny to actors [41]. According to Pozzi et al. [42:5], affordances are defined as "the potential for behaviors associated with achieving an immediate concrete outcome and arising from the relation between an object (e.g., an It artifact) and a goal-oriented actor".

In information systems, affordances look at the actual use, similar to animals, which use an object instead of thinking about what the object is [43, 44]. The focus of affordances is on action possibilities by considering features of technology and people's goals [45]. The described focus put technology in its empirical reality, which shows its capabilities, and people's uses of it [46, 47].

Treem and Leonardi [43] related four affordances: visibility, editability, persistence, and association. *Visibility* referred to the need of people to locate, access and seek out information, which technology provided in an easy- and effortless manner [48]. According to Salmon [49:151], technology makes a "person's knowledge visible". In the BI literature, visibility is loaded with control [50] and information [17, 51] to increase the capability of BI and improve decision making [52]. Visibility provides means, methods and opportunities for people to see information mainly through front-end application of BI [19, 53]. Visbility is related to visualisation, which relates to interfaces (badges, leadersboards, and points), design patterns and mechanics (challenges, progress time constraints), and game design methods (physical awards) [2]. *Editability* is the manner by which people have the capability to change data and information gathered. *Persistence* refers, in the context of BI systems, to the length at which a system provides data and information. *Associations* are circulating around the question of how related the content of the BI system is to the user (e.g., individual data, which is customised for the seller).

Technology offers certain methods of control for managers through it affordances: visibility, editability, persistence, and association [43]. According to Hamari et al. [2:3030], the "sporadic nature of usage might not be compatible with persistent gameful affordances."

3 Methodology

The single case study played in the sales process of a car manufacturer. The business affords to satisfy customer in a process which is usually standardised and routinised. In the sales process, a BI system is installed which measures the sales process based on key performance indicators (KPIs). According to the director of sales, the aim with the KPIs is to "honest customer feedback and help the dealer to make better decisions. This strengthens the relationship between sellers-and-buyers." For example, the BI system used 'overall satisfaction with purchase experience' as KPI, which can be compared between sellers in an integrated league table resulting in different rankings of sellers. Top sellers are at the top of the ranking, and receive a physical reward [54]. The BI system supports decisions of the seller, who gets through the reward recognition, and reputation for their work in the sales process.

The *data collection* at the car manufacturer had a qualitative approach over a three-year period. The qualitative research compiled 35 semi-structured interviews with 21 respondents [55, 56]; 92 h of observations in the social context [57]; and 32,586 datasets of the BI system. The *data analysis* of the collected data was documented and analysed from a BI system and gamification perspective [58–60]. The data was analysed in a triangulation between interviews, observation, and BI systems, which involved coding into sub-codes (e.g., data sources, data warehouse, front-end application, and game design elements) [61].

4 Findings

4.1 BI System and Affordances

The BI system at the car manufacturer is a multisided tool, which combines analysis, databases and techniques to support decisions [15–17]. The sales process of the car manufacturer is linked to a BI system, which measures different KPIs to evaluate and analyse customers' experience and satisfaction. The BI system combined different technologies, which develop different affordances for sellers (Table 1):

Table 1. BI system and affordances free after Treem and Leonardi [43]

Technology	Example	Affordance for sellers			
BI SYSTEM	Case company	Visibility	Editability	Persistence	Association
Data sources	Call center: ETL tool	High	Low	High	High
Data warehouse	Siebel: manage & report	Low	Low	High	High
Front-end application	BI portal: analysis & report	High	High	High	High

BI systems technology consists of data sources, a data warehouse, and front-end application [19, 62]. *Data sources* are at the case company ETL tools (extract-transform-load) [62], which gather data of customer experience and –satisfaction through phone calls and online forms. Sellers have high visibility, persistence, and association of data sources because of their individual access and unlimited storage in the BI system. The editability for sellers is low as data is filled in by the call center agents and is deposited in the BI system's interface [43]. The *data warehouse* stores and queries data sources, which merges multiple data (e.g., customer or cars) into one database [19]. The database is connected with data sources, which support different formats (e.g., excel, voice file and online interface), and access levels. Sellers have low visibility and editability because the car manufacturer manages and modifies the data warehouse. The data warehouse enables a high persistence and association with the data, because data of sellers can be accessed individually. *Front-end application* enable content and documentation management for analysis, reporting and decision-making [19]. At the case company, front-end applications enable text mining, work groups, and interactive visualisation tools like ad-hoc queries, dashboards, and spreadsheets (cf. Olszak [62]). The front-end application enables high visibility, editability, persistence, and association through the BI portal, which makes data accessible, and people have the possibility to see their data.

4.2 Gamification and Affordances

The BI system shows characteristics of gamification, which consider components, dynamics, and mechanics of games comprised in game design elements [27]. The game design elements of game interface design, design patterns and mechanics, design principles and heuristics, and game design methods [29, 31] are presented in Table 2:

Table 2. Use of gamification and affordances at case company free after Deterding, et al. [31] and Treem and Leonardi [43] - *Low/high – BI system features have a low/high affordance for user(s)*

Technology	Example	Affordance for sellers			
Game design elements	Case company	Visibility	Editability	Persistence	Association
Game interface design pattern	Point system, leaderboard, reward	High	Low	High	High
Design patterns and mechanics	Limited resources, time constraints, turns	High	High	High	High
Design principles and heuristics	Clear goals, enduring playing, variety of game styles	High	Low	High	High
Game models	Challenge, mechanics, game design atoms	High	Low	High	High
Game design methods	Centric design, play testing, value conscious game design	High	High	High	High

Visibility is an affordance which is heavily presented in game design elements. For example, in game interface design patterns are design patterns giving solutions to known problems, which increases the interaction between people and technology [29]. The interaction at the case company is triggered through leaderboards, points, and rewards, which afford people to take actions. The visibility is high because leaderboards and points are integrated into the BI system, and the reward plays a central role as it is partially in the BI system and multiple documents. The points are shown on a 5-Likert scale and reflect on leaderboard ranking, which results in the reward. The sales expert described the process and explained that "…at the end of the year, we sent out mails to inform about the current ranking and how close they [sellers] are to each other."

Editability is an affordance which is perceived as a high point in design pattern and mechanics, and game design methods, and low in game interface design pattern, design principles and heuristics, and game models. For example, in game interface design pattern is the leaderboards, points and rewards preset in the BI system, which offers limited chances for sellers to edit or manipulate them. A similar argumentation for editability exists for design principles and heuristics, and game models.

Persistence is an affordance, which is high for all game design elements. For example, the game interface design gave points, motivated people through leaderboards and influenced people on an operational level. Beyond the operational level is the reward that belongs to a strategic level as it makes use of the BI system and a certain strategy of winning necessary. The director of sales (2016) describes the strategic situation as follows: "An 'internet-affine' CEO with an aggressive price strategy does not have the time to consider the BI system [...]. The good deals know that the BI system is an important tool and know how to use it." The operational and strategic level developed a certain persistence which affords certain actions of people.

Association is an affordance, which has a high influence on game design elements. For example, in the game interface design patterns are rewards recognised in the BI system as a non-financial measurement. The sales expert described that the reward was introduced in the case company as follows: "...we decided in the group not to make the award bonus relevant." The sellers developed an emotional association with the reward and the brand, as both are recognised in the design of the BI system. This develops through symbols and logos in the BI system a high association with the case company.

5 Discussion

5.1 VEPA Affordance Model in an Organisation

According to Te'eni [5:474], affordances and an organisational context are forcing people to "think how particular patterns of using technology, potential or actual, change organisational structure and practice to affect future behavior and to design new systems". Both, behaviour and new design of systems is supported by the affordances of visibility, editability, persistence, and association resulting in a VEPA affordance model.

The VEPA affordance model structures affordances in an organisational context. The organisational context provides different motivational affordances, which each come into play when considering gamification. The VEPA affordance model could present a way to develop, design, and implement an IS further. It takes visibility, editability, persistence, and association and shows what IS affords users to do to progress in their process. The process is standardised, and automised by the BI system as they guide and control people.

People take action triggered by BI systems. A BI system affords people to take certain actions based on visual impulses (visibility), changes they have to make (editability), longitudinal data availability (persistence), and that the data and information belong to them (association). In the case studied, gamification triggered an action or response by using different features in a BI system. As Table 2 shows high visibility, persistence, and association, which afford certain actions with the BI system. The actions are triggered by five game design elements: game interface design pattern, design patterns and mechanics, design principles and heuristics, game design and game design methods as game design elements. Those game design elements require continuously individual adjustments and the input of a seller to make better decisions in the sales process.

Furthermore, the VEPA affordance model helps to design a BI system, which uses game design elements, increases the use of people of BI, and implements the right feature to trigger an action (e.g., game interface design pattern, rules or constraints).

A VEPA affordance model simplifies a BI system by highlighting affordances, which plays a role in a process and acts as a basis for improving certain game design elements. The case featured design principles and heuristics (e.g., clear goals, enduring playing, variety of game styles) low editability, which could be improved. For example, different game styles could be improved or certain steps, which aim that people log-into the BI system more often. In this way, the VEPA affordance model is a way of looking at the current stage of a BI system, and ways of changing and improving it.

5.2 Change is Coming

Affordances and the VEPA affordances model lead to technological- and social changes, which come from implementing game design elements into BI systems. In the case studied, changes occurred throughout the whole sales process. The sales process gets transparency and visibility for sellers, which is a result of increasing data availability and analysis. The increasing availability and analysis produces larger amounts of data in the sales process, which differs in value, variety, velocity, veracity, and volume [63]. In the case studied, the KPIs in the sales process give a picture of the experience and satisfaction of customers with the capability for analysis and reporting. According to the director of sales, the next changing step is to "connect the data with each other," which follows features like data- and text analytics and other features (e.g., crosstabs, follow-up impact report, and the hot alert closing time report).

In earlier times, the process of selling cars was in the car manufacturing industry an in-transparence process, which, through data analytics, gets more comparable within an organisation and their sellers. The evaluation of experience and satisfaction changed how people perceive individual expertise and decision making in the sales process. The increasing amount of data is a result of gamification and technology advances, which impact two important actors: seller and customer. On the one hand, the seller participates in increasing numbers in providing data and information in the BI system. On the other hand, customers provide their data willingly, which results in almost every sold car getting feedback. Seller and customer change their behaviour, which leads to social change, because the seller understands actual needs of the customer, which modifies and optimises sales processes through the use of gamification in a BI system.

6 Conclusion

The research question *"How do new affordances lead to gamification in a BI system?"* can be answered by saying that game design elements contribute to the discussion of affordances. Affordances used at the BI system have a certain visibility, editability, persistence and association to people working with that specific technology. The study introduced a proposition for a VEPA affordance model, which helps in improving and understanding technology like a BI system.

The assembling of BI, gamification and affordance implies through the empirical case that they are inter- and intra-correlated, which followed and contributed to the call of Te'eni [5]. Future research could apply the VEPA affordance model and use it for implementing, design or studying current BI systems.

The paper has certain managerial implications, concerning the design, implementation and development of systems. The VEPA affordance model could be a tool to look at the status quo or a desired output with a technology. The presented empirical study could give impulses and help design new BI systems that use game design elements.

The illustration of the board game could furthermore be a visual picture for using technology that has game design elements.

References

1. Huotari, K.A.H., Hamari, J.: Defining gamification: a service marketing perspective. In: Presented at the Proceeding of the 16th International Academic MindTrek Conference (2012)
2. Hamari, J., Koivisto, J., Sarsa, H.: Does gamification work?–a literature review of empirical studies on gamification. In: 2014 47th Hawaii International Conference on System Sciences (HICSS), 2014, pp. 3025–3034. IEEE (2014)
3. Deterding, S.: The lens of intrinsic skill atoms: a method for gameful design. Hum.-Comput. Interact. **30**(3/4), 294–335 (2015)
4. Augustin, K., Thiebes, S., Lins, S., Linden, R., Basten, D.: Are We Playing Yet? A Review of Gamified Enterprise Systems (2015)
5. Te'eni, D.: Contextualization and problematization, gamification and affordance: a traveler's reflections on EJIS. Eur. J. Inf. Syst. **25**(6), 473–476 (2016)
6. Rodrigues, L.F., Costa, C.J., Oliveira, A.: Gamification: a framework for designing software in e-banking. Comput. Hum. Behav. **62**, 620–634 (2016)
7. King, D., Greaves, F., Exeter, C., Darzi, A.: 'Gamification': Influencing health behaviours with games. J. R. Soc. Med. **106**(3), 76–78 (2013)
8. Denny, P.: The effect of virtual achievements on student engagement. In: Presented at the Proceedings of CHI 2013: Changing Perspectives, Paris, France, 27 April–2 May 2013 (2013)
9. Moise, D.: Gamification - The NEW GAME in MARKETING. Rom. J. Mark. **2**, 29–33 (2013)
10. Blohm, I., Leimeister, J.M.: Gamification: design of IT-based enhancing services for motivational support and behavioral change. Bus. Inf. Syst. Eng. (BISE) **5**(4), 275–278 (2013)
11. Xu, F., Weber, J., Buhalis, D.: Gamification in Tourism. In: Xiang, Z., Tussyadiah, I. (eds.) Information and Communication Technologies in Tourism 2014, pp. 525–537. Springer, Cham (2013). doi:10.1007/978-3-319-03973-2_38
12. Chen, H., Chiang, R.H., Storey, V.C.: Business intelligence and analytics: from big data to big impact. MIS Q. **36**(4), 1165–1188 (2012)
13. Wixom, B.H., Yen, B., Relich, M.: Maximizing value from business analytics. MIS Q. Executive, **12**(2), 111–123 (2013)
14. Kane, G.C., Palmer, D., Phillips, A.N., Kiron, D., Buckley, N.: Strategy, not technology, drives digital transformation - becomig a digitally mature enterprise (2015). http://sloanreview.mit.edu/projects/strategy-drives-digital-transformation/?utm_source=twitter&utm_medium=social&utm_campaign=dlrpt15. Accessed 25 May 2016
15. Turban, E., Pearson, E.: Business Intelligence: A Managerial Approach. Pearson Education Limited, Harlow (2014)
16. Clark, J.T.D., Jones, M.C., Armstrong, C.P.: The dynamic structure of management support systems: theory development, research focus, and direction. Mis Q. **31**(3), 579–615 (2007)
17. Polites, G.L., Karahanna, E.: The Embeddedness of information systems habits in organizational and individual level routines: development and disruption. MIS Q. **37**(1), 221–246 (2013)
18. Gangadharan, G.R., Swami, S.N., Business intelligence systems: design and implementation strategies. In: 26th International Conference on Information Technology Interfaces, 2004, pp. 139–144. IEEE (2004)
19. Chaudhuri, S., Dayal, U., Narasayya, V.: An overview of business intelligence technology. Commun. ACM **54**(8), 88–98 (2011)

20. Chen, H., Chiang, R.H.L., Storey, V.C.: Business intelligence and analytics: from big data to big impact. MIS Q. **36**(4), 1165–1188 (2012)
21. Quagini, L., Tonchia, S.: Performance Measurement: Linking Balanced Scorecard to Business Intelligence. Springer-Verlag, 2010
22. Harman, K., Koohang, A., Paliszkiewicz, J.: Scholarly interest in gamification: a citation network analysis. Ind. Manage. Data Syst. **114**(9), 1438–1452 (2014)
23. Tynan, K.: How Gaming is Shaping the Future of Work (2016). https://hbr.org/2016/05/how-gaming-is-shaping-the-future-of-work. Accessed 20 Aug 2016
24. Saran, C.: A business case for gameplay at work. Comput. Weekly, 19–22 (2015). 20-26 August 2013
25. Meister, J.: Gamification: Three Ways to use Gaming for Recruiting, Training, and Health & Wellness (2012). https://www.forbes.com/sites/jeannemeister/2012/05/21/the-future-of-work-how-to-use-gamification-for-talent-management/#6e80583698d3. Accessed 25 July 2017
26. Robson, K., Plangger, K., Kietzmann, J.H., McCarthy, I., Pitt, L.: Is it all a game? Understanding the principles of gamification. Bus. Horiz. **58**(4), 411–420 (2015)
27. Cheong, C., Filippou, J., Cheong, F.: Towards the gamification of learning: investigating student perceptions of game elements (in English). J. Inf. Syst. Educ. **25**(3), 233–244 (2014)
28. Dale, S.: Gamification: making work fun, or making fun of work? (in English). Bus. Inf. Rev. **31**(2), 82–90 (2014)
29. Morford, Z.H., Witts, B.N., Killingsworth, K.J., Alavosius, M.P.: Gamification: the intersection between behavior analysis and game design technologies (in English). Behav. Anal. **37**(1), 25–40 (2014)
30. Werbach, K.A.H., Hunter, D.: For the Win How Game Thinking Can Revolutionize Your Business. Wharton Digital Press The Wharton School, University of Pennsylvania, Philadelphia (2012)
31. Deterding, S., Dixon, D., Khaled, R., Nacke, L.: From game design elements to gamefulness: defining gamification. In: Presented at the 15th MindTrek Conference, Tampere, Finland (2011)
32. Fuchs, M., Fizek, S., Ruffino, P., Schrape, N.: Rethinking gamification. meson Press by Hybrid Publishing Lab, Lüneburg (2014)
33. Jung, J.H., Schneider, C., Valacich, J.: Enhancing the motivational affordance of information systems: the effects of real-time performance feedback and goal setting in group collaboration environments. Manage. Sci. **56**(4), 724–742 (2010)
34. Mollick, E.R., Rothbard, N.: Mandatory fun: consent, gamification and the impact of games at work. The Wharton School Research Paper Series (2014)
35. Garcia-Penalvo, F.J., et al.: Learning services-based technological ecosystems. In: Presented at the Proceedings of the 3rd International Conference on Technological Ecosystems for Enhancing Multiculturality, Porto, Portugal (2015)
36. Braunstein, D.: Gamification: An Introduction to its Potential (2016). http://www.huffingtonpost.com/danya-braunstein/gamification-an-introduct_b_3167566.html. Accessed 01 Sept 2016
37. Rapp, A.: Beyond gamification: enhancing user engagement through meaningful game elements. In: FDG, 2013, pp. 485–487 (2013)
38. Kapp, K.M.: The Gamification of Learning and Instruction: Game-Based Methods and Strategies for Training and Education. Wiley, New York (2012)
39. DomíNguez, A., Saenz-De-Navarrete, J., De-Marcos, L., FernÁNdez-Sanz, L., PagéS, C., MartíNez-HerráIz, J.-J.: Gamifying learning experiences: practical implications and outcomes. Comput. Educ. **63**, 380–392 (2013)

40. Gibson, J.J.: The Ecological Approach to Visual Perception. Lawrence Erlbaum Associates, Hillsdale (1986)
41. Gibson, J.J.: The Ecological Appraoch to Visual Perception. Houghton Mifflin, Boston (1979)
42. Pozzi, G., Pigni, F., Vitari, C.: Explaining big data impact on healthcare organizations: a technology affordance approach (2014)
43. Treem, J.W., Leonardi, P.M.: Social media use in organizations: exploring the affordances of visibility, editability, persistence, and association. Ann. Int. Commun. Assoc. **36**(1), 143–189 (2013)
44. Faraj, S., Azad, B.: The materiality of technology: an affordance perspective. In: Materiality and Organizing: Social Interaction in a Technological World, pp. 237–258 (2012)
45. Markus, M.L., Silver, M.S.: A Foundation for the study of IT effects: a new look at DeSanctis and Poole's concepts of structural features and spirit. J. AIS **9**(10/11), 609–632 (2008)
46. Leonardi, P.M.: Theoretical foundations for the study of sociomateriality. Inf. Organ. **23**(2), 59–76 (2013)
47. Leonardi, P.M.: When flexible routines meet flexible technologies: Affordance, constraint, and the imbrication of human and material agencies. MIS Q. **35**(1), 147–167 (2011)
48. Brown, J.S., Duguid, P.: Knowledge and organization: a social-practice perspective. Organ. Sci. **12**(2), 198–213 (2001)
49. Salmon, C.T.: Communication Yearbook 36 (in English). International Communication Association, Washington, DC (2013)
50. Verkooij, K.I.M., Spruit, M.: Mobile business intelligence: key considerations for implementations projects. J. Comput. Inf. Syst. **54**(1), 23–33 (2013)
51. Popovič, A., Hackney, R., Coelho, P.S., Jaklič, J.: Towards business intelligence systems success: effects of maturity and culture on analytical decision making. Decis. Support Syst. **54**(1), 729–739 (2012)
52. Boyer, J., Frank, B., Green, B., Harris, T., Van De Vanter, K.: Business intelligence strategy: a practical guide for achieving BI excellence. Mc Press, LLC (2010)
53. Bregman, A., Haythornthwaite, C.: Radicals of presentation: visibility, relation, and co-presence in persistent conversation. New Media Soc. **5**(1), 117–140 (2003)
54. Malmi, T., Brown, D.A.: Management control systems as a package—opportunities, challenges and research directions. Manage. Acc. Res. **19**(4), 287–300 (2008)
55. Ritchie, J., Lewis, J., Nicholls, C.M., Ormston, R.: Qualitative Research Practice: A Guide for Social Science Students and Researchers. Sage, London (2013)
56. Seidman, I.: Interviewing as qualitative research: a guide for researchers in education and the social sciences. Teachers college press, New York (2013)
57. Czarniawska, B.: Shadowing: And Other Techniques for Doing Fieldwork in Modern Societies. Copenhagen Business School, Denmark (2007)
58. Eisenhardt, K.M.: Building theories from case study research. Acad. Manage. Rev. **14**(4), 532–550 (1989)
59. Bryman, A.: Integrating quantitative and qualitative research: how is it done. Qual. Res. **6**(1), 97–113 (2006)
60. Saunders, M., Lewis, P., Thornhill, A.: Research Methods for Business Students, 6th edn. Pearson, Harlow, New York (2012)
61. Pentland, B.T.: Building process theory with narrative: from description to explanation. Acad. Manage. Rev. **24**(4), 711–724 (1999)
62. Olszak, C.M.: Toward better understanding and use of business intelligence in organizations. Inf. Syst. Manage. **33**(2), 105–123 (2016)
63. Frizzo-Barker, J., Chow-White, P.A., Mozafari, M., Ha, D.: An empirical study of the rise of big data in business scholarship. Int. J. Inf. Manage. **36**(3), 403–413 (2016)

SPI in Industry 4.0

A Design Process Approach to Strategic Production Planning for Industry 4.0

Andreas Riel[1(✉)] and Martina Flatscher[2]

[1] Grenoble Alps University, 46 av. Félix Viallet, 38031 Grenoble, France
andreas.riel@grenoble-inp.fr
[2] ZF Friedrichshafen AG, 38038 Friedrichshafen, Germany

Abstract. The fourth industrial revolution confronts existing industrial organisations with fundamental manufacturing innovation challenges. The high levels of risk and uncertainty linked to corporate strategic planning activities are driven by the necessity of reacting to the rapidly increasing innovation pressure exerted on manufacturing companies in particular in technology-driven sectors such as automotive. This research deals with the creation of a structured methodological approach to strategic production planning that is essentially based on the systematic leveraging of the creativity and experience of a vast diverse network of employees in order to establish an actionable and living integrated manufacturing-driven innovation road mapping process. The process approach has strongly been inspired by process approaches to new product development (NPD). The results have been validated within the industrial environment of one of the biggest German automotive tier-1 suppliers.

Keywords: Planning process · Technology planning · Innovation planning · Technology roadmapping · Industry 4.0

1 Introduction

Manufacturing industries are confronted with exceptional challenges in an era which is frequently called the "Fourth Industrial Revolution". Modern manufacturing paradigms such as Added-Value and Knowledge-based Manufacturing are mainly characterised by the fact that production is increasingly driven by integrated information technology systems, rendering manufacturing systems more autonomous, flexible and configurable. Megatrends are driving new manufacturing technologies and processes at a speed never experienced before. Additive manufacturing and lightweight materials processing are only two representative examples for technologies confronting manufacturing industries with new and complex challenges. More than ever before these industries have to invest early in know-how and infrastructure to implement production technologies, and adapt them timely both to the rapid technology development and the ever changing product requirements. Industries are therefore looking for methods and tools helping them plan such investments systematically, reliably, and with a holistic view.

With software and embedded being at the very heart of cyber-physical production systems, the field of Software Process Improvement (SPI) is rapidly gaining relevance in the field of manufacturing systems. Concepts of product engineering design are carried over to the latter field, thereby facilitating the complete integration of product and process development along a seamless digital value chain.

This article proposes a systematic yet highly creative process for strategic production planning (SPP) that is entirely based on concepts of integrated design [1]. Its objective is the integrated design of technology roadmaps which are an established decision support tool for long-term technology planning in industrial organisations. Section 2 explains the context, the research objectives and methodology. Section 3 summarizes the state of the art of SPP with a particular regard to technology roadmapping. Section 4 presents the integrated design principles based approach to SPP that we have developed. Section 5 elaborates on the validation of this approach in the context of one of the worldwide largest automotive tier-1 suppliers in Germany. Section 6 concludes with a summary of the key contributions and an outlook.

2 Objectives and Methodology

The objective of this research is to elaborate a systematic and actionable approach that helps industrial organisations plan their future investments and activities in modern production technology and the related processes and organisations. Having led and participated in numerous technology planning sessions, our fundamental hypothesis is that Strategic Production Planning in an Industry 4.0 context has a lot of characteristics in common with creative integrated design processes for new products, services and processes (NPD) [2]:

1. the outcome of the planning is unknown at process start,
2. the artefacts to be designed are highly interdisciplinary in their nature thus requiring experts from several different trades to actively participate in the process,
3. only a relatively small number of key requirements to the process and the final outcome are given at the beginning, whereas the identification and formalisation of requirements and constraints is part of the design process.
4. The outcome of the process is subject to evolution, driven by requirements changes as well as the changing context.

Hence, our quite natural idea and assumption is to find a means to carry out SPP as a creative integrated design process, bringing together experts from diverse organisational units. To validate this hypothesis based on published and own experiences, we designed a novel structured ideation process taking into account the constraints we face in stage-gate process driven organisations, and for the particular objective of SPP, and applied it in a pilot project at an automotive tier-1 supplier over one year.

In terms of the planning instrument, we decided for technology roadmaps, since they are widely spread in industry. Technology roadmapping (TRM) is an effective tool for technology planning and coordination which fits within a broader set of planning activities [GAR1997].

3 State of the Art

In order to analyse the state of the art of SPP with a particular regard to TRM, we have carried out a systematic literature review using bibliometric analysis facilitated by Cite-Space. We can only present very few key insights of this analysis here.

Motorola was the first to publish about the use of a technology roadmap as a tool for better integration of business and technology strategy [3]. Over the last few years, roadmapping has been gaining momentum as a strategic management tool for organisations to better adapt themselves to modern marketplaces [4]. While the roadmap is fairly simple in structure and concept, its content is the result of complex processes (Fig. 1).

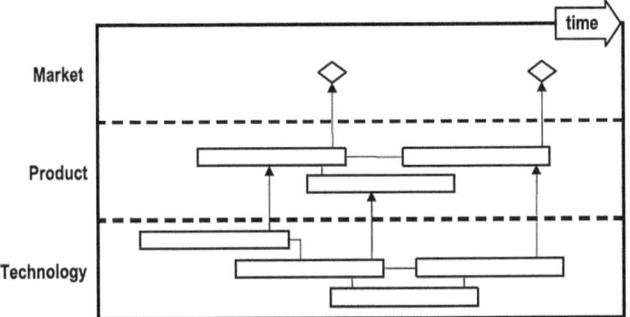

Fig. 1. Technology roadmapping example [5]

Implementing these processes and measuring their performance represents a huge challenge for organisations. There is a lack of practical guidelines for all roadmapping steps, in particular for the regular update of an already implemented roadmap [6]. Ioannou et al. insist on the importance of the fact that for TRM to be successful, the strategic decision-making process has to be a collaborative one [7]. Thus, roadmapping has to take a mediating and networking approach which can happen by the integration of suppliers in the TRM process, a cross-functional approach to product and technology planning and vision building, as well as the ongoing coordination between corporate laboratories and business units [8]. Team members from different departments including both technical and commercial functions such as R&D, product development, manufacturing, marketing, finance, and human resources are involved in a consensus building process, which connects an expected future (descriptive) with a desired future (normative) [9]. Tolio et al. confirm this by investigating the co-evolution of products, processes and production systems in order to address challenges like new regulations, new materials, technologies, services and communications [10]. Putnik et al. discuss the scalability in manufacturing systems design and operation, using advanced and emerging design and management approaches and information and communication technologies to support their effective and efficient deployment in practice [11]. None of these articles, however, deal with a systematic and actionable approach to implement TRM for SPP in an industrial organisation.

Holmes et al. confirm our own finding that the evolution of roadmapping as a strategic decision support tool has been led by management practice rather than by theory [12]. Publications covering TRM are in general focused on explaining the value of roadmaps as decision support tool and the typical difficulties encountered during their deployment, rather than on practically usable approaches and/or best practice experience reports. In particular, we could not find any explicit treatment of TRM for strategic production planning in literature. Neither could we identify any collaborative or integrated design based approach to TRM and SPP in general. This represents a real problem for industries struggling to prepare themselves timely for the challenges, opportunities and risks that the fourth industrial revolution is about to bring along [13].

4 A Creative Design Process Approach to SPP

In the context of a clearly structured and stage-gate process driven organisation, the entry challenge of executing a SPP project as a creative design process [14] is to propose a clear design process structure allows for a high degree of dynamics at the same time. Our approach is based on the model of problem solving published by Geschka [15] (Fig. 2).

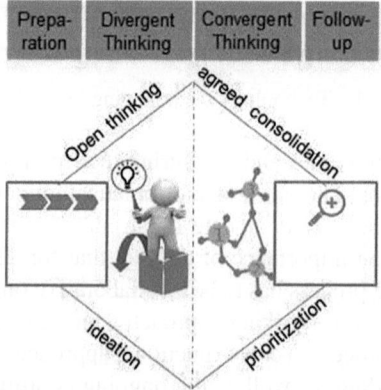

Fig. 2. Fundamental ideation process model based on Geschka [15]

The fundamental idea underlying this model is that in an integrated design process, the involved stakeholders shall run through a series of phases of divergent and convergent thinking. Every phase of divergence is a phase of idea generation and out-of-the-box thinking related to topics defined and prepared before. Experts from different domains work together in moderated creativity workshops, where the moderator's principal function is to help participants open up their minds to be able to get out of their boxes (i.e., contexts). The numerous ideas have to be consolidated and evaluated in the subsequent convergence phase whose principal objective is to decide how to proceed with each single idea generated during the previous phase. In moderated idea selection workshops, participants have to apply techniques facilitating idea evaluation.

A design process based on this fundamental ideation process element would be composed of an enchainment of several such elements, each element leading most notably to an increased level of concretization of the ideas [16]. Typically, there are also multiple parallel paths, each path representing a particular set of ideas being worked out further. For the particular design problem of SPP, the authors proposed the schema depicted in Fig. 3.

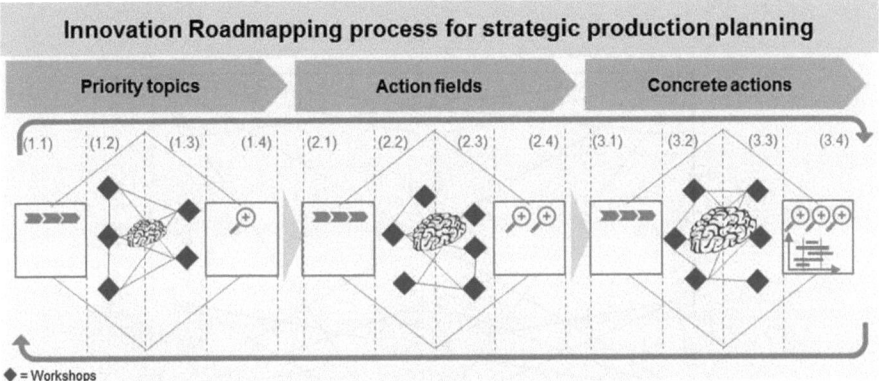

Fig. 3. Innovation Roadmapping (IRM) process model

SPP seeks to find a creative yet systematic way to derive concrete actions to carry out to respond to trends that influence the organization. These trends are manifold and related to several fields, such as technology, economy, ecology and society. The first process element deals with the identification of key topics derived from a list of (mega-)trends collected in the preparation phase, typically on the basis of relevant studies. Opening up the mind-set for the potential impacts these trends will have on the company is the key success factor for the divergence phase of this process element. Techniques like brainwriting, extreme scenarios, etc. are well suited to achieve this [17]. In the convergence phase, topics are prioritized, typically based on the company strategy, which requires the participation of top management representatives in the ideation team. The ranked topic list serves as the primary input for the subsequent process elements which deal with the particular challenges linked with each topic. Several such second-level elements might be triggered in parallel, depending on the process requirements and constraints in terms of time, resources and completeness.

For each selected topic, challenges (linked to a specific e.g. technology trend) have to be identified by the group during the subsequent divergence phase. Here, it is important to involve experts on a program management level, i.e. experts having collected experience in numerous projects. For each challenge the group identifies, fields of action addressing these challenges shall be defined in the convergence phase. In this process element, the timing of action fields shall not yet be taken into account. The focus has to be on what has to be done rather than on when. The who is also important to consider in both process elements, since it has strong implications on the ideation team composition of each subsequent ideation session (Fig. 4). The objective of the final process element is to define concrete projects addressing the fields of action per challenge. The divergence phase delivers relevant project ideas which are subsequently elaborated as project sheets containing key project data (objectives, motivation, resources, timing, budget, dependencies, etc.) that will be used for updating the company's strategic long-term strategic planning instrument, typically roadmaps.

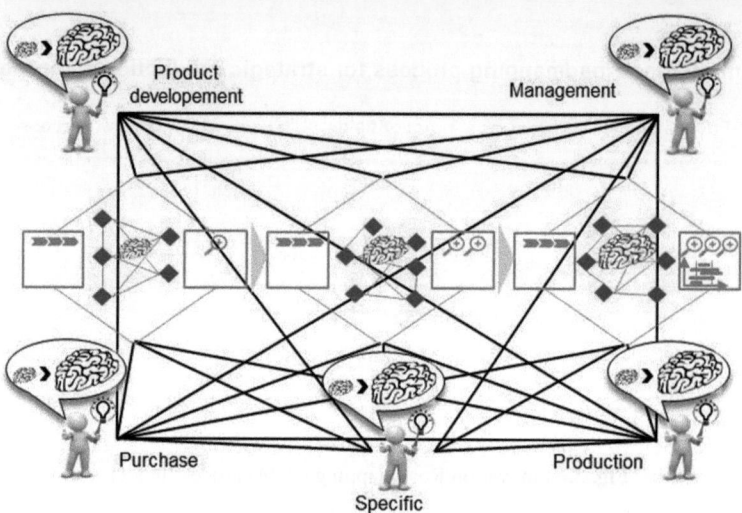

Fig. 4. Networked involvement of diverse experts in the innovation roadmapping process

It is important to highlight that the suggested SPP process is to be seen as a model which need to be implemented and adapted to specific organization's context. Each of the three process elements does not necessarily correspond to one single ideation session. There may be several ideation sessions per process element, and the phases of divergence and convergence may be ran through in different sessions. Key success factors we found are the following:

1. Full bi-directional traceability of all the results over all sessions: this is essential for sustaining the stakeholders' motivation and for understanding the decision history.
2. Consequent analysis of the interrelationships between results: building a network of topics rather than independent lists help understanding dependencies.
3. Excellent moderation and facilitation: experts have to be guided for stepping out of their boxes in order to capitalize on their expertise and creativity potentials.
4. Team composition: diversity in represented departments and personal traits in all the collaborative activities is the essential ingredient of any integrated design process.
5. Perfect preparation and post-processing of each session: key preparation factors include the (strategic) selection of the ideation team members as well as the objectives and techniques to achieve those. Post-processing has to make sure that all results are properly documented, even intermediate ones if they are useful for traceability.

6. Regularity of sessions: ideation sessions need to be organized in a regular rhythm over the year so as to maintain the spirit of the process and the teams.
7. Constructive ambience and environment: while critical analysis of ideas can be useful at certain stages in the process, a constructive way of communicating is vital for fostering creativity and active participation.
8. Governance: the process should be owned and driven by a steering team that assures its organization-wide impact. Networking the SPP process with relevant other strategic activities in the company helps assure the management attention necessary for sustaining the process and implementing its results.

Thanks to its strictly subsequent phases of divergence, convergence, and consolidation, the proposed process model intrinsically renders the progress measurable, which is very important in industrial organizations.

5 Automotive Case Study

We applied the SPP process model in the context of one of the largest worldwide automotive tier-1 supplier who was looking for a systematic approach to SPP for their worldwide production network [18]. For evident confidentiality reasons, we are not allowed to present any details about the process and the results obtained during its execution in the course of our pilot project over one year. We will therefore focus on presenting the key steps and the main insights we could get from them.

One key challenge was to integrate stakeholders of production, development and procurement in this effort. A core team was established which was both part of the steering consortium and the ideation teams. The team size varied between 8 and 15, depending on the experts' availabilities and the roles and expertise required for the particular objectives of each session. Influential representatives of the three areas production, product development and procurement have been part of this core team, which was a significant change with respect to existing practices in the organization. The production experts were in the leading position, since the whole initiative was driven by them with the key objective to introduce a sustainable systematic strategic planning process that starts from megatrends and ends up in concrete project ideas placed in the production technology roadmap. A major requirement to the result was that it should reflect the holistic, integrated view of the three involved areas on the production planning, leveraging the role of modern production technology as a driver for innovation both of products, processes, and the company's global organizations including suppliers.

Moderated ideation sessions with integrated design character have been carried out about every 5 weeks over one year in a way that the three process elements have been traversed exactly once over this time period. The duration of each session was half a day or an entire day, with the team composition remaining stable over the complete duration. Each session was prepared very carefully in terms of the selection of the detailed objectives, the topics chosen, the experts to be invited and the roles they should assume, and the methodology to be applied. Likewise, the results and experiences made in each session have been consolidated and documented in a systematic manner. During each session, tool support was deliberately kept basic in order to maximize the efficiency of human interaction. Mind maps had a key role, including the representation of links between dependent ideas. A focus was set on parallel group work, and the common discussion of all group results to take idea generation and/or selection even further. In this way, all the results have been produced entirely by the expertise and creative power of the ideation team members who were all employees of the company. The external moderator's role was only that of a facilitator of the application of integrated design approaches to ideation for planning purposes.

The ZF-specific pilot application of the IRM is depicted in Fig. 5. The point of departure was a regularly updated set of about 40 societal, economic and technological megatrends that serves as a basis of any strategy definition in the entire company. The session's key objective was to derive by voting from this vast list of trends three trend clusters having the highest relevance for the company's production technology. The result was subsumed in three artificial terms: Glocalisation (the target conflict between Globalisation and Localisation), Flexagility (being flexible and agile), and Hybridisation (combination of several technologies in the products). In a next step, the experts worked together in small groups in order to ideate about topics they consider particularly relevant for these selected trends, as well as for organisation and cost (constraints imposed by steering team). About 130 ideas have been generated and consolidated in about 30 topics and six mutually linked clusters (processes, employees, competences, production network, external collaborations, infrastructure). To illustrate one concrete example, the balancing of the complete (internal and external) production network was one of the topics selected for further investigation.

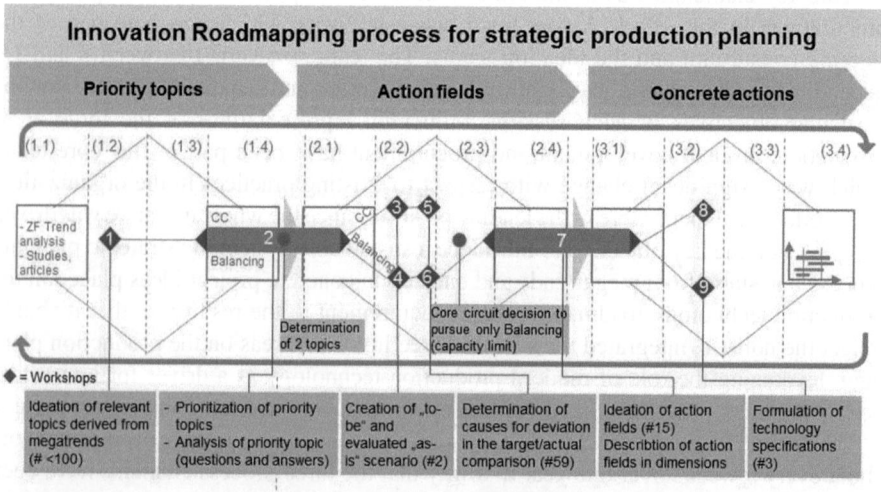

Fig. 5. Pilot application of the IRM at ZF

The following ideation methodology was applied to each of the selected topics during the next phase:

1. Getting a common understanding of the topic.

2. Designing a target scenario for the topic ("to-be" scenario).
3. Describing the actual situation ("as-is" scenario).
4. Identifying the deviations between the two scenarios (using suitable rating scales) and the causes for these deviations.
5. Clustering the causes for the derivation of fields of action.
6. Describing each field of action and identifying resources required to define concrete actions related to the field.

One of the about 15 action fields linked to the example topic is the improvement of the support by the organisation and the process for the flexible use of plant and equipment within the global network ("Balancing" in Fig. 5). For each of these action fields, the affected organisational units, as well as a rough effort classification have been determined. This was important for including experts from the affected units in the ideation sessions of the subsequent ideation process phase.

The objective of the final process element was the definition of concrete actions related to the fields of action based on the guiding thought: what needs to be done in order to address the respective field of action. Actions were then packaged into project sheets having the following rough outline structure: problem description, measurable objectives and indicators for success, methodology, opportunities and risks, estimated cost, key stakeholders, and timeframe. Another key information to be made explicit on these sheets is the relevant links to other projects, in particular (company-wide) strategic projects. This is essential especially for determining the importance of a particular project with respect to others, as well as its impact on a global level. About two to three projects per action field have been defined. Key data for all these project sheets have been elaborated in the teams during the ideation sessions, and elaborated in greater detail in the post-processing phase.

At the end of this process the project sheets were sufficiently detailed for being placed in the TRM. Thanks to the consistent involvement of product development and procurement representatives, the SPP roadmap could be easily networked with the development and purchase roadmaps, leading to an integrated innovation roadmap (IRM) which results in a holistic decision support instrument for the strategic long-term planning representing a significant progress with respect to previous instruments and practices. This added value was much appreciated by decision makers from various organizational units and from different management levels, mainly thanks to the strong involvement in the establishment of both the process and the IRM.

6 Conclusions and Outlook

We have proposed a strategic production planning process based on core principles of integrated design and compliant with key requirements imposed on strategy processes by big global industries. The fundamental process element is a sequence of guided and facilitated divergent and convergent thinking of ideation teams that are composed of company experts from different domains, most notably from production, development, and procurement. Three serial process steps are required to take ideas from megatrend-level of concrete projects. This has been validated with great success in a pilot project carried out in a business unit of one of the worldwide largest automotive suppliers. Together with this supplier, we are currently working on the definition of KPIs (key performance indicators) for both the efficiency and effectiveness of the process, which is absolutely necessary for its management and continuous improvement. These indicators will go beyond existing KPIs for process performance in that they shall measure the extent to which the process achieves the integration of stakeholders, and the consequences of this on the process output.

Our initial hypothesis that core principles of integrated design approaches applied to strategic planning activities in industrial organizations can significantly outperform existing practices, has clearly been confirmed. Although adequate performance measures are still a subject of further research, the benefits we observed are obviously significant and multi-dimensional. Thanks to its focus on systematic human interaction and diversity, the integrated design approach can take strategic technology and innovation planning to a level that has not been experienced with traditional approaches. The simple yet powerful systematic structure that we propose tackles the difficult challenge of guiding all stakeholders in the process and rendering the process manageable while still being generic enough to be deployed in various different organizations.

Although the planning process has been conceived and validated for innovation roadmapping in manufacturing environments, the essential concepts we propose are not focused on Industry 4.0 by their very nature. The essential thing is that the process systematically links manufacturing departments with experts representing both downstream and upstream life cycle phases, in particular product development, procurement, and most notably information technologies.

References

1. Tichkiewitch, S., Brissaud, D.: Methods and tool for co-operative and integrated design. Kluwer Academic Publishers, Dordrecht (2004). ISBN 1-4020-1889-4
2. Khurana, A., Rosenthal, S.R.: Towards holistic "front ends" in new product development. J. Prod. Innov. Manage **15**(2), 57–74 (1998)
3. Willyard, C.H., McClees, C.W.: Motorola's technology roadmap process. Res. Manage. **30**, 13–19 (1987)
4. Gerdsri, N., Kongthon, A., Vatananan, R.S.: Mapping the knowledge evolution and professional network in the field of technology roadmapping: a bibliometric analysis. Technol. Anal. Strategic Manage. **25**(4), 403–422 (2013)
5. EIRMA. Technology roadmapping - delivering business vision, Working group report, European Industrial Research Management Association, 52, Paris (1997)
6. Phaal, R., Farrukh, C.J.P., Probert, D.R.: Technology roadmapping – a planning framework for evolution and revolution. Technol. Forecast. Soc. Change **71**, 5–26 (2004)
7. Ioannou, C.A., Panagiotopoullos, P., Stergioulas, L.: Roadmapping as a collaborative strategic decision-making process: shaping social dialogue options for the European banking sector. World Acad. Sci. Eng. Technol. **54**, 770–776 (2009)
8. Kappel, T.A.: Perspectives on roadmaps: how organizations talk about the future. J. Product Innov. Manage. **18**(1), 39–50 (2001)
9. Zweck, A., Holtmannspötter, D.: Technology roadmapping: turning hype into a systematic process. Int. J. Technol. Intell. Plan. **5**(1), 55–72 (2009)

10. Tolio, T., Ceglarek, D., ElMaraghy, H.A., Fischer, A., Hu, S.J., Laperriere, L., Newman, S.T., Vancza, J.: SPECIES – co-evolution of products, processes and production systems. CIRP Ann. Manuf. Technol. **59**(2), 672–693 (2010)
11. Putnik, G., Sluga, A., ElMaraghy, H.A., Teti, R., Koren, Y., Tolio, T., Hon, B.: Scalability in manufacturing systems design and operation: state-of-the-art and future developments roadmap. CIRP Ann. Manuf. Technol. **62**(2), 751–774 (2013)
12. Holmes, C., Ferrill, M.: The application of operation and technology roadmapping to aid Singaporean SMEs identify and select emerging technologies. Technol. Forecast. Soc. Change **72**(3), 349–357 (2005)
13. Brettel, M., Bendig, D., Keller, M., Friederichsen, N., Rosenberg, M.: Effectuation in manufacturing: how entrepreneurial decision-making techniques can be used to deal with uncertainty in manufacturing. Procedia CIRP **17**, 611–616 (2014)
14. Lutters, D., van Houten, F., Bernard, A., Mermoz, E., Schutte, C.: Tools & techniques for product design. CIRP Ann. Manuf. Technol. **63**(2), 607–630 (2014)
15. Geschka, H.: Das Offene Problemlösungsmodell (OPM) und andere Problemlösungsstrategien. In: Preiß, L. (ed.) Jahrbuch der Kreativität, Köln (JPKM), pp. 82–100 (2010)
16. Le Masson, P., Weil, B., Hatchuel, A.: Strategic Management of Innovation and Design. Cambridge University Press, New York (2010). ISBN 978-0-521-18243-0
17. Geschka, H.: Creativity techniques in product planning and development: a view from West Germany. R&D Manage. **13**, 169–183 (1983). doi:10.1111/j.1467-9310.1983.tb01143.x
18. Flatscher, M., Riel, A., Kösler, T.: The need for a structured approach towards production technology roadmaps in innovation-driven industries. In: Barafort, B., O'Connor, Rory V., Poth, A., Messnarz, R. (eds.) EuroSPI 2014. CCIS, vol. 425, pp. 251–261. Springer, Heidelberg (2014). doi:10.1007/978-3-662-43896-1_22

Industry 4.0 as Digitalization over the Entire Product Lifecycle: Opportunities in the Automotive Domain

Eric Armengaud[1(✉)], Christoph Sams[1], Georg von Falck[1], Georg List[1], Christian Kreiner[2], and Andreas Riel[3]

[1] AVL List GmbH, Graz, Austria
{eric.armengaud,Christoph.Sams,georg.vonfalck, georg.list}@avl.com
[2] Graz University of Technology, Graz, Austria
christian.kreiner@tugraz.at
[3] Grenoble Alps University, Grenoble, France
andreas.riel@grenoble-inp.fr

Abstract. Industry 4.0 is an important trend aiming at increasing competitiveness and rebalancing value creation in global networks. It targets the reduction of production costs while improving product quality and production scalability and individualization by means of digitalization of product and production. Products as well as their production are becoming cognitive and can therefore better adapt to given customer needs or production variations. In this paper, we discuss impacts of Industry 4.0 along the entire automotive supply chain. In particular, we illustrate that Industry 4.0 in the automotive context has a high cross-impact between development, production, operation and maintenance, thus requiring innovative solutions along the entire value creation chain.

We enhance the commonly understood scope of Industry 4.0 towards digitalization over the entire product lifecycle and introduce data-driven business models to support exploitation of opportunities coming from this digitalization over the supply chain. We also propose a seamless cost engineering discipline in the automotive context for enabling a more systematic analysis and monitoring of the foreseen production costs from early development phase until SOP. This leverages system optimization to fulfil customer expectations from a functional, contextual and from an affordability point of view.

Keywords: Industry 4.0 · Automotive · Big data · Product lifecycle · Simultaneous cost engineering · PLE

1 Introduction

Europe is a major player in the automotive market. According to [1] Europe has produced 20% of the motor vehicles worldwide in 2015 (18.4 million units produced in Europe out of 91.5 million motor vehicles produced worldwide). This industrial sector has an important impact on employment since it ensures 5.6% of the EU employed population (12.2 million of jobs), for an added value of 139.4 billion € (10.4% of the manufacturing sector). In 2015, 6.6 million of vehicles were exported from the EU, leading to a trade surplus of

100.4 billion €. Parallel to that, automotive demand is evolving fast (e.g., BRIC countries) and is leading to a re-organization of the market with consolidation, globalization, competing with new entrepreneurial start-ups and players in new technologies.

The product vehicle is highly complex (amount of components, heterogeneity of the skills required to build the product), highly mature (vehicles have been on the road for more than 100 years) and subject to worldwide competition. Consequently, a strong trend exists since several decades to globalize production networks and offshore production plants to move more parts of the value creation to non-European countries with lower factor costs. *"Industry 4.0"* concept and technologies in this context can be used to emphasize the attractiveness of European production supported by high level of innovation, rebalanced value creation, more effective global networks and work shares, and supporting smart individualized products.

The first contribution of this paper is the analysis of the Industry 4.0 concept from the automotive point of view. Especially, we show that Industry 4.0 has a high cross-impact between development, production, in-use phase and maintenance – targeting global optimization instead of local improvement – and thus requiring innovative solutions along the entire value creation chain. This, requires tailored solutions from the original equipment manufacturer (OEM), with the support of its development team and finally from its engineering partner. Another important aspect is the need for appropriate tool chains to create a digitized world of development linking development, production, in-use phase and maintenance together, and thus mapping these skills and information more closely together. A second, related contribution of this paper is the introduction of data-driven business models – as complement to more traditional business models to exploit this digitalization. The third contribution of this paper is related to the introduction of a seamless cost engineering discipline in the automotive context. Hence, thanks to higher availability of development data as well as related context information, a more systematic analysis of foreseen production costs can be performed already early in the development phase and further monitored until production starts. This enables the optimization of the system to fulfil customer expectations both from the function and from the costs point of views. Our fourth contribution is the use of the digitalization over the lifecycle as an enabler for forward and backward control of variants and variation. This forward and backward control shall finally enable a higher a customer driven, individualized production and eventually enabling adaption and cognitive products.

The paper is organized as follows: Sect. 2 summarizes the definition of Industry 4.0 according to the literature and derives an enhanced definition targeting the digitalization of production and product over the entire product lifecycle. In Sect. 3 opportunities and approaches for data-driven business models are presented. Section 4 introduces seamless cost engineering as a method to better monitor expected production costs already in the development. After that, the opportunities for forward and backward control of variants and variation of the production are discussed in Sect. 5. Finally, Sect. 6 concludes this work.

2 Industry 4.0 as Digitalization over the Product Lifecycle

2.1 Industry 4.0 as a Holistic Concept

This section argues the holistic nature of Industry 4.0 based on different definitions of Industry 4.0 from the literature. According to [2] *Industry 4.0* means higher degree of digitalization for products, value creation chain and business models. In this paper, digitalization is stated as an answer to higher cost pressure, shorter innovation cycles, more complex and individualized, even adaptive and cognitive products, needs for reduction of energy and row materials during production process. Digitalization of the production targets an improved internal and cross-company steering by means of horizontal integration of the value creation chain supported by IT solutions. This shall enable enhanced exchange of data (also real-time) and insights throughout value chain and product lifecycle, which leads to increasing productivity and turnover as well as to being an important enabler for revolutionary business models. Two main impacts of Industry 4.0 are listed in the paper: "re-shoring" and "next-shoring", as the capability to rebalance value creation work shares and to enable the development of highly modern production facilities.

According to [3] *Industry 4.0* is defined as a new organization and steering approach for the entire value creation chain over the products' lifecycles. It relies on the four following pillars: (a) horizontal integration over the value creation chain, (b) seamless engineering over the entire life cycle, (c) vertical integration and networking of the production systems as well as (d) continuous development of underlying and connective technologies such as wireless communication, security and safety, or reference architecture and service oriented architectures.

According to [4] *Industry 4.0* is defined as the comprehensive introduction of information and communication technology (ICT) as well as their connection to an internet of things, services and data, which enables a real-time production. This shall enable a fast and flexible reaction to customer requests as well as large number of variants by low number of units – therefore enabling customization and individualization.

According to [5] *Industry 4.0* is defined as a smart integration from product and processes in the industrial added value. It relies on five technological pillars: embedded systems, smart factory, robust networks, cloud computing and IT security. The expected impact for the automotive sector is 15 billion € (1.5% per year until 2025). Key technologies to be developed are (a) higher production scalability by integration and use of real-time data, (b) more intuitive human-machine interfaces and (c) flexible automation.

According to [6], the digital transformation of the industry is relying on four pillars (a) digital data by the capacity of gathering, managing and analyzing the data, (b) automation to provide cognitive products and environment able to work autonomously and organize themselves, (c) connectivity to synchronize supply chains and shorten innovation cycles, and (d) digital customer access for more transparency and new services. Further, the digitalization will lead to a major market re-organization by shifting from rigid value chains to dynamic value-added networks, thanks to connected players able to communicate with each other in real-time.

According to the previous definitions, Industry 4.0 strongly focuses on a higher degree of **digitalization of the production** (supported by IT solutions) and connection to the development process to improve production scalability and reduce costs. In the following, we suggest the enhancement of this definition towards **bi-directional digitalization of the entire development lifecycle** including in-use and service phase, thus supporting **global optimization of all the phases within the lifecycle,** and finally **targeting added value and cost reduction for customers,** as well as more efficient **integration of new technologies and management of quality, legislation and emission targets** – see Fig. 1. The final targeted impact of product and production optimization with respect to costs, quality and scalability is even higher, given increased flexibility of the production system to higher individualization, faster and more effective response to deviations, self-adjusting product and production improvement cycles.

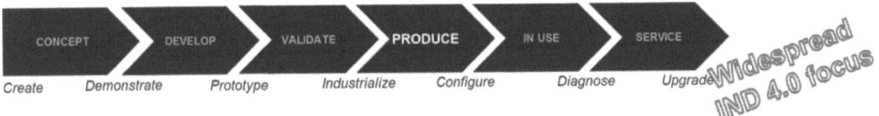

Industry 4.0: gather information along the entire lifecycle and generate knowledge out of the raw data to *improve the production w.r.t. costs and product quality and to increase flexibility* (incl. safety, durability, reliability)

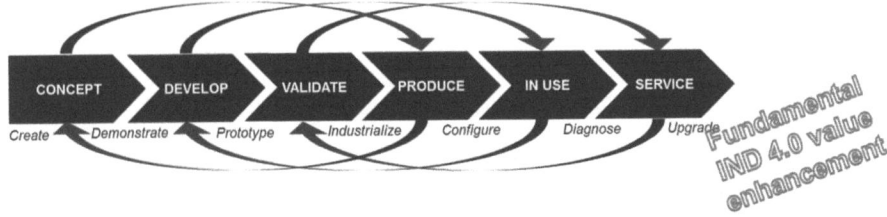

Fig. 1. Industry 4.0 enhancement proposal

This enhancement targets two additional benefits: First the iteration back from the production to earlier development phases shall lead to more effective (continuous) innovation cycles between product development and production. Second, the information during in-use and service shall be integrated into this digitalization in order to cover all the aspects of the product and therefore better understand the customer use as well as possible improvement potentials. This would allow anticipating usage of information into production (e.g., late configuration, real time to individual usage patterns or remote product upgrades). This would further increase efficiency and flexibility through consistency of the information over the entire product lifecycle (single source of truth between development, production, in-use, service).

2.2 Seamless Collection and Analysis of Information Covering Development, Production and Application for the Automotive Domain

The automotive domain is challenged by heterogeneous sources of requirements coming from multiple domains and leading to highly complex targets for the development and validation of products such as the powertrain, see Fig. 2. End-user requirements (e.g., usability, reliability, costs, time to market, features) as well as legal requirements (emissions, safety, liability) lead to high-level vehicle targets to be identified at the begin of the development, to be managed consistently during development and validation, and finally to be fulfilled after production. These requirements usually add complexity and increase costs. This is even more stringent due to the limitation of using specific, traditional technologies. At the same time, manufacturer requirements (e.g., cost effectiveness, faultless process, warranties, company image) are more targeted to the production steps, while also impacting the development.

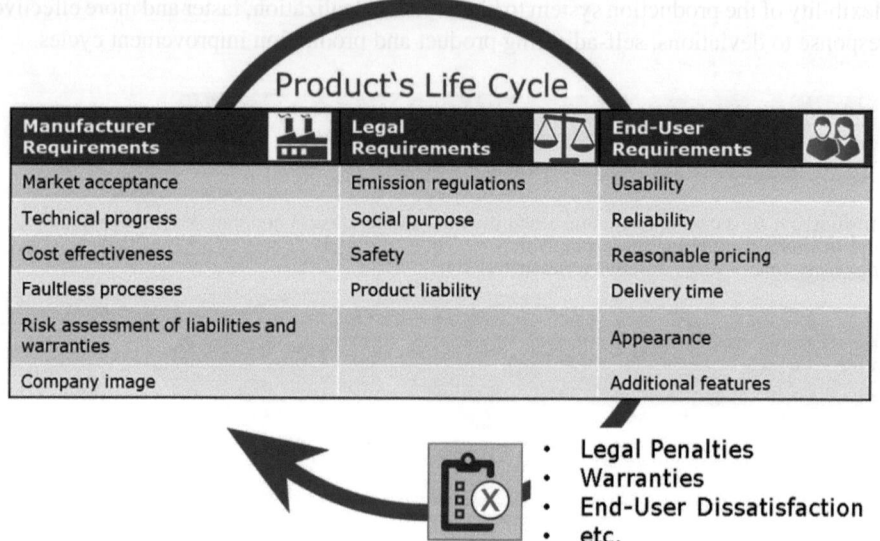

Fig. 2. Automotive context: heterogeneous sources for requirements leading to complex vehicle targets

One important challenge is therefore to provide an efficient and consistent management of all these requirements over the entire product's lifecycle as well as over the institutions involved. The reaction time to a change of a requirement is a critical factor. The challenge is to analyze ideally in "real-time" the impact of a changed requirement and adapt accordingly the digitalized product and supply chain over the entire product lifecycle. The final benefit is then the reduction of both time-to-market and total cost of ownership (TCO), while ensuring high degree of customization of the produced powertrain. Major potential for improvement is to provide solutions to reduce silos – both at company level between the different departments and/or product lifecycle (e.g., between development and production), but as well within the supply chain between OEM and suppliers.

There is a consensus in the literature that Industry 4.0 is a major trend relying on digitalization along the product lifecycle and over the supply-chain and having strong potential to increase competitiveness and generate new business opportunities [7–9].

Especially, digitalization of the existing value chain is an enabler for cost reduction through improved data quality and insights as well as for data-driven innovation. These aspects aim at enabling better decisions by using more and better data, at reducing fragmented information and insights from organization silos, as well as at discovering game-changing relationships hidden in the data by using advanced data analytics [7]. At the same time there is a consensus that the identification of new value propositions is a challenging task since it requires the collaboration between domain experts (technical domain knowledge), IT experts (data scientists, IT infrastructure) and business experts (link investments to clear business case) [8], see Fig. 3. This collaboration targets the identification of new value proposition with "physical product at the core, augmented by digital interfaces and data-based, innovative services" [9].

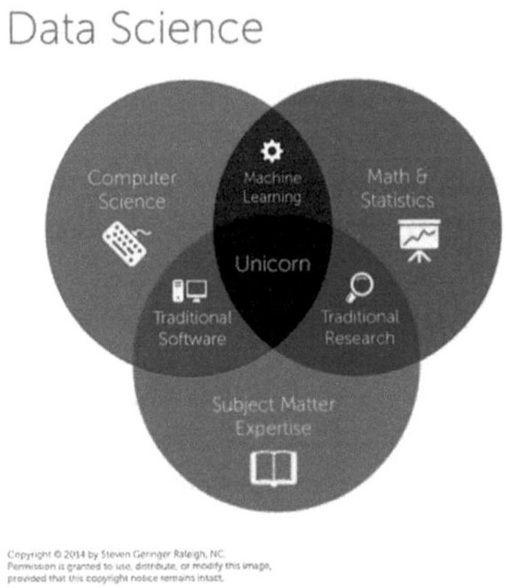

Fig. 3. Data science as convergence between computer science, math & statistics, and domain expert [10]

2.3 Cybersecurity as a Key Challenge of Data-Driven Life Cycles and Business Models

As argued above, digital manufacturing and smart, completely customizable product-service systems go hand in hand in Industry 4.0, and are driven by a seamless end-to-end information flow as a "digital thread" spanning the complete product/service/system life cycle. The key element enabling and driving these paradigms is the high integration of complex interconnected embedded systems of electronics and software in traditional manufacturing systems and products. Through this integration, such cyber-physical systems (CPS) are increasingly taking over control of essential value-added functions. In applications like automotive, aeronautics, medical, nuclear power plants, etc. such functions are often safety-critical, i.e. any failures linked to these functions might harm human health. The same applies to manufacturing environments where high levels of automation and autonomy of machines and robots lead to the necessity of taking safety criticality into account in the very design of Industrial Control Systems (ICS) and their operating environments. While not every secure system is necessarily safety-critical, the opposite always holds true: safety-critical systems have to be secure as well, otherwise the built-in safety features might be compromised by intruders.

At the same time, safety-critical embedded systems are increasingly part of networks of systems which interact among each other in order to provide added-value functions on system level. This interaction takes place via computer networks which are either private to the system, or linked to an information technology (IT) cloud, or both. A key challenge of such networks is the assurance of cybersecurity and trust, i.e. the protection of these networks against malicious intrusions aiming at modifying the intended behaviour of the network and/or the linked devices and services. The Industrial Internet of Things (IIoT) and the growing reliance on automation and big data have rendered cybersecurity the biggest risk factor in manufacturing [11]. Due to the seamless digital thread approach, the vulnerability of CPS is significantly increased with respect to traditional, less networked systems. This requires new approaches to establishing and protecting trust domains in highly distributed organisations, products, services, and processes.

3 Opportunities and Approaches for Data-Driven Business Models in the Context of Industry 4.0

3.1 Potential for Value Creation Enabled by Big Data/Infonomics

Large data sets are already today's reality: Around 2.5 quintillion bytes of data are created every day, and this amount of data is increasing by 40% each year. This large amount of data represents an important opportunity for today's and tomorrow's value creation. Possible aspects encompass cost reduction in the daily business, productivity gains (relying on data-driven decision making), eco-design or supply chain analysis, finally leading to expected annual net savings of €600 billion only for the EU business. This situation is evolving fast; indeed, the digital assets across the entire economy doubled over the past 15 years, and European companies expect a growth from 28% (today) to 71% (by 2020) of their achievement in advanced levels of digitalization [12].

The societal impact is huge. Beside the estimated additional EU-GDP of 206 billion € by 2020, the usage of big data is expected, e.g., to support CO_2 reduction by more than 2 gigatonnes [13]. At the same time the successful deployment of big data related business require advances in multiple dimensions:

- Data: Availability of the data and access to data sources
- Skills: Capability to train the engineers to enable value creation based on big data in their respective (native) application domains
- Legal: Different legal issues – such as ownership, protection and privacy, liability, cybercrimes, IPR - arise from using data as core asset for value creation
- Technical: Capability to provide appropriate framework (methods, tools and solutions) for e.g., real-time analytics, ETL, new and rich user interfaces
- Business: Capability to generate business innovation by understanding value creation based on data and by enhancing traditional business models with data-driven business models

An important challenge for big data is the capability to assess the business value behind the data, in order to deploy the appropriate budget and resources to create the business. The concept of infonomics[1] has been introduced in this context to assert economic significance to information and provide the framework for businesses to measure, manage and monetize information as a real asset. In fact, according to today's literature, there is no consensus to quantify and provide business value of a data. Instead, guidelines are available to support business development experts to quantify their own data in their respective (application domain) context [14]:

- The cost and effort of preparing or acquiring it?
- The cost of storing it and managing it vs. re-acquiring it?
- The context in which it has been used in the past, or how it may be used in the future?
- Its rarity or brevity or accuracy?
- The lifecycle of its relevance
- How often it has been accessed and referenced and by whom?
- Who it is relevant to?
- The frequency of its access? (If I create a piece of information and 5 other people use it, is it 5 times more valuable?)
- The length of time that it retains its value, and the related potential for real-time data analytics?
- At what point does its value peak and when does it wane?
- The risk it carries, by its existence or by its absence?
- Is the value absolute, or relative to other information?

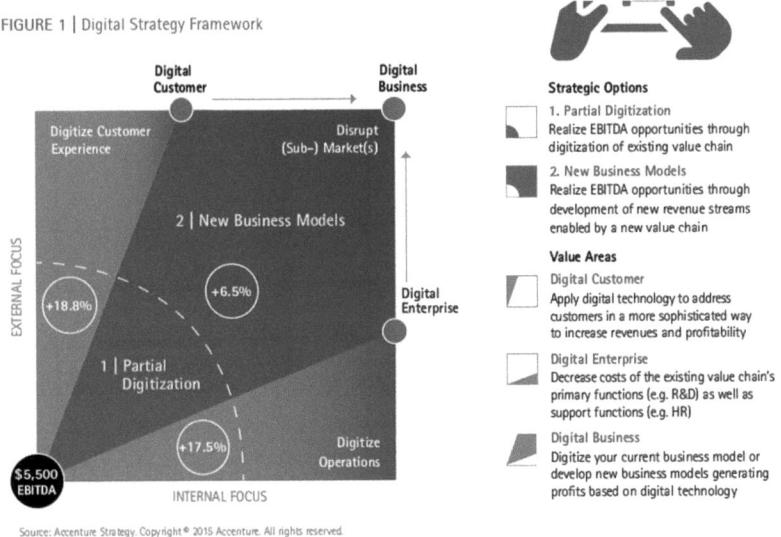

Fig. 4. Digital Strategy Framework [15]

---

[1] https://en.wikipedia.org/wiki/Infonomics.

The main challenge is to identify value areas and apply typical types of data-driven business models to enhance existing portfolios accordingly. The strategy strongly relies on the convergence of traditional business models with IT expertise. Different improvements can be achieved with digitalization. Especially, three main value areas are identified [15] (see Fig. 4 as well):

- Digital Customer: Apply digital technology to address customers in a more sophisticated way to increase revenues and profitability
- Digital Enterprise: decrease costs of the existing value chain's primary functions (e.g. R&D) as well as support functions (e.g., human resources)
- Digital Business: Digitize your current business model or develop new business models generating profits based on digital technologies

While going to a data-driven business model, the importance of data becomes very central and consequently different roles and responsibilities need to become more explicit. This new business model organization foresees different roles, see Fig. 5:

- Data producer, generating the relevant data and receiving earning for the information (payback according to amount of data, relevance of data…). Trust is required at data producer side that the payback is in relation to the data consumed and that no confidentiality issue arise (e.g., unintended communication of confidential information).
- Data consumer, receiving the consolidated data against payment. Trust is required at data consumer side that the quality of data received is in relation to their payment, and that efficient access to the large dataset can be provided while no confidentiality issue arise at their site.
- Data broker, in charge of interacting with data producer and data consumer, providing a technical and legal framework for the exchange of the information, and in charge of merging and consolidating the dataset accordingly.

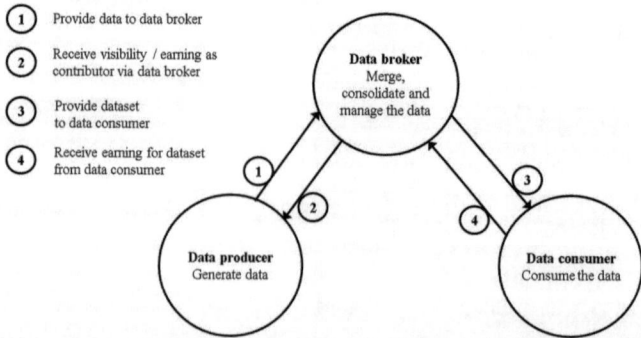

Fig. 5. Data-driven business model - role of data broker

As depicted previously, trust is a central enabling aspect – respectively show-stopper – for data-driven business models. Historically, the role of data brokers was implicitly integrated at data producer or data consumer side. All participants are part of a single sphere of trust (see Fig. 6–A) supported by legal frameworks (e.g., Non-Disclosure Agreements –

NDA, terms and conditions) as well as technical frameworks (e.g., databases and secure connections to exchange the data). However, these structures are not scaling well for a growing number of participants in such business. This is especially true when different partners have different contributions (e.g., different amount/quality of data produced, or consumed).

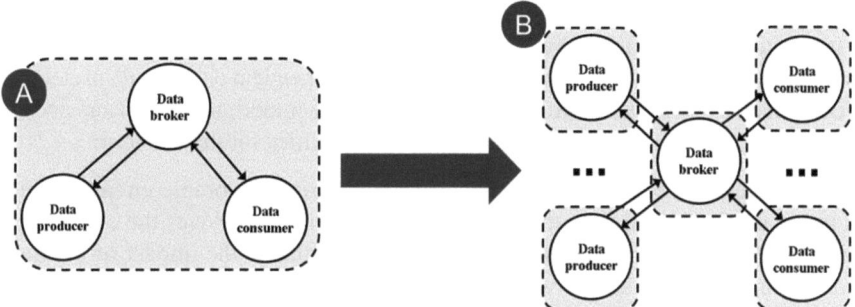

Shift from one common sphere of trust to partial aggregation of spheres of trust

Fig. 6. Different supply chain organization leading to different scenarios for sphere of trust

Hence, a shift to partial aggregation of different spheres of trust (see Fig. 6–B) is required. From a technical aspect, partial access to the data set shall be possible (e.g., due to different needs from consumers or different contributions from producers). From a legal point of view, a personalized sphere of confidences shall be provided to ensure that only the expected partner(s) can access to only the expected dataset(s). Ideally, an accompanying assessment capability by independent third party shall be provided to further strengthen the trust in this proposed sphere of confidence.

Summarizing, the shift toward data-driven business models and the resulting growing complexity by terms of number of participants and higher business relevance, it is evident that the role of data broker must become more explicit and specialized.

3.2 Potential of Digitalization over the Product Lifecycle for the Automotive Market

The automotive market can be described as follows [1]:

- Worldwide market with 91 million units vehicle produced by year, of which 18.4 million (20%) produced in Europe, and 290 millions vehicles in use within EU28.
- Important pillar for the European economy with 12 million (direct and indirect) jobs within Europe and a trade balance of over 100 billion euro, as well as fiscal income of 401 billion euro.
- Highly competitive and capital intensive market with a focus to reduce production costs while improving vehicle quality (including reliability, availability) as well as customisability.

- Highly segmented market with complex supply chains, making global system optimization very challenging due to the number of persons and skills involved, significant transaction costs, as well as IPR and confidentiality issues.
- Market re-organization due to disruptive technologies such as electrification or autonomous driving. This leads to strong corporate re-organization of traditional players (introduction of a "vehicle business unit") as well as the appearance of new market entrant (e.g., Tesla).
- Innovation strongly driven by cyber-physical systems: it is estimated that 80% to 90% of the key differentiating competitive features are dependent on the built-in electronic components and systems with a strongly increasing importance of sensors and software [16] enabling adaptive or cognitive functionalities for the end user.

Consequently, the automotive context is providing a favorable environment for the usage of digitalization ta to improve the competitiveness over the entire supply chain and to develop new applications. More particularly, the impact of big data – by mapping different stages within a product lifecycle and by bridging different application domains – solves industrial challenges in the automotive domain is huge. The opportunity for new or enhanced value proposition can be represented as matrix between the digitalization supply chain (from digitalization platforms up to smart products) and the product supply chain, see Fig. 7.

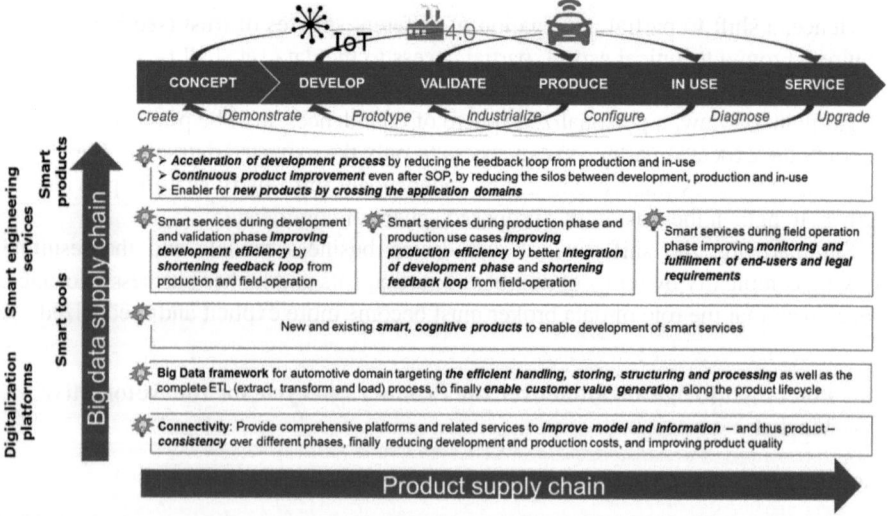

Fig. 7. Value proposition for big data solutions in the context of digitalization of the product lifecycle

4 Combining Systems- and Cost Engineering for Improved TCO Monitoring Already During Development Phase

In addition to commonly known design and development tasks, methods and tools for cost prediction in an early development phase will play an increasingly important role [17]. To meet this demand, the integrative approach of the methodology presented goes beyond commonly known methods by not just covering production requirements such as Design for Manufacturing or Design for Assembly but also proactively incorporates in-field requirements. The consideration of cost information in the early development and design stages ensures that trend-setting decisions can be taken very early in the development process. Therefore, this methodology helps to optimize the total cost of ownership (TCO) for e.g. different powertrain architectures.

The declared goal of the TCO principle as a method of considering total costs is to not solely align a purchase decision with the purchase price, but with all costs associated with the acquisition, use, repair, maintenance, reuse and disposal [18]. Figure 8 identifies the decisive role of the effect of the early development phase on the costs occurring later in the use phase. The temporal and causal interactions between the influence on cost, cost determination and cost accrual are visualized based on the observation timeline of the integrated product lifecycle related to the lifecycle of a passenger car, commercial truck, and off-road and generator applications [19].

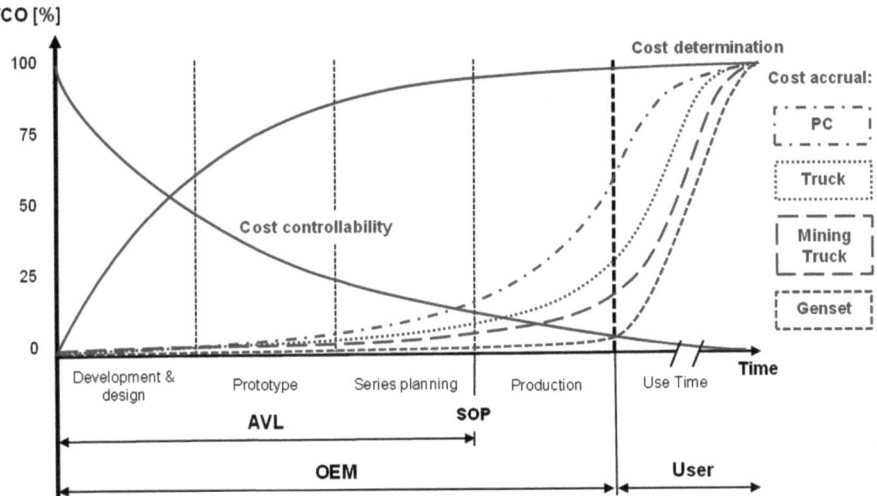

Fig. 8. Schematic representation of TCO determination, accrual and controllability using examples of passenger car, commercial truck, mining truck and genset applications (based on [20, 21])

The contribution presented in this paper supports AVL's methodology for the calculation of the total cost of ownership of powertrains that simulates the visualized dependencies at the beginning of product development and hence can support technological decision-making [22]. The basis for this simulation is a consistent data backbone, ensuring that information is managed, or linked and accessible, in a central manner (e.g., using databases and/or specific architecture description language such as SysML) and strongly increasing the consistency over the involved technologies.

The main target of the combined systems- and cost engineering methodology, illustrated in Fig. 9, is to perform a holistic analysis and assessment of function-oriented powertrain configurations in the early development phase. Functional orientation shall ensure that the increase in complexity (e.g. similar development targets can be realized by ever more powertrain and vehicle functions which can be again implemented by various powertrain architectures) can be structured, assessed and managed in a reproducible way.

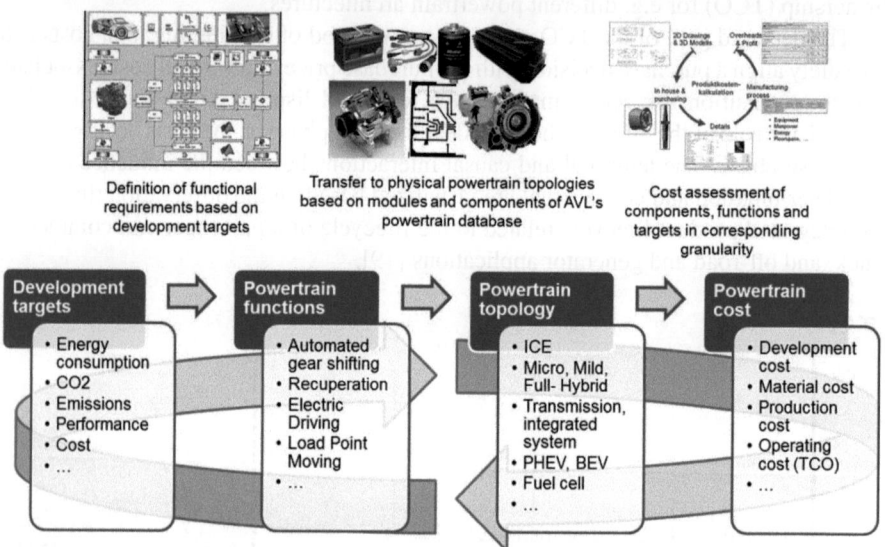

Fig. 9. Combined systems- and cost engineering

One important challenge for the method presented is to interface to different engineering domains and to control the complexity originating from the crosslinking of development activities [23]. For that reason, following aspects need to be taken into account, further developed and integrated:

- Definition of technical and financial development targets.
- Technical concept specification under consideration of functional requirements based on these development targets.
- Analysis of correlations between technical parameters and product cost. This will be based depending on data availability either by deterministic approaches or big data analysis.
- Investigation of various tools (e.g. DoE) to optimize multidimensional parameters regarding costs, energy consumption, CO_2 at defined emission boundary conditions.

- Assessment of significant correlations between development targets, functionalities, product architectures and costs in an early development phase.
- Identifying technical parameters which need to be known in powertrain development which allow an early and sound cost assessment.

Figure 10 exemplarily shows how design of experiment methods can be applied to assess and optimize multidimensional influencing factors. Before running optimization algorithms, the correlations of multiple technical parameters and product costs need to be understood. The most promising enabler to cope with this challenge is the digitalization of the powertrain lifecycle and the seamless analysis of big data covering development, production and application.

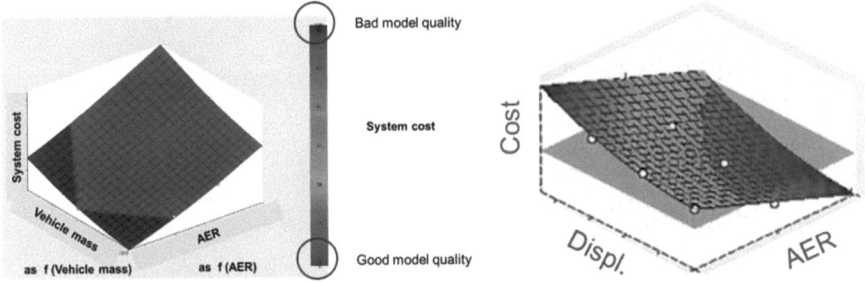

Fig. 10. DOE based optimization method: modelling, visualization and optimization

5 Early Industry 4.0 Scenarios – Processes and Information Infrastructure for Forward and Backward Control of Variants and Variation

Individual product variation can be wanted or unwanted. In both cases, systematic control is necessary to manufacture and deliver components or complete end-customer products. While wanted product variation concerns mainly significantly differing made-to-order product variants based on a reuse platform, unwanted variation is mainly associated with imperfect production repeatability – both in variance (process capability, CpK) and centering (process performance, PpK).

Systematic variant management builds on a reuse platform dedicated to configure a range of product variants for a certain domain. Variant control by configuration can be characterized as **forward acting control**, and includes consistent variant management in all required disciplines of system, and all lifecycle phases. Important phases are customer-specific product variant engineering (including integration and verification), and/or their mass production with individual configuration. E.g. engineering of customer-specific ECU models, and configuring their individual part's IDs and secrets for trustworthy and secure interoperability when integrated in the assembled car's environment.

Continuing with this example, Fig. 11 shows such trust provisioning steps in a multi-supplier chain. Its main prerequisites are a supporting architecture for later injection of parameters, and tools for use at the point of configuration (e.g. end-of-line, or repair). In addition to the forward-directed sub-product's lifecycles, apparently there are also **lateral cross cutting** processes to ensure consistent configuration and parameterization of sub-products across suppliers. Effective "lateral" process synchronization and distribution of individual product data across OEM and suppliers is key for a friction-less integration. Such supplier-distributed processes can be supported by a mutually trusted cloud service architecture as described further above.

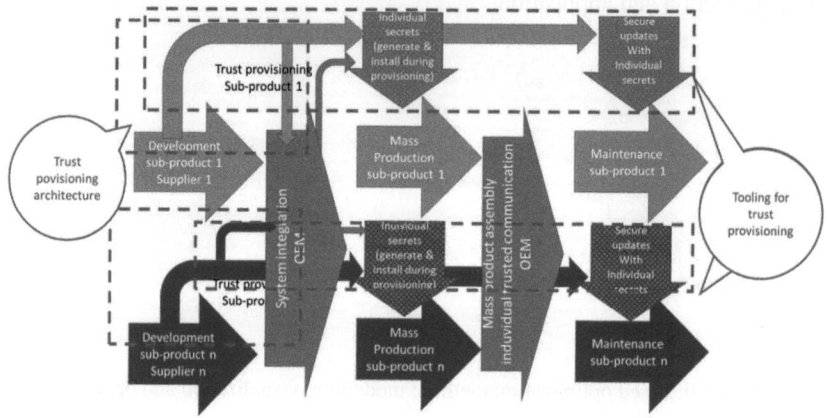

Fig. 11. Main trust provisioning interactions in a complex supply chain

Thinking beyond classical Six Sigma statistical control of mass production, a fully digitalized production environment can **measure individually varying** product and production properties in earlier stages (e.g. random production variations) for **forward compensation and as individual fingerprints** in order to

- systematically compensate in later stages to achieve significantly better variation and centering, and
- use several of these individual "parts fingerprints" as a way to securely prove identity (remote attestation), eliminating the need to incorporate dedicated electronics for that purpose.

This scenario also benefits from **feed-back control**. Real end user mission profiles, field monitoring of maintenance cases call for usage and incident monitoring. Such kind of data is best collected by the (sub-) product itself, as that has the best and most complete perception of its operation conditions and environment. Again, trusted cloud services can help in offloading product data to collection services. Feed-back information can be used to continuously

- re-align product platforms to market needs,
- trigger improvement processes to tweak integrated design parameters and production/testing steps for better production repeatability and fast-efficient EoL testing,

- acquisition of mission profile dependent fleet parameter like Real Driving Emissions, and of course,
- the validation of failure rates (safety) as well as lifetime model data.

Cross cutting processes like in Fig. 11 also makes a fundamental challenge in Industry 4.0 adoption apparent: neither a sub-product's lifecycle nor a consistent configuration process can be the primary "intelligent" backbone process in the overall picture – at least not without compromises. One inevitable transformation in Industry 4.0 is to move information ownership from processes to the (sub-) products, those becoming then **cognitive products**, i.e. as inseparable product-information duality through process steps of potentially many organizations throughout their lifecycle.

Process coupling and trust is established nowadays mostly between organizations at their interface (clearing) points on a coarse business process level, linked to business transactions on ERP level (delivery and replenishment). In Industry 4.0 supply chains, it might become even necessary to establish interfacing and trust much more fine granular for each process step. At the same time, access is only granted to information necessary for processing and mutual trust, i.e. access to all other information is restricted, like that needed for another process steps & trust relations. Enabling fine-grained reconfiguration of supply chains in this way, they become more agile and resilient. As illustrated in Fig. 12, this transformation calls for (reconfigurable!) inter-organization communication not just on ERP level, but at least also in MES and SCADA levels. In future service oriented control architectures also PLC and sensor level could be offered in a trusted cloud architecture.

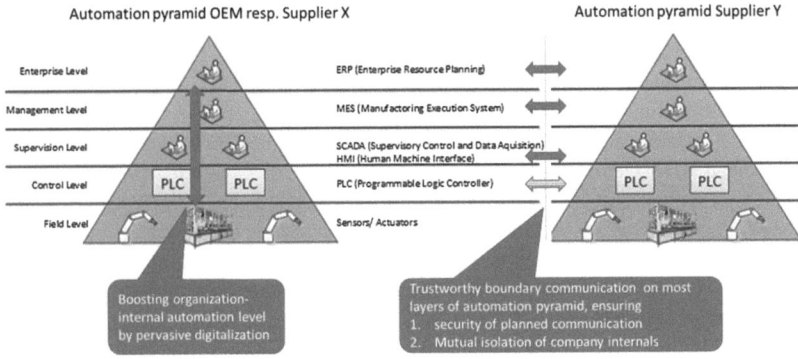

Fig. 12. Industry 4.0 improvements on automation pyramid and supply chain communication

6 Conclusion

Industry 4.0, understood as the digitalization over the entire product lifecycle, has the capability to revolutionize the industry. Hence, the information backbone has the capability to reduce silos – both at company level between the different departments and/or product lifecycle (e.g., between development and production), as well as within the supply chain between customer and suppliers. This has two major impacts: First, the complex product can be understood and analysed as a whole, over the technologies, expertise, company structure, market or customer boundaries. This enables to understand complex relationships and finally optimize the product and its production for an individualized customer need and for a given industrial and legal context. Second, the resulting cognitive product, together with its cognitive development, production and in-field environments, is able to automate decisions and to finally act in a more pro-active way in its given environment. This includes for example automated ordering when a warehouse is close to be empty, or strategies for predictive maintenance to reduce down-time.

Acknowledgments. The research leading to these results has received funding from the ECSEL Joint Undertaking under grant agreement n° 692466 (project SemI40), from the respective national funding authorities, and from the Austrian funding agency (FFG) under grant agreement n° 858656 (P2-Opti).

References

1. The automotive industry – Pocket guide 2016–2017. European Automobile Manufacturers Association. http://www.acea.be/publications/archives/category/acea-pocket-guide
2. Industry 4.0 - Österreichs Industry im Wandel, PwC Österreich GmbH Wirtschaftsprüfungsgesellschaft, June 2015
3. Industry 4.0 – Whitepaper FuE-Themen, Platform Industry 4.0, April 2014. http://www.plattform-i40.de/blog/industry-40-whitepaper-fue-themen-stand-7-April-2015
4. Spath, D., Ganschar, O., Gerlach, S., Hämmerle, M., Krause, T., Schlund, S.: Produktionsarbeit der Zukunft – Industry 4.0, Fraunhofer IAO (2013). ISBN 973-3-8396-0570-7
5. Bauer, W., Schlund, S., Marrenbach, D., Ganschar, O.: Industry 4.0 – Volkswirtschaftliches Potenzial für Deutschland, BITKOM/Fraunhofer IAO (2014). https://www.bitkom.org/Bitkom/Publikationen/Publikation_2753.html
6. The digital transformation of the industry, Roland Berger Strategy Consultants, commissioned by the federation of German Industries (BDI), February 2015. https://www.rolandberger.com/publications/publication_pdf/roland_berger_digital_transformation_of_industry_20150315.pdf
7. Gissler, A., Oertel, C., Knackfuß, C.: Driving digitalization in the auto industry, Franziska Kupferschmidt, accenture strategy (2016). https://www.accenture.com/t20160321T000505__w__/us-en/_acnmedia/PDF-10/Accenture-Strategy-Driving-Digitization-Auto-Industry-1.pdf
8. Wee, D., Breunig, M., Kelly, R., Mathis, R.: Industry 4.0 after the initial hype - Where manufacturers are finding value and how they can best capture it, McKinsey Digital (2016). http://www.mckinsey.com/~/media/mckinsey/business%20functions/operations/our%20insights/getting%20the%20most%20out%20of%20industry%204%200/mckinsey_industry_40_2016.ashx
9. Geissbauer, R., Vedso, J., Schrauf, S.: Industry 4.0: Building the digital enterprise, PWC (2016). https://www.pwc.com/gx/en/industries/industries-4.0/landing-page/industry-4.0-building-your-digital-enterprise-april-2016.pdf
10. Sivaraj, A.: Data Science Venn's diagram, Copyright©2014 Steven Geringer Raleigh, NC) of Data Science Buzzwords Demystified, July 2015. https://indico.io/blog/data-science-buzzwords-demystified/

11. BDO Manufacturing Risk Factor Report (2016). https://www.bdo.com/insights/industries/manufacturing-distribution/2016-bdo-manufacturing-riskfactor-report. Accessed 08 Jan 2016
12. European Commission, DG Internal Market, Industry, Entrepreneurship and SMEs, Big data and B2B digital platforms: the next frontier for Europe's industry and enterprises, April 2016. http://ec.europa.eu/growth/tools-databases/newsroom/cf/itemdetail.cfm?item_id=8800
13. Big Data Value Association, Big Data Value Strategic Research and Innovation Agenda, January 2016. http://www.bdva.eu/sites/default/files/EuropeanBigDataValuePartnership_SRIA__v2.pdf
14. Executive Leadership Council, Infonomics, how do you measure the value of information – Summit on Infonomics, Summer 2016. http://info.aiim.org/infonomics-how-do-you-measure-the-value-of-information
15. Redman, T.C.: Business Models for the Data Age. Harvard Business Review (2015). https://hbr.org/2015/05/4-business-models-for-the-data-age
16. ECSEL Joint Undertaking, 2017 Multi Annual Strategic Research and Innovation Agenda for ECSEL Joint Undertaking (2017). https://artemis-ia.eu/publication/download/masria2017.pdf
17. Braess, H.H., Seiffert, U. (eds.): Vieweg Handbuch Kraftfahrzeugtechnik, 7th edn. Springer, Wiesbaden (2013). doi:10.1007/978-3-8348-8298-1
18. Geißdörfer, K.: Total Cost of Ownership (TCO) und Life Cycle Costing (LCC): Einsatz und Modelle: Ein Vergleich zwischen Deutschland und USA. LIT Verlag Dr. W. Hopf, Berlin (2009)
19. Sams, C., von Falck, G., Glensvig, M., Lind-Braucher, S.: Entwicklung einer Total Cost of Ownership Methodik für AVL List. In: Sustainability Management for Industries 6, Leoben (2015)
20. Bubeck, D.: Life Cycle Costing (LCC) im Automobilbau. Verlag Dr. Kovac, Hamburg (2002)
21. Ehrlenspiel, K., Kiewert, A., Lindemann, U.: Kostengünstig entwickeln und Konstruieren: Kostenmanagement bei der integrierten Produktentwicklung. Springer, Heidelberg (2014). doi:10.1007/978-3-642-41959-1
22. Glensvig, M., Sams, C., von Falck, G., Finnigan, B.: Simulation der Lebenszykluskosten in einer frühen Entwicklungsphase. In: ATZextra Prüfstände und Simulation für Antriebe, September 2015
23. Arnoscht, J.: Beherrschung von Komplexität bei der Gestaltung von Baukastensystemen. Apprimus Wissenschaftsverlag, Aachen (2011)

Chances for Virtual and Augmented Reality Along the Value Chain

Sonja Hammerschmid(✉)

IMC Krems, Donau, Austria
sonja.hammerschmid@imc-krems.eu

Abstract. In this paper readers receive an overview of the opportunities for using virtual and augmented reality (VR and AR) in a standardized value chain in various industries. The main objective is to show different possible applications for companies to use VR and AR. Literature research is the basis for the findings in this paper. Results were found in the fields of sales, marketing, training, product design and development, logistics and manufacturing. There are many possibilities for companies to become more efficient and cost-saving. In addition, employees can benefit from additional help and time-saving training. At the moment, the most potential is found in the field of marketing and sales due to the fact that customers will be directly influenced by the technologies. Nevertheless, it depends on the company which opportunity suits them the best.

Keywords: Virtual reality · Augmented reality · Value chain · Sales · Product design · Product development · Manufacturing · Training · Logistics

1 Introduction

As virtual reality and augmented reality (VR and AR) are a part of Internet 4.0 it is interesting explore where these two technologies could be used throughout a (standardized) value chain to gain additional benefit. In this paper, readers have the opportunity to find different examples of usage for various industries. First of all, there is a short introduction about definitions and future expectations of VR and AR. Followed by an explanation of the method used. In the last part, the opportunities throughout a standardized value chain are shown.

1.1 Definition of Virtual and Augmented Reality

The As VR a relatively new term, there is not only one definition. However, there are some characteristics defined to describe VR. First, VR is a computer based reality in 3D likely with sound. VR could be used with a large screen, special rooms, or special glasses. The main difference to normal 3D videos is that users can look around, move and interact in the virtual world (Bendel 2017).

The definition of AR from Azuma (1997) is well-established. He specified AR as a combination of reality and virtuality which is interactive and in real-time. From a perspective view AR is described as an extension of the real surrounding with virtual aspects. Furthermore, it should be so well done that the user cannot distinguish between real and virtual impressions. (Broll 2013). All of these new technologies VR, AR and mixed reality (MR), which is a combination of VR and AR, use special output devices, such as headsets, to alter human perception and take users somewhere or enable them to see something that otherwise would be invisible (O'Brien 2016).

1.2 Future Expectation

The report of Gartner's Hype Cycle serves strategists and planners with an assessment of the maturity business benefit and future direction of more than 2,000 technologies grouped into 98 areas (Gartner 2013).

In Fig. 1 the Hype Cycle 2016 from Gartner is displayed. Throughout the curve technologies are placed depending on their development phase. The symbols that are used represent when the specific technology is likely to penetrate the market. In the past these expectations were relatively exact. In Fig. 1 it is illustrated that VR and AR will penetrate the market in the next five to ten years (Dumont 2015).

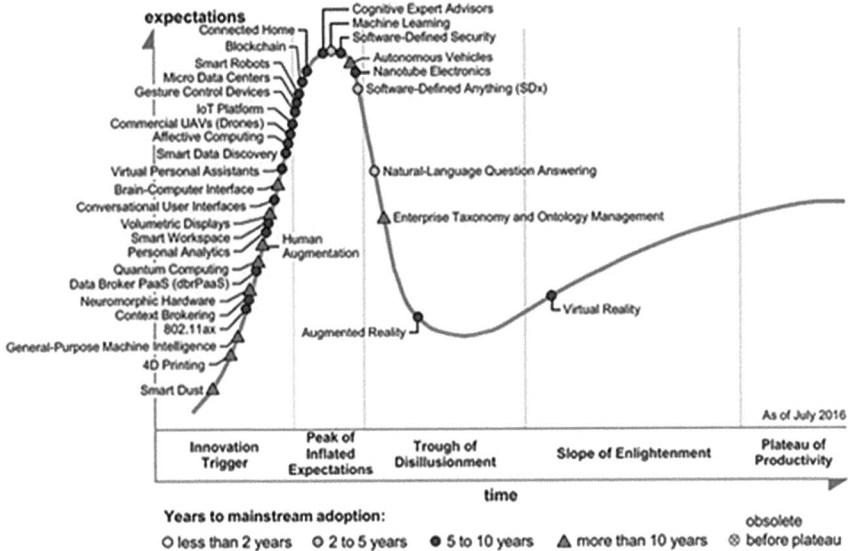

Fig. 1. Gartner's Hype Cycle (Gartner 2017)

Research from KPMG shows that the market for VR and AR will dynamically develop due to the fact that complementary technologies will occur. Moreover, the study points out that probably all industries will profit from the innovation for example by increasing in turnover, cost savings or more efficient processes (Erbert et al. 2016).

2 Methodology

This paper aims to do an extensive literature research. This research was made throughout a project of an Austrian office furniture manufacturer who wants to implement VR and/or AR along their value chain. The scope of this paper is to find use cases along the value chain in various branches. In the next step of the project is to find a suitable opportunity for the project partner. Afterwards, case studies with other companies will be made to find similarities or differences between various industries.

When the boundaries between the phenomenon being studied and the context within which it is being studied are not unambiguous, case studies are used. Multiple sources of evidence and theoretical propositions are consultant to improve the research method. In addition, a number of case studies could strengthen the findings (Yin 2014).

3 Capabilities Through the Value Chain

The study from KPMG has shown that the potential of VR and AR has not yet come to a peak. Nevertheless, a detailed prediction is not possible to make. However, it is certain that more and more areas of application will develop. In the study 260 use cases were analyzed and in Fig. 2 the frequency of current application is illustrated (Erbert et al. 2016).

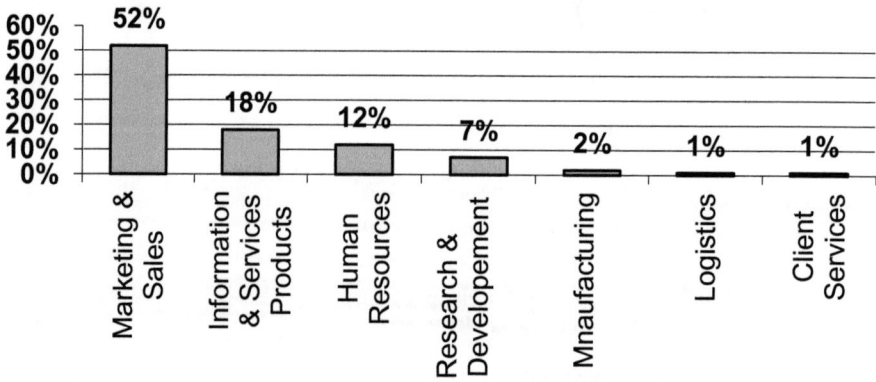

Fig. 2. standarized value chain (Erbert et al. 2016)

As we can see at the moment more than half of the usage of VR and AR is in Marketing and Sales. Around 20% of the companies which are already working with these technologies deploy them in the field of information and services of products (Erbert et al. 2016).

3.1 Marketing and Sales

3.1.1 Virtual Meetings

As VR-technologies could lift conferences, screen-sharing-tools, etc. to a new level. As an avatar other colleagues, customers or even providers could come to a virtual table to look at (new) products and discuss them. This could be a solution for meetings in person. Even with these expectations there could be some problems regarding acceptance of the different stakeholders (Neidel 2016). The preparation for a virtual meeting is almost the same as for personal meetings. One of the big differences is that participants are less connected because they are not in the same room, due to that fact, more empathy and thoughtfulness is needed. Another problem could be that non-verbal cues such as whether people have questions or would like to enter the conversation, are not seen. In view of a good meeting more leadership approach is required (Axtell 2016).

3.1.2 Presentation of Products

Audi is conducting a project to bring more customers back to their car dealerships. Customers can configure their dream car and with VR-Glasses they have the opportunity to look at their vehicle from all perspectives even in other surroundings. Furthermore, with VR customers come into another emotional state, Audi does not sell more cars but more facilities (Ilg 2017) (Figs. 3 and 4).

Fig. 3. Audi VR (Remco 2016)

Since 2014 Google has been working on a project called Tango. With this app clients can measure their room or house and have the possibility to arrange the furniture in it. After planning, customers could talk to vendors and buy the furniture which fits them best. Another opportunity of Tango is to obtain information about samples in museums. Visitors just hold their smart phones above a sample and get more information about it (Google Tango 2017).

IKEA is testing a virtual tour through their furniture stores and can show the chosen furniture as it would look in a potential customer's home. Furthermore, customers can have a look from different perspectives for example how the kitchen looks from a

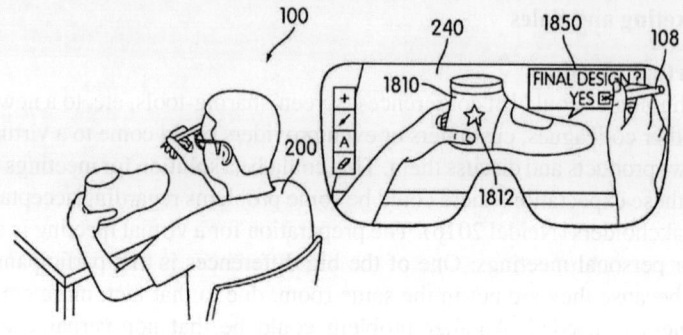

Fig. 4. Nike's shoe design (Murphy 2015)

perspective of a child (Neidel 2016). Another chance of a virtual showroom could be the installation of a VR-CAVE, this is a room with screens and projectors everywhere, to give the feeling to a customer that he/she is in this virtual world (Geert 2013).

3.2 Training and Further Education

Seminars and workshops will become location independent but can take place together with other participants even a virtual trainer could hold the seminars or workshops. A European study shows that 10.6% of further education costs are due to traveling (Erbert et al. 2016).

Surgeons at UCLA are using VR technology to run highly technical and sensitive surgeries before they operate on patients (O'Brien 2016).

For industries where employees are in dangerous surroundings, VR is being widely used to train staff. For example VR headsets are used by the military soldiers can be tested and trained in challenging combat scenarios within a safe virtual world. Althought, this application could help to train some companies are still skeptical about the benefit of virtual training. Another point of virtual training is that people across different destinations can be trained (Lyons 2016).

Daily work can benefit from AR because information can be seen through devices such as glasses or smart phones. In other words, if there are problems during routine tasks, workers have the possibility to react and address the problem. Additionally, with interactive applications a positive learning effect will be recognized (Erbert et al. 2016).

3.3 Product Design

Companies with complex and difficult to produce products can benefit significantly from the usage of VR-Technologies. First of all, designers can build a new product in a virtual world without using any material resources. Another benefit is that designers and engineers from all over the world can work together on one project (Erbert et al. 2016).

John Deere is using VR for product development and the integration of elements into existing designs (John Deere 2014). Ford designers and engineers use VR to test elements of new cars, saving $8 million in one year by using these technologies (O'Brien 2016). In a virtual reality prototypes can be established and as many test people as the company wants can try it without producing anything, therefore it is cost saving (Erbert et al. 2016). Nike gives the opportunity to their customers to design individual shoes with a model in their hand and a VR-headset (Murphy 2015).

Procter & Gamble has 20 centers of visualization for Research & Development with which they reduced the time of penetration to the market by 50% (Accenture 2017).

3.4 Logistics

AR-Technology could help to increase efficiency by navigating employees through the streets. Statistics shows that traffic jams reduce European economic performance by one percent per year (Erbert et al. 2016).

Furthermore, AR can make processes more efficient and new employees have the opportunity to receive an excellent training. Moreover, the warehouse can be optimized. With a pick-by-vision solution employees get information displayed directly on their glasses and they have free hands to work with. A field test showed that around 40% of failures will be reduced by using VR-Glasses (Glockner et al. 2014).

DHL completed a pilot project in the Netherlands in co-operation with RICOH. Employees were equipped with AR hard- and software. The main objective of the project was to check if efficiency and quality of order picking could be enhanced by means of smart glasses, compared to working with hand-held scanners or paper pick lists. The results gathered were very convincing. Performance increased by 25% by each picker and time-savings per task were significantly higher compared to the control group that used hand-held devices. Furthermore, the feedback of the pickers was encouraging as, they benefit from the hands free picking process (Kückelhaus 2015).

3.5 Manufacturing

Product processes will be eased with automatic target-performance comparison. The check is in real-time due to the fact that nonperforming production can be identified and repaired immediately. Nonperforming production costs rise exponentially the later they are identified (Erbert et al. 2016).

Maintenance can occur before it comes to a blackout. Furthermore, AR-technology can support employees by repairing machines without an expert coming locally (Erbert et al. 2016). Users are shown information relevant to the specific task at hand at the appropriate time with AR technology. Thus, AR has potential application in maintenance, service, inspection and repair of complex machinery. Manuals with text and pictures are less understandable than computer-generated step-by-step instructions in front of the machinery (Feiner et al. 1993).

Assembling of products could be inefficient and expensive. Therefore, AR could help to reduce time and errors. In other words, assembly information, such as a step-by-step instruction, can be displayed on the operators' device (e.g. head-mounted-display). Another advantage for employees is that they do not have to change their position if they need information while operating on a product (Ong et al. 2008).

4 Conclusion

This paper shows that VR and AR have a lot of potential in various fields of industries. Not every company could use all possibilities. Organizations which wants to apply VR or AR, must know their core competences and the additional benefit from using these technologies. At the moment, some opportunities are very theoretical without any real case in the industry. Hence, it will take some time before implementing them into a system. The most realistic scenarios and use cases can be found in the field of Marketing and Sales. Nevertheless, it depends on the company and industry which of the use cases is appropriate for them. Organizations must get an overview of their initial situation before implementing VR and/or AR. The additional benefit for a company is one the most important part of introducing new technology.

References

Accenture: Procter & Gamble: Virtual solutions BPO Services Case Study. Von accenture, 22 März 2017. https://www.accenture.com/us-en/success-procter-and-gamble-virtual-solution-bpo abgerufen

Axtell, P.: What everyone should know about running virutal meetings. Harvard Bus. Rev. 1–6, 14 April 2016

Azuma, R.: A survey of augmented reality. Teleoperators Virtual Environ. **6**, 335–385 (1997)

Bendel, O. (kein Datum): Gabler Wirtschaftslexikon. (S. G. Verlag, Herausgeber) Abgerufen am 05. March 2017 von Virtuelle Realtiät: http://wirtschaftslexikon.gabler.de/Archiv/-2045879784/virtuelle-realitaet-v1.html abgerufen

Broll, W.: Augmentierte Realität. In: Dörner, R., Broll, W., Grimm, P., Jung, B. (eds.) Virtual und Augmented Reality (VR/ AR), pp. 241–294. Springer, Heidelberg (2013). doi:10.1007/978-3-642-28903-3_8

Dörner, R., Jung, B., Grimm, P., Broll, W., Göbel, M.: Einleitung. In: Dörner, R., Broll, W., Grimm, P., Jung, B. (eds.) Virtual und Augmented Reality (VR/ AR), pp. 1–31. Springer, Heidelberg (2013). doi:10.1007/978-3-642-28903-3_1

Dumont, A.: Cebit. Von Garnter Hype Cycle, 25 November 2015. http://www.cebit.de/de/news-archiv/digital-insights/die-tops-und-flops-des-gartner-hype-cycle/ abgerufen

Erbert, D., von der Gracht, H., Lichtenau, P., Reschke, K.: Neue Dimensionen der Realität - Eine Analyse der Potenziale von Virtual und Augmented Realtiy. KPMG Wirtschaftsprüfgesellschaft (2016)

Feiner, S., MacIntyre, B., Seligmann, D.: Knowledge-based augmented reality. Commun. ACM **36**, 52–62 (1993)

Gartner: Gartner. Von Hype Cycle, 16 März 2017. http://www.gartner.com/newsroom/id/3412017 abgerufen

Gartner hype cycle maps out human-machine relationship. NetworkWorld Asia, pp. 10–11, 1 September 2013

Geert, M.: Die aixCAVE an der RWTH Aachen University. In: Dörner, R., Broll, W., Grimm, P., Jung, B. (eds.) Virtual und Augmented Reality (VR/AR), pp. 297–300. Grundlagen und Methoden der Virtuellen und Augmentierten Realität. Springer Verlag, Berlin Heidelberg (2013)

Glockner, H., Jannek, K., Mahn, J., Theis, B.: Augmented Reality in Logistics. DHL Customer Solutions & Innovations, Troisdorf (2014)

Google Tango. (9 März 2017). Von Places with Tango: https://get.google.com/tango/places/ abgerufen

Ilg, P.: Zeit Online. Von Vorsprung durch Virtual Reality, 24 January 2017. http://www.zeit.de/mobilitaet/2017-01/audi-virtual-reality-autohaus-vertrieb-verkaufsprozess abgerufen

John Deere: John Deere Pressemeldungen. Von John Deere nutzt Vorteile der "Virtual Reality"-Welt, 12 Dezember 2014. https://www.deere.de/de_DE/our_company/news_and_media/press_releases/2014/corporate/jd_virtual_reality_welt.page abgerufen

Kückelhaus, M.: Eleven reasons to consider augmented reality in logistics. In: Logistics & Transport Focus, pp. 14–17, April 2015

Lyons, M.: Virtual Reality. Training J. 20–22, August 2016

Murphy, M.: Quartz. Von Nike may let you design your next pair of shoes using virutal realty, 17 February 2015. https://qz.com/344522/nike-may-let-you-design-your-next-pair-of-shoes-using-virtual-reality/ abgerufen

Neidel, M.: Cloudero. Von Virtual Reality im Vertrieb, 15 July 2016. https://cloudero.de/virtual-reality-im-vertrieb/ abgerufen

O'Brien, J.M.: The race to make virtual reality an actual (business) reality. Fortune **173**(6), 126–133 (2016)

Ong, S.K., Yuan, M.L., Nee, A.C.: Augmented reality applications in manufacturing: a survey. Int. J. Prod. Res. **46**(10), 2707–2742 (2008)

Rao, L.: Inside Google's next ecosystem: virtual Reality. Fortune **173**(7), 39–42 (2016)

Remco, V.: The impact of Virtual Reality on Audi's next gen. showroom experience is huge! Von LinkedIn, 28 December 2016. https://www.linkedin.com/pulse/impact-virtual-reality-audis-next-gen-showroom-experience-remco-vroom abgerufen

Yin, R.K.: Case Study Research: Design and Method. Sage, London (2014)

Supporting the Integration of New Security Features in Embedded Control Devices Through the Digitalization of Production

Tobias Rauter[✉], Johannes Iber, Michael Krisper, and Christian Kreiner

Institute of Technical Informatics, Graz University of Technology,
Inffeldgasse 16, 8010 Graz, Austria
{tobias.rauter,johannes.iber,michael.krisper,
christian.kreiner}@tugraz.at

Abstract. Security is a vital property of Industrial Control Systems (ICS), especially in the context of critical infrastructure. In this work, we focus on distributed control devices for hydro-electric power plants. Much work has been done for specific lifecylce phases of distributed control devices such as development or operational phase. Our aim here is to consider the entire product lifecycle and the consequences of security feature implementations for a single lifecycle stage on other stages. At the same time, recent trends such as the digitization of production is an enabler of production process extensions that support the integration of such security features during the operational phase of a control devices. In particular, we propose a security concept that enables assurance of the integrity of software components and product configuration of other control devices in the same network. Moreover, we show how these concepts result in additional requirements for the production stages. We show how we meet these requirements and focus on a production process by extending previously proposed methods that enable the commissioning of secrets such as private keys during the manufacturing phase. We extend this process by extracting information about the configurations of the actually produced devices during production. Based on this information, the proposed security techniques can be integrated without considerable overhead for bootstrapping.

1 Introduction

The growth of the renewable energy sector has a high impact on the technology of hydropower plant unit control systems [7]. Today these must react to power grid changes in time to achieve overall grid stability. As a consequence, control devices (depending on the provided functionality, they are also referred to as Remote Terminal Unit (RTU) or Programmable Logic Controller (PLC)) in single power plants, as well as control devices of different power plants have to cooperate in order to achieve the system-wide control goal. These requirements lead to networks of small, embedded control devices and heavyweight Supervisory Control and Data Acquisition (SCADA) servers and clients. At the same time, these power plants represent critical infrastructures that have to be protected against the recently emerging risk of security attacks [4,8].

The actual control devices (i.e., the Remote Terminal Units (RTUs)) are basically embedded computing devices. They are, however, not atomic with regard to their configuration. They are composed of different sub-components. A central processing component, consisting of a relatively powerful CPU, is in charge to execute the actual control application and provides the interface to the internal plant network. In order to interact with the physical environment (the sensors and actuators), additional components provide the required interfaces. Such components may provide digital I/Os, analog I/Os for voltage or current measurement or even specialized hardware for specific types of sensors and actuators. The full product, the RTU, is a composition of such sub-components. The final configuration (i.e., what components and how much of them are put together), however, strongly depends on the actual project. Malicious parties could aim to change the product configuration at any time after the production process. By doing so, they could be able to change the behaviour of the device, what could lead to a loss of availability of the correct function. Moreover, they could insert single components that are not certified by the Original Equipment Manufacturer (OEM) of the original device. In both cases, the manipulated device may behave adversely. Since state-of-the art control systems consist of several networked control devices and human operators, all other system entities should be informed about this unauthorized change of configuration. Otherwise, they could take decisions based on wrong information received by the compromised device.

Much work in the field of security for control systems has already been done. During run-time, methods to detect intrusion on the process, device and network level have been proposed [9,14]. Since many security mechanisms such as device authentication rely on public key cryptography, the initial provisioning of device secrets during the production process is also a main focus (e.g., [10]). Based on such initial establishment of trust into control devices, it is also possible to assure the integrity of their software configuration during run-time [11]. In this paper, we propose to build upon these previous approaches to introduce assurance of the RTU configurations during the operational phase of the run-time.

In particular, this paper contributes the following:

- We discuss an approach to adapt existing software configuration

integrity reporting techniques to enable a step towards the assurance of full hardware and software product configurations by remotely verifying the configuration of the RTU components.

- This requires each RTU to know the initial (certified) configuration of their peers. Therefore,
    - we briefly describe state of the art methods that are used to bootstrap the initial authentication information for each component during the production process, and

- discuss how to adapt the production process to not only augment the produced device with information but also to extract information from each produced device in order to enable the proposed configuration reporting method.

The rest of this paper is organized as follows: Sect. 2 provides the required background and related work for the proposed security method. Section 3 analyzes the requirements such a method raises and describes how we tackled these challenges in both lifecycle stages and Sect. 4 concludes the paper.

2 Background and Related Work

2.1 Trusted Computing and Remote Attestation

In order to mitigate the problem of compromised devices, mechanisms to establish trustworthiness in the software configuration (i.e., the running software components and their configurations) and the hardware configuration of remote devices have to be ensured. Trustworthiness, in this context, means that the device behaves demonstrably compliant with its intended functionality. Assuming that the initial system configuration represents the intended functionality, a system is trustworthy if its integrity is not violated. In order to establish trustworthiness, integrity reporting where a *prover* reports its integrity to a *challenger* is used as shown in Fig. 1.

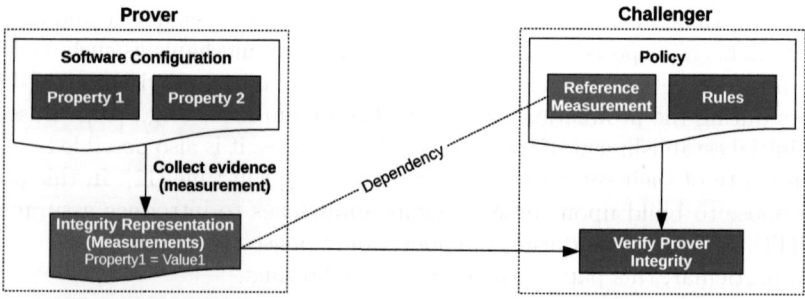

Fig. 1. Remote Attestation: The prover collects evidence of its software configuration (*measures* its configuration) by storing values of properties that reflect the current system state. The challenger compares the measurement to a reference in order to verify the integrity of the prover.

The *prover* collects evidence of the integrity of its configuration. In the trusted computing context, this process is called *measurement* [3]. In order to do so, the prover identifies system properties that can be used as integrity proof later on. One example of such *integrity properties* is the content of the program memory. This property reflects the executed program code and can therefore be used to detect integrity violations in the system. In order to ensure that malicious software components cannot forge the measurement lists, they are usually protected by some kind of security hardware. In this work, we used a Trusted Platform Module (TPM) that provides special registers, called Platform Configuration Register (PCR), to achieve this task.

Based on a policy that defines rules and reference values, the challenger is able to verify the prover's integrity. In the exemplary use of memory content as integrity property, the policy would consist of a reference value of the memory content (i.e., a copy) and a rule that defines this reference as valid system state. Whenever the executed software on the prover is changed, the challenger would detect the integrity violation. Thus, the value of the reference depends on the prover's system state.

In the context of trusted computing, this process is called *remote attestation*, is well known and still a research topic. Its application in real-world systems, in particular in embedded devices, is, however, limited. The main problems concern the maintenance of the reference measurements [6]. Especially in distributed embedded systems such as in typical Industrial Control System (ICS) architectures, these references have to be distributed to all possible communication partners of each proving device. Moreover, every time the prover's configuration is updated, all references have to be redeployed. This is a tedious task and not feasible in real-world distributed systems.

2.2 Remote Attestation Methods

In order to attest the integrity of different devices to each other, the integrity of their configuration has to be measured. Basically, the configuration is represented by the software components running on the device. A variety of schemes and implementations that tackle this problem exist in the literature. Remote attestation methods for binaries, properties, security policies and platform-specific permission-systems have been introduced. However, the mapping of these concepts into the ICS domain is not a trivial matter due to resource and connectivity constraints.

The Integrity Measurement Architecture (IMA) [13] generates a measurement list of all binaries and configuration files loaded by the system. The cumulative measurement (i.e., hash) of the measurement list is extended into a PCR. To attest the system's state, the prover sends the measurement list to the challenger and proves its integrity with the help of the TPM. Binary measurement approaches are not suitable for systems with many different or dynamic configurations because each challenger has to maintain a comprehensive list of known 'good' configurations. Especially when system updates or backups are taken into account, the set of possible configurations may grow to an unmaintainable size. In this work, we mitigate this problem by exploiting the fact, that all software components are delivered by the same vendor which could digitally sign the executables.

Property-based attestation [1,12] overcomes some issues of binary-based methods. A challenger is only interested in whether the prover fulfills particular security properties (e.g., strict isolation of processes). Therefore, a set of possible platform configurations is mapped to different properties. This approach eliminates the need for comprehensive lists of reference configurations on the challenger by the introduction of a Trusted Third Party (TTP) which is in charge of the mapping. Similar approaches focusing on privacy-preserving features [2] do not need a TTP and use ring-signatures to protect the prover's configuration from exposure. In this paper, we use this concept to sign reference measurements. In our work, the device vendor represents the trusted party. He is able to authorize software components (with executable signatures). Moreover, we add the product configuration as attestable property to assure not only the integrity of the software modules but also the device configuration in terms of installed sub-components.

3 Product Configuration Attestation

This section discusses the integrated approach of software and product configuration integrity assurance based on remote attestation. For the software part, we use state-of-the-art IMA, which was described in the last section. Therefore, this section only discusses the required changes to enable the attestation of the product configuration. This section therefore motivates the need of process adaptions during production to enable products with certain security properties during operation based on a specific method.

3.1 RTU Architecture and Product Configuration

Figure 2 shows the existing system architecture. Each RTU consists of a central component. This component is in charge to execute the actual control application and provides the interface to other network participants via the internal plant network. Moreover, there exist a number of peripheral components that may provide input or outputs, as well as specific functionality. These peripheral components also consist of a (more lightweight) microcontroller and a firmware. For communication with the central component, an internal bus is used. Each component has an unique identifier (ID). This ID also encodes the component type. Moreover, for component authentication, which is described later, each

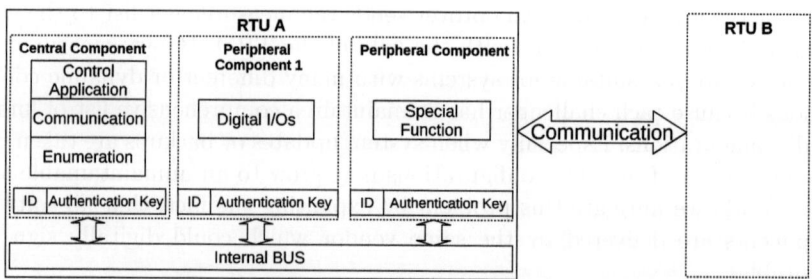

Fig. 2. Overview of the proposed system architecture

component securely (e.g., protected by some kind of security hardware) stores an authentication key. Whenever another RTU initiates a connection to exchange information, it wants to ensure, that both the software and product configuration of its communication partner is intact. In order to do so, the targeted control device, which is the prover in this case, has to reflect this information in an integrity measurement and the other device, the challenger, has to know how to verify this information.

3.2 Integrity Measurement Process

In this use-case, the integrity of an RTU comprises the integrity of the executed software on the central component, as well as the IDs of all build-in components. Although it would be possible to also integrate the software configuration of the peripheral components into this measurement, we do not consider them here for the sake of simplicity.

In order to collect evidence about the central component's software configuration, cryptographic hashes of all executed software components are calculated and securely stored (on a TPM) with IMA. Here, we propose to add an additional software module to the central component that enumerates all connected peripherals at boot-time. In order to do so, it collects a list of IDs from all peripheral components and the central component and appends it to the list of software integrity measurements of IMA. This is done by enumeration requests which are sent to the bus. Each authorized component answers with its ID and unauthorized components (with an unknown ID or an ID that reflects an component that is not intended to be in this RTU) are also reflected in the integrity measurement. Here, two important aspects have to be considered:

First, a potentially malicious component could forge its ID and simply pretend to be another component. In order to tackle this problem, each component cryptographically signs its ID with its unique private authentication key.

The second problem are replay attacks. A malicious component could record the bus communication and intercept a cryptographically signed ID of an authorized component. Later, it could simply authenticate itself with this previously recorded information to pretend to be the authorized component. Such attacks can be prevented with fresh random numbers that are used as challenge from the enumeration component on the central device. The peripherals do not only have to sign their ID, but also the random number. This ensures that each answer to an enumeration request is only valid once.

For completeness, the security properties of this method have to be mentioned here: First, it inherits the properties of IMA. Only the execution of unauthorized or modified software modules are reflected in the integrity measurement. Whenever an attacker is able to use an exploit in existing modules and execute arbitrary code without spawning a new process on the central device, the attack remains undetected. Concerning hardware modifications, only the insertion or removal of components is detected. If an attacker is able to modify an existing, authorized component in a way that it behaves harmful and uses the existing ID and authorization key, the attack also remains undetected. Also hardware modifications of the internal bus can be used to circumvent the system. A malicious module could forward (relay) an enumeration request to a authorized component that is not connected to the bus and use the message received from the authorized component to authenticate itself. While some of these types of attacks can be mitigated with existing technologies, these extensions remain open for future work.

In summary, the method collects information about both, the software configuration of the central component as also the connected peripherals.

3.3 Integrity Verification Process

Based on the collected information, another device, the challenger, wants to verify the product configuration of the prover. In order to securely exchange this information, remote attestation based on a TPM, as described in the background section, is used. Now, the challenger has the list of integrity measurements of the prover, containing the executed software modules, as well as the connected peripheral components.

For the verification of the software components, we slightly adapted the IMA method. We exploit the fact, that all software modules are installed by the same company that created the RTU, the OEM. This avoids the need of reference measurements (i.e., reference hash values for all software modules) on the challenger. The OEM can cryptographically sign the hashes of the software modules it installs on the RTUs. The challenger can request this signatures from the prover and simply checks whether the component is authorized by the OEM by verifying the signature with the public OEM key. Since no other party is allowed to install software on the RTUs, only one verification key is needed at each challenger.

For the verification of the product configuration (i.e., the composition of the components), we use a similar method. At some point in time, the OEM authorizes the RTU configuration by signing the composition of the whole device. Basically, it authorizes that the RTU with the ID ID_{RTU} consists of the components $ID_{C1}, ..., ID_{Cn}$. Based on this information, the challenger is able to verify whether the prover's product configuration has been authorized by the OEM by checking whether the current configuration matches the initial one.

4 Product Lifecycle - Production Processes

The proposed remote attestation method contributes to improving the security during operation. However, in order to actually integrate such methods, adaptions during earlier lifecycle stages have to be conducted. Figure 3 shows a simplified lifecycle model of an embedded device. First, the *OEM* develops the system. When the system is ready for use, it is manufactured by a *contracted manufacturer*, which could be a different company. A *customer* uses the device during the operational phase. After disposal, the gathered information can be used to refine future designs. This model deliberately omits additional stages such as deployment or maintenance for the sake of simplicity. In this paper, we focus on the prerequisites for the

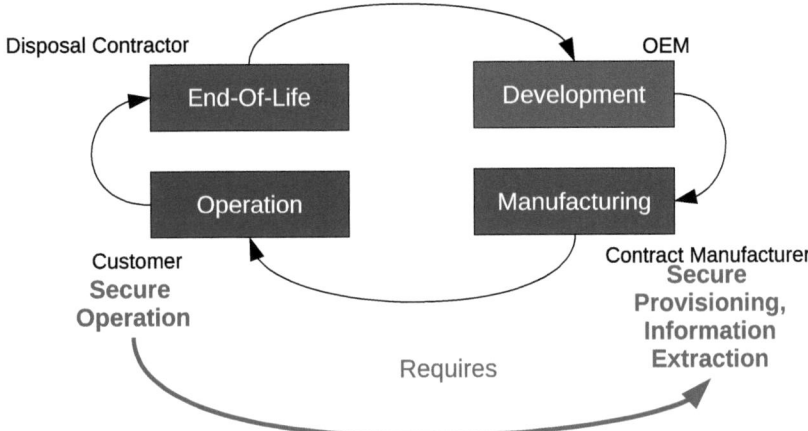

Fig. 3. The basic product lifecycle model and the stakeholders which are in place at every stage. Figure adapted from [10].

operational phase and propose fulfilling them during production phase. Therefore, the simplified model is detailed enough for the discussion.

As indicated by the green arrows in Fig. 3, the integration of a remote attestation method has an impact on other lifecycle stages. Many security enhancing technologies (e.g., remote attestation, secure channels, secure firmware updates etc.) rely on public key cryptography which itself rely on securely distributed secrets. Therefore, we use a previously proposed approach to integrate a *secure provisioning* process that determines how to create and deploy such secrets during the manufacturing phase [10]. In this process, the produced device is augmented with information during production. In this paper, however, we show how the extraction of information of the produced devices during production time can be an enabler for the product configuration attestation proposed before.

In addition to private keys used for authentication and signatures, the proposed method relies on information about the initial (authorized) software and product configuration of each RTU. This section first briefly describes the state-of-the-art secure provisioning process and then discusses how we adapted it to fit our needs.

4.1 Secure Provisioning

In order to enable authentication and remote attestation mechanisms, secrets, or more generally, security credentials have to be deployed on each device. The lifecycle of the security credentials typically consists of four steps [5]: First, cryptographic keys which represent the secret have to be generated (1). With an certification (2), keys are bound to a device[1]. Moreover, they have to be distributed (3) and

---

[1] Here, certification is achieved through using public-key cryptography. The private part of the key represent the device secret. The public part signed by the OEM and augmented with meta-information to generate the certificate.

stored (4) on the device. In [10], it has been proposed to integrate the four steps into the manufacturing process. Hence, two main challenges must be faced: First, even the manufacturer who is often an external company may be (partly) compromised. Thus, we have to ensure that the access to secret key material is as difficult as possible during the production process. Moreover, a large number of different and customized devices has to be built and provided with keys: In our scenario, a RTU consists of a variety of different components. They all have some similarities (e.g., an MCU executing a specific firmware) but vary in features, configuration and also security requirements. In [10], both challenges have been discussed. The second problem of product variants is tackled by using a manufacturing tool that uses techniques from the model based testing domain to enable the application of one generic secure provisioning process to a variety of device types. Here, we only focus on this generic process.

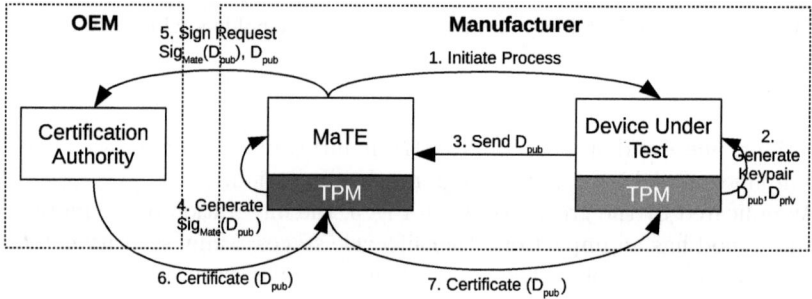

Fig. 4. Overview of the secure provisioning process. Figure adapted from [10].

Figure 4 illustrates the previously proposed secure provisioning process. The OEM commissions different contract manufacturers to produce the devices. At each manufacturing location, hard- and software components are assembled to produce the control devices. Ultimately, the certified devices are shipped to the customer. Since even a manufacturer may be compromised, the process should protect the key material in a manner that makes it impractical to reveal it for the manufacturer. Therefore, we propose integrating the framework for the manufacturing process on an OEM-controlled and trusted device called Manufacturing and Test Environment (MaTE). Based on MaTE, the OEM is able to trust the manufacturing process at the contract manufacturer's site. The proposed approach is based on three concepts: local key generation, local certification and global certification.

Local Key Generation. As shown in Fig. 4 (steps 1 and 2), the secrets (i.e., private keys) are directly generated on the produced device. Therefore, no unnecessary exposure of key material takes place at any time. Usually, neither the manufacturer nor the customer have access to the generated secrets. Optionally, the keys can be generated on hardware security components to protect keys from adversaries with direct hardware access.

Local Certification. In order to attach a meaning to the generated secrets, the OEM has to create certificates that enable binding private keys to a specific device (i.e., signing the public part of the produced device's identification key, steps 3 and 4). If the device secret would be certified in an uncontrolled way, a possibly compromised manufacturer would be able to create certificates, or at least signing requests at its will. Due to the trusted manufacturing device, the OEM has, however, full control over the locally signed certificates. Based on hardware security components such as a TPM, it can be ensured that the process is secured from tampering by malicious parties who intercept the manufacturing process.

Global Certification. In order to track all produced devices globally, the device secret is additionally sent to the OEM, together with the certificate created by MaTE (steps 5 to 7). The OEM is able to verify the validity of the created device by checking the local certificate. After additional examinations, such as checking the orders placed for the specific manufacturer to prevent them from creating cloned devices, the OEM creates the actual certificate which is used to authenticate the device during operation.

4.2 Device Configuration Certification

As mentioned before, the proposed method not only rely on the certification of private keys used for authentication, but also on the certification of authorized product configurations. Here, we propose to integrate this step into the previously described secure provisioning process by extracting information of the initial device configuration. In order to do so, two steps have to be conducted:

- (Sub-)Component provisioning: For the production of each sub-component, the secure provisioning process has to be conducted. This ensures that each peripheral component initially contains its authorization key and enables a secure extraction of the overall RTU configuration.
- Product configuration certification: Whenever a customer orders an RTU, it is composed of the previously produced subcomponents. At this stage, the decision of what software and hardware components are integrated is taken and this is therefore the earliest possible point in time to conduct the authorization by the OEM.

Figure 5 illustrates the extended process. During the production process, the produced device conducts actions similar to the measurement actions during operation. First, it creates a measurement list by collecting information of the installed software by taking hashes of the executed software components (I). Then it enumerates the connected peripheral components. Similar to the provisioning process, this is directly generated on the device and locally signed by the devices private key to hinder manipulations of these values. Also, the local certification step on the MaTE is augmented to certify that the configuration represented in the measurement list is actually produced legitimately (II, III).

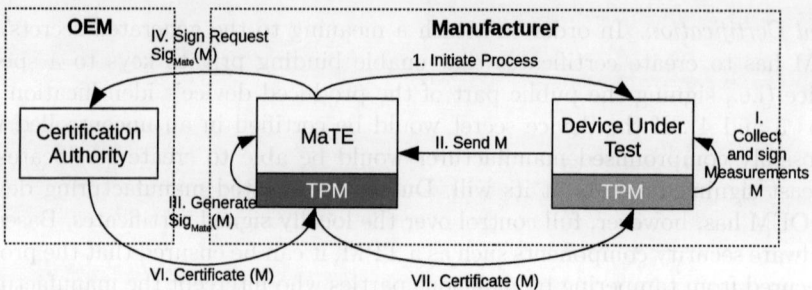

Fig. 5. Overview of the extended secure provisioning process with product configuration certification.

The OEM receives the list and checks it against the order of the customer. After assuring that there exist an corresponding order and the produced product fulfills the requirements for this order, it certifies the measurement list with an cryptographic signature and sends it back to the contract manufacturer (IV, V, VI). The resulting signature is stored on the produced device (VII) and is used during the operation phase to prove the validity of the devices software and hardware configuration.

5 Discussion and Conclusion

Due to recent trends, control devices in ICS have to meet ever higher security properties. While there exist a number of techniques to enable these properties, they raise demands for earlier product lifecycle changes.

In this paper, we proposed to extend existing remote attestation techniques such as IMA to provide integrated assurance of software and hardware configurations of RTUs. In particular, remote systems are able to ensure that the product configuration of their communication partner corresponds to the initial configuration intended by the OEM.

It is not enough, to consider the operational phase only when integrating such techniques. Therefore, we discussed the requirements that are risen for earlier product lifecycle stages. We showed how to adapt existing ideas for secure provisioning to extract information from the actually produced devices. Trends such as the digitization of production have been an enabler for such more complex manufacturing processes. Due to existing internet connectivity, the OEM can now have full control over the produced devices, their certification and their configuration, even if the production takes place at a contracted third party. As shown in this specific use-case, exploiting such trends enable an relatively easy integration of more sophisticated security techniques whose integration would have been too complex in traditional processes.

References

1. Ceccato, M., Ofek, Y., Tonella, P.: A protocol for property-based attestation. Theory Pract. Comput. Sci. 7 (2008). http://portal.acm.org/citation.cfm?doid=1179474.1179479, http://link.springer.com/chapter/10.1007/978-3-540-77566-9_8
2. Chen, L., Löhr, H., Manulis, M., Sadeghi, A.-R.: Property-based attestation without a trusted third party. In: Wu, T.-C., Lei, C.-L., Rijmen, V., Lee, D.-T. (eds.) ISC 2008. LNCS, vol. 5222, pp. 31–46. Springer, Heidelberg (2008). doi:10.1007/978-3-540-85886-7_3
3. Coker, G., Guttman, J., Loscocco, P., Herzog, A., Millen, J., O'Hanlon, B., Ramsdell, J., Segall, A., Sheehy, J., Sniffen, B.: Principles of remote attestation. Int. J. Inf. Secur. **10**(2), 63–81 (2011)
4. Sharing, E.I., Center, A.: Analysis of the cyber attack on the ukrainian power grid. Technical report (2016)
5. Fischer, K., Gesner, J.: Security architecture elements for IoT enabled automation networks. In: International Conference on Emerging Technologies and Factory Automation (2012)
6. Kylänpää, M., Rantala, A.: Remote attestation for embedded systems. In: Security of Industrial Control Systems and Cyber Physical Systems (2015)
7. Liserre, M., Sauter, T., Hung, J.: Future energy systems: integrating renewable energy sources into the smart power grid through industrial electronics. IEEE Ind. Electron. Mag. **4**(1), 18–37 (2010). http://ieeexplore.ieee.org/lpdocs/epic03/wrapper.htm?arnumber=5439057
8. Miller, B., Rowe, D.: A survey SCADA of and critical infrastructure incidents. In: Annual Conference on Research in Information Technology p. 51 (2012). http://dl.acm.org/citation.cfm?doid=2380790.2380805
9. Mitchell, R., Chen, I.R.: A survey of intrusion detection techniques for cyber-physical systems. ACM Comput. Surv. (CSUR) **46**(4), 1–29 (2014)
10. Rauter, T., Höller, A., Iber, J., Kreiner, C.: Development and production processes for secure embedded control devices. In: Kreiner, C., Connor, R., Poth, A., Messnarz, R. (eds.) EuroSPI 2016. Communications in Computer and Information Science, vol. 633, pp. 119–131. Springer, Cham (2016). doi:10.1007/978-3-319-44817-6_10
11. Rauter, T., Iber, J., Krisper, M., Kreiner, C.: Integration of integrity enforcing technologies into embedded control devices: experiences and evaluation. In: The 22nd IEEE Pacific Rim International Symposium on Dependable Computing (2017)
12. Sadeghi, A., Stüble, C.: Property-based attestation for computing platforms: caring about properties, not mechanisms. In: Proceedings of the 2004 Workshop on New Security Paradigms, pp. 67–77 (2004). http://dl.acm.org/citation.cfm?id=1066038
13. Sailer, R., Zhang, X., Jaeger, T., van Doorn, L.: Design and implementation of a TCG-based integrity measurement architecture. In: USENIX Security (2004)
14. Urbina, D.I., Giraldo, J., Cardenas, A.A., Tippenhauer, N.O., Valente, J., Faisal, M., Ruths, J., Candell, R., Sandberg, H.: Limiting the impact of stealthy attacks on industrial control systems. In: 23rd ACM Conference on Computer and Communications Security (2016)

A Conceptual Mixed Realities (AR/VR) Capability Maturity Model – With Special Emphasis on Implementation

Sonja Hammerschmid[1(✉)], Gerhard Kormann[1], Thomas Moser[2], and Michael Reiner[1]

[1] IMC University of Applied Sciences, Piaristengasse 1, 3500 Krems, Austria
sonja.hammerschmid@imc-krems.eu
[2] University of Applied Sciences St. Pölten, Matthias Corvinus - Straße 15, 3100 St. Pölten, Austria

Abstract. This paper investigates the promoting and opposing factors which determine implementation paths (or process improvements) of mixed reality applications in industrial companies. Mixed realities are defined as the combined application of virtual and augmented reality technologies. We review maturity model-related literature to ascertain which reference models are available and how mixed reality phenomena have been treated. The Capability Maturity Model (CMM) is the starting point of our analysis. The authors aim at setting the foundation of a mixed reality readiness/maturity model that take into consideration the scientific relevance and the actual requirements of the practical application. The conceptual model incorporates the companies' technological, organisational and industry value chain-related maturity-levels. To consider empirical implications, we applied a case study approach based on the real-life implementation projects in industrial companies.

Keywords: Mixed reality · Maturity model · CMM · Automotive spice

1 The Mixed Reality Framework – From a General CMM to a Mixed Reality Specific CMM Model

A maturity model can be viewed as a set of structured levels that describe how well the behaviors, practices and processes of an organization can reliably and sustainably produce required outcomes. Therefore, a maturity model can be used as a benchmark for comparison and as aid to understanding - for example, for comparative assessment of different organizations (Yoon et al. 2015).

Nowadays, maturity models are becoming increasingly important in any technology-driven discipline. However, the current scientific activities primary focus on the development of rigor methods for defining such maturity models rather than putting the focus on the contribution of a developed maturity model for addressing and/or solving relevant real-life problems of industrial companies (CCMI Product Team 2006).

In this paper, we start from the well-established generic Capability Maturity Model (CMM) and derive a mixed reality specific CMMI (the so called MR-CMM) that is highly relevant for real-life mixed reality implementation projects in industrial companies. The original CMM is a development model created after study of data collected from organizations that contracted with the U.S. Department of Defense, who founded the original research. The term "maturity" relates to the degree of formality and optimization of processes, from ad hoc practices, to formally defined steps, to managed result metrics, to active optimization of the processes. The model's aim is to improve existing software development processes, but it can also be applied to other processes (Paulk 2009).

CMM contains essential elements of effective processes for one or more disciplines and describe an evolutionary improvement path from immature processes to mature processes with improved quality and effectiveness (CCMI Product Team 2006).

1.1 Levels of CMM

Choosing processes for CMM is relatively flexible. CMM can be used for every process in a company. Defining the goal of a process development with milestones is one of the core elements of CMM. To measure to which extent a process is as good as best practice capability levels can be used. CMM covers process areas like product and development, systems engineering, integrated teaming, integrated supplier management, organizational environment for integration and decision analysis and resolution. (Sassenburg and Kitson 2006) There are six different levels to rate these processes. In Table 1, the different Levels of CMM can be seen. Level 0 is incomplete this means that there are no implementations. On the other hand Level 5 is the stage of optimizing. So, the company is able to reduce operating costs by improving processes or find innovative solutions for process oriented problems (Herndon et al. 2003).

Table 1. Capability levels CMM

Capability level	Implementation in an organization
Level 0: Incomplete	The organization does not provide specific practices
Level 1: Performed	Lack of necessary processes
Level 2: Managed	Managing and reacting but no strategically prediction
Level 3: Defined	Anticipation of change but still lack of forecasting
Level 4: Quantitatively Managed	Statistical forecasts and performance management against costs, schedule, etc.
Level 5: Optimizing	Reduction of operating costs by improving processes or introduction of innovations

The new developed MR-CMM focus on three different types of maturity, namely (a) the technological and process maturity: e.g., availability of digital blueprints, availability of digital process documentation and content, etc.; (b) the organisational maturity: e.g., mind-set, innovation culture, etc.; and (c) the Industry value-chain-related maturity: e.g., compelling events/applications by competitors, suppliers and customers, etc. The capability Levels of CMM are used to define on with stage the companies are.

1.2 Automotive SPICE (ISO/IEC 33xxx)

The Automotive SPICE (Software Process Improvement and Capability dEtermination) is based on a two-dimension framework. The process dimension (first dimension) provides processes defined in a reference model, like supplier monitoring, supply, measurement and reuse program management. (Sassenburg and Kitson 2006) The capability dimension (second dimension) consists of capability levels that are further subdivided into process attributes. (VDA QMC Working Group 13/Automotive SIG 2015) The relationship between the two-dimensions is shown in Fig. 1:

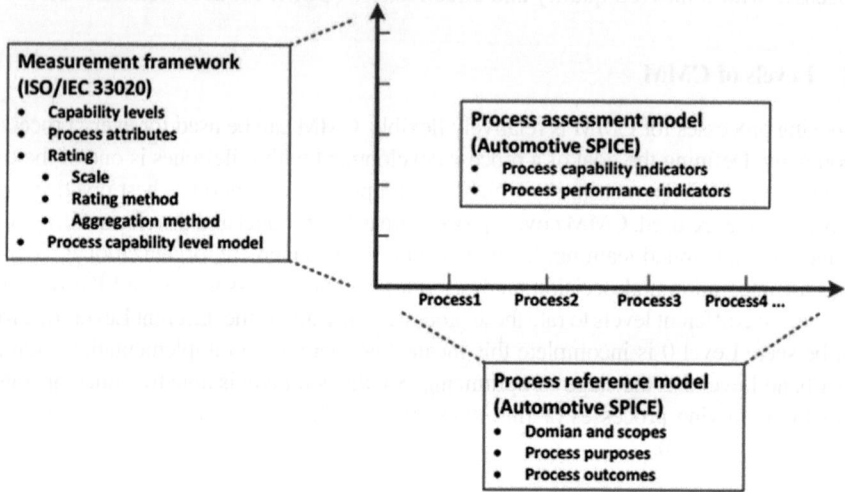

Fig. 1. Process assessment model relationship (VDA QMC Working Group 13/Automotive SIG, 2015)

The capability dimension contains of the necessary requirements for the measurement framework. With this framework assessors can determine the capability level of given processes. The process capability levels are identical to those in ISO/IEC 33020. (ISO/IEC 33020:2015 2015) There are six capability levels in ISO/IEC 33020 shown in Table 2.

1.3 Usage for MR-CMM

Both frameworks consider different processes. For the MR-CMM framework the research team wants to focus on technological, organizational and value-chain oriented processes and maturity. The measurement framework of ISO/IEC 33020 is very similar to the capability Levels of CMM. Because of this both systems can be used for the MR-CMM to measure VR/AR processes in an organization.

As the research team is at the beginning of developing this new MR-CMM framework there is no model available yet. With the help of a pilot project (mentioned in Chap. 2) the MR-CMM framework will be tested and worked out in detail.

Table 2. Process capability levels according to ISO/IEC 33020

Capability level	Implementation in an organization
Level 0: Incomplete process	No implementation of the process or the purpose is not achieved
Level 1: Performed process	The process purpose is achieved
Level 2: Managed process	The performed process is implemented in a managed fashion
Level 3: Established process	The defined process is capable of achieving its process outcomes
Level 4: Predictable process	The established process operates predictively within defined limits. Measurement data is collected and analyzed to identify causes of variation
Level 5: Innovating process	The predictable process respond to organizational change and is continually improved

2 Research Method, Findings and Project

This paper aims to develop and test a longitudinal case-study-based research design. At this pilot stage, the study will be based on a single partner firm. The next step will involve studying more companies based on a cross-case study approach. Case study research is often used when the boundaries between the phenomenon being studied and the context within which it is being studied are frequently ambiguous. Case studies relies multiple sources of evidence, in addition, it benefits from theoretical propositions. Several case studies could strengthen the findings more than just one case study (Yin 2014).

The partners within this project were researchers from IMC University of Applied Sciences Krems and researchers from University of Applied Sciences St. Pölten. As an approach the project decided to have a hands-on experience at a company. For this, partners were looking for a possible approach and found an Austrian office furniture manufacturer to pursuit a joint project. The company engaged a student to analyze both their internal business processes and possibilities to improve them by applying mixed reality technologies.

During the pre-study, the internal and external team identified the relevant business processes of major interest and the respective technological status concerning the availability of 3D digital blueprints of plans and designs. While discussing the topic of needed data and prerequisites came up and it became clear that the office furniture manufacturer as a company already has lots of data in digital versions. Since bene is already planning and designing all of its products in 3D, the data for 3D models needed for VR/AR is already there.

The agreed next step was to have a short workshop about possibilities in VR/AR. This awareness workshop was based on practical use and try-out of current versions of VR/AR devices (HTC Vive, Oculus Rift, Smartphones for AR). The participants (senior management and company experts) developed applicable ideas about realizable options. Because of the 3D data available, it was possible to show some small demo with the office furniture manufacturer specific data. The participants were able to try out and "walk" through a showroom based on their own product data. Additionally, this demo included some showcases from competitors or companies working in similar fields (ie. Ikea).

As a next step, the involved master student worked out detailed analyses on the primarily identified application options starting with the "obvious" (e.g. product presentation for Marketing & Sales) and later on "latent" (e.g. trainings for new employees) possibilities to eventually list a complete variety of possibilities on where to use VR/AR in the internal value chain of the office furniture manufacturer. The research team decided with the office furniture manufacturer that they have a high level of capability concerning product data. The first pilot will be in the field of product presentation because it can be implemented relatively fast without extraordinary costs.

Additionally, a Cost-benefit analysis was applied to check competitors positioning and advantages as well as technical issues (e.g. AR being not in need of too many details, difference between production data and 3D data for visualization…), and the required additional (external) data. This resulted in several possible scenarios of how and where a VR/AR solution can be applied in the business processes of the office furniture manufacturer.

The research team decided together with the partner company that applications with data from products are easier and faster to implement than opportunities with other data.

The scope of this research should be that a special MR-CMM framework will be developed. In other words, companies should be able to rate their status quo for VR and/or AR along their supply chain by themselves or with the help of the research team. After rating, recommendations should help the companies to implement mixed reality in the fields that are most appropriate for them.

By discussing our results, concepts and findings with the EuroSPI researcher community, the research team will have the opportunity to receive valuable feedback on the project design as well as to meet potential partners for further research in the field of industrial mixed reality applications.

3 Conclusion

The pilot project in combination with the office furniture manufacturer is not finished yet. Analyzes and workshops were made to find the best VR/AR application for the project partner. The research team wants to find a way to make this process more efficient. Due to the fact they want to introduce a special maturity framework for VR/AR almost all companies could use the so called MR-CMM.

A MR-CMM framework will help companies to measure their status quo when it comes to the implementation of VR and AR. Different processes and maturities will be measured with the help of capability levels. The next level can only be reached by fulfilling the stage before.

References

CCMI Product Team: CMMI for Development Version 1.2. Carnegie Mellon University, Pittsburgh (2006)

Herndon, M.A., Moore, R., Phillips, M., Walker, J., West, L.: Interpreting Capability Maturity Model Integration (CMMI) for Service Organizations - A Systems Engineering and Integration Service Example. Carnegie Mellon University, Pennsilvania (2003)

ISO/IEC 33020:2015. Information technology - Process assessment - Process measurment framework for assessment of process capability. ISO/IEC (2015)

Paulk, M.C.: A history of the capability maturity model for software. ASQ Softw. Qual. Prof. **12**(1), 5–19 (2009)

Sassenburg, H., Kitson, D.: A Comparative Analysis of CMMI and Automotive SPICE. Carnegie Mellon Software Engineering Institute – Europe, Frankfurt/Main, Germany (2006)

VDA, QMC Working Group 13/Automotive SIG: Automotive SPICE Process Reference Model/Process Assessment Model. VDA Quality Management Center, Germany (2015)

Yin, R.K.: Case Study Research: Design and Method. Sage, London (2014)

Yoon, B., Lee, K., Yoon, J.: Development of an R&D process model for enhancing the quality of R&D: comparison with CMMI, ISO and EIRMA. Total Qual. Manage. Bus. Excellence **26**(7–8), 746–761 (2015)

Best Practices in Implementing Traceability

Graceful Integration of Process Capability Improvement, Formal Modeling and Web Technology for Traceability

Miklós Biró[1,3(✉)], Felix Kossak[1], József Klespitz[2], and Levente Kovács[2]

[1] Software Competence Center Hagenberg, Hagenberg, Austria
{miklos.biro, felix.kossak}@scch.at
[2] Óbuda University, Budapest, Hungary
klespitz.jozsef@phd.uni-obuda.hu,
kovacs.levente@nik.uni-obuda.hu
[3] Johannes Kepler Universität, Linz, Austria

Abstract. This paper discusses the need and leveraging potential of formal modeling and web technology for progressing towards the goal of automating the establishment, maintenance and assessment of the completeness of traceability and the consistency of the requirements. The generic Augmented Lifecycle Space method, devised in an earlier paper, is applied as the approach to improve the capability of software processes requiring bidirectional traceability as well as consistency of the requirements in either homogeneous or heterogeneous development environments capitalizing on the emerging Open Services for Lifecycle Collaboration (OSLC) initiative. One of the important features of the presented new approach is that it allows for the so called "graceful integration" of formal modeling. Formal modeling is fundamentally necessary for securing completeness and consistency, but customarily rejected due to the usually prohibiting up-front effort needed to formally process all artifacts of an already established traditional system; Graceful integration can considerably lower this threshold.

Keywords: Application lifecycle management · Process assessment · Process improvement · Formal modeling · Open services for lifecycle collaboration · Tools integration · Heterogeneous tool environment · Requirements traceability · Requirements consistency

1 Introduction

The ultimate need addressed in this paper is functional safety extensively discussed in the IEC 61508 series of international standards setting out "the requirements for ensuring that systems are designed, implemented, operated and maintained to provide the required safety integrity level (SIL)" [19]. The use of systems in all industries, including automotive, transportation, medical, manufacturing, nuclear industries for instance, involves a foreseen level of risk of causing harm that must always be reduced to a level "as low as reasonably practicable" (ALARP) as required by ethics, regulatory regimes, and standards.

The key requirements of processes producing safety-critical systems, addressed in this paper, are the completeness of bidirectional traceability and the consistency of the requirements of the system under assessment which appear in all process assessment and improvement models [24]. As already highlighted in [10], traceability is fully recognized as a key issue by the agile community as well [2, 3].

The addressed software development processes naturally involve artifacts that can only be created by humans (customers, sales, marketing, etc.). Yet, there are other artifacts which can hardly be managed manually, including, for example, the documentation of low level test results or results of automated testing (e.g. static and/or dynamic code analysis). Similarly, the number of relationships, including traceability links, between the different artifacts becomes prohibitive even in the simplest practical cases [8, 9], so the handling and maintenance requires automated support which is the direct goal of our research [29, 30].

The commercially available tools supporting the above mentioned processes are called Application Lifecycle Management systems (ALMs) which do not only cover the implementation, but the whole process starting from the initial idea, closing with the end of the product's life [12]. When a company chooses to set up an ALM, it can choose among numerous off-the-shelf or third party software systems and/or can decide to develop needed elements and optionally complement them with other management tools. And adapting Murphy's law to this case, whatever can happen will happen, so many companies are effectively using a heterogeneous variety of ALM tools as pointed out for example in [21, 26, 28].

People and process challenges as well as fundamental logical and technical barriers for assessing and improving the completeness of traceability and verifying the consistency of the requirements in either homogeneous or heterogeneous tool environments were discussed in [10] also referring to [13, 16]. The Augmented Lifecycle Space approach was introduced in [10] as a generic method building on an arbitrary model containing traceability and consistency requirements, allowing the automation of the assessment, and facilitating the improvement of the completeness of traceability as well as the verification of the consistency of the requirements in either homogeneous or heterogeneous tool environments.

In this paper, we present the initial development phases of the system we call Requirements Traceability and Consistency checking Tool (RTCT) planned to integrate the latest achievements independently evolving in the fields of process capability improvement, formal modeling, and web technologies. It is interesting to remark that these fields clearly match the process areas of organization (O), methodology (M) and technology (T) devised in the historically significant European BOOTSTRAP software process assessment and improvement methodology [7].

Beyond the general goals, Sect. 2 presents use cases that RTCT must be able to handle exploiting OSLC technology and leading to the capability of automatically checking bidirectional traceability and consistency of the requirements in a possibly heterogeneous lifecycle management system under assessment, and proving that all of its necessary artifacts are available and properly linked.

The traceability and consistency requirements shall be based on the V-model of the software development lifecycle also applied in the Automotive SPICE standard [5] as depicted in Fig. 1. All of the arrows represent bidirectional traceability

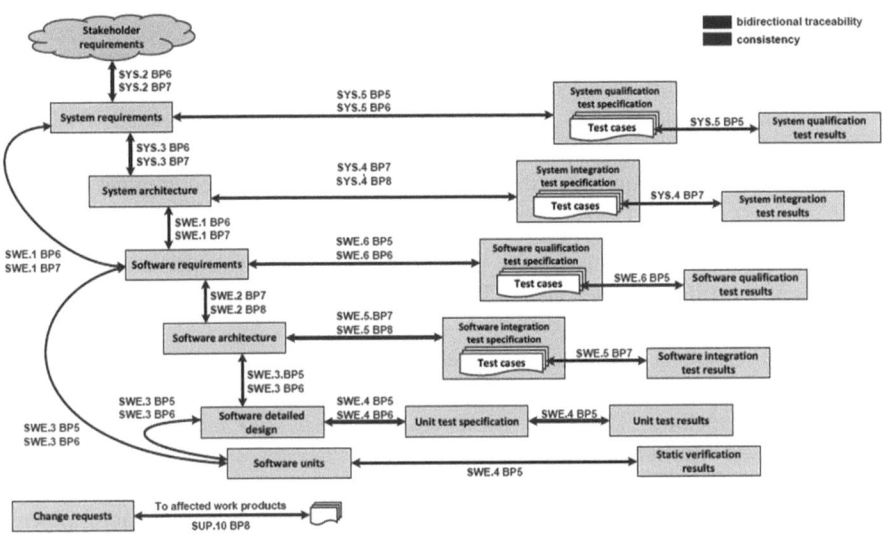

Fig. 1. Bidirectional traceability and consistency requirements of Automotive SPICE [5]

requirements; arrows that have two labels depict consistency requirements as well (see the lower labels).

One of the features of the new approach, of high importance for actual applications but rarely considered by promoters of formal modeling, is that it is possible to introduce the newly designed requirements management system incrementally, so that only new or changed requirements are affected and traced. This means that only new or changed requirements need to be formally modeled at the start, making the operational introduction of the new system practically feasible.

Let us use the term "graceful integration" for the above capability of incrementally introducing formal modeling. Formal modeling is fundamentally necessary for securing completeness and consistency, but customarily rejected due to the usually prohibiting up-front effort needed to formally process all artifacts of an already established traditional system; Graceful integration can considerably lower this threshold. In contrast to the established term "graceful degradation" for the ability of a system to maintain functionality when portions of the system break down, "graceful integration" means the ability of a system to be incremented so that its functionality is improved without significant disruption.

For consistency checking, a formalized representation of all relevant requirements will have to be available however. The need for the feature of the incremental introduction of the formal modeling based system originates from an actual safety-critical software development environment providing the fundamental industrial background of this research.

The proposed RTCT prototype shall have the following features:

- Create a collection of artifacts (typically corresponding to a project; possible artifacts include requirements and test cases, for example).
- Add an artifact to a collection or actually a link to an artifact/URI.

- Add a traceability link between artifacts.
- Show which test cases (etc.) are linked with a requirement and that each requirement is linked with at least one test case (etc.).
- Show which requirement(s) a test case or another artifact belongs to.
- Check whether all requirements of a given collection are mutually consistent.
- Check whether all required artifacts are linked with a given requirement.

The desired requirements traceability tool (RTCT) is illustrated in more detail in the next section. Single elements of the envisaged RTCT software have already been investigated by different researchers. The present work is based on [10] which also gives an overview over the topic.

Regarding models for trace completeness, [27] study models for realizing requirements traceability but do not consider process models as a source for trace completeness checking. The same holds e.g. for [18], who make suggestions for document-based requirements tracing.

Regarding requirements consistency checking, [20] state that "only few requirements tools are available in the market to provide facilities for the validation process especially for verifying and checking the requirements qualities, such as the completeness and consistency". This paper gives a good overview over approaches and tools for heuristic and formal requirements consistency checking as well as mixed approaches. However, most of the cited approaches or tools do not seem applicable for the setting envisaged by us. Some approaches address high-level structure consistency only, some will obviously yield highly incomplete results e.g. because they rely on natural language analysis, and others appear to be rather demanding for users and require special modelling that cannot be reused in implementation.

An exception is [Sousa et al., 2010], who use the formal method B for requirements consistency checking in a way which fits our approach in principle, except for questions of tool integration. Interestingly, they consider use cases rather than imperative, constraint-like requirements statements. They see consistency checking as checking that the actions of use cases preserve invariants (i.e. constraints); however, at least in the paper, they do not consider consistency (feasibility) of the invariants themselves.

The structure of the rest of this paper is as follows. In Sect. 2, we describe the envisaged Requirements Traceability and Consistency checking Tool (RTCT) by selected use cases. We discuss the most important and novel features in more detail and provide an example to better understand key ideas. In Sect. 3, we comment on available technologies for implementation. We conclude in Sect. 4.

2 RTCT: General System Description and Use Cases

2.1 General Goal Description

The general goal we want to address in our work is the improvement of tool support for requirements engineering. The specific goal of this paper is to describe major requirements for a requirements traceability and consistency checking tool (RTCT) with a user interface, in the sequel referred to as RTCT-UI, which allows to

- Manage artifacts involved in the development of software or combined hardware-software systems and possibly residing on different platforms, of different types and at least including requirements, design and implementation artifacts, test cases, and test results;
- Manage traceability links between requirements and other artifacts (possibly including other requirements, especially in the case of decomposition or refinement, including formalization);
- Check whether all requirements pertaining to one product are mutually consistent; and
- Check whether each requirement is linked to all expected other artifacts according to a given requirements traceability model.

We will further discuss approaches of implementing such a tool (at least in prototypical form). The described tool may be considered as part of or add-on to a more comprehensive requirements engineering tool, or even as part of a comprehensive systems engineering tool. We will describe the major requirements in the form of use cases, rather than in the form of a formal specification, in order to provide a well readable impression which is not cluttered by technicalities.

2.2 General Constraints

The RTCT software shall be built under the following constraints:

- The Augmented Lifecycle Space approach shall be implemented (see [10]).
- Consequently, OSLC shall be employed to integrate different platforms and the OSLC standard, including its terminology, shall be used wherever applicable (see [OSCL, 18]).
- It shall be possible to introduce the new system incrementally, that is, only for new projects or new requirements for existing projects.

2.3 RTCT Use Cases

The following use cases informally describe the key features of the RTCT prototype to be implemented. Selected features and an example illustrating the rationale of the use cases will be discussed in more detail in subsequent sections. There are features of the system which are naturally needed and included for the sake of completeness. Those features, which determine the novelty value of RTCT with respect to the features of existing systems, are marked with a bold asterisk (*) at the beginning of the corresponding text.

U1. Create a new artifact collection. A user creates a new collection (project) with a custom name by means of RTCT-UI.

- The new collection is displayed in RTCT-UI.

U2. Add a new requirement to an empty collection. A user searches a requirement artifact within a given search space (possibly comprising different platforms) and adds it (as a link) to a selected, empty collection.

- Available meta-data are displayed (such as title, artifact type: Requirement, etc.). If relevant meta-data are missing, the user is prompted to enter them.
- * Based on a given lifecycle model (e.g. the V-schema), RTCT determines which other artifacts are required to be linked to the new requirement (such as implementation artifacts to fulfil and test cases to test the requirement).
- * For each required artifact, RTCT either creates a workflow for the creation of the artifact, or creates a stub artifact from a template, or creates a stub artifact plus a workflow for further work.

U3. Add a new requirement to a non-empty collection. A user adds a requirement artifact to a collection which already contains at least one other requirement artifact.

- As in (U2), with the following addition:
  * If the new requirement is formal, RTCT automatically checks its consistency with all other formal requirements in the same collection. If consistency cannot be proved, or an inconsistency is detected, RTCT issues a warning to the user.

U4. Add an artifact other than a requirement to a collection. A user adds an artifact other than a requirement to a selected collection which already contains at least one requirement artifact.

- Available meta-data are displayed (such as title, artifact type: Test case, etc.). If relevant meta-data are missing, the user is prompted to enter them.
- The user is asked to which existing requirement (or intermediate artifact) the new artifact should be linked. A respective bidirectional link is established after selection.

U5. * Check completeness of links. A user shall be able to check for a selected requirement, or for all requirements of a selected collection, whether all required links already exist. The check is triggered by a user and performed by RTCT.

U6. * Check consistency of requirements. A user shall be able to check for a selected collection whether all its formal requirements are mutually consistent. The check is triggered by a user and performed by RTCT.

U7. * Refine a requirement. A user selects a requirement to refine.

- A copy of the selected requirement is made by RTCT for further work by the user, with a new unique requirement identifier (URI), and/or a workflow for creating/editing the new requirement is created.
- Alternatively, the user can add an existing requirement as the formalized version of the selected requirement.
- A new bidirectional traceability link of type "refines" (respectively "isRefinedBy") is automatically generated between the selected requirement and the new (refining) requirement. The list of required traceability links is shifted from the refined requirement to the refining requirement, unless the refinement was required by the model used.

U8. * Decompose a requirement. A user selects a requirement to decompose.

- A user-specified number of copies of the selected requirement is made by RTCT for further work by the user, with new unique requirement identifiers (URIs), and/or a workflow for creating/editing the new requirements is created.
- Alternatively, the user can add existing requirements as decompositions of the selected requirement.
- New upstream bidirectional traceability links are automatically generated as in U7, for each new requirement, but of type "decomposes" (respectively "isDecomposedBy"). The list of required traceability links of the selected requirement is deleted (unless the decomposition was required by the model used) and new lists of required traceability links are created for each new requirement (further steps as in U2).
- Advanced (OPTIONAL): RTCT allows the user to search for existing blocks for reuse in the decomposition.

U9. * Formalize an informal requirement. A user selects an informal requirement to formalize.

- As in U7, with the following differences:
- A property "isFormal" of the new artifact is automatically set to TRUE.
- The type of the upstream traceability link is automatically set to "formalizes", the corresponding oncoming link to "isFormalizedBy".
- When the new, formal requirement is committed, an automatic consistency check with existing formal requirements in the same collection is performed.

In the following, we will describe key and novel features contained in these use cases in more detail.

2.4 Traceability Link Completeness

In order to determine whether a requirement has been fully satisfied by implementation and testing, we need to know not only which design, implementation and testing artifacts (and possibly other artifacts) relate to the requirement in question, but also whether all artifacts we should expect to relate to this requirement actually exist and are linked to the requirement. [32] have presented empirical evidence that traceability completeness actually has a major impact on software quality.

Which traceability links to other artifacts we should expect, or actually require, can be determined from any appropriate model addressing traceability (see [10] for details). For instance, the version of the V-model applied in the Automotive SPICE standard (see Fig. 1 above) explicitly depicts required traceability links between artifacts associated with different project phases.

2.5 Stub Artifacts and Automatic Workflow Creation

Considering the model addressing traceability, it can be automatically determined which artifacts are necessary to satisfy a traceability requirement. In order to make sure that all of these artifacts are actually created and linked, we can offer the user at least twofold support: First, we can create stub artifacts of the required types from templates, and secondly, we can create a workflow (or separate workflows for all required artifacts) which have to be allocated to appropriate development project members for completion. Both measures can be combined or applied alternatively. With traceability link completeness checking and automatic workflow generation for missing links, we implement the Augmented Lifecycle Space approach introduced in [10].

2.6 Requirements Consistency Checking

If requirements are formalized, we can move a step further in the early discovery of inconsistencies which would otherwise be usually detected only during design or implementation. It is well known that not only a major proportion of the deficiencies in software is introduced in the early project phases including requirements analysis, but that those deficiencies are typically the most costly to remediate. When such deficiencies are only detected during design or even implementation, then the requirements analysis phase and all subsequent lifecycle phases have to be at least partly reenacted, while elements of the already performed design and implementation phase may become obsolete. (Cf. [20] on the importance of requirements consistency.)

Formally modeled requirements within a project – or, more generally, any given collection – can be automatically checked for mutual logical consistency at least partially, provided they use a common data model, such as common variables. For instance, if we add a requirement which requires a certain pressure to be within a given window, but another requirement has already ruled out such a pressure, we must use the same pressure variable to detect this inconsistency. Standard verification can be performed e.g. with model checking or static analysis like satisfiability checking (SAT-checking). Complete models comprising all requirements in a more systematic way can be checked more comprehensively, using e.g. semi-automatic verification tools or more sophisticated model checking using custom temporal properties to be checked (see [20], Sect. 2.2.2 for some possible approaches; see also the example in Sect. 2.8 as well as Sect. 3 on implementation below).

Model checking may become difficult for large models, but may still be possible using appropriate model decomposition. Semi-automatic verification can take considerable effort, but may still pay off in many cases considering the potential cost of errors which are detected late or even after deployment. Note that others have considered heuristic, non-formal consistency checking, see e.g. [20] (Sect. 2.2.1); however, we do not consider this approach to be reliable and sufficiently automatable.

2.7 Decomposition, Refinement, and Formalization

A complication which is not fully visible in a model addressing traceability is the need for decomposition and refinement. We can see in Fig. 1 that stakeholder requirements must be refined to system requirements, for example. Stakeholder requirements are usually not precise enough, are incomplete (tacitly assuming domain knowledge, for instance), and may even be inconsistent, as they are often compiled from the desires of different stakeholders with different roles and professional and educational backgrounds. Yet they form the basis for the system requirements, and thus the respective traceability links have to be established.

Beyond this refinement step, however, often more of such steps are required, as well as decomposition. Decomposition may be necessary, for instance, when comprehensive or general requirements will affect different parts or aspects of the desired system and/or will require different test cases, if overview would become lost during refinement of such a comprehensive requirement, or if consistency checking can be facilitated by decomposition.

Consider, for example, the following requirement: ***Rx***. *RTCT-UI SHALL allow to search for and add new artifacts to collections and to add new relations between existing artifacts. New artifacts may exist on external data stores (repositories) and shall remain there, except from a local reference and possibly a local copy of metadata.* This requirement may be decomposed as follows:

- **Rx.1.** RTCT-UI SHALL allow to search for and add new artifacts to collections.
- **Rx.2.** RTCT-UI SHALL allow the addition of new relations between existing artifacts.
- **Rx.3.** If an artifact residing in an external repository is added to a collection in RTCT, then only a link SHALL be added to the collection as well as (OPTIONALLY) a local copy of metadata. The artifact itself SHALL remain in its original location and SHALL NOT be copied.

Formalization is a special case of refinement. The core of the result must be entirely formulated in a formal language suitable for automated verification (including model checking). A formal requirement must also be explicitly flagged as such in order to signal that it shall be checked for consistency with other formal requirements within the same collection (typically corresponding to a project). Whenever a new formal requirement is added to a collection, pairwise consistency checks shall be performed with all other formal requirements already in that collection.

Also certain types of formal requirements (especially model-based formalizations) may still be refined in order to allow for simulation for the sake of validation. Thereby already abstract, specification-level models can be interpreted and animated to allow domain experts assess whether the specified system behaviour meets their expectations. This way, many otherwise costly misunderstandings can be detected at an early stage.

2.8 An Example

We illustrate the important use cases by an example taken from [23] concerning the development of software for active medical devices. Let's consider a hypothetical project, "Hemodialysis Safety System (HDSS)". We assume an RTCT collection "HDSS" already exists and we have to increment it with the following requirement: *The software shall monitor the critical flow in the extra-corporeal circuit and if no flow is detected for more than 120 s then the software shall stop the critical flow pump and execute an alarm signal.*

We add an artifact containing this text to our collection. We are asked for metadata. Let us give a title: "Monitor critical flow", artifact type: "Software requirement", set flag "is-formal" to FALSE. Other metadata can be set automatically: A URI must already exist anyway for RTCT so that it can access the artifact; a serial number (let's say "R.HDSS.126"), can be automatically generated, while time, author, etc. are readily available to the tool.

Now RTCT will ask us whether this new artifact has an upstream dependency (e.g. was derived from another requirement). As this is a software requirement, it should depend on some system requirement (see the V-schema depicted in Fig. 1 above), so we select an existing system requirement, let's say "R.HDSS.16", and give its type by "refines/refined-by" (or, alternatively, "decomposes"/"decomposed-by"). By the act of selection, the new requirement replaces a stub software requirement which was automatically generated when system requirement R.HDSS.16 was added, and the respective workflow is marked as closed.

Next, RTCT determines that the new requirement requires two downstream links: one to a software qualification test case, and another to a software architecture artifact. The respective stub artifacts are created and bidirectional links are established; workflows are created. The resulting artifact dependencies are depicted in Fig. 2.

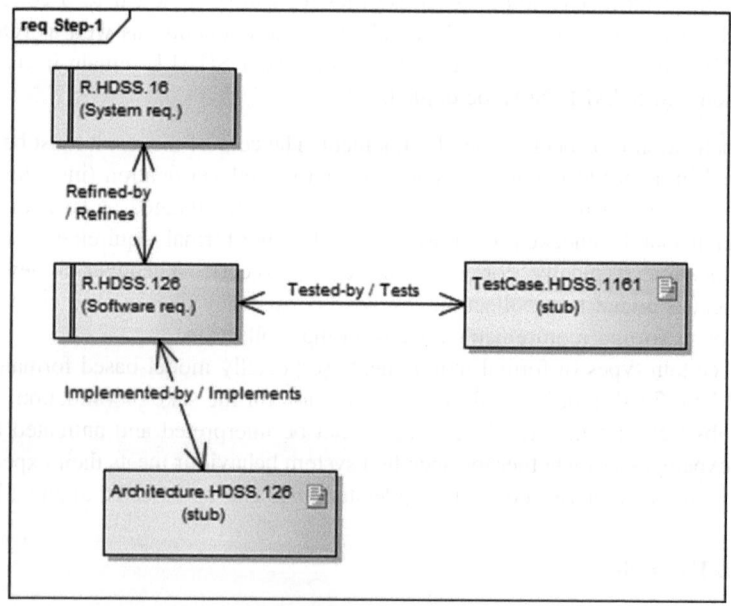

Fig. 2. Example artifact dependencies (Step 1)

In order to check the consistency of the new requirement with existing requirements, it needs to be formalized. A formalization of this informal requirement in Event-B, as given in [23], consists of two different files (artifacts), called a context and a machine:

CONTEXT
  C0
SETS
  criticalFlowPumpingValues , Alarms
CONSTANTS
  Start , Stop, noFlowMaxTime, ALM382, NULL
AXIOMS
  tec1 partition (criticalFlowPumpingValues , {Start}, {Stop})

  tec2 partition (Alarms, {ALM382}, {NULL})

  typ1 noFlowMaxTime ∈ N

  pro1 noFlowMaxTime = 120
END

MACHINE
  M0
SEES
  C0
VARIABLES
  noFlowDetectionTime, alarm, criticalFlowPumping
INVARIANTS
  inv1 noFlowDetectionTime ∈ N // Typing

  inv2 noFlowDetectionTime > noFlowMaxTime ⇒ alarm = ALM382

  /* If no flow is detected in 120s then the alarm should be executed */

  inv3 alarm ∈ Alarms // Typing

  inv4 criticalFlowPumping ∈ criticalFlowPumpingValues // Typing
EVENTS
  Event INITIALISATION // Initialization values
    Then
      act1 noFlowDetectionTime := 0
      act2 alarm := NULL
      act3 criticalFlowPumping := Stop
    End
  Event stopCriticalFlowPumping // Stop critical flow pumping event
    Where
      grd noFlowDetectionTime > noFlowMaxTime ∧ criticalFlowPumping = Start
    Then
      act1 alarm := ALM382
      act2 criticalFlowPumping := Stop // Stop critical flow pumping
    End
  Event startCriticalFlowPumping // Start critical flow pumping event
    Where
      grd criticalFlowPumping = Stop
    Then
      act1 criticalFlowPumping := Start
    End
  Event flowDetectionClock // The clock to simulate the time for flow detection
    Where
      grd noFlowDetectionTime < noFlowMaxTime ∧ criticalFlowPumping = Start
    Then
      act1 noFlowDetectionTime := noFlowDetectionTime + 1
    End
END

(Note that in the machine above, the event "startCriticalFlowPumping" is not explicitly specified in the informal requirement; we will not pursue this issue here, however). We could either add these two artifacts to the collection separately or add the whole Event-B model (such as generated by the Rodin tool), e.g. in the form of a ZIP-file. We opt for the latter. So we add a new artifact: we select the URI where this ZIP-file can be found and add appropriate metadata; in particular, we set "is-formal" to TRUE. Let us call the new requirement "R.HDSS.127". RTCT will ask us for an (optional) upstream dependency. Now we select R.HDSS.126 (the informal counterpart) and set the *link type* to "formalizes/formalized-by".

Now two things should happen automatically: First, existing downstream links of parent R.HDSS.126 have to be rerouted to the new R.HDSS.127: now the only downstream link of R.HDSS.126 is to R.HDSS.127, of type "formalized-by", and the previously generated links to a test case and an architecture artifact are now downstream links of the new R.HDSS.127. Figure 3 shows how the traceability graph has changed by this step.

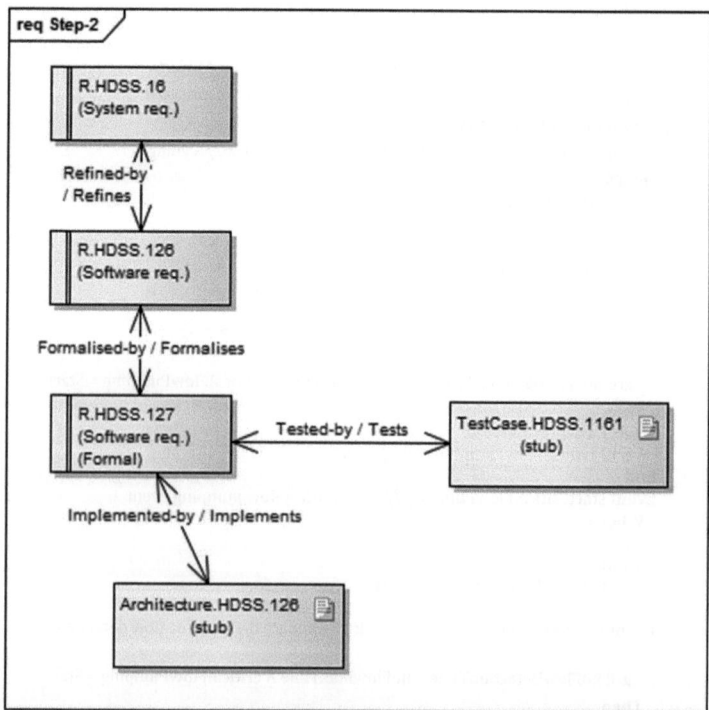

Fig. 3. Artifact dependencies after adding a formalization of R.HDSS.126.

Secondly, as R.HDSS.127 is a *formal* requirement, RTCT will need to check its mutual consistency with all other formal software requirements which are already within the collection HDSS. The outcome of this check will be reported to us. If the system requirement R.HDSS.16 (the parent of R.HDSS.126) also has a formal counterpart, also consistency with this formal parent can be checked.

For instance, there might exist an requirement stating that "the critical flow pump MUST NOT be stopped during treatment", obviously contradicting the new requirement that "if no flow is detected for more than 120 s then the software shall stop the critical flow pump …". This consistency can only be detected if both requirements, in their formal versions, use the common variable "criticalFlowPumping" (plus a few other variables and constants).

Given that R.HDSS.127 is formal, a potential third step would be to automatically generate one or more test cases for it. There are tools which are capable of test case generation from formal models, e.g. Asmeta (see the next section). We could have proceeded differently, by the way. For instance, requirement R.HDSS.126 could have been decomposed before formalization (though this might seem rather artificial in this particular case). We could (in theory) decompose into monitoring, stopping the pump at a particular monitoring event, and executing an alarm at the same monitoring event.

In such a case, three new requirements would be added, each with links of type "decomposes" to R.HDSS.126. In this case, the existing downstream links of R.HDSS.126 as well as their targets would become invalid; instead, for each of the new requirements, new stub artifacts – test cases and architecture artifacts – together with the respective traceability links as well as workflows will have to be created. Figure 4 depicts the respective portion of the new traceability graph. Note that Test Case HDSS.1161 and Architecture artifact HDSS.126 have disappeared.

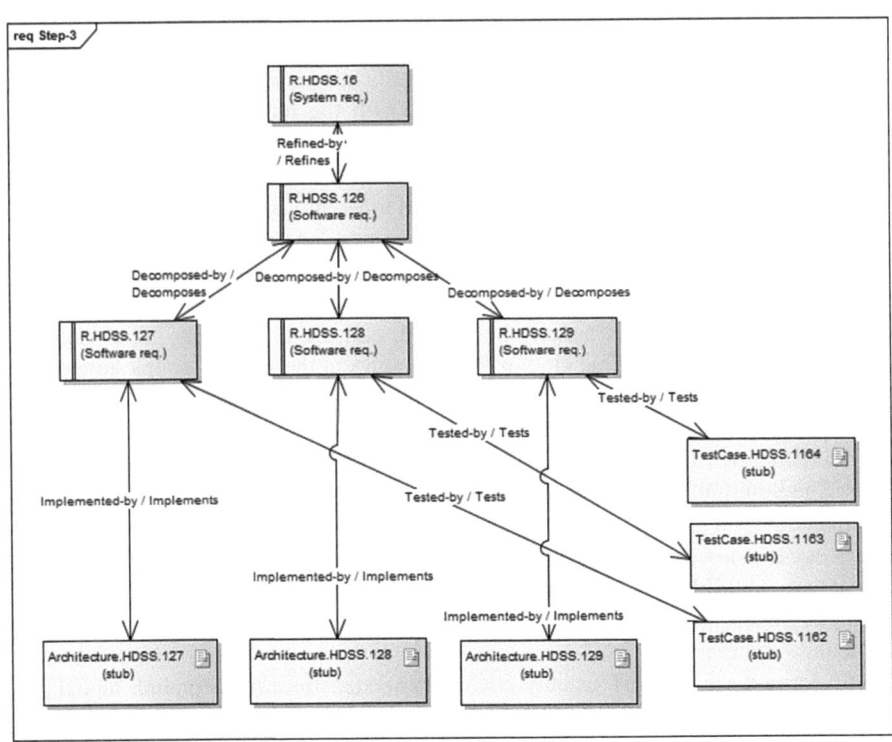

Fig. 4. Artifact dependencies after decomposition of R.HDSS.126.

3 Implementation

As OSLC is based on web technologies, RTCT is best implemented as a web service. The core implements an OSLC client which can access different artifact repositories via OSLC adapters. The user interface of RTCT (RTCT-UI) is best implemented as a web interface using the RTCT service. There exists an OSLC reference Software Development Kit (SDK) called OSLC4 J and provided by the project Eclipse Lyo [22]. This is explicitly recommended on the OSLC web page [25]. It is Java-based and builds on the Wink library for RESTful web services [35]. It provides a library for implementing both OSLC servers and clients.

The RTCT core must also be able to access resources like a lifecycle model and a verification tool (e.g. a model checker). A Java-based implementation platform is helpful for this purpose as there exist Java libraries for tasks like verification, but also e.g. for test case generation from abstract models. Examples are the tool Asmeta [4], which is based on the Abstract State Machine (ASM) method [11, 17], or the tool Rodin [33] for Event-B [1]. For various other tools, e.g. Python interfaces or even OSLC adapters exist.

Regarding formal modelling, there exist several implementations on the market which address parts of the issues targeted by the above use cases. One of the market leaders is Mathworks, with the related systems MatLab Simulink® and Polyspace®. Simulink models are not only implementations, but also abstractions of problems [15]. As Simulink models can usually not run on the target device, code has to be generated. Analysis can be performed in three different ways. First, the compliance with (corporate) guidelines can be checked with the Verification and Validation toolbox. This toolbox contains a rule base which complies with the most relevant standards (i.e. DO-178, ISO 26262, and IEC 61508). These rules contain design patterns corresponding to best development practices. By following and checking modelling guidelines, unsafe situations can be avoided and inherently safe design can be achieved (similarly to using MISRA rules in the programming language C).

For example, data flow can be restricted in a certain way to improve readability. If data flow is detected which does not comply with the restriction, a warning is given. Similarly, initial conditions have to be defined, and the lack of any initial condition again leads to a warning. This kind of analysis stays at the level of simple rule checks or pattern analysis, which is certainly useful but its capability is limited.

Second, the Simulink model can be interpreted as a formal description: the blocks have well defined (formal) descriptions together with the necessary boundary conditions. The Simulink Design Verification and Validation toolbox is capable of analyzing the model in such a manner and highlighting the weaknesses. It cannot only find certain errors but test cases can be generated with its help, where the use of formal methods guarantees the full test coverage at least at model level. Furthermore, dependencies can be highlighted, which helps identify the implementation artifacts corresponding to particular requirements.

As formerly mentioned, usually code is generated from the Simulink model. The generated code may fulfill certain standards [14] guaranteed by MathWorks (the manufacturer). Still, Polyspace can be utilized to check the generated code. This third analysis again uses formal methods as a tool to find bugs which were inserted during code generation or were overlooked previously. These three steps provide an analysis as complete as can be expected, and they also support the documentation process of certain standards (mostly DO-178, ISO 26262 and IEC 61508). MathWorks also realized the importance of integration. Therefore, Simulink models can be linked directly to numerous tools used for requirements management. These tools include, among others, Rational DOORS. Yet it is important to highlight that Matlab uses a unique method via URIs to create the connection. Using OSLC compliant connections would further improve the usefulness of these well-build tool packages. There actually exist OSCL adapters for Simulink by third parties, see [6, 31], giving evidence for the interest for the integration of Simulink in tool chains.

In summary, the major building blocks necessary for creating the RTCT system exist, and have been independently developed in the fields of process capability improvement, formal modeling, and web technologies. The addressed challenge is the achievement of the collaboration of these building blocks, allowing the incremental improvement of the efficiency and effectiveness of safety-critical software development in practice, exploiting OSLC (Open Services for Lifecycle Collaboration).

4 Conclusion

We have presented major steps in realizing the Augmented Lifecycle Space approach for requirements management presented in [10] in a tool prototype which we call Requirements Traceability and Consistency checking Tool (RTCT). The approach considers cross-platform traceability exploiting OSLC, trace completeness checking based on a process model, and requirements consistency checking in order to considerably ease the requirements management process, to reduce major and costly defects in the requirements engineering phase, and to better support the verification of requirements satisfaction and thereby certifiability of the respective processes and products.

RTCT should not be seen as a standalone application, but as a kind of middleware providing particular services for engineering software that shall ultimately be integrated with other ALM-related software.

One of the important features of the new approach, of high importance for actual applications, is that it allows for the so-called "graceful integration" of formal modeling. Formal modeling is fundamentally necessary for securing completeness and consistency, but customarily rejected due to the usually prohibiting up-front effort needed to formally process all artifacts of an already established traditional system; Graceful integration can considerably lower this threshold.

In future work, amongst others, systems engineering aspects could be considered in RTCT, and RTCT could be integrated into a toolchain covering much of systems engineering activities. For instance, SysML requirements diagrams [34] could be used to depict the dependencies between requirements, and SysML associations can be used to depict traceability links between requirements and other artifacts.

Acknowledgement. The authors are grateful for the support of Research and Innovation Center of Óbuda University. The work is supported by the European Research Council Starting Grant ERC-StG 679681.

The research reported in this paper has been supported by the Austrian Ministry for Transport, Innovation and Technology, the Federal Ministry of Science, Research and Economy, and the Province of Upper Austria in the frame of the COMET center SCCH.

References

1. Abrial, J.-R.: Modeling in Event-B System and Software Design. Cambridge University Press, Cambridge (2010)
2. Ambler, S.: Tracing your design. Dr. Dobb's J. World Softw. Dev. (1999). http://www.drdobbs.com/tracing-your-design/184415675. Accessed 08 Apr 2016)
3. Ambler, S.: Agile Requirements best practices. In: Agile Modeling (2014) http://www.agilemodeling.com/essays/agileRequirementsBestPractices.htm. Accessed 08 Apr 2016
4. University of Milan: "Asmeta". http://asmeta.sourceforge.net/. Accessed 31 Mar 2017
5. Automotive SIG. VDA QMC Working Group 13: Automotive SPICE Process As-sessment/Reference Model, v3.0 (2015). http://www.automotivespice.com/fileadmin/software-download/Automotive_SPICE_PAM_30.pdf. Accessed 08 Apr 2016
6. Biehl,M.: OSLC-Style Tool Adapter for MATLAB/Simulink. http://open-services.net/pub/Main/PLMWorkgroupWorkingMeetingJune282011/simulink-oslc-demo-2.pdf. Accessed 07 Apr 2017
7. Biró, M., Feuer, É., Haase, V.H., Koch, G.R., Kugler, H.J., Messnarz, R., Remzső, T.: BOOTSTRAP and ISCN: a current look at the European software quality network. In: Sima, D., Haring, G. (eds.) Proceedings of the Conference on the Challenge of Networking: Connecting Equipment, Humans, Institutions (CON 1993), R. Oldenbourg Verlag GmbH, pp. 97–105 (1993). http://dl.acm.org/citation.cfm?id=200895.200906. Accessed 07 Apr 2017
8. Biro, M.: Open Services for software process compliance engineering. In: Geffert, V., Preneel, B., Rovan, B., Štuller, J., Tjoa, A.M. (eds.) SOFSEM 2014. LNCS, vol. 8327, pp. 1–6. Springer, Cham (2014). doi:10.1007/978-3-319-04298-5_1
9. Biró, M.: Functional safety, traceability, and open services. In: Madeyski, L., Ochodek, M. (ed.) Software Engineering from Research and Practice Perspective. Wyd. Nakom, Poznan, pp. 73–82. ISBN 978-83-63919-16-0
10. Biró, M., Klespitz, J., Gmeiner, J., Illibauer, C., Kovács, L.: Towards Automated Traceability Assessment through Augmented Lifecycle Space. In: Kreiner, C., O'Connor, R., Poth, A., Messnarz, R. (eds.) EuroSPI 2016. CCIS, vol. 633, pp. 73–82. Springer, Cham (2016)
11. Börger, E., Stärk, R.: Abstract State Machines. A Method for High-Level System Design and Analysis. Springer, Heidelberg (2003)
12. Chapman, D.: What is application lifecycle management? (2010) http://www.davidchappell.com/writing/white_papers/What_is_ALM_v2.0–Chappell.pdf. Accessed 08 Apr 2016
13. Cleland-Huang, J, Gotel, O. C., Huffman Hayes, J., Mäder, P., Zisman, A.: Software trace-ability: trends and future directions. In: Proceedings of the on Future of Software Engineering, pp. 55–69. ACM (2014)
14. Generate C and C++ code optimized for embedded systems. https://www.mathworks.com/products/embedded-coder.html

15. Ferrari, A., Fantechi, A., Gnesi, S., Magnani, G.: Model-based development and formal methods in the railway industry. IEEE software **30**(3), 28–34 (2013). (https://doi.ieeecomputersociety.org/cms/Computer.org/dl/mags/so/2013/03/figures/mso20130300281.gif), (source of the mentioned picture)
16. Gotel, O., Cleland-Huang, J., Hayes, J.H., Zisman, A., Egyed, A., Grünbacher, P., Dekhtyar, A., Antoniol, G., Maletic, J.: The grand challenge of traceability (v1.0). In: Cleland-Huang, J., Gotel, O., Zisman, A. (eds.) Software and Systems Traceability, pp. 343–409. Springer, London (2012)
17. Gurevich, Y.: Sequential abstract state machines capture sequential algorithms. ACM Trans. Comput. Logic **1**(1), 77–111 (2000)
18. Ibrahim, S., Idris, N.B., Munro, M., Deraman, A.: Implementing a document-based requirements traceability: a case study. In: IASTED International Conference on Software Engineering, pp. 124–131 (2005)
19. Functional safety. International Electrotechnical Commission®. http://www.iec.ch/about/brochures/pdf/technology/functional_safety.pdf. Accessed 31 Mar 2017
20. Kamalrudin, M., Sidek, S.: A review on software requirements validation and consistency management. Int. J. Softw. Eng. Appl. **9**(10), 39–58 (2015)
21. Lacheiner, H., Ramler, R.: Application lifecycle management as infrastructure for software processes improvement and evolution: Experience and insights from industry. In: Biffl, S., Koivuluoma, M., Abrahamsson, P. (eds.) Proceedings of the 37th EUROMICRO Conference on Software Engineering and Advanced Applications - SEAA 2011, pp. 286–293. IEEE, August/September 2011
22. Eclipse Lyo: Enabling tool integration with OSLC. http://www.eclipse.org/lyo/. Accessed 31 Mar 2017
23. Mashkoor, A., Biro, M., Dolgos, M., Timar, P.: Refinement-based development of software-controlled safety-critical active medical devices. In: Winkler, D., Biffl, S., Bergsmann, J. (eds.) SWQD 2015. LNBIP, vol. 200, pp. 120–132. Springer, Cham (2015). doi:10.1007/978-3-319-13251-8_8
24. McCaffery, F., Casey, V., Sivakumar, M.S., Coleman, G., Donnelly, P., Burton, J.: Medical device software traceability. In: Cleland-Huang, J., Gotel, O., Zisman, A. (eds.) Software and Systems Traceability, pp. 321–339. Springer, London (2012)
25. Open Services for Lifecycle Collaboration: an open community building practical specifications for integrating software. http://open-services.net/. Accessed 31 Mar 2017
26. Pirklbauer, G., Ramler, R., Zeilinger, R.: An integration-oriented model for application lifecycle management. In: Proceedings of the 11th International Conference con Enterprise Information Systems (ICEIS 2009), pp. 399–403. INSTICC (2009)
27. Ramesh, B., Jarke, M.: Towards reference models for requirements traceability. IEEE Trans. Software Eng. **27**(1), 58–93 (2001)
28. Ramler, Rudolf, Lacheiner, Hermann, Kern, Albin: Rule-Based Detection of Process Conformance Violations in Application Lifecycle Management. In: Winkler, Dietmar, O'Connor, Rory V., Messnarz, Richard (eds.) EuroSPI 2012. CCIS, vol. 301, pp. 37–48. Springer, Heidelberg (2012). doi:10.1007/978-3-642-31199-4_4
29. Regan, Gilbert, Biro, Miklos, Mc Caffery, Fergal, Mc Daid, Kevin, Flood, Derek: A traceability process assessment model for the medical device domain. In: Barafort, Béatrix, O'Connor, R.V., Poth, Alexander, Messnarz, Richard (eds.) EuroSPI 2014. CCIS, vol. 425, pp. 206–216. Springer, Heidelberg (2014). doi:10.1007/978-3-662-43896-1_18
30. Regan, G., Biro, M., Flood, D., McCaffery, F.: Assessing traceability—practical experiences and lessons learned. J. Softw. Evol. Process **27**(8), 591–601 (2015). http://dx.doi.org/10.1002/smr.1728. Accessed 31 Mar 2017

31. Reichwein, A.: Java-based Implementation of OSLC Simulink Adapter. https://github.com/ld4mbse/oslc-adapter-simulink. Accessed 07 Apr 2017
32. Rempel, P., Mäder, P.: Preventing defects: the impact of requirements traceability completeness on software quality. IEEE Trans. Softw. Eng. **PP**(99), 1 (2016)
33. Event-B and the Rodin Platform. http://www.event-b.org/. Accessed 31 Mar 2017
34. OMG: OMG Systems Modeling Language (OMG SYSMLTM), Version 1.4. http://www.omg.org/spec/SysML/1.4/. Accessed 31 Mar 2017
35. Apache Wink. https://wink.apache.org/. Accessed 31 Mar 2017

Good and Bad Practices in Improvement

The SPI Manifesto Revisited

Eva Breske[1(✉)] and Tomas Schweigert[2(✉)]

[1] BOSCH Engineering GmbH, Abstatt, Germany
eva.breske@bosch.com
[2] SQS AG, Cologne, Germany
tomas.schweigert@sqs.de

Abstract. The paper shows a new view on SPI given from the perspective of organisations research especially from the view of Marvin Weisbrod. It takes the trend analysis of Weisbrod and maps approaches like the SPI Manifesto and the agile Manifesto in the roadmap of Weisbrod. It also analyses the thesis of Weisbrod in detail by reflecting the history of industrial work in the last century. It shows how the Agile and the SPI Manifesto fit into trends of organisational change management and it provides a very simple understanding of process quality.

Keywords: Organisational change management · SPI manifesto · Agile manifesto · Improvability · Process improvement · Reengineering · Process quality

1 Introduction

2010 the SPI Manifesto was launched. It contains the PI knowledge of many leading experts of PI (Figs. 1 and 2). Everybody being in Alcala that year thought that this paper would have great impact on the evolution of PI. However –compared to the agile manifesto- the SPI Manifesto is something for expert clubs and did not have real impact. The paper creates an Idea Why.

The SPI Manifesto at a glance.

For PI experts it sounds trivial. But what was the Problem the SPI manifesto aimed at?

It was the process bureaucracy caused by the CMMI driven SEPG. It was a "no" to ivory towers where unsuccessful project managers and clueless beginners met in order to define the software development and testing processes of an organisation. Producing process descriptions that created very interesting sites on the intranet. The authors of the SPI manifesto were right to oppose this way of PI but they did not reflect the complete scenario.

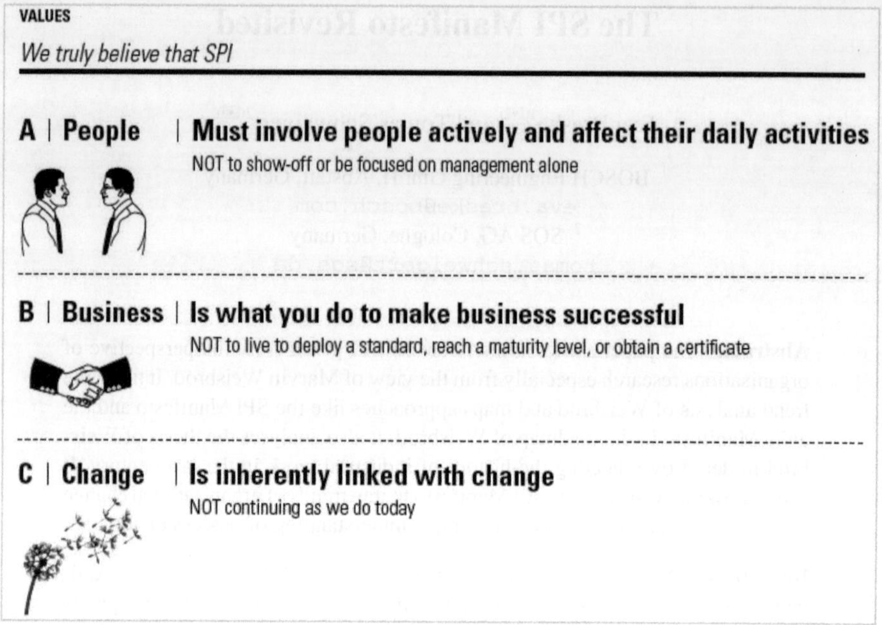

VALUES

We truly believe that SPI

A | People | Must involve people actively and affect their daily activities
NOT to show-off or be focused on management alone

B | Business | Is what you do to make business successful
NOT to live to deploy a standard, reach a maturity level, or obtain a certificate

C | Change | Is inherently linked with change
NOT continuing as we do today

Fig. 1. SPI Manifesto values

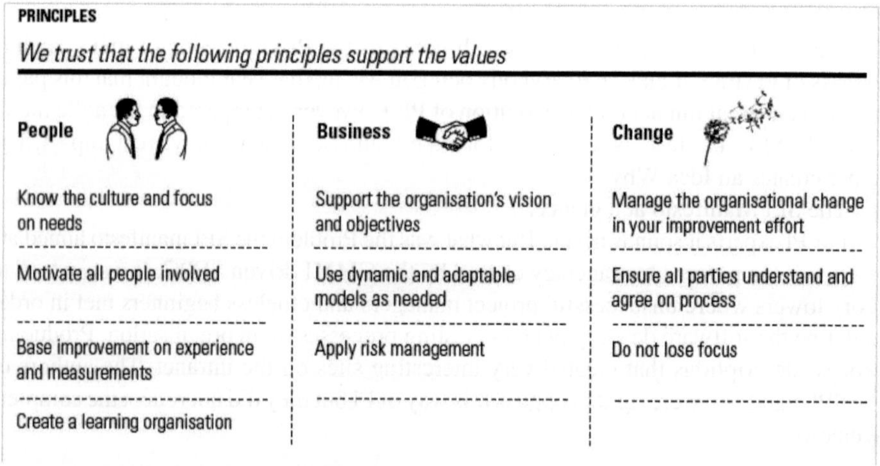

PRINCIPLES

We trust that the following principles support the values

People	Business	Change
Know the culture and focus on needs	Support the organisation's vision and objectives	Manage the organisational change in your improvement effort
Motivate all people involved	Use dynamic and adaptable models as needed	Ensure all parties understand and agree on process
Base improvement on experience and measurements	Apply risk management	Do not lose focus
Create a learning organisation		

Fig. 2. SPI Manifesto principles

2 The Evolvement of Organisations and the Empowerment of People

To understand the trend and the current situation of PI we need to look at the core discipline of which PI is a part of: The theory of organisations.

Looking at one influencer, Marvin Weisbord (Weisbord 1987), we see his fundamental view on the learning curve of organisations (Fig. 3):

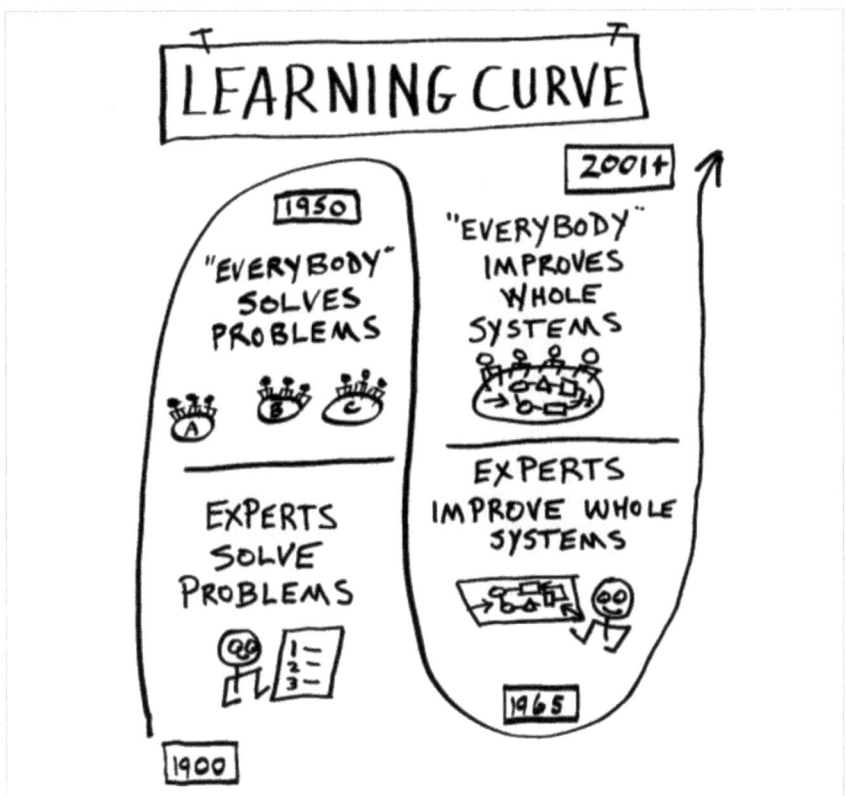

Fig. 3. Learning curve according to Weisbord

One trend in this learning curve is that every member of an organisation now performs tasks formerly performed by experts.

We see that the Capability Maturity Model (CMM) was published in 1991.

We also see that the SPICE (Software Process Improvement and Capability dEtermination) started in 1993.

Last but not least we see the Bootstrap Approach published 1994.

They all contribute to the paradigm of that time: Experts improve whole systems.

They all had to deal with the new paradigm expected to step in 2000: Everybody improves whole systems.

And what happened 2001: The agile manifesto was published. By giving back the centre stage to the software developer, it seemed to be a perfect fit to this new paradigm.

2010 the SPI Manifesto was published written by experts who had a broad experience in improving organisations (Pries-Heje and Johansen 2010). However, the prognosis of Weisbrod was that in this time everybody has the task to improve whole systems.

Summarizing the provocation: The SPI Manifesto was the summary of expert knowledge in SPI but was outdated when written. Therefore, it had no practical impact and remained an academic footnote.

2.1 Was Weisbord Right and Does the Agile Manifesto Really Fit into His Paradigms?

When discussing the learning ladder of organisations as described by Weisbord, we need to have a look at his core cornerstones: Everybody. Improves. Systems.

Everybody. The word seems to be trivial but it isn't. The problem arrives when we see the timeframe in the prognosis of Weisbord: 1900 to 2000. Looking at 1900, industrialization meant employing unskilled people in a plant or an office, organizing their work and letting them perform very little steps of the process (e.g. fasten a screw or add numbers). This time has gone. Currently we face completely automated back offices, and we see skilled workers with lot more authority and responsibility than even a team, lead in 1900, would have even dreamed about. Looking at this fact it becomes reasonable that "Everybody" improves whole systems because "Everybody" has rapidly changed, in the financial industry there are only some subject matter experts remaining as "Everybody".

Improve, this word looks great, but again, we need to revisit. Everybody "Improves" whole Systems. What does it mean? Is every improvement of the individual work sphere also an improvement for the system? Certainly not. By learning how to deal with linear systems of equations, matrix calculation we learn that in a true system the optimum for a system is not the optimum for a factor. Therefore, every local improvement, often declared as low hanging fruit, hampers the total performance of a system. Also when frame conditions are complex and rapidly changing, how does one rate a change as an "Improvement"?

System, also this topic needs revisiting. In 1900 a system was a car and maybe a plant. But in 2000 we see system of systems and looking at European air travel we see systems of systems of systems. So what is the system that has received an improvement? How can someone make sure that an improvement in a low-level system also causes improvements in overarching systems?

So when we shortly analyze the paradigms of Marvin Weisbord, they still look attractive and helpful but also somewhat fuzzy.

2.2 The Agile Manifesto – Revisited

Revisiting the agile manifesto (Beck 2001), there could be doubts whether this manifesto really fits into the modern time paradigm of everybody improving whole systems.

The agile manifesto focuses on "teams". A team can be understood as a system and with stand up, reviews and retrospectives there are tools for improvement available. Looking in team level it is a perfect fit. However, if the system is a whole organisation it turns out, that there are big doubts. If teams in an organisation come to different conclusions on how to work then these teams tend to work differently, measure their progress differently and deliver at a different cost. This causes a dilemma: By sticking to the team approach, the organisation might risk a decrease in performance. If the organisation decides to introduce guiderails, two questions remain. Namely, who it is to define the guide rails and who is in charge to control their effective implementation. At the end, it turns out that the same "everybody" who improved the Team System has to reject the improvement on the level of an organisational system. Therefore, at the end there are real doubts if the agile manifesto really fits into Weisbord paradigm. The agile community has developed several approaches to deal with this issue. One of these is the scaled agile framework: (Gerush 2017; Powell Horse 2017). See Fig. 4.

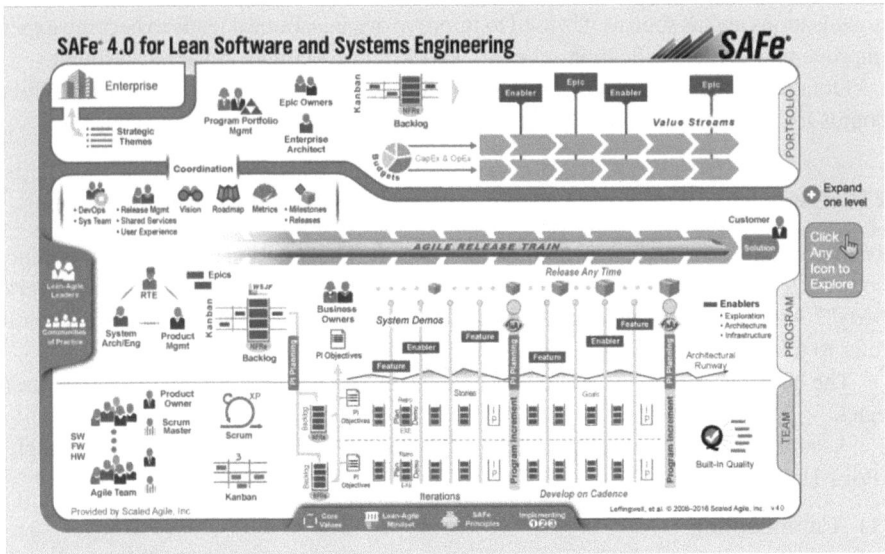

Fig. 4. Agile framework

It is easy to see that this framework and the related certification scheme is a step back to expert driven process improvement.

The same impression is delivered by the disciplined agile framework (see Fig. 5).

The issue of team vs organisation focus is unsolved and subject to debate (Mitchell 2013).

Disciplined Agile 2.0

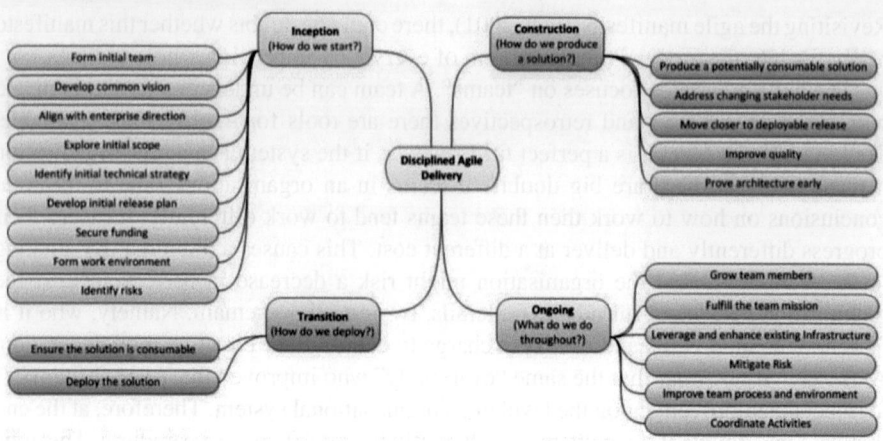

Fig. 5. Disciplined Agile 2.0

At the end it could be summarized that agile in its core is not a tool to improve organisations and as soon as it is used to improve organisations it tends to become expert improvement with certification schemes, and strict procedures in the background.

Organisations, which want to enable their people and try to move ahead in Weisboards learning curve, will find agile a plank road or even worse a dead end.

2.3 Comparing Weisbords Learning Curve with Typical Change Strategies

To improve an organisation means also to change it. The question is: Is there a difference between a system that is improved by experts and a system that is improved by "Everybody"? Are the underlying change strategies different? A possible answer is to refer to refer to the improvability approach.

The book describing the approach contains also a section dealing with change strategies

According to the research presented in this book the most typical change strategies (Pries-Heje 2013), are:

(1) **Commanding**

Change is driven and dictated by (top) management (owner, sponsor and change agent).

(2) **Employee driven**

Change is driven from the bottom of the organizational hierarchy.

(3) **Exploration**

Change is driven by the need for flexibility, agility, or a need to explore news.

(4) **Learning driven**

Change is driven by a focus on organizational learning, individual learning.

(5) **Metrics driven**

Change is driven by metrics and measurements.

(6) **Optionality**

Change is driven by the motivation and need of the individual or group.

(7) **Production organized**

Change is driven by the need for optimization and/or cost reduction.

(8) **Reengineering (BPR)**

Change is driven by fundamentally rethinking and redesigning the organization.

(9) **Socializing**

Change in organizational capabilities is driven by working through social relationships. Diffusion happens through personal contacts rather than through plans and dictates.

(10) **Specialist driven**

Change is driven by specialists (professional, technical, or domain knowledge).

The research in this topic was driven by IT-University, Copenhagen, Denmark, DELTA and 4 companies in a 3-year project.

Checking which of these strategies might more fit to an expert driven improvement or an "everyone" driven improvement, it becomes obvious, that commanding is really a tool from the 20th century but all other need a high level of collaboration, e.g. analyzing Metrics and as well analyzing potential impacts of measures. It is also obvious that the strategies "employee driven" and "socializing" fit best to the stage "Everybody improves whole systems" of the Weisboard approach.

3 The Customer as a New Factor in SPI Projects

In the last few years, a new strategy has emerged:

Customer Driven
This change was introduced in the last years mainly in the German automotive market and in the Dutch construction market.

In the German automotive market the Original Equipment Manufacturers (OEM) face the need to get the software parts of car components under control in the Dutch construction market the change was driven by Rijkswaterstaat (RWS) in order to implement the Design, Build, Finance and Maintain (DBFM) approach.

This seems to be a loop back to the start of the story where the US Department of Defense (DoD) tried to achieve control over underperforming software suppliers by pushing them into CMMI.

While the need is similar, RWS and the German OEM use different tools:

German OEM challenge their suppliers to fulfill Automotive SPICE® Requirements while RWS uses ISO/IEC 15504 Part 6:2013 – Systems engineering.

There is one big difference in both approaches:

OEMs use Automotive SPICE® to create pressure on the software engineers, which make them feel that they are threatened by only living to deploy standards, rather than employing the principles, which support business values.

RWS is aiming at the management system of its suppliers (van Loon 2012a) (Which is reasonable recognizing that a DBFM contract includes a maintenance period of 20 to 30 years). Even if RWS has difficulties in formulating reasonable improvement roadmaps (van Loon 2012b) for the DBFM contractor, its approach is a great success story, including huge infrastructure projects like Poort van Bunnik, Poort van North, OpenIJ and SAA1.

The other big difference is how contractors deal with the challenge: While German OEM contractors often do not see the business chances of process improvement with Automotive SPICE® the huge Dutch companies started to use the approach of RWS to improve their business and to create competitive advance.

Nevertheless, the customer on the driver seat has an impact of the role of (S)PI professionals.

4 Closing the Loop I: What Is Process Quality

Process quality can be expressed in very complex terms like capability diagrams including lots of information for (S)PI experts and hard to understand for the major parties (Workers, managers, customers).

Simplifying process quality from their perspective means

Worker: I step in, complete my tasks and step out, no time consuming disturbance, no over hours, no weekend work
Manager: I make money with a reliable business
Customer: I get what I want with an acceptable quality for an acceptable price.

Closing the loop to Weisbrod: When we ask, who is the everybody who improves whole systems than workers, managers, and customers are part of the group named "everybody".

So what is the new role of the SPI expert in an organization on the top of Weisbords learning curve?

Currently hierarchy and silos define organizations. Often processes do not reflect the work but the organizational boundaries. Mike Hammer (Hammer 2007) defined the ability of an organization to define processes across silos even across formal boundaries of legal entities as one major tool for organizational maturity. Even if this is a key ability for process capability, neither the old framework of ISO/IEC 15504 nor the new Framework of ISO/IEC 33003/33020 require cross boundary process designs.

When transforming a silo organization and helping the organization to make the next step in the learning curve, the SPI expert needs organizational background knowledge. The SPI expert has to have the capability to organize cross silo and cross boundary cooperation to empower people by giving them tools for problem solution. The SPI expert also understands the needs of systems at different levels, creating customer satisfaction and thus constantly assuring management commitment to SPI activities.

SPI experts will also face the challenge to help organizations, which are misled by so-called agile evangelists to get back to sustainable IT business.

5 Closing the Loop 2: The Learning Curve of Organizations and the SPI Manifesto

When revisiting the thesis of Weisbrod, it becomes clear that using his scheme to categorize his work, Weisbrod is an expert, an expert in organizational learning. His work is a perfect fit into his learning curve but still he is an expert who wants to improve organizations but he wants to improve y empowering people. Otherwise, there would be no progress and his prognosis that everyone will improve systems will become a fairytale.

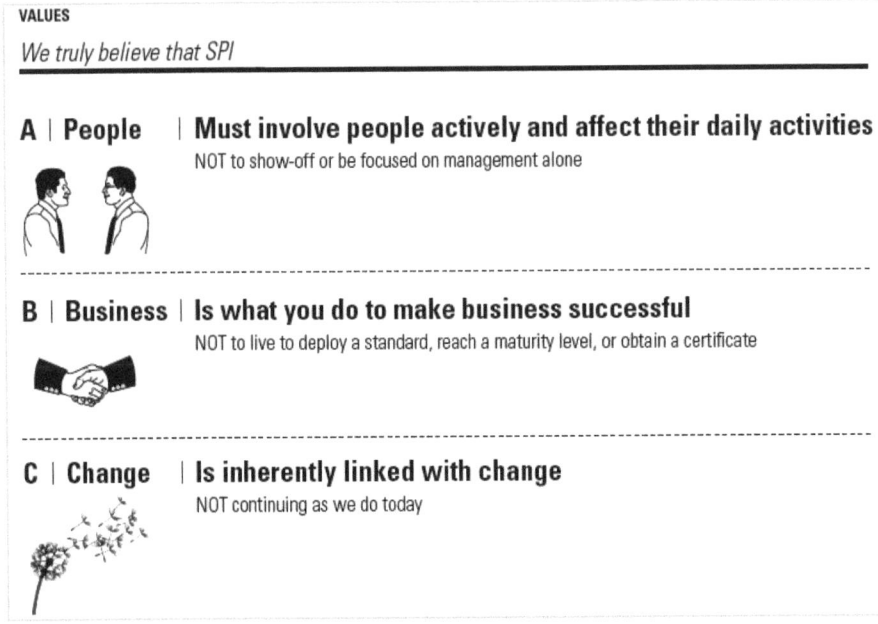

Fig. 6. The values of the SPI Manifesto revisited

So differentiating the author from the message there is a huge overlap between the prognosis of Weisbrod and the SPI Manifesto because the SPI Manifesto is focused on People (Fig. 6).

As a conclusion, driving an organization through the learning curve is not a matter of Methods. It is a matter of orientation (Empowering or commanding) and a matter of skills.

The SPI manifesto and the related PI manager training by delivering the necessary principles, values and tools will help the (S)PI professionals to deal with these challenges and successfully help organizations to improve their business y empowering their people.

But the SPI community should not lose the focus on implementing and improving the SPI manifesto.

References

van Loon, H.: Concrete, steel and ISO 15288. In: Mas, A., Mesquida, A., Rout, T., O'Connor, R.V., Dorling, A. (eds.) SPICE 2012. CCIS, vol. 290, pp. 269–272. Springer, Heidelberg (2012a). doi:10.1007/978-3-642-30439-2_29

van Loon, H.: Using target process profiles in the real world. In: Mas, A., Mesquida, A., Rout, T., O'Connor, R.V., Dorling, A. (eds.) SPICE 2012. CCIS, vol. 290, pp. 286–288. Springer, Heidelberg (2012b). doi:10.1007/978-3-642-30439-2_33

Pries-Heje, J., Vinter, O.: Selecting change strategies in IT organisations – proof of strategy. In: Pries-Heje, J., Johansen, J. (eds.) ImprovAbility™ - Success with Process Improvement, Delta, Horsholm (2013). ISBN: 978-87-7398-139-9

Pries-Heje, J., Johansen, J. (eds.) MANIFESTO Software Process Improvement eurospi.net, Alcala, Spain (2010). http://www.iscn.com/Images/SPI_Manifesto_A.1.2.2010.pdf

Beck, K., et al.: Manifesto for Agile Software Development, Snowbird Ski Ressort (2001). http://agilemanifesto.org/

Hammer, M.: The process audit - a new framework, as comprehensive as it is easy to apply, is helping companies plan and execute process-based transformations. Harvard Business Review, p. 111, April 2007. https://hbr.org/2007/04/the-process-audit

Weisbord, M.R.: Productive workplaces: organizing and managing for dignity, meaning and community. In: The Jossey-Bass Management Series, vol. xxv, p. 405. Jossey-Bass Productive workplaces: Organizing and Managing for Dignity, Meaning and Community, San Francisco, CA, US (1987)

Gerush, M.: Agile in Large, Complex Organizations (2017). http://www.blueprintsys.com/blog/scaled-agile-framework-increase-agility/

Powell-Morse, A.: Scaled Agile Framework: What Is It And How Do You Use It? (2017). https://airbrake.io/blog/sdlc/scaled-agile-framework

Mitchell, I.: Method Wars: Scrum vs SAFe (2013). https://dzone.com/articles/method-wars-scrum-vs-safe

Documentation of Improvement Competences

Jørn Johansen[1(✉)], Karsten Kristensen Back[2], Morten Korsaa[1],
Jan Pries-Heje[2], and Tomas Schweigert[3]

[1] Whitebox, Hørsholm, Denmark
{jj,mk}@whitebox.dk
[2] Roskilde University, Roskilde, Denmark
{kkback,janph}@ruc.dk
[3] SQS, Cologne, Germany
Tomas.Schweigert@sqs.com

Abstract. This paper demonstrates how a report used in a Master in Project management and Process improvement training at Roskilde University Denmark can be used to evaluate if a student can pass the ECQA SPI Manager exam. It also demonstrates how the structure of the report addresses all necessary competences, which should or could be brought into play during the project – and therefor also in one way or another addresses the quality of the activated competences in the improvement project – a kind of qualification. The clue is that the structure of the report follows the units and element in the SPI Manager job role, which is based on the SPI Manifesto and the ImprovAbilityTM model (part of ISO/IEC 33014 Guideline for Process Improvement) among other types of knowledge and research.

Keywords: Process improvement · SPI Manifesto, ImprovAbility[TM] · ISO/IEC 33014 · ECQA SPI manager job role

1 Introduction

Software Process Improvement Manager (SPI Manager) is one of the topics in European Certification and Qualification Association ECQA. The development of the SPI Manager training and certification scheme has been done in many small steps so far by several specialists in Europe. The current version of the SPI Manager skill set is mainly based on software, systems and service processes and their related reference models. It includes the SPI Manifesto [1] and ImprovAbilityTM [3] as the main structure for the training course [2].

It has for a long time (we are talking about years) been a wish to combine the ECQA SPI Manager training and certificate with a Master degree from a university. In this paper, we describe how this is realized – with the focus on how to evaluate the competences learned at a course and documented in a report, which was the basis for the evaluation and the certification [11].

2 Context and Background

At Roskilde University Denmark (RUC), you can take a Master in Project Management and Process Improvement – for persons who has a relevant job. It takes place in 4 3-day-modules, including weekends. Module 3 is about Process Improvement and includes maturity models, improvement, SPI Manifesto, ImprovAbility™, ISO/IEC 33014 and other relevant theories and models.

This education has taken place for many years now, and more than 130 persons have now taken the education, with an exam based on exercises and improvement projects performed in the companies they were employed at. Passing this exam gives a normal RUC Master degree certificate.

The latest exam for Module 3 in February 2017 included the possibility of taking an ECQA SPI Manager exam and get an ECQA SPI Manager Certificate.

It was up to the students if they would like to complement their RUC Master certificate with a ECQA SPI Manager exam and certificate or not. At the training course, there were 6 students, and three of them decided to take an ECQA exam. It was then up to the students if they would take the standard ECQA multi choice test for SPI Manager or write a report, which demonstrated they could use the new competences required in the ECQA SPI Manager Job Role description. All three of them chose to write a report.

3 Problem Statement

It is an often-discussed problem how to evaluate competences learned during training courses. Do you need a demonstration from a real-world project, documented in a report and discussed through an oral exam? And what if the real-world project doesn't include elements required in the set of learning goals form the course?

Here we had a situation, where the students worked on real-world improvement projects in an organization. We also had a very well defined set of competences the students need to have to get a ECQA SPI Manager certificate, defined in the associated Job role description.

The students choose to document their competences by writing a report.

So, the challenge was how to write a report, which fulfilled the two requirements:

1. The report (seen from a student's point of view) can be used to document the improvement work in the organization and at the same time demonstrates the student's competences required from the ECQA Job role description.
2. The report (seen form an evaluator's point of view) must be concrete enough to document the student's competences – and if the competences are not used in the improvement work, the report must demonstrate that the student understands the competence and can describe how it should be used if necessary.

The question was, if the structure in the Job role description was usable for the students as a template for the report and for the evaluator as a tool for evaluation.

You can find links to the relevant ECQA pages in references [4, 5].

4 Approach

It was not a very well-considered decision we took at the training course – more a practical decision. If the evaluator should be able to perform the evaluation during a minimum use of time, the report must have a structure, which matches the units and elements in the Job role description.

The ECQA Job role description was presented for and discussed with the students, and they found it interesting and could see it was relevant in relation to their education. They also accepted to use it as a template for the report (Table 1).

A requirement for the report was also a size not less and not much larger than 20 pages. The very good question was how well the template would do during the writing, which the students had 3 weeks to complete.

Table 1. ECQA Unit and Elements for the SPI Manager Job Role description

Unit 1: PI Involvement and Commitment Issues
Element 1: PI Team-working Skills
Element 2: Multicultural PI Teams
Element 3: Organizational Culture Influencing PI
Element 4: Modern Group Motivation Techniques for PI
Unit 2: Improvement Models
Element 1: Process and Life Cycle Models
Element 2: Process Improvement Models
Element 3: Process Design & Process Description Models
Unit 3: Managing Process Improvement
Element 1: Supporting Top Manager for Organizational Change Management
Element 2: PI Drivers Analysis
Element 3: Alignment of PI Goals to Business Goals
Element 4: Process Measurement, Data Collection and Analysis
Element 5: PI Leadership
Unit 4: Implementation
Element 1: Planning Improvement
Element 2: Deployment of PI
Element 3: Reporting SPI & Awareness Creation
Element 4: Experience and Good Practice Sharing

5 Example 1

The next two sections gives two examples from one of the students at the training course, Karsten Kristensen Back. The only difference from the report [7] is, that the organization Karsten has worked for is anonymous. Example 1 is the Unit Improvement Models: Element 2: Process Improvement Models. In Sect. 7 Karsten Kristensen Back gives his experience on how it was to use the SPI Manager Job role Unit and elements as the content of the report.

In Table 2 is the description of the ECQA SPI Manager unit: "Improvement Models" second element "Process Improvement Models". Here you can see the relevant performance criteria (PC) that defines what the student must know be capable of.

Table 2. ECQA SPI Manager Job role Unit 2, Element 2

Unit 2: Improvement Models: Element 2: Process Improvement Models		
17131	SPI.U2.E2.PC1	She/he knows the established models of SPI, their content, outcomes and their structure
17132	SPI.U2.E2.PC2	She/he knows the most common elements of the established SPI models
17133	SPI.U2.E2.PC3	She/he knows the success factors of the most common SPI models
17134	SPI.U2.E2.PC4	She/he knows implications of having products on the market on the enterprise
17135	SPI.U2.E2.PC5	She/he can estimate the efforts necessary to transform a prototype into a product

Next chapter 5.2 is an example for the student report [7]. Here you can follow how the competences are demonstrated in use – and if not, how they are explained to a degree where the student show how well he knows or would use the competence.

Unit 2: Improvement Models: Element 2: Process Improvement Models

The SPI Manifesto recommends that, in PI, models are used according to the organization's objectives and needs, and that part of different models can be used to resolve specific challenges ([8] Pries-Heje & Johansen, 2010). The process in the organization has been built on that specific principle, even if the PDCA cycle, based on Total Quality Management, was the dominating process improvement model. The most common, internationally used models are CMMI® and ISO/IEC 15504 (SPICE). Only parts of these models have been used in the process improvement at the organization, and this is because of the fact that this is a rather small-scale process improvement, whereas SPI projects are normally large-scale, organization-wide change initiatives.

The ImprovAbility^{TM} model (part of ISO/IEC 33014; based on SPICE), for instance, was applied as an initial check in the PDCA cycle to gather facts on company visions and goals, to analyses and deduce abilities, to compile recommendations, and finally: to recommend improvements on the tactical and operational levels of ISO 33014. We learned from our qualitative interviews and the ImprovAbility^{TM} assessment shown in Figs. 1 and 2 below that the organization has challenges within three foundation parameters: Organizational culture, Knowledge management, and Management competence. Furthermore, they have challenges in one In use parameter: Deployment strategy and in one Projects parameter: Project competence and knowledge.

Figure 1 below shows the results of the assessment, and Fig. 2 shows the parameter selection matrix that was filled in by the director at the organization – in order to decide what set of recommendations they found useful – and to tailor these recommendations

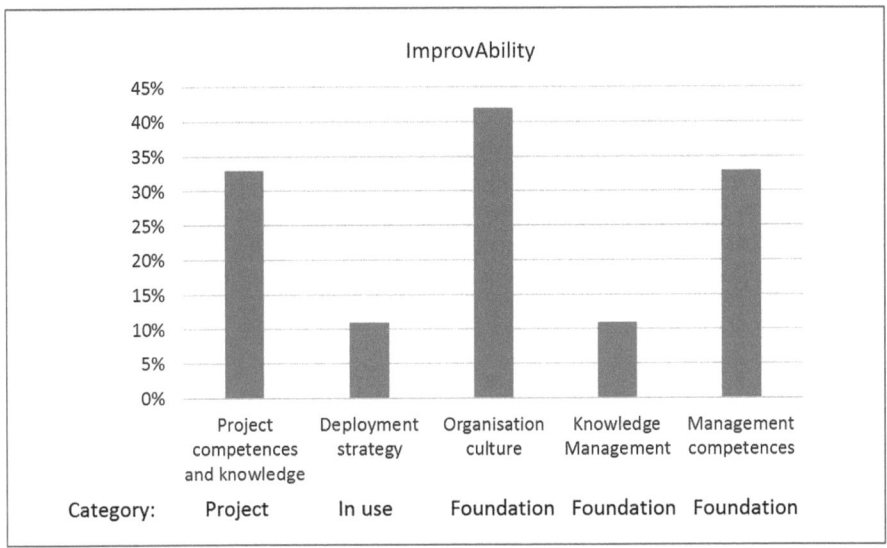

Fig. 1. ImprovAbility.

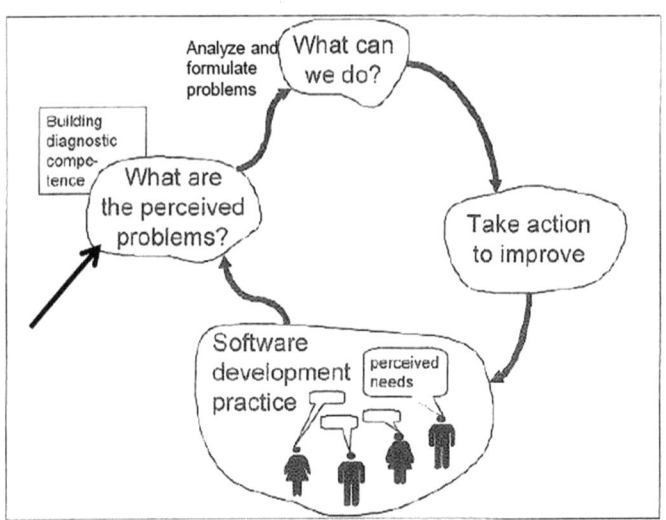

Fig. 2. Iproblem Orientated SPI.

to fit the organizational needs for improvement. These needs were investigated in the workshops that constituted intervention (addressed in another chapter in the report).

Based on this initial check, a problem-oriented approach seemed to be the most appropriate approach to PI in the organization ([9] Mathiasen et al., 2001). Relying on semi-structured interviews, rich-picture techniques known from Soft Systems Methodology, and an overall AR approach in the plan stage (cf. Deming), our main objectives were to give a diagnosis of existing problems, out-line different, competing viewpoints and find ways to implement new or better practices in the collaboration with project partners.

The perspective that has driven the entire process improvement project in the Organization can be characterized as the situated-balancing dimension of agenda types, because the focus has been on identifying different perceptions of the problems in the current procedure, and on making inquiry into understandings and values to decide what actions to improve and what constituted a desirable outcome ([10] Pries-Heje & Baskerville, 2010). In the plan stage of the PDCA circle, the SSM techniques have proven themselves to be valuable tools, as they work well within the approach and focus.

6 Example 2

Example 2 is another unit, element form the ECQA SPI Manager Job role description. In Table 3 is the description of the ECQA SPI Manager unit "Managing Process Improvement" first element "Supporting Top Manager for Organizational Change Management". Here you can see the relevant performance criteria that defines what the student must know be capable of.

Table 3. ECQA SPI Manager Job role Unit 2, Element 2

Unit 3: Managing Process Improvement: Element 1: Supporting Top Manager for Organizational Change Management		
17142	SPI.U3.E1.PC1	She/he must know the split of responsibilities between support and management
17143	SPI.U3.E1.PC2	She/he must appreciate what structural/hierarchical power is needed for a person to implement a given change
17144	SPI.U3.E1.PC3	She/he must know the business priorities of top management
17145	SPI.U3.E1.PC4	She/he must know how top management see PI to support business objectives
17146	SPI.U3.E1.PC5	She/he must know how PI supports top management priorities
17147	SPI.U3.E1.PC6	She/he must know which process measures that will be most valuable for top management

Next is an example from the student report [7]. Here you can follow how the competences are demonstrated in use – and if not, how they are explained to a degree where the student show how well he knows or would use the competence.

Supporting Top Manager for Organizational Change Management

As mentioned before, the organization is a very small organization where top management and employees are in contact on a daily basis and work very closely together. Because of this, it has been quite easy to involve the top management in the interventions, which in itself has been a huge advantage for supporting the top management for organizational change and for "managing the organizational change in [the] improvement effort" ([8] Pries-Heje & Johansen, 2010: 14).

The Action Research approach also gave many opportunities in that respect, as the foundation and the team of researchers have worked closely together and produced and analyzed learning outcomes together, for instance when talking about the strategic game plan in intervention 5. In creating the strategic game plan and describing the vision of the PI, a constructive dialogue about how PI supports top management priorities was created. In addition, in the intervention with the organization, we have talked a lot about the business priorities of the top management when designing our PI.

Not only do the interventions in themselves seem to be advantageous in supporting the top manager because of the management involvement and commitment in the interventions. The clan culture characteristics of teamwork and cohesion in the organization also encourage support of the top manager, as they have a relationship built on trust. As we would assume that clan culture is also positively related to support of the top manager because of this relation of trust and cohesion, we would also assume that the clan culture provides a secure foundation for a person to implement the change we are aiming for in the organization.

Seen from a CMMI perspective, these conditions have especially had a positive effect on process and product quality assurance (PPQA), because both staff and management have been in direct con-tact and dialogue about both process and the typology tool that was the output artefact of the PI initiative. Speaking about management in the CMMI model, especially project planning (PP), risk management (RSKM), and project monitoring and control (PMC) have been positively associated with the AR design of the PI initiative, because researcher and researched (both the top management and staff members) have worked so closely together in managing the change initiatives. Integrated Project Management (IPM) has been positively associated with the interventions to some extent, but one has to take into account that only part of the stakeholders has been involved in the change initiative. Decision analysis and resolution have partly been touched upon in intervention 7, where open observation was a method to formally evaluate the process, but alternatives were not really identified in that formal evaluation. Interventions 6 and 7 were ways to provide a CHECK/ACT of the output artefact and will be elaborated on when process measurement is described below.

7 Discussion and Next Steps

If we look at the requirements for the report in Sect. 3, we would like to discuss if the content of the report in a more general way could be used to document improvement work in an organization – maybe as a kind of checklist.

The best answer for this would be to ask the different stakeholders, which is done in the following chapters, starting with the student.

7.1 Seen from a Student Point of View - Karsten Kristensen Back

I attended the course of "Process Improvement – Advanced" at module 3. Applying the values and principles of the SPI Manifesto as well as the SPI Manager Job Role description was an eye-opening experience. In the process of writing the report, it was interesting to experience how theory about classic project management, change management theory, and process improvement theory join forces in the job role descriptions and together provide an effective toolbox for managing Process Improvement in an organisation.

The job role descriptions constitute a valuable framework for both documenting and evaluating my SPI initiative in the organisation. Even though I found most of the descriptions universal, I also experienced that the job role description for managing multicultural teams was not applicable in my particular context. However, it was useful to reflect on possibilities of managing multicultural teams if this organisation had multicultural teams – and the Master in Project Management and Process Improvement provides an excellent basis for that kind of reflection.

That the descriptions of personal competences in the job role descriptions are accompanied with short, precise information also provides a useful checklist for completing the report and documenting any PI initiative, as it's quite easy for the student to understand how a PI initiative can be characterised as successful.

7.2 Seen from a Trainer Point of View – Jørn Johansen

I was the trainer at module 3 together with Jan Pries-Heje. I was responsible for the training including e.g. ECQA SPI Manager Job role, ISO/IEC 33014 Guide for process improvement [6] and maturity assessments in organizations.

My experience was, that the students easily understood the ECQA SPI Manifesto Job role, and found it natural that they could be able to demonstrate the addressed competences.

It was not my job to evaluate the reports, but I took part in the RUC examination, before which I had read the reports. I was impressed. The reports seemed from my point of view to give a coherent description of the improvement work the students have done in their organizations, and also demonstrate how they have worked with the taught competences in the training course.

7.3 Seen from an Evaluation Point of View – Morten Korsaa

I was by the ECQA organization chosen as the evaluator and found the report interesting to read and the structure gave a natural grouping of the information.

However, it was not a straight relation between the chapters and the relevant information for assessing the performance criteria. Often positive aspects where demonstrated in other chapters that was relevant for the assessment, but the benefit from the overall structure made it easy to manage. The information flow in the report did not suffer much from the structure, even though the structure was not made for this purpose. Maybe changing a little on the order of elements would improve this. To be considered.

Compared with other evaluation cases, where the structure was not given as part of the assignment, this approach was much more straight forward. I spent 1/3 of the time and I felt much more confident that I had captured the learnings of the student.

7.4 Seen from a Trainer and Evaluation Point of View – Tomas Schweigert

I frequently deliver trainings for the SPI manager Certification and do case study evaluations as well. I was not involved in the training and the evaluation described in this paper. From this independent perspective, I really agree with the idea to develop a case study template from the skill card. Experience from several evaluated case studies show, that, without a template candidates face difficulties to describe their work in the underlying SPI project in a way that shows their thoughts, plans and delivered work completely and that there where potential enrichments that were not delivered because of missing request. As an example, the question of national culture was often a missing point in the provided case studies, even if we know that also national culture must be considered when defining a PI project.

7.5 Seen from the Responsible for the Training – Jan Pries-Heje

As head of Studies for the Master in Project Management and Process Improvement I had some considerations before, and after. Before the training I worried about and considered two issues. First, would this be of interest to our students that typically are practicing project managers from many different organizations? I presented the idea to the students early and receive a very positive response. Especially they liked the idea of getting a formal certificate. Second, I worried about whether the level of knowledge was right for master-level students at a University? Here my answer was the addition of five state-of-the-art papers to the mandatory curriculum which made me certain that the level requirements were satisfied.

After the training took place we did two things. First, we had an oral exam to satisfy the formal exam requirements in the study regulations for the Master. Here 5 out 6 students passed and one failed. That is well within the acceptable. Second I followed with interest how many out of the 6 students that found the extra time required to make the report. The answer was 50% which was less than expected. However, it is quite understandable that it can be hard to find extra time on top of a full-time job and a half-time Master-study.

In conclusion, we will certainly offer this training again next year as part of the Master in Project Management and Process Improvement.

8 Conclusion

Many specialists have taken part in development of the ECQA SPI Manager Job role description as well as all the knowledge and experience in e.g. the SPI Manifesto and the ImprovAbiltiy^{TM} model, which is the basis for the Job role description.

The ECQA SPI Manager Job role is a kind of tool to structure all the knowledge presented in the SPI Manifesto, ImprovAbility™, maturity models, and so on, into a set of competences described in units and elements. Does it make this representation of competences useful as a template for a report about an improvement project? Can this be used as an evaluation of the learned competences for a student at a Master training course?

We can conclude, that the structure makes sense for the main stakeholders: the student and the evaluator – described in Sect. 7. For the student, it was a challenge to use the structure as a template for the report – but it gave a lot of learning, and it was possible.

For the evaluator, it was useful, because most of the competences was addressed in the report corresponding the units and elements, which made it much easier to score. We have used this report based method on 3 student evaluations and presented examples from one of the evaluations. The response form the 2 other students were more or less the same: It was difficult but made sense. We need to continue to use this method in the future for more evaluations to consolidate experience.

It would also be of interest if a student would take both the multi-choice and the report evaluation, which enable comparison of the two methods. The only problem in this is the quality of the questions in the multi-choice evaluation tool, which can disturb the conclusion.

Whether the structure in the ECQA SPI Manager Job role description can be used as kind of checklist for an improvement project – to check if the right competences are brought into play - is difficult to answer. But it appears to be feasible since the correct competence are more likely to succeed. If it is sufficient to look at competences may require a second study.

References

1. SPI Manifesto
2. ECQA SPI Manager training
3. ImprovAbility™ book
4. (ECQA homepage). http://www.ecqa.org/
5. (SPI Manager Job role hompe page). http://www.ecqa.org/index.php?id=37
6. ISO/IEC 33014:2013 Information technology – Process assessment – Guide for process improvement
7. ECQA Report, Karsten Kristensen Back, RUC, 16 December 2016
8. Pries-Heje, J., Johansen, J.: SPI manifesto. Version A 1.2.2010. In: European System & Software Process Improvement and Innovation (2010)
9. Mathiassen, L., Nielsen, P.A., Pries-Heje, J.: Learning SPI in Practice, pp. 3–21. Addison-Wesley, Boston (2002)
10. Pries-Heje, J., Baskerville, R.L.: 5 Design and management. In: Design Research: Synergies from Interdisciplinary Perspectives, p. 63 (2010)
11. Korsaa, M., Biro, M., Messnarz, R., Johansen, J., Vohwinkel, D., Nevalainen, R., Schweigert, T.: The SPI Manifesto and the ECQA SPI manager certification scheme. J. Softw. Evol. Process **24**(5), 525–540 (2012)

Experiences with SQIL – SW Quality Improvement Leadership Approach from Volkswagen

Richard Messnarz[1(✉)], Maik Sehr[2], Ingrid Wüstemann[2], Joachim Humpohl[3], and Damjan Ekert[1]

[1] ISCN GesmbH, Graz, Austria
{rmess,dekert}@iscn.com
[2] BOSCH Automotive Steering, Schwäbisch Gmünd, Germany
maik.sehr@bosch.com
[3] HELLA, Lippstadt, Germany
Joachim.Humpohl@hella.com

Abstract. SQIL stands for SW Quality Improvement Leader. This is a new schema by Volkswagen where improvement agents are trained at suppliers to trace the quality of the processes, the quality of the product, and a set of metrics to track the progress of the development. The idea is to create a synergetic collaboration between suppliers and Volkswagen. Volkswagen defined so called KGAS (Konzerngrundanforderungen Software, in English: Group Basic Requirements Software) requirements which extend the scope of Automotive SPICE by a number of consistency requirements for engineering. The SQIL knows these requirements, usually has an Automotive SPICE Assessor qualification and correctly interprets the VW additional criteria to coach the improvement programs.

Keywords: Improvement · KGAS · SQIL · Automotive SPICE®

1 The Need for an Extension of Automotive SPICE by Additional KGAS Criteria

Vehicles nowadays are not only understood as a set of components to be integrated but as a set of vehicle functions which are linked with sub-functions/features at component level [3]. A steering system, for instance, delivers the correct movement of the steering rack and angle position of wheels and sends the steering angle on the bus, the ESP uses this input (besides more inputs like speed, yaw rate, etc.) to slow down the inner wheels, the second axle steering system uses the steering angle to set a supporting steering angle at the second axle, the torque vectoring uses that input to speed up the outer wheels, the active damper system configures the right characteristic curve based on that steering angle, speed etc. to keep the car stable in the curve, and so forth. So it is usually not possible to assign one function to only one component. Vehicle functions define a sequence of component functions/features and provide a bus specification with defined messages and timing to support the real time sequence of interactions of component functions/features. For manufacturers it is important to manage this complexity, at VW this principle is called **FUN (function-oriented development)**.

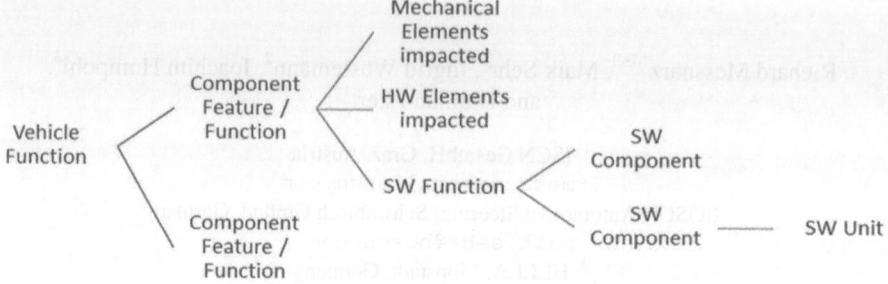

Fig. 1. FUN - Functional decomposition to create a consistent path from high to low level

In the next development step of ADAS (Autonomous Driving Assistant, test tracks are currently established, e.g. a test track at A2 in Graz, Austria) [9] cloud functions will be added to this schema so that the functional hierarchy will even get one level more complex. When driving a car on a specific road section, for instance, the cloud will deliver the typical steering angle, which other cars used, the steering angle of neighbouring cars, information if obstacles were identified by cameras of cars who went through the road section in the last 10 min, etc. The cloud can also set a defined speed and steering angle in full self-driving mode.

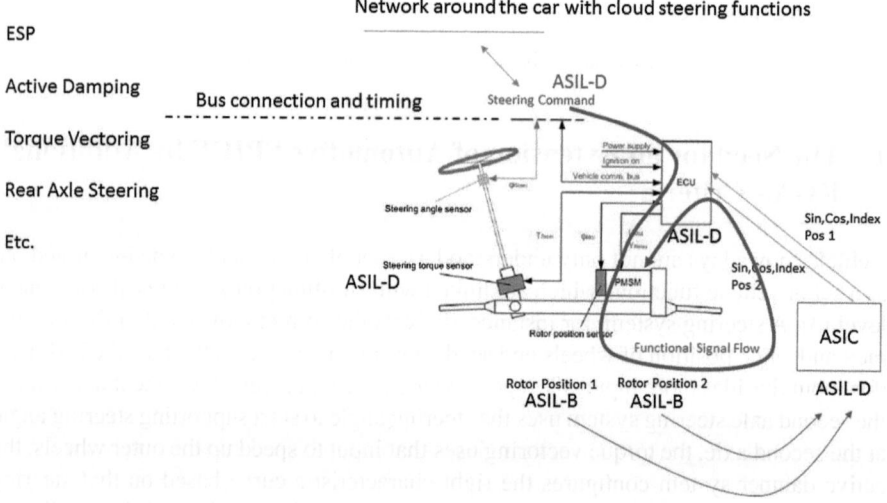

Fig. 2. FUN – Steering function in a self-driving networked car

In addition, the safety goal will change in a self-driving car environment (Fig. 2).

Safety Goal: Do not steer more than requested by the command. Commands then include a requested steering angle, this is translated in the ECU to a requested torque and the achieved angle position (internal steering angle) is then compared with the external requested steering angle [2, 4, 9] (Fig. 2).

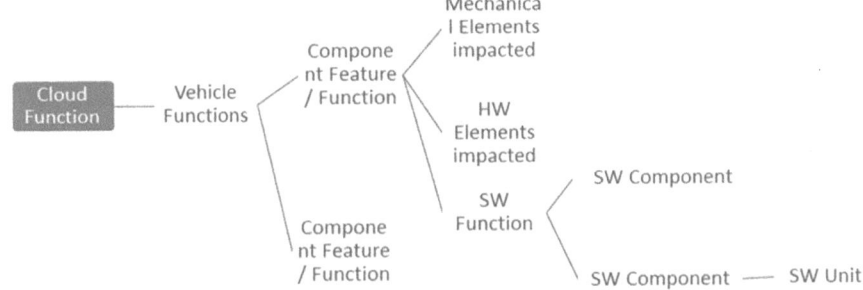

Fig. 3. FUN – Extended Functional decomposition including cloud functions

Why Functional Safety is not enough: If a system is developed by ASIL D (based on ISO 26262) the electronic and software has to prove an architectural metric, in form of a 10 FIT (Failure in Time rate based on operating hours for single point faults). 1 Fit is 10^{-9} and 10 FIT means 1 hazardous fault in 10^8 operating hours in the fleet.

Usually a passenger car is driven in the lifetime 10^4 h. So far ca. 35 million Golf cars were produced, makes $35 * 10^6$. Let us assume that only the last 2 generations of Golf cars are counted and we use approx. 10 million cars, i.e. $10 * 10^6 = 10^7$. The fleet has then $10^4 * 10^7 = 10^{11}$ h. That means that even when developing the whole design based on ASIL – D requirements 10^3 (1000) hazardous faults would appear in the field with that fleet size. Therefore VW needs a rigorous design approach which even extends the scope of Automotive SPICE and functional safety [2, 5–9].

The Quality of the Requirements Drives the Quality of the System: In KGAS (version 3.0, from 3.11.2015, [3]) there are a number of requirements about how to describe a requirement, extending the scope of Automotive SPICE. The underlying idea is that requirements are verifiable (clear input condition and result that can be tested), atomic (e.g. clear functional decomposition), unambiguous (e.g. no different interpretations possible), measurable, etc. Also certain attributes for the analysis are required by KGAS, such as risk (e.g. assigned ASIL level), feasibility (feasibility is described in the new base practice "Evaluate" in Automotive SPICE 3.0, with guidance in the VDA yellow book for the interpretation of ASPICE 3.0).

KGAS examples:

- KGAS_3193: All requirements must be evaluated in terms of risks and feasibility.
- KGAS_3247: All requirements must be unambiguous.
- KGAS_3248: All requirements must be self-consistent.
- KGAS_3249: All requirements must be understandable.
- KGAS_3250: All requirements must be feasible.

Moreover, KGAS asks you to formulate requirements with a clear IF <condition> THEN <event> syntax that helps to fulfil the above mentioned criteria.

KGAS example: KGAS_3267: Each specification of system and software requirements and software as well as system and software elements and components must follow a defined schema (e.g. [Condition] [the system or software or component] [shall or must do] [action or procedure or interface requirement]).

A Strategy assures that all engineers work towards the same process goals: n VW assessments, it is important to present a how-to-guide or process plan document with a strategy per process. Meanwhile a VDA yellow book [10] (1st edition, February 2017) provides guidance about how to rate the strategy base practice in SWE.4 SW Unit Verification to SWE.6 SW Qualification Test, SYS.4 System Integration and Integration Test to SYS.5 System Qualification Test, SUP.1 Quality Assurance, SUP.8 Configuration Management, SUP.9 Problem Resolution Management, and SUP.10 Change Request Management processes. Example Checklist for SW Unit Test Strategy SWE.4 BP1:

Moreover, the Yellow book [10] defines dependencies so that down rating BP1 automatically leads to further down rating of other BPs (Base Practices) (Fig. 5).

The expectations for a software unit verification strategy cover these aspects:
a) A definition of the verification objects
b) A definition how specific requirements regarding verification and testing (e.g. test-specific stakeholder requirements, ISO 26262, HIS-Metrics, MISRA) are covered.
c) A definition of the methods for test case and test data development derived from the detailed design and the non-functional requirements (e.g. development of positive/negative tests, equivalence class analysis).
d) A definition of the methods and tools for static verification and for reviews
e) A definition of the test environment regarding each test method
f) A definition of the test coverage in relation to project and release plan
g) A definition of entry and exit criteria for the software unit verification
h) A documentation of sufficient test coverage of each test level, if the test levels (e.g. software qualification test, software integration test and unit test) are combined
i) An approach for the handling of failed tests, failed static verifications (e.g. justification for failed MISRA-check or compiler warnings) and review findings.

Fig. 4. VDA yellow book – Checklist for strategy underlying SWE.4 BP1

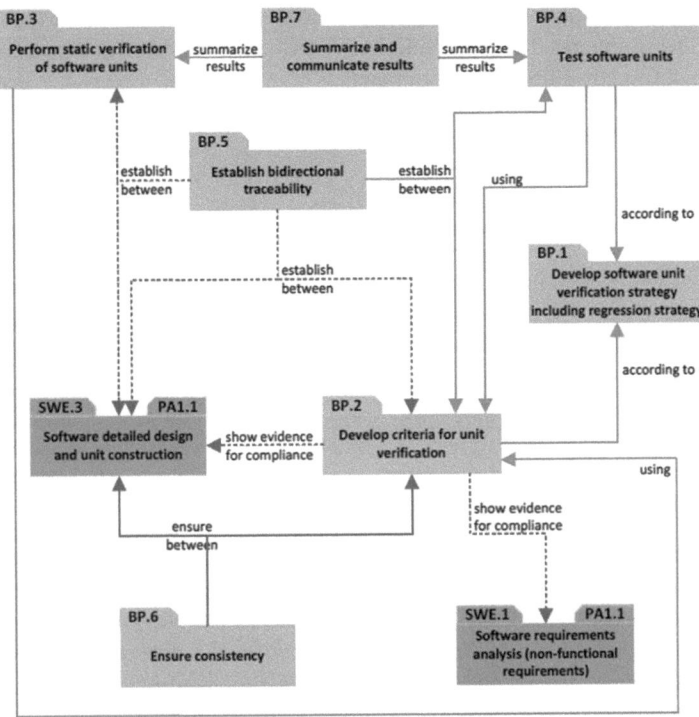

Fig. 5. VDA yellow book – Dependencies for Rating

Breaking down to a manageable size of a unit and traceability: In the KGAS [3] the idea is that, the linking concept (see Fig. 1) allows to trace SW requirements to a manageable size of a code block in the source code. Usually this would be e.g. a C-function or a block (with input – output transitions) in a model based development with defined maximum size of the source code.

KGAS examples: KGAS_3322: For software units with cyclomatic complexity smaller or equal than 10 bidirectional traceability between the unit (at least header level) and the software detailed design must be available. KGAS_3323: For software units with cyclomatic complexity greater than 10 bidirectional traceability between the software unit elements and the software detailed design must be available.

The cyclomatic complexity tells how many paths are possible through the software. Every if, else, else if, switch-case statement increases the cyclomatic complexity.

This figure therefore tells how many test vectors are needed as a minimum to cover all paths. The above definition means that a cyclomatic complexity 10 is manageable and the unit can be linked as a whole, when the unit is more complex the inside of the unit must be linked upward (with blocks inside the unit that again should be lower than 10 cyclomatic complexity).

There are many more such system engineering principles which are the root cause for KGAS requirements. In total, the KGAS Version 3.0 from November 2015 contains more than 400 such additional requirements.

2 The SQIL Report

The report of the software quality as part of the SQIL [3] activities should include:

(a) The fulfilment of the process quality according to Automotive SPICE®
(b) Findings of the requirements consistency check
(c) Metrics indicating the progress of the product development and test coverage.

The SQIL report should reported regularly (monthly) to the quality department of Volkswagen. In the next chapters, each of the activity will be explained in more detail.

2.1 Process Reviews and KGAS

Most of companies have already implemented some kind process reviews according to process checklists, where they check if the project activities are compliant with their process. In Automotive SPICE® 3.0 this is reflected with following base practice: *SUP. 1.BP3: Assure quality of process activities. Perform the activities according to the quality assurance strategy and the project schedule to ensure that the processes meet their defined goals and document the results.*

When performing process reviews, the additional KGAS requirements, can be incorporated in the existing checklists, lowering the effort of performing additional reviews against the KGAS. In the below example, the question referring to the project schedule is extended to fulfil the KGAS requirements:

Process review question: *The project schedule is updated weekly and consistent with the project milestones*

Relevant KGAS requirements:

- KGAS_3164: A schedule based on the project structure plan must be created
- KGAS_3176: The Schedule must be based on the effort according to the estimations of activities
- KGAS_3173: Each activity planned in the schedule must have a start date, end date, duration, and effort, degree of fulfilment, resources and dependencies
- KGAS_3182: The schedule must contain the software, hardware, customer, functional safety and quality assurance milestones.
- KGAS_3184: The schedule must not contain any activities with a duration longer than a working week
- KGAS_3597: The schedule must not contain any activities with an effort higher than a working week

Combined process review question: *The project schedule is updated weekly and consistent with the project, system and subsystem milestones. All activities are planned with an effort and duration of less than 40 h and contain the degree of fulfilment, an assigned resource and dependencies.*

The process reviews should be performed according to the KGAS_3477 at least each 2 months and reported to the quality department of Volkswagen.

2.2 Consistency Check of Requirements

With Automotive SPICE® 3.0 [1] the traceability and consistency of requirements are addressed by separate base practices. Where the traceability refers to the links between requirements, design, code, and test cases, the consistency addresses content and semantics [9]. In Fig. 6, the bidirectional traceability and consistency concept is shown:

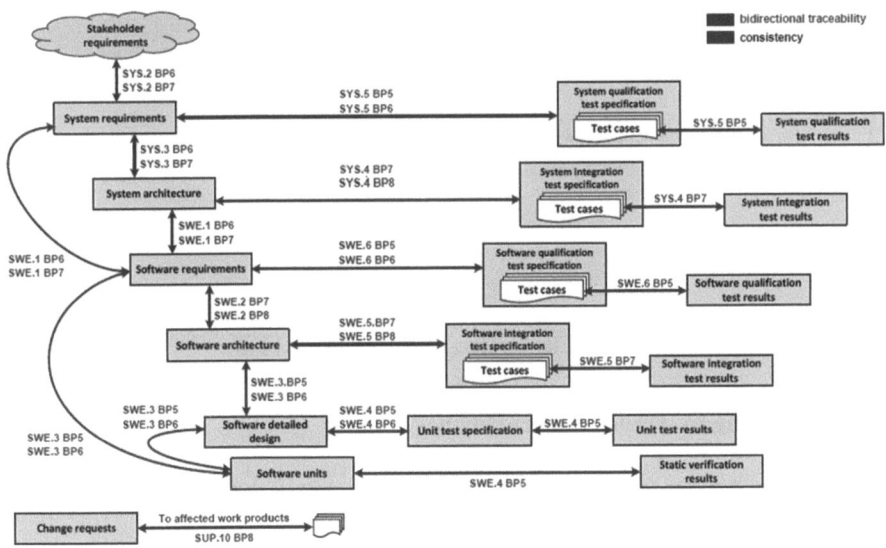

Fig. 6. Bidirectional traceability and consistency [10]

Traceability is usually measured and tracked by using metrics and trends, where the consistency of requirements can be checked only with reviews. In projects even with a high test coverage (100% traceability from requirements to tests), problems and bugs are found due to poor written requirements or test cases only covering parts of the requirements.

Therefore one of the goals of the SQIL review is also to check the content of the requirements, design, code and test cases and if they are consistent to each other. A typical review starts by selecting a customer function/sub-function in the customer requirements specification. The links are then followed to the requirements specification, architecture, and detail design documents to the code section, continuing with links to the test cases. The consistency from the code to the requirements is checked by selecting a function and following the links through to the initial requirement. Each step should be documented with a screenshot, the path to the work product and the identifier of the objects or work product (e.g. requirement SYS_ID182, detailed design for the function …). The findings should be then confirmed by an expert (Fig. 7).

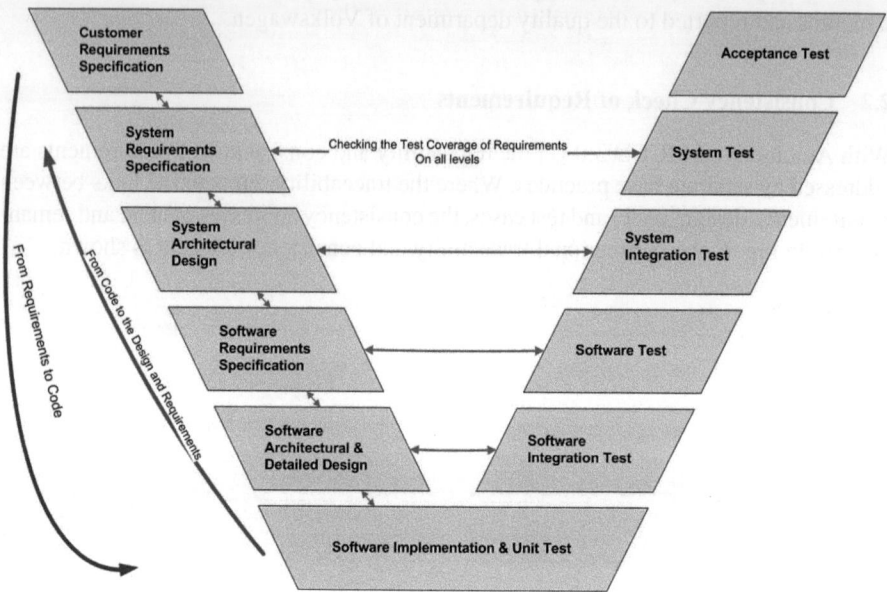

Fig. 7. Consistency check

2.3 Monitoring by Trends of Performance

Many of the metrics collected and reported to VW base on the traceability model in Annex D of Automotive SPICE 3.0. The annex D [1] describes the key concept criteria for understanding Automotive SPICE ® (see Fig. 6).

When working in VW projects a dashboard must be created, filled with data, and reported as a trend. Most of the data base on the traceability aspects in Automotive SPICE (see Fig. 4). The measurements are done monthly and once you have two measurement points you can calculate a vector, with three measurement points a trend can be estimated. The coverage metrics are rated with symbols such as:

↘	Performance is decreasing
↗	Performance is increasing
→	Coverage is the same as before

The SQIL collects the following data in reviews and evaluate the performance: Number based metrics:

- No. of System/SW Features planned
- No. of System/SW Features implemented
- No. of System/SW Features positively verified
- No. of Customer requirements implemented
- No. of Customer requirements implemented and linked to system requirements
- No. of Software related System requirements reviewed
- No. of SW related System requirements linked to system element(s)
- No. of SW related System requirements linked to SW requirements
- No. of SW requirements reviewed
- No. of SW requirements linked to SW elements
- No. of SW requirements linked to SW units
- No. of SW components linked to SW detailed design ↓
- No. of SW component interfaces specified in SW architecture
- No. of SW units in SW specified in detailed design
- No. of SW units implemented according to SW detailed design
- No. of SW units verified
- No. of SW units positively verified
- No. of SW units in SW detailed design linked to SW unit test cases
- No. of SW component interfaces verified
- No. of SW component interfaces positively verified
- No. of SW component interfaces specified in SW architecture linked to SW integration test cases
- No. of SW requirements verified
- No. of SW requirements positively verified
- No. of SW requirements linked to SW test cases ↓
- No. of System interfaces verified
- No. of System interfaces positively verified
- No. of System interfaces linked to System integration test cases
- No. of System requirements verified
- No. of System requirements positively verified
- No. of System requirements linked to System test cases ↓
- Number of all customer requirements

   Coverage based metrics for development process:

- Impl. Coverage: Customer Requirements
- Linking Coverage: Cust. Reqs. –> Sys. Reqs.
- Review Coverage: System Reqs.
- Linking Coverage: Sys. Reqs. –> Sys. Elements
- Linking Coverage: Sys Reqs. –> SW Reqs.
- Review Coverage: SW Reqs.
- Linking Coverage: SW Reqs. –> SW Arch.
- Linking Coverage: SW Reqs. –> Units
- Linking Coverage: SW components –> SW DD
- SW units impl. Specified in DD
- Impl. Coverage: SW units acc. DD spec.

Coverage based metrics for testing process:

- SW Units verified
- SW Units positively verified
- SW units in DD linked to test cases
- SW component interfaces verified
- SW component interfaces positively verified
- SW component interfaces linked to SW integration test cases
- SW Requirements verified
- SW Requirements positively verified
- SW Requirements linked to SW Test Cases
- System interfaces verified
- System interfaces positively verified
- System interfaces linked to sys. Integration test cases
- System Requirements verified
- System Requirements positively verified
- System Requirements linked to System Test Cases

In Volkswagen projects requirements are grouped to features (most suppliers called it function; e.g. lane assist function of a steering system) and the performance per function/feature is tracked. Figure 8 shows an actual template for a functional performance evaluation used at BOSCH AS.

Function	Traceability	Technical Consistency	Trend
Function name X	●	●	↗
Path	Filter in DOORS for feature "X"		
Traceability		Checking the technical consistency	
not all safety critical requirements are analysed in the customer requirements and linked from the technical safety requirements.		Reviews have been performed, further reviws needed together with the safety manager	

Fig. 8. Performance Evaluation per Function/Feature

3 Experiences and Hints from Industry Partners

3.1 Bosch AS Experience with KGAS Implementation

Automating the Metrics is Important: BOSCH AS (Automotive Steering Systems) developed in the VW MQB project an automated Q-Report in 2010, which was then used in VW projects until 2013 and then rolled out to all projects in the company. The Q-report already contained the traceability and coverage metrics for requirements and test levels and has two variants. In the "released" report, only released requirements are counting and in the "development" report, all analysed requirements are counting.

From 2013 to 2016 the report has been further refined. The Volkswagen data are then generated from the data of the Q-report plus additional data from the development environment. Experience shows that such data must be automated so that 2-weekly or latest monthly a progress overview can be generated.

Achieving a High Level of Coverage by a Baukasten/Tool Kit: In the VW MQB project a Baukasten of requirements and design elements as been set up with a set of re-usable links. System functions have been agreed among all steering system variants and a re-usable mother of a system specification has been set up. System requirements are grouped by system functions. SW functions are defined in a Baukasten SW concept and SW functions relate to SW components and SW units. SW requirements have been grouped by SW functions. Also standard system test catalogues have been created for vehicle verification, test bench and HIL test and re-usable test specifications are linked with the requirements. Similar it works on SW level where for each SW function there is a directory with SW requirements, design requirements, HIL test specifications etc. and completely linked. If you select a function you drag all requirements, test specifications, etc. into the project (a child derived from a mother module).

This Baukasten is adaptable to different projects by a placeholder {..} concept where in the text of the requirement a measurable parameter (e.g. {max-voltage}) is named generically within brackets and in a data file the project enters the value (e.g. 30 V) and then the requirements specification generates the right text with the project specific value. This way the same specification in a generic way can be adapted by parameters. Also due to the Baukasten concept ca. 86% of links have been re-usable.

Tracking Safety and Non-Safety Coverage Separately: The development of steering systems with a servo motor is highly safety critical and it includes safety goals with an ASIL-D classification (highest possible safety integrity level in Automotive). The automated Q-report of BOSCH AS generates three types of trend metrics, one for the overall coverage, one for safety and one for non-safety coverage. This means that, for instance, for the system test coverage the Q-report displays the coverage of all system requirements as a percentage, the coverage of all safety classified (ASIL-A to ASIL-D) requirements in system test, and the coverage of non-safety relevant (e.g. with QM classification) system requirements.

This strategy is used to create a synergy between VW technical audits, functional safety assessments, and ASPICE assessments.

Using the Dashboard Strategy in all Projects as a Standard: The VW Dashboard was first introduced at Bosch AS in 2014. A large number of the VW Dashboard metrics have been taken directly from the Q-Report (developed in the VW MQB project in 2009 to 2013). It was possible to re-use a large number of metrics from the Q-report by small adaptions/changes of the Q-Report to provide the needed metrics to VW.

Currently BOSCH central quality is establishing a standard for a dashboard (BBM metrics) which will be used for all projects concern wide and agrees this dashboard with Volkswagen. In BOSCH AS first external SQILs were used in 2015, and since 2016 in

BOSCH AS internal SQILs have been trained to support the process and dashboard optimization, and more SQILs will be trained in 2017.

3.2 HELLA Experience with KGAS Implementation

Using the Dashboard and Trends to Track the Quality Performance: In HELLA the standard VW dashboard has been implemented and standard data and trends are reported monthly. Quality managers with an Automotive SPICE assessor background are trained as a SQIL and act as improvement coordinator in VW projects.

Some of the dashboard trends are explained in the below Figs. 9 and 10. However, these figures are only an example and do not display a real project. Figure 9 displays a feature coverage trend. In VW projects, the software and system requirements are assigned to features. Features are planned by integration releases and the maturity of features is tracked.

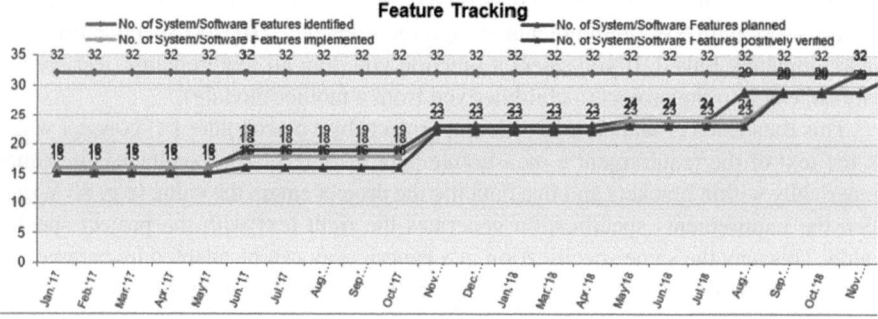

Fig. 9. Tracking the maturity of features/functions in total

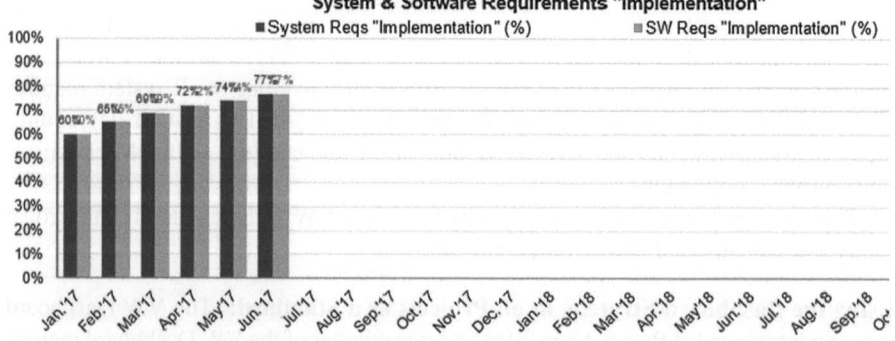

Fig. 10. Trend of systems and software requirements implementation

Figure 10 displays a trend of software and system requirements implementation coverage. In VW projects, this implementation trend is to be tracked to display the progress in the development.

Using a Process Compliance Coverage Trend:

In HELLA a standard process review tool is used to rate the compliance of each process in the project at least quarterly. Based on that tool a process coverage trend can be tracked. In addition, the process review checklist is based on ASPICE and additional VW specific KGAS questions.

4 Outlook

Volkswagen is currently promoting a new version of the dashboard concept, which defines the documentation required by SQILs. This includes:

1. Process Check
2. Consistency Check
3. Monitoring Metrics

Figure 11 shows a process check where the field WP Quality is linked with specific metrics in the dashboard. Project management, for instance is related to the customer requirements implementation and linking. The progress of plan is linked with reaching the agreed target coverage, and the trend field shows if the related metrics show an increase, decrease or no change in the performance.

Project overview / Main emphasis		SQIL Analyzed	WP Quality	Progress of plan	Trend
< TEXT >		Harveyball / %	red yellow green	red yellow green	→↗↘

Process overview A-SPICE (V2.5 / V3.0)		SQIL Analyzed	WP Quality	Progress of plan	Trend
MAN 3	Project Management	Harveyball / %	●/●/●	●/●/●	→↗↘
SUP 1	Quality Assurance	Harveyball / %			
ENG 2 / SYS 2	System Requirement Analysis	Harveyball / %			
ENG 3 / SYS 3	System Architetural Design	Harveyball / %			
ENG 4 / SWE 1	Software Requirement Analysis	Harveyball / %			
ENG 5 / SWE 2	Software (Architectural) Design	Harveyball / %			
ENG 6 / SWE 3	Software Construction / Software Detailed Design an Unit Construction	Harveyball / %			
SWE 4	Software Unit Verification	Harveyball / %			
ENG 7 / SWE 5	SoftwareIntegration / Software Integration and Integration Test	Harveyball / %			
ENG 8 / SWE 6	Software Test / Software Qualification Test	Harveyball / %			
ENG 9 / SYS 4	System Integration Test / System Integration and Integration Test	Harveyball / %			
ENG 10 / SYS 5	System Test / System Qualification Test	Harveyball / %			
SUP 8	Configuration Management	Harveyball / %			
SUP 9	Problem resolution Management	Harveyball / %			
SUP 10	Change Request Management	Harveyball / %			

Fig. 11. Tracking the Progress per Process

The concept of consistency check was described in Sect. 2.2 of the paper. In addition, the monitoring metrics have been listed in Sect. 2.3 of the paper.

5 Relationship with the SPI Manifesto

The SPI manifesto [11] has been developed in 2009 at an international workshop attached to EuroSPI 2009 in Alcala, Spain. It describes 3 values and 10 principles which make SPI really work.

The following principles of the SPI manifesto have a direct relationship with the SQIL approach.

5.1 Base Improvements on Experience and Measurement

Section 2.3 describes a number of metrics used to track the progress of a development project in the Automotive area (based on Automotive SPICE 3.0 and VW KGAS requirements).

5.2 Support the Organisations Needs and Vision

Section 1 of the paper describes a number of system engineering paradigm which are specific for working in Volkswagen projects. They reflect the understanding of the organisation when working in the organisation.

Some of them are (see Sect. 1):

- The FUN principle.
- The FUN principle will be extended with self driving cars.
- The Quality of the Requirements Understanding with clear KGAS criteria which criteria must be met.
- Etc.

In general the KGAS [3] requirements represent a VW (adapted for projects in this organisation) specific understanding of the needs when using Automotive SPICE.

5.3 Apply Risk Management

Section 1 of the paper describes the paradigm "Why Functional Safety is not enough" together with a risk calculation why the additional VW KGAS requirements are needed.

Also the monitoring approach and dashboard are used to display a progress trend and based on the trend a projected performance is calculated. The biggest risk (with a he financial impact) in Automotive projects is the delay of an SOP (Start of Production). This trend based metric approach allows projects to anticipate risks by projected trends and the illustration of expected performance.

5.4 Ensure All Parties Agree and Understand the Process

Section 2.1 of the paper describes the process reviews approach where quarterly reviews are done for all processes in scope (based on Automotive SPICE) and a process performance trend is created during the project lifetime showing the improvement in the processes until full coverage is reached.

References

1. Automotive SPICE 3.0, VDA AK13, July 2015. www.automotivespice.com
2. Messnarz, R., Kreiner, C.J., Riel, A.: Integrating automotive SPICE, functional safety, and cybersecurity concepts: a cybersecurity layer model. Softw. Qual. Prof. **18**(4), 13–23 (2016)
3. KGAS (Konzerngrundanforderungen SW, Group Basic Requirements Software, Version 3.0, Volkswagen (2015)
4. Kreiner, C.J., Macher, G., Riel: Integrating automotive hazard and threat analysis methods: how does this fit with assumptions of the SAE J3061?. Softw. Qual. Prof. **18**(4), 37–46 (2016)
5. Messnarz, R., Kreiner, C., Riel, A., Tichkiewitch, S., Ekert, D., Langgner, M., Theisens, D.: Integrating functional safety, automotive SPICE and Six Sigma – the AQUA knowledge base and integration examples. In: Barafort, B., O'Connor, R.V., Poth, A., Messnarz, R. (eds.) EuroSPI 2014. CCIS, vol. 425, pp. 285–295. Springer, Heidelberg (2014). doi:10.1007/978-3-662-43896-1_26
6. Kreiner, C.C., Messnarz, R., Riel, A., Ekert, D., Langgner, M., Theisens, D., Reiner, M.: Automotive knowledge alliance AQUA – integrating automotive SPICE, six sigma, and functional safety. In: McCaffery, F., O'Connor, R.V., Messnarz, R. (eds.) EuroSPI 2013. CCIS, vol. 364, pp. 333–344. Springer, Heidelberg (2013). doi:10.1007/978-3-642-39179-8_30
7. Messnarz, R., Kreiner, C.J., Bachmann, O., Riel, A., Dussa-Zieger, K., Nevalainen, R., Tichkiewitch, S.: Implementing functional safety standards - experiences from the trials about required knowledge and competencies (SafEUr). In: EuroSPI Conference on European Systems and Software Process Improvement and Innovation 2013, pp. 323–332 (2013)
8. Riel, A., Bachmann, V.O., Dussa-Zieger, K., Kreiner, C., Messnarz, R., Nevalainen, R., Sechser, B., Tichkiewitch, S.: EU Project SafEUr – Competence Requirements for Functional Safety Managers. In: Winkler, D., O'Connor, R.V., Messnarz, R. (eds.) EuroSPI 2012. CCIS, vol. 301, pp. 253–265. Springer, Heidelberg (2012). doi:10.1007/978-3-642-31199-4_22
9. Macher, G., Messnarz, R., Armengaud, E., Riel, A., Brenner, E., Kreiner, C.: Integrated Safety and Security Development in the Automotive Domain. SAE Technical Paper 2017-01-1661, USA (2017). doi:10.4271/2017-01-1661
10. VDA Yellow book, Automotive SPICE Guidelines, 1st edn. (2017)
11. The SPI Manifesto, EuroSPI 2009, Alcala, Spain (2009). http://2017.eurospi.net/images/Documents/spi_manifesto.pdf. Accessed 7 Jun 2017

Safety and Security

Need for the Continuous Evolution of Systems Engineering Practices for Modern Vehicle Engineering

Richard Messnarz[3], Alexander Much[4], Christian Kreiner[5], Miklos Biro[1(✉)], and Jenny Gorner[2]

[1] SCCH, Hagenberg, Austria
Miklos.Biro@scch.at
[2] KNOWIT, Göteborg, Sweden
[3] ISCN GesmbH, Graz, Austria
rmess@iscn.com
[4] ELEKTROBIT, Erlangen, Germany
Alexander.Much@elektrobit.com
[5] TU Graz, Graz, Austria
christian.kreiner@tugraz.at

Abstract. Cars of the future (ADAS – Autonomous self-driving assistant) will need to cover a number of new standards for mechatronic design and networking of the car in the cloud. This includes job roles for ISO 26262, IEC 61508 (functional safety), SAE J3061 (cybersecurity), etc. For instance, a car driving on a street will exchange information with neighbouring cars and learn the right steering angle, speed, etc. while the driver is using the car like a work place. Manufacturers plan to produce from 2030 only cars which have such a self-driving function incorporated. The design of new electric cars will require new infrastructures, new energy management, new battery concepts, and also new materials design (light weight and still resistant), and the job role pool will include these key skills as well. The production of cars will be with connected plants, robots to be programmed, and central production servers to coordinate the industry 4.0 type of production virtually across the world. And the new cybersecurity norm SAE J3061 will develop further in the next years because by moving the cars to the cloud and the production to industry 4.0 leaves Europe's industry vulnerable to attacks if this is not handled. Also the medical systems move towards an IoT (Internet of Things) approach where people receive implants which read out the data and transport them to the mobile which forwards the data to a medical service in the cloud where data are used by states and hospitals.

Keywords: Strategy projects · Vision of networked services · Change towards a service driven architecture in automotive and other domains like the medical device industry · AQUA · Safety · Security

1 The Ecosystems Layer Model

Figure 1 below illustrates an integrated layer model of eco systems that impact the future dependent vehicle design highlighting two aspects whose criticality is amplified by the current and forthcoming changes in the Industry 4.0 era. In our view, targeting safety [1–3, 5, 6, 8] means protecting the environment (including humans) from the system.

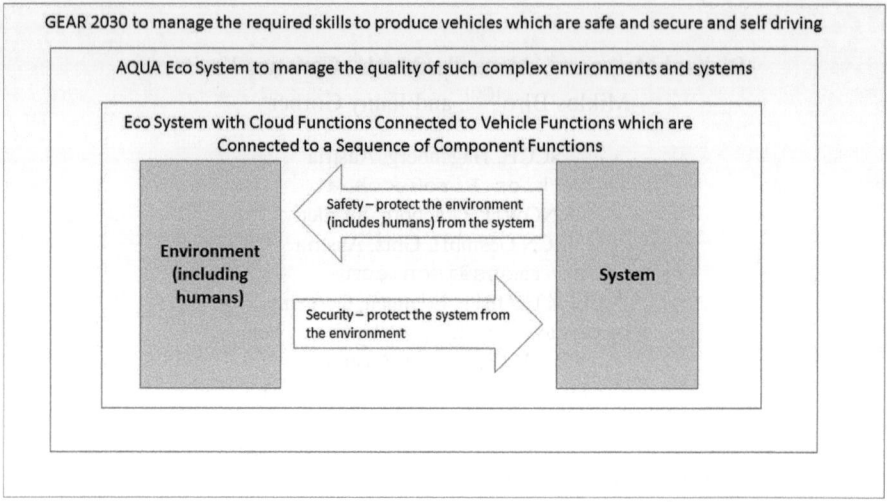

Fig. 1. Layers of ecosystems that impact the future dependent vehicle design

Targeting security [1, 4, 7] means protecting the system from the environment. Ecosystem with connected functions [5, 7]: The traceability schema will be extended to map cloud functions onto vehicle functions and further onto features of components in the car.

AQUA ecosystem [1–4, 9, 13, 18]: AQUA (Knowledge alliance for Quality in Automotive engineering) integrates different norms and standards related to Functional safety, Automotive SPICE, APQP, Cybersecurity to manage the complexity of the systems and to achieve quality, safety, and security in the vehicle. AQUA created a new job role of a quality engineer that can integrate these methods and standards.

Gear 2030 [23]: The initiative includes the European Automotive manufacturer association, the European Automotive supplier association, key players in Automotive education to develop the skills needed for future dependent vehicles in a complex ecosystem and environment as outlined in Fig. 1. However, Gear 2030 extends the scope with material design (in future light-weight materials are needed), energy management (new battery designs, new industry 4.0 networked production design, etc.) and so forth.

Systems engineering is an extensively developed discipline. In Automotive currently many of the systems engineering principles are re-invented, most of them transform proven in use principles to the connected and dependent vehicle domain.

New buzzwords are coming up and the issues and problems are similar to those identified before. In many cases, the Automotive industry needs to go back to the already working concepts, re-engineer and adapt them for the dependent vehicle ecosystems. New technologies are coming up but the approaches for solving the problems are essentially the same.

2 Existing Initiatives, Standards and Norms for the Ecosystem

The GEAR 2030 [23] initiative on EU level: The GEAR 2030 Human Capital Project Team was established to "Identify the impact on employment in the EU, prepare approaches for mitigating possible negative consequences and develop a strategy for ensuring that the necessary skills will be available in 2030" for the EU automotive industry. The work has assessed the landscape of existing initiatives across the EU, looked at what trends will impact the sector up to 2030 and developed recommendations and actions to support the development of the automotive sector and the future skills required to ensure its continued success.

The automotive industry is undergoing technological change at an unprecedented rate. As it moves towards a new era facing new challenges, human capital will be the driver of the change. People's skills lead the evolution of vehicle manufacturers, suppliers, after-market, and service providers. These actors of the automotive value chains can only succeed with the right skilled workforce.

GEAR 2030 has support from the ACEA European Automobile Manufacturers' Association and the CLEPA European Association of Automotive Suppliers. Results are restricted for the purpose of supporting the competitiveness of European manufacturers.

The AQUA-ecosystem [1–4, 9] was first developed in the AQUA (Knowledge alliance for Automotive Quality) skills alliance where a tool kit with training materials was developed to teach and implement functional safety (ISO 26262, IEC 61508), Automotive SPICE®, and Six Sigma in an integrated approach. This integrated previous ECQA (European Certification and Qualification Association, www.ecqa.org) job roles such as ECQA certified functional safety manager, ECQA certified lean six sigma yellow/orange/green/black belt, and the INTACS certified assessor education). Based on AQUA further projects were performed to developed the ECQA certified Automotive engineer (mechatronics), the Automotive Quality Universe project where Automotive engineering universities joined forces and teach the knowledge at master level (TU Graz, FH Joanneum, FH Düsseldorf, TUOstrava, Grenoble INP).

The SOQRATES (www.soqrates.de) [1–4, 9, 24] initiative was founded in 2003 and leading Automotive and electronic suppliers from Germany and Austria established task force teams to work on new challenges like functional safety, cybersecurity, traceability throughout the entire life cycle etc. Outcomes from those working parties are best practice models about how to implement functional safety or cybersecurity, what is seen as state of the art, and how the different standards can be integrated into one engineering life cycle.

- Various standards and guidelines have been developed to address these issues.
- Quality and Safety Related Standards and Guidelines (see [7]):

The most essential approach for ensuring product quality in software engineering is an established quality management system, which is usually based on ISO 9001 and for the automotive domain additionally on ISO/TS 16949. Well established in the automotive domain are process audits which are based on ISO 12207 [14], ISO 15504 [17] and Automotive SPICE [25]. Basically all related software engineering standards for software engineering, safety and security need to be aligned with established quality management and process assessment procedures.

For coding guidelines usually the MISRA-C [26, 27] and MISRA-C++ [28] standards are used for electronic control units. For large infotainment systems CERT-C and ISO17961 [19] is used if security requirements are allocated to the system.

In modern vehicles the number of functions realized by E/E/PE (Electrical/Electronic/Programmable Electronic) systems which are safety-relevant is rising. During the last years, ISO 26262 [20] has been introduced in development organizations, a standard which is derived from IEC 61508 [10]. Engineering and quality organizations have found ways to merge the established quality management and audit approaches with the requirements from those safety standards. Technical risk management is performed in safety-related projects in the form of safety analysis and safety cases in ISO 26262.

Security Related Standards and Guidelines (see [7]): There is no commonly accepted automotive security standard but there are established standards in other domains. In avionics, the DO-326A is a risk-based standard for security processes on a system level which details the relation to other standards in avionics. In the automation domain the standard series IEC 62443 can be used as reference, however the work on these documents is still ongoing. For IT systems the standard series ISO 27000 [21, 22] is established and can be taken as reference. There are many specific guidelines or even checklists from NIST, FIPS, BSI and others.

Next to standards and guidelines, there are a large number of open or quasi standards for security, such as the Microsoft SDL [29], OpenSAMM [30] and others. All these approaches are valid input for future standardization for automotive security.

In the last years many research programs for automotive security have been performed, such as EVITA [31], HEAVENS [32] and others. In January 2016, a working group on cybersecurity at SAE International (initially established as Society of Automotive Engineers) published their results in the form of a guidebook [4, 33]. Its aim is "to provide a cybersecurity process framework and guidance to help organizations identify and assess cybersecurity threats and design cybersecurity into cyber-physical vehicle systems throughout the entire development lifecycle process". It is not meant to be a standard or normative document. It provides "high-level guiding principles", "information on existing tools and methods" and "the foundation for further standards development". The primary domain is the automotive domain and the motivation is the connected car with its increased attack surface.

As there are already many standards and practices in the automotive domain a new guidebook can only be established by taking these into account. Hence the life-cycle of development processes is based on the safety processes as defined in the ISO 26262. For a quick introduction on the high-level similarities, see e.g. [34]. As system, safety and security experts need to interact and synchronize at defined mile-stones, sharing a common life-cycle is essential.

Established standards for software development focus mainly on the development phase as the interaction between different roles is more frequent. The SAE J3061 follows the ISO 26262 and many public security approaches and extends into the operations phase by defining maintenance activities, an incident response process and a field monitoring process.

Similar to the life-cycle of the ISO 26262 the life-cycle of the SAE J3061 is divided into a concept phase, product development at system level and then splits into the hardware and software levels. The output of the concept phase are defined cybersecurity goals, threat and risk assessment and functional cybersecurity requirements. This pattern then repeats on each level with added risk analysis and sometimes additional verification or validation activities.

As the guidebook is meant to be high-level, only a rough description of possible steps, using defined methods, is detailed. A large part of the guidebook is taken up by annexes and the process descriptions often point there. Most annexes contain a collection of techniques, references to methods and other established cybersecurity standards, examples and publicly available research programs. The working group of SAE International did a great job at collecting and summarizing such a wealth of information.

The annexes not only contain pointers to other material, but they also extend to a classification or a discussion of their relevance to the automotive domain, including a summary of publicly accessible results of research programs and even tools which are potentially relevant for the domain. An interesting aspect is that a lot of standardization has been done in the US, whereas nearly all research programs have been conducted in Europe. There seems to be a need for closer cooperation on the topic.

As one of the aims of the guidebook is to serve as "[…] foundation for further standards development" it needs to be mentioned that automotive organizations have started the process for a new work item proposal in the working group ISO/TC 22 "Road Vehicles" for a standard about "Automotive Security Engineering".

3 Change in Architectural Frameworks

This chapter outlines a number of key factors that will change the future design and architectural frameworks of systems.

Principle: A Car Is Understood as a Set of (Safety Critical) Signal Flows/Functions [4, 5]: The interfaces, functions and signal flows and safe states will change when connecting the car to the cloud using an ADAS (Autonomous Driving Assistant) program.

In the current system design the safe electric steering systems are limiting the torque so that not more torque than requested by the driver can be put onto the motor by the ECU. Therefore it is clear that the torque sensor is ASIL-D as well (see Fig. 3).

A command can come from the network (networked car) or from a central ECU in the car, and then even the safety goal will change.

> *Safety Goal: Do not steer more than requested by the command. Commands then include a requested steering angle, this is translated in the ECU to a requested torque and the achieved angle position (internal steering angle) is then compared with the external requested steering angle.*

Also the safe state will change, because in ADAS full implementation (at least from 2030) it is expected that we cannot give the control back to the driver any more. Therefore 6 to 12 phase e-motors are needed to continue driving and safe state would become a kind of limp home mode to the garage with the car passenger (formerly a driver).

Another bigger change is the distribution of ASIL values. While in earlier solutions the typical scope of a supplier of the external steering angle sensor was not in scope, and ASIL-D rating related to the internal steering angle provided as a message on the bus, in ADAS the functional signal flow will change as outlined in Fig. 2.

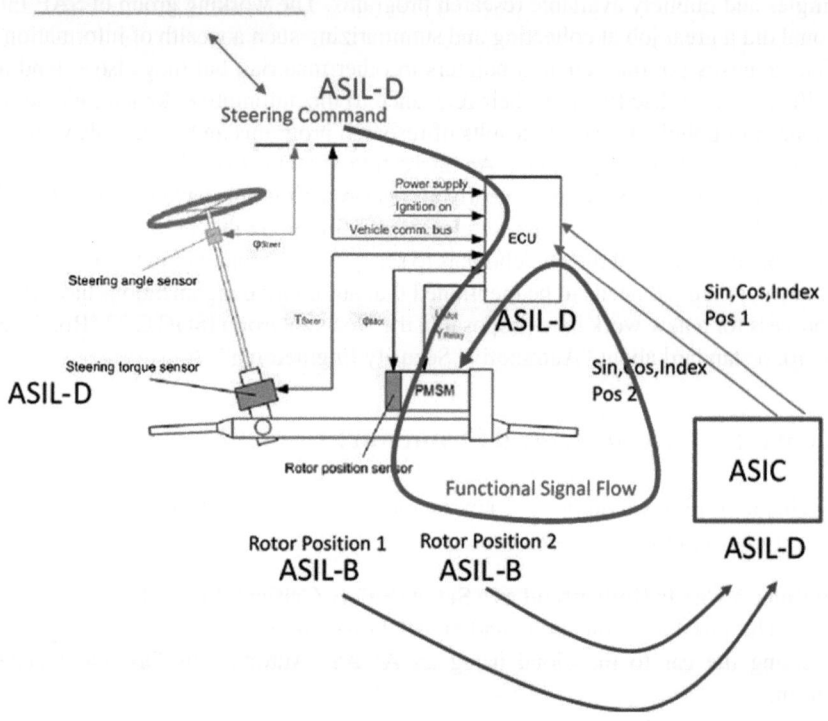

Fig. 2. Future ADAS changing the safety critical signal flow

Principle: A Car Becomes Part of a Service Architecture [1, 5, 7]: In a connected ADAS scenario, cars are connected to global services (see Fig. 3) as part of their infrastructure. Connection technologies base on established mobile internet technologies, base stations and mobile antenna built along the motorways and servers and functions in the cloud.

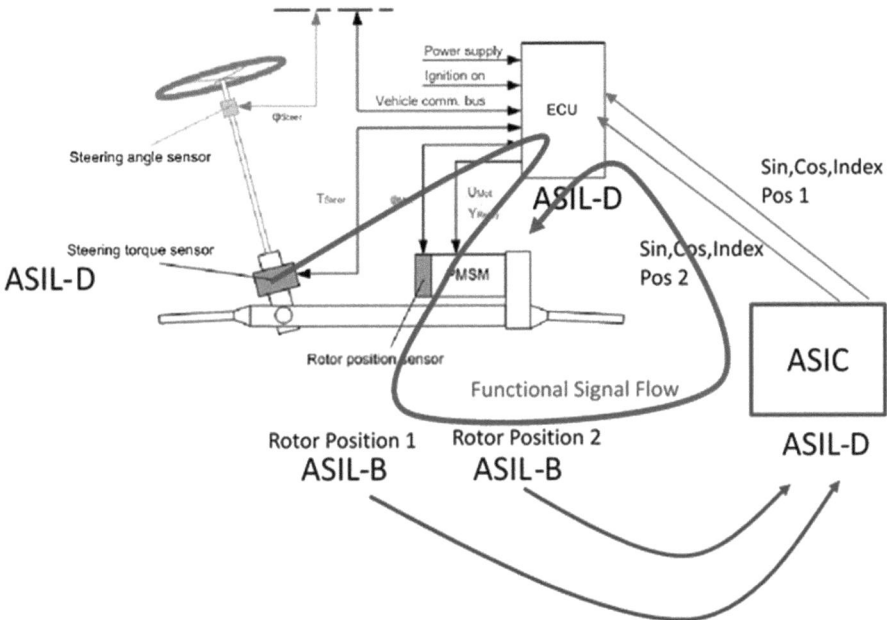

Fig. 3. Typical safety critical signal flow in current system designs

Applying this service for the example in Fig. 2 a car driving a certain road part receives information about the typically selected steering angle in this section of the road, any obstacles recently reported by cameras of cars, the steering angle of neighboring cars, and adjusts speed and steering angle accordingly.

A future car will have (in 3 years 8 cameras, in 2030 32 cameras are planned) a large number of cameras with overlapping sight, cameras recently get developed with ASIL B (D) and 2 overlapping cameras will deliver an ASIL D safe evaluation of the presence of an obstacle. So many cameras will be built in that for every space around the car there are minimum 2 overlapping ASIL B(D) cameras.

Moreover ECUs will combine lidar, radar, cameras and depending on the speed of the car the car will automatically set a specific priority in using the signals. At high speed, for instance, the cameras are too low and the radar will be priority 1 while at low speed and medium speed the cameras will take priority 1.

A car will even be connected to a Google User account, credit car account (the more you pay the more functions can be configured) and user profiles can be configured.

In medical device industry [11] Telecom industry [12] develops a new chip that can be implanted into people, that reports blood pressure, identity, pulse, alcohol in blood, etc. to the mobile that can exchange data with the car. The pure presence of the person will open cars, doors etc. or a certain alcohol in the blood will automatically disallow the driver to take over any of the functions (Fig. 4).

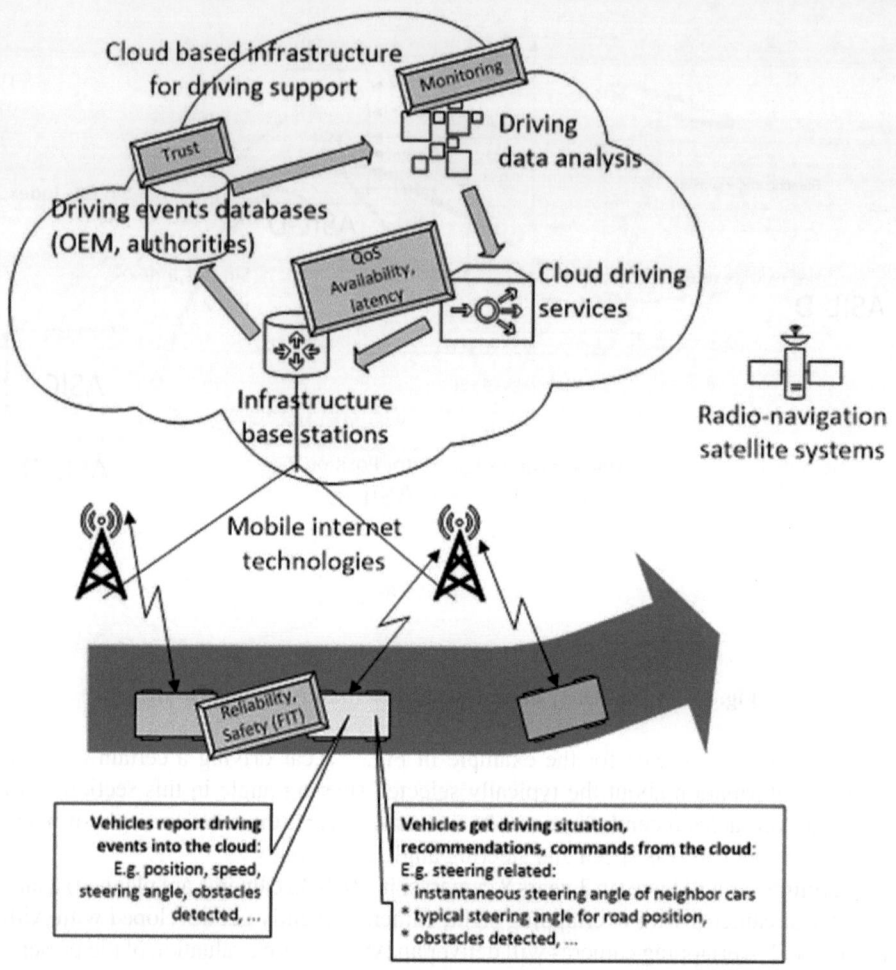

Fig. 4. A car is part of an overall service infrastructure

Principle: A Complex Set of Skills and Industries are Interconnected in the Future [23]: The GEAR 2030 initiative mentioned before widens this future service and networked functions vision by a vision of interconnected disciplines to create a complete new service model for Automotive industry.

They also include e.g. energy related associations (developing new fuel concepts, battery management, North Sea energy plants with new technology at sea ground level), material design (new light weight but stable materials for cars), technology for industry 4.0 automation, programming of robots and control via production servers (managing it world wide), etc. and the mechatronic function based system is only part of the overall picture.

Principle: Layer Models are Needed for Managing Cybersecurity [4, 5, 7]: A secure platform (see Fig. 5) is usually built around a special-purpose security hardware and on top of this a soft-ware solution. In the automotive domain the hardware part is often realized as a hardware security module (HSM) which supports hardware protected secure key storage and cryptographic functions and is hardened against tampering. Nowadays many silicon vendors offer an HSM as part of their standard control units. This means that the software solution can be based on established software architectures such as the OSEK or AUTOSAR [ASR15] standards.

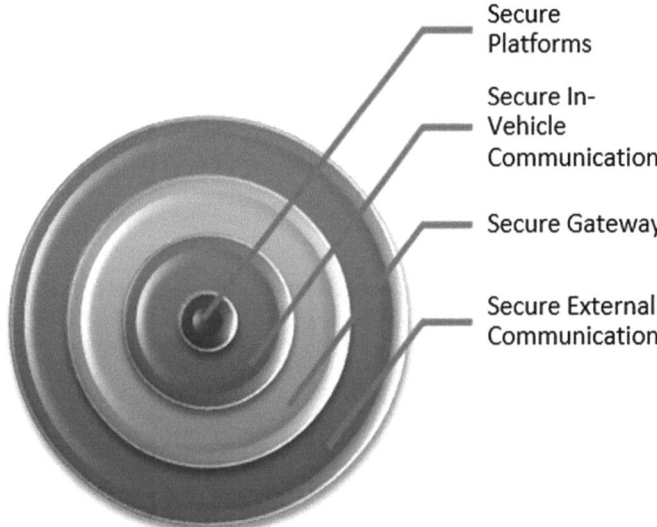

Fig. 5. Cybersecurity layers in vehicle design

Principle: New Static and Dynamic Design Views Needed: Such layer models lead to system engineering principles of Automotive DEfense Layers as outlined in Fig. 6 below.

After the attacker (layer 1) retrieves access data, he can send commands on the bus (layer 2), these can influence an ECU behavior (layer 3), and in layer 4 the attacker eventually tries to control the vehicle behavior. On each interface between the layers, defense mechanisms are placed. Only if the attacker can pass all layers, he can facilitate an effect on the overall vehicle level. Figure 6 provides some examples of such assignments. And functions (impact chains across cloud functions and vehicle functions and component features) can be modelled and dynamic signal flows can be tracked and controlled (see Fig. 7).

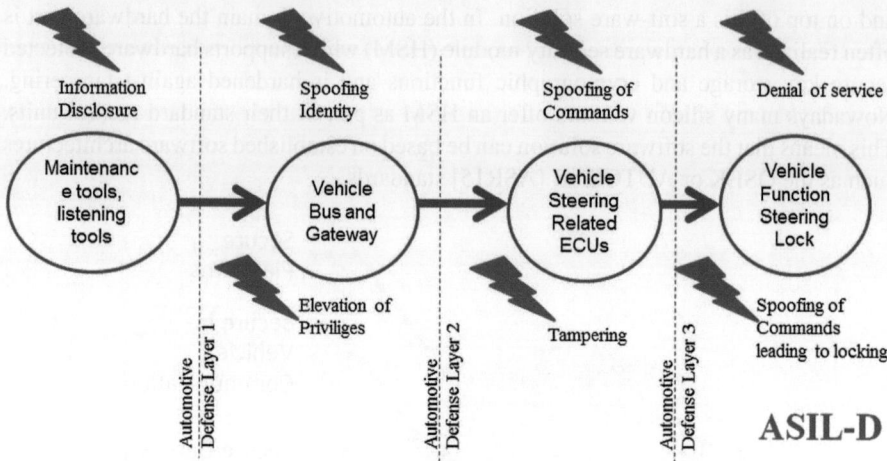

Fig. 6. Static architecture of the cyberattack defense model (AutoDLs)

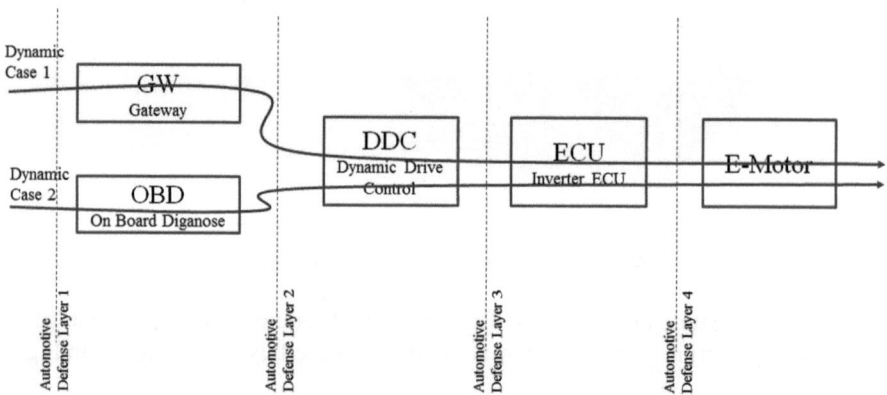

Fig. 7. Modelling functional attacks chains across the layers

4 Major Environmental Changes Expected

New Commercial Models Need: In the past people bought cars. Nowadays they lease cars. In future users will lease functions and have a user profile and cars will be provided as a service and automatically (self driving, configured with the right user profile) appear at the door step. This will require new commercial models.

New Ethics Guidance Needed: Data about a person (see above described example about the implanted chip) will be automatically stored and retrieved including medical data. A car would then see users on the road by the RFID reflection and the personal data. However, these data can easily be misused and so the rules of ethics and data protection law must be updated.

New Laws Need for Insurance of Systems: While so far the driver must have an insurance, in future the car (when it is self driving) must be insured. The cars will have a black box, ECUS will deliver failure data and in case of an accident the black box will be analysed and the supplier causing the problem will pay with his insurance. The insurance cost will be added to the service fee that users will pay in the future commercial models.

Integration of Different Product Aspects and Skills Needed [7]: Safety and security are not enough. A car, for instance, can receive upgrades during drive and maintainability needs to be developed differently from the past. Also cars will be used by more than one user and user profiles can be configured and adjusted, and also user data are stored in the cloud, so that confidentiality becomes a major issue as well, etc. (Fig. 8).

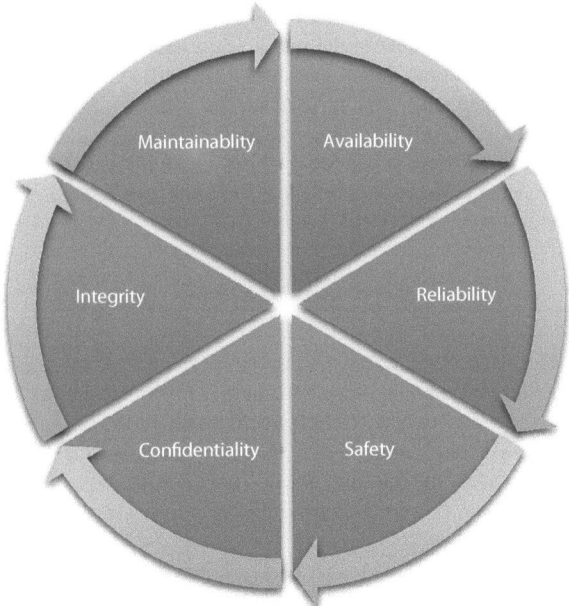

Fig. 8. All product aspects must be integrated

5 Conclusion of the Vision

Quality management and development processes in the last years in the automotive domain have been focused on safety-critical systems. But the connected car with autonomous functions cannot simply focus on safety, the other aspects such as availability, reliability, confidentiality, integrity and maintain-ability need to be addresses as well. These attributes are sometimes conflicting each other, but it is clear that new approaches to product and service development are needed.

Also the Gear 2030 initiative outlines that for developing such an environment an integration of new skills is needed including safety, security, reliability, but also new infrastructure design (energy, industry 4.0, changing whole fuelling concepts, light—weight materials, and more).

This will lead to new job roles, new companies, new networks, new solutions, and new dependent vehicle concepts.

However, it is interesting to observe that many of the previous system engineering principles [15, 16] of service based architectures are used and transformed to this new ecosystem. So instead of buying a car, users in future will buy a service in an infrastructure which is part of an eco-system driven environment.

Acknowledgements. Elektrobit Automotive GmbH, TU Graz, and ISCN GesmbH are part of the SOQRATES [24] working group and we are grateful to the experts who have contributed to the working groups and to the design principles in this paper. We are also grateful to the European Commission which has funded some of the initiatives referenced in this paper such as GEAR 2030, ECQA Certified Functional Safety Manager (2012 2014), ECQA Certified Automotive Quality Engineer Integrated and AQUA (Knowledge Alliance for Quality in Automotive Engineering, 2013–2015), and AQU (Automotive Quality Universities, 2015–2017). The research reported in this paper has also been supported by the Austrian Ministry for Transport, Innovation and Technology, the Federal Ministry of Science, Research and Economy, and the Province of Upper Austria in the frame of the COMET center SCCH.

References

1. Kreiner, C.J., Macher, G., Riel, A.: Integrating automotive hazard and threat analysis methods: how does this fit with assumptions of the SAE J3061? Softw. Qual. Prof. **18**(4), 37–46 (2016)
2. Messnarz, R., Kreiner, C., Riel, A., Tichkiewitch, S., Ekert, D., Langgner, M., Theisens, D.: Integrating functional safety, automotive SPICE and six sigma – the AQUA knowledge base and integration examples. In: Barafort, B., O'Connor, R.V., Poth, A., Messnarz, R. (eds.) EuroSPI 2014. CCIS, vol. 425, pp. 285–295. Springer, Heidelberg (2014). doi:10.1007/978-3-662-43896-1_26
3. Kreiner, C., Messnarz, R., Riel, A., Ekert, D., Langgner, M., Theisens, D., Reiner, M.: Automotive knowledge alliance AQUA – integrating automotive SPICE, six sigma, and functional safety. In: McCaffery, F., O'Connor, R.V., Messnarz, R. (eds.) EuroSPI 2013. CCIS, vol. 364, pp. 333–344. Springer, Heidelberg (2013). doi:10.1007/978-3-642-39179-8_30
4. Macher, G., Messnarz, R., Armengaud, E., Riel, A., Brenner, E., Kreiner, C.: Integrated safety and security development in the automotive domain. SAE Technical Paper 2017-01-1661, USA (2017). doi:10.4271/2017-01-1661
5. Messnarz, R., Kreiner, C., Riel, A.: Integrating automotive SPICE, functional safety, and cybersecurity concepts: a cybersecurity layer model. Softw. Qual. Prof. **18**(4), 13–23 (2016)
6. Messnarz, R., Kreiner, C., Bachmann, O., Riel, A., Dussa-Zieger, K., Nevalainen, R., Tichkiewitch, S.: Implementing functional safety standards – experiences from the trials about required knowledge and competencies (SafEUr). In: McCaffery, F., O'Connor, R.V., Messnarz, R. (eds.) EuroSPI 2013. CCIS, vol. 364, pp. 323–332. Springer, Heidelberg (2013). doi:10.1007/978-3-642-39179-8_29

7. Much, A.: Automotive security: challenges, standards, and solutions. Softw. Qual. Prof. **18**(4) (2016)
8. Riel, A., Bachmann, V.O., Dussa-Zieger, K., Kreiner, C., Messnarz, R., Nevalainen, R., Sechser, B., Tichkiewitch, S.: EU project SafEUr – competence requirements for functional safety managers. In: Winkler, D., O'Connor, R.V., Messnarz, R. (eds.) EuroSPI 2012. CCIS, vol. 301, pp. 253–265. Springer, Heidelberg (2012). doi:10.1007/978-3-642-31199-4_22
9. Santer, C., Messnarz, R., Much, A., Ekert, D., Riel, A.: Integrating assessment models for ASPICE, functional safety, and cybersecurity. Softw. Qual. Prof. **18**(4), 24–36 (2016)
10. International Electrotechnical Commission (IEC): IEC 61508 2nd ed: Functional safety of electrical/electronic/programmable electronic safety-related systems – Parts 1–7 (2010)
11. International Electrotechnical Commission (IEC): IEC 62304: Medical device software – Software life cycle processes (2006)
12. International Electrotechnical Commission (IEC): IEC 62443: Industrial communication networks – Network and system security (2008–2013)
13. International Organization for Standardization (ISO): ISO 9001 - Quality management systems – Requirements (2015)
14. International Organization for Standardization (ISO): ISO 12207 - Systems and software engineering - Software lifecycle processes (2008)
15. International Organization for Standardization (ISO): Systems and software engineering – Systems and software assurance (2011, 2013, 2015)
16. International Organization for Standardization (ISO): ISO/IEC 15408: Information technology – Security techniques – Evaluation criteria for IT security – Parts 1–2 (2008, 2009)
17. International Organization for Standardization (ISO): ISO/IEC 15504 – Information technology – Process assessment – Parts 1–10 (2004–2010)
18. International Organization for Standardization (ISO): ISO/TS 16949 – Quality management systems – Particular requirements for the application of ISO 9001:2008 for automotive production and relevant service part organizations (2009)
19. International Organization for Standardization (ISO): ISO/IEC TS 17961: Information technology – Programming languages, their environments and system software interfaces – C secure coding rules (2013)
20. International Organization for Standardization (ISO): ISO 26262. Road vehicles – Functional safety – Parts 1–9 (2011)
21. International Organization for Standardization (ISO): ISO/IEC 27001: - Information technology - Security techniques - Information security management systems – Requirements (2015)
22. International Organization for Standardization (ISO): ISO/IEC 27002: Information technology - Security techniques. Code of Practice for Information Security Controls (2008)
23. GEAR 2030, European Commission, Commission launches GEAR 2030 to boost competitiveness and growth in the automotive sector (2016). http://ec.europa.eu/growth/tools-databases/newsroom/cf/itemdetail.cfm?item_id=8640
24. SOQRATES. http://soqrates.eurospi.net/index.php. Accessed 15 May 2017
25. Automotive SPICE – Process Assessment Model v2.5 (2010), and v3.0 (2015). www.automotivespice.com
26. MIRA Limited: MISRA-C:2004, Guideline for the use of the C language in critical systems (2004)
27. MIRA Limited: MISRA C:2012, Guidelines for the use of the C language in critical systems (2013)
28. MIRA Limited: MISRA C++: 2008, Guidelines for the use of the C++ language in critical systems (2008)

29. Microsoft Security Development Lifecycle. https://www.microsoft.com/en-us/sdl/. Accessed 10 Mar 2016
30. OWASP Project, OpenSAMM, Software Assurance Maturity Model. http://www.opensamm.org/. Accessed 15 May 2017
31. EVITA project, E-safety vehicle intrusion protected applications. http://www.evita-project.org/index.html. Accessed 15 May 2017
32. HEAVENS, HEAling Vulnerabilities to ENhance Software Security and Safety, Deliverable D2 Security models. HEAVENS Project, Deliverable D2, Release 1, December 2014, https://research.chalmers.se/en/project/5809. Accessed 15 May 2017
33. SAE International, SAE J3061: Cybersecurity Guidebook for Cyber-Physical Vehicle Systems, January 2016
34. Czerny, B.: System security and system safety engineering: differences and similarities and a system security engineering process based on the iso 26262 process framework. SAE Int. J. Passeng. Cars Electron. Electr. Syst. **6**(1) (2013). doi:10.4271/2013-01-1419

Automotive Quality Universities – AQU – Integration of Modular Content into the Higher Education Studies

Svatopluk Stolfa[1(✉)], Jakub Stolfa[1], Miran Rodic[2], Mitja Truntic[2], Christian Kreiner[3], and Richard Messnarz[4]

[1] Department of Computer Science, FEECS, VSB-Technical University of Ostrava, 17. Listopadu 15, 708 33 Ostrava-Poruba, Czech Republic
{svatopluk.stolfa,jakub.stolfa}@vsb.cz
[2] Faculty of Electrical Engineering and Computer Science, University of Maribor, Smetanova Ulica 17, 2000 Maribor, Slovenia
{miran.rodic,Mitja.truntic}@um.si
[3] Institute of Technical Informatics, Graz University of Technology, Rechbauaerstrasse 12, 8010 Graz, Austria
christian.kreiner@tugraz.at
[4] University of Applied Sciences Joanneum, FH Joanneum, Alte Poststrasse 152, 8020 Graz, Austria
rmess@iscn.com

Abstract. This paper introduces and discuss the integration of originally modular VET course AQUA (original idea about integrating teaching of Automotive SPICE, Functional Safety and Six Sigma content) into the higher education studies. The goal is to integrate industry courses to higher education learning, provide certification and examination appropriate for the higher education learning without extensive practical experience and thus prepare the students for their future jobs and trainings in automotive development in these fields. An idea about combination of industry and higher education levels learning, certification and examination is presented. Example of possibilities and experiences of integrated teaching from the universities involved in Automotive Quality Universities (AQU) project is also presented and discussed.

Keywords: Automotive · Automotive SPICE · Functional Safety · Six Sigma · Integrated approach · AQU · AQUA

1 Introduction

Currently the labour market in Automotive has a large demand on engineers with electronics and software background. Especially engineers with a background in integrated (multi-disciplinary) and globally collaborative engineering, as well as functional safety standards are needed. Already more than 70% of the car functionality is controlled by electronics and software and several studies predict this share to grow to 90% and more in the future [1], and since the ISO 26262 norm for Functional Safety in passenger cars came out recently, many systems (especially in the driving dynamics area) have been classified as safety critical. Functional Safety, just as Quality and Reliability largely addresses the architecture of systems and significantly impacts the hardware, the sensors and the software. All these are subjects that can only be implemented effectively on an organizational level, impacting many different stakeholders from different expert departments, as well as different management levels.

International standards and norms about Development Quality (Automotive SPICE®, ISO/IEC 15504 [2]), Functional Safety (ISO 26262 [3], IEC 61508 [4]) and Six Sigma [5] (production and process quality) form the backbone of the European automotive and supplier industry. These standards make the smooth coupling of the different companies along the supply chain possible, and enable the successful integration of all parts and subsystems. In order to be eligible for OEMs, suppliers have to implement and master all these standards. The European automotive industry, however, is confronted with a lack of qualified specialists and even more so of interdisciplinary "all-rounders" that can act as the links between different expert groups.

Attempts to develop a new educational approach for automotive engineers already begun. The EU Erasmus+ Sector-Skills-Alliance project AQUA (Automotive Knowledge Alliance AQUA – Integrating Automotive SPICE, Six Sigma, and Functional Safety, 2013-2014) first developed a curriculum (skill card), training material, and certificate for an "Automotive Quality Engineer Integrated" on Vocational education and training level (hereinafter VET) [6, 7]. This is based on a consistent and modular kit ("Baukasten") of training modules for Functional Safety, Automotive SPICE and Six Sigma, as well as on their integration that was developed (which is completely new on the training market) [6, 8, 9]. As a European Skills Alliance project, AQUA received high visibility by the European Commission, Automotive clusters, and industry.

The basis for the new educational approach in form of integrated teaching of standards and approaches was established [6, 10] and now is the time to do the next step - AQUA alliance evolution - in terms of geographic coverage, by extending the initial focus on vocational training to cover also university and technical school education programmes, as well as extending the scope of topics, e.g. incorporating security design in practice to harden Automotive systems against malicious attacks. Follow-on project "Automotive Quality Universities" is currently rolling out and extending AQUA skills to Universities across Europe - to grow and strengthen the AQUA alliance.

In this paper, Automotive Quality Universities (hereinafter AQU) extension concept of AQUA to higher education level is described and next development and visions about a possible orientation to the future is discussed. Section 2 presents the AQUA establishment idea and basic principles. Section 2 introduces the AQUA basic idea and principles. Section 3 describes the AQU project goals and achievements and Sect. 4 Adapting the Originally VET Oriented Courses for the Higher Education Level Studies describes the solution for the teaching of AQUA at the universities and Sect. 6 Conclusion then summarizes the results and future extension of the concept.

2 AQUA – Automotive Quality Integrated

In the past, the role of an Automotive quality manager was based on standards like IEC 16949 and the implementation of a quality management system.

With the growth of complexity of car functionality and the increased use of electronics (more than 100 ECUs in cars are connected by a bus and each car function is mapped onto an ECU cluster) other rules came into existence. Automotive SPICE (ISO 15504) knowledge is meanwhile an important skill to assess Automotive systems which include both, electronics and software. Most of the manufacturers demand a SPICE level 3 from the suppliers.

Faults of electronic devices and software can lead to hazards (e.g. blocking wheels, unintended steering, no brake force, etc.) so that a new standard functional safety ISO 26262 has to be implemented. Systems that might cause a hazard get classified by an ASIL-A to D level. Therefore quality managers that have to release a product to the market must be familiar with the functional safety as well.

Quality management (specified in IEC 16949) has a responsibility for the entire product life-cycle, including the production part. Six Sigma is nowadays the most well-known method and statistical toolbox for quality control in production.

AQUA (Knowledge Alliance for Training, Quality and Excellence in Automotive) project, a pilot in the Erasmus+ Sector Skill Alliances Program under the project number EAC-2012-0635, is the very first European qualification and certification program that addresses exactly this need and established an innovative modular teaching platform integrating following three dimensions on VET level:

- Automotive SPICE® (ISO/IEC 15504): Quality linked to the development process of software and electronics.
- Functional Safety (ISO 26262): Quality associated with the achievement of Functional Safety requirements.
- Design for Six Sigma: Focus on the reliability and robustness of products and production processes.

A Base layer of core modules was established and allows an integrated complementary view about these three approaches. Figure 1 illustrates the AQUA concept.

Specific content layers (Automotive SPICE, Functional Safety and Six Sigma) represent the particular approaches and the knowledge that is necessary for the specific element. The additional Integration AQUA layer then presents the integrated view, where common principles and paradigms of all approaches are linked, forming the holistic understanding of the presented contents.

This modular strategy allows companies to select each method separately or also to gain an advanced insight into how these methods in fact are joined together in advanced engineering companies. The AQUA unit content covers all the necessary knowledge: introduction of the approaches, product development, quality and safety management, and measurement.

In AQUA the concept of a new education for "Automotive Quality Manager with AQUA Skills" is formed and quality managers for the integrated understanding of the above three methods are trained [6, 12, 13].

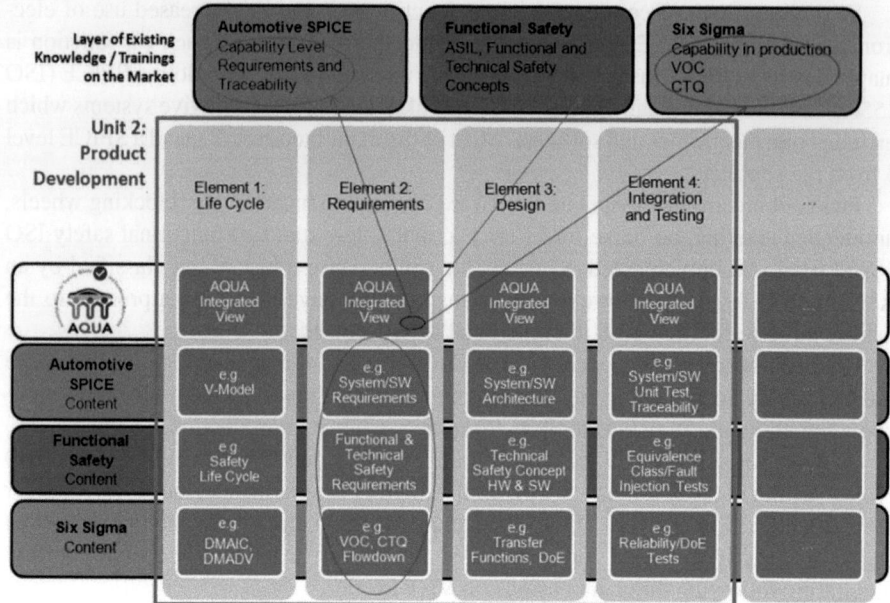

Fig. 1. Modular AQUA concept - unit 2 product development.

3 AQU – Automotive Quality Universities

In the Automotive Quality Universities (Automotive Universe, hereinafter AQU) a ERASMUS+ project on Strategic Partnership for higher education, it was planned to launch the AQUA education at the universities, where ECTS (European Credit Transfer System) will be agreed to among a set of universities in Europe [14]. The Automotive area is one of the European lead industries and employers, thus to provide the proper skills for staying competitive at the university level is a high demand across all member states.

Schematic view of relations between AQUA, automotive industry, universities and AQU project are depictured in the Fig. 2. On the top left of the figure universities as a provider of higher education are depictured. Universities provide graduates to the automotive industry, however like it was mentioned in the introduction, it is possible to identify some kind of knowledge gap in the area of automotive spice, functional safety and six sigma that are widely used and form the backbone of quality assurance in the automotive industry. Previously mentioned AQUA helps to increase knowledge level directly in the automotive industry by educating employees. AQU's goal is to reduce the knowledge gap between graduates of universities and required engineering and management skills in the industry. Anyway, the need for the application of selected approaches is relatively new even in the industry, so sometimes there are no engineers in the company, who would be skilled in this direction. With the combination of AQUA trainings at the industry and AQU courses at the universities, prepared by AQU project, it is possible to bring a synergistic and homogenous solution to education of Automotive SPICE, Functional Safety and Six Sigma in the automotive area.

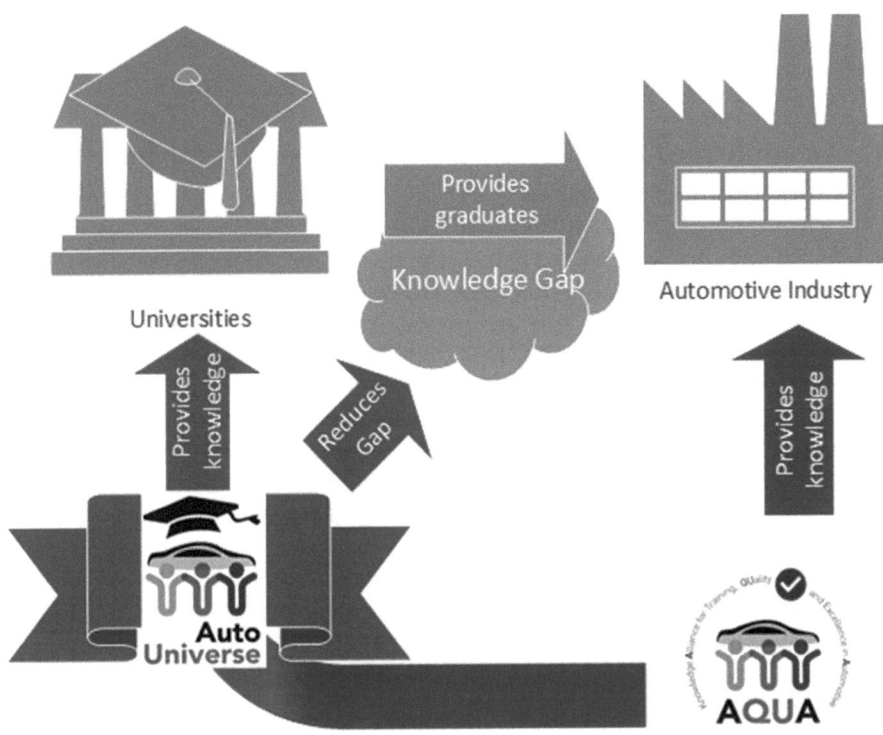

Fig. 2. Schematic view of AQUA, automotive industry, universities and AQU project relations

The goal of AQU project was to establish the AQUA training at different universities as Automotive Quality Engineering oriented lectures. All universities agreed to provide ECTS for the lectures and also agree to recognize ECQA as a supplementary industry certificate for the students. AQU project consortium includes:

- VŠB - Technical University of Ostrava, Czech Republic
- University of Technology Graz, Austria
- University of Applied Sciences Joanneum, Graz, Austria
- University of Maribor, Slovenia
- EMIRACLE (European Innovation in Manufacturing Association), Belgium, teaching students e.g. at Grenoble Institute of Technology, as well as professors and students in several French Engineering Schools (Ecole Centrale de Nantes, ENSAM ParisTech Aix en Provence, Université de Technologie de Troyes, Ecole Centrale de Lyon)
- ISCN/ECQA Online Campus for Industry

To prepare an integrated homogenous environment for an AQU teaching we had to challenge the two following topics:

1. Adapting the originally VET oriented courses for the higher education level studies.
2. Prepare a proper certification scheme for the certification of university studies and industry trainings.

4 Adapting the Originally VET Oriented Courses for the Higher Education Level Studies

In [15], the steps that were needed to be performed for the adoption of original AQUA courses at the higher education studies are presented. An analysis that was performed at the universities shown that there are two possible and requested options of an integration to higher education studies. First, to have and AQU as a separate course, in bachelor, master and doctoral studies. Second option that is natural for the AQUA courses modular content is to integrate some module content into the current subjects. Both approaches have their pros and cons. AQU as a separate course can serve as a good overall explanation how specific topics like ASPICE, Functional Safety and Six Sigma affects or can affect the development of the product, but student has to be experienced enough to be able to adjust his other subjects learned knowledge to fulfil the requirements of these standards and methods. On the other hand, integration of some modules into current subjects at the university directly adjusts the knowledge of specific subject as needed, but in that case, especially when these subjects are learned in different years or semesters, students might be missing the overall understanding of inclusion of these topics to the specific fields like design etc.

Anyway, both ways are possible and the negative aspects of both approaches can be minimized. E.g. if AQU is lectured as a separate course, practical examples and student's own development of examples for almost all modules reduces the risk of inclusion of new content to the learned approaches without AQU content. In case of integrated teaching, the AQU introductory modules gives an overall overview of the application of standards and methods and its whole integration.

4.1 Integration into the Partner Universities

Project partner universities integrated the AQU content and new style of teaching of standards and related methods to their study programs. Both approaches were used – AQU as a separate course and integration of AQU content in to the current related subjects that are development and/or quality oriented.

Integration of the AQUA to the current programmes and new courses:

VŠB-TU Ostrava

- *Process Modeling and Standards (PMS)* – master level, ECTS 4; second year; summer semester, Computer Science and Technology Branch of Master Degree Programme - Information and Communication Technology

- *Introduction to the quality management of automotive electronic systems* (IQM) (Úvod do řízení kvality AS) – bachelor level, ECTS 3, second year, summer semester, new study programme Automotive electronic systems
- Quality management of AES (QMA) – ECTS 4; first year; summer semester, new study programme Automotive electronic systems

University of Maribor

- *Digital Signal Controllers in Automation* – ECTS 6; third year (Electrical Engineering and Mechatronics, Bachelor study); summer semester – AQUA content will be partially integrated into the lectures.
- *Software Engineering for Control Systems* – ECTS 6; first year (Electrical Engineering, Master study); winter semester – AQUA content will be integrated into the lectures.
- *Optimization of Business Processes* – ECTS 6; first year (Informatics and Technologies of Communication, Master study); summer semester – AQUA content will be partially integrated into the lectures.

Grenoble Institute of Technology

- *Integrated Design for Innovative Products and Services (iDesigner)* – ECTS 4; third year; winter semester, Industrial Engineering – Product Development specialisation.

FH Joanneum

- *Introduction to Quality Management* (Bachelor Level, 1 ECTS), Automotive Engineering study programme
- *Logistics in the Automotive Sector* (Bachelor Level, 2 ECTS), Automotive Engineering study programme
- *Quality Management* (Master level, 2 ECTS), Automotive Engineering study programme

Graz University of Technology

- Set of courses "*Industrial Software Development and Quality Management*" VO+UE (3 + 1,5 ECTS, course no. 448.068 and 448.069). Listed as elective course in the curriculum Information and Computer Engineering. AQUA content established within the elective course catalogues of "C01 Secure and correct Systems" and "C06 Embedded and Automotive Systems". As free subjects for students of Computer Science, Software Engineering and Management, Electrical Engineering, Mechanical Engineering (vehicle technologies)
- The full AQUA curriculum will be established as University course via the Life-Long-Learning center of TU Graz.

4.2 Prepare a Proper Certification Scheme for the Certification of University Studies and Industry Trainings

ECQA certificates are issued to the students that passed the exam. Exam is a combination of multiple choice questions and practical example that has to be done by the student

[11–13]. As well as in the VET courses, there are listed just modules that were examined and there is a proof that student understands the content and/or can apply the knowledge on the development example if applicable. Except the VET certificate, it is clearly stated on the certificate that it is the student's certificate. If the student provides an evidence in the future that he can apply his knowledge on the real development examples and this is approved by the examiners of the AQUA job role the same way as a VET course certificates, then the practitioner certificate can be issued.

As the AQUA learning materials, e.g. norms content, is evolving all the time, versioning and release management is used as well. AQUA skills definition and learning materials are versioned and the release version is stated on the certificate as well

5 Experience from the Universities: University of Maribor Example

The teaching based on the created materials was performed for the first year (school year 2016/2017) at the University of Maribor in the frame of the subject *Software engineering for control systems*. The subject is taught at the Master level of the study programme *Electrical Engineering*. It is not a mandatory subject, but can be chosen by students from all three study directions (Automation and Robotics, Power Engineering and Electronics), with the most of students choosing it coming from the study direction Automation and Robotics.

The participating students therefore have a good knowledge regarding electrical and electronic systems and devices, but much less knowledge in the field of software engineering. In fact, they are able to program in C and C++, as well as in Matlab/Simulink, but lack the knowledge regarding the software engineering, which they are to obtain in the frame of this subject.

The software engineering contents can be a very abstract matter for non-specialists, which was experienced in the lectures held in previous years. What was missing most were practical example and it was extremely hard to give a rationale without a practical example that would be generally understood. However, automotive applications proved to be an excellent solution. Namely, every young student (this is especially true in Slovenia) likes cars and will readily swallow any information related to them. It even gives them a possibility to have an interesting theme at social events. Thus their motivation is much improved. The ability to see the reasons and ways of solution (risk and hazard analysis) gave them a necessary motivation to handle less fascinating issues (Hardware-Software interface).

In the following text the use of AQUA materials in the teaching will be presented. First the basic presentation of lectures used will be given, followed by the performance of exercises. Some results made by students Gregor Drakšič and Jernej Medved will be presented and commented.

The lectures were focused most on the *Functional safety* materials, mainly due to the knowledge and preference interest of lecturer. They formed a core of the subject. The systemic insight was made by the *Integration* materials. This was of special importance, because the students of electrical engineering are used to be presented with

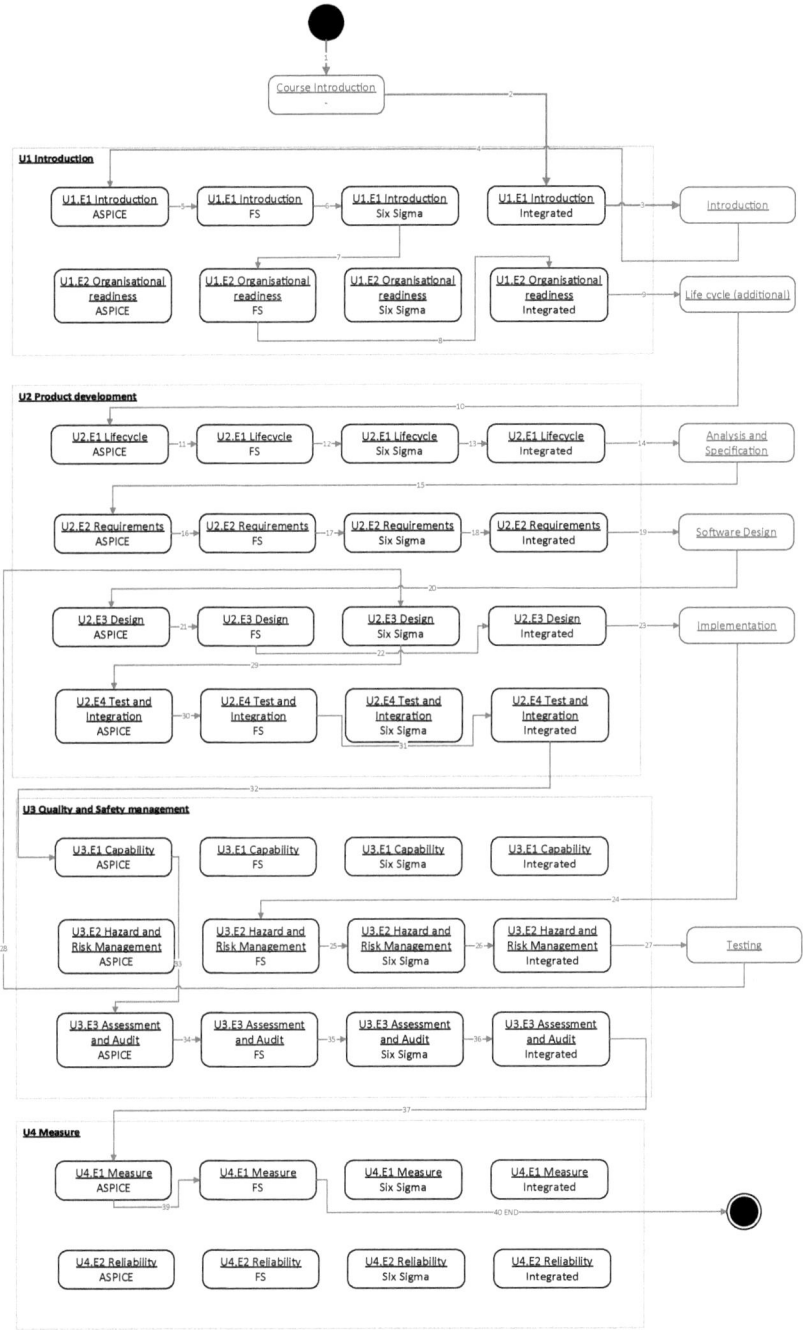

Fig. 3. AQUA learning plan as applied at University of Maribor (Color figure online)

connections and are used to the system approach. The *ASPICE* materials were applied to give a presentation of the process. Finally, *SixSigma* was just briefly mentioned, since its tools and methods are extensively taught in other subjects, focused on quality and reliability of hardware. In this subjects they also learn calculations of FIT rates and in the frame of mathematical subjects they have a very good coverage of probability (it is essential for electrical engineers of all study directions). The learning plan is presented in Fig. 3.

Additional materials (featured red in Fig. 3) were required to enable the understanding. Again, it needs to be understood that students of Electrical Engineering lack some knowledge related to Software engineering, so it has to be presented to them, at least briefly. Thus the following teaching materials were included (created locally at the University of Maribor):

- Introduction (system and software engineering, v-model – basic introduction, software engineering, software system engineering, some basics regarding quality, some basics regarding languages (C, assembly, UML, ...), verification and validation),
- Life cycle (development models: waterfall, code-and-fix, big-bang, spiral cycle),
- Analysis and specification (problem domain - software domain, functional and non-functional requirements, requirements engineering),
- Software design (software architecture, abstraction, encapsulation, modularity),
- Implementation (defensive coding, naming, - technical issues of coding in safe systems, reusability).

The exercises were performed in two steps. First lecturer presented the matter in front of the blackboard, using slides (partially from AQUA, rest self-made) on practical example of four-wheel vehicle with all of the wheels independently driven (with in-wheel motors). Then the students, with the help of instructor, repeated the exercise on the example of their choice. Since exercises were held weekly, they had the rest of the week available, when they could improve their work. In the first hour of every week's exercises the work of the previous exercise was presented to all participants and commented by instructor. In final week students prepared a short presentation, showing some typical results. This presentation contained discussion, in which comments were not only given by instructor, but also by students.

The examples chosen by students were:

- Adaptive headlights (will be presented in more details in the following text),
- Anti-Lock Braking System (ABS),
- Airbag system,
- Battery Management System,
- Collision prevention system,
- Cruise control, and
- Electronic stability program (ESP).

The adaptive headlight system, which was chosen by students Gregor Drakšič and Jernej Medved, was one of the best done, and is further quite interesting for the presentation. The figures are directly copied into this paper, by the permition of the students, therefore some names used are based on the Slovenian language. Thus it is possible to directly observe the students' work and results.

In the frame of exercises following was done:

- Item definition,
- Risk and hazard analysis,
- ASIL determination,
- Requirements – functional and safety requirements,
- Hardware-Software interface, and
- FMEA.

The presented system (Fig. 4) of adaptive headlights changes the direction of lighting based on the information of four sensors:

S_H1.1 – vehicle speed sensor,
S_N1.1 – front level sensor,
S_N1.2 – rear level sensor,
S_Z1.1 – steering wheel position (turning) sensor.

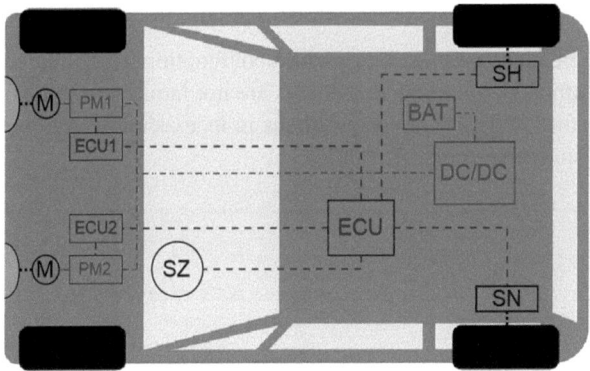

Fig. 4. Representation of vehicle and headlight (Gregor Drakšič and Jernej Medved, University of Maribor) (Color figure online)

Position of headlights can be set in two directions, horizontal and vertical, by two actuators:

A_M1.1 – motor in x-axis,
A_M1.2 – motor in y-axis.

Sensors and actuators will not be discussed further here, since they are typical devices used for that purpose.

The power for the system was provided from the vehicle battery and adjusted to the system requirements using DC/DC converter. Power connections and elements are marked in red. The information infrastructure was based on CAN and is presented in green.

The item definition is presented in Fig. 5. It presents the easiest task for students, since they are quite used to draw the block schemes.

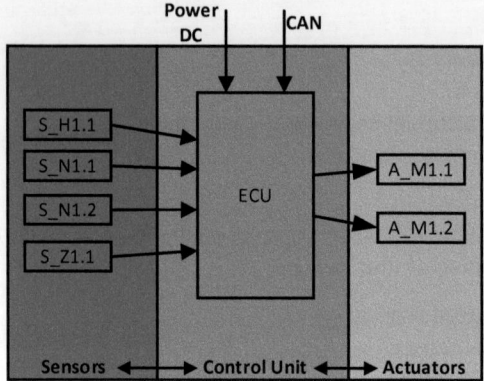

Fig. 5. Item definition (Gregor Drakšič and Jernej Medved, University of Maribor) (Color figure online)

The more interesting task was determination of functional requirements. This subject does not get a sufficient attention, so students are not familiar with its formal performance. However, they had only minor problems in its execution. An excerpt of requirements made by students is presented in Fig. 6.

ReqID	Reference	Type	Status	Requirement	Verification Crit	Domain	System-Part
System_01		R	new	EDC voltage (12 V) shell not deviate for more than allowed tolerance	System test: check controller settings, connections.	System	Main
HW_01	System_01	R	new	Additional control voltage (12 V) for the connection with the software supervision system.	Voltage is measured with the voltage sensor	HW	Power connection
SW_01	System_01	R	new	DC voltage of inverter is signaled to ECU through two signals - analogue and CAN.	Both connections are checked at vehicle startup.	SW	ECU-SW
HW_02	System_01	R	new	Current is in between 50 and 2000 mA	Current is measured usingf sensor.	System	Power connection

Fig. 6. Requirements (Gregor Drakšič and Jernej Medved, University of Maribor)

The most popular and interesting task for students was the determination of the ASIL. A presentation of an example resulting in chosen ASIL level (B) is shown in Fig. 7. Students enjoyed this exercise and were quite impressed with the straightforwardness of the process. They also understood that the worst-case scenario is the right solution. This was made easier by the fact, that this is usually the case in electrical Engineering. On the other hand, they understood the necessity to keep the ASIL as low as possible, due to the reduction of cost and effort to produce the product.

Component	Adaptive headlights	
Possible malfunction	ECU failure disables the setting of headlights, which remain in extreme sideways position.	
Situation	Fully loaded vehicle, high speed.	
S	Reduced visibility, severe injuries are possible.	2
E	Normal use of vehicle.	4
C	Can be handled by an average driver.	2
ASIL	B	
Safety Goal	Headlights should not remain in extreme sideways position.	

Fig. 7. ASIL determination (Gregor Drakšič and Jernej Medved, University of Maribor)

The rest of the exercises will not be presented at this point, but it has been proven that FMEA and risk and hazard analysis don't cause the problem for students of electrical engineering. What basically has to be taught is the tool, its use is easily understood and learned.

The exercises were considered by students as a nice experience and they got the feeling that they obtained a lot of useful and interesting knowledge. They also got to understand the reasons for learning some theory, which seemed quite useless to them previously.

The results of using the AQUA materials were even better than expected. At the start there was a question, if the students will be able to get involved fully, due to some missing knowledge. This was not a problem at all. Partly because of the additional materials and rest due to the highly interesting subject matter. The expected advantages of Electrical Engineering students (good understanding and mastering of probability issues, from the theoretical and implementation viewpoint, understanding of system approach; and familiarity with systems, in general and ones of automotive field) prove to be true.

Finally, the use of AQUA materials was a success and the same approach with only minor changes will be applied next year. The only issue we have to think about is the possibility to work in smaller groups (typically now the group has up to 16 students, but up to 8 would be much better).

6 Conclusion

Integration of AQUA content into the study programmes at the Universities is gladly accepted by the staff and potential employers of graduates. Since the development of electronics and software systems for automotive is growing in the last years, there is a big demand for graduates both software and electronic branches of study. According to the employers, graduates that will start their career there should know the methods and approaches of software or electronics system development, know foreign language and have some background about standards and approaches that are needed for the development. Employers especially mention that they would like to hire graduates with at least basic knowledge things like V-Model, functional safety standards requirements, application of methods and tools that help to fulfill standard's requirements. This need is very well covered by the AQUA integration of ASPICE, Functional Safety and SixSigma and its inclusion into the study programmes is very welcomed.

As we can see, there is a difference between the university study programmes. Some programmes are more software oriented, some more electronic oriented and some programmes concern is general vehicle engineering. Anyway, all graduates then must deal with the same topics in industry and therefore there is raising a question, how to compare or judge the employee knowledge if the background is so different. The answer is skill oriented learning and training that is highly and naturally supported by the AQUA approach. It does not matter from which university graduates will come, because they are having a certificate that proves the skills that they have learned.

As for an AQUA content, ASPICE, ISO 26262 and Six Sigma content is taught and integrated currently. However, the rapid development of the electronics and new challenges considering e.g. environmental issues rise very quickly new topics that for sure must be considered during a development of the system and therefore future engineers should know and practice. Some examples that are already considered and being prepared to be integrated into the AQUA learning materials is Security, Sustainability, Reliability etc.

Acknowledgement. This research was financially supported by the European Commission in the AQUA (Knowledge Alliance for Training, Quality and Excellence in Automotive) project as a pilot in the Erasmus+ Sector Skill Alliances Program under the project number EAC-2012-0635. The special aspect of adapting the training program to higher education level, and its deployment in five European universities is financially supported by the European Commission in the Erasmus + Strategic Partnership project 2015-1-CZ01-KA203-013986 AutoUniverse (Automotive Quality Universities). This publication reflects the views only of the authors, and the Commission cannot be held responsible for any use which may be made of the information contained therein.

This research has been also supported by the internal grant agency of VSB-Technical University Ostrava, project No. SP2017/133.

Authors would like to also express the thanks to the ECQA and other project team members, namely to Richard Messnarz (ISCN), Damjan Ekert (ISCN), Ales Hace (UM), Milan Zorman (UM), Andreas Riel (EMIRACLE), Serge Tichkiewitch (EMIRACLE), Kurt Steiner (FHJ), Eugen Brenner (TUG), and others that are working on the fulfilment of the project goals and also supporting this effort.

References

1. Oliver Wyman Automotive: Car Innovation. A comprehensive study on innovation in the automotive industry (2015). http://www.car-innovation.com. Accesed 11 Dec 2013
2. International Organization for Standardization: ISO/IEC 15504 International Standard Information Technology – Software Process Assessment (2008)
3. ISO, Road vehicles – Functional safety, ISO 26262, part 1 – 10, International standard under publication, Geneva (2011)
4. International Electrotechnical Commission, IEC/EN 61508: International standard 61508 functional safety: safety related systems: Second Edition, Geneva (2010)

5. Theisens, D.: How Green is your Black Belt. In: Riel, A., O'Connor, R., Tichkiewitch, S., Messnarz, R. (eds.) EuroSPI 2010. CCIS, vol. 99, pp. 257–267. Springer, Heidelberg (2010)
6. Kreiner, C., Messnarz, R., Riel, A., Ekert, D., Langgner, M., Theisens, D., Reiner, M.: Automotive knowledge alliance AQUA – integrating automotive SPICE, Six Sigma, and Functional Safety. In: McCaffery, F., O'Connor, R.V., Messnarz, R. (eds.) EuroSPI 2013. CCIS, vol. 364, pp. 333–344. Springer, Heidelberg (2013). doi:10.1007/978-3-642-39179-8_30
7. The Vocational education and training level, http://ec.europa.eu/education/opportunities/vocational/index_en.htm. Accesed 08 Apr 2016
8. Messnarz, R., König, F., Bachmann, V.O.: Experiences with trial assessments combining automotive spice and functional safety standards. In: Winkler, D., O'Connor, R.V., Messnarz, R. (eds.) EuroSPI 2012. CCIS, vol. 301, pp. 266–275. Springer, Heidelberg (2012)
9. SOQRATES Safety Team, Messnarz, R., Ross, H.-L., Habel, S., König, F., Koundoussi, A., Unterrreitmayer, J., Ekert, D.: Integrated automotive SPICE and safety assessments. SPIP **14**(5), 279–288 (2009). Wiley
10. Messnarz, R., König, F., Bachmann, V.: Experiences with trial assessments combining automotive SPICE and functional safety standards. In: Winkler, D., O'Connor, R.V., Messnarz, R. (eds.) EuroSPI 2012. CCIS, vol. 301, pp. 266–275. Springer, Heidelberg (2012). doi:10.1007/978-3-642-31199-4_23
11. Rosnah, M.Y., Wan Nurul Karismah, W.A., Zulkifli, N.: Quality management maturity and its relationship with human resource development strategies in manufacturing industry. AIJSTPME **3**(3), 53–63 (2010)
12. Riel, A., Tichkiewitch, S., Messnarz, R.: Qualification and certification for the competitive edge in integrated design. CIRP J. Manuf. Sci. Technol. **2**(4), 279–289 (2010). Special Issue on Competitive Design
13. The European Qualifications Framework (EQF). http://ec.europa.eu/education/lifelong-learning-policy/eqf_en.htm Accessed 8 Apr 2016
14. BE-TWIN: Toolkit Bridging ECVET and ECTS – A Guide for Pedagogical Staff. http://www.ecvet-projects.eu/Documents/BeTWIN-Toolkit%20for%20trainers.pdf Accessed 8 Apr 2016
15. Stolfa, J., Stolfa, S., Riel, A., Tichkiewitch, S., Kreiner, C., Messnarz, R., Rodic, M., Gaisch, M.: Automotive quality universities – AQUA alliance extension to higher education. Commun. Comput. Inf. Sci. **633**, 176–187 (2016)

Experiences with Agile and Lean

Lean and Agile Software Process Improvement - An Overview and Outlook

Alexander Poth[1(✉)], Susumu Sasabe[2], and Antònia Mas[3]

[1] Volkswagen AG, Berliner Ring 2, 38436 Wolfsburg, Germany
alexander.poth@volkswagen.de
[2] Union of Japanese Scientists and Engineers (JUSE),
1-2-1 Koenji-Minami, Suginami-ku, Tokyo 166-0003, Japan
sasabe@mue.biglobe.ne.jp
[3] Department of Mathematics and Computer Science,
University of the Balearic Islands, Ctra. de Valldemossa, km 7.5, Palma, Spain
antonia.mas@uib.es

Abstract. Agile and lean approaches are disruptive approaches for the established software development approaches. Furthermore agile approaches are going step by step out of the software area into other areas like individual services outside the production, which is the root of lean. In this work we present an overview and outlook about agile and lean approaches to help to find answers to some questions: What is the difference between agile and lean? What kind of continuos improvement is inherent in agile and lean? How can lean and agile approaches be combined with software process improvement approach?

Keywords: Agile · Lean · Software process improvement (SPI) · Established environment

1 Introduction

Lean principles have had decades of success in lean manufacturing, logistics, and construction. Agile software development methods are interrelated with Lean principles. Agile&Lean principles are well established and mostly used in IT sector, however, the question is: Is it possible to integrate these principles in well-established and process dependent environments like Automotive, space, medical devices and other industries where safety is a critical issue?

The company culture of established organizations favors standardization and is process driven. The introduction of Agile methods in these environments is a challenging process and many research is conducted to identify key success factors facilitating the integrations of both paradigms.

The remainder of this paper is structured as follows: Sect. 2 presents the background of agile and lean approaches. Furthermore, principles of Lean Software Development and Agile frameworks are introduced. Section 3 outlines SPI in the context of agile and lean approaches. Section 4 discusses how established software process improvement approaches can be combined with Agile&Lean principles. Section 5 concludes the article.

2 Historical Background of Agile and Lean Approaches

Through the historical background of agile and lean approaches we can identify inherent approach which has essential characteristics for agility among various agile and lean software development practices in the world. Better understanding the historical background also helps us when we apply the inherent approach to improve software quality and business performance.

The origins of the agile and lean approaches can be traced back to the product quality studies in Japan after the Second World War. In 1950, Edward Deming was invited from the United States. With his lectures on quality management, Japanese industry leaders learned mindset of responsibility for product quality and started to implement organization-wide quality improvement activities.

TQC (Total Quality Control) is management activities, originated in Japan, for the organization-wide quality improvement implementation [1]. The applications of TQC spread from product manufacturing industry to various other domains of industry, such as construction, power utility, services, and software [2]. Such spread in multiple industry domains was due to a general nature of TQC. TQC was evolved in 1970s and 1980s, focusing firstly on statistical quality control, secondly on process improvement, and then thirdly on new product development, adapting to changes in market and economic situations. In 1997, the concept of TQC was inherited to a new quality management activities called TQM (Total Quality Management), where emphasis was extended to corporate business management beyond quality management [3].

TQC/TQM is equipped with various practical methods and tools: for example, (i) involvement of front-end workers, (ii) QC (Quality Control) circle - small team for quality improvement activity, (iii) use of various systematic problem-solving and visualization tools called 7 (seven) QC tools. The continuous improvement, known as KAIZEN [4], is core part of TQC/TQM. The KAIZEN improves quality of product, process, and capability of work by closing a feedback-loop after implementation of work on such objects and repeating the PDCA cycles step-by-step in an incremental way towards improvement goals. Necessary steps for solving quality problems were evolved to the Deming cycle, or PDCA cycle, which is a tool for conducting quality improvement in Japan.

In the Japanese automotive industry, for example, Toyota introduced the TQC/TQM approach for improving their production system of cars and created their own Toyota Production System (TPS) with the philosophy of removing waste ("Muda") via KAIZEN. The "Just in time" concept and the "Kanban" method were invented and practiced by Taiichi Ohno [4]. TPS realized a car production system to fit the Japanese automotive market situations and showed flexibility in adapting to the customer requirement changes.

In 1980s, TPS was benchmarked by the US experts of industrial engineering and business management. One example is a book titled "The Goal: A Process of Ongoing Improvement" written by Eliyahu Goldratt and Jeff Cox in 1986 [5]. They developed the "Theory of constraints", which is a theoretical explanation for reducing inventories and production lead time. Another example is a book titled "The machine that changed the world: The Story of Lean Production "by James Womack, Daniel Jones, and Daniel

Roos in 1991 [6]. The term "Lean" became well-known in the US and world-wide. James Womack and Daniel Jones showed the concept of lean production can be applied to any enterprise by their book "Lean Thinking" in 1996 [7].

In mid 1980s, excellent companies evolved their new product development to realize enhanced-speed because time-to-market of innovative new product impacts their revenue and profit. In 1986, two Japanese professors, Hirotaka Takeuchi and Ikujiro Nonaka, published their report in the Harvard Business Review (HBR) [8]. The report is a case study about new product development performed at several successful Japanese and US companies. The enhancement of development speed achieved by overlapping multiple development processes within organization and by highly interactive team play from concept phase to delivery phase to customer. This development model was named as "Rugby Model" with an analogy of rugby team handling ball interactively and rushing together to their goal.

In 1990s, software industry had a programming paradigm shift from procedural approach to object oriented approach in order to realize flexibility in software functions and enhanced speed of development. The internet created new business models and demanded enhanced speed of business. Extreme Programming (XP) [9] and SCRUM [10] are examples in this trend.

Kent Beck created XP, a software development methodology which focused on a collaborative and iterative design process. The Rugby model described above is root of SCRUM. The rugby model inspired Jeff Sutherland to begin formulation of the SCRUM framework for enhancing software development speed and flexibility of software functions realization when he read the article of the HBR [10]. Jeff Sutherland and Ken Schwaber presented their SCRUM framework in OOPSLA '95 in Austin, Texas [11]. In 2001, seventeen software developers including Kent Beck, Jeff Sutherland, and Ken Schwaber, published the Manifesto for Agile Software Development [12]. The manifesto highlights four thinking in the agile software development; individuals and interactions, working software, customer collaboration, and responding to change.

From a point of view of the Theory of Constraints (TOC) and lean approach, David Anderson wrote a book titled "Agile Management for Software Engineering: Applying the Theory of Constraints for Business Results", in which reducing work in progress (WIP) and maximizing throughput in software development were highlighted [13]. In 2010, David Anderson wrote a book titled "Kanban" [14] in which lean approach adapted much more explicitly to the software development (Fig. 1).

Two streams of approach, agile and lean, were interrelated each other. Mary Poppendieck and Tom Poppendieck applied lean principle to software development with thinking tools to help software development leaders as they develop the agile practices. In 2003, they wrote a book and used two keywords, agile and lean, together for the first time in their book title [15]. This trend of interrelationship between agile and lean approaches still continues today.

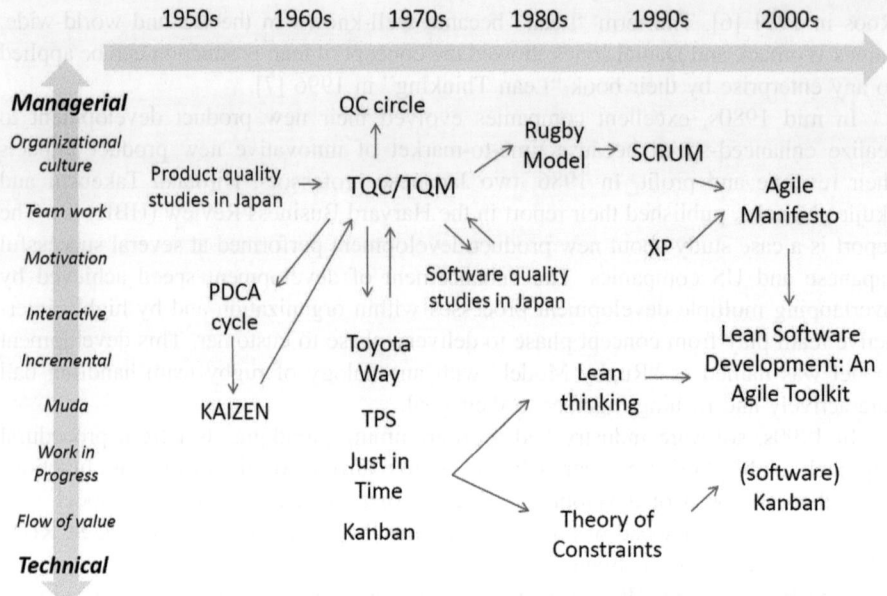

Fig. 1. Historical background of Agile and lean approaches.

2.1 Key Principles of Lean Software Development

The key principles of Lean Software Development that Mary and Tom Poppendieck published in [15] are introduced in this section. Principles are guiding ideas and insights about a discipline, while practices are what to perform in order to carry out principles [16]. Principles are universal, but it is not always easy to see how to apply them to a particular environment. Practices provide specific guidance on what to do, but they need to be adapted to a particular domain.

Table 1 summarizes the seven key principles of Lean Software Development and the support tools.

Lean Development further expands the theoretical foundations of agile software development by applying well known and accepted lean principles for software development.

2.2 The Agile Manifesto

Agile Manifesto was published in 2001 as a result of a seventeen-experts meeting to talk on most agile methods used in the market such as: Extreme Programming (XP), Scrum, Dynamic systems development method (DSDM), Adaptive Software Development (ASD), Crystal, Feature-Driven Development, Pragmatic Programming and other rapid development evangelist. They all agreed to the need for an alternative to documentation driven, heavyweight software development processes convened. What

Table 1. Key principles of Lean Software Development and support tools.

Key principle	Description	Support tools
P1. Eliminate waste	Waste is anything that does not add value to a product, value as perceived by the customer. The ideal is to find out what a customer wants, and then make or develop it and deliver exactly what they want, virtually immediately. Whatever gets in the way of rapidly satisfying a customer need is waste. Eliminating waste is the most fundamental lean principle, the one from which all the other principles follow. Thus, the first step to implementing lean development is learning to see waste	T1. Seeing waste T2. Value Stream Mapping
P2. Amplify learning	Development is an exercise in discovery, while production is an exercise in reducing variation, and for this reason, a lean approach to development results in practices that are quite different than lean production practices. Soft-ware development is best conceived of as a similar learning process with the added challenge that development teams are large and the results are far more complex than a recipe. The best approach to improving a software development environment is to amplify learning	T3. Feedback T4. Iterations T5. Synchronization T6. Set-based development
P3. Decide as late as possible	Development practices that provide for late decision making are effective in domains that involve uncertainty, because they provide an options-based approach. Delaying decisions is valuable because better decisions can be made when they are based on fact, not speculation. A key strategy for delaying commitments when developing a complex system is to build a capacity for change into the system	T7. Options thinking T8. The last responsible Moment T9. Making decisions
P4. Deliver as fast as possible	Rapid development has many advantages. With-out speed, you cannot delay decisions. Without speed, you do not have reliable feed-back. In development, the discovery cycle is critical for learning: Design, implement, feedback, improve. The shorter these cycles are, the more can be learned. Speed assures that customers get what they need now, not what they needed yesterday. It also allows them to delay making up their minds about what they really want until they know more	T10. Pull systems T11. Queuing theory T12. Cost of delay

(*continued*)

Table 1. (*continued*)

Key principle	Description	Support tools
P5. Empower the team	Involving developers in the details of technical decisions is fundamental to achieving excellence. The people on the front line combine the knowledge of the minute details with the power of many minds. When equipped with necessary expertise and guided by a leader, they will make better technical decisions and better process decisions than anyone can make for them	T13. Self-determination T14. Motivation T15. Leadership T16. Expertise
P6. Build integrity in	Perceived Integrity is affected by the customer's whole experience of a system. A system is perceived to have integrity when a user thinks, "Yes! That is exactly what I want. Somebody got inside my mind!" Market share is a rough measure of perceived integrity for products, because it measures customer perception overtime. Conceptual integrity means that the system's central concepts work together as a smooth, cohesive whole, and it is a critical factor in creating perceived integrity. Research has shown that integrity comes from wise leadership, relevant expertise, effective communication, and healthy discipline; processes, procedures, and measurements are not adequate substitutes	T17. Perceived integrity T18. Conceptual integrity T19. Refactoring T20. Testing
P7. See the whole	Integrity in complex systems requires a deep expertise in many diverse areas. One of the most intractable problems with product development is that experts in any area have a tendency to maximize the performance of the part of the product representing their own specialty rather than focusing on overall system performance. A system is not just a sum of its parts, it's a product of those interactions. When individuals or organizations are measured on their specialized contribution rather than overall performance, sub-optimization is likely to result. So, the focus should be on optimizing the whole rather than optimizing departments/sub- departments/individuals	T21. Measurements T22. Contracts

emerged was the Agile Software Development Manifesto [17], with four basic values encapsulating the agile methods:

- Individuals and interactions over processes and tools.
- Working software over comprehensive documentation.

- Customer collaboration over contract negotiation.
- Responding to change over following a plan.

The 12 principles of Agile Software Development are:

1. Our highest priority is to satisfy the customer through early and continuous delivery of valuable software.
2. Welcome changing requirements, even late in development. Agile processes harness change for the customer's competitive advantage.
3. Deliver working software frequently, from a couple of weeks to a couple of months, with a preference to the shorter timescale.
4. Business people and developers must work together daily throughout the project.
5. Build projects around motivated individuals. Give them the environment and support they need, and trust them to get the job done.
6. The most efficient and effective method of conveying information to and within a development team is face-to-face conversation.
7. Working software is the primary measure of progress.
8. Agile processes promote sustainable development. The sponsors, developers, and users should be able to maintain a constant pace indefinitely.
9. Continuous attention to technical excellence and good design enhances agility.
10. Simplicity–the art of maximizing the amount of work not done–is essential.
11. The best architectures, requirements, and designs emerge from self-organizing teams.
12. At regular intervals, the team reflects on how to become more effective, then tunes and adjusts its behaviour accordingly.

Agility can be defined as the ability to create and to respond to change in order to create value in turbulent business environment. It is based on several business principles like continuous innovation, product adaption, shortening delivery times, adjustment of people and processes, and get-ting reliable results. Therefore, it is common to say that agility is also the ability to balance between flexibility and stability. Adaptability is the key characteristic of agile approach even more important than predictability, which is the basis of the traditional approach.

3 Software Process Improvement (SPI) in the Context of Agile Approaches

The root of many agile methods are derivations are the lean development principles and the agile manifesto. We can identify different agile approaches. Some approaches are more methods other are more models. The message is mostly all agile approaches have an inherent mechanism to improve their outputs. Table 2 shows some agile approaches with their improvement mechanisms.

Notable is that many agile approaches have as core concept for SPI the iterative and incremental product development with more or less formal retrospectives. From the SPI side this inherent approach of the agile SPI approach is usable to create a platform or connection point for systematic SPI in agile environments.

Table 2. Agile approaches with their improvement proposals.

Name	Usefull for	Approach based on	Effect/Outcome	Key success factor	Inherent SPI aspect
Design Thinking [18]	innovation	Ideation approach to solve issues or develop new things	Get the creative potential of the team	Creative freedom	Iterative and incremental approach
Lean StartUp [19]	Business models	Validate fast hypothesis about business idea	Get early realistic feedback	Openness & brave	Iterative and incremental approach
Scrum [20]	Development projects	Framework for product development	Self-optimizing team	"Safe area" for the team	Iterative and incremental approach with retrospective as ritual for SPI
Kanban [14]	Service teams	Modell for effective service delivery	Optimize flow, predictable services	Understand lean principles	Outcome driven improvement by WIP reduction etc.
Scrumban [21]	Development & service teams	Combines benefits of Scrum and Kanban	Reach service levels and optimize team	Openness for continuous improvement	See Scrum and Kanban
Less [22]	Development programs	Framework to scale Scrum teams	Coordination of teams	Big jobs are brake down to small	Retrospective, Communities etc.
Safe [23]	Research and development organizations	Framework to scale agile & lean into entire organizations	Teams are working prioritized on enterprise objectives	Agile & lean mind-set	Iterative & incremental with "reuse" of Scrums retrospective
Lean Production [4]	Production of goods	Principals for optimize production by reducing waste and variance	Eliminate waste	Involve all affected parties	continuous improvement concept

3.1 Bridge the Gap from Established SPI to Agile Improvement Demands

For the retrospective existing many methods and tools like starfish [24], mood-curve [25] and on many other toolboxes – many are using gamification aspects to identify improvement potentials. The traditional SPI approaches oriented on SPICE [26] and CMMI [27] are using more formal ways to reach their goals. They have in Level 4 and

5 requirements defined to set up and establish the continuous improvement procedures. Both methods have the same goal: improve the product by improving procedures[1] of the product and services delivery. However, on the other side the approaches are completely different: SPICE and CMMI come with well-defined maturity levels and formal proofs as assessments.

The agile approaches comes with "try something, search effects and improve it" – without any formal requirements and proofs only reaching the goal gradually is enough feedback-loop to iterate with this greedy algorithm to the goal. This is driven by the observation, that in complex environments long term planning is not effective because there are too much parameters, which are interfering and which cannot be adequately predict. Compare his with tactical military teams – independent, self-organized and empowered to be effective, but with a clear objective in focus. This does not mean not to know what you are doing – there are some pattern or methods which are applied for example in retrospectives, which are working to optimize the current parameter values, but you have to go incrementally ahead to show their side effects in the complex environment. The environment will react to the change and depending on the type of reaction; you will try your next step by selecting one of your SPI methods.

SPI approach in Agile organisations should be focused on function teams, which differ from SPI approach in traditional (established) organisations where focus is to improve established organisational procedures or processes.

These two approaches – the agile/lean and the established SPI - derived by the different approaches to handle people in organizations. Based on Conways-Law [28] teams are influencing the architecture of their products and supporting structure and reverse. Taylorism [29] plans all options of the end-to-end value chain[2] and the organization "uses" people as actors. Agile organizations are people-centric by definition in the manifesto [17] "Individuals and interactions over processes and tools". Their people are responsible and self-organized[3] in end-to-end function teams. End-to-end in function teams significate that the team has contact to the customer with its demands and is responsible for the delivery to the customer and the technical stuff behind the delivery-procedure. Organizational procedures in agile organizations existing as "optional" support-functions to accelerate product delivery – the function team can choose acceleration options. The mindset of the self-organized agile function team is the team has the right skills and does it right.

---

[1] The term procedure is used instead of process because the ISO 9000:2015 defines procedures as optional documented to emphasis the more formal character. This makes the term procedure more adequate for agile teams because many teams do not focus on too much consolidation and reinforcement of processes to be able to change them easier if needed.

[2] The value chain is a core business procedure to make money. In agile environments, teams are organized around a value chain in independent teams to deliver entire functions to the value chain. In a web-shop a value chain could be "search product", "put it on the shopping card", "check out/buy" depending on complexity additional functions like "manage customer profile" etc. are also individual function teams instead of be part of check out "shipping address fields".

[3] Self-organized teams are setup and organized to act business centric and autonomy. They are empowered with their comprehensive know how to decide and act self-organized and independent from other teams – for fast reaction on incidents etc.

With the background of the argumentation above SPI in agile environments is more adaption of procedures to make them useful in the feature-team context. The feature teams[4] do not expect an abstract and generic procedure – they want a context adapted support procedure. SPI have to design for example systematic QM methods for embedding to the agile approaches to identify product specific quality risks [30] and assure the overall demanded compliance to external quality standards. The feature team wants to do what is needed to deliver adequate quality for their product and fit with the product all relevant quality regulations. The feature team will not see the verification management as a direct product value driver or core competence. The feature team will be open for supporting procedures to prevent resource intensive knowledge mining about the regulations. This demands individual procedures or highly adaptable procedures to fit the team specific demands to find their acceptance. Furthermore, for a SPI initiative the maturity level form the spiral dynamics model [31] of the target environment is important to get acceptance for the SPI actions. The spiral dynamics model makes transparent that established organizations mostly are 2 or 3 levels below good agile teams. This makes it difficult to communicate between teams of different levels [32].

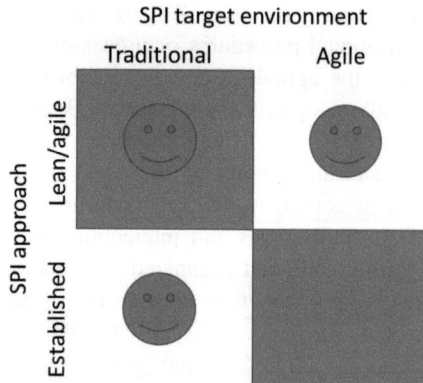

Fig. 2. Matching of SPI approaches into target environments.

3.2 Know How Transfer from SPI Changes to Agile Transition Management

A SPI initiative can be separated into two dimensions in an agile context. The first dimension is the SPI target environment, in which the SPI is applied. There is an agile or a traditional environment for application. The second dimension is the SPI approach, which is applied to change the SPI target environment. The SPI approach can be

---

[4] Feature or function teams are agile teams to handle a business functionality. Focus is to bring all relevant know how to run a "part" of business in an end-to-end fashion in the team. This is orthogonal to many IT setting with stacking teams in for example 3-tier applications in a frontend, business logic-and database-team to group specialists into competence teams.

distinguished into an established and a lean/agile approach. Figure 2 shows the two dimensions and their compatibility. The 4 cases are described as follows:

1. The lean/agile approach fits with an agile target environment. There is no problem to improve an agile environment with agile methods – the acceptance is given by design because no difference between the spiral dynamics maturity levels exists.
2. The established approach fits with a traditional environment. There is no problem to improve a traditional environment with established SPI methods – acceptance is given by design because no difference between the spiral dynamics maturity levels exists.
3. The lean/agile approach can easy applied in a traditional environment, because the iterative and incremental steps can be included into the traditional long-term SPI project management – some aspects of agile will be lost like early release-feedbacks but it works in a traditional environment with some risks caused by the lacking aspects. To compensate the loss of some aspects selected methods form the established approach can be used. But there is an additional mental effort the SPI team to "downgrade" their behavior/actions to the spiral dynamics maturity of the target environment. The observation of the authors is that it is not easy to find acceptance in the agile and lean environments for established SPI approaches. This is mostly motivated, that SPI is associated with SPICE or CMMI initiatives. Many people were involved in such initiatives and they remember that the main outcome was a process framework with regulations – this is the opposite of what the people expect from agile and lean.
4. It is more difficult to integrate long running established actions into sprints. One approach could be to break down the outcomes into MVPs to deliver also into agile environments. But the acceptance in the agile target environment for "hack"-MVPs will not be high and will be a high risk to fail with entire SPI initiative - SPI lives from the "user-acceptance". In this combination, it is more difficult to bridge the levels of the spiral dynamics model between the SPI approach and target environment peoples mindset because the established SPI approach team has to climb up levels to communicate adequate to the target environment teams for acceptance.

Now SPI scenarios can be discussed with their individual aspects depending on the SPI approach and target environment. For experienced SPICE or CMMI SPI managers the new demand is to be much more functions specific in the solutions. For agile SPI managers, often named transition[5] managers, the demand is to establish comprehensive procedures on organization level. With this focus SPI is also in agile environments a facilitator capability, which is needed if more teams have to work together.

Bigger organizations needs more procedures to manage the interfaces and interactions [32] between more or less independent agile teams. This observation leads to more procedures in bigger organizations and with the iterative and incremental working fashion SPI will be an important element in growing agile organizations. These agile

---

[5] Transition: The way from the status quo to an ideal agile organization is often called transition or agile transition. By definition, a transition never ends because something is always to optimize to have a better agile organization.

organizations will struggle with similar change resistance issues as established organizations because the feature teams are independent value chains which will only accepted procedures if they can see explicit benefits for the (organizational) value chain. The strength of agile organizations is that the iterative and incremental mindset never should close the door for test improvements about procedures. Based on this insight we can transform SPI knowledge from established change to transition managers and reverse.

The following example shows this: The Volkswagen AG is working with the internal change management team to transform organizational units from traditional to agile working procedures. The change management team is involved in a consulting fashion to reflect and develop ideas and concepts of the transition approaches but the operational lead of the transition is mostly by the agile guides. However, in 2016 the "recruiting" of agile guides from established change managers starts with a common annual event. The main topic is the mindset of agile – to get high acceptance the transition needs an agile guide, which has the lean and agile values always on focus. To develop the know-how and mindset is the challenge before the recruiting of established change managers works for agile transitions. The Fig. 2 shows that topic – the know-how background and experience of traditional change managers is good but at the end the agile guide and transition manager exemplify agile values and mindset. For the agile guides the know-how sharing with the change management team is also valuable because they have so much experience with the established culture and mindset which helps to predict "system" reactions for planned transition steps especially in environments with many teams and established processes.

4 Discussion

As seen in Sect. 2 the evolution of lean and agile is driven by many quality management approaches. The presented agile and lean approaches of Chap. 3 are including inherent continuous improvement. The instantiation can differ between the approaches, but there is a starting point for inherent software process improvement with the interactive and incremental working fashion.

4.1 Discussion on the Result

We have to keep in mind that some standards are not negotiable for many industries. An example is safety and security standards like the ISO 27000, which are defining a process framework to address security risks. In this context, agile teams have to satisfy the processes of the company's safety and security standard. The approaches to deal with the compliance requirements have started – see [33, 34]. A point to become formal correct and lean would be to find out how many procedures in teams can be accepted by the company's safety and security processes. Depending on the attitude to agile of the auditors, more or less procedures will be accepted. This area has to be analyzed in future work to give some recommendations for interpretation in agile environments like CMMI.

4.2 Related Discussions and Future Work

Another aspect for SPI in agile target environments is what can be handled by a good tool-set [35] and what should be integrated into automated procedures [36]? Furthermore, there is room for more statistical and empirical analysis for agile vs. traditional SPI like [37] for agile projects. Last but not least agile SPI should by analyzed more comprehensive on the publications which are made in the past like [38] it does for agile project success factors to improve the agile SPI approaches more holistic.

The bi-directional expertise of SPI from the established and agile/lean environments could be more investigated. Many concepts behind the process frameworks about rollout and chances are useful also in the agile and lean environments. At this point a mindset topic have to addressed in future works by identify methods and tools which are applicable in both environments.

5 Conclusion

This work demonstrates that SPI is part of agile and lean approaches. Many concepts behind established SPICE and CMMI initiatives are also valid for agile transitions. It is a chance for SPI to become a key-driver for the improvement of agile and lean approaches. Important for SPI is that it comes in a fashion that is integrating the operative methods and tools of SPI into the fashion of the agile/lean target environment to get acceptance as part of the "inspect & adapt" mechanism of the target environment for sustainable SPI. The sustainable integration into the target environment gives SPI the chance to be inherent in the agile teams. The inherent SPI approach stimulates and helps established SPI teams to rethink their strategy about supporting the holistic organizational SPI, because the agile teams will setup on demand actions between organizational units if they need it – self organized as lean and agile make things happen.

References

1. Ishikawa, K.: What is Total Quality Control? The Japanese Way. Prentice Hall, Upper Saddle River (1988)
2. [SQU07] The SQuBOK Project Team, SQuBOK (Software Quality Body of Knowledge) Guide, Version 1, 42 (2007). (in Japanese)
3. The TQM Committee: Total "Quality" Management in the 21st century. JUSE Press (1998). (in Japanese)
4. Ohno, T.: Toyota Production System: Beyond Large-Scale. Productivity Press (1988). ISBN: 978-0915299140
5. Goldratt, E.M., Cox, J.: The Goal: A Process of Ongoing Improvement. North River Press, Great Barrington (1992)
6. Womack, J.P., Jones, D.T., Roos, D.: The Machine That Changed the World: The Story of Lean Production. Harper Collins, New York City (1991)
7. Womack, J.P., Jones, D.T.: Lean Thinking. Simon & Schuster, New York City (1996)

8. Takeuchi, H., Nonaka, I.: The New New Product Development Game. Harvard Business Review, January–February 1986
9. Beck, K.: Extreme Programming Explained: Embrace Change. Addison-Wesley, Boston (1999)
10. Sutherland, J.: Scrum: The Art of Doing Twice the Work in Half the Time. Crown Business, New York (2014). ISBN: 978-0385346450
11. Sutherland, J.: SCRUM Development Process 10th Annual Conference on Object-Oriented Programming Systems, Languages, and Applications Addendum to the Proceedings. OOPS Messenger 6:4, pp. 170–175. ACM/SIGPLAN, October 1995
12. (2001). http://agilemanifesto.org/history.html
13. Anderson, D.J.: Agile Management for Software Engineering: Applying the Theory of Constraints for Business Results. Prentice Hall, Upper Saddle River (2003)
14. Anderson, D.J., Reinertsen, D.G., Kanban: Successful Evolutionary Change for Your Technology Business. Blue Hole Press (2010). ISBN: 978-0984521401
15. Poppendieck, M., Poppendieck, T.: Lean Software Development: An Agile Toolkit. Addison-Wesley, Boston (2003)
16. Senge, P.: The Fifth Discipline: The Art and Practice of the Learning Organization. Currency – Doubleday, New York (1990). ISBN: 0-385-51725-4
17. The Agile Manifesto (2001). https://www.agilealliance.org/agile101/the-agile-manifesto/
18. Plattner, H., et al.: Design Thinking: Understand, Improve. Apply. Springer, Heidelberg (2010)
19. Ries, E.: The Lean Startup: How Today's Entrepreneurs Use Continuous Innovation to Create Radically Successful Businesses. Crown Business, New York (2011). ISBN: 978-0-307-88789-4
20. scrumguide.org
21. Ladas, C.: Scrumban: Essays on Kanban Systems for Lean Software Development. Modus Cooperandi Press (2009). ISBN: 978-0578002149
22. Larman, C., Vodde, B.: Large-Scale Scrum: More with LeSS, 1st edn. Addison-Wesley Professional, Boston, 20 August 2016. ISBN: 978-0321985712
23. www.scaledagile-frame-work.com
24. http://www.funretrospectives.com/starfish/
25. http://www.scrummingman.com/2014/09/scrum-retrospective-technique-mood-chart/
26. ISO IS 15504
27. CMMI Dev V1.3. http://www.sei.cmu.edu/reports/10tr033.pdf
28. Conway, M.E.: How do committees invent? Datamation **14**(5), 28–31 (1968)
29. http://www.gutenberg.org/cache/epub/6464/pg6464-images.html
30. Poth, A.: Sunyaev. Effective quality management: value- and risk-based software quality management. IEEE Softw. **31**(6), 79–85 (2014)
31. Beck, D.E., Cowan, C.: Spiral Dynamics: Mastering Values, Leadership and Change. Wiley-Blackwell, Hoboken (2005). ISBN: 978-1-4051-3356-2
32. Drobietz, M., Poth, A.: A new approach: not agile vs. traditional QM but applying the best of both. In: Stolfa, J., Stolfa, S., O'Connor, R.V., Messnarz, R. (eds.) EuroSPI, pp. 486–494. Springer, Heidelberg (2017)
33. Poth, A., Wolf, F.: Agile Procedures of an automotive OEM – views from different business areas. In: euroSPI (2017)
34. Doss, O., Kelly, T., Stålhane, T., Haugset, B., Dixon, M.: Integration of the 4+1 Software Safety Assurance principles with Scrum. In: Stolfa, J., Stolfa, S., O'Connor, R.V., Messnarz, R. (eds.) EuroSPI, pp. 72–82. Springer, Heidelberg (2017)

35. Mesquida, A.L., Karać, J., Jovanović, M., Mas, A.: A game toolbox for process improvement in agile teams. In: Stolfa, J., Stolfa, S., O'Connor, R.V., Messnarz, R. (eds.) EuroSPI, pp. 302–309. Springer, Heidelberg (2017)
36. Kösling, M., Poth, A.: Agile development offers the chance to establish automated quality procedures. In: Stolfa, J., Stolfa, S., O'Connor, R.V., Messnarz, R. (eds.) EuroSPI, pp. 495–503. Springer, Heidelberg (2017)
37. Siqueira, A.A., Reinehr, S., Malucelli, A.: Using a statistical method to compare agile and waterfall processes performance. In: euroSPI (2017)
38. Aldahmash, A., Gravell, A.M., Howard, Y.: A review study on the critical success factors of agile software development. In: EuroSPI (2017)

A New Approach: Not Agile vs. Traditional QM but Applying the Best of Both

Mirko Drobietz[1(✉)] and Alexander Poth[2(✉)]

[1] Volkswagen Group IT Services GmbH,
Major-Hirst-Straße 11, 38442 Wolfsburg, Germany
mirko.drobietz@vwgis.de
[2] Volkswagen AG, Berliner Ring 2, 38436 Wolfsburg, Germany
alexander.poth@volkswagen.de

Abstract. During the long and arduous journey of the Volkswagen group IT towards a better quality culture we have established a better understanding of product quality. We were distressed about our internal struggle whether the traditional or the agile approach of quality management is the only way of life. The authors were involved in these struggles, Alexander for the traditional approach and Mirko for the agile way until we discovered that our goals were exactly the same: how do we produce high quality products with an optimal cost and effect ratio. While reading this paper we want to show our starting point of the discussion about traditional and agile QM and how we evolved the discussion to an integrated QM-Concept which got farer than software development only.

Keywords: Agile software development · Agile transition · Quality management · Quality assurance (QA) · Qualification · Integrated quality approach

1 Description Traditional Believes in TQM

Total Quality Management (TQM) is the core concept of most established quality management systems. TQM developed in the 1980s to improve the quality of manufacturing. Many standards [BSI92] or [TSE06] and recommendations [CEC96] or [TSE06] existing with the subject TQM. However, there is no single definition of what TQM is about or what it is not about. Mostly all instantiations believe in the following key aspects:

Customer: TQM is customer centric. The needs of the customer define the quality requirements. Based on the quality requirements TQM optimizes the value streams.

Responsibility: TQM starts with a top management initiative/commitment for quality. For the quality, every employee is responsible.

Process: TQM is process centered. The processes are run by individuals. They have to be trained, but the main "key" for the delivery quality is the process. Focused on this idea, employees have a mindset that the reason of defects is an imperfect process instead of themselves.

Improvement: TQM is based on continuous improvement. The idea behind leads to the optimization of processes, which can be run to guarantee a zero defect rate. Kaizen [IMA86] is based on this manufacturing delivery approach.

Based on the strong process believe with continuous improvement the zero defect approach is a logical consequence. Believing in strong processes with a continuous improvement it is a logical consequence to bring quality to a zero defect rate.

Cross-functional: TQM implements cross-functional teams up to improve the quality. However, the teams are mostly driven to handle quality issues that have to be sustainable fixed. The concept of Taylorism is deeply integrated in the manufacturing paradigm.

Supply-Chain: TQM works with selected suppliers as partners to establish a high quality of the processes. The partners have to have an implemented TQM approach to assure adequate process integration.

Based on these key aspects TQM is a quality philosophy with a methodological approach to reach the goal of continuous process improvement. This leads to models and awards like [EFQM], which are focusing on operative excellence.

TQM and its concepts is the base for many other quality approaches like six sigma (from Motorola) or lean initiatives (derived from Toyota Production System [TPS88]), which leads to the agile approach described later.

2 Agile Believes in Culture and Interacting People

The basics of the agile quality approach are submitted in the agile Manifesto [AGMA]. It is stated "[…] we have come to value: […] working software over comprehensive documentation […] That is, while there is value in the items on the right, we value the items on the left more." That means by no way that agile processes work without documentation, we simply take in consideration that a document without working software is meaningless and therefore the effort in building the product is more important. What I have seen in many discussions is a half-hearted approach in implementing this manifesto.

For those, who want a better grasp in the meaning of the manifesto, there are the twelve agile principles for clarification [AGPI]. We can read "Working software is the primary measure of progress" and "Continuous attention to technical excellence and good design enhances agility" for example.

Reading this should lead everyone to the realization, that high product quality is mandatory in agile development approaches.

Process quality is also addressed in the manifesto: "Individuals and interactions over processes and tools" does not mean agility uses no processes. In contrary it is stated in the principles "At regular intervals, the team reflects on how to become more effective, then tunes and adjusts its behavior accordingly". That means, that correctly implemented agile environments can reach a CMMI or SPICE Level of 5 (in short defined processes with a defined improvement cycle). For most traditional organizations and QM-approaches such a high level is nearly unreachable.

For those, who find the idea of agile processes for high quality products and processes still hard to believe I recommend the rule-books of the two largest agile practices:

- Scrum [SCRUM, SCRUMM]: In my words: A process-framework with a distinct role description, process description and defined product- and process-improvement-events.
- Kanban [KANBAN]: Quotation from the Intro: "A method for defining, managing and improving services that deliver knowledge work […]".

3 Joining Both Approaches

As it can easily be seen out of the previous descriptions, there are no real differences between these two approaches. In our perception, the differences are made up out of a misunderstanding of the primary goals of both approaches for high quality products and processes.

Based on the theory of the Spiral Dynamics model [BEC05] we implemented another approach for addressing a quality understanding. Table 1 shows the defined levels and key aspects of the perception of business reality for our teams.

Table 1. Levels of the spiral dynamics model

Level	Context
Turquoise	Collective individualism – deal with multi-dimensional trans-rational issues
Yellow	World-centric – Live fully and responsibility and integrate diversity with discernment
Green	Social democracy – inner peace and consensus in communities
Orange	Capitalistic democracy – act self-interest driven to win
Blue	Nation states – follows given rules and individual life their roles
Red	Feudal empire – Alignment based on power; not long-term stable
Purple	Tribal order – Establish a spirit in a tribes to have a safe "area"
Beige	Survival bands – Individual actions/reactions

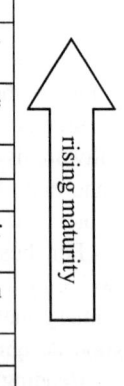

rising maturity

For many traditional teams the blue or also the red level can be observed as their level of interacting with each other. It is difficult for such a team to interact with another team more than one level above because they cannot understand the approaches of teams above to reach (quality) goals.

On the other side, it is difficult to work with teams which are multiple levels below their own perception, because a team with the high maturity has to downgrade the quality assurance mindset to a lower and in their perception unwanted quality level.

We observed that in agile teams at least the green maturity level is the basis of working together.

After we realized this, we decided to start a blog in the internal social media of Volkswagen and en-forced this in various community meetings to emphasis the common ground for both business units. To polarize the positions in the blog we played the roles classic and agile "evangelist". Mirko played the agile and Alexander the classic QM evangelist to make the different mindsets transparent and to start reflection by the people based on their team maturity to go ahead and to bring them together. The red and blue teams should see that the green teams are not against quality assurance and management (and vice versa). Only the application of methods varies to fit their respective mind set for excellence in quality topics. But the fundamental principles behind the applied methods are the same for both groups.

Here is an extract out of the quality blog of Volkswagen IT.

3.1 Preamble

No fighting, no disrespect any more – whether traditional or agile projects, together we want to reach our goal.

With this blog we want to encourage all developer, in which way you could improve the quality of your project.

In regular intervals we want to post real life problems and possible solutions, collected from our trainings and consultant work with the projects.

We are curious about your feedbacks and ideas for further articles.

3.2 Testing Reduces Product Costs

Ever heard this: Business: Why should I pay so much for testing? I pay for developers!

Common reason for this question: In many cases, the development department has a "monkey on the shoulder" from the business side. For those who are not familiar with this picture: with a "monkey on the shoulder" we have taken the problem from another person or another group. It happens quite often without us realizing such an act, so the monkey crawled up our back or was placed there secretly.

In many of the cases we reviewed, the developers who implemented new features were fixing the software bugs as well. Therefore, as a development team if you take the example of the monkey for deciding in which way to split your capacity either for new feature implementation or for bug fixing you will get a conflict with the business expectations very often. At the Volkswagen IT the budgets are released and fixated by business departments for the development of new functionality and therefore customer satisfaction is mandatory. For many projects, this is a no win situation.

An idea out of the situation: Give the monkey back to the business departments! Implement the customer in the development process and let him decide where the actual priorities between feature implementation and bug fixing are. The business side will be far better in deciding, whether the actual product quality is sufficient for the end-customers or if we should spend more work on higher product quality.

A word of warning: When you try to send the monkey back in the same secret manner you received it, you will likely fail in reaching customer satisfaction. Be open and courageous about it and discuss the problem and the consequences with your business representative. In this way we reached numerous agreements and more stable development processes.

It could be helpful to discuss the total cost of ownership of a product. In most cases it is not helpful to think in extremes of quality management. The usefulness of the first QM-activities is enormous but will decrease with rising numbers. In a similar fashion the cost of the first QM-activities is in most cases moderate to low but will steeply increase as you can see in the following diagram:

In most Cases the target to reach is the optimal cost and effect ration for quality management (Fig. 1 – sweet spot).

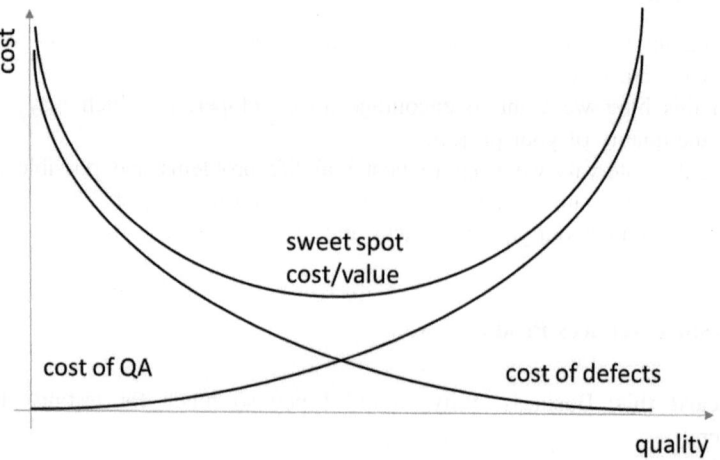

Fig. 1. Cost of quality efforts and sweet spot of cost/value for QA activities

Take-Aways

- responsibility for the balance of new features vs. bug fixing is up to the customer
- discuss with the customer the best cost and effect ratio for your QM-endeavours
- take the low hanging fruits of quality management by early integration of quality mechanisms.

3.3 Zero Known Bugs for a Release – Implementing the Rule of Ten

Ever heard this: Business: You really suggest going live with this bunch of bugs? Have you ever tested before the user acceptance test?

Common reason for this question: In many projects the testing and bug correction for a fundamental scope is still planned at the end of longer development cycles (e.g. integration at the end of a release-cycle) and cause the nearly unsolvable problem that either the bug fixing ("We don't" want to touch this module, because finding the bug in this complex structure will take ages!") or the retest of the corrected modules ("Ok, bug fixing is done in five minutes, no problem. But we don't know which side-effects will occur…") is not economical accomplishable.

These development teams in many cases either don't know or have forgotten the implication of the rule of ten. For anybody who is not familiar with the term: the rule of ten shows that later bug-fixing will lead to exponential higher cost (interesting side fact: the original thesis of an exponential factor of ten was never proven but is still the name-giver of the idea – compare with Fig. 2).

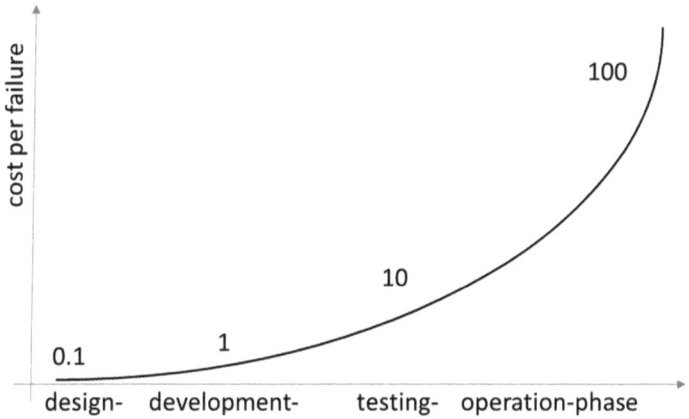

Fig. 2. Cost of fixing bugs depends on product life-cycle phase

An idea out of the situation: After sensitization and training of development teams we have come to the conclusion, that often a consideration is quite easy. Success factors besides the training are sufficient contract negotiations and planning in the development cycle.

Our most successful teams are co-located with a proximity to the customer representatives (often in the business department). This leads to understanding of the requirements much more in depth and often even before the first line of code. This is the earliest possible intervention-point and according to the rule of ten the cheapest way to correct bugs.

The next success-factor is the integration of test-know-how in the development teams (according to the scrum-idea [SCRUM, SCRUMM]: "Scrum recognizes no sub-teams in the Development Team, regardless of particular domains that need to be addressed like testing or business analysis"). We often see this Sentence misunderstood: it might be necessary to integrate test-know-how in the development team, but it is a good idea to understand testing as a team effort and not an activity of few team members (also stated in [SCRUM, SCRUMM]: "Individual Development Team members may have specialized skills and areas of focus, but accountability belongs to the Development Team as a whole."). Keeping this idea in mind you set testing *directly* at the end or even *during* coding. When the developer is still into his feature development it is a minimum of additional cost to fix the first bugs. Such things as spelling errors disappear in seconds and the retest is equally fast.

These two steps can be implemented without additional tool support and in nearly every development environment.

Enriching this with intelligent toolchains (e.g. continuous basis auf automated regression tests, treat each feature as a branching point and testing on virtual servers) it is possible to reach new levels of product quality. One of our review results was, that quite a lot of developer and tester are not familiar with state of the art for actual test methods (e.g. session based testing) and tools (e.g. FitNesse, JBehave, Cucumber) and therefore need training of this knowledge.

Another positive effect of strictly following the rule of ten is the greatest possible reduction in tracking work for defects. In projects where this principle is the leading guideline there is nearly no need for meetings for defect-classification and rework-planning, escalation meetings with management attention, etc. Naturally, not all problems especially in integrating complex products can be resolved in this manner, but with a clear focus on integration problems this project phases can become tremendous more effective.

Take-Aways

- Co-Location of important project members (e.g. tester and developer)
- Integration of test activities in the development process
- become state-of-the art with automation and actual development tools, especially for regression testing
- prevent waste in defect management (i.e. focus on solutions and working software and not on defect tracking).

4 Conclusion: There Is no Mismatch

TQM as a quality approach from the 1980 is the root of many established QM and QA settings, which are inspired by the well-working and established TQM methods and philosophy.

The newer approach of agile initiative is using concepts of TQM like continuous improvement. Agile was initial focused on IT but gradually it becomes a generic focus. This generic focus of Scrum and other agile methods and frameworks are possibilities to establish high quality in areas, which are not manufacturing based by their history. We see agile as an approach to bring quality management into knowledge-based individual products and service, which historically often were difficult to reach with explicit holistic QM approach.

Both ways optimize quality to reach the goal of effective product development and adequate quality in the field or for service operation. The agile teams improve the quality in smaller steps by quick iterations, which need less long-term planning by the short iterations of sprints, but the quality objectives with the optimization targets have to be understood by the team.

In more than 100 teams we trained in reaching a better quality understanding we observed the following facts:

- about half of that (50 teams) are organized in an agile fashion
- the part of the teams, which are organizing their processes and procedures around the quality mindset with the objective of reaching the highest quality is significant higher in agile teams
- the objective of highest quality is measured with the following KPI's
  - known defects before release date nearly 0
  - defects after start of operation without significant impact for the product
  - considerably better product understanding between business and development with greatly reduced quota of escalation needs (nearly 0)
  - considerably enhanced level of trust due to reliable commitments to deliverables (quota of keeping release dates at nearly 100%)

We observed teams, which reached the goal, but we also see that it is constant work to keep the level. The work is to deal with that key-players leave the team, the environment changes with impacts to the team etc.

The key for our resume is that agile procedures mostly have an inherent QM approach with the iterative and incremental improvement. This approach focuses on both the product and process quality. These two aspects help to establish QM also in not process driven business – but systematically they will discover the processes to assure better product quality.

The wording in the established agile approaches sometimes differs, but the objectives about the product and process quality are equivalent.

References

[AGMA]   Sutherland, J., et al.: http://www.agilemanifesto.org
[AGPI]   Sutherland, J., et al.: http://agilemanifesto.org/principles.html
[BEC05]   Beck, D.E., Cowan, C.: Spiral Dynamics: Mastering Values, Leadership and Change. Wiley-Blackwell, Hoboken (2005). ISBN: 978-1-4051-3356-2
[BSI92]   Total Quality Management: Guide to Management Principles, London, England: British Standards Institution (1992). ISBN 9780580211560, OCLC 655881602, BS 7850
[CEC96]   Electronic Components Committee: Guide to Total Quality Management (TQM) for CECC-Approved Organizations, Brussels, Belgium: European Committee for Electrotechnical Standardization, CECC 00 806 Issue 1 (1994)
[EFQM]   http://www.efqm.org/
[IMA86]   Imai, M.: Kaizen: The Key to Japan's Competitive Success. Random House, New York (1986)
[KANBAN] Anderson, D.J., Carmichael, A.: Essential KANBAN Condensed. http://leankanban.com/guide/
[SCRUM]   Sutherland, J., Schwaber, K.: The Official Scrum Guide. http://scrumguides.org/

[TPS88]   Ohno, T.: Toyota Production System: Beyond Large-Scale. Productivity Press, Portland (1988). ISBN: 978-0915299140
[TSE06]   Total Quality Management: Guide to Management Principles, Turkish Standards Institution (TSE), TS 13133 (2006)
[SCRUMM]   http://www.scrumguides.org/scrum-guide.html

Agile Development Offers the Chance to Establish Automated Quality Procedures

Marc Kösling(✉) and Alexander Poth(✉)

Volkswagen AG, Berliner Ring 2, 38436 Wolfsburg, Germany
{marc.koesling,alexander.poth}@volkswagen.de

Abstract. In large enterprises, it is not a trivial feat to establish well-defined quality processes and procedures. Agile development needs automated procedures to realize the iterative product development. This automation demand can be a starting point to setup automated quality procedures for product testing during the continuous integration of the product development. This work shows the way to a testing as a service environment for a private cloud infrastructure. The service environment is motivated by up-coming challenges, agile teams are developing cloud applications with a focus on product specific quality assurance.

Keywords: Agile software development · Agile transition · Quality management · Quality assurance · Cloud · Micro-services

1 The Agile Context from the Quality Assurance Perspective

Agile sets a good environment for quality assurance (QA) by its iterative and incremental product development. The core principal of quality assurance – the Deming circle [DEM82] – is an inherent procedure of many agile frameworks and established for example in Scrum rituals like from sprint planning to identify (quality) tasks as planning, sprinting as do, check is established with the retrospective and act are the measures from the retro in the next sprint for improvement. The manual procedure of iterative and incremental procedures is supported by automated procedures of the continuous integration and continuous deployment chain (CI/CD) for the product delivery [HUM10].

The quality assurance in agile environments can be optimized with methods like IPDCA cycle (Fig. 1) and with automated procedures. The IPDCA cycle is an iterative way to identify and mitigate prod-uct quality risks [POT14]. This is important to identify product quality risks, which can be addressed manually (with the gained time by optimizing tasks with the CI/CD chain) or with more automated re-gression tests.

To generate more degrees of freedom for the agile team we are presenting the approach of the Volkswagen AG group IT to support the agile transition from a quality assurance perspective. We are offering automated testing via self-services in the hybrid cloud of the Volkswagen group. The presented software process improvement (SPI) approach uses the knowledge of the expectations of agile teams about value focus and the need of methods and tools to perform with current technologies, which are used by agile teams. The next chapter shows the objectives of agile teams to deliver value

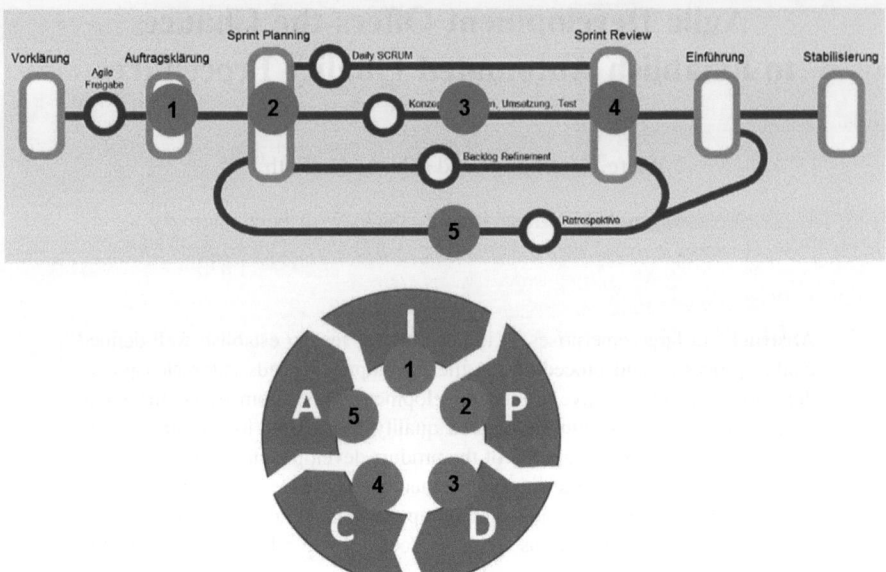

Fig. 1. The agile procedure of the group IT mapped to IPDCA cycle shows the iterations (German words are not relevant to show the concept)

with performance. Chapter 3 shows how to design automated procedures to deliver performance benefits for agile teams. The last chapter sums up progress as of now and looks into the future.

2 The Objectives of an Agile Team

Agile teams are set up as a feature team. This leads to the effect that agile teams are optimizing their autonomy by being an independent feature team. The responsibility objective of an agile team is to be able to deliver functionality end to end without dependencies on other teams [SCRUM]. The Team optimizes everything that is needed to deliver fast and efficient business value. With the focus on business value or functionality, the agile team wants to get rid of non-valuable elements from the business perspective (Fig. 2). This focus opens up the chance for supporting services – also for quality assurance supporting services. The capacity-gain can be used to build more business value or to be faster (start later).

To design supporting services two objectives have to be in top of the agenda:

- Agile teams want the freedom to choose their methods and tools to do their job efficiently
- Agile teams are open for automated support-services, which are not "core-competence" for their function-responsibility

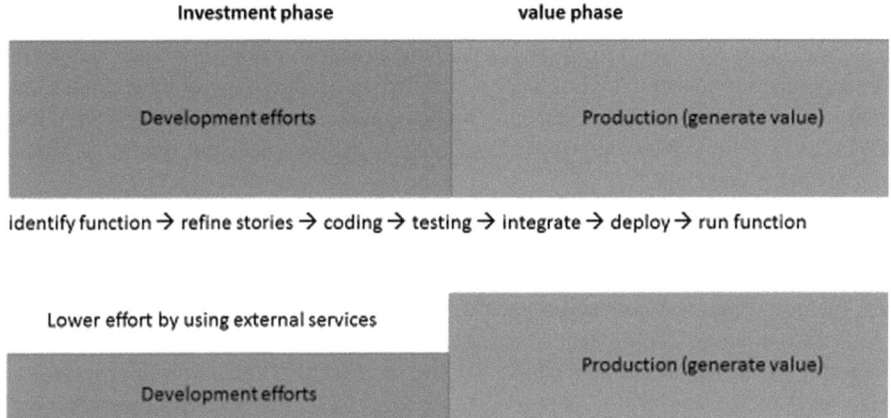

Fig. 2. External service can reduce development efforts in the agile team

We observed that if these two aspects are fulfilled agile teams would accept quality assurance methods and tools if they are helping to reach their objectives and can be included in the team's procedures in a self-service fashion. Bigger service providers like AWS provide a CI/CD chain to their customers. These chains are out of the box but are more deployment pipelines than CI/CD chains. For a complete CI/CD chain adequate test-actions have to be integrated. Third-party providers offer some additional testing services which can be added. For private clouds, these AWS and third-party tools are mostly not useable and have to be rebuild for the private cloud. In the next chapters we show how the Volkswagen group IT established for the hybrid cloud a more holistic approach for QA, which includes self-services into the CI/CD-chain.

3 Automated Workflows for Procedures

The cloud philosophy is to manage resources via self-service portals and automatism [NIST11]. This fits to the mindset of agile teams to be autonomous and independent with high focus on the business value stream. The cloud technology brings some more "nice stuff" to the agile teams to get rid of high team resource allocations:

- Setup of infrastructure via configuration makes it easy to create equal environments in all stages
- Setup of new deployments is "fast" by using software defined infrastructure and network
- Micro-services [NEW15] are bounded contexts, which limit the impact of failures to the bounded context
- Core resilience aspects are delivered by cloud technology – auto restart, scaling etc.

Based on these cloud features the need for heavy testing procedures over long periods is not necessary because you focus on your main risks during testing. Non critical aspects with low product quality impact are not tested in detail because it is easy to correct them with a bug fix deployment. To realize this quality assurance and testing strategy an automated CI/CD chain is needed to ensure reproducible builds and deployments, which are guaranteeing improvement and not more bugs with each deployment. The CI/CD chain operationalizes or includes inherent quality assurance and testing procedures.

Continuous Integration can be triggered after every code commit and delivers a fast feedback to the developer via the results of the tests.

Continuous Delivery has some manual action before productive-delivery, which can include some manual user acceptance tests.

For Continuous Deployment no manual actions are needed before productive usage – see Fig. 3, which shows an example for stages of a CI/CD chain. In both variants, a high level of test-automation is needed to perform CI/CD in a reliable manner.

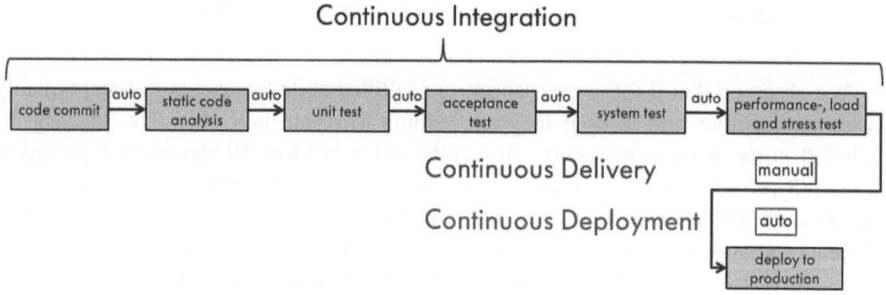

Fig. 3. CI/CD-chain schemata

Some standard aspects that are addressed in an operational QA-strategy of an agile team, which develops cloud applications in a micro-service context:

- Zero defect strategy to fix a bug at the moment when the bug is discovered – this definition does not say that the product has no bugs – only no known bugs
- Test methods for different aspects are defined and implemented for example from the static code analysis to the end to end test
- Early automation focus on fast deployment cycles with high quality because in short cycles it is impossible to test enough to be sure that all important things are "checked"
- User involvement (acceptance) is done early and often – this can be carried out by deployments which are only visible for a sub-set of users
- Check performance and load demands early to assure that the system has the capability to serve the load

Based on these insights quality assurance and testing services can be designed to fit the demands of agile teams.

3.1 Agile Quality Management Supported with Testing as a Service

Agile teams have the full responsibility for their software product and therefore an interest in good quality in their work because they get the blame and have to fix errors themselves. The team normally has a quality strategy for micro-service based cloud applications similar to:

Quality-Management is set up to manage the service quality. The development team of ProductX uses the IPDCA cycle to manage the service quality. ProductX dosn't guarantee SLAs, but ProductX is designed to be a reliable service in functionality, availability and performance from users perspective and maintainability from the developer perspective.

Based on the product quality risk analysis, stories with product impact are reflected about their quality risks to set up specific quality actions to mitigate the story-specific quality risks. Defects and other technical debts are fixed quickly to have a small cost of delay for ProductX service changes. This approach leads to fast response to fix bugs in production and is a balance between "over-testing" and "unappropriated quality".

Quality-Assurance is to reduce quality risks in a front-loading fashion before the service is in production. The development team of ProductX uses constructive and analytic methods to mitigate the quality risks.

Constructive quality assurance methods and techniques:

- micro-service approach to bound the impact space of a failure
- API-first approach to define well-known and early testable interfaces
- resilience approach via self-diagnostic to reset "unhealthy" micro-services

Analytic quality assurance methods and techniques:

- static code analysis
- unit testing
- acceptance testing
- Integration testing (also with consumer driven contract testing (CDCT))
- System test (with specialized endpoint testobject-stub)
- Performance-, load- and stress test

The test activities are driven by the product quality risks from the IPDCA cycle. High test coverage is not the main objective, because the constructive actions make it possible to act fast if defects or other unexpected issues enforce reactions to defects etc.

This leads to analyze what is easy to setup for the agile team and what needs high effort to establish. Static code analysis is easy to integrate in the CI/CD chain, e.g. via SonarQube. For unit testing it's the same. Acceptance testing is driven by the acceptance criteria of the individual story and can be realized in different test stages with different tools. Integration testing is based on different methods and tools, but should be done on a common test dataset. Test data could be provided on a generic way. System test should be technical and UI-driven. The UI-part could be done in a generic way. Not all Use Cases can be tested in an automated way. Some need the expertise of a user or not all external system can be mocked. The performance- load and stress-test needs special test environments and tools. This is not easy to set up and a good point for generic solution.

Based on this analysis the topics that should be generic are good starting points for testing services. The other topics are done in more or less the standardized CI/CD chain. For example, SonarQube can be configured centralized with a ruleset for languages like Java or JavaScript.

3.2 Implementation of the Developer Testing Service

The implementation of the identified demands for testing services is realized in the group IT cloud (GITC) of Volkswagen AG. The private part of the GITC is a cloud solution for applications, which cannot be hosted in public cloud environments. These types of applications also have quality requirements. This leads us to set up a testing as a service portfolio, which currently addresses performance-, load- and stress-testing to integrate the micro-service to the business processes. Further, a WAN-simulation is offered to test the "feeling" of the applications on remote locations or mobile connections with limited bandwidth and/or high latency. The WAN-simulation makes it possible to quickly identify with a cloud internal testing environment how the real world will experience the application performance without complex test scenarios with mobile devices with limited bandwidth etc.

Core requirements for the TaaS solution

- Self service capability
- Test resources on demand (pay per use)
- Scaling with the service customers (horizontal scaling – each customer gets an individual in-stance)
- Service runs on each cloud instance/side of the GITC
- Starting functionality is extendable to new features and functions
- Openness to our hybrid cloud users (if the market can't offer cheaper or better solutions)

The implementation is made in an open stack environment via kubernetes and docker containers to be flexible for future extensions of the testing services. To realize the testing functionality jmeter [JMET] and traffic control is used. Traffic control is currently an architectural issue, because the configuration is made in the open stack [OSTA] environment and not on higher abstraction layer. The selection of these tools was driven by the availability under open source licenses, which make it easier to setup the service in different cloud locations without difficult license management actions. Furthermore, the open source tools makes it easier to scale without additional costs. The figure below shows the logical architecture for the testing as a service solution. The architecture is designed to be a generic API service for all testing solutions for projects. Once the projects are registered, they can use all services of the TaaS solution for functional and non-functional tests via their build pipelines for their applications.

Only providing technical services is not enough to be a good partner for the agile teams. We also offer know-how by providing a service How-To and other related information which is important for a successful service integration. Figure 4 shows the environment for the cloud testing services in the con-text of additional service information. The most important aspect of load testing within a micro-service architecture is the knowledge about the dependencies of the test object in the service chains. The idea of load testing is not to accidentally make implicit a denial of service (DoS) attack to other ser-vices in the service chain (yellow and red traffic). The agile team can write the test scripts if they have the knowledge and time or they can use offered services also for outsourcing the work of write and maintain test scripts. The agile team can choose what the adequate way for efficient testing is.

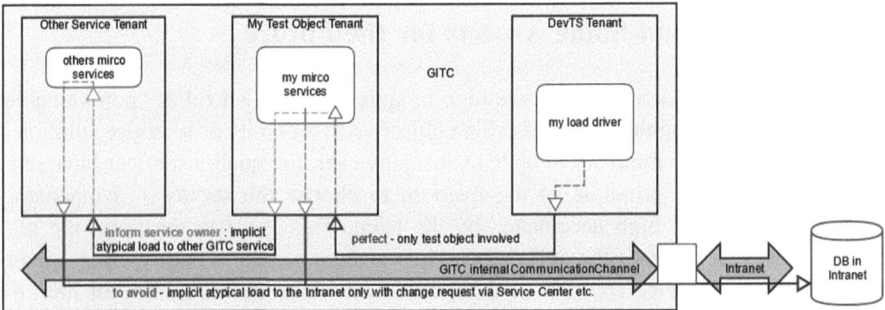

Fig. 4. Integration of testing as a service in the GITC – and possible side effects of tests (Color figure online)

Services under development are currently test data management and transfer to test objects and functional testing services on UI-level, which are easy to add into Kubernetes [KUB] cluster with Docker [DOCK] containers (Fig. 5). However, for

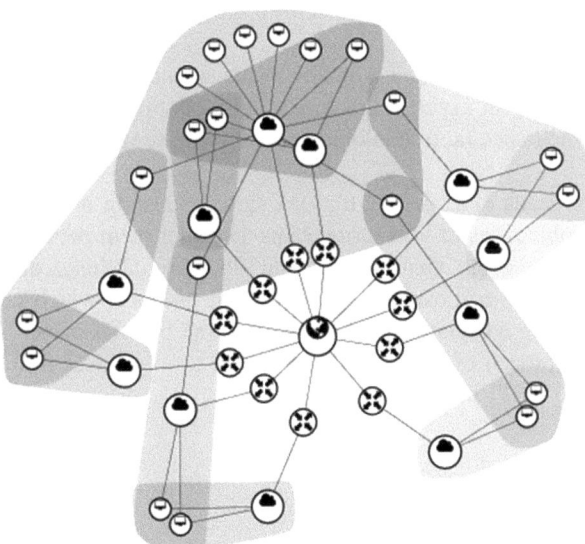

Fig. 5. The Open Stack network view by running 4 test clusters and one under construction

functional services the cloud foundry environment with the spring boot framework offers specific functional test solutions. The specific framework with specific testing solutions are an issue for generic testing services. Trade-offs have to be done and decisions about what is provided as service and what is a specific team demand and have to be handled in the agile teams. We also have a similar function for browser testing, because we cannot test each browser in all versions - we have to define an adequate sub-set to demonstrate that all applications (of our private cloud with a limited browser support) are compatible with key versions of the browser's.

4 Conclusion and Some Aspects for the Future

The acceptance of XaaS solutions are high in agile teams to get rid of "non-valuable" tasks to focus more on their business value objective. If a quality as a service solution is offered this fits to the mind-set of agile teams. However, the quality services have to be compatible with the principle of the freedom to choose the service – a mandatory service will not find high acceptance by the team. This leads to the point the high quality self-expectation of the agile teams have to support with a highly fitting quality and testing as a service solution to their demands. If the demands are not met, the solution will not be chosen. In the context of compliance and regulations, the freedom is not given to choose, but in most cases, the team makes its decisions which QM, QA and testing strategy are adequate.

We observed with the services, the central test and quality assurance team notified "new" customers after offering the cloud testing service. An effect for the customers/user is the integration into their CI/CD-chain, without dependencies to manual setup of a load test environment by the central test and quality assurance team, which makes the round-trip time of tests much shorter. The change for the teams is now that they do not have to setup testing systems nor do they have to wait for support by a centralized testing team.

However, the main challenge for quality management, quality assurance and testing will be more diversity in expertise, methods and tools to fit the different agile teams' demands about their specific technologies, which they are using to realize the business value.

These insight leads to a strategy for QM, QA and testing in the future: keep your attention on the objectives of your agile teams and offer them perfect support services to reach their quality goals. Quality gates and other formal things don't drive quality now – quality is now in most cases a supporting instance, which could be a good partner for delivering adequate product quality to the product owner and users. With the automation approach of CI/CD are many other process areas in focus and can be accompanied with a SPI initiative.

References

[DEM82] Deming, W.E.: Out of the Crisis. Massachusetts Institute of Technology. Cambridge University, Cambridge (1982)
[DOCK] https://www.docker.com/
[HUM10] Humble, J., Farley D.: Continuous Delivery: Reliable Software Releases through Build, Test, and Deployment Automation. Addison-Wesley (2010). ISBN 978-0321601919
[JMET] http://jmeter.apache.org/
[KUB] http://kubernetes.io/
[NEW15] Newman, S.: Building Microservices. O'Reilly Media, (2015). ISBN 978-1491950357
[NIST11] Mell, P., Grance, T.: The NIST Definition of Cloud Computing (2011). doi:10.6028/NIST.SP.800-145
[OSTA] http://openstack.org/
[POT14] Poth, A., Sunyaev, A.: Effective quality management: value- and risk-based software quality management. IEEE Softw. **31**(6), 79–85 (2014)
[SCRUM] http://www.scrumguides.org/scrum-guide.html

A Review on the Critical Success Factors of Agile Software Development

Abdullah Aldahmash[✉], Andy M. Gravell[✉], and Yvonne Howard[✉]

School of Electronics and Computer Science, University of Southampton, Southampton, UK
a.aldahmash@soton.ac.uk, {amg,ymh}@ecs.soton.ac.uk

Abstract. Given the evolution and increasing usage of agile methods and practices, the successful adoption of agile is crucial. During the last decade, the critical success factors (CSFs) of agile development research developed rapidly. This paper aims to review the research on CSFs of agile software development in the last ten years (2006–2016) which used empirical methodologies to identify the success factors. In this paper, eight factors are selected as critical success factors for agile software development. A taxonomy which maps these eight CSFs into Technical, Organizational, People, Process categories is introduced in this research.

Keywords: Success factors · Agile development · Software development · Agile success

1 Introduction

The success of implementing agile development practices has been investigated by many researchers over the last decade. According to Sjoberg, Dyba, and Jorgensen [1], in the future software engineering research should focus more on empirical studies. Such empirical research will likely lead to established scientific knowledge regarding how the different software engineering methods, tools, and techniques are being used. In the case of agile development, empirical studies should enable a better understanding regarding how agile principles and practices are adopted and their impact on project success. Important factors associated with agility, such as people, process, and organizational culture, are unlikely to be addressed without solid empirical research. Kitchenham et al. [2] did a systematic review about the status of systematic literature review (SLR) in software engineering and 20 SLRs have been selected. There are some SLRs covering aspects of agile development such as requirement engineering [3]. However, there was no SLR focused on the success factors of agile software development. In light of this, there is a need for more SLRs to study the status of the success in agile development.

This paper is aiming to review the literature on the critical success factors (CSFs) of agile software development over the past ten years. The focus in this paper will be only on the studies which use empirical methodologies to identify the success factors of agile software development in the last decade. Eight papers have been selected which investigated the CSFs of agile development dated from 2006 to 2016. We then include all the success factors which were mentioned in at least two of these eight papers.

The success factors identified by this process are Delivery strategy, Team capability and training, Agile development techniques, Customer involvement, Project management process, Organizational culture, Communication, and Top management support. This paper also introduces a taxonomy which maps these eight CSFs into Technical, Organizational, People, Process categories.

This paper is organized as follows: Sect. 1 is an introduction, and Sect. 2 is a background. Section 3 shows the research methodology, Sect. 4 presents the findings and gives more details about each success factor. Section 5 provides conclusion and suggestions for future work some of which is on-going.

2 Background

Agile practices have been developing since the late 1990s. The agile momentum in the software industry started with the Agile Manifesto [4]. In 2001, a group of software practitioners introduced the Agile Software Development Manifesto. According to Conboy [5], agility denotes "the continual readiness of an information system development (ISD) method to rapidly or inherently create change, proactively or reactively embrace change". According to agile principles, the focus should be on adding value rather than following the plan. Delivering working software to the users frequently and in a short period of time can add a value for the users [6]. Agile development expects the software development team to deliver early and then gain feedback early, meaning it can make changes more easily, improve quality, and conduct constant testing.

The agile mindset supports changes during the development rather than discouraging them. It also encourages feedback from the users as early as possible. Agile practices address two of the toughest challenges facing business and technology nowadays: firstly, the need for an innovative approach in developing software and, secondly, the need for a work environment which is dynamic in responding to frequent changes [7].

The agile encourages the overlapping of roles and tasks within the development team. Such overlapping will likely lead to skills improvement among the team members. This overlapping of roles and redundancy of skills will probably enhance the team's ability to respond to changing requirements throughout the development project [8].

Cockburn and Highsmith [9] claimed that the agile philosophy places more emphasis on the people factor than traditional software development approaches. A skilled team is crucial, and so each individual team member adds more value to the agility of the development process. Thus, agility not only reduces the documentation effort in a development project, but also focuses on building a highly-skilled team capable of using any technique or tool to achieve its objectives.

In addition to this, Boehm and Turner [10] identified several barriers preventing the implementation of agile practices in a legacy organization. They divided the barriers into three categories, the first of which is software development conflicts, which are linked to the process of developing the software itself. Since the agile methods and the traditional methods differ, the process of requirement gathering, designing, implementation... etc. will require new approaches which will, in turn, require new techniques, tools, and skills to develop software. The second category is related to business process conflicts. Because agile development is evolutionary or iterative, there will be tremendous changes in the way business processes are built or managed. The third category is people conflicts. People conflicts constitute the most critical barrier standing in the way of development. The people factor is a vital aspect of agile movement, since agile relates to motivated individuals and flexibility in a supportive environment [10].

Gandomani et al. [11] claimed that the obstacles in agile transformation originate from the organizational culture and structure. It is suggested that organizations attempting to move to agility should pay attention to the efforts involved in moving from a process-centric model to a people-centric model.

Begel and Nagappan [12] from Microsoft Research, conducted a survey with 487 respondents, all of whom were asked what they felt were the top benefits and problems associated with agile development. The top three benefits were the improvement of communication and coordination among the development team, faster delivery and release, and quicker response to changes/design flexibility. On the other hand, the top three problems were the difficulties with large-scale projects, many required meetings, and management buy-in, the latter of which means being strict with dates.

According to Leidecker and Bruno [13], the critical success factors are those factors, conditions, variables and attributes that, when properly addressed, managed and sustained, have a huge impact on the success of the work. Kloppenborg, Manolis, and Tesch [14] stated that a project is considered successful if it meets the traditional success measures of cost, time and scope constraints. However, Bytheway [15] claimed that unless a software project addresses organizational needs, it cannot be deemed successful. Shenhar, Dvir, Levy, and Maltz [16] introduced a multidimensional concept of project success. This concept introduced four measures of project success: project efficiency (meeting time, cost and scope constraints), customer satisfaction, business or organizational success, and future preparation.

3 Research Methodology

According to Kitchenham [17], one of the reasons for undertaking a systematic review is to summarize the existing evidence about a technology or a phenomenon. In this paper, the reason for undertake a study review is to summarize the empirical evidence of the critical success factors of agile software development during the last ten years. The literature reveals a large number of studies which have examined the success factors of implementing agile practices in an organization. We did a review to search for the studies of agile CSFs in the last ten years (2006–2016) which used empirical methodologies to identify the success factors of agile development. Previous empirical studies [18, 19, 20, 21, 22, 23, 24, 25] have been selected to review in this paper. Indeed, a number of success factors in agile development have been proven as a result of these studies. The selected journals and conferences which are the ones recognized for publishing high quality papers on agile development are shown in Table 1.

Table 1. Selected journals and conferences proceedings

Source	Number of selected studies
Journal of Systems and Software	3
Journal of Software Engineering and Applications	1
European Conference on Software Process Improvement	1
International Journal of Project Management	1
The Eighth International Workshop on Cooperative and Human Aspects of Software Engineering	1
SoutheastCon, 2007. Proceedings. IEEE	1
Empirical Software Engineering Journal	0

4 Findings

The criteria for selecting the critical success factors in this study are: (i) to be validated by an empirical study; (ii) to be mentioned in at least two different studies. The selected critical success factors for agile development and the corresponding literature are listed in Table 2. There are other success factors which we did not include in this paper because they were mentioned only in one study. For example, Livermore [25] indicated that the organization size is a success factor for agile development. Another example, Stelzmann et al. [19] claimed that the change response strategy is a success factor for agile development. A taxonomy of the critical success factors is shown in Fig. 1.

Table 2. CSFs of agile software development

Success factors	Literature
Delivery strategy	[18, 19]
Team capability and training	[25, 18, 20, 22, 21]
Agile development techniques	[18, 22, 19]
Customer involvement	[18, 20, 19]
Project management process	[18, 19, 23]
Organizational culture	[20, 22, 21, 24]
Communication	[19, 24]
Top management support	[25, 24]

This taxonomy of the success factors is driven by the classical approaches of project management and ISO21500 were the success factors classified into technical, process, and organizational categories. According to [26], projects success factors could be classified into four categories as follows:

- Project initiation and pre-contract activities
- Project preparations, design policy, technological infrastructure, design methods
- Planning and control processes
- Organizational and management environment

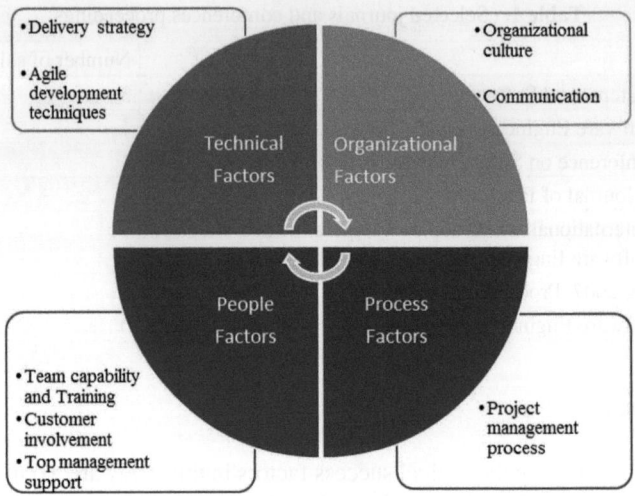

Fig. 1. Agile development success factors taxonomy

In light of this, these categories proposed by [26] could be labeled as Process, Technical, and Organizational categories. With categories I and III to be merged as Process. And category II could be labeled as Technical and category IV could be viewed as organizational category.

In the case of agile projects success factors. With the concentration of the agile manifesto values [4] on individuals and the people role in agile software development. There is a need to add a new category of the success factors of agile development which is people category. Therefore, this paper categorized the eight identified success factors of agile development from the literature into Technical, Process, People, and Organizational categories Fig. 1.

4.1 Delivery Strategy

In order to have an effective delivery strategy in agile development projects, two points must be assured. Indeed, there must be frequent delivery of working software and the most important features should be delivered first [18]. The delivery strategy should be clear within the project team, and each member should know his/her role in the strategy.

4.2 Team Capability and Training

Agile development should be built on motivated individuals. Having the right people is essential for any project, and in agile projects it is even more important, since agile projects depend on the individuals' competency. There should be an emphasis on training and continuous learning during the agile development project [20]. In order to maximize the benefits of the team capability factor, agile development should be built on a talented team. Moreover, all necessary steps should be taken to ensure that the team has the training needed and that all members are empowered; this will lead to high levels of trust, and will ultimately result in success on the agility journey. According to Livermore [25], there is a significant relationship between successful agile implementation and receiving training on the implemented agile methods or practices.

4.3 Agile Development Techniques

Before using an agile method or technique, it is essential that the project members are familiar with the selected method or technique. The tools, ideas, and terminologies used by the selected agile method or practice must be clear to all agile development project team members [19].

4.4 Customer Involvement

Customer involvement is crucial during agile software development. Delivering frequent releases of working software and welcoming the changes in the requirements depend heavily on the involvement of customers. The more involved customers are, the more satisfied they will be with the agile development. Customer collaboration and commitment are believed to have an impact on the successful implementation of agile software [20].

4.5 Project Management Process

During the early stages of the agile development project, it is essential to launch the project plan, which must be correctly sized. The selection of an appropriate project management process contributes to the success of agile development projects in term of developing quality software [18]. According to Sheffield and Lemétayer [21], the project factor is considered to be an indicator of the agility in software development. The selected project management process should empower the project team and address the talents of the development team. The nature of agile projects which embrace changes and deliver many iterations requires a flexible project management approach.

4.6 Organizational Culture

Organizational culture can be defined as a set of organization's factors or variables which may influence the development of agile software in an organization. Organizational culture factor is a vital factor in the transition into agility. The organization should have a dynamic culture to respond to the frequent changes during the agile development life cycle [20]. According to Wan and Wang [22], three aspects of organizational culture may affect agile development, the first of which is the overtime culture. This is followed by the culture of no trust in an organization, and finally the lack of mutual collaboration culture.

4.7 Communication

Communication is essential to the success of any project. In agile development, communication factor is playing a vital role to the success of agile projects. The nature of agile project which includes involvement of the customers, frequent feedback, dynamic changing and self-organizing teams will require an efficient communication between the project's members and with the customers. Stelzmann et al. [19] stated that in agile development it is necessary that the communication being as direct as possible. Since direct communication will eventually lead to foster the communication process in agile development projects.

4.8 Top Management Support

According to Livermore [25] study, there was a significant relation between the support of top management and the success of agile projects. The management involvement and support is crucial to the success of agile projects.

5 Conclusion and Future Work

The last decade has produced a great deal of research focused on identifying the factors that influence the success of agile software development. This paper aims to do a review of the critical success factors of agile software development research in the last decade (2006–2016). Eight previous studies have been selected because they used empirical methodologies to validate the CSFs. The selected studies identified many success factors for agile software development. Of which eight factors have been selected in this paper because they were identified by more than one study. The eight factors are delivery strategy, team capability and training, agile development techniques, customer involvement, project management process, organizational culture, communication, and top management support. The selected factors have been classified into a taxonomy of factors which include Technical, Organizational, Process and People categories.

Future research might work on the proposed taxonomy and explore how those success factors are related to each other. Future work may study the importance of these CSFs and the weight for each factor. There is an on-going survey to collect data from agile practitioners around the world to explore the importance of the eight identified success factors. We received responses from 131 agile practitioner. The relation between the number of completed iterations in the agile project and the importance of the success factors will be investigated. The role of individual's experience and organizational experience with agile in the perception of the identified success factors will be explored. Using factor analysis, we will investigate the relationships among the identified eight success factors.

References

1. Sjoberg, D.I., Dyba, T., Jorgensen, M.: The future of empirical methods in software engineering research. In: 2007 Future of Software Engineering, pp. 358–378 (2007)
2. Kitchenham, B., Brereton, O.P., Budgen, D., Turner, M., Bailey, J., Linkman, S.: Systematic literature reviews in software engineering–a systematic literature review. Inf. Softw. Technol. **51**(1), 7–15 (2009)
3. Inayat, I., et al.: A systematic literature review on agile requirements engineering practices and challenges. Comput. Hum. Behav. **51**, 915–929 (2015)
4. Beck, K., Beedle, M., Van Bennekum, A., Cockburn, A., Cunningham, W., Fowler, M., Grenning, J., Highsmith, J., Hunt, A., Jeffries, R., et al.: Manifesto for Agile Software Development (2001)
5. Conboy, K.: Agility from first principles: reconstructing the concept of agility in information systems development. Inf. Syst. Res. **20**(3), 329–354 (2009)
6. Dingsøyr, T., Nerur, T., Balijepally, V., Moe, N.: A decade of agile methodologies: Towards explaining agile software development. J. Syst. Softw. **85**(6), 1213–1221 (2012)
7. Highsmith, J., Cockburn, A.: Agile software development: the business of innovation. Computer **34**(9), 120–122 (2001)
8. Nerur, S., Balijepally, V.: Theoretical reflections on agile development methodologies. Commun. ACM **50**(3), 79–83 (2007)
9. Cockburn, A., Highsmith, J.: Agile software development, the people factor. Computer **34**(11), 131–133 (2001)
10. Boehm, B., Turner, R.: Management challenges to implementing agile processes in traditional development organizations. IEEE Softw. **22**(5), 30–39 (2005)
11. Gandomani, T., Zulzalil, H., Ghani, A.A., Sultan, A.B., Nafchi, M.Z.: Obstacles in moving to agile software development methods; at a glance. J. Comput. Sci. **9**(5), 620 (2013)
12. Begel, A., Nagappan, N.: Usage and perceptions of agile software development in an industrial context: an exploratory study. In: First International Symposium on Empirical Software Engineering and Measurement (ESEM 2007), pp. 255–264 (2007)
13. Leidecker, J.K., Bruno, A.V.: Identifying and using critical success factors. Long Range Plann. **17**(1), 23–32 (1984)
14. Kloppenborg, T.J., Manolis, C., Tesch, D.: Successful project sponsor behaviors during project initiation: an empirical investigation. J. Manag. Issue. pp. 140–159 (2009)
15. Byteway, A.J.: Guest Editor's introduction: successful software projects and how to achieve them. IEEE Softw. **16**(3), 15 (1999)
16. Shenhar, A.J., Dvir, D., Levy, O., Maltz, A.O.: Project success: a multidimensional strategic concept. Long Range Plann. **34**(6), 699–725 (2001)
17. Kitchenham, B.: Procedures for performing systematic reviews, vol. 33, pp. 1–26. Keele University, Keele, UK (2004)
18. Chow, T., Cao, D.B.: A survey study of critical success factors in agile software projects. J. Syst. Softw. **81**(6), 961–971 (2008)
19. Stelzmann, E., Kreiner, C., Spork, G., Messnarz, R., Koenig, F.: Agility meets systems engineering: a catalogue of success factors from industry practice. In: European Conference on Software Process Improvement, pp. 245–256 (2010)
20. Misra, S.C., Kumar, V., Kumar, U.: Identifying some important success factors in adopting agile software development practices. J. Syst. Softw. **82**(11), 1869–1890 (2009)
21. Sheffield, J., Lemétayer, J.: Factors associated with the software development agility of successful projects. Int. J. Proj. Manag. **31**(3), 459–472 (2013)

22. Wan, J., Wang, R.: Empirical research on critical success factors of agile software process improvement. J. Softw. Eng. Appl. **3**(12), 1131 (2010)
23. Stankovic, D., Nikolic, V., Djordjevic, M., Cao, D.B.: A survey study of critical success factors in agile software projects in former Yugoslavia IT companies. J. Syst. Softw. **86**(6), 1663–1678 (2013)
24. Kelle, E.V., Visser, J., Plaat, A., Wijst, P.: An empirical study into social success factors for agile software development. In: 2015 IEEE/ACM 8th International Workshop Cooperative and Human Aspects of Software Engineering, pp. 77–80 (2015)
25. Livermore, J.A.: Factors that impact implementing an agile software development methodology. In: Proceedings 2007 IEEE SoutheastCon, pp. 82–86 (2007)
26. Dvir, D., Lipovetsky, S., Shenhar, A., Tishler, A.: In search of project classification: a non-universal approach to project success factors. Res. Policy **27**(9), 915–935 (1998)

Agile Procedures of an Automotive OEM – Views from Different Business Areas

Alexander Poth[✉] and Fabian Wolf[✉]

Volkswagen AG, Berliner Ring 2, 38436 Wolfsburg, Germany
{alexander.poth,Fabian.wolf}@volkswagen.de

Abstract. In large enterprises, it is not trivial to establish new procedures in a standardized manner. We show how agile procedures are becoming step by step state of the art in different business areas of Volkswagen AG. A key point is that all want to improve the same with agile methods, but all demand different instantiations of agile methods to reach them. Business acceleration is the paradigm, but in a different business environment with different "business rules" – some have to be more innovative while others have to fit to more or new standards and regulations in the near future etc. We show an approach to support these different means of business acceleration with agile methods and we try to figure out some generic aspects of the acceleration journey.

Keywords: Agile software development · Agile transition · Quality Management (QM) · Quality Assurance (QA) · Software Process Improvement (SPI)

1 Agile to Accelerate Product Delivery

Business units or areas want to be more agile to deliver faster. The acceleration of time to market is mostly the driver for different business areas to start their agile transition. Often over years, bureaucratic processes and workflows are established, i.e. to satisfy normative regulations in the development of safety or emission relevant systems. People in these procedures are trained to standardize workflows and escalate non-conformance to the procedures to their managers. These bureaucratic fashion of work demands management decisions for each exception of the well-defined procedures, which become a bottleneck.

In these organizations, all people are busy to satisfy the given and established procedures. The focus of the busy people is on individual efficiency by supporting the procedure. The overall effectivity and efficiency is assured on another level – the end-to-end responsibility of the procedures is often not in scope due to the necessity to fulfil mandatory methods and process steps to release services or products like a car to the road. Local improvements to help the engineers with adopted real-life process descriptions and checklists to be used in everyday-business have been introduced at Volkswagen [Wolf17]. The result is an intranet SharePoint-based system (KEEP: Komponenten Elektromechanik Entwicklungsprozess) that is tailored to different projects including only the necessary process steps.

Even with this simplified approach to fulfil normative regulations, individuals in the procedures notice these performance potentials but are not able to change it in the Taylorism workflows. In addition, they notice that the environment demands more and more exceptions to the standardized procedures to assist fast prototype delivery, task forces and other escalation mechanisms. The exceptions are often killing potential efficiency gains of the well-defined procedures by their focus on speed. The demand to speed up their business by accelerating their product or service delivery starts the request for agile methods.

Agile breaks this fashion of working. Agile methods are focusing on an end-to-end responsibility of products or services. They focus on effectivity on short time and only if a procedure is often repeated the iterative and incremental fashion of agile methods improves continuously the workflows behind the delivery – an example shows Fig. 1 oriented on the IPDCA cycle [POT14]. Learning from these agile methods, the tailoring mechanism of the KEEP process platform is extended to agile methods where they are possible and necessary, which is decided during the tailoring.

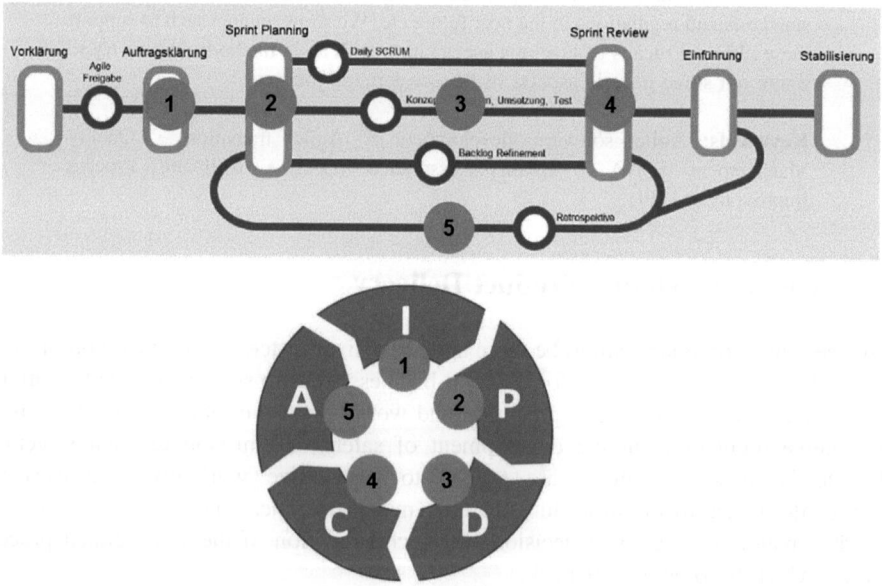

Fig. 1. The agile procedure of the group IT mapped to IPDCA cycle shows the iterations (German words are not relevant to show the concept)

2 What's Accelerate You Won't Accelerate Me

As identified in the chapter before the driver on the enterprise-level to implement an agile methodology is optimize the time to market. A closer look shows that different demands and needs to accelerate the business areas have to be addressed by implementing agile methodologies. Some examples are presented to demonstrate these different aspects:

2.1 Example from the Group IT - Deal with Established Workflows

The group IT of the Volkswagen AG build and run IT service. In the last years, the pressure to reduce time to market came to the group IT via demands from their business partners. Most applications are developed without special regulation requirements like banking or safety. These "normal" IT services can be handled with state of the art agile development methods. The group IT select Scrum and Kanban as the two first supported agile methodologies. The scrum methodology is linked to the official and generic product/service development procedure, called IT PEP, of the group IT. The IT-PEP exists in the traditional V-model and Scrum fashion. This offers the choice for all projects to select the agile instance of the IT-PEP for the product development. The big amount of projects with their business area specific products and services implement different styles of Scrum. Small projects implement a Scrum for one team big programs with more Scrum teams also implement scaling methods of Scrum. The IT-PEP do not define which kind of scaling like Less [LESS], Safe [SAFE] or another method should be used. These projects can use what is useful to fit their demands. Often a simple Scrum of Scrum is implements to synchronize 2 or 3 teams. To have an information flow between the projects about their experience with agile methods different know-how sharing options are existing. They can use the monthly agile community, which is a physical "meeting", or social media like for ex-ample the group wiki. What often is implicit expected but not explicit mentioned is better quality of the products. On one side, the co-working of the developers with the customers' product owner supports this. But on the other side if the product owner does not explicit demand quality by QA activities while focusing on feature implementation the quality activities will not done – agile makes only what is explicit demanded via stories and acceptance criteria in combination of the definition of done. This observation is important to keep in mind that time to market accelerated with a minimal viable product (MVP) by focusing only on features. However, in later phases of the product development all not early discovered and fixed bugs and technical debts of the quick hacks have to be reworked which costs performance of the developer team. Often product owner does not keep these cost of delay [REI09] in mind during the first phases of the product development – Fig. 2.

Often the development teams are not exclusive for the development of one product. In many cases, they also have to do some other not good estimable stuff to do like operating issues. This constraint makes it also for Scrum difficult to plan sprints. Often a Kanban [SHI89] approach is used to deal with these kind of issues. In some cases, it leads to Scrumban [LAD09] to accelerate the product development and make transparent what brakes.

The main topic for the transition phase is that team are mostly not full end to end oriented from the business perspective. This comes from the established Taylorism and the team have to learn to be end to end responsible. This identifies that most teams initial do not have the know-how of full stack developers to implement the business demanded functionality end to end. Further the organization around have to learn to take over responsibility into the agile teams. One big impediment to optimize the time to market in the first phase is that one procedure stage of the established Taylorism in the value chain of the agile team blocks their speed down to this stage. The development team have to

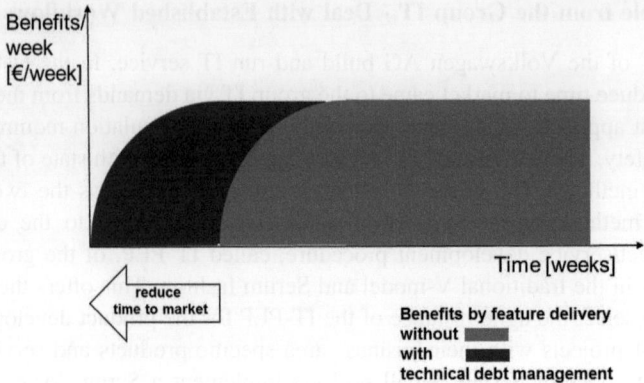

→ Less technical debt implies faster feature delivery

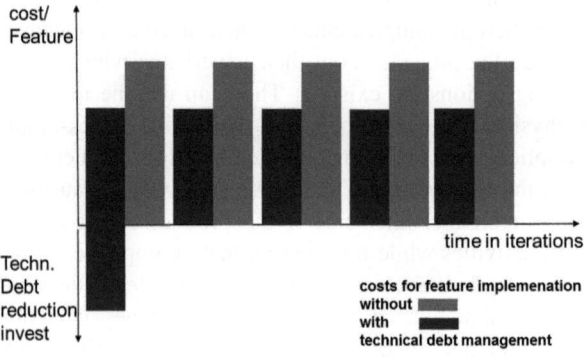

→ With starting the 3rd iteration savings are realized (product life-cycle view)

Fig. 2. Focus on feature development without adequate quality delays future features.

find out how many dependencies to for example technical competence areas they will accepted be-cause a full stack developer will not be specialist in some basis technologies – a full stack developer is a generalist. This opens the door to offer self-services to the agile teams for all non-business specific IT aspects. These services make them independent and fast and on the other side, the technical competence areas can do what they can best: optimize efficiency by centralized service delivery – this could be the balance between the efficiency of Taylorism and fast delivery by agile methodology de-pending on the demands of the specific business area.

2.2 Example from Financial Services - Deal with Regulations

The finance and insurance sector have to fulfill many regulations. The regulations are established and growing since the finance crisis driven by political forces and the European Central Bank. The regulation makes is more and more difficult to bring up fast new IT services. Different strategies are currently applied to be fast on the market. One is to invest in small start-ups called Fintechs. Another approach is to setup small units with startup character for new digital services. Both approaches have to fulfill the compliance requirements, which makes it important to show exactly what kind of services are developed and select exactly the necessary requirements to fit to the regulations. However, by this approach it is possible to define new procedures that starts with minimal and lean development procedures. They can choose the technology stack and frameworks, which are most adequate for the business demand without focus on established and "over-compliant" systems, which make extensions more difficult and slow down time to market. In such a development unit the procedures are oriented on ISO 9000 aspects and only product specific quality aspects (including regulation). The two dimensions are shown in Fig. 3. The Level of Done (LoD) dimension is for organizational quality and the product quality risk analysis identifies the product specific aspects, which have to be mitigated with product individual additional quality assurance actions. This approach empowers teams to act self-organized and agile in the context of their product. The product owner is responsible for the compliance about legal/regulation aspects and for the product quality. Some organizational aspects are de-pending from hosting and operations models – this is the reason for Product2 in Fig. 3 to do "less" organizational actions. The LoD are a kind of Definition of Done. The content is aligned on the finance and insurance market furthermore, it is assigned to agile procedures and the product responsible team workflows. For product quality risk identification a design thinking optimized method of [POT14] is used. With these two dimensions for identify the quality scope a lean approach for fast product

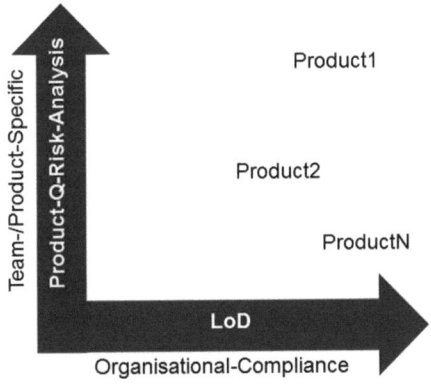

Fig. 3. Products are in fitting the organizational and specific quality requirements.

development is given to the product team compared to traditional waterfall development procedures. Based on this quality framework the teams can choose adequate methods and tools for quality assurance activities. The team can share know-how in wikis etc. to improve their efficiency and gain from projects lessons learned by high autonomy of each agile product team.

2.3 Example from Component Development - Deal with Safety

The development of electromechanical systems – an example shows Fig. 4 - including embedded hardware-software systems is one of the most difficult engineering challenges. Especially handling software complexity and safety aspects are main factors for project success. Software process quality is an important factor and should be a main focus. In the automotive domain, software features are a major part of the cars functionality while software size and complexity rise continuously. As a solution for rating process quality Automotive SPiCE [ASP2, HIS] was established in the automotive industry for more than a decade. Additionally, for safety relevant development like steering or braking systems the ISO 26262 [ISO2] is of high importance and a 'must have' for the product development. The engineering context is safety critical systems containing Automotive Safety Integrity Level D (ASIL D).

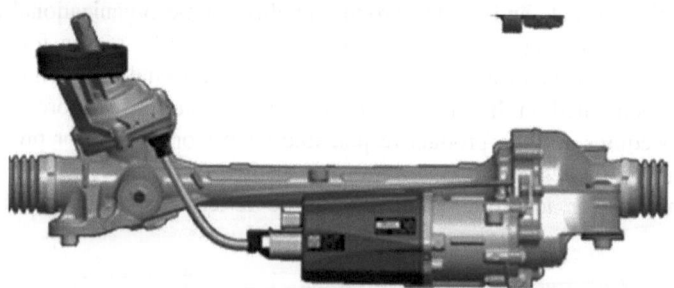

Fig. 4. Electromechanical steering system

The development experiences are documented in a web-based process management system called KEEP ('Komponenten Elektromechanik Entwicklungsprozess') – see Fig. 5 for an overview - including about 60 processes, 500 activities, 50 roles, 120 method descriptions and 250 document tem-plates with a total of more than 3000 chapters. As a novelty, all three disciplines (hardware, software, and mechanical engineering) are fully covered and deployed at development teams working in different locations and domains. Even supporting non-engineering processes like quality assurance and risk management are modelled.

Such a comprehensive process model handling that complexity and simultaneously giving the opportunity of an individual process tailoring for every project and focussing on user experience is – to our knowledge - unique in the automotive domain.

KEEP builds upon Microsoft SharePoint combined with Microsoft Visio for graphical modelling. The basic structures and functions for this system are enabled by

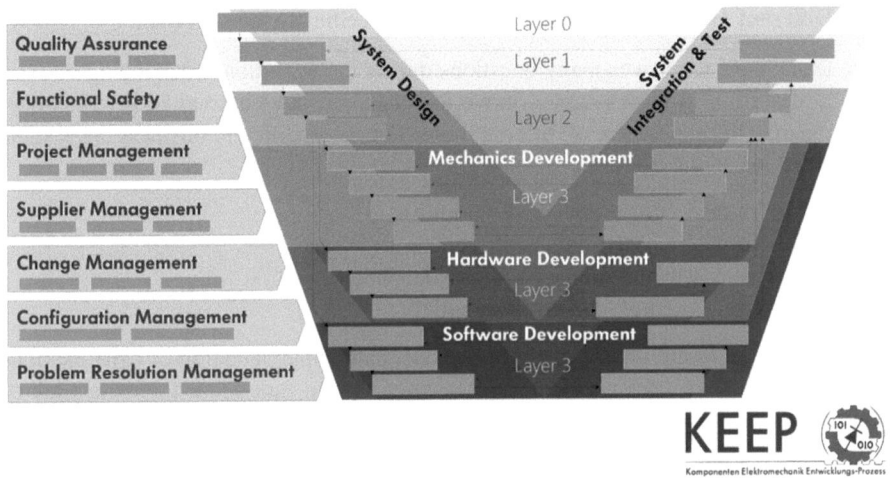

Fig. 5. KEEP – Komponenten Elektromechanik Entwicklungsprozess

an additional software suite. This combination enables active directory integration, bidirectional connections between different elements, different context types and workflows.

Pragmatic help for the engineers with established working descriptions and checklists including a defined lessons-learned process to be used in everyday development is established at Volkswagen [WOL17]. The intranet SharePoint-based system KEEP and the underlying process descriptions is subject to continuous improved and the adoption of the described agile methods where they can be applied even in safety-relevant development, e.g. for the releases of prototypes or subsystems for tests.

3 Setup of Individual Accelerators

The ACE (Agile Center of Excellence) is facilitator around agile topics for brands and business areas in the Volkswagen AG. The concept of the ACE is to "offer" agile guides to identify the individual demands and objectives of the agile transition. The agile guide develops with the people involved into the agile transition an individual and adequate transition path to reach the expected transition goals. Furthermore the ACE offers a wide spectrum of agile trainings to support the people during the transition with know how about agile methods to assure the sustainability of the transition. Each agile guide has the objective to empower the people of the transition to run the agile transition by their own. After the empowerment to organize their transition self-organized the agile guide leaves the team. The guides are recruited from different organizational units. Some are working in their units by supporting in "part-time" transitions others are "full-time" agile guides. However, all agile guides are organized in the guide guild to share know-how and plan the next transitions and assign an adequate skilled agile guide. All agile interested people can use different networks to share their experiences and knowledge around the agile community.

3.1 Different Demands for Acceleration in Specific Business Areas

Agile teams have to answer many questions during the transition – depending on their focus as described in the examples above the questions have individual prioritization. To summarize the experience of different transitions from different business areas some often asked questions (Q) are:

- Q1: How to deal with established workflows?
- Q2: How to deal with compliance (regulation) aspects?
- Q3: How to deal with complex product-dependencies?
- Q4: Setup new technologies to push agile?

These questions are important to find an adequate implementation of agile methods in the business area, because each business area has an individual focus on each of these questions, which has to be addressed by the agile methods. The questions can used to identify generalized answers and les-sons learned.

3.2 Some Generic Lessons Learned to Accelerate Your Business

Some generic practices from the experience of accompany many transitions in an enterprise environment, which is running business acceleration bottom up by business areas:

Practice	Description	Related
Know-how pooling in the agile guide guild	the guild of the agile guides is a platform for networking and know-how sharing. This is needed because our agile guides are from different organizational units and they need a platform in which they are under colleagues to learn from successful steps and mistakes	Q1, Q2, Q3, Q4
"Provisioning" of specialized know-how with a suitable agile guide to start the transition	To identify and plan/schedule agile guides for transitions are "resource allocation" of agile guides is needed. Provisioning considers the individual know how and interests of agile guides to realize a successful transition	Q1, Q2, Q3, Q4
Sharing know-how in networks around agile topic	Know-how sharing via social media and cyclic community meetings. Offer to all involved people of a transition the space to interact about the agile topic to be informed and cross-linked	Q1, Q2, Q3, Q4

(continued)

(continued)

Practice	Description	Related
Offer trainings for know-how transfer with training concepts for different professional levels	To address the demand of people to get background know how (from beginner to guru) on specialized topic around agile like leading in agile environments, scale more agile teams, etc. trainings are offered with know-how from external agile coaches and from internal agile guides. Use this practice also to establish and train new technologies like cloud etc.	Q1, Q2, Q4
Define a kind of "readiness list" before starting the transition to avoid a "bad start"	To assure a good start into the transition some basics should be set before the transition starts about the key stakeholders and the environment. Also use this check-points to reflect your progress and be honest to you if during the starting phase of a transition some key-parameters go into the wrong direction – be transparent and stop the transition if success is not visible (often the organizational environment outside the transition area is a dependency issue)	Q3
Cut established procedures by for example re-organize workflows and teams	It is important that it is possible during the transition to cut established procedures if needed to start from stretch if needed. Often a focus on acceleration about time to market and value chain focus is only limited in established structures and workflows	Q1, Q4
Care about the individual expectations about the transition to fit the demands	The individual expectations and ideas for tailored accelerations of the involved people while keeping the necessary regulations have to be addressed to keep the motivation for the "extra mile", which has to be gone during the transition	Q2, Q3

With these generic lessons learned, the ACE is able to support different business areas with their individual objectives about business acceleration by using agile methods. These generic lessons learned do not differ from the SPI Manifesto [EURO] – they confirm it also for agile transitions as a kind of SPI.

4 Conclusion and Some Aspects for the Future

The generic demand at the beginning of agile transitions is the same: give me agile to accelerate my time to market. Each business is different and agile methods have adequately instantiated to fit the business domain. The work is not to rollout agile methods quick – the work is a qualitative instantiation of agile methods to fit the specific needs of the business. Agile methods can even help to accelerate the development of traditional automotive systems. The tailoring mechanisms in different development areas can be extended to agile methods where they are possible and necessary as we have shown for the process platform KEEP. This is supported by identifying their specific demands about acceleration. This leads to individual transitions for each business unit or area. Some aspects are generic and can be addressed by answering some questions and keep in mind some lessons learned – as we show above. For the future the open point is how many self-organization could be established or in other words, how less Taylorism works on an enterprise level? This balance has to be find out – enterprise overall efficiency vs. local business areas speed.

References

[ASP2]   Automotive SPICE® Process Assessment Model; PAM 2.5: The Procurement Forum/Automotive SIG. http://www.automotivespice.com/fileadmin/software-download/automotiveSIG_PRM_v45.pdf. Accessed 10 May 2010
[EURO]   euroSPI, et al.: SPI Manifesto (2009). euroSPI.net
[HIS]   Results from the HIS (Herstellerinitiative Software) Woking-Group 'Process Assessment'. http://portal.automotive-his.de/images/pdf/ProcessAssessment/his_process-scope_automotivespice_v01.pdf
[ISO2]   ISO 26262 Road vehicles – Functional safety; Part 1-10 (2011–2012)
[LAD09]   Ladas, C.: Scrumban: Essays on Kanban Systems for Lean Software Development. Modus Cooperandi Press (2009). ISBN: 978-0578002149
[LESS]   https://less.works/
[POT14]   Poth, A., Sunyaev, A.: Effective quality management: value- and risk-based software quality management. IEEE Softw. 31(6), 79–85 (2014)
[REI09]   Reinertsen, D.: The Principles of Product Development Flow (2009). ISBN: 1-935401-00-9
[SAFE]   http://www.scaledagileframework.com/
[SHI89]   Shingō, S.: A Study of the Toyota Production System from an Industrial Engineering View-point, p. 30. Productivity Press (1989). ISBN: 0-915299-17-8
[WOL17]   Wolf, F., Lackmann, P., Steinmann, C.: Process Management for Electromechanical Systems Development on SPICE Level 3 and ASIL-D at VW. Wiley (2017). Euro-SPI special issue of the Journal of Software: Evolution and Process

Using a Statistical Method to Compare Agile and Waterfall Processes Performance

Alexssander A. Siqueira[✉], Sheila Reinehr, and Andreia Malucelli

Pontifical Catholic University of Parana, Curitiba, PR, Brazil
`alexssander_as@hotmail.com, sheila.reinehr@pucpr.br, malu@ppgia.pucpr.br`

Abstract. The agile principles and methods have become an important contribution in the Software Engineering area. Several works reported successful cases of agile adoption in the software industry and academic environment. Organizations can adopt the agile methods into their software development process using incremental or big bang approaches. The incremental approach allows the team members and stakeholders to assimilate the agile principles and techniques progressively. However, the use of this approach can omit supporting agile practices. In this case, process specialists usually recommend the big bang approach that allows teams to have a full agile practices experience. The current work contributes reporting an alternative approach based on the parallel development of projects using plan-drive and agile based processes. In this case, two development teams using different processes developed each project simultaneously. A set of ten real small projects were successfully delivered using this proposed approach and their respective results analysis, in terms of spent hours and defects, was performed using the Wilcoxon signed-rank test that consists in a nonparametric statistical method.

Keywords: Agile software development · Process improvement · Wilcoxon signed-rank test

1 Introduction

The agile methods and good-practices have been employed by several organizations to support their software development processes. In the software industry, there is a significant pressure to continuously improve business processes in order to stay competitive. The companies' productivity is directly impacted by their software development process's effectiveness [1].

In practice, few organizations are technically able to adopt agile development approaches immediately and adopt them successfully over a short period of time. A complete transition often takes a few years [2]. As the continuous agile methods adoption, there are emerging patterns of success and failure. Organizations can adopt the agile methods using an Incremental [3] approach that allows the team members and stakeholders to assimilate the agile principles and techniques progressively. In this case, the software development organization can resume their agile transition. These organizations would have conventional processes with the use of some agile techniques, not achieving a complete agile development process with the main agile practices and principles adoption.

The Big Bang [4] approach is a wholesale agile process adoption that is recommended by process specialists due to the team's need to experience the synergy of agile practices and the danger of omitting supporting practices when using the incremental approach. An agile process adoption rollout is a progressive and evolutionary flow that requires certain organization investment, especially in cultural changes to allow the agile principles and practices acceptance [5]. However, this one-way approach can cause several impacts when not successfully implemented.

A previous experience report [6] described a parallel development approach that employed a spare team of developers to initiate the agile transition in a telecommunication services company. That experience is a compromise between the Incremental and the Big Bang approaches, once the organization and development teams received the necessary training and experienced the agile techniques in real projects. However, the results analysis was not performed using any consistent method.

The current paper describes a second experience report based on parallel development that was performed in the same organization. This time, a set of ten projects were developed and the results analysis was performed with the Wilcoxon signed-rank test.

The Wilcoxon signed-rank test is a nonparametric statistical method whose application is suitable to perform data analysis from two-paired groups with different conditions [7]. The "W" test allows researchers to calculate and analyze the difference between the paired samples [8]. This nonparametric test approach was previously employed by [9] to perform software development effort estimation when encountering missing historical data sets issues. In this research, as there were a set of data measures from the same set of projects, the research group employed the Wilcoxon test to evaluate the action-research results after the projects development and their respective processes performance.

2 Research Method

The reported experience took place within a telecommunication company in Brazil. A research group was composed by an external researcher and two employees (company's internal process specialists). In this case, the suitable research method was the Action-Research (see Fig. 1). This method is an interactive approach that requires intensive researcher involvement and is composed by three types of steps [10]:

- **Pre-step:** research's context and purpose understating and definition.
- **Six main steps:** based on the context data information to elaborate an action plan that will be implemented and evaluated.
- **Meta-step:** monitoring the execution of the six main steps and identify the need for additional cycle planning and execution.

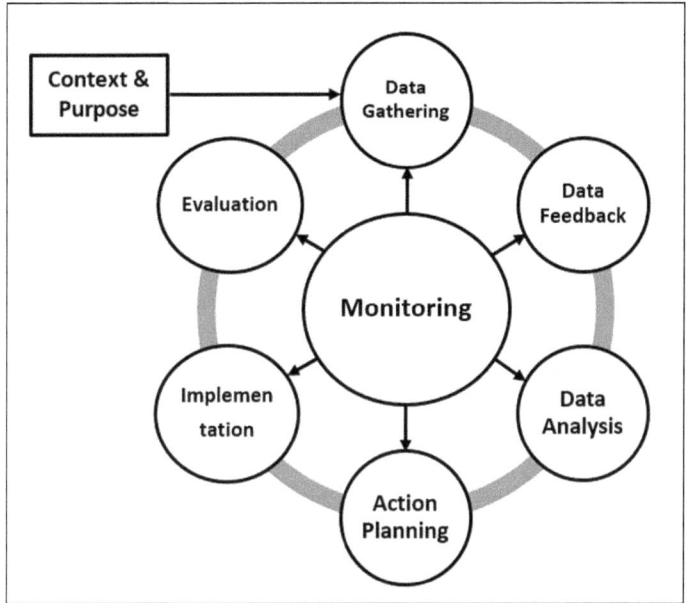

Fig. 1. Action-research method development cycle [10].

3 Research Development

A complete action-research development cycle was successful performed and described in this section.

3.1 Context and Purpose

The company had adopted in the past years many plan-driven development approaches such as the waterfall, spiral and a RUP based process. The main concerns were the difficulties to accept customer's change requests. A high number of software defects were found in the integration test and the projects costs were impacted by the unnecessary rework generated during the development phase. The main company's software development process (that it is the company's traditional process reference) was a waterfall-based process that has 5 simple phases: Business Analysis, Solution Design, Development, Integration Test and User Acceptance Test.

The development process was started with the internal customer writing the Initial Business Requirement document that contained the project's general scope that is described in functionalities and business constraints that must be implemented. Then, the development processes were performed as following:

- **Business Analysis:** A business analyst reviews the Initial Business Requirement document to describe in detail the new requirements in the Final Business Requirement document and identify any additional business constraint that must respected,

other functionalities, and projects that can be impacted by the change request. To complete the Final Business Requirement document, the business analyst informs the test cases that will be executed during the Test phase.
- **Solution Design:** A system architect reviews the Final Business Requirement document to describe the necessary changes in the involved components and databases. The architect output is the Solution Proposal document that will provide guidance to the developers during the Development phase.
- **Development:** The developers will execute the necessary changes in the identified components and databases using the Solution Proposal document as reference. The updated source code is uploaded into a specific source code repository to further deployment in the test environment.
- **Integration Test:** The project's source code is merged with other projects' source codes and deployed in the test environment. The test cases are executed as was previously informed in the Final Business Requirement document.
- **User Acceptance:** The internal customer representative checks if the delivered solution was developed as requested in the Initial Business Requirement document. After obtaining the users acceptance, the solution is deployed in the production environment for general availability.

The waterfall based process and its issues were discussed in the next action-research steps.

3.2 Data Gathering, Feedback and Analysis

The waterfall based process was presenting some issues during the project development that impacted the projects development performance (extra effort to projects completion, delivery delays) and quality (a high number of defects found during the integration test). The main issues were:

- **Documentation:** The communication channel to share information among the team members was the project's documentation. As the communication was very formal the requirements and the technical solution details were extensible documented. Even with the available documentation, architects had problems to design the solution using the project's requirements. Developers had problems to understand and implementing the solutions described by the architects. The quality of the software produced was impacted by defects that are generated during the solution coding and implementation.
- **Change Requests:** Any minimal change or update in the project's scope, was impacting the project development. The previous process phases were re-executed to support the necessary changes in the documents and components source code. In this case, changes in the project scope used to impact the cost and the project delivery date was usually postponed.
- **User Acceptance:** The business representatives (internal customer) were deeply involved in the beginning of the project when the Initial Business Requirement document was received and reviewed by the business analyst. However, during the project development the business representatives were not involved.

The adoption of agile methods is an alternative to mitigate the previously mentioned issues. A new agile development process was a suitable solution to the described organization context.

3.3 Action Planning

Due to listed productivity and quality issues that the company's traditional software development processes have presented in the last years, the company was looking for an alternative software development process to replace the traditional ones.

In this case, the necessary actions to achieve a software development proposal employing agile as an approach to solve the mentioned plan-drive issues are:

- **Action 1:** Provide the necessary agile awareness and training sessions.
- **Action 2:** Define an agile software development process proposal.
- **Action 3:** Develop 10 selected projects using the plan-drive and agile based processes.

These actions development are described in the next action-research step.

3.4 Implementation

Initially, the research group arranged a set of awareness and training sessions (Action 1) to support the use and understanding of the most important agile methods previously mentioned by [11], such as Scrum, XP (eXtreme Programming), TDD (Test-Driven Development) and PP (Pair Programing).

Then, to define an agile based development process (Action 2), the research group arranged a workshop with the development team. The result is an agile process proposal based on the core XP practices [12], such as:

- **Planning Game:** the iterations planning and control must use Scrum. The stories (activities) progress are visible for the project team and the internal customer representative (product owner). The iteration duration is 2 weeks. It is necessary to arrange a planning meeting in the iterations' beginning, daily meetings, and a final meeting in the iterations' end to verify its completion and discuss about the main goals and issues found.
- **Metaphor:** the business requirements have to be described using a simple and direct language (customer friendly language).
- **Small Releases:** all iterations should produce a software artifact that may be part of the architectural solution or a functional feature (working software) that will tested by the Test Team (Integration Test).
- **Simple Design:** the solution proposal document must have the fewest possible classes and methods. Just the minimal information to clarify the problem solution and to define a set of technical stories that will be addressed to the developers in the planning game (Scrum meetings).
- **Tests:** the source code development must be started with the elaboration of a test case. The TDD agile method supports the developer's activities.

- **Pair Programming:** this practice is applied just when a story involves a critical component change or development. This practice allows knowledge and experience sharing between two developers when working with a complex solution.

The research group organized the projects development by two different teams. All team members were newcomers to this development department. All of them, have similar skills, technological expertise and academic background. They were trained in the organization tools and technologies. However, they did not have any previous contact with the organization's waterfall based software development process.

Before starting the projects development, the following assumptions were stated as rules:

- **Parallel Development:** the same project must be developed using the waterfall based life-cycle and the agile development process. The start date was the same for both initiatives.
- **Team Member Assignment:** as the projects must be implemented in parallel, the team members would be assigned for only one of the projects implementation. It was important to balance the number of traditional and agile projects that each team member is assigned.

All selected projects were successfully executed in three months. The research assumptions were respected and followed. The parameters were registered as planned and the comparative study started analyzing the effort (hours) expended to develop the projects.

3.5 Evaluation

The initial analysis was focused on the necessary effort (hours) to deliver the project using both software development processes (see Table 1). Observing the hour's average spent in the projects, it could be possible to affirm that the agile process is more expensive than the waterfall one.

However, it is necessary to check if this difference in effort is statistically significant. The employment of a nonparametric statistical method is suitable alternative as previously described in Sect. 1. The test regarding the processes performance considered the following hypotheses:

- **Hypotheses 1:** The agile process is more expensive than the waterfall based one.
- **Hypotheses 2:** The agile process performance is not significant different from the waterfall based one.

To use the Wilcoxon test to evaluate the processes regarding their effort in hours, the following steps were performed as indicated in Table 1:

- **Step 1:** Firstly, it was calculated the difference between each value of hours by project.
- **Step 2:** Then, ignoring sign of the difference, each value was ranked starting from the smaller (Project 09 = 12) value to the highest one (Project 05 = 160). In this case, there was a match with 3 different projects with the value of 16, it was necessary to

Table 1. Wilcoxon test for projects effort analysis.

Wilcoxon Signed-Ranking Test- Analyzing Projects Effort (Hours)							
Project	Waterfall	Agile	Difference	Rank	Rank Sum		
01	112	128	16	(2) 3	Positive	37	
02	600	680	80	8	Negative	18	
03	836	960	124	9		❸	
04	708	672	-36	7			
05	400	560	160	10	Values		
06	228	244	16	(3) 3	W	18	❹
07	488	456	-32	6	N	10	❺
08	272	288	16	(4) 3	α < 0.05	8	❻
09	240	252	12	1			
10	672	648	-24	5			
Average	455,6	488,8	❶	❷			

sum their respective ranking values (2 + 3 + 4) and divide by 3, obtaining the average value of 3 for their ranks.
- **Step 3:** Next, the sum of positive and negative sign ranks was calculated (Positive = 37 and Negative = 18).
- **Step 4:** As the negative score is the smaller one, it was selected as value of "W" (W = 18).
- **Step 5:** As there was not any difference value equal to zero, the "N" value is number of projects (N = 10).
- **Step 6:** Finally, consulting the Wilcoxon's table of critical values, considering the value of "N" the result value is 8 for the significance level of 0.05 ($\alpha \leq 0.05$).

By the Wilcoxon signed-rank test, a calculated "W" is significant if it is less than or equal to the critical value [8]. The obtained value of 18 is larger than 8, in this case the Hypotheses 2 must be assumed as true, because there was no significant difference between the effort spent in the waterfall and agile based processes.

Checking the processes' average number of defects, the waterfall process produced more defects during the integration test. The Wilcoxon test was employed to verify if this average difference is statistically significant. The test regarding the number of defects identified in the processes considered the following hypotheses:

- **Hypotheses 1:** The waterfall process produces more defects than the agile one.
- **Hypotheses 2:** The number of defects produced by the waterfall process is not significant different from the agile one.

Then, the following steps were performed as indicated in Table 2 to execute the Wilcoxon signed-rank test:

- **Step 1:** The difference was calculated between each project's hours value.
- **Step 2:** Then, ignoring sign of the difference, each value was ranked starting from the smaller (Project 05 = 1) value to the highest one (Project 08 = 16). In this case, there were two matches; the first match was between the projects with difference value of 8. The rank value for both was updated to 3.5. The second match occurred with the difference value of 14, obtaining the average value of 7.5 for both ranks.
- **Step 3:** Next, the sum of positive and negative sign ranks was calculated (Positive = 0 and Negative = 55).
- **Step 4:** As the positive score is the smaller one, it was selected as value of "W" (W = 0).
- **Step 5:** As there was not any difference value equal to zero, the "N" value is number of projects (N = 10).
- **Step 6:** Finally, consulting the Wilcoxon's table of critical values, considering the value of "N" the result value is 8 for the significance level of 0.05 ($\alpha \leq 0.05$).

Table 2. Wilcoxon test for projects number of defects analysis.

Wilcoxon Signed-Ranking Test - Analyzing Projects Defects							
Project	Waterfall	Agile	Difference	Rank	Rank Sum		
01	16	4	-12	6	Positive	0	
02	8	0	-8	(3) 3,5	Negative	55	
03	16	2	-14	(7) 7,5	❸		
04	19	5	-14	(8) 7,5			
05	8	3	-5	1	Values		
06	13	6	-7	2	W	0	❹
07	13	5	-8	(4) 3,5	N	10	❺
08	19	3	-16	10	α < 0.05	8	❻
09	12	3	-9	5			
10	19	4	-15	9			
Average	14,3	3,5	❶	❷			

The obtained value of 0 is smaller than 8, in this case the Hypotheses 1 can be assumed as true, because there was a significant difference between the number of software defects that were identified during the integration test.

3.6 Results Analysis

The agile development process consumed more hours to deliver the same set of projects, but it is not possible to affirm that the proposed agile process is more expensive than the waterfall process. In this case, it is necessary to consider testing the number of identified defects in each project, once this is a company issue reported during the action-research previous steps of Data Gathering, Feedback and Analysis (Sect. 3.2). As the defects average score for the waterfall process is larger than the proposed agile process, it is possible to affirm that the use of agile methods such as TDD and PP can improve the software quality as employed in the company new agile development process. However, the PP was employed when the teams had complex solutions to be developed. In fact, the PP supported the share knowledge among the team members due to its collaborative and interactive approach.

4 Conclusion

The experience reported in this work, compared the performance of two different software development processes, using a nonparametric statistical method that allowed the test and analysis of data provided by the different measures obtained by the same set of projects. Instead of performing a simple analysis on the obtained averages values, the test identified if there was a statistically significant difference between the measured values. In this case, the Wilcoxon signed-rank test become an important contribution to compare process's performance indicators.

This research was possible due to the use of an alternative parallel approach that consists of the development of selected set of projects in parallel using two different processes and separated teams of developers.

The use of real projects was possible once the new employees were not engaged in projects and they were available to receive the technical training. As a similar context of having spare development teams is very unusual to happen in a corporative environment, a similar experience could be developed in an academic environment using active methodologies such as Project-Based Learning or Problem-Based Learning approaches.

An important research limitation was the teams' size and projects' scope extension. Some small projects were performed in just one single sprint. In this cases, the team members were not fully assigned to these projects. They completed their activities working less than 40 h/week. This is not a recommended practice, however this was not an issue to the research development. Further work, should consider all projects with a minimum number of three sprints. Then, the research group will be able to register the teams' feedbacks and sprints retrospective properly.

References

1. Kukko, M., Helander N., Virtanen, P.: Knowledge management in renewing software development processes. In: Proceedings of the 41st Hawaii International Conference on System Sciences, Waikoloa, Big Island, pp. 1–9 (2008). doi:10.1109/HICSS.2008.229
2. Qumer, A., Henderson-Sellers, B.: A framework to support the evaluation, adoption and improvement of agile methods in practice. J. Syst. Softw. **81**, 1899–1999 (2008). doi:10.1016/j.jss.2007.12.806
3. Hodgetts, P.: The impact of refactoring the development process - experiences with the incremental adoption of agile practices. In: Proceedings of the Agile Development Conference, pp. 106–113. IEEE Computer Society, Salt Lake City (2004)
4. Mencke, R.: A product manager's guide to surviving the big bang approach to agile transitions. In: Proceedings of the 2008 Agile Conference, pp. 407–412. IEEE Computer Society, Toronto (2008). doi:10.1109/Agile.2008.65
5. Roche, G., Vaquez-McCall, B.: The amazing team race - a team based agile adoption. In: Proceedings of the 2009 Agile Conference, pp. 141–146. IEEE Press, Chicago (2009). doi:10.1109/AGILE.2009.67
6. Siqueira, A., Reinehr, S., Malucelli, A.: Agile adoption - developing projects in parallel with agile and traditional life-cycles. In: Proceedings of the 24th European System, Software and Service Process Improvement and Innovation Conference, pp. 54–66. Publizon, Luxembourg City (2014)
7. Corder, G.W., Foreman, D.I.: Nonparametric Statistics: A Step-by-Step Approach, 2nd edn. Wiley, Somerset (2014)
8. Graham Hole Research Skills: Wilcoxon hand out. http://users.sussex.ac.uk/~grahamh/RM1web/WilcoxonHandoout2011.pdf. Accessed 25 May 2010
9. Idri, A., Abname, I., Abran, A.: Missing data techniques in analogy-based software development effort estimation. J. Syst. Softw. **117**, 595–611 (2016). doi:10.1016/j.jss.2016.04.058
10. Coughlan, P., Coghlan, D.: Action research for operations management. Int. J. Oper. Prod. Manag. **22**, 220–240 (2002). doi:10.1108/01443570210417515
11. Dingsøyr, T., Nerur, S., Balijepally, V., Moe, N.B.: A decade of agile methodologies: towards explaining agile software development. J. Syst. Softw. **85**, 1213–1221 (2012). doi:10.1016/j.jss.2012.02.033
12. Beck, K.: Embracing change with extreme programming. Computer **32**, 70–77 (1999)

Standards and Assessment Models

Development of the 2nd Edition of the ISO 26262

Gerhard Griessnig[✉] and Adam Schnellbach

AVL List GmbH, Graz, Austria
{gerhard.griessnig,adam.schnellbach}@avl.com

Abstract. In 2011 the automotive standard ISO 26262:2011 for the development of safety critical systems has been officially released. This standard has been successfully applied by various companies in the automotive supply chain and is the framework of the development of safety related systems and of their components. There is a regulation of the International Standardization Organization (ISO) that valid and published standards shall be periodically reviewed. Now the time has come to update and extend the existing standard, to make it applicable for future systems and technologies. The main motivations for the 2nd edition of ISO 26262: are the experiences gathered with the 1st edition; the extension of the scope to other vehicle categories; the inclusion of a semi-conductor guideline and the inclusion of guidance on fail-operational systems. This paper presents the key changes and updates and the motivation behind them.

Keywords: ISO 26262 · ISO 26262:2018 · SOTIF · Functional safety · Automotive

1 Introduction

The development and publication of the ISO 26262:2011 [1] was a big step forward for the automotive industry. Before 2011 safety related automotive systems were developed in accordance with the IEC 61508 [2], since no other applicable standard existed. This demanded significant compromises from the automotive developers due to the fact that this is a generic safety standard. The particularities of the safety lifecycle of automotive systems and the different state-of-the-art in terms of methods and techniques made the application of the IEC 61508 challenging. Therefore, the automotive industry has been decided to develop a domain specific standard for the development of safety critical systems. This domain specific standard, the ISO 26262:2011 has introduced a tailored hazard analysis and risk assessment technique; state-of-the art techniques, methods and principles and an automotive safety lifecycle including production and decommissioning. In accordance with the ISO regulations a review of the standard was required 5 years after the publication of the 1st edition [1]. In that time various reasons for a re-work have surfaced. This lead to a significantly improved and extended standard.

2 Motivations for the 2nd Edition

The main motivation behind the 2nd edition of the standard is the fact that by working with the standard, a lot of improvement potential has been identified. The advances in methods and techniques allowed the automotive sector to use different and more efficient processes than captured in the 1st edition. Besides that, the need of further clarification and optimized wording arose.

Another motivation to extend the standard has been clear for a long time: the extension of the scope. In the 1st edition, the scope was limited to passenger cars up to 3,5t. It was clear from the start that the extension of the scope to similar vehicles is reasonable and should be planned for the 2nd edition. That's the reason why motorcycles, trucks and busses are included.

Another domain that needed further explanation and guidance is the development of semiconductors. Due to ISO 26262:2011 part 5 deals with hardware development in general and it is difficult to apply this part to a semiconductor development because various aspects have not been addressed there.

With the advance of automated and autonomous driving functions the trend towards fail-operational systems is inevitable. Since the 1st edition has been created for mainly with fail-safe systems in mind, it had to be investigated whether the standard's concepts can be carried over to fail-operational applications. In addition to that further specific guidance was intended, wherever necessary.

The increasing importance of cyber security and safety of the intended functionality (SOTIF) with clearly existing interfaces to functional safety, the working group also decided to address these topics. The way of addressing them is significantly different, though, as it can be seen in chapter 4.

3 Timeline for the 2nd Edition

As already indicated, the ISO regulations require a 3 years' period from the publication until a revision starts. Figure 1 "Timeline of the ISO 26262 2nd edition" shows the timeline starting from the revision. The ISO directives offer three timelines to choose from (24, 36 or 48 months). The working group decided for the standard timing, meaning that 3 years are available from the start of the revision until the publication.

As it can be seen in the figure above, the standard goes through various iterations before it gets published. It starts with the committee draft (CD) phase, then the draft international standard (DIS) phase and finally the (optional) final draft international standard (FDIS) phase. In the CD and DIS phases technical and editorial comments are created in the corresponding ballots, then debated and resolved in the comments resolution phase. In the FDIS phase, on the other hand, only editorial comments are allowed. ISO CS denotes the phases where the ISO Central Secretariat (CS) is reviewing and adapting the document.

The new version of the standard is expected to arrive at the beginning of 2018.

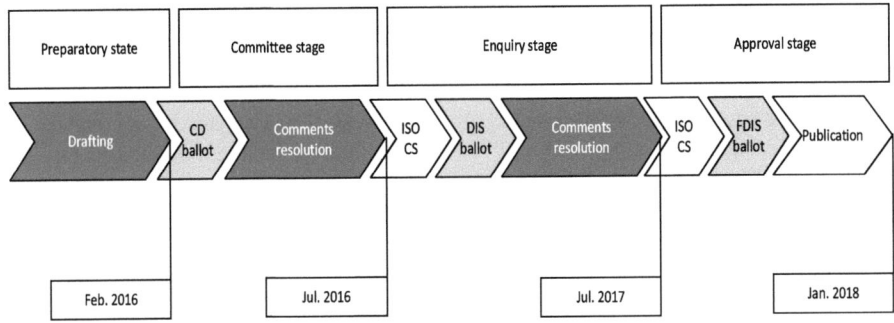

Fig. 1. Timeline of the ISO 26262 2nd edition

4 Description of the Changes

Due to various reasons, this paper is not intended to give a complete list of all changes in the standard. The goal is to highlight the most important changes and to provide background information and rationale to them.

4.1 Generic Changes Affecting All Parts

First of all, due to the new parts that have been included in the 2nd edition (see in Fig. 2 marked grey), the structure of the standard is slightly changed. There are certain changes affecting basic concepts or generic content that has affected all parts. First of all, the scope has been significantly extended, as shown in comparison with the former version, in Table 1.

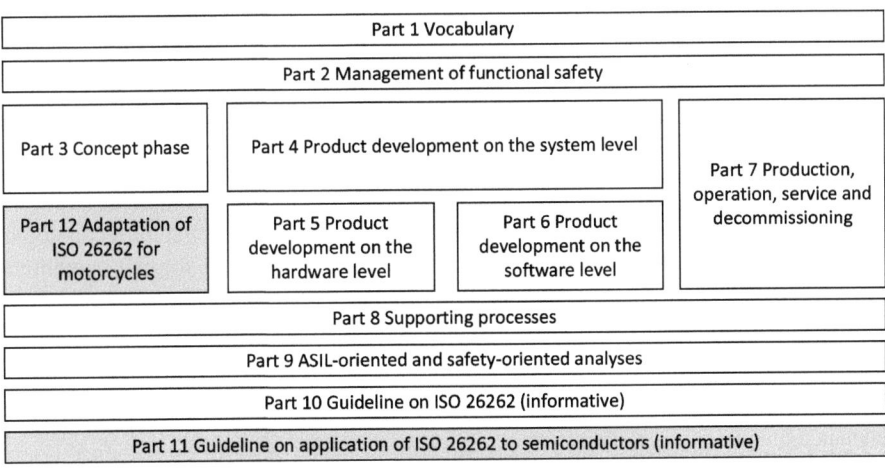

Fig. 2. Structure of the ISO 26262 2nd edition

Table 1. Extended scope of the 2nd edition

New scope [3]	Old scope [1]
ISO 26262 is intended to be applied to safety-related systems that include one or more electrical and/or electronic (E/E) systems and that are installed in series production road vehicles, *excluding mopeds*. ISO 26262 does not address unique E/E systems in special vehicles such as E/E systems designed for drivers with disabilities. *NOTE: Other dedicated application-specific safety standards exist and may complement ISO 26262 or vice versa*	ISO 26262 is intended to be applied to safety-related systems that include one or more electrical and/or electronic (E/E) systems and that are installed in series production passenger cars with a maximum gross vehicle mass up to 3 500 kg. ISO 26262 does not address unique E/E systems in special purpose vehicles such as vehicles designed for drivers with disabilities

Whereas a new part has been introduced for motorcycles, the specific requirements for the trucks and busses are fully integrated into existing parts. It is beneficial to know that requirements related to truck and busses 'T&B' are collected in subchapters in the different parts.

Another important clarification is the better elaboration of the objectives sections in each clause. These support the new goal definition and focus of safety assessments in part 2 (Management of functional safety).

In order to eliminate redundancies in the standard, the clauses "Initiation of the safety lifecycle [...]" of parts 3 (Concept phase), 4 (Product development at the system level), 5 (Product development at the hardware level) and 6 (Product development at the software level) have been removed and merged into part 2 (Management of functional safety). The reason for this is that these clauses were mainly concerned with the further refinement of the safety plan.

4.2 Changes in ISO 26262-Part 1 (Vocabulary)

The definitions in ISO 26262-Part 1 'Vocabulary' [3] have been updated and extended due to three reasons:

- Certain definitions were optimized regarding their clarity and comprehensibility.
- Certain definitions needed updates due to the application to different technologies (e.g. the definition of the fault tolerant time interval (FTTI) for fail-operational systems).
- Certain definitions have been newly introduced due to the extension of the scope (e.g. trucks and busses) or due to new application fields (e.g. fail-operational).

However, the majority of the existing definitions of the 1st edition remain unchanged.

4.3 Changes in ISO 26262-Part 2 (Management of Functional Safety)

The ISO 26262-Part 2 'Management of functional safety' [4] has been updated mainly based on the 5 years' experience with management of functional safety. First of all, the clause "Impact analysis" from part 3 has been moved to part 2 (Management of functional safety). The reason for this is that the impact analysis work product is one of the key inputs for creating the safety plan.

In order to allow more flexibility, the list of tailoring options has been extended: phases can be performed concurrently, and phases that are not applicable can be omitted.

Besides that, the requirements regarding confirmation measures have been significantly reworked. First, their focus has changed, by putting more emphasis on content and its sufficiency to argue functional safety in order to get a kind of a pre-assessment. Second, to correct a weakness in the 1st edition, some confirmation measures are also required for QM (e.g. that of the 'Hazard Analysis and Risk Assessment'). Third, based on practical experiences, the 2nd edition will allow that confirmation measures are supported by assistants with lower level of independence (to compensate the lack of specific knowledge of an I3 assessor).

Another major improvement is that functional safety assessment's scope has been shifted from requirements to objectives.

An important structural improvement is that the release for production and functional safety assessment clauses from part 4 have been shifted into part 2 (Management of functional safety) for better comprehensibility and to emphasize that they apply independently of the development domain (system, hardware or software).

Further an own chapter has been introduced about the management of safety anomalies. This chapter summarizes the safety anomaly process, responsibilities and the necessary communications.

Additionally, Part 2 (Management of functional safety) has been extended by two new annexes. Annex C describes confirmation measures in detail, is now extended and adapted to the new scope of confirmation measures. Annex F gives guidance on the interaction and interfaces with cyber security. Cyber security is still outside of the scope but (mainly) part 2 (Management of functional safety) gives informative guidance on the interfaces between the two domains that need our attention. The goal was definitely to be as limited in content as possible but to give enough guidance on the interfaces. This includes the management of safety and security; coordinated field monitoring (incident reporting, tracking and resolution); considerations of the interfaces between the 'Hazard Analysis and Risk Assessment' and the 'Threat Analysis' (communication of safety goals, information about hazards); coordination of safety and security related measures in the design and harmonization of safety and security analyses.

4.4 Changes in ISO 26262-Part 3 (Concept Phase)

The main content of ISO 26262-Part 3 'Concept phase' [5] is the description of the 'Hazard Analysis and Risk Assessment' (HARA) and the functional safety concept, therefore it was essential to incorporate changes here related to trucks and busses. Especially the hazard analysis and risk assessment needed to reflect the specifics of these vehicle classes. The basic concept and the normative part of the HARA did not change, but the Annex B (containing informative examples for the severity, exposure and controllability ratings) has been extended accordingly.

Besides the extension for trucks and busses, the hazard analysis and risk assessment has been reworked further. An important change is that E1/S3/C3 is allowed to lead to QM if E1 is the result of the combination of several unlikely situations. The clause addressing the functional safety concept received only minor changes, updates and clarifications.

One of the key content in part 3 (Concept phase) is definitely Annex B, giving guidance on the HARA. Here the main modification is that the tables are simplified, the number of examples is notably reduced. Reason for this was to avoid the impression that these lists are exhaustive and to emphasize that these are only examples. In various cases for certain target vehicles and markets these examples were even inappropriate.

4.5 Changes in ISO 26262-Part 4 (Product Development at the System Level)

As already mentioned in chapter 4.3, some clauses of ISO 26262-Part 4 'Product development on the system level' [6] (initiation of safety lifecycle, functional safety assessment, release for production) have been moved into part 2 to improve clarity and comprehensibility.

A major change compared to the 1st edition is that clauses 6 (Specification of the technical safety requirements) and 7 (System design) are merged into one clause to eliminate redundancies and to reflect current industrial practice. The steps of defining the system level technical safety requirements, designing a system architecture and allocating the defined requirements to hardware, software or both are performed in parallel and iteratively. This is much better reflected by the new merged clause 6.

Furthermore, the clause focusing on system integration and testing has been improved. Tables containing test methods and methods for deriving test cases have been slightly extended and merged wherever necessary, to improve the comprehensibility of this clause. Additionally, the clause has been renamed into System and item integration and testing to reflect that it can and needs to be also applied at the item level.

4.6 Changes in ISO 26262-Part 5 (Product Development at the Hardware Level)

ISO 26262-Part 5 'Product development on the hardware level' [7] did not face any fundamental changes, modifications intend to improve comprehensibility and clarity. For instance, in clause 8 now a more accurate description is included how field data can be used for determining base failure rates.

A very important clarification has been added to clause 9 (Evaluation of the safety goal violations due to random hardware failures) defining that for distributed systems the Probabilistic Metric for Random Hardware Failures (PMHF) target values (100/100/10FIT) can be used for each subsystem of the distributed system separately. This reflects the original intent. Besides that, a note reflects the common industrial practice that a qualitative evaluation of the residual risk can be used as argument if the PMHF target value has been exceeded. Annex F gives an example how this can be reasonably performed.

4.7 Changes in ISO 26262-Part 6 (Product Development at the Software Level)

The main changes in ISO 26262-Part 6 'Product development on the software level' [8] intend to improve comprehensibility and clarity. Only few new content has been added.

In clause 7, addressing software architectural design, Tables 4 and 5 have been slightly extended and their wording improved.

A major improvement compared to the 1st edition is the more pragmatic and holistic view on verification activities on the unit and integration levels. In this sense, on the unit level, static verification from clause 8 (Software unit design and implementation) has been moved to clause 9 (Software unit verification) to reflect that these two method domains closely interact and complement each other. This allows the application of intelligent mixed verification concepts that are already in use by various companies. The unit verification methods are therefore integrated into one table.

The same principle has been applied to software integration and testing (clause 10). In modern software development landscapes, some aspects of the integration verification are handled by static verification methods (e.g. interface consistency can be checked by a tool). Therefore, these methods have been included in Table 12 to allow mixed verification concepts. Also in order to improve comprehensibility, clause 11 has been renamed to "Testing of the embedded software". Besides that, the implicit reference to methods in clause 10 (Software integration and verification) has been replaced by dedicated method tables.

Two annexes have been significantly extended and improved: Annex B for model-based development and Annex E for software safety analyses. Both intend to give more guidance on these important topics and to reflect current industrial practices.

4.8 Changes in ISO 26262-Part 7 (Production, Operation, Service and Decommissioning)

ISO 26262-Part 7 'Production, operation, service and decommissioning' [9] has been slightly re-structured and some clauses, notes and examples rephrased for better comprehensibility.

4.9 Changes in ISO 26262-Part 8 (Supporting Processes)

Since ISO 26262-Part 8 'Supporting processes' [10] is a heterogeneous collection of supporting processes, the changes separate clauses are explained separately. First of all, clauses 6, 7, 8, 10 and 14 (Specification and management of safety requirements, Configuration management, Change management, Documentation management and Proven in use argument respectively) have not been notably changed.

In clause 5 (Interfaces within distributed developments) the key change is the more extended description of the job-split between customer and supplier regarding safety assessments. Besides that, more elaborated description of the provision and feedback regarding exchanged safety requirements has been introduced.

In clause 9 (Verification) there is one interesting new content among the minor editorial changes: a recommendation has been added that test cases should be reviewed by a different person than the test case's author.

The normative part of clause 11 (Confidence in the use of software tools) has not been significantly altered. But as a major improvement, the generic section of the clause now includes a detailed informative description of the different aspects of developing and using a tool.

In order to strengthen the requirements on qualified software components, clause 12 (Qualification of software components) introduced several changes. First of all, requirements on the specification of the qualified software components have been significantly extended, now including the requirements on of the component, description of its configuration, the application manual, etc. On the other side of the V-model, specific requirements have been introduced on the expected verification results of the component. These changes are intended to ensure that even if a software component is not developed in accordance with the ISO 26262-6, it can be safety integrated into safety relevant software.

In clause 13 (Evaluation of hardware elements) a new method and process has been introduced, focusing of three classes of hardware components. Basic principle remained basically the same (with low, medium and high complexity) but the classification criteria became much clearer.

4.10 Changes in ISO 26262-Part 9 (ASIL-Oriented and Safety-Oriented Analyses)

Regarding the Automotive Safety Integrity Level (ASIL) decomposition, there is one major change in ISO 26262-Part 9 'ASIL-oriented and safety-oriented analyses' [11]: the confirmation measures do not need to be performed in accordance with the original ASIL any longer. This change eliminates the unnecessarily high requirement that was unreasonable for lower ASIL components that are developed as Safety Element out of Context (SEooC).

Another major change is the extended definition of the analysis of dependent failures. The normative part allows that the rigor and level of detail is tailored based on the ASIL, system architecture, etc. Besides that, Annex C provides a dependency model including 7 types of dependent failure initiators that can be used on any abstraction level (i.e. system, hardware and software). The 7 dependent failure initiators are:

- Shared resources (e.g. common clock for two microcontrollers)
- Shared information inputs (e.g. global variables for software)
- Environmental influences (e.g. mechanical shock)
- Systematic coupling (e.g. identical algorithms used by two redundant functions)
- Components of identical type (e.g. same sensor used by two channels)
- Communication (e.g. data exchange between two software components)
- Unintended impact (e.g. crosstalk between signal lines)

This model can support analyses of dependent failures on all abstraction levels and can be easily tailored for the particular application.

4.11 Changes in ISO 26262-Part 10 (Guideline on ISO 26262)

Since ISO 26262-Part 10 'Guideline on ISO 26262 (informative)' [12] is an informative guidance on the application of the normative parts of the ISO 26262, it has been extended significantly. Since this paper focuses on the normative changes of the ISO 26262, only the most important new content of part 10 is highlighted here:

- The timing model (incl. the explanation of the FTTI) has been extended, mainly driven by the demand to address fail-operational systems. Especially the architectural variants where an emergency operation is included are of great importance.
- The simplified PMHF calculation method (relying on Failure Mode, Diagnostics and Effects Analysis (FMEDA) instead of a Fault Tree Analysis (FTA) based calculation) is more elaborated and can address more typical safety mechanism patterns.
- Extensive guidance on fault tolerant (i.e. fail-operational) E/E systems is given, addressing various aspects of the safety lifecycle that need special attention when developing such products.

4.12 Introduction of ISO 26262-Part 11 (Guideline on Application of ISO 26262 to Semiconductors)

Although ISO 26262-Part 5 of the standard addresses the development on the hardware level, its applicability to semiconductor products is limited. The process and methods applied there are difficult to tailor for a semiconductor development. Due to this reason, ISO 26262-Part 11 'Guideline on application of ISO 26262 to semiconductors (informative)' [13] was initiated as an informative part to provide guidance on the application on the ISO 26262 for semiconductor technologies.

ISO 26262-Part 11 [13] consists of two clauses and five annexes:

- Cause 4: Semiconductor component and its partitioning
- Clause 5: Specific semiconductor technologies and use cases
- Annex A, giving examples on digital failure modes for evaluating the diagnostic coverage
- Annex B, giving examples on the dependent failure analysis.
- Annex C–E, providing examples on quantitative analyses of different semiconductor product types.

Clause 4 gives guidance on semiconductor-specific issues that are not addressed in part 5 (Product development at the hardware level). This includes the handling of IP, calculation of failure rates for these components, specific guidance on dependent failure analyses, different applications of fault injection and specific guidance on the production.

Clause 5 on the other hand elaborates the guidance for different types of semiconductor products: digital, analogue, mixed signal components, programmable logic devices, multi-core microcontrollers, sensors and transducers.

The annexes, as mentioned above, give specific examples.

4.13 Introduction of in ISO 26262-Part 12 (Adaptation of ISO 26262 for Motorcycles)

The main reason for ISO 26262-Part 12 'Adaptation of ISO 26262 for motorcycles' [14] is that the state-of-the-art of motorcycles is significantly different from that of passenger vehicles. Therefore, certain aspects of the ISO 26262 need adaptions before applying it to motorcycles. Note, that part 12 only applies to motorcycles but not to mopeds (<50 km/h top speed, <50 cc displacement).

The main content of part 12 is the slightly different 'Hazard Analysis and Risk Assessment' method. The rationale for this is that the dynamic behavior and the emphasis on the rider are different than in case of passenger vehicles. The basic concept of part 12's 'Hazard Analysis and Risk Assessment' is that a MSIL (Motorcycle Safety Integrity Level, from A to D) is determined in the first step. Then this MSIL is converted into an ASIL where each MSIL is allocated to an ASIL one level below, e.g. MSIL B is converted to ASIL A. Besides that, the standard protective environment prescribed in the user manual is always assumed to be in use. Part 12 also gives practical guidance to 'Hazard Analysis and Risk Assessment' by examples in the annexes B and C.

From the process point of view a major simplification is that for the confirmation measures of part 2 (Management of functional safety), the level of required independence is less strict. Due to the smaller company size in the motorcycle industry, the original requirements would have been way beyond the state-of-the-art.

4.14 Safety of the Intended Functionality (SOTIF)

SOTIF is a topic closely related to functional safety. A new work item proposal has been issued in 2016 to create a standard addressing this scope. This **ISO PAS 21448** 'Road vehicles – Safety of the intended functionality' [15] is currently developed and maintained by the same working group as the ISO 26262, and the option is still open to merge this standard into a later edition of the ISO 26262.

Figure 3 shows the scope of SOTIF, in relation with functional safety. As it can be seen, in both cases malfunctioning behavior and resulting risk are addressed. The difference between the two domains lies within the causes of these malfunctions. In case of functional safety, the cause always needs to be fault or failure in an E/E component, e.g. a short circuit of a capacitor or a buffer overflow in the software. Whereas in case of SOTIF, the cause lies within the shortcomings of the technology or the system definition, e.g. in the image recognition accuracy or in the disturbance resistance of a radar. In case of SOTIF, no faults or failures are present.

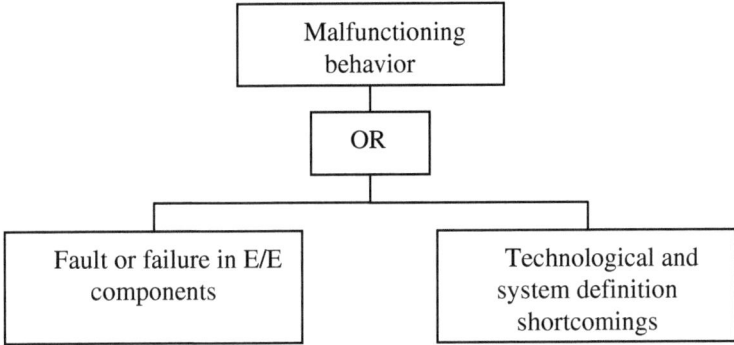

Fig. 3. Fault tree representing the relation of SOTIF with functional safety

The importance of SOTIF increases rapidly with the trend towards autonomous and automated driving. In order to be able to ensure the safety of these systems, a holistic view on safety is necessary. SOTIF is definitely a key aspect of this holistic view.

The PAS (which is currently under construction), offers an extension to the V-model of the ISO 26262, including a SOTIF HARA, a SOTIF concept and verification and validation activities related to SOTIF. These process steps will then be further detailed and elaborated in the clauses and in the annexes of the PAS. Since the work is still in progress, further details cannot be given currently.

5 Summary and Outlook

Many changes have been introduced with the update and extension of the 1st edition of the ISO 26262:2011. The main reasons for the 2nd edition of ISO 26262:2018 are in the lessons learnt by application of the 1st edition, the extension of scope, the consideration of evolved process methods and tools and the new challenges with advanced driving functions. All parts of the standards are accordingly updated and 2 additionally parts are introduced.

Due to the increasing pace in the development of technology in the automotive industry it is quite easy to predict that we are facing interesting and big challenges in the domain of functional safety and SOTIF. The 2nd edition of the ISO 26262 will address many of these and will give necessary guidance. Nonetheless, the state of the art will evolve rapidly in the next 5–10 years. This automatically implies the necessity of a revised 3rd edition. The SOTIF PAS will be surely converted into an international standard in the next 5 years, either as integral part of the ISO 26262 or separately. This international standard will definitely need a rework after the experiences with autonomous and automated driving are gathered.

Therefore, the development of the related standards remains a continuous task, providing guidance to an industrial domain that is facing one of its biggest challenges so far.

References

1. International Organization for Standardization. ISO 26262:2011 - Road Vehicles - Functional safety - Part 1 to Part 10, ISO (2011)
2. International Electrotechnical Commission. IEC 61508, Functional Safety of Electrical/Electronic/Programmable Electronic Safety-Related Systems, part 1–7 (2002)
3. ISO TC 22/SC 32/WG 8: ISO/DIS 26262-1 - Road Vehicles - Functional safety - Part 1: Vocabulary: ISO (2016)
4. ISO TC 22/SC 32/WG 8: ISO/DIS 26262-2 Road vehicles - Functional safety - Part 2: Management of functional safety: ISO (2016)
5. ISO TC 22/SC 32/WG 8: ISO/DIS 26262-3 Road vehicles - Functional safety - Part 3: Concept phase: ISO (2016)
6. ISO TC 22/SC 32/WG 8: ISO/DIS 26262-4 Road vehicles - Functional safety - Part 4: Product development at the system level: ISO (2016)
7. ISO TC 22/SC 32/WG 8: ISO/DIS 26262-5 Road vehicles - Functional safety - Part 5: Product development at the hardware level: ISO (2016)
8. ISO TC 22/SC 32/WG 8: ISO/DIS 26262-6 Road vehicles - Functional safety - Part 6: Product development at the software level: ISO (2016)
9. ISO TC 22/SC 32/WG 8: ISO/DIS 26262-7 Road vehicles - Functional safety - Part 7: Production, operation, service and decommissioning: ISO (2016)
10. ISO TC 22/SC 32/WG 8: ISO/DIS 26262-8 Road vehicles - Functional safety - Part 8: Supporting processes: ISO (2016)
11. ISO TC 22/SC 32/WG 8: ISO/DIS 26262-9 Road Vehicles - Functional safety - Part 9: Automotive Safety Integrity Level (ASIL)-oriented and safety-oriented analyses: ISO (2016)
12. ISO TC 22/SC 32/WG 8: ISO/DIS 26262-10 Road vehicles - Functional safety - Part 10: Guideline on ISO 26262: ISO (2016)
13. ISO TC 22/SC 32/WG 8: ISO/DIS 26262-11 Road vehicles - Functional safety - Part 11: Guidelines on application of ISO 26262 to semiconductors: ISO (2016)
14. ISO TC 22/SC 32/WG 8: ISO/DIS 26262-12 Road vehicles - Functional safety - Part 12: Adaptation of ISO 26262 for motorcycles: ISO (2016)
15. ISO TC 22/SC 32/WG 8: ISO WD PAS 21448.1-SOTIF-20170224: ISO (2017)

Improvements in Functional Safety of Automotive IP Through ISO 26262:2018 Part 11

Alison Young[1] and Alastair Walker[2(✉)]

[1] Lorit Consultancy, Glasgow, Scotland
alison.young@lorit-consultancy.com
[2] Lorit Consultancy, Edinburgh, Scotland
alastair.walker@lorit-consultancy.com

Abstract. In early 2018, the second edition of ISO 26262:2018 [1] automotive functional safety standard, is due for release. At the time of writing, the draft international standard (DIS) version is out for comment and review. One significant change over the original version of the ISO 26262:2011 [2] standard is part 11, which brings detailed information to support semiconductor manufacturers develop ISO 26262 compliant intellectual property (IP). In the original version, information available to semiconductor companies was limited. This forthcoming release will bring significantly more information to support semiconductor and silicon IP suppliers in the areas of digital and analogue components, programmable logic devices (PLD), multi-core processors and sensors. Tips, recommendations and practical examples are illustrated. However, there are certain areas that still not well represented, diagnostic coverage for analogue components for example is not defined in detail and there is a shortage of supporting information. Part 11 could also provide more worked examples to give design and functional safety teams a better insight into estimation techniques. The final draft international standard (FDIS) is due for publication in autumn 2017, and certain aspects of part 11 will be enhanced.

Keywords: Functional safety · Intellectual property · Diagnostic coverage · Dependent failures analysis · Transient faults

1 Introduction

When ISO 26262:2011 was released, it brought a lot more information than was in IEC 61508 [3] covering the areas of system, hardware and software development, to support design and functional safety teams in the automotive industry. However, for many semiconductor suppliers, the information represented in the first edition of ISO 26262 did not capture the requirements or considerations that are relevant to them in comparison with original equipment manufacturers (OEMs) and design teams at tier 1 or 2 level suppliers.

As many semiconductor devices are developed as Safety Element out of Context (SEooC) the end application is unknown and assumptions on the final implementation, safety goals and Automotive Safety Integrity Levels (ASIL) need to be made. While design teams implementing the Item can define and assess system level safety mechanisms and diagnostic coverage it is not so easy for semiconductor suppliers. Many concerns for semiconductor manufacturers are centred around transient failures of components, something that was not well addressed in the first edition of ISO 26262, equally part 11 brings enhanced information to support dependent failures analysis (DFA).

Part 11 would also be a very useful reference source for teams in the aviation industry as it expands greatly on some of the topics covered in DO-254 [4].

In this paper, the solutions proposed in the DIS ISO 26262:2018 are reviewed and discussed in terms of how they enhance the detail and act as an adjunct to the first edition.

2 ISO 26262 Part 11 Concepts

There is a good comparison between the suggested techniques in part 5 and part 11 of ISO 26262 and more over part 11 can also provide additional information for teams designing products that are not deemed to be IP.

Good references are made in part 11 to JEDEC [5] standards for understanding failure mechanisms and reliability of semiconductors additionally, equally the introductions to reliability standards, IEC TR 62380 [6], SN 29500 [7] and FIDES [8] are also very informative.

Conversely part 11 repeats a number of topics that are addressed in other parts of ISO 26262 and relates them to IP, the size of part 11 could have been restricted if the information was referenced from other parts of the standards e.g. Section 4.10 Interfaces within distributed developments.

2.1 Transient Fault Quantification

Part 11, includes a more detailed definition of transient faults, than was given in the original version of ISO 26262. As defined in section 4.6.2 of part 11, there are many considerations regarding transient faults including α, ß, neutron, or γ radiation sources. The first edition of ISO 26262 did not provide much support in this subject area.

2.2 Component Package Failure Rate

Section 4.6.2.2 of part 11 discusses the strengths and weaknesses of different reliability standards in relation to component package failure rates, it also addresses considerations relating to the device packaging and pins, topics that are not easily understood nor addressed to any great extend in the original version of ISO 26262.

2.3 Permanent Base Failure Rate Calculation Using Industry Sources

Part 11 addresses the topic of base failure rate distribution in a concise manner, introducing the reader to the techniques for calculation of failure rates based on die and package. The die calculation methods using either area or number of equivalent gates. Figure 1 illustrates the typical factors contributing to the hardware component failure rate.

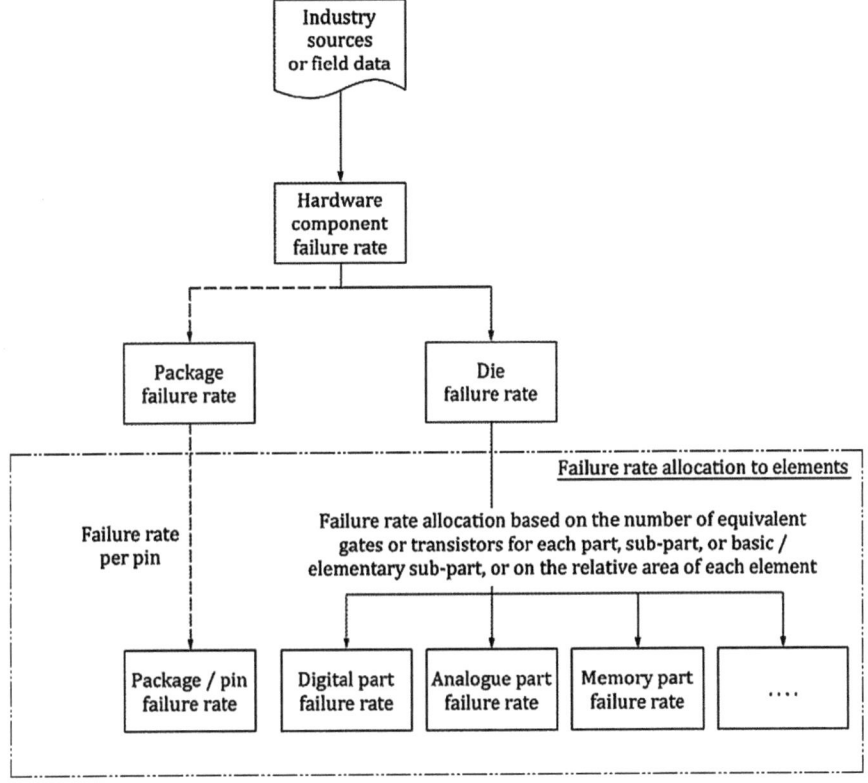

Fig. 1. Base failure rate distribution

Section 4.6.3.5, introduces the topic of Multi-Chip Modules, but does not unfortunately give much guidance on what this referring to.

2.4 Diagnostic Coverage

Part 11 is still weak in supporting the definition of analogue diagnostic coverage, this is conceded in the document that accurate estimation of analogue diagnostic coverage is not easily achieved. The techniques used in other standards such as the ISO 13849-1 [9] are potentially superior, where application specific examples of diagnostic coverage are given in Annex E, this however would be more complex to realise in the wide variety of automotive applications. There are better examples of calculating diagnostic coverage for digital components e.g. the Direct Memory Access (DMA) controller given in Annex A.

2.5 Dependent Failures Analysis (DFA)

The DFA section of part 11 provides guidelines for the identification and analysis of possible common cause and cascading failures between given elements, the assessment of their risk of violating a safety goal (or derived safety requirements) and the definition of safety measures to mitigate such risk if necessary. This is done to evaluate potential safety concept weaknesses and to provide evidence of the fulfilment of requirements concerning independence or freedom from interference identified during coexistence analysis (see ISO 26262-9:2018, Clause 6).

Section 4.7.4 of part 11 also addresses the topic of the difference between common cause failures and cascading failures in semiconductor devices and highlights that in a given failure scenario the differentiation is not always possible or useful. This is a distinct difference from other parts of ISO 26262.

The Dependent Failures Initiator (DFI) represents the root cause of dependent failures in safety scope. A list of DFI is provided as a starting point, considering different systematic, environmental and random hardware issues see Fig. 2 for the table of environmental issues.

DFI examples	Measures to prevent dependent failures from violating the safety goal	Measures to prevent the occurrence of dependent failures during operation
Temperature Vibration Pressure Humidity / Condensation Corrosion EMI Overvoltage applied from external Mechanical stress Wear Aging Water and other fluids intrusion	Diversification of impact (e.g. clock delay between master & checker core, diverse master and checker core, different critical paths) Direct monitoring of environmental conditions (e.g. temperature sensor) or indirect monitoring of environmental conditions (e.g. delay lines used as dependent-failure sensors)	Fault avoidance measures (e.g. conservative specification / robust design) Physical separation (e.g. distance of the die from a local heat source external of the die) Adaptive measures to reduce susceptibility (e.g. voltage/operating frequency decrease) Limit the access frequency or limit allowed operation cycles for sub-parts (e.g. specify the number of write cycles for an EEPROM) Robust design of semiconductor packaging

Fig. 2. Systematic dependent failures initiators due to environmental conditions

A good definition of the relationship between DFA and safety analysis is given: While the safety analysis primarily focuses on identifying single-point faults and dual/multiple-point faults to evaluate the targets for the ISO 26262 metrics and define safety mechanisms to improve the metrics if required, the DFA complements the analysis by ensuring that the effectiveness of the safety mechanisms is not affected by dependent failures initiators.

2.5.1 DFA Workflow

Part 11 gives a very good approach to identifying DFI, if the DFI is adequately captured, identifying the necessary safety mechanisms and ensuring these are also adequate. The techniques listed could benefit teams working on automotive systems which are not necessarily restricted to semiconductors or IP (Fig. 3).

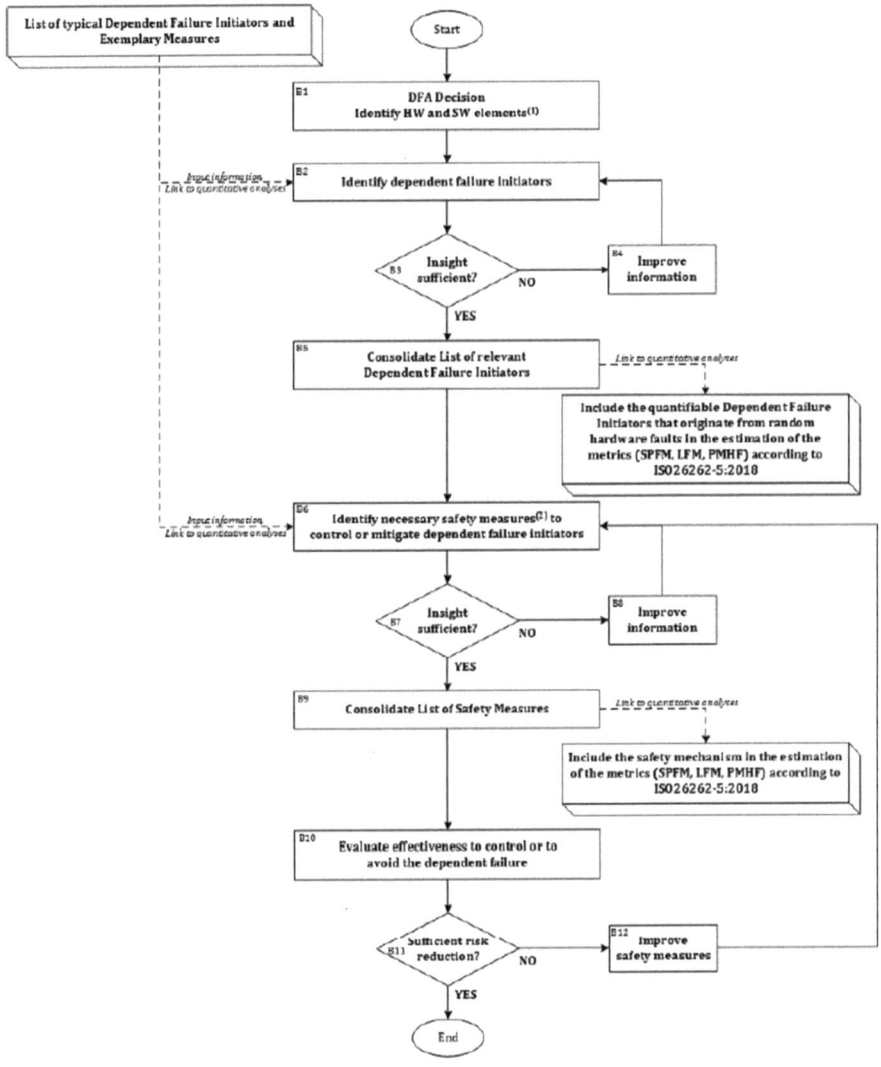

Fig. 3. Dependent failures analysis workflow

2.6 Fault Injection

Good guidance is given in part 11 on the potential benefits and usage of fault injection, e.g. on verification planning, and techniques. Where part 11 is maybe a bit weaker is on the definition of when and how often to use fault injection testing i.e. more to verify the effectiveness of safety mechanisms rather than to justify diagnostic coverage.

3 Semiconductor Technology Categories and Use Cases

3.1 Digital Components

The handling of digital components and memories is arguably the strongest area in part 11. Detailed definition and guidance on fault models of components such as memories, failure modes of common digital blocks, transient analysis and estimation of diagnostic coverage are documented. For teams developing purely digital components part 11 is an extremely helpful reference. Part 11 also supports the processes and is a suitable adjunct to the information already documented in part 5 of ISO 26262.

3.2 Analogue and Mixed Signal Components

Regarding analogue components there is good coverage of potential failure modes in part 11, particularly in Table 35. Likewise, the discussions on Analogue Single Event Transients (ASET) are very good. The weakness in part 11 is the lack of information on diagnostic coverage. Annex D gives a good example of a quantitative analogue assessment, however under and overvoltage detection is given 99.9% diagnostic coverage, without any rationale on how this was calculated. Typical examples of circuits and the estimated or calculated diagnostic coverage would be very helpful.

3.3 Programmable Logic Devices (PLD)

The lifecycle mapping of PLDs as indicated compares well with the SEooC mapping given in ISO 26262, showing clearly the hardware assumptions generated by the PLD manufacturer, that must be validated by the PLD user. Part 11 documents a good relationship between PLD die failure rates and IEC TR 62380, giving complete examples of FIT rates based on logic, memory etc. and giving derating figures. Also, there are good references to JESD89A [10] for transient fault considerations (Fig. 4).

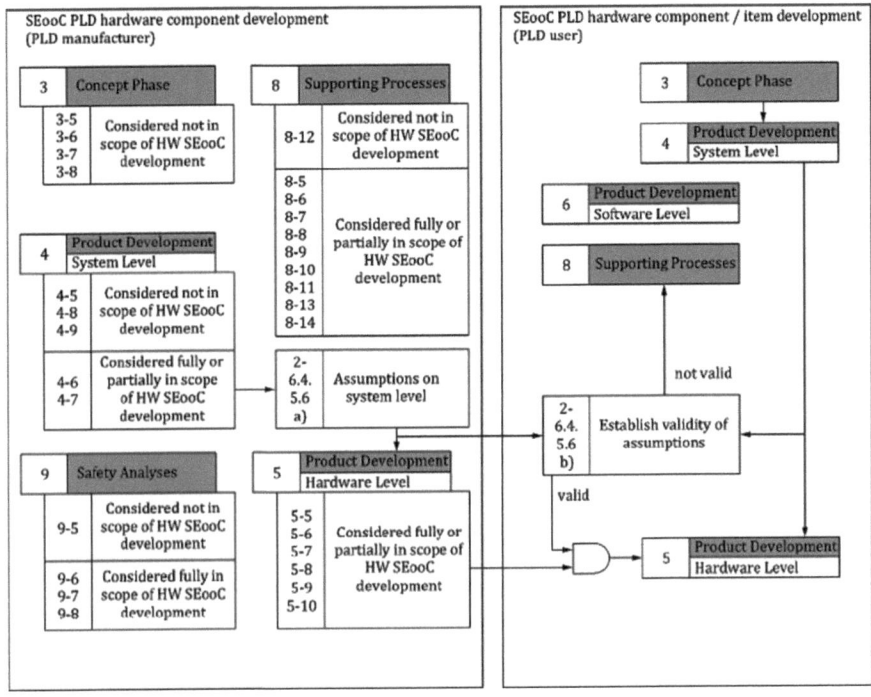

Fig. 4. ISO 26262 lifecycle mapping to PLD

3.4 Multi-core

The analysis of multi-core components gives a good overview of simplistic multi-core applications and supports this well with decomposition discussions. However, this section of part 11 does not elaborate on the techniques such as software lock-step or loosely coupled lock-step, as these are deemed to be out with the scope of part 11. As microcontroller technology advances, we now have standard automotive devices with 3 or more cores [11]. How these cores interact and are assessed in the context of functional safety requires a significantly more detailed evaluation than that given in part 11. Part 11 does give an introduction to the topic of multi-core components as indicated in Figs. 5 and 6 below.

Multi-core component type	Description
Homogeneous multi-core component	Homogeneous multi-core components include only identical PE
Heterogeneous multi-core component	Heterogeneous multi-core components have non-identical PEs, typically with different Instruction Set Architecture (ISA)

Fig. 5. Types of multi-core components

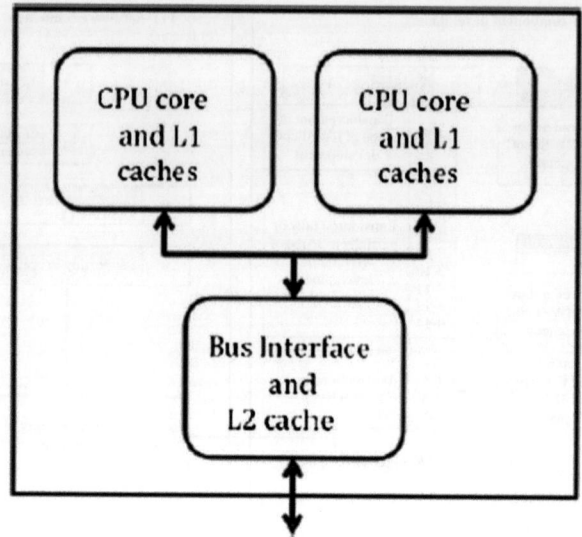

Fig. 6. Generic diagram of a dual-core system

As described in Section 5.4 of part 11, shared resources are a known DFI. For a software element, a shared resource can be a hardware element (e.g. RAM, cache) as well as a software element (e.g. drivers). Within a multi-core the issue caused by shared resources (e.g. memory, time, execution or exchange of information interferences) can be resolved by assigning the corresponding software elements to independent programmable elements (PE) without the same shared resources. Other issues (e.g. shared memory, commonly used software elements) are addressed analogously to a single core system (e.g. memory encapsulation via MPU by the OS, developing the commonly used software elements compliant with the initial ASIL). Techniques such as hypervisors [12, 13] can help to achieve software partitioning, are introduced, but the reader of part 11 would require much more detailed investigation to establish the benefits.

3.5 Sensors and Transducers

Section 5.5 gives a good general overview of sensors, failure modes, production processes. Several examples are given of different stages of a Micro Electro Mechanical Systems (MEMS) functional safety evaluation, looking at the safety analysis, safety measures, DFA and specific failures of the component parts. This section does give a good introduction to the topics but again very much at an introductory level (Fig. 7).

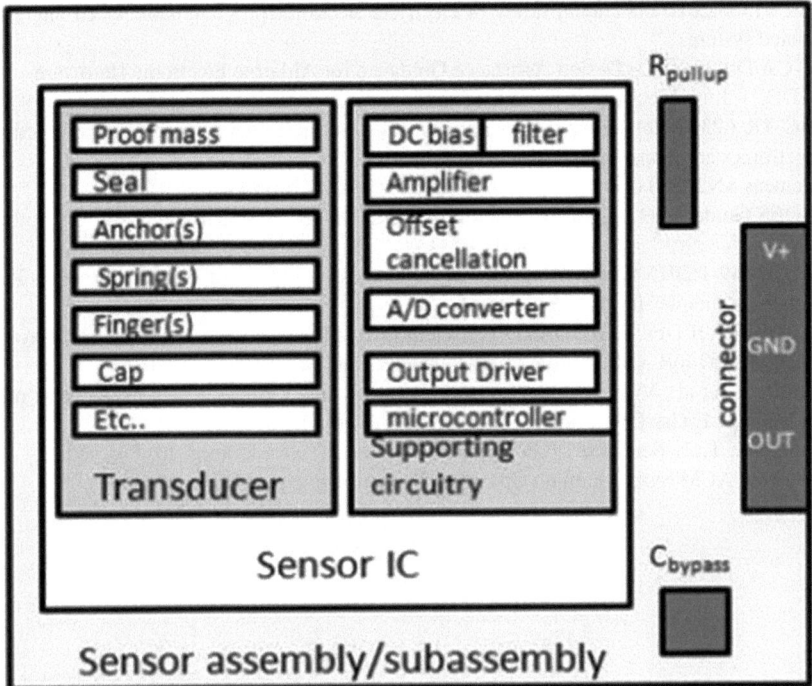

Fig. 7. Example of sensor complex hierarchical sensor

4 Conclusion and Future Work

ISO 26262:2018 gives additional supporting information to design and functional safety teams, in areas that were not too well supported in ISO 26262:2011, particularly how to evaluate hardware failure rates and DFA. Much of the additional information in part 11 focuses on introduction topics, rather than delving into subjects in more detail. Particularly the area of diagnostic coverage of analogue components is not well represented, and the 2011 version of the standard gave better support to teams in this area. Part 11 will generally be a helpful reference to design and functional safety teams and not only in the automotive sector, the aviation sector for instance could find this to be a valuable source of information.

Lorit Consultancy in cooperation with partner organisations, is currently preparing training material based on the concepts in this paper. These shall be reviewed, updated and expanded upon as the final version of part 11 is released.

References

1. ISO DIS 26262:2018 Road vehicles – Functional safety
2. ISO 26262:2011 Road vehicles – Functional safety

3. IEC 61508:2010 Functional safety of electrical/electronic/programmable electronic safety-related systems
4. RTCA/D0-254:2000 Design Assurance Guidance for Airborne Electronic Hardware
5. JEDEC – Joint Electronic Device Engineering Council. https://www.jedec.org/
6. IEC TR 62380 Reliability data handbook – Universal model for reliability prediction of electronics components, PCBs and equipment
7. Siemens SN29500 Component Failure Rate data (parts 1 to 14)
8. FIDES Guide 2009 Edition A: Reliability Methodology for Electronic Systems, September 2010
9. ISO 13849-1:2015 Safety of machinery – safety related parts of control systems – Part 1: General principles for design
10. JESD89-2A JEDEC STANDARD Test Method for Alpha Source Accelerated Soft Error Rate
11. NXP MPC5746R – SPC5746R Microcontroller Data Sheet Rev. 5 10/2016
12. Niimi, Y., et al.: Virtualization Technology and Using Virtual CPU in the Context of ISO 26262: The E-Gas Case Study. SAE Technical Paper, April 2013
13. Bressoud, T.C., Schneider, F.B.: Hypervisor-based fault tolerance. In: Proceedings of the Fifteenth ACM Symposium on Operating Systems Principles, pp. 1–11 (1995)

Using the ISO/IEC 27034 as Reference to Develop an Application Security Control Library

Alexssander A. Siqueira(✉), Sheila Reinehr, and Andreia Malucelli

Pontifical Catholic University of Parana, Curitiba, PR, Brazil
`alexssander_as@hotmail.com`, `sheila.reinehr@pucpr.br`,
`malu@ppgia.pucpr.br`

Abstract. Secure software development allows the development of solutions considering information security aspects in the project's scope, avoiding malicious users to attack system's vulnerabilities. In this case, security controls must be integrated into the application's solution design. The standard ISO/IEC 27034 provides the necessary guidance to the development of application security in any interested organization. An important standard's concept is the Application Security Control (ASC) Library that may provide a central repository of security controls specification and design. The ASC Library can support the organization's projects secure development considering their main characteristics and providing the necessary security controls references. This work reports an action-research developed in an international bank that adopted the ASC Library concept after reviewing its previous applications security risk assessments and identifying several missing security controls. The main contribution of this work is a process to identify, specify and document the organization security controls based on the ASC Library concept.

Keywords: Secure development · Application security · ISO/IEC 27034

1 Introduction

The world's community is increasingly relying on complex software and systems. In several industries such as finance, banking, automotive and medical devices, systems play a critical role and require high assurance. A failure caused by an attacker could lead to a catastrophic loss in terms of costs, reputation, environment damage, or even human life [1].

Secure software development is an engineering area that allows the development of software systems that can avoid malicious users to attack these systems using harmful software technologies that can affect systems' features operation [2].

There are frameworks, best practices and standards to support organizations in assessing their security risks, establishing their security management system, implementing the appropriate security controls, complying with governance requirements and security regulations. However, the security attacks techniques are in frequent evolution and becoming more sophisticated. Information security must be always aware of new threats, along with the available methods, techniques, policies, guidelines, educational and training approaches and technologies used to combat them [3].

Secure development has two large acceptable approaches. The first approach consists in implementing security in a reactive manner, where the security aspects are integrated in the produced software after its development. However, this approach is costly due to the effort to fix security defects that can require a rework in terms of analysis, design, coding and testing activities. The second approach addresses security as a proactive process, where the security aspects are largely integrated in the development lifecycle since the initial phases [4].

This work was developed in an organization that has a proactive process that includes security controls into the projects' scope in the software development process. However, the activity of security control recommendation was not being properly performed, once the security specialists did not have a central repository with a simplified security controls catalogue. In this case, the projects risk assessment activities were not considering all necessary controls to mitigate the possible applications vulnerabilities.

1.1 Secure Software Development

The security standard ISO/IEC 15408 (Common Criteria for Information Technology Security Evaluation) also known as Common Criteria (CC) provides a common set of security requirements for IT products. In addition, the standard provides the necessary guidance for assurance and evaluation of the security requirements employment [5]. The standard ISO/IEC 15408 can be combined with the standard ISO/IEC 12207 (Systems and software engineering - Software life cycle processes) that defines a common framework for software life cycle processes with a well-defined terminology that can be referenced by the software industry. The resulted combination is a set of tailored secure development processes [6].

The secure development process maturity can be evaluated using the standard ISO/IEC 21827:2008 that specifies the Systems Security Engineering - Capability Maturity Model® (SSE-CMM®), which describes the essential process management characteristics and security engineering process activities that must exist to ensure the security engineering practice in an organization. The ISO/IEC 21827 does not prescribe a particular process or sequence. However, the standard presents a set of good practices generally observed in industry. This standard has a relationship with the ISO/IEC 15504 especially with ISO/IEC 15504-2 that was recently replaced by ISO/IEC 33002:2015, as both are dedicated to process improvement and capability maturity assessment. Once, the standard ISO/IEC 15504 is focused on software development process assessments and the ISO/IEC 21827 is focused on security engineering practices evaluation and improvement into organizations [7].

The SSE-CMM do not prescribe or support the creation of a secure software development process. Then, the software industry employed the CC to adapt their development process to secure development.

1.2 ISO/IEC 27034

A specific standard for secure software development was finally released in 2011. The ISO/IEC 27034 provides guidance to assist organizations in the integration of security aspects into their software development processes. This standard is flexible and can be applied to in-house developed applications, applications acquired from third parties, and where the development or the operation of the application is outsourced [8].

The standard main element is the Organization Normative Framework (ONF) that is composed by the Application Security Control (ASC) Library and the Application Normative Framework (ANF).

The ONF supports the secure development process management, providing the necessary guidance to map the organization context and environmental elements, such as regulatory laws, technologies, security policies and application specification. This information allows the definition of security requirements that will result in security controls to mitigate any potential application risk. The ASC Library is a central repository that is part of the ONF structure and contains all security controls specifications.

The ANF structure is a subset of the ONF, when starting a new project, it is necessary to analyze the project scope and context to identify which ONF's elements will be applied on the new project (see Fig. 1). For instance, a payments software project may have different regulatory laws that could be not applied to a stock options system. In this case, the ANF for the payments project will consider just the necessary constraints regarding this specific domain.

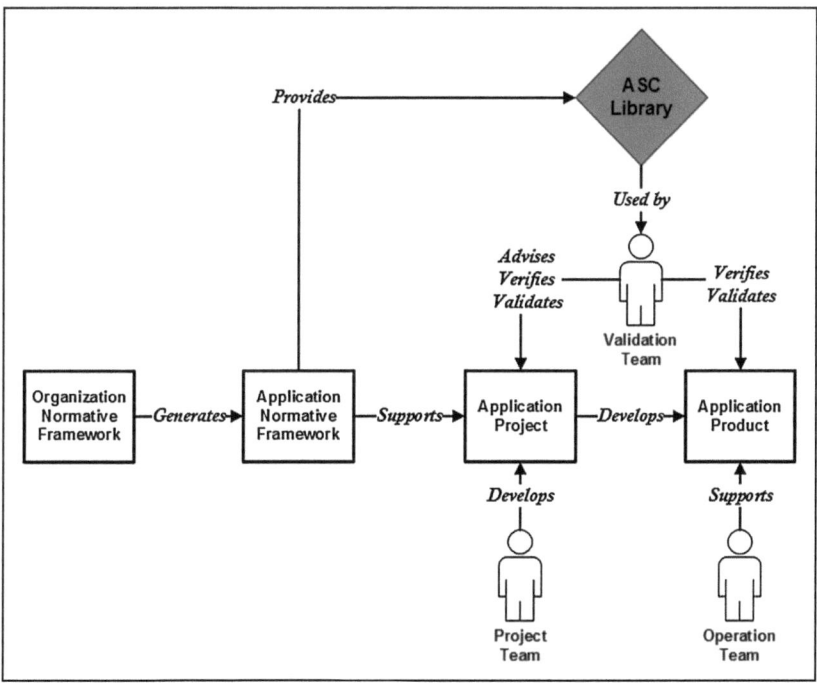

Fig. 1. Project impact by the use of ISO/IEC 27034 standard [8].

The selection of ASC Library elements to the specific project's ANF is performed considering which security controls are recommended to that specific project. In addition, it is necessary to identify the application's Target Level of Trust (TLT) that consists in a scale of risk that is acceptable by the organization to the applications that will be part of the project's solution. An ASC Library example is presented in Fig. 2.

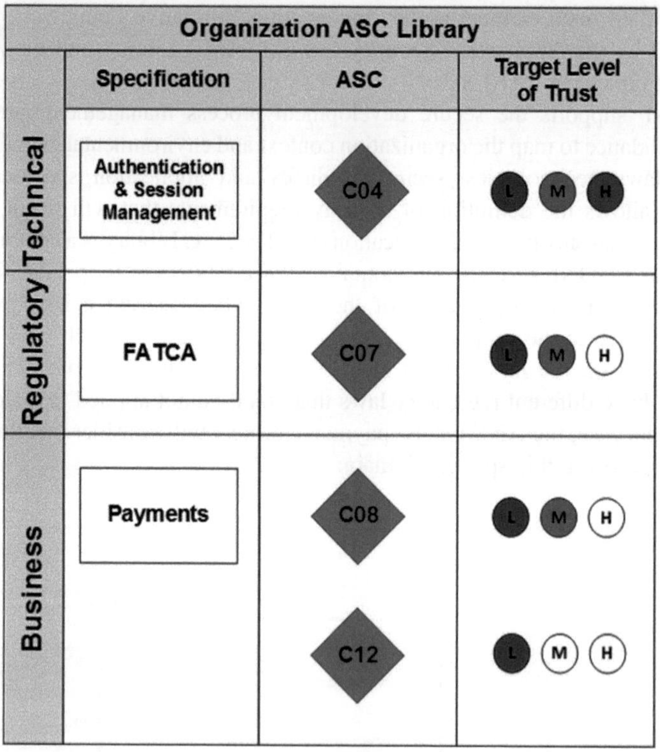

	Specification	ASC	Target Level of Trust
Regulatory / Technical	Authentication & Session Management	C04	L M H
	FATCA	C07	L M (H)
Business	Payments	C08	L M (H)
		C12	L (M) (H)

Fig. 2. Application security control library structure [8].

From this library will be selected the ASCs needed for any specific business application project. An organization could use the TLT to identify the set of necessary controls for a specific project, considering the technical, regulatory and business contexts. The organization must define its own range, or scale, of TLT that can be selected as a target for business applications [8].

2 Research Method

The reported experience was developed in an international banking company with a branch office in Brazil. A research group was composed by 3 employees (company's internal application security specialists). In this case, the suitable research method was the Action-Research (see Fig. 3) that it is an interactive approach that requires an intensive researcher involvement and it is composed by three types of steps [9]:

- **Pre-step**: Research's context and purpose understanding and definition.
- **Six main steps**: Based on the context information to elaborate an action plan that will be implemented and evaluated.
- **Meta-step**: Monitoring the execution of the six main steps and identify the need for additional cycle planning and execution.

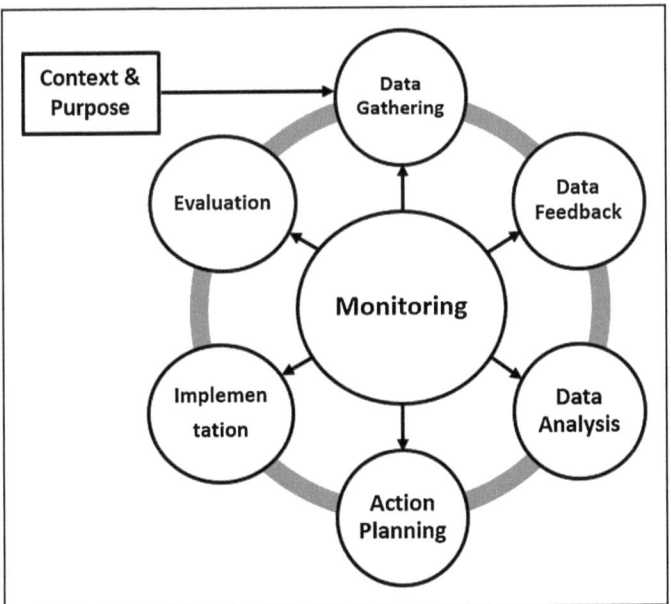

Fig. 3. Action-research method development cycle [9].

3 Research Development

A complete action-research development cycle was successful performed and described in this section.

3.1 Context and Purpose

The research was developed in a company that has offices and operations in 70 countries in all continents, serving about 51 million customers. To offer all banking services, the organization has a complex system platform composed by several applications that are deployed in different countries and regions.

All applications must be developed using the security aspects. The secure development process is performed and its outputs are shared with the project teams. At the end of the secure development, all necessary evidences and findings are documented and reported to the senior managers and project teams.

3.2 Data Gathering, Feedback and Analysis

The organization information security department did not have a central repository with all recommended security controls specification and design. To perform a risk assessment analysis, the application security specialists were used to recover previous Risk Assessment (RA) documents to identify controls that other specialist had recommended in the past. The RA document list all application security controls and how the project team worked to implement each one, providing the necessary evidences of risks and threats mitigation.

Without a central repository of security controls, all the application security reviews could be impacted in terms of quality, allowing the occurrence of possible security threats. In this case, the security specialists could miss important security controls. There was not any assurance mechanism that could support the selection of correct and suitable security controls for the organization's applications.

The main contribution of this experience is the ASC Library implementation to support the organization secure software development process. An initial set of basic controls was necessary to support the projects development. In this case, the main contribution of this work is a process to identify, specify and document the necessary security controls that would be applied in real projects in an international bank company.

3.3 Action Planning

The research group elaborated an action plan to implement an ASC Library:

- **Action 1**: Define a process to identify, specify and document a security control backlog before registering it into the central repository.
- **Action 2**: Select a specific business domain, identify their main applications and obtain the last Risk Assessment document version of each application from the selected business domain.
- **Action 3**: Apply the process designed in the Action 1 to produce a first version of the ASC Library.
- **Action 4**: Compare the number of security controls specified in the previous RA documents and the amount identified after the process implementation.

The next section described these actions implementation.

3.4 Implementation

The Action 1 implementation resulted in a process design (see Fig. 4) to identify potential ASC items from the previous projects' RA documents, allowing in this case the creation of a library based on a security controls backlog.

To implement the Action 2, the research group selected the business domain of insurance systems. Then, a set of 12 applications were identified as part of the core insurance platform for a specific set of countries (South America) where the company provide insurance services. Next, implementing the Action 3, the RA documents of the last projects of these applications were recovered from a document repository.

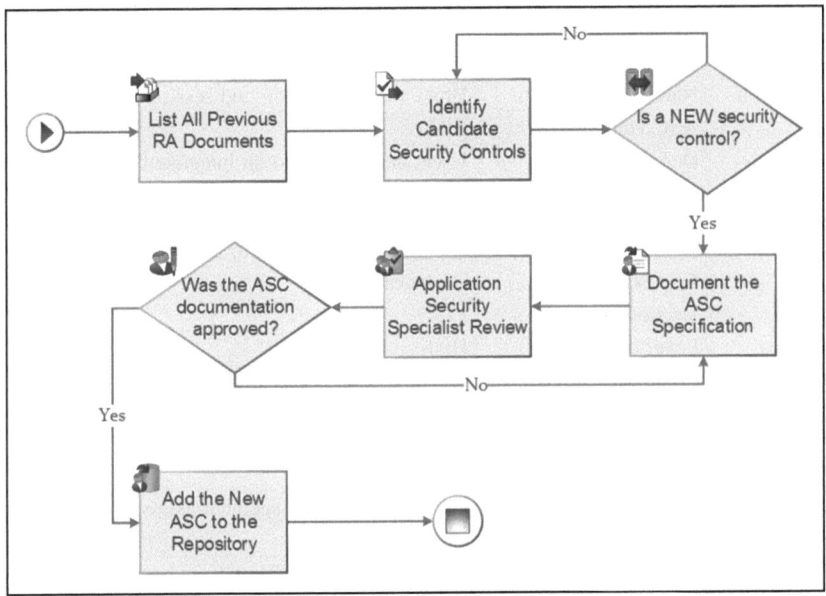

Fig. 4. General process to identify, specify and document ASC Library elements.

An ASC Library requests a TLT value to select which security controls are suitable for a specific application. The research group identified the necessary security controls and classified them using three TLT scores (Low, Medium and High), as presented in Table 1.

Table 1. Security controls x Target level of trust matrix.

TLT	Security Controls																					Total
	C01	C02	C03	C04	C05	C06	C07	C08	C09	C10	C11	C12	C13	C14	C15	C16	C17	C18	C19	C20	C21	
Low	x			x	x	x					x	x		x		x					x	9
Medium	x			x	x	x	x	x			x	x	x		x		x				x	12
High	x	x	x	x	x	x	x	x	x	x	x	x	x	x	x	x	x	x	x	x	x	21

The security control C01 is recommended to all TLT scores. However, C02 is applied only to TLT with High value. The controls are accumulative, being the High score the most complete level of security.

The standard presents a security control documentation format that it is composed by a set of fields that describe the ASC identification, objectives, activity and measure. Table 2 presents an example of ASC that covers the Broken Authentication and Session Management security risk that was identified as the second most critical risk for broad array of organizations [10].

Table 2. An ASC documentation example.

Category	Field	Value (example)
Identification	Name	Broken authentication and session management.
	ASC Unique ID	C04
	Description	Users have access to an integrated platform of services and applications. Then, attackers can use leaks or flaws in the authentication or session management functions to impersonate users
	Context	Technical context
	Version	v1.1
Objectives	Level of trust	High
	Purpose	Avoid session management hijacking
	Associated standards & best practices	OWASP Top 10 (2013) – Security Risk A2
Activity	Activity name	Protect session management assets
	Activity unique ID	C04-A01
	Activity description	Assure that user credentials and session IDs are properly protected. Must use the organization approved solution
	Artifact	Source-code: project sessionprotection (CVS repository)
	Expected results	For each user request, the application must protect all session management assets
Measure	Method name	Test session management hijacking
	Method Unique ID	C04-T01
	Method description	Access the application and verify if its supports URL rewriting and try to obtain the user's session ID attribute
	Method artifact	OWASP Session management cheat sheet reference guide
	Method results	All application's URL must avoid the session ID attribute

Next, as the selected business domain has a High TLT, it was necessary to consider 21 security controls for all 12 applications. Then, it was possible to calculate the difference (see Table 3) between the current (As Is) number of controls that were identified in the original RA documents and the expected value (Should Be) as requested by the Action 4 implementation.

The actions were implemented as planned and the research group identified an issue regarding the number of security controls. An outstanding difference is regarding to the project P05 that had 10 controls missing, there were 7 of 12 projects with similar issue.

Table 3. Security controls difference analysis.

Projects	P01	P02	P03	P04	P05	P06	P07	P08	P09	P10	P11	P12
As Is	12	15	21	16	11	21	12	21	21	16	16	21
Should Be	21	21	21	21	21	21	21	21	21	21	21	21
Difference	9	6	0	5	10	0	9	0	0	5	5	0

3.5 Evaluation

The current organization secure development process received a punctual change that consisted in the use of the ASC Library during the project's RA document elaboration. In this case, for each project a list of recommended security controls will be obtained from the ASC Library, instead of searching in previous documentation, the security specialists have to use the library as reference. The development teams will also have access to the ASC Library, after receiving a RA document they will be able to consult the controls specifications before implementing them.

Then, the process proposed by the Action 1, must be executed in parallel to the projects development process. It is possible to identify a set of security controls before the projects kick-off, during the risk assessment new controls can be requested and after the project delivery new threats could be identified by the production support area, demanding in this case a new security control request.

The difference calculated in Table 3, it is an important warning about RA documents quality that must be hold by the organization application security team. It is not possible to affirm that the applications were not protected. The missing security controls should be included in the applications scope in further projects development. After that, security specialists must perform penetration tests and other security reviews to assure the mitigation of risks identified in this research.

4 Conclusion

The ASC Library adoption is an important concept to the secure development process. Due to a lack of similar researches, this experience report can be a contribution to support other organizations to aggregate a similar library to their secure development process. The organizations can identified missing security controls and work to mitigate possible applications vulnerabilities.

Further work will report an entire ISO/IEC 27034 standard implementation that will contribute to provide more details about the challenges of adopting the ONF and ANF structures and the necessary changes in the organization environment, culture and work to produce secure applications.

References

1. Ponsard, C., Massonet, P., Rifaut, A., Molderez, J.F.: Early verification and validation of mission critical systems. Formal Methods Syst. Des. **30**, 233–247 (2007). doi:10.1016/j.entcs.2004.08.067
2. El-Attar, M.: From misuse cases to mal-activity diagrams - bridging the gap between functional security analysis and design. Softw. Syst. Model. **13**, 173–190 (2014). doi:10.1007/s10270-012-0240-5
3. Futcher, L., Solms, R.: Guidelines for secure software development. In: Proceedings of 2008 Conference of South African Institute of Computer Scientists and Information Technologists (SAICSIT), pp. 56–65. SAICSIT in Association with ACM, Port Elizabeth, South Africa (2008). doi:10.1145/1456659.1456667
4. Khan, R.A., Mustafa, K.: From threat to security indexing - a causal chain. Comput. Fraud Secur. **5**, 9–12 (2009). doi:10.1016/S1361-3723(09)70059-4
5. ISO/IEC 15408: 2009 - Information technology - Security techniques - Evaluation criteria for IT security Information technology. International Organization for Standardization/International Electrotechnical Commission, Geneva (2009)
6. ISO/IEC 12207: 2008 Standards Catalogue - Systems and software engineering - Software life cycle processes. International Organization for Standardization/International Electrotechnical Commission, Geneva (2008)
7. ISO/IEC 21827: 2008 Standards Catalogue - Systems Security Engineering - Capability Maturity Model® (SSE-CMM®). International Organization for Standardization/International Electrotechnical Commission, Geneva (2008)
8. ISO/IEC 27034: 2011 Part 1 - Information technology - Security techniques - Application security - Overview and concepts. International Organization for Standardization/International Electrotechnical Commission, Geneva (2011)
9. Coughlan, P., Coghlan, D.: Action research for operations management. Int. J. Oper. Prod. Manage. **22**, 220–240 (2002). doi:10.1108/01443570210417515
10. OWASP Top 10 (Release 2013) – The Ten Most Critical Web Application Security Risks. https://www.owasp.org. Accessed 24 May 2017

Analysis of the Practices for the CMMI-SVC in an ISO/IEC 20000-1 Certified Organization

Ayşegül Ünal[✉], Rabia Burcu Karaomer, and Onur Kaynak

INNOVA IT Solutions, Ankara, Turkey
ayunal@innova.com.tr

Abstract. CMMI-SVC (Capability Maturity Model Integration for Services) is a process models for service provider organizations and ISO/IEC 20000 is ITIL based service management system standard. These are mature and accepted internationally. CMMI-SVC and ISO/IEC 20000 are tools for companies to develop their processes. Companies use these to increase quality of their services and productivity of teams and to decrease maintenance cost and time. Although, CMMI-SVC is a process model and ISO/IEC 20000 is a standard there is some similarities between them. In this study, we described the relationship between CMMI-SVC and ISO/IEC 20000 and the roadmaps of the two tools and gave pairing of systems according to these roadmaps. In this work, the aim is to define extra things to do for an organization that already has ISO/IEC 20000 certification, to get CMMI-SVC level 3 certification.

Keywords: ISO/IEC 20000 · CMMI for services · ITSM

1 Introduction

IT Service Management (ITSM) can defined as a management system of organizational resources and capabilities for providing value to organizational customers through IT services. As there are some standards and guide models to provide good quality for production, there are some standard and guide models for providing services. The ITIL best practice framework provides excellent guidance for transformation of IT into an IT service-oriented organization, which delivers services aligned with business needs in a cost-effective manner. However, implementation of ITIL does not provide any guarantee that implementation itself is done in the most consistent and best way possible across the service portfolio. It simply provides information regarding what should be done, and there are no "must be done" statements within it. This makes the quality of ITIL implementation hard to measure, and ITIL certification for organizations impossible. ISO 20000, on the other hand, is a standard with clearly defined requirements that must be met in order to certify that a minimum of best practice standards are met. ISO 20000 is ITIL based, and ITIL is designed with ISO 20000 in mind; therefore, they complement each other well. ISO/IEC 20000 is one of the standards that has used for providing service and CMMI-SVC is a guide model for increasing the quality of services. Although ISO/IEC 20000 and CMMI-SVC have some common specifications, they have some differences too [1].

INNOVA Information Technologies provides services with ISO/IEC 20000 standard since 2010 and it has decided to investigate about CMMI-SVC because of possible customer expectations and competitive market in the future. As the first thing to investigate, this work has done to compare ISO/IEC 20000 and CMMI-SVC. We listed process areas that are common in ISO/IEC 20000 and CMMI-SVC and what differences in these areas. In addition, the process areas that is included in CMMI-SVC but not included in ISO/IEC 20000 have investigated.

As a result, the similarities and differences between ISO/IEC 20000 and CMMI-SVC defined and especially the steps that should be done to get CMMI-SVC for a company that has ISO/IEC 20000 certifications are provided in this work.

INNOVA Information Technologies first established an ISO 9001 based quality management system. Because of statutory and competition motivation need for different process improvement and certification is raised and ISO/IEC 20000 based systems are defined and integrated with the existing quality management system. The motivation in this work comes from, as the quality assurance team, preparing our company for possible situations and comparing already had certificates with other models, in this increasing competition market in addition we want to show how an organization which has ISO/IEC 20000 certification can cover CMMI-SVC Level 3 practices.

As a result, the similarities and differences between ISO/IEC 20000 and CMMI-SVC defined and especially the steps that should be done to get CMMI-SVC for a company that has ISO/IEC 20000 certifications are provided in this work.

2 ISO/IEC 20000 versus CMMI for Services

ISO/IEC 20000 Information Technologies Management System standard is a guidance to the information technology companies or units for choosing method and how to apply this to meet inside and outside customers' expectations, to improve and develop their situations and performances continuously, to manage their operation and to provide services. It specifies requirements for the service provider to plan, establish, implement, operate, monitor, review, maintain and improve an SMS. The requirements include the design, transition, delivery and improvement of services to fulfil service requirement. According to ISO/IEC 20000, a service is an intangible product of a process where there are interaction of supplier and customer activities [3, 4].

The CMMI-SVC model guides service-providing organizations on applying CMMI best practices. How to provide quality services to customers have focused by best practices in this model. The CMMI-SVC combines indispensable knowledge for a service provider. According to CMMI-SVC, service is a product that is intangible and no storable delivered through service systems designed to satisfy service requirements. The basic feature of service that separates it from a product is having no property of the produced output in a service [3, 5] (Fig. 2).

Although ISO/IEC 20000 and CMMI-SVC has the same purpose and some similarities, they have some differences too [3]. The process areas in CMMI-SVC that are covered by ISO/IEC 20000 is shown in the Fig. 1 roughly. As can be seen in the Fig. 1, for a company that has ISO/IEC 20000 certification, Organizational Process Focus,

Organizational Process Definition, Organizational Training, Integrated Management, Decision Analysis and Resolution, Strategic Management and Service System Management processes should be defined and applied according to CMMI-SVC models to get CMMI-SVC Level 3 certification. In addition, there should be improvement in the other process areas according to CMMI-SVC (Fig. 3).

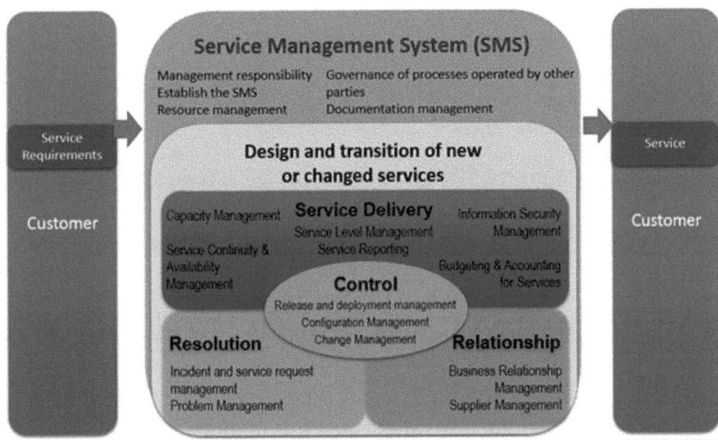

Fig. 1. ISO/IEC 20000 processes

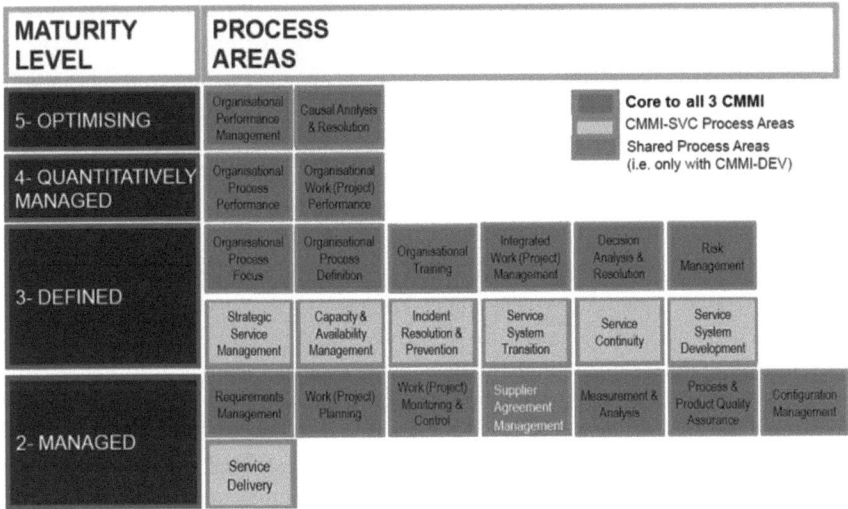

Fig. 2. CMMI SVC processes

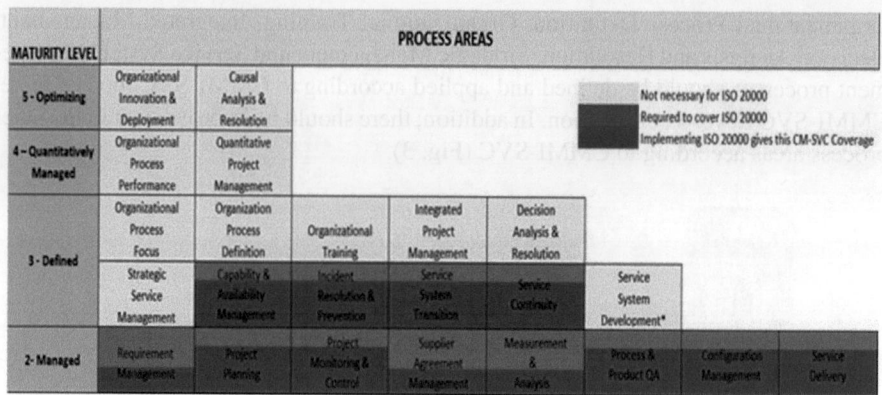

Fig. 3. Difference between CMMI-SVC and ISO/IEC 20000

3 How Much CMMI-SVC Requirements Meet in INNOVA

For CMMI-SVC [5], In Service Delivery process, the service agreement between a service provider and a customer is established and maintained. To succeed in maintaining collaboration between the service provider and customer, it is important to define the responsibilities of both parties. It is also important to set realistic expectations for service levels, which requires defining measurable, achievable service levels. Our company has "IT Service Catalogue Management Process" for all new services and changes to services with the potential to have a major impact on services or the customer. "IT Service Request Form" has prepared for all new, changed or removed services. This form includes all requirements of "ISO/IEC 20000-1:2011 Clause 5 Design and transition of new or changed services" section. Service requests are come from e-mails, SM tickets and actions of IT SMS committee or changing technologies. IT SMS Manager manages this form and presents to IT SMS committee meetings. Service Level Agreements have prepared by using "Service Level Agreement Form". Our company analyzes existing service agreements and service data to prepare for expected new agreements by using "Service Catalogue Management Process". For analyzing the capability to supply requested services we refer to "Capacity Management Process". Refer to the "Operation Supplier Management Process" process area for more information about managing the acquisition of products and services from suppliers. We define criteria for determining service requests in "IT Service Request Form", The service delivery approach resources, processes, and interfaces that are essential to successful service delivery over time is defined in "IT Service Catalogue Management Process".

In CMMI-SVC [5], Requirements Management processes manage all requirements received or generated by the work group, including both technical and nontechnical requirements as well as requirements levied on the work by the organization. In our company, "IT Service Level Management Process" holds new service or change service requirements and for every new/changed service, we use "Service Level Agreement Form". Changes, release and deployment activities we use "Change and Release

Management Process". All change requests for services are open on Service Management System (SMS). We can track our changes on SMS; if any service is change then SLA's and Service Catalogue has changed. When the change request is opened, the title, description, cause, field, priority, effect, risk, configuration item, start date, end date, implementation plan, risk assessment plan, test plan, return plan information are entered. Other considerations affecting service requirements can stem from the customer's agreements with other supplier, our company use "Operation Supplier Management Process". We use supplier agreements for these requirements. Our improvement for this process area should be documenting requirements changes and their rationale and maintaining bidirectional traceability between source requirements, all product and product component requirements, and other specified work products.

In CMMI-SVC [5], Planning is one of the keys to effectively managing work. The Work Planning process area involves, developing the work plan interacting with relevant stakeholders appropriately and getting commitment to the plan maintaining the plan. In our company, we prepare "Service Management Plan" for describing "Scope of IT Service Management System (SMS)", "IT Service Management System Methodology", "Service Management Goals", "Restrictions That Can Affect Service Management System", "IT Service Management System Requirements", "IT Service Management System Processes", "Authority, Role and Responsibilities of IT Service Management System", "IT Service Management Policy, Standards, Laws and Regulations", "Planning and Budgeting of IT Service Management System Resources (Human, Technical, Information and Financial)", "Risk Assessment Methodology", "Managing IT Service Management Plan Changes", "Technology(s) Supporting IT Service Management System", "Internal Audit of IT Service Management System", "Continuous Improvement Activities".

In CMMI-SVC [5], a documented work plan is the basis for monitoring activities, communicating status, and taking corrective action. Appropriate visibility of progress enables timely corrective action taken when performance deviates significantly from the plan. In our company, each service request is monitoring by SMS and for each process, we prepare performance reports, which mentioned in measurement and analysis process area. "Corrective/Preventive Action Request Process" handles deviation form Service Management Plan. During monitoring and control, risks handled in the direction of risk management process. Progress Reviews handled through process performance reports.

In CMMI-SVC [5], The Measurement and Analysis process area involves the following activities; Specifying objectives of measurement and analysis so that they are aligned with identified information needs and work, organizational, or business objectives, Specifying measures, analysis techniques, and mechanisms for data collection, data storage, reporting, and feedback, Implementing the analysis techniques and mechanisms for data collection, data reporting, and feedback Providing objective results that can be used in making informed decisions and taking appropriate corrective action. In our company measurement objectives are driven from SLAs and management reviews. Metrics are defined in Service Management Plan. We generate performance report for each process. The measurement values of the related targets and the results of the measurement values follow the IT Operation Process Performance Report. If there are deviations from the target values, the reasons examined and the necessary actions are taken by IT Operation. Reports to the top management regarding the realization status of the targets are made in the Committee and Management Review Meetings. These reports are "Configuration Management Performance Report", "Change and Release Management Performance Report", "Incident Management Process Performance Report". These reports are published in our portal and they are analyzed by review meetings. These data and results are stored in portal.

In CMMI-SVC [5], The Process and Product Quality Assurance process area supports the delivery of high quality products by providing work group staff and managers at all levels with appropriate visibility into, and feedback on, processes and associated work products throughout the work. The Service Management System is inspected according to the Management Systems Internal Auditing Process according to the requirements of the IT-System standard in terms of compliance with company processes, plans, policies and procedures. Internal audit reports are prepared for nonconformities. Corrective and Preventive Actions are determined is determined and followed according to "Corrective/Preventive Action Request Process."

In CMMI-SVC [5], The Configuration Management process area involves the following activities, identifying the configuration of selected work products that compose baselines at given points in time, controlling changes to configuration items. Building or providing specifications to build work products from the configuration management system, Maintaining the integrity of baselines, Providing accurate status and current configuration data to developers, end users, and customers. Our Company's quality management system is based on the ISO 9001. ISO 27001 and ISO/IEC 20000 systems are defined and integrated with the existing quality management system for Documentation management process and record control process. Documentation requirements are managed with Microsoft SharePoint Library system. PIT was created service policy and objectives for service management, service management plans, service catalogue, SLAs, service management processes. Baselines are established in "Configuration Management Process". We prepare for tracking performance of this process "Configuration Management Performance Report" and "Change and Release Management Performance Report". The CM process is audited by the Configuration Manager over a period of 3 months and the actions are planned and the actions taken are reported so that the identified problems are resolved. Changes are tracked by using "Change and Release Management Process".

In CMMI-SVC [5], the scope of Supplier Agreement Management process area addresses the acquisition of products, services, and product and service components that can be delivered to the service's customer or included in a product or service system. This process area's practices can also be used for other purposes that benefit the service. Supplier management was a practice based on ISO 9001. Evaluating suppliers already done periodically. But alignment of SLA breach times, basis for charging, service targets, and interfaces between service management processes operated by the supplier and other parties and define relationships between suppliers added to contracts. We were developed contracts with our law department. Customer's agreements with other supplier, our company use "IT Operation Supplier Management Process". Supplier agreements are established by using Service Level Agreement with suppliers. We accept the acquired product/service before any IT system is purchased, through criteria which

Analysis of the Practices for the CMMI-SVC   573

mentioned in process are evaluated by IT Operation. Evaluation results are shared with IT Operation Manager and registered in the portal.

The organization's processes include all processes used by the organization and its work groups. Candidate improvements to the organization's processes and process assets are obtained from various sources, including the measurement of processes, lessons learned in implementing processes, results of process appraisals, results of product and service evaluation activities, results of customer satisfaction evaluations, results of benchmarking against other organizations' processes, and recommendations from other improvement initiatives in the organization.

In CMMI-SVC [5], Organizational process assets enable consistent process execution across the organization and provide a basis for cumulative, long term benefits to the organization. In INNOVA our process is defined, our templates are established.

In CMMI-SVC [5], Organizational Training addresses training provided to support the organization's strategic business objectives and to meet the tactical training needs that are common across work groups and support groups. Training needs identified by individual work groups and support groups to meet their specific needs. In our company, organizational training plan is prepared annual and deliver training according to this plan, and establish training records. Effectiveness of the training is measured.

In CMMI-SVC [5], the purpose of Integrated Work Management (IWM) is to establish and manage the work and the involvement of relevant stakeholders according to an integrated and defined process that is tailored from the organization's set of standard processes.

In CMMI-SVC [5], The Decision Analysis and Resolution process area involves establishing guidelines to determine which issues should be subject to a formal evaluation process and applying formal evaluation processes to these issues. A formal evaluation process is a structured approach to evaluating alternative solutions against established criteria to determine a recommended solution.

In CMMI-SVC [5], Risk Management is a continuous, forward-looking process that is an important part of work management. Risk management should address issues that could endanger achievement of critical objectives. A continuous risk management approach effectively anticipates and mitigates risks that can have a critical impact on work activities. Risk assessment guide is prepared by IT Operation. Guide was prepared for ISO 27001 requirements but changes at ISO/IEC 20000:2011 version expectance was managing service risks. By the way, service risks calculated periodically and if there were, some risks improvements and changes implemented.

In CMMI-SVC [5], The Incident Resolution and Prevention process area involves the following activities, Identifying and analysing service incidents Initiating specific actions to address incidents Monitoring the status of incidents, tracking progress of incident status, and escalating as necessary Identifying and analysing the underlying causes of incidents Identifying workarounds that enable service to continue Initiating specific actions to either address the underlying causes of incidents or to provide workarounds, Communicating the status of incidents to relevant stakeholders Validating the complete resolution of incidents with relevant stakeholders, The reasons for Incident and problem management processes are different. In INNOVA, Incident Management is concerned with reserving the service to the user as quickly as possible. Problem

Management is a process related to determining the underlying causes of an event, resolving it, and preventing its repetition. Incident management operations begin with the end user registering through the Service Portal. "IT Incident Request" link on the main page at service portal. The following basic fields are sufficient for registration: a short title (mandatory field) describing the call, mandatory field), detail information of the call content (mandatory field), urgency level (mandatory field), additional files describing the problem (optional). Each incident is assigned and prioritized. If the IT operation personnel who the incident log is assigned fails to perform diagnosis and resolution, the incident is escalated to the "Problem Management Process". In the meantime, if possible, the user tries to solve the problem by suggesting an alternate or temporary solution. If permanent solution is possible, solution will be provided and tested. The incident log is closed and the status of the call log is set to "closed" by the operator. Then operator will get approval from the user for resolution. We prepare "Incident Management Process Performance Report" for tracking and improve the process.

In CMMI-SVC [5], The Service System Transition process area addresses all aspects of planning, communicating, managing, deploying, and confirming that service system components effectively make the transition to the delivery environment. The scope of this process area covers both new components and significant changes to existing components. In our company, we use "Service Catalogue Management Process" for new service or changed service. In our company, analyst analyses the new or changed service request, defines milestones, risks, test schedule and delivery schedule. After realization, service will be tested. Then request is send to live environment.

In CMMI-SVC [5], Service Continuity is the process of preparing mitigation for significant disruptions to service delivery so that delivery can continue or resume, although perhaps in a degraded fashion. These practices describe how to prepare service systems and the resources they depend on to help ensure that a minimum critical level of service can continue if a significant risk is realized. Part of service continuity is identifying which services cannot be disrupted and which can be disrupted and for what amount of time. In our company, PIT created Service Continuity and Availability Plans for IT SMS. Periodically this plan controlled and improved by using disaster plans and reports feed backs. Awareness is increasing about service up times. We use "Determining Accessibility and Business Continuity Process". Critical business functions for customers are determined by the IT Operations Manager and addressed for inclusion in Disaster Recovery Plans, taking into account criteria including Service Level Commitments as specified in the Service Level Agreement (SLA) to determine Accessibility and Business Continuity requirements and Service Level Commitments as defined in the Service Catalog. Accessibility and Business Continuity Plan is established and risks are identified. Accessibility Measurement Reporting and Unplanned Critical interruption and Corrective Actions are defined in this process. Business Continuity Plan is updated and changes is track by "Change and Release Management Process". Training the staff who will be involved in executing is defined in "Determining Accessibility and Business Continuity Process". IT operation team reviews "Service Continuity Plan". Designed, planned, and established for possible disaster situations using system monitoring tools to meet the requirements for services that need to be maintained. The IT Operation team tests disaster recovery plans. In addition, the tests are repeated after the major changes affecting the plans. To maintain test records, Disaster Recovery Test Reports are generated as a result of each Disaster Recovery Plan Test and these records are stored.

In CMMI-SVC [5], The Service System Development (SSD) process area focuses on the following activities, Collecting, coordinating, analysing, validating, and allocating, stakeholder requirements for service systems, Evaluating and selecting from alternative service system solutions, Designing and building or composing (as needed), integrating, and documenting service systems that meet requirements, Verifying and validating service systems to confirm they satisfy their intended requirements and they will satisfy customer and end user expectations during actual service delivery. SSD is an "Addition". As such, it is at the organization's discretion whether to implement SSD, and, whether to include SSD in a SCAMPI appraisal.

In CMMI-SVC [5], The Strategic Service Management process area involves the following activities, analysing capabilities and needs for services that span multiple customers and agreements, Establishing and maintaining standard services, service levels, and descriptions that reflect these capabilities and needs. In our company at yearly management review, strategic service needs are determined. We create annual service management plan. Properties of Standard Services and Service Levels Service Catalogue and Descriptions of Standard Services are defining in Operational Service Catalogue.

In CMMI-SVC [5], The Capacity and Availability Management process area involves establishing and maintaining capacity and availability at a justifiable cost and with an efficient use of resources. Capacity and availability management activities can be performed at different levels of the organization, including across different services. Capacity management plan is created periodically. This plan includes projects and improvements capacity calculations, storage, memory, line, server, backup, network switch capacities and change management effects. After creating that plan, we can manage time-scales and thresholds, and it causes less costs. In our company, we prepare Capacity Plan, Capacity reports and statistics, Current Capacity Plan for Monitor and Analyze Availability and capacity.

4 Conclusion

We analysed our processes (the ones related to ISO 20000) for achieving CMMI-SVC level 3 by conducting a high-level analysis at our organization to reach our business goal to show how an organization which has ISO/IEC 20000 certification can cover CMMI-SVC Level 3 practices. Our findings and analyzes in this context are written below. While doing this analysis, we inspected all written processes and work product that have developed through these processes.

CMMI-SVC processes such as, Service Delivery, Organizational Training, Configuration Management, Process and Product Quality Assurance, Strategic Service Management and Risk Management Processes practices have met through our company's ISO 20000, ISO 9001 and ISO 27001 processes. We do not need any additional improvements in our company for achieving these CMMI-SVC processes.

In Requirement Management process, our process improvement is documenting requirements changes and their rationale and maintaining bidirectional traceability between source requirements, all product and product component requirements, and other specified work products.

We may have improvements for "establish estimates of work product and task attributes, define lifecycle phases, estimate effort and cost" specific practices in Work (Project) Planning process for CMMI-SVC achievement. Further we may have improvements for "Monitor Commitments, Monitor Data Management, Monitor Stakeholder Involvement, Conduct Milestone Reviews" specific practices in Work (Project) Monitoring and Control process for CMMI-SVC achievement. Also we may have improvements for "Assess and Control the Impacts of the Transition" specific practice in Service System Transition process, "Analyse Results of Verification and Validation of the Service Continuity Plan" specific practice in Service Continuity process for CMMI-SVC achievement.

We may have improvements for "Determine Acquisition Type, Select Suppliers, Ensure Transition of Products" specific practices in Supplier Agreement Management process for CMMI-SVC achievement. Also we may have improvements for "Establish a Capacity and Availability Management Strategy" specific practice in Capacity and Availability Management process for CMMI-SVC achievement.

In Measurement and Analysis process, updating procedures of measurements nee to be defined. Metrics traceability to information need to be defined too. In Organizational Process Focus, Integrated Work (Project) Management and Decision Analysis and Resolution processes, we need to have improvements for all practices for CMMI-SVC achievement. In Organizational Process Definition process, we should improve "Establish Lifecycle Model Descriptions, Establish Tailoring Criteria and Guidelines, Establish the Organization's Measurement Repository, Establish Work Environment Standards, Establish Rules and Guidelines for Teams" specific practices for CMMI-SVC achievement.

In Incident and Resolution Prevention process, we should improve reusable solutions such as workarounds are important mechanisms that enable service delivery to continue in spite of the occurrence of an incident. Therefore, it is important that workarounds and other reusable solutions to be documented and confirmed for being effective before they used to address incidents with customers and end users.

In our company "Institutionalization" is fully covered by ISO 9001 and ISO 20000 requirements fulfilment. In CMMI-SVC, Institutionalization is an important concept in process improvement. When mentioned in the generic goal and generic practice descriptions, institutionalization implies that the process is ingrained in the way the work is performed and there is commitment and consistency to performing (i.e., executing) the process. In INNOVA, "Establish an Organizational Policy, Plan the Process, Control Work Products, Establish a Defined Process, Provide Resources, Assign Responsibility, Identify and Involve Relevant Stakeholders, Monitor and Control the Process, Objectively Evaluate Adherence, Review Status with Higher Level Management, Train People, Collect Process Related Experiences generic practices are covered in our processes.

References

1. Mora, M., Raisinghani, M., O'Connor, R.V., Gomez, J., Gelman, O.: An extensive review of it service design in seven international ITSM processes frameworks: Part I. Int. J. Inf. Technol. Syst. Approach. **7**(2), 83–107 (2014)
2. Sahin, Ö., ve Kaynak, O.: Experience report: implemental on of ISO/IEC 20000 information technology service management system. In: EuroSPI (2015)
3. ECCI Group: CMMI-SVC & ISO 20000 Perspectives on Service Management. www.eccinternational.com/iNugget/CMMIISO20000.pdf. Accessed Jan 2017
4. TS, ISO/IEC 20000:2011 Information Technology - Service Management
5. Chrissis, M.B., Konrad, M., Shrum, S.: CMMI-SVC Version 1.3. CMMI for Services Guidelines for Process Integration and Product Improvement, 3rd edn.

A Lightweight Software Process Assessment Approach Based on MDevSPICE® for Medical Device Development Domain

Özden Özcan-Top[1(✉)] and Fergal McCaffery[1,2]

[1] Regulated Software Research Centre and Lero,
Dundalk Institute of Technology, Dundalk, Ireland
{ozden.ozcantop, fergal.mccaffery}@dkit.ie
[2] STATSports Group, Dundalk, Ireland

Abstract. Software process improvement is challenging in the medical device development domain, as significant constraints exist such as ensuring conformance to regulations while improving software quality. The regulations that medical products are subject to may be overwhelming for organisations as a variety of international standards have to be implemented in order to address regulatory compliance. MDevSPICE® is a framework developed to overcome this challenge by integrating different international regulatory standards' requirements with generic software development best practices. Keeping the complexity of the domain in mind, the formal process assessments performed based on MDevSPICE® are highly detailed and require significant resource and effort investment. With the MDevSPICE® lightweight software process assessment approach, we aim to obtain maximum benefit from an assessment within a limited time by assessing all processes within MDevSPICE®, specifying and presenting major issues in projects, prioritizing such issues and progressing to the improvement stage as early as possible. The approach has designed to be a solution to improve feedback time and motivation to move forward for software process improvement actions. In this experience paper, we describe the development of the lightweight MDevSPICE® assessment method and its implementation in four companies.

Keywords: Lightweight assessment · Medical device software development · Regulatory requirements · Safety critical · MDevSPICE®

1 Introduction

Systems developed in medical, automotive, military-aviation, food, nuclear, pharmaceutical and railway domains are significant parts of our daily lives and are subject to heavy regulatory demands due to their safety critical characteristics. This is particularly the case in the medical domain, where the purpose of the regulations is to ensure that developed systems will not harm patients.

Medical device manufacturers in the US as well as in the EU must satisfy the associated regulatory demands of the region that the device will be marketed in. A variety of international standards have to be implemented in order to ensure regulatory requirements for a medical device. Such standards include IEC 62304:2006 (software life cycle processes for medical device software) [1], ISO 13485:2003 (quality management system requirements) [2] and ISO 14971 (risk management) [3] but there are many more.

An integrated framework for medical device software development MDevSPICE® has been developed by one of the authors to assist software development organisations in the medical device domain to achieve regulatory compliance [4, 5]. MDevSPICE® integrates generic software development best practices with medical device standards' requirements enabling robust software process assessments to be performed against an organisation's current software development practices. Either self-assessments or assessments against a standard are important in terms of creating action plans for improvement [6]. These process assessments may be used in different ways: (a) to ensure that the medical device software being developed by an organization conforms to regulatory software requirements for the industry which are across a spectrum of medical device standards (but defined in one place within MDevSPICE®) (before regulatory audits) (b) to use as a guidance for process improvement activities, and (c) to obtain support for action in developing better products.

In this experience paper, we present a light weight process assessment approach that allows practitioners to achieve significant results from the limited time that is available for performing an assessment. As part of this research we have performed MDevSPICE® based process assessments in four Irish software development companies, three of which are in medical device development domain. This approach was developed in an iterative and incremental way with the experiences we had after each assessment and has been evolved as a result of learnings in each assessment.

The paper is structured as follows: In the next section, the MDevSPICE® framework is presented. Following this, we present the literature survey on software process assessment. In Sect. 4, we present the lightweight process assessment approach along with the development stages. Details of the implementation are also discussed in Sect. 4. Finally, an overall conclusion is presented.

2 MDevSPICE® Framework

MDevSPICE® has been developed with the purpose of reducing the demanding and costly overhead associated with preparing for regulatory audits. It is a process capability assessment model which supports the performance of medical device software process assessments in accordance with the requirements of ISO/IEC 33002:2015 [7].

It has been built upon a wide number of medical software development and software engineering standards some of which are 'IEC 62304:2006: Software life cycle processes for medical device development [1] '; 'ISO/IEC 12207:2008: Software life cycle processes' [8], 'ISO/IEC 33002:2015: Requirements for performing process assessment' [7], 'ISO 14971:2009: Application of risk management to medical devices' [3], and 'ISO 13485:2003: Medical devices — Quality management systems — Requirements for regulatory purposes' [2].

MDevSPICE® consists of two-dimensions: The first dimension is the process dimension in which the processes are defined and the second dimension is the capability dimension in which the process attributes constitute the process capability levels.

Each process in the process dimension is described in terms of a purpose statement. Satisfying the purpose statements of a process represents the first step in building a Level 1 process capability where the expected outcomes are observable. A list of specific outcomes are given in relation to process purpose statements. Each outcome is associated with at least one of the safety classes mentioned above which is a critical information to show mandatory outcomes to achieve the specific classes.

The list of processes in MDevSPICE® process assessment model is given in Fig. 1.

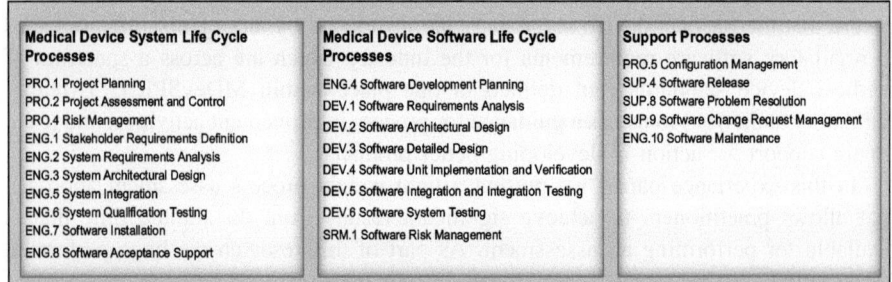

Fig. 1. MDevSPICE® processes

3 Literature Review on Formal and Lightweight Approaches to Software Process Assessment

In this section, we present the formal and lightweight software process assessment methods and the challenges in performing assessment associated with those methods over a literature review.

The first phase of method based software process improvement (SPI) studies is the process assessment where the purpose is to identify process gaps and weaknesses that exist within an organization or a project. These specified gaps and weaknesses play a significant role in success of improvement endeavors as they are used as a basis for improvement actions.

Software process assessment and improvement methods can be classified into two main categories: descriptive and prescriptive methods [9]. The descriptive methods aim to answer the question "how software is being actually developed?". Improvements are performed through gaining a thorough understanding of the current practices that are implemented in projects. There is no initial assessment or comparison with a pre-defined set of practices [10]. The prescriptive methods answer the question of "how software should be developed?" based on the best practices of the software industry [11]. Common SPI frameworks such as CMMI [12] and ISO/IEC 15504 (SPICE) [13] are also prescriptive models that are quite challenging to implement as they are too comprehensive [14].

Previously, the Regulated Software Research Center in DkIT published four lightweight software process assessment methods: Adept [15], Med-Adept [16], Med-Trace [17] and MDevSPICE-Adept [18]. Adept was developed in 2006 to assist small and medium sized Irish software organizations that have little or no experience of SPI [15]. It aims to diagnose weaknesses in a company's software processes and to provide a roadmap based on the business goals and specified weaknesses. The method uses a process assessment model adapted from CMMI® and ISO/IEC 15504 models. Twelve process areas may be assessed using the Adept Method, four of which are mandatory in an assessment: Requirements Management, Configuration Management, Project Planning, and Project Monitoring & Control. An onsite interview-based one day assessment is limited to six process areas using the Adept Method.

Med-Adept expends the Adept method for the medical device software development industry including processes for IEC 62304 [1]. In the overall, Med-Adept provides coverage of 11 CMMI® process areas, 12 ISO/IEC 15504-5 and 11 IEC 62304 processes. Med-Trace [17] was developed to analyze a mandatory component of medical device software development: traceability. The method aims to help evaluation and establishment of traceability linkages as there is no specific guidance within the medical device standards and documentation. A specific light-weight assessment model was required for MDevSPICE®. The aim when developing the MDevSPICE-Adept [18] method was to select a limited number of processes from out of the 23 processes that would be most beneficial and relevant to companies and to provide an onsite process assessment that lasted no longer than 2 days. Consequently, 11 processes were included in the method.

Pettersson et al. [14] published a lightweight software process assessment and improvement planning approach regardless of any specific framework to enable practitioners' to base improvement efforts on the issues that are the most critical for the specific organizations. The approach they suggested facilitates sampling of projects, roles and practitioners, and describes how to perform interviews and gives guidance on choosing an appropriate prioritization method.

Wiegers and Sturzenberger [19] discuss that CMM-based appraisals are quite expensive and time consuming and many companies find it difficult to perform these assessments regularly. They propose a mini-assessment method (MMA) to overcome this challenge. The method proposes multiple options that are available for most assessment steps such as using questionnaires based on (a) CMM practices, sub-practices, (b) All CMM key practices, (c) Institutionalization factors only. MMA doesn't include suggestions for follow-up action planning and action plan tracking activities or provide details on questionnaires used.

Success factors related to software process improvement (SPI) activities from a general perspective include management support, motivation and commitment of other employees, a systematic implementation strategy, standards and procedures, training and mentoring and experienced staff [6, 20–22]. It was shown by Rainer et al. that training and mentoring, and standards and procedures are considered as two factors having a major impact on SPI by low maturity companies. Mature companies having more detailed understanding of SPI additionally think that internal leadership, inspections, executive support, and internal process ownership have important impact on SPI success [21].

Although numerous studies have explored the success factors of SPI initiatives, there are no studies specifically exploring the success factors of software process assessment. However, new approaches to process assessment were suggested in the literature [23, 24]. Dyba and Moe mention that what is important for assessments are the identification of critical problems and establishment of improvement priorities [24]. In this study, a participative approach to assessment was adopted where data was collected from everyone in the organization and action planning was done by teams at all levels were suggested. Significant findings of this study which could be a guide for software process assessment could be summarized as follows:

- Involvement of different groups within the assessment increases the possibility of having multiple views and discovery of issues.
- Waiting too long before the assessment feedback session, may lead to a loss of SPI focus in the department/company.
- The data analysis and feedback session shouldn't be ended without identifying concrete areas for improvement.
- Holding a presentation for the assessment participants, provides motivation for the assessment, and ensures that everybody has the same understanding of the questions and the goals of the assessment.

Senior managers' active participation in assessment meetings is thought to add the necessary momentum to the initiative by Stelzer and Mellis [6], however, based on our opinions, this might cause pressure on the participants in assessment interviews and may prevent reveal of critical issues.

4 The Lightweight Software Process Assessment Approach

In this section, we describe the lightweight software process assessment approach developed based on MDevSPICE® for medical device software development domain. This approach aims to obtain maximum benefit from an assessment within a limited time by covering all processes within MDevSPICE®, specifying and presenting the major issues in projects, prioritizing these issues and starting improvement actions as early as possible.

4.1 The Structure of the Approach

Both formal and lightweight assessment approaches of MDevSPICE® are performed based on the high level flow shown in the BPMN diagram in Fig. 2. The process starts with identification of assessment needs by sponsor. Based on the defined assessment needs, assessment scope, projects to be assessed, resources and team members are specified by the sponsor and lead assessor. The sponsor establishes the assessment plan and informs the assessment participants about the plan. Process and product artefacts are observed as evidence of achievement of base practices during interviews with process owners. During the next step, issues, challenges and strengths are reported by the assessment team. The report is validated during a findings reporting session where sponsor and process owners are involved.

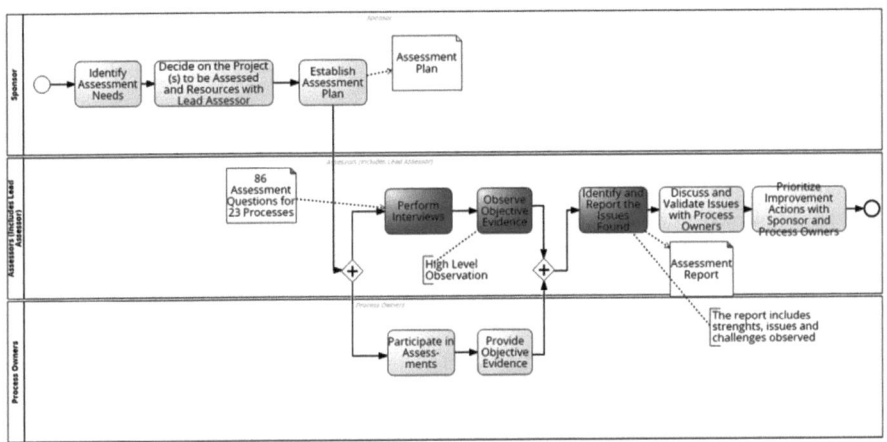

Fig. 2. High level flow of MDevSPICE® based light weight process assessment approach (Color figure online)

The difference of the formal and lightweight assessment approaches lie in the three activities shown with orange in Fig. 2: "Perform Interviews", "Observe Objective Evidence", and "Identify and Report the Issues Found".

The "Perform Interviews" activity is a question and answer session where the responses from the process owners are recorded by assessors for analysis. A scripted question set is defined by assessors prior to this activity. The formal assessment approach of MDevSPICE® is so comprehensive that the scripted question includes 758 questions across 23 processes. Software Risk Management, Software Development Planning, Software Requirements, Software Unit Implementation and Testing and Software Architecture processes have larger number of questions, with 108, 78, 61, 51 and 43 respectively. As an example, it takes approximately 3 h to discuss the Software Requirements Process having 61 questions with the process owners. A whole assessment takes approximately 37 h. This requires having 6 business days of assessments back to back. For small organisations, such an uninterrupted dedication for assessments would not be possible. The assessment sessions usually take place with 2 to 3 h sessions daily or 4 to 6 h sessions on weekly basis. Such an implementation would result in a formal assessment being completed in months and prevent a rapid start to improvement activities.

With the motivation to reduce SPI initiation and to capture as many as issues possible within a limited time, we have updated the question set mentioned above to include a total of 86 questions for the 23 processes.

Question examples from the Software Risk Management process are shared in Tables 1 and 2 to show how detailed questions differ from the lightweight questions:

The lightweight questions allows process owners' to describe the process flow and focus on the challenges and issues. These questions led the assessment process being performed as a descriptive approach rather than a prescriptive approach.

The **"Observe Objective Evidence"** activity involves a high level observation of the process artifacts rather than finding evidences for each question. The formal

Table 1. Software risk management process formal question & sub-questions for base practice #1

SRM.1.BP1.Q1: Describe how you identify software items that can contribute to hazardous situations?
Do you identify hazardous situations that can arise as a direct result of software failures? [Class: B, C]
Do you identify hazardous situations that can arise as a result of failures of risk control measures implemented in software? [Class: B, C]
Do you document software items contributing to hazardous situations in the risk management file? [Class: B, C]
Where do you identify software items as contributing to hazardous situations, identify the potential causes of the contribution. [Class: B, C]
Do you identify any non-specified SOUP software (e.g. word processors, games) that could cause a hazardous situation to arise?
Do you define risk control measures that could prevent the operation of non-specified SOUP software? (e.g. in system design, preventative measures, or labelling)
Is input from unnecessary sources prevented? (e.g. disabling floppy/CD/tape drives, modems)

Table 2. Light weight questions for software risk management process

What do you understand by software risk management as opposed to medical device risk management?
Do you track software risks throughout the development lifecycle?
Do you include 3rd party software anomalies as risks?
What challenges do you face in relation to this process?

approach would of course include finding supporting evidence and ensuring that they are adequately recorded for presentation in regulatory audits.

The **"Identify and Report the Issues found"** activity includes analyzing the assessment session with the assessors and reporting the issues, challenges and strengths for 23 processes. The major difference of this activity from the formal assessment is that it does not include any *process attribute rating*.

4.2 Development of the Approach and Lessons Learned

The approach and the experiences that were described in this paper have evolved within the scope of a research project, the purpose of which is to adapt agile software development practices into highly regulated environments in order to achieve higher productivity levels and product quality. Four software development companies from regulated domains, based in Ireland, have been visited several times for the first phase of the project: MDevSPICE® based software process assessment for gap analysis. The profiles of these companies are given in Table 3.

We have started implementing the MDevSPICE® formal process assessment method in Company A, Company B and Company C. The assessment needs were specified by the sponsors and discussed with the lead assessor. The needs specified were "identify the process gaps from medical device development regulations

Table 3. The companies that the approach has been implemented

Company A	Company A develops medical applications for iOS, Android, Windows 8 and Web Browser. It was formed in 2011 and since 2012, it has been developing medical device software. The products that they developed are classified as Class B based on IEC 62304:2006. It's a small company including 7 people whom are developers, testers, a product manager and clinicians
Company B	Company B develops software that is currently not safety critical but the organisation has demands placed upon them from their industry as it has to be always accurate, reliable and consistent. It includes 50 employees
Company C	Company C develops personalized safety critical applications for patients to support them in behavior change and improve patient engagement with healthcare practitioners. It's a large scale company employing more than 150 people across three main offices in Ireland, Poland and the US
Company D	Company D develops mobile and web applications to assist patients who are recovering from injury or operations or are dealing with chronic pain. The products that they developed are classified as Class B based on IEC 62304:2006. It is based in Ireland and 10 people work in the company

perspective" and "understand how the gaps could be fulfilled with implementing agile practices". We commenced the assessment sessions and followed the flow in processes of the basic software development life cycle. Very detailed questions were asked to process owners, the answers were recorded and evidences observed. After 3 to 4 sessions over a two to three week time period, 1/3 of the processes still remained not assessed, but in the interests of timeliness we decided to present the partial results to Company A and Company B.

The companies were willing to proceed with the improvement phase while leaving the rest of the assessment to a later time. However the challenge with the results is that they don't represent the complete picture for the workflow. We feel that the success of the process improvement activities rely upon working on the right processes at the right time. Spending effort and resources on trivial improvements while unwittingly ignoring the ones which will have a greater effect on the quality of a process and a product would decrease the impact of the improvement initiative and the motivation for such an endeavor.

As we had already performed the formal assessments for five MDevSPICE® processes in Company C and with the lessons learned mentioned above, we have developed the lightweight approach, and proposed it to the company sponsor and agreed upon proceeding with the new approach. It took 11 h to complete the full assessment with 23 processes, 5 of which were assessed with the formal approach and 18 of which were assessed using the lightweight approach. If the assessment had been performed using the formal approach, it would take 37 h as the rationale for this effort was described above. Compared to a full formal assessment approach, with 11 h we have gained 70% from the actual time required. This would even be much more when the interruptions between the assessment sessions are considered. The major strength of this assessment is that the complete lifecycle picture of the processes and issues were assessed for the project. We then prioritized the improvement needs and defined improvement actions with relevant process owners (Fig. 3 and Table 4).

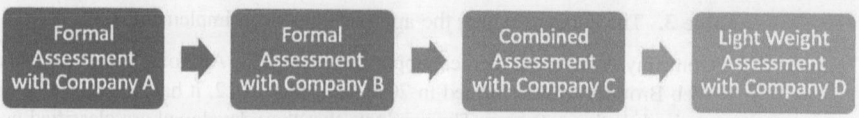

Fig. 3. Evolution of the assessment approach based on lessons learned

Table 4. Effort spent for each assessment

	Company A	Company B	Company C	Company D
# Of processes assessed	9 Processes were assessed with the formal approach	5 Processes were assessed with the formal approach	5 Processes were assessed with the formal approach	23 Processes were assessed with the lightweight approach
			18 Processes with the lightweight approach	
Spent effort	12 h for the assessment	9 h for the assessment	11 h for assessment	6 h for assessment
			8, 5 h for reporting	3 h for reporting

After obtaining positive feedback from the sponsor and the process owners on implementation of the lightweight approach in Company C, we then implemented it in Company D. It took 6 h to assess all 23 processes in Company D. We were able to schedule a back to back 2 day session with the Company, as we estimated that less time would be required for the assessment. After the assessment, we were able to point out the major issues regarding the MDevSPICE® processes in the assessed project, prioritize improvement needs and begin identifying which agile practices would be most suitable for resolving the issues specified.

5 Conclusion

MDevSPICE® has been developed as a prescriptive process assessment and improvement framework for medical device development domain. The purpose of which is to ensure the conformance to regulatory requirements of a variety of regulatory standards whilst improving process and product quality and required safety. The formal process assessment approach of MDevSPICE® has built upon ISO/IEC 15504-Part 2. The approach includes highly detailed questions to be asked and specific evidences for base practices to be observed. This approach ensures a project's full conformance to medical regulatory requirements. However, when the major purpose of the assessment is to understand the issues in the overall lifecycle development and to proceed with the improvement actions as quickly as possible, the formal approach proves overwhelming. MDevSPICE-Adept, on the other hand proposes a detailed assessment with limited scope.

In this regard, we have developed a lightweight process assessment approach that looks across all processes at a high level rather than looking deep at a few processes with the purpose of gaining a good understanding of the overall workflow within a project or an organization. We have provided a remedy for the main shortcoming of the formal software process assessment method which is waiting too long before the assessment feedback session that leads to loss of SPI focus.

While major activities in the formal workflow remain the same such as: identification of assessment needs, selecting the processes to be assessed, establishing the assessment plan, reporting the issues and prioritization; the way we have performed these activities has significantly changed. Instead of performing the assessment over 758 questions, we now perform it over 86 questions in the light weight approach. The approach focuses upon identifying appropriate improvement opportunities rather than capability level ratings for processes. Although we no longer provide a detailed analysis for each process, the new approach provides a significant gain in terms of the time required for a full assessment and nothing is overlooked in terms of issues and challenges at the lifecycle level. It should be noted that the light weight approach cannot be used as a readiness check before a formal regulatory audit as this requires deeper assessment of objective evidences.

To sum up, the achievements obtained with the light weight approach are:

- Specifying the issues in software development projects quicker through enabling a higher level view of the complete software development lifecycle
- Significantly reduced time to start MDevSPICE based SPI activities
- Higher motivation to proceed with the SPI activities

The future work regarding this study is to perform the approach in more regulated companies and to observe the successes achieved on SPI activities that are initiated after the light weight assessment.

Acknowledgment. This research is supported by Science Foundation Ireland under a co-funding initiative by the Irish Government and European Regional Development Fund through Lero - the Irish Software Research Centre (http://www.lero.ie) grant 13/RC/2094. This research is also partially supported by the EU Ambient Assisted Living project – Maestro

References

1. IEC 2006. IEC 62304: Medical Device Software - Software Life-Cycle Processes
2. ISO 2003. ISO 13485: Medical Devices - Quality Management Systems - Requirements for Regulatory Purposes
3. ISO 2009. ISO 14971 - Medical Devices - Application of Risk Management to Medical Devices
4. Lepmets, M., Clarke, P., McCaffery, F., Finnegan, A., Dorling, A.: Development of MDevSPICE®–the medical device software process assessment framework. J. Softw. Evol. Process **27**(8), 565–572 (2015)
5. Lepmets, M., Mc Caffery, F., Clarke, P.: Piloting MDevSPICE: the medical device software process assessment framework. In: Proceedings of the 2015 International Conference on Software and System Process, pp. 9–16. ACM (2015)

6. Stelzer, D., Mellis, W.: Success factors of organizational change in software process improvement. Softw. Process Improv. Pract. **4**(4), 227–250 (1998)
7. ISO/IEC 33002:2015, Information technology – Process assessment – Requirements for performing process assessment (2015)
8. ISO/IEC 12207:2008 Systems and software engineering – Software life cycle processes (2008)
9. Acuna, S.T., Juristo, N., Moreno, A.M., Mon, A.: A Software Process Model Handbook for Incorporating People's Capabilities. Springer Science & Business Media, Heidelberg (2006)
10. Basili, V.R.: The experimental paradigm in software engineering. In: Rombach, H.D., Basili, V.R., Selby, R.W. (eds.) Experimental Software Engineering Issues: Critical Assessment and Future Directions. LNCS, vol. 706, pp. 1–12. Springer, Heidelberg (1993). doi:10.1007/3-540-57092-6_91
11. Lonchamp, J.: A structured conceptual and terminological framework for software process engineering. In: 1993 Second International Conference on the Software Process, Continuous Software Process Improvement, pp. 41–53. IEEE (1993)
12. Capability Maturity Model Integrated-Development (2010)
13. ISO/IEC 15504–5:2012 Information technology – Process assessment – Part 5: An exemplar software life cycle process assessment model (2012)
14. Pettersson, F., Ivarsson, M., Gorschek, T., Öhman, P.: A practitioner's guide to light weight software process assessment and improvement planning. J. Syst. Softw. **81**(6), 972–995 (2008)
15. Mc Caffery, F., Richardson, I., Coleman, G.: Adept–a software process appraisal method for small to medium-sized Irish software development organisations (2006)
16. Mc Caffery, F., Casey, V.: Med-Adept: a lightweight assessment method for the Irish medical device software industry (2010)
17. Casey, V., Mc Caffery, F.: A lightweight traceability assessment method for medical device software. J. Softw. Evol. Process **25**(4), 363–372 (2013)
18. McCaffery, F., Clarke, P., Lepmets, M.: A lightweight assessment method for medical device software processes. In: Mitasiunas, A., Rout, T., O'Connor, V., Dorling, A. (eds.) Software Process Improvement and Capability Determination, pp. 144–156. Springer, Heidelberg (2014)
19. Wiegers, K.E., Sturzenberger, D.C.: A modular software process mini-assessment method. IEEE Softw. **17**(1), 62–69 (2000)
20. Kauppinen, M., Vartiainen, M., Kontio, J., Kujala, S., Sulonen, R.: Implementing requirements engineering processes throughout organizations: success factors and challenges. Inf. Softw. Technol. **46**(14), 937–953 (2004)
21. Rainer, A., Hall, T.: Key success factors for implementing software process improvement: a maturity-based analysis. J. Syst. Softw. **62**(2), 71–84 (2002)
22. Niazi, M., Wilson, D., Zowghi, D.: Critical success factors for software process improvement implementation: an empirical study. Softw. Process Improv. Pract. **11**(2), 193–211 (2006)
23. Ares, J., García, R., Juristo, N., López, M., Moreno, A.M.: A more rigorous and comprehensive approach to software process assessment. Softw. Process Improv. Pract. **5**(1), 3–30 (2000)
24. Dybå, T., Moe, N.B.: Rethinking the concept of software process assessment. In: European Software Process Improvement Conference (EuroSPI), Pori, Finland (1999)

The Current Status of the TestSPICE® Project

Klaudia Dussa-Zieger[1(✉)], Mohsen Ekssir-Monfared[2], Tomas Schweigert[3], Michael Philipp[3], and Monique Blaschke[3]

[1] imbus AG, Möhrendorf, Germany
klaudia.dussa-zieger@imbus.de
[2] SQS Software Quality Systems, Vienna, Austria
[3] SQS Software Quality Systems, Cologne, Germany

Abstract. The paper presents the TestSPICE approach showing the content of the current version of TestSPICE, the transition to Scalable TestSPICE and the agile extension of TestSPICE. In addition it describes the relationship of TestSPICE to the ISO Standard ISO/IEC/IEEE 29119 and the ISO/IEC 15504 family of process assessment standards. The ECQA SPI Manager training which supports the implementation of TestSPICE is also presented.

Keywords: Testing process · SPICE · TestSPICE · Process assessment · Process improvement · ECQA · INTACS · ISO 29119 · ISTQB · SPI Manager

1 Introduction

Agile times provide some challenges for testing professionals. Testing is usually the last step, always under time and budget pressure. But even if the test engineers work hard to execute all planned tests, due to high frequency of deliveries, it often happens that a last minute build is produced by the development team which causes the consequence that the build that is delivered is not the build that was tested. Test engineers are then held responsible for poor quality in the field. In order to respond to this thread testing processes need to be clearly understood and transparent. The TestSPICE model supports test engineers and test managers to understand the current status of testing and to identify and understand optimization options. The paper will describe a short history of the evolution of TestSPICE. It will present the model as is and the upcoming mechanisms for scalability. It will also show the content and structure of the agile extension as well as the content of the ECQA SPI Manager Skill Card.

2 History and Development of TestSPICE®

The starting point for TestSPICE was an SQS initiative launched in 2009. Its objective was to create a test assessment approach as close as possible to ISO/IEC 15504 (SPICE). The initial architectural decision was just to replace the Engineering Process Group (ENG) of SPICE with a specific Testing Process Group (TST) for TestSPICE. The approach was presented at the SPICE Days 2010 in Stuttgart. At the same place representatives of other SPICE and testing service provider showed great interest in the assessment model and agreed to form a special interest group (SIG) to drive the further development of TestSPICE.

The TestSPICE SIG decided some major architectural changes specially regarding technical testing processes and launched TestSPICE 2.0 in 2012. At this point TestSPICE was the only testing PAM that was compliant with ISO/IEC 15504 Part 2 and verified by the International Assessor Certification Scheme INTACS. After this launch the TestSPICE SIG started planning for TestSPICE V3.0 with focus on:

- Re-Arrangement of the relationship to ISO/IEC 15504-5 in order to avoid duplicate processes
- Alignment to the test process in ISO/IEC/IEEE 29119-2
- Additional technical testing processes e.g. Test Automation & Test Data Management.
- TestSPICE 3.0 is active since 2013, but new questions came up:
- How to make assessments more efficient without losing information
- How to allow TestSPICE to be combined with other models, e.g. Automotive SPICE®
- How to combine TestSPICE with different measurement frameworks
- How to incorporate the strategic aspects of agile transition into the agile extension
- How to make TestSPICE more flexible to allow an enhanced assessment-scaling with respect to customer needs

The TestSPICE SIG is still working on these issues, but some ideas become more and more clear. Progress was made when TestSPICE 3.1 was launched in 2014.

3 The Structure of TestSPICE 3.1

TestSPICE 3.1 takes several approaches into account that are available on the market:

- The requirements for process reference models (PRM) and the requirements for process assessment models (PAM) as stated in ISO/IEC 15504 Part 2
- Testing best practices as described in the ISTQB® Syllabi (Foundation Level)
- Test process as described in ISO/IEC/IEEE 29119-2
- Test techniques as described in ISO/IEC/IEEE 29119-4

These inputs are synthesized in the TestSPICE PAM. It includes:

- TestSPICE PRM including processes described in terms of ID, Name, Purpose and Outcomes
- TestSPICE PAM including
  - indicators (practices and work products)
  - the measurement framework as stated in ISO/IEC 15504 Part 2

There are additional features that are not described in the TestSPICE® PAM which are typically used:

- The assessment process as described in ISO/IEC 15504 Part 2
- Assessor training and certification standard as defined by INTACS
- Independence requirements stated by ISO/IEC/IEEE 15504 Part 7 and supported by the INTACS trustworthiness approach

This feature set was found adequate. During all discussions in the TestSPICE SIG no additional feature was required.

4 The TestSPICE® 3.1 Process Reference Model

The TestSPICE 3.1 Process Reference model is composed of four processes categories: Business Life Cycle Processes, Technical Life Cycle Processes, Agreement Life Cycle Processes and the Agile Extension Processes. All categories are further composed of process groups, see also Fig. 1.

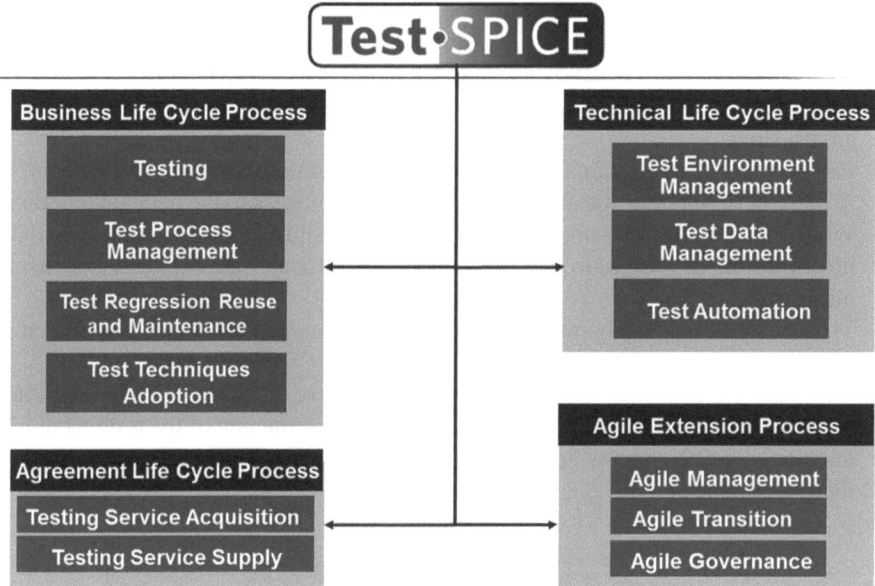

Fig. 1. Overall structure of TestSPICE

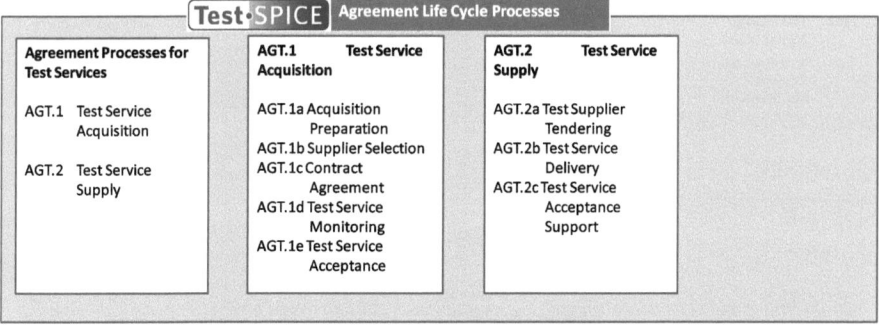

Fig. 2. Agreement life cycle processes

Looking at a more detailed level TestSPICE 3.1 looks as follows.

- The Agreement processes for testing services (AGT): The Agreement for Testing Services Process Category consists of processes to be used for acquisition and supply of testing services.
- The Agreement for Testing Services process category (AGT) consists of processes that are performed by the customer, or by the supplier even when acting as a customer for its own suppliers, in order to acquire or supply a test service.
- Any contract performed will be managed by processes in the Test Process Management process group (TPM) and executed by the processes in the Testing process group (TST).
- Each group has an overarching process (Testing Service Acquisition and Testing Service Supply) and detailed processes where a mapping is in place between the indicators of the overarching process to the detailed process.
- The Business Life Cycle Process Category consists of processes to be used for operative testing.
- Each group has an overarching process and detailed processes where a mapping is in place between the indicators of the overarching process to the detailed process.
- While planning an assessment a clear decision should be taken if the overarching process or the detailed processes are in the scope. Mixtures are explicitly not recommended.
- The detailed mapping between overarching and detailed processes is declared in Annex N of the TestSPICE PAM.
- The process group Test Techniques Adoption is one of the links between TestSPICE and ISO/IEC/IEEE 29119. TestSPICE does not advocate any of the test techniques mentioned in this process group, but advocates explicit decision making regarding these techniques.

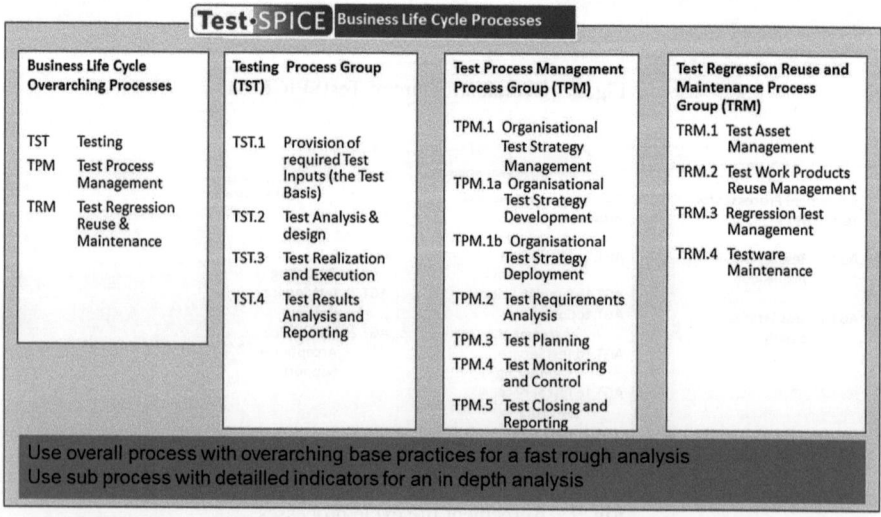

Fig. 3. Business life cycle processes (part I)

- The Technical Life Cycle Process Category consists of processes to be used for the technical enabling of testing.

Each group has an overarching process and detailed processes where a mapping is in place between the indicators of the overarching process to the detailed process. When planning an assessment a clear decision should be taken if the overarching process or the detailed processes are in scope. Mixtures are explicitly not recommended. Details on the processes within the different process group can be found in the TestSPICE Model itself [4]. The model was found suitable to assess testing processes of any kind (Figs. 3 and 4).

Test·SPICE Business Life Cycle Processes

Test Techniques Adoption Process Group (TTA)

TTA.1	Adoption of Equivalence Partitioning	TTA.9	Adoption of Scenario Testing
TTA.2	Adoption of Classification Tree Method	TTA.10	Adoption of Error Guessing
TTA.3	Adoption of Boundary Value Analysis	TTA.11	Adoption of Random Testing
TTA.4	Adoption of State Transition Testing	TTA.12	Adoption of Statement Testing
TTA.5	Adoption of Decision Table Testing	TTA.13	Adoption of Branch Testing
TTA.6	Adoption of Cause-Effect Graphing	TTA.14	Adoption of Decision Testing
TTA.7	Adoption of Syntax Testing	TTA.15	Adoption of Condition Testing
TTA.8	Adoption of Combinatorial Test Techniques	TTA.16	Adoption of Data Flow Testing

Fig. 4. Business life cycle processes (part II)

5 Determine Assessment Scope

When determining the scope of an assessment based on TestSPICE a focus should always be on the technical life cycle processes. Especially the test data and test environment management processes are key processes to provide an undisturbed and smooth work environment for the test. Thus, they build the base to support the business life cycle processes defined in TestSPICE.

Focusing on test data management the TDM process group combined with the Testware Maintenance process (TRM.4) provides a set of base practices and work products that covers the various problems projects and organizations have to face in dealing with test data usage. While the TDM process group addresses the initial requirement setup and provisioning of test data, the Testware Maintenance process supports the maintenance and deletion of test data. Only in combination of the two the whole test data life cycle is covered adequately (Fig. 5).

Since test data management is a challenge for most organizations especially in shared test environments, a fast and easy test data set up is essential for test automation and agile testing. Therefore the test data relating processes should be part of every assessment to support the quality of the tests and reduce issues regarding test data.

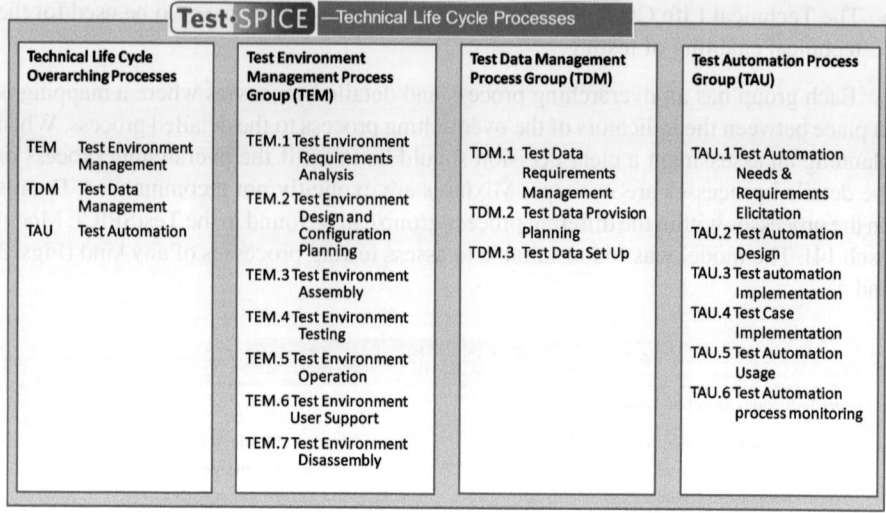

Fig. 5. Technical life cycle processes

6 Scalable TestSPICE®

Even if the process assessment model of TestSPICE is suitable for standard SPICE Assessments, there is a remaining challenge. The assessment cannot completely be adjusted to customer needs. An organization might decide to analyze a process or not. But there is nothing in between. TestSPICE shares this challenge with other models like TPI NEXT or TMMI. As a result, many so called health checks can be found in the internet that promise (and deliver) faster overarching results by less effort.

Mostly these health checks address some critical points without having a theoretical background or an understanding of measurement frameworks or generic practices.

To explain this a little deeper, health checks focus often on a pragmatic and quick understanding of momentary process quality or related questions in order to get a first impression on improvement needs. Therefore, health checks can be a quick way to adopt guidelines such as best practices. As a response to this challenge, the TestSPICE SIG decided to check if the model could be made more efficient for assessors by making it more scalable. One potential solution can be found in the Agreement for Test Services process group (AGT), see also Fig. 2.

While AGT.1 Testing Service Acquisition serves as an overarching process, processes like AGT.1a Acquisition Preparation serve as sub processes. Looking at the content of AGT.1 it becomes clear that the overarching process has the sub processes as base practices:

- Prepare Acquisition
- Select Supplier
- Agree on contract
- Monitor the testing service
- Accept the testing service

It is easy to see that the sub process AGT.1a Acquisition Preparation details the base practice "Prepare Acquisition" of the overarching AGT.1 process providing low level practices as indicators:

- Establish the needs
- Define the requirements
- Review requirements
- Develop acquisition strategy
- Define selection criteria
- Communicate the need

To adopt this architecture to the complete TestSPICE model a transformation has to be done:

- Transform former process categories to process groups
- Transform former process groups to overarching processes
- Transform former process to sub processes.

Doing so the following scalability options are at hand:

- "Overarching" assessment using only the overarching processes. This gives a rough indication of the current status in about 3 days including kick off and final results presentation.
- Mixed assessment of overarching processes and sub processes according to customer needs. That means using for one process group the overarching process and for another process group the sub processes. Using Overarching and sub processes of the same process group will lead to confusion and is explicitly not recommended.
- Complete assessment on sub process level. This assessment gives more insights but will also cause more effort and a longer duration.
- Deep dive assessment that not only uses sub processes but also checks on content level if the information, required in the work product characteristics is provided completely and adequate. Even if this is a deep dive level, it is explicitly not a review, as it is not checked if the content is correct.

Currently the TestSPICE SIG is discussing a draft and some technical problems have to be solved until scalable TestSPICE will be released. As soon as the TestSPICE SIG decides to bring the scalable approach into public discussion the PAM will be published at www.testspice.info. Currently available are the TestSPICE PAM 3.0 and 3.1.

7 Combining TestSPICE® with Other Models

There are other models in the market like ISO/IEC 15504 Part 5:2013, Automotive SPICE® and CMMI. All this models do not provide a very deep insight into testing. TestSPICE allows combined scoping. If an organization uses Automotive SPICE in order to check the development processes it can also choose TestSPICE for testing processes, include them into the assessment scope and check the whole scope during one assessment [1]. This works with all types of SPICE models but also with CMMI continuous model. The advantages of this approach are clear. An organization, which wants to check the capability of its processes, does not need to learn interpretations or do mappings just use the framework the organization is familiar with and gain a consistent understanding of process capability across all domains of systems and software engineering (Figs. 6 and 7).

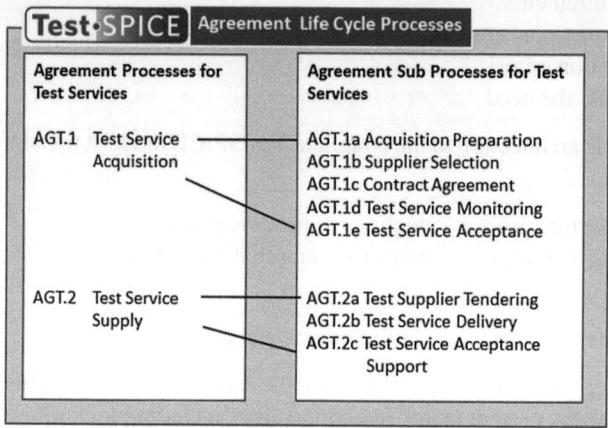

Fig. 6. Agreement life cycle processes

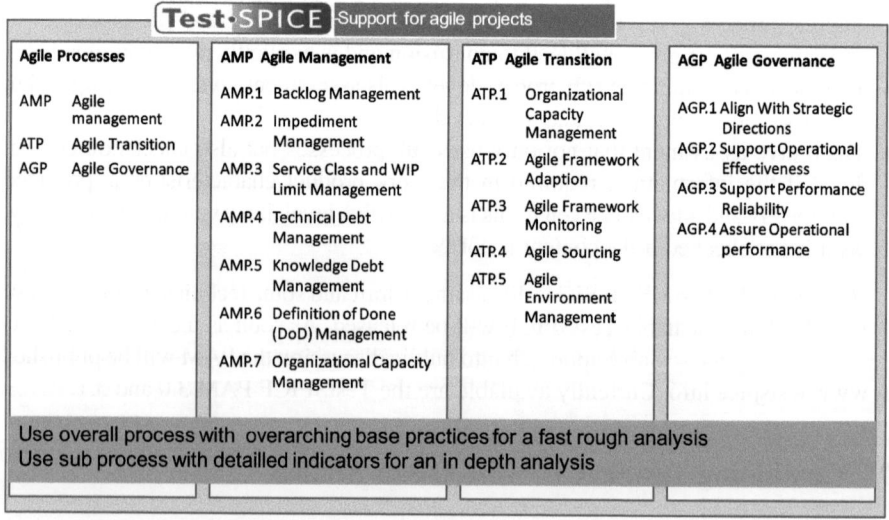

Fig. 7. Agile Extention of TestSPICE

8 Supporting Agile

In order to support agile organizations TestSPICE provides an agile process reference and assessment model in an annex. The agile PAM is aiming to provide useful practices on project level but also on strategic and tactical level of organizations [2]. In the context of TestSPICE the Agile Extension Processes category is an optional category which is provided in the annex of the TestSPICE model. The category consists of three process groups:

- One of the influencing factor behind this model is that organizations often see agile more as a kind of fashion for developers rather than as a serious business issue. Therefore agile is introduced bottom up instead by clearly setting, managing and monitoring expectations in a top down approach.
- This problem causes a loss of control and as a result also a loss of time resources and money.

9 Assessor Training and Certification

TestSPICE is recognized by INTACS as a conformant PAM. As a result of this TestSPICE training and certification follows the rules of INTACS. For details see www.intacs.info)

The first step in the assessor career is to become provisional assessor. This can be achieved in the following ways:

- Undergo a complete provisional assessor training (TestSPICE Syllabus)
- Undergo an upgrade training (provisional status e.g. AutomotiveSPICE® is a prerequisite)

As a provisional assessor you are eligible as a team member having basic knowledge of the assessment model but are well trained in assessor behavior and team member duties e.g. notes taking. Being a provisional assessor you can start collecting experience evidences. These experience evidences are not only granted for taking part in a TestSPICE assessment but also for any type of learning e.g. taking a presentation at a conference or taking special trainings. Experience evidences are also granted for lectures or paper presentation.

If a candidate has collected enough experience evidences the candidate can take part in a competent assessor training and certification. A competent assessor is eligible for planning and leading an assessment. Further if a candidate contributes to the further development of TestSPICE additional experience evidences will lead to the status Principal Assessor. Many organizations require a principal assessor as team lead for bigger assessment campaigns.

10 Process Improvement

TestSPICE does not have an own process improvement guideline. Due to the policy of the TestSPICE SIG, to focus on testing processes, topics that create unnecessary redundancy are kept out of scope. Knowledge about process improvement is documented in ISO/IEC 33014:2015. Lots of the content of this standard is covered by the ECQA Software Process Improvement (SPI) Manager training and certification [3].

The SPI Manager Training strongly focusses on the needs of people managing SPI. It was assumed that managing process improvement (PI) needs a broader view on the PI related issues such as culture and change. The training consists of a series of learning blocks make sure that the attendee of the SPI manager training is capable to do a complete implementation of the SPI manifesto [5].

11 Conclusions and Further Work

As shown, it is possible to analyze the testing process in way that supports the development approach of a huge bandwidth of organizations. It is necessary that test engineers and test managers become more aware that testing is not only a matter of technology or a matter of testing methods but also a matter of process capability.

TestSPICE delivers a complete but scalable approach of test process assessment. TestSPICE also supports the assessment of the status of agile transition therefore adding value to any type of SPICE assessment. Training of assessors and process improvers is also assured by INTACS and ECQA. Currently there is no indicator that something is missing in the core PAM of TestSPICE. TestSPICE scalable PAM version 3.33 will be released soon. There are some recommendations to transform the agile extension of TestSPICE to an own process reference model "Agility SPICE" but currently there is no special interest group formed to transform and maintain Agility SPICE. Potential further work is to describe the relationship between TestSPICE and other Models (e.g. ISO/IEC/IEEE 29119 or AutomotiveSPICE).

References

1. Schweigert, T., Nehfort, A., Ekssir-Monfared, M.: The feature set of TestSPICE 3.0. In: Barafort, B., O'Connor, R.V., Poth, A., Messnarz, R. (eds.) EuroSPI 2014. CCIS, vol. 425, pp. 309–316. Springer, Heidelberg (2014). doi:10.1007/978-3-662-43896-1_28
2. Schweigert, T., Ekssir-Monfared, M., Ofner, M.: An agile management process group for TestSPICE®. In: McCaffery, F., O'Connor, R.V., Messnarz, R. (eds.) EuroSPI 2013. CCIS, vol. 364, pp. 228–236. Springer, Heidelberg (2013). doi:10.1007/978-3-642-39179-8_20
3. Nevalainen, R., Schweigert, T.: A European scheme for process improvement manager training and certification In: 9th International Conference on SPICE (2009)
4. TestSPICE PAM v3.1: www.testspice.info
5. The SPI Manifesto: EuroSPI 2009, Alcala, Spain (2009). http://2017.eurospi.net/images/Documents/spi_manifesto.pdf. Accessed 7 June 2017

Towards a Survival Analysis of Very Small Organisations

Xabier Larrucea[(✉)] and Izaskun Santamaria

TECNALIA, Bizkaia, Spain
{xabier.larrucea,izaskun.santamaria}@tecnalia.com

Abstract. Very small entities are gaining relevance with the emergence of the ISO/IEC 29110, and with its lightweight approach. However there are still facing some barriers for its adoption, and some VSEs have abandoned their software process improvement initiatives. This paper provides a survival analysis of very small entities when they are implementing an improvement initiative. This study is based on non-parametric (e.g. Kaplan-Meier) and semi-parametric models (e.g. Cox models), and it is useful for practitioners in order to identify the ideal duration of an improvement initiative. These survival functions are applied to our database containing 90 software process improvement initiatives.

Keywords: Survival analysis · ISO/IEC 29110 · Cox model

1 Introduction

During these recent years a special attention has been devoted to very small entities (VSE) in the context of software process improvement [1–3]. Traditional approaches such as Capability Maturity Model Integration (CMMI) and Software Process Improvement and Capability Determination (SPICE) approaches are being considered as not appropriated for very small entities [4]. In this context, the ISO/IEC 29110 [5] has been an enabler for this kind of organisations which are embarked on improvement activities. Several improvements initiatives promoted by governments such as [1] or promoted by specific projects [6] have revealed several benefits for small entities. Industry is applying this ISO/IEC 29110 [7] with specific basic profiles [5, 8, 9] and some extensions for project management aspects [10, 11] including project management body of knowledge (PMBOK) [12].

This kind of improvement initiatives, including CMMI or SPICE, requires a relevant investment on efforts among other aspects. Financial aspects and appropriate skills are some of the main hurdles which VSEs are facing nowadays [13], and they used to be the main reasons for setting aside improvement activities. As result these organisations usually abandon these initiatives because they do not have a clear foresight. Recently it has been published the main hurdles this kind of entities are facing when they are embarked on process improvement initiatives [13]. In this sense, Is there any survivability study related to VSEs adopting ISO/IEC 29110? A survival analysis is perceived not only as a retrospective analysis tool of what they have done, but also as a tool for helping stakeholders to decide on what are the main critical aspects during the deployment of these initiatives. Survival analysis has been used in economics [14] and health sector [15] but it can also be used for analysing survivability based on specific events. In other domains these events are related to death such as in the health domain, or to a failure in the engineering domain.

From an industrial perspective there is an interest to provide an answer to the following questions:

1. How can be defined a survival analysis study in software process improvement initiatives?
2. Is there any preliminary study related to survival analysis of software process improvement initiatives?

This paper is structured as follows. First section provides a background on ISO29110 experiences and on survival analysis. Secondly we define a preliminary survival analysis approach for software process improvement based on our experience. Thirdly we provide our first results applying this survival approach to our experience. Finally, we provide a conclusion and we outline future works.

2 Background

2.1 Very Small Entities

A Very Small Entity (VSE) is defined in [16], but, in short, it is a group of up to 25 people developing software or related to implementation activities. The ISO/IEC 29110 [16] has been assessed in industrial settings [17] and several experiences have been reported [1–3, 18, 19]. Some of these experiences provide a general perception on the ISO/IEC29110 adoption [11, 20]. Researchers have contributed from several perspectives to ISO/IEC29110. For example, authors in [21] define composition trees for modelling processes. Other authors [19] propose a semantic wiki for documenting management aspects in VSEs context.

But this paper is focused on the survivability analysis of this kind of small entities when they are starting a software process improvement initiative. To the best of authors' knowledge, there is no study related to survivability analysis of VSEs applying ISO/IEC29110. Our study is related to previous research works [13, 22] performed during these recent years for analysing very small entities involved in process improvement initiatives. Figure 1 summarizes an experience applying ISO/IEC 29110, and it shows the main assessments results based on the basic profile elements. In fact, these data are part of our study presented in this paper where we analyse 90 organisations where 74 are VSEs. These assessments are based on the ISO/IEC29110 basic profile: project management process activities and software implementation process activities. This figure highlights some weaknesses, and the areas posing the most problems are software implementation, verification and validation, test cases, test procedure, software components, and software architecture and detailed design [13].

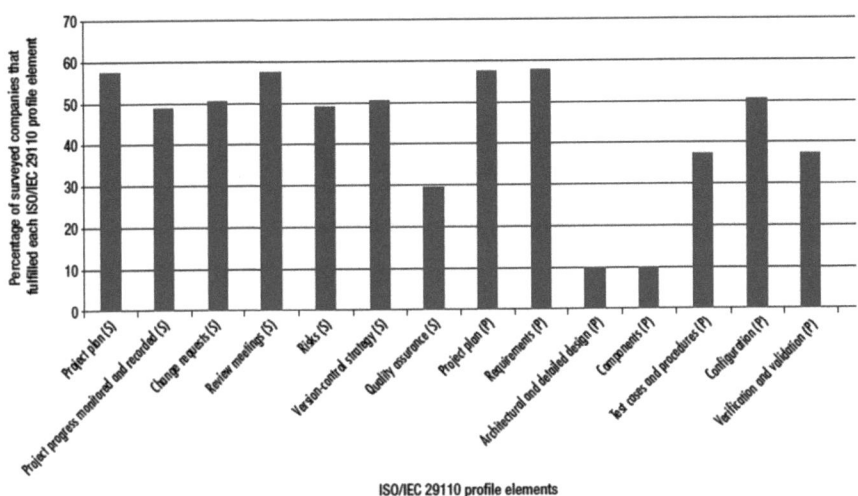

Fig. 1. Results from ISO/IEC 29110 assessments of 74 very small entities (VSEs) [13]

2.2 Survival Analysis

Recently, a special issue on survival analysis [23] noted the following: *Survival data consists of observations that are time to certain event, such as length of life or time to disease in bio-statistical settings or time to break down of a system in reliability settings*. In our context the event is whether an organisation is meeting the ISO/IEC 29110 requirements. In this sense, our approach is similar to [24] where the survival time is the duration time until an event is occurred. Instead of the traditional approach where the event is a negative fact (e.g. death or failure), we consider the event as a positive event: to meet requirements defined by ISO/IEC 29110. In this survival analysis context we used to study parametric (e.g. lognormal, Weibull, etc.), non-parametric (or semi-parametric) approaches (e.g. Kaplan-Meier), semi parametric (e.g. Cox Proportional Hazard Regression model) [25] and other models such as competing risks model. Parametric models have been used in several domains, but always when the event we are looking at follows a normal distribution. Non-parametric models are suitable when we cannot make an assumption about the population and about its distribution, and it used to manage ordinal data.

Semi-parametric approaches are a blend of these approaches, and they are used for exploring the association of covariates with survival time. In our context we use a semi-parametric approach because the distribution is unknown, and the time to the event is not fully observed. This specific characteristic suggests us to use semi-parametric models. In fact software process improvement (SPI) assessments used to be limited only to certain intervals where the assessments are carried out. In addition some initiatives are abandoned or failed during the interval of observation. Therefore we need to censor the data falling outside the limits of our study. The events occured before the starting time interval are called left truncated data. And the events occured after the ending time interval are called right censored data (example on Fig. 2).

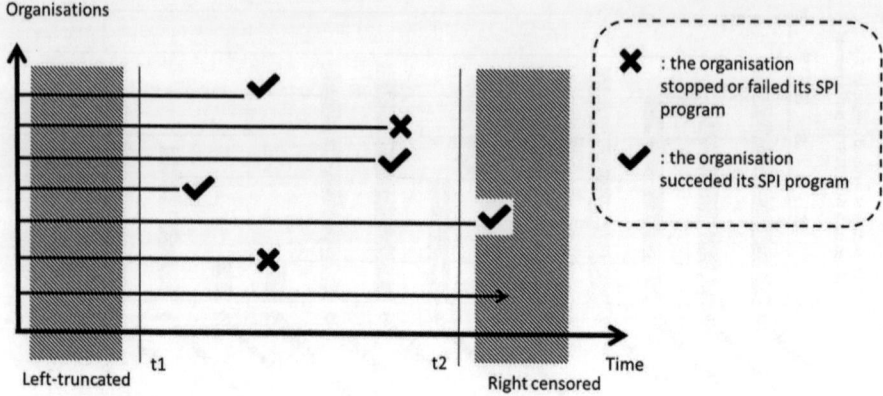

Fig. 2. Failure/success possibilities identified including right censored data.

3 Defining a Survival Analysis

There is a wide set of survival analysis approaches which can be used, and we are going to use non-parametric models and a semi-parametric model called Cox proportional hazards regression model [26] because we are studying SPI assessments, and these SPI assessments between an interval of time. First of all we need to introduce the non-parametric models. Second we need to interpret and adapt the Cox Proportional Hazard Regression model to our study. Third we analyse the scenario, and we need to specify which software process improvement initiatives are taken into account or not.

3.1 Non Parametric Models

There are several survival functions and methods used by the community, but we are going to be focused on two non parametric models: Kaplan-Meier [27] and Nelson-Aalen estimators. Kaplan-Meier is one of the most non-parametric models used, and its formulae is the following

$$\hat{S}(t) = \frac{1}{n}\sum_{i=1}^{n} I\{t_i > t\} \quad (1)$$

Where I is an indicator function evaluating whether $t_i > t$ is True or not.

Another survival function approach is the Nelson-Aalen which is used when we consider estimating the cumulative hazard.

$$\hat{\Lambda}(t_{(i)}) = \sum_{j=1}^{i} \frac{d_j}{n_j} \quad (2)$$

This function accumulates (sum) the hazard from time = 1 to time = i.

Both functions are used in our study for analysing the stuiable duration of software process improvement initiatives in VSEs.

3.2 Semi-parametric Model: Cox Proportional Hazard Regression Model

We are going to use the semi–parametric Cox proportional hazards regression model [26] which is an extension of the Kaplan-Meier estimator because we can use numerical variables, and because we do not know the distribution behind the software process improvement initiatives.

$$h_i(t) = h_0(t) * \exp(\beta * X(t)) \quad (3)$$

where $h_i(t)$ is a hazard rate for a subject "i", $h_0(t)$ depends on time (not on the covariates) with unspecified baseline hazard function that describes the instantaneous risk of experiencing an event at some time, t, when the values of all covariates are zero. $\exp(\beta * X(t))$ depends on the covariates (not the time). X(t) is a vector of possibly time-varying covariates that are collected at each event occurrence that may or may not have predictive power over the time to the event. This vector is composed by several parameters such as the ISO/IEC 29110 basic profile elements. β. a vector of regression coefficients (i.e., one coefficient for each covariate)

In some cases there is an interest to compare two different initiatives. The main difference between 2 subjects under study (two software process improvement initiatives) only depends on their covariate values as described in formulae 4.

$$\frac{h_i(t)}{h_j(t)} = \frac{h_0(t) * \exp(\beta * X_i(t))}{h_0(t) * \exp(\beta * X_j(t))} = \exp\left(\beta * \left(X_i(t) - X_j(t)\right)\right) \quad (4)$$

Our aim is not to provide a depth explanation of the mathematics behind the Cox's model. In this paper we explain the Cox's model formulae for our purpose. We would like to mention that we use the R studio [28] and the Cox's model implementation in the R [29] package survival [30] for calculating the results explained in this paper.

3.3 Considering a Survival Scenario

As stated before software process improvement initiatives requires a high comittment on efforts. And sometimes this aspect is critical for VSEs. So we will have different types of events (Fig. 2):

(1) Starting event – the first observation that a software process improvement initiatives has started.
(2) Succeeding/Failing software process improvement initiative – the event of interest
(3) Censoring event – an event that is falling outside the interval of study. This event can be left-truncated data or right censored data. Left truncated data is not considered on this study because we do not know whether the organisations started or not an improvement initiative before the time t1 (Fig. 2). Right censored data is the data falling behind t2, and it does not matters whether this organisation obtained or failed on their SPI initiatives.

4 A Survival Analysis in Practice

4.1 Data

We have analysed and observed 90 organisations which started a software process improvement initiative. Some of them obtained a specific CMMI level or an ITMark certification. Most of them (74) are VSEs, and we carried out a ISO/IEC 29110 assessments of 74 very small entities (VSEs) [13]. For each observation on each organisation, we have collected the following data from the assessments results (Table 1):

- Duration: this is the time taken by each initiative (organisation) to succeed or to fail.
- Event: we have defined three types of events.
- Censor: type of event which is not taken into account because it is outside of the observed interval.
- Itmark: this element is to indicate whether the organisation was certified ITMark.
- Cmmi: this element is to indicate whether the organisation obtained a specific level of CMMI.
- Vse: this element is to indicate whether the organisation is a very small entity or not.
- PM1: this element indicates the percentage of ISO/IEC 29110 basic profile element fulfilment related to the Project Plan
- PM2: this element indicates the percentage of ISO/IEC 29110 basic profile element fulfilment related to progress of the project monitored against the Project Plan and recorded in the Progress Status Record.
- PM3: this element indicates the percentage of ISO/IEC 29110 basic profile element fulfilment related to Change Requests
- PM4: this element indicates the percentage of ISO/IEC 29110 basic profile element fulfilment related to review meetings
- PM5: this element indicates the percentage of ISO/IEC 29110 basic profile element fulfilment related to risks
- PM6: this element indicates the percentage of ISO/IEC 29110 basic profile element fulfilment related to software Version Control Strategy
- PM7: this element indicates the percentage of ISO/IEC 29110 basic profile element fulfilment related to Software Quality Assurance
- SI1: this element indicates the percentage of ISO/IEC 29110 basic profile element fulfilment related to Project Plan.
- SI2: this element indicates the percentage of ISO/IEC 29110 basic profile element fulfilment related to Software requirements
- SI3: this element indicates the percentage of ISO/IEC 29110 basic profile element fulfilment related to Software architectural and detailed design
- SI4: this element indicates the percentage of ISO/IEC 29110 basic profile element fulfilment related to Software components
- SI5: this element indicates the percentage of ISO/IEC 29110 basic profile element fulfilment related to TestCases and Test Procedures.
- SI6: this element indicates the percentage of ISO/IEC 29110 basic profile element fulfilment related to A Software Configuration
- SI7: this element indicates the percentage of ISO/IEC 29110 basic profile element fulfilment related to Verification and Validation.

Table 1. Chunk of the data used for the analysis

Duration	Event	Censor	Itmark	Cmmi	Vse	PM1	PM2	PM3	PM4	PM5	PM6	PM7	SI1	SI2	SI3	SI4	SI5	SI6	SI7
15	1	0	1	0	1	55.05	57.74	63.27	79.2	45.95	54.68	24.06	55.94	52.29	2.78	16.92	30.28	54.48	39.48
20	1	0	1	1	1	45.13	53.83	46.78	70.1	48.82	43.84	26.34	54.49	43.3	12.7	17.96	39.4	43.34	40.79
19	1	0	1	0	1	59.06	51.16	43.5	52.83	46.89	44.71	29.18	66.35	60	7.23	7.2	40.43	49.68	34.82
18	1	0	1	1	1	58.24	63.98	37.81	55.74	50.3	46.87	26.14	58.5	63.97	9.6	8.8	33.89	49.94	36.92
13	1	0	1	1	1	40.32	45.13	54.52	62.67	49.82	41.81	24.05	55.47	67.69	14.96	17.38	37.24	50.89	40.24
19	1	0	1	0	1	56.83	45.68	64.38	50.96	48.42	46.6	25.28	59.39	65.34	13.83	7.39	43.91	48.01	30.99
17	1	0	1	1	1	49.92	33	61.9	58.77	48.91	50.24	32.7	56.32	62.82	16.74	10.59	32.3	55.74	34.04
21	1	0	1	1	1	57.42	52.72	57.66	45.76	50.33	42.29	23.49	52.56	65.72	9.76	12.3	33.67	42.17	30.02
17	1	0	1	0	1	57.7	54.94	46.42	56.6	49.87	41.18	29.22	53.24	53.98	11.15	13.66	41.47	53.28	38.78
19	1	0	1	0	1	51.59	34.9	62.9	59.7	46.71	53.81	29.57	65.91	48.43	6.98	17.06	40.05	52.83	33.81
17	1	0	1	1	1	47.28	45.77	60	52.81	48.9	51.21	28.47	57.86	61.47	7.76	5.75	42.14	42.39	38.64
22	1	0	1	0	1	64.28	47.88	46.7	58.13	49.34	48.91	29.7	56.81	57.6	9.94	9.05	40.04	51.63	37.2
19	1	0	1	1	1	57.98	53.97	66.88	44.41	48.22	50.22	27.61	60.87	72.54	17.52	13.29	37.17	43.95	32.9
22	1	0	1	1	1	52.45	72.74	56.29	47.86	51.37	56.05	31.59	66.31	33.95	14.14	13.09	35.54	49.21	34.62
15	1	0	1	0	1	64.71	40.21	80.64	47.69	46.42	45.32	32.35	59.84	49.54	9.4	14.24	38.52	52.03	35.84
19	1	0	1	1	1	46.2	45.09	26.19	55.85	47.12	47.46	23.95	53.77	54.33	14.55	10.91	41.16	60.36	32.8
24	1	0	1	1	1	65.44	63.14	33.77	59.75	50.43	56.33	26.23	63.56	60.75	8.23	13.72	47	54.48	40.59
......																			

4.2 Results

First of all we generate the results for the non-parametric models: Kaplan-Meier (KM) and Nelson Allen. This Table 2 shows the results for KM. Those software process improvement initiatives which duration is 11 months have the highest survival ratio. If these initiatives are taken longer than 11 months their survivability decreases. We can analyse why this situation is happening, but in general organisations, and more precisely people which is undertaken these initiatives are loosing interest, or they are facing new hurdles or barriers for their adoption.

One of the first conclusions from this Fig. 3 is that Nelson Allen and Kaplan Meier models are similars. From this figure we can conclude that initiatives with the highest survival probabilities are those taken less than 11 months.

Table 2. Kaplan-Meier data results

Time	n.risk	n.event	Survival	Std.err	Lower 95% CI	Upper 95% CI
11	78	1	0.9872	0.0127	0.96253	1
13	77	6	0.9103	0.0324	0.84899	0.976
14	70	2	0.8842	0.0363	0.81591	0.958
15	68	7	0.7932	0.0461	0.70790	0.889
16	60	8	0.6875	0.0530	0.59111	0.800
17	52	14	0.5024	0.0573	0.40170	0.628
18	38	9	0.3834	0.0558	0.28823	0.510
19	28	8	0.2739	0.0516	0.18932	0.396
20	20	7	0.1780	0.0445	0.10909	0.290

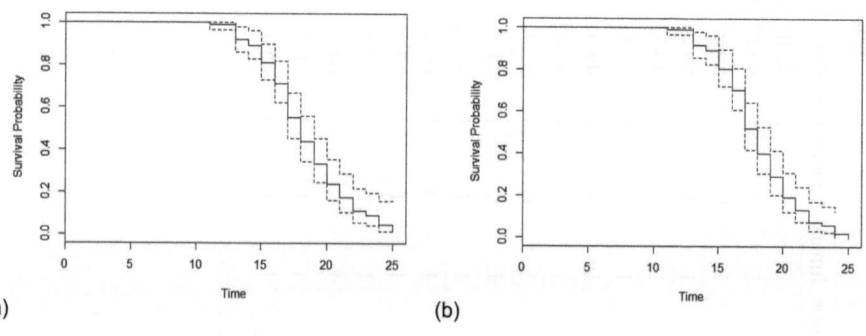

Fig. 3. (a) Plot of the Nelson Allen [31] non parametric analysis; (b) Kaplan Meier estimator

Concerning the semi parametric model (Cox model) we have included as covariates the assessments results for each ISO/IEC29110 basic profile element. We obtained a set of coefficients for each ISO/IEC 29110 basic profile element: pm1 = 1.0138, pm2 = 1.0038, pm3 = 1.0342, pm4 = 1.0057, pm5 = 0.9812, pm6 = 1.0318, pm7 = 1.0273, si1 = 0.9597, si2 = 1.0059, si3 = 0.9850, si4 = 0.8821, si5 = 0.9768, si6 = 1.0268, si7 = 1.0380

Figure 4 clearly highlights that when these initiatives are taking more than 15 months their variability increases. So it seems that VSEs aiming to implement an improvement initiative should devote between 11 and 15 months.

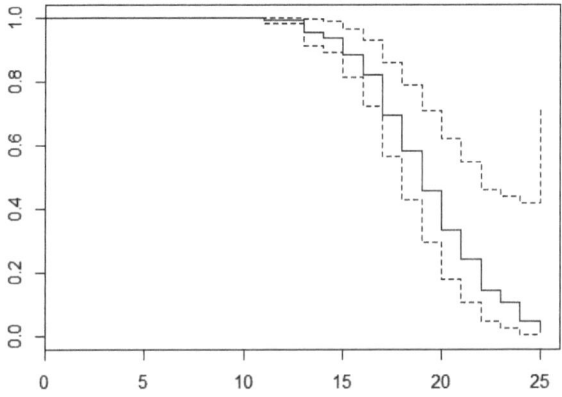

Fig. 4. Plot of the Cox model

Additionally from the Cox model we obtained a concordance = 0.729 (se = 0.046), a Rsquare = 0.286 (max possible = 0.997), a likelihood ratio test = 30.31 on 14 df, p = 0.006917, Wald test = 24.94 on 14 df, p = 0.03514, and score (logrank) test = 29.63 on 14 df, p = 0.008588.

5 Conclusion

VSEs are facing different hurdles [13] when they are starting software process improvements initiatives. We are building a database with knowledge from different quality models such as ITMark (https://tinyurl.com/larnc8q). In this sense we are gathering different aspects related to assessments, duration of each initiative, and so on. And some of these aspects are used for providing this survival analysis.

Based on this knowledge, this paper presents a first survival analysis of VSEs embarked on a software process improvement initiative. In this sense we identified a set of non-parametric and semi parametric models which are used in several domains, and we defined how to proceed with a survival analysis in our context (*1. How can be defined a survival analysis study in software process improvement initiatives?*). This approach is applied to our database containing information about software process improvement initiatives (*2. Is there any preliminary study related to survival analysis of software process improvement initiatives?*)

From this study there are some interesting outcomes:

- When these initiatives are taking more than 15 months their variability increases. This means that there are more chances to fail.
- The ideal duration is 11 months or less because it has the highest survival probability.
- When an initiative is taken too much time their survival probability decreases

One of the future research works is to generalise this approach, and to analyse the representativeness of the study group with regards to the whole population.

As a future work we will be focused on analysing why this situation is happening. As researchers and consultants we can figure out some reasons such as they are loosing interest, or they are facing new hurdles or barriers for their adoption. But these are just subjective facts.

References

1. O'Connor, R.V., Sanders, M.: Lessons from a pilot implementation of ISO/IEC 29110 in a group of very small irish companies. In: Woronowicz, T., Rout, T., O'Connor, R.V., Dorling, A. (eds.) SPICE 2013. CCIS, vol. 349, pp. 243–246. Springer, Heidelberg (2013). doi:10.1007/978-3-642-38833-0_23
2. Polgar, P.B., Kazinci, F.: Report on an assessment experience based on ISO/IEC 29110. J. Softw.-Evol. Process **26**(3), 313–320 (2014)
3. Mesquida, A.-L., Mas, A.: A project management improvement program according to ISO/IEC 29110 and PMBOK (R). J. Softw.-Evol. Process **26**(9), 846–854 (2014)
4. Pino, F.J., García, F., Piattini, M.: Software process improvement in small and medium software enterprises: a systematic review. Softw. Qual. J. **16**(2), 237–261 (2008)
5. ISO/IEC, ISO/IEC 29110-2. Software engineering — Lifecycle profiles for Very Small Entities (VSEs), vol. 2011 (2011)
6. Mendoza, R.C., et al.: Supporting the Software Process Improvement in Very Small Entities through E-learning : the HEPALE ! Project, pp. 221–231 (2009)
7. O'Connor, R.V., Laporte, C.Y.: Deploying lifecycle profiles for very small entities: an early stage industry view. In: O'Connor, R.V., Rout, T., McCaffery, F., Dorling, A. (eds.) SPICE 2011. CCIS, vol. 155, pp. 227–230. Springer, Heidelberg (2011). doi:10.1007/978-3-642-21233-8_27
8. ISO/IEC, ISO/IEC 29110-4-1. Software engineering — Lifecycle profiles for Very Small Entities (VSEs), vol. 2011 (2011)
9. ISO/IEC, ISO/IEC TR 29110-3. Software engineering — Lifecycle profiles for Very Small Entities (VSEs), vol. 2011 (2011)
10. Ribaud, V., Saliou, P., O'Connor, R.V., Laporte, C.Y.: Software engineering support activities for very small entities. In: Riel, A., O'Connor, R.V., Tichkiewitch, S., Messnarz, R. (eds.) EuroSPI 2010. CCIS, vol. 99, pp. 165–176. Springer, Heidelberg (2010). doi:10.1007/978-3-642-15666-3_15
11. O'Connor, R.V.: Early stage adoption of ISO/IEC 29110 software project management practices: a case study. In: Mitasiunas, A., Rout, T., O'Connor, R.V., Dorling, A. (eds.) SPICE 2014. CCIS, vol. 477, pp. 226–237. Springer, Cham (2014). doi:10.1007/978-3-319-13036-1_20

12. Mas, A., Mesquida, A.L., De, U., Balears, I.: Gestión de proyectos de software en pequeñas y micro empresas. Software project management in small and very small entities
13. Larrucea, X., O'Connor, R.V., Colomo-Palacios, R., Laporte, C.Y.: Software process improvement in very small organizations. IEEE Softw. **33**(2), 85–89 (2016)
14. Fenech, J.P., Yap, Y.K., Shafik, S.: Modelling the recovery outcomes for defaulted loans: a survival analysis approach. Econ. Lett. **145**, 79–82 (2016)
15. Althouse, A.D.: Basic principles of survival analysis with composite endpoints: why you must use the 'first' event, not the 'worst' event. Int. J. Cardiol. **201**, 319–320 (2015)
16. ISO/IEC, ISO/IEC TR 29110-1. Software engineering — Lifecycle profiles for Very Small Entities (VSEs), vol. 2011 (2011)
17. O'Connor, R.V.: Evaluating management sentiment towards ISO/IEC 29110 in very small software development companies. In: Mas, A., Mesquida, A., Rout, T., O'Connor, R.V., Dorling, A. (eds.) SPICE 2012. CCIS, vol. 290, pp. 277–281. Springer, Heidelberg (2012). doi:10.1007/978-3-642-30439-2_31
18. O'Connor, R.V., Laporte, C.Y.: Software project management in very small entities with ISO/IEC 29110. In: Winkler, D., O'Connor, R.V., Messnarz, R. (eds.) EuroSPI 2012. CCIS, vol. 301, pp. 330–341. Springer, Heidelberg (2012). doi:10.1007/978-3-642-31199-4_29
19. Ribaud, V., Saliou, P.: Using a semantic wiki for documentation management in very small projects. Metadata Semantic Res. **108**, 119–130 (2010)
20. Basri, S., O'Connor, R.V.: Understanding the perception of very small software companies towards the adoption of process standards. In: Riel, A., O'Connor, R.V., Tichkiewitch, S., Messnarz, R. (eds.) EuroSPI 2010. CCIS, vol. 99, pp. 153–164. Springer, Heidelberg (2010). doi:10.1007/978-3-642-15666-3_14
21. Wen, L., Rout, T.: Using composition trees to validate an entry profile of software engineering lifecycle profiles for very small entities (VSEs). In: Mas, A., Mesquida, A., Rout, T., O'Connor, R.V., Dorling, A. (eds.) SPICE 2012. CCIS, vol. 290, pp. 38–50. Springer, Heidelberg (2012). doi:10.1007/978-3-642-30439-2_4
22. Larrucea, X., Santamaría, I., Colomo-Palacios, R.: Assessing ISO/IEC29110 by means of ITMark: results from an experience factory: Assessing ISO/IEC29110 by means of ITMark. J. Softw. Evol. Process **28**(11), 969–980 (2016)
23. Datta, S., del Carmen Pardo, M., Scheike, T., Yuen, K.C.: Special issue on advances in survival analysis. Comput. Stat. Data Anal. **93**, 255–256 (2016)
24. Sentas, P., Angelis, L., Stamelos, I.: A statistical framework for analyzing the duration of software projects. Empir. Softw. Eng. **13**(2), 147–184 (2008)
25. Kitchenham, B., et al.: Robust statistical methods for empirical software engineering. Empir. Softw. Eng. **22**(2), 579–630 (2017)
26. Cox, D.R.: Regression models and life-tables. J. Roy. Stat. Soc.: Ser. B (Methodol.) **34**(2), 187–220 (1972)
27. Kaplan, E.L., Meier, P.: Nonparametric estimation from incomplete observations. J. Am. Stat. Assoc. **53**(282), 457–481 (1958)
28. R Studio. https://www.rstudio.com/
29. The R project of statistical computing. http://www.r-project.org
30. Therneau, T.M.: Survival Analysis. https://cran.r-project.org/web/packages/survival/survival.pdf
31. Kalbfleisch, J.D., Prentice, R.L.: The Statistical Analysis of Failure Time Data: Kalbfleisch/The Statistical. Wiley, Hoboken (2002)

Team Skills and Diversity Strategies

A Model to Integrate Highly Effective Teams for Software Development

Mirna Muñoz[1(✉)], Luis Hernández[1], Jezreel Mejia[1], Adriana Peña[2], Nora Rangel[3], Carlos Torres[3], and Gabriele Sauberer[4]

[1] Centro de Investigación en Matemáticas,
Av. Universidad no 222, 98068 Zacatecas, Mexico
{mirna.munoz,luis.hernandez,jmejia}@cimat.mx
[2] Centro Universitario de Ciencias Exactas e Ingenierías (CUCEI)
de la Universidad de Guadalajara, Blvd. Marcelino García Barragán #1421,
esq. Calzada Olímpica, C.P. 44430 Guadalajara, Jalisco, Mexico
adriana.pena@cucei.udg.mx
[3] Centro de Estudios e Investigaciones en Comportamiento de la Universidad
de Guadalajara, Calle Francisco de Quevedo # 180, Col. Arcos Vallarta,
C.P. 44130 Guadalajara, Jalisco, Mexico
norarangel@cucba.udg.mx, jtorres@cencar.mx
[4] Forum European Diversity Mangement, Sulzweg 9/3, 1190 Vienna, Austria
gabriele@fedm.eu

Abstract. Software development is not always a successful task, mainly for human related reasons. This situation highlights the importance of focusing on the human factor to help organizations in reducing the risk of failure due to this factor. As a solution, this paper presents a model that aims to help organizations in the integration of highly effective teams for software development, based on three factors: skills, interactive styles and knowledge. The paper includes the development of the model steps and the proposal of an environment we are developing to implement the model using gamification so that it will present an attractive way to integrate the teams.

Keywords: Effective teams · Software development teams · Human factor · Software development organizations

1 Introduction

Nowadays a lot of organizations have discovered that working in groups allows for a higher people commitment and a faster implementation of changes, so that most of the software is developed by teams. However, even when this way generates benefits to the organizations, not all the teams provide the expected results due to the human factor. Besides, failures in software projects have been claimed to be the result of teamwork factors more than technical factors [1].

A team is a group of individuals working together and performing a work that involves a project, so that each member has specific knowledge in specific subjects and with specific skills to carry out that work [2]. This highlights the fact that the success of a team is highly reliant on the human factor. Moreover, it appears that human aspects can become more relevant than technological ones in the team's performance [3, 4]. Therefore, within a set of soft skills expected from a software engineer, one of the essential is the capability to work in a team [1, 5].

The software development in both environments academy and industry, is performed by teams which unfortunately have not worked effectively since the beginning of their activities. This research work arose from the premise that a not proper team performance may be the product of a not proper members' composition [6]. Because, there are factors that intervene in the behavior and performance of a team beyond the technical skills, known as soft-skills [7] and a team must have a variety of personalities to get a correct group [8].

In this context, an adequate integration of teams has high influence in team performance, so that, it is necessary to integrate teams in a way in which it can be possible to complement each member's abilities, knowledge, and interactive styles in order to get a high effective team.

The hypothesis of this research work is that if we can help organizations in the identification of the right people according to the team's needs, the organization will be able to improve the team's performance in a short time. Then, the goal of this paper is to show the development of a model, based on three factors: skills, interactive styles and knowledge, to integrate high effective teams for software development as well as the environment we are proposing to implement the model.

The rest of the paper is organized as follows: Sect. 2 provides an overview of the model elements; Sect. 3 presents related works; Sect. 4 describes the activities performed to develop the method; and Sect. 5 presents a discussion, conclusions, and future work.

2 Model Elements

The required steps to integrate teams are not as obvious as it could be expected, and frequently new teams spend a lot of time working on teamwork techniques [1]. In this context, this research work aims to develop a model for integrating highly effective teams for software development.

The base of the model is not in analyzing the personalities but the skills, interactive styles and knowledge. Besides, it aims to provide an adequate environment using gamification to make it more attractive and efficient than questionnaires. Then, the elements that compose the model are:

- *A set of software development phases:* it refers to a set of phases and the activities provided by the TSP methodology [7, 8] that was taken as reference framework. The phases included in the model are launch, strategy, planning, requirement, design, implementation, test and postmortem [9, 10].
- *A set of team roles:* it refers to the set of software development roles provided by the TSP methodology [11, 12] that was taken as reference. The roles included in the model are team leader, planning manager, quality manager, support manager, design manager, implementation manager and test manager.

- *Knowledge:* it refers to the knowledge that an individual must have to perform specific tasks throughout the phases of the software development cycle.
- *Skills:* it refers to the capacity of an individual to easily make something in a correct way.
- *Interactive Styles:* it refers to a metric of the natural preferences of each person related to the way in which an individual behaves in specific situations.
- *Gamification:* it refers to a set of gamification elements that will help us to provide an attractive way to be integrated in environments that allow analyzing individuals to collect information about their knowledge, skills and interactive styles.
- *Environment:* it refers to a set of sceneries that will provide the main challenges to be solved by a person or a set of people. They simulate the activities and decisions that a team should take throughout the phases of the software development cycle, and enable us to collect the individuals' knowledge, skills and interactive styles.

Detailed definitions about the model elements are provided in [6]. Besides, it is important to mention that the model was developed to focus on the human factor, therefore, it can be used to integrate teams in both environments academy and industry:

- *Academy environment*: the model supports the integration of teams with no more that 6 members to increase an effective participants' interaction in software development activities.
- *Industry environment*: the model supports the integration of software development teams with no more than 8 members, so that they can reinforce their knowledge and communication skills. Due to its nature, the model can be used without restriction of organization type or work culture.

3 Related Works

This section provides a description of works related to the integration or reinforcement of teams.

- Latulipe C., Long N.C. and Seminario C.E. in *"Structuring Flipped Classes with Lightweight Teams and Gamification"* present an approach to make more social and effective classes in the computer science area. This paper focuses on applying gamification to lightweight teams combined with blended classes, which aim to support the learning and increment the commitment of activities by the students. Their results showed a slight difference with respect to other courses that do not use their approach. However, they highlight that students using their approach make more friends during the course, achieving one of their goals [13].
- Rozman T., Stjepanovic T.K. and Rspor A., in *"An analysis of web-based document management and communication tool usage among project managers"* explore how to use the communication tools and management systems as motivational factors to support the decision making in teams. Besides, they have been studied some tools to manage virtual teams that help to solve problems in the team such as: knowledge management, coordination, collaboration, socio-cultural distance and lack of trust within the teamwork. The paper goal is researching the behavior of projects

managers in virtual teams regarding the use of information technologies tools. As result, they identify, among others, security concerns and lack of abilities as barriers to use online communication tools [14].

4 Activities Performed to Develop the Model to Integrate Highly Effective Teams

This section provides an overview of the activities performed to develop the model.

4.1 Identify the Specific Knowledge Expected by Each Role Throughout the Set of Software Development Phases

To identify the specific knowledge, three model elements were used: (1) a set of software development phases (each one with specific task to be performed by each role); (2) a set of team roles (each role should perform a set of specific practices depending on the software development phase); and (3) the knowledge (the specific knowledge to be identified by analyzing the phase and roles).

To identify the specific knowledge, the next steps were performed:

1. Map the activities described in the phases forms and the activities described in the roles forms to be performed in each phase.
2. Identify the activities in which a role is "responsible", "addresses" or "leads". This activity was performed for all phases and roles.
3. Extract the main verbs of each activity, then these verbs were related to the "main activity" which is knowledge required to execute the activities of each phase.

Table 1 shows an example of the mapping performed.

Table 1. Mapping between phases & roles to identify the specific knowledge.

Role	Specific activities to be performed in the planning phase according to the phases forms	Activities to be performed by each role in the planning phase according to the role forms	Summary of the total main activities without those in which the role "participate"	Main verbs (without participation)
TSP team leader	N/A		N/A	
		1-Participate in making the development plan	N/A	
		2-Participate in making the quality plan	N/A	

(continued)

Table 1. (*continued*)

Role	Specific activities to be performed in the planning phase according to the phases forms	Activities to be performed by each role in the planning phase according to the role forms	Summary of the total main activities without those in which the role "participate"	Main verbs (without participation)
TSP development manager	N/A		N/A	
		1-Participate in making the development plan	N/A	
		2-Participate in making the quality plan	N/A	
TSP planning manager	1-Enter the size estimates in form STRAT		1-Enter the size estimates in form STRAT	Enter
	2-Produce the task plan		2, 10-Lead the team effort to produce the task list	Lead
	3-Produce the schedule plan		3-Produce the schedule plan	Produce
	4-Produce the individual engineer plans		4-Produce the individual engineer plans	Produce
	5-The planning manager helps the engineers make personal plans		5, 15-The planning manager helps the engineers make personal plans	Help
	6-Identify workload imbalances		7-Reallocating task to minimize the schedule	Reallocate
	7-Reallocating task to minimize the schedule		8-Producing the consolidated team plan	Produce
	8-Producing the consolidated team plan		9-Lead the work to identify the project's products and sizes	Lead

(*continued*)

Table 1. (*continued*)

Role	Specific activities to be performed in the planning phase according to the phases forms	Activities to be performed by each role in the planning phase according to the role forms	Summary of the total main activities without those in which the role "participate"	Main verbs (without participation)
		9-Lead the work to identify the project's products and sizes	11-Lead the team in estimating the task hours	Lead
		10-Lead the team effort to produce the task list	12-Obtain engineers' estimates for their weekly hours	Obtain
		11-Lead the team in estimating the task hours	13-Produce the preliminary team plan	Produce
		12-Obtain engineers' estimates for their weekly hours	6, 16-Lead the team in balancing team workload	Lead
		13-Produce the preliminary team plan	17-Produce final team and individual engineer plans	Produce
		14-Participate in making the quality plan		
		15-Help each engineer make a personal plan		

4.2 Identify the Skills Expected by Each Role Throughout the Set of Software Development Phases

To identify the skills, three model elements were used: (1) a set of software development phases (each one with specific task to be performed by each role); (2) a set of team roles (each role should perform a set of specific practices depending on the software development phase) and (3) the skills (the capacity of an individual to easily make something in a correct way to be identified by analyzing the roles' activities).

Besides, to identify the skills we took the definitions of the six roles necessary for the change: inventors, entrepreneurs, integrators, experts, managers and sponsors [15]. Table 2 shows the definition of each role necessary for the change.

Table 2. Roles for change.

Inventors (IV)	He/she visualizes the big picture. Therefore, he/she focuses on integrating trends and data into concepts, models and plans.
Entrepreneurs (ET)	He/she seeks for new opportunities. Therefore, he/she focuses on identifying critical issues and new possibilities.
Integrators (IT)	He/she forges alliances. Therefore, he/she focuses on gaining personal acceptance and helping to gain acceptance for the team and their program.
Experts (EP)	He/she explains information in a logical way. Therefore, he/she focuses on taking responsibility for the technical knowledge
Managers (M)	He/she gets the job done at all cost. Therefore, he/she focuses on simplifying, delegating and assign priorities.
Sponsors (S)	He/she communicates where the change fits in the overall organization vision. Therefore, he/she focuses on enduring support and resources from the highest levels of the organization.

To identify the skills, the next steps were performed:

1. Analyze the mapping performed in the last step and identify per phase the primary and secondary roles (see Table 3).
2. Classify the activities in which a role: "lead", "help", "produce". This activity was performed for all roles.
3. Assign values to the roles for change.
4. Map the roles activities classification with the roles for change. Table 4 shows an example of mapping the planning manager role with the roles for change. As Table 4 shows, at the end of the table there are the scores expected for a person able to develop a planning manager role.

Table 3. Analysis of the roles forms to identify primary and secondary roles.

Phase	Main role	Count activities	Secondary role	Count activities
Launch	Team leader	6	Planning manager	3
Strategy	Development manager	10	Support manager	3
			Planning manager	1
			Quality processes manager	1
Planning	Planning manager	8	Quality processes manager	5
Requirements	Development manager	10	Quality processes manager	5
			Team leader	2
			Support manager	1
Design	Development manager	8	Quality processes manager	3
			Team leader	2
			Support manager	1

(*continued*)

Table 3. (*continued*)

Phase	Main role	Count activities	Secondary role	Count activities
Implementation	Development manager	7	Team leader	8
			Planning manager	6
	Quality processes manager	8	Support manager	7
Test	Development manager	5	Team leader	1
Postmortem	Team leader	6	Development manager	1
			Planning manager	1
			Quality processes manager	1
			Support manager	1

Table 4. Mapping between planning manager role and the roles for change.

Phase	Activities	IV	ET	IT	EP	M	S
Launch	Data required from every team member every week	–	1	1	–	1	–
	Reports to be generated and provided the team from these data	–	–	1	–	1	–
Strategy	Participate in developing and reviewing the strategy	1	–	2	–	–	–
	Size and time estimates for all the next-cycle products	–	–	–	1	–	–
Plan	Lead the work to identify the project's products and sizes	–	1	–	–	–	–
	Lead the team effort to produce the task list	–	–	1	–	1	–
	Lead the team in estimating the task hours	1	–	1	1	1	–
	Obtain engineers' estimates for their weekly hours	–	–	1	–	–	–
	Produce the preliminary plan	1	–	1	1	–	–
	Participate in making the quality plan	1	–	2	–	–	–
	Help each engineer make a personal plan	–	2	1	–	–	–

(*continued*)

Table 4. (*continued*)

Phase	Activities	IV	ET	IT	EP	M	S
	Lead the team in balancing team workload	–	–	–	–	2	–
	Produce final team and individual engineer plans	1	1	2	1	–	–
	Lead the team through producing balanced engineer plans	1	2	1	1	–	–
	Lead the team through reallocating task to minimize the schedule	–	–	–	–	1	–
	Lead the team through producing the consolidated team plan	1	2	1	1	–	–
Requirement	Participate in analyzing and clarifying the requirements	1	–	–	–	–	–
	Produce the assigned parts of the SRS	1	–	–	1	–	–
	Participate in producing the system test plan	1	–	2	–	–	–
	Participate in inspecting the SRS and system test plan	1	–	2	–	–	–
Design	Participate in developing the SDS	1	–	–	1	–	–
	Participate in producing the integration test plan	1	–	2	–	–	–
	Participate in inspecting the SDS and integration test plan	1	–	2	1	–	–
Implementation	Participate in planning the implementation work	1	–	–	1	–	–
	Produce and review detailed designs	1	–	2	1	–	–
	Produce and review the unit test plans	1	–	2	1	–	–
	Participate in inspecting detailed designs and unit test plans	1	–	–	1	–	–
	Produce unit test materials	–	–	–	1	–	–
	Implementation and review programs	–	–	1	–	1	–
	Compile programs	1	–	–	–	–	–
	Participate in inspecting programs	1	–	2	1	–	–
	Unit-test programs	1	–	2	1	–	–
Test	Participate in test development task	1	–	2	1	–	–
	Participate in building the product	1	–	2	1	–	–
	Participate in integrating the product	1	–	2	1	–	–

(*continued*)

Table 4. (*continued*)

Phase	Activities	IV	ET	IT	EP	M	S
	Participate in system-testing the product	1	–	2	1	–	–
	Participate in producing the user documentation	1	–	2	1	1	–
Postmortem	Participate in reviewing team performance and producing a report on the least development cycle	1	–	3	1	1	–
	Complete a peer review for the planning manager's role and for all the other team roles using form PEER	1	–	3	1	1	–
Total score		27	8	48	23	11	0

4.3 Identify the Interactive Styles to Be Evaluated

An interactive style is a consistent mode of behavior in particular situations [16]. To identify the interactive styles, a set of meetings, in which the interactive styles were explained and discussed, were performed with some of the researchers of this paper with high experience in the human behavior topic. During the meetings the experts explained the types of interactive styles.

Next, a list of the interactive styles to be included in the model is presented:

- *Achievement or persistence*: it analyzes the option of maintaining or executing under specific conditions; an increasing requirement or a major requirement with a relative or absolute response.
- *Decision making and risk*: it analyzes the possibility to give in time a single response to contingencies that imply uncertain or competitive stimulus.
- *Signal dependence*: it analyzes the adjustments of response to repetitive or eventual signals that are redundant to contingency, and the effects in a stable execution, when the signals are removed without changing the criteria to manage the consequences.
- *Change flexibility*: It analyzes the response to change in the face of a finite number of contingencies not indicated or non-specifically identified in alternation or random.
- *Tolerance to ambiguity*: It analyzes antagonistic and/or different functional properties between the signal and the supplementation, inability to discriminate the relationship contingency-non-contingency, or the irrelevance of the signal with respect to the contingency.
- *Conflict reduction*: It analyzes the response in the face of concurrent signals or in the face of response options that imply opposite or competitive concurrent consequences.
- *Tolerance to frustration*: It analyzes the maintenance of the performance under unnoticed conditions of interference, decrease, loss or delay of consequences.

4.4 Gamification Techniques

The gamification term is applied to the use of game elements in a non-game context, getting a better experience and commitment of the participants [17]. To select the gamification techniques, the authors of this paper performed a systematic review to identify those techniques used to integrate teams [18]. The results of a sample of 31 primary studies showed that there is evidence of the factors that support the collaborative work and the accomplishment of the assigned tasks, but none of them have been applied to create or integrate work teams or to establish work profiles [18].

However, it was possible to identify the most used elements that are: (1) leaderboard, (2) points system, (3) badges, (4) levels and (5) progress bar. Besides, reviewing the Octalysis framework developed by Yu-Kai [19], others gamification elements such as narrative, beginner's luck from the epic meaning and calling area; boosters and milestone unlock from the empowerment of creativity & feedback and water coolers from the social influence and relatedness area will be included.

Besides, it is important to highlight that the combination of 2 or more gamification elements produces good results. Therefore, the implementation of one or more of these elements should be taken into account to define the environments.

4.5 Building Environments

To build the environment a search of activities that reinforce the teamwork was performed. The set of criteria established for the selection of the activities were: 1) the activity goal; 2) the quantity of participants needed; 3) the time required to develop the activity; 4) the required materials; and 5) the process to perform the activity.

It resulted that most of the activities found required from 20 to 30 participants. So the list of candidate activities was reduced to those that only need from 5 to 12 participants. Besides, the selection was performed based on the main goals to achieve the activity and focusing on those that support the identification of the team roles of TSP based on the performed activities. Finally, the candidate activities that were taken as reference are showed in Table 5.

Table 5. Set of candidate activities taken as reference.

Activity	Goal	No of participants	Dev. time
Align by influence	Identify an impartial team leader	12	60 min
Team work	Show the efficiency of working in group	5 to 7	30 min
Pulse	Integrate a member into a team	N/A	N/A
Space situation	To relate among others	N/A	15 min
Rube Goldberg machine	Strengthen the team work	Min 3	N/A
The car rise	Show the efficiency of work in group	5 to 7	20 min
Team building	Increase the cohesion and the identity of working in group	8	30 min

The selected one was the Rube Goldberg machine, it commonly has a particular target that can be considered as very simple to perform, but it needs to follow a set of steps to perform it. Rube Goldberg machines were designed to push the team work and the solution of problems in people of all ages. They start with a simple switch and perform a set of multiple chain reactions to achieve the target. Some examples of challenges to achieve are: cook a burger, turn off an alarm, toast a slice of bread, open an umbrella and water a plant.

The main characteristics taken into account to select the Rube Goldberg machine were: (1) it allows the integration of 7 participants; (2) it provides flexibility to understand how to solve a problem; (3) it promotes communication activities, and (4) it encourages the participation among team members. Therefore, the Rube Goldberg machine will allow us to adapt a set of activities according to the task that should be performed by an individual in a TSP team. Moreover, developing a Rube Goldberg machine will enable us to assign rules or conditions to adapt the situations contemplated in the interactive styles. As Fig. 1 shows, the way it is possible to classify both situations, that is on the one hand, by mapping the activities provided by phases with the interactive styles and on the other hand, by mapping the interactive styles with the participants.

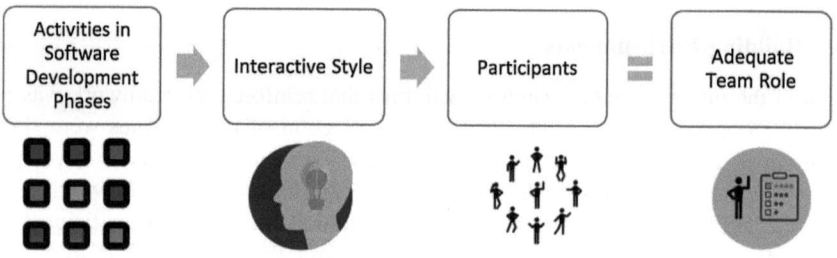

Fig. 1. Proposal of the Rube Goldberg machine adapted to the model.

Based on the above mentioned, our environment proposal consists on giving to the participants the challenge to create a Rube Goldberg machine focused on lighting a candle, within a set of common elements such as books, chairs, balls, dominoes cards, paper rolls, etc. Then, based on the TSP roles showed on Table 3, there is defined a set of expected behaviors we expect from the participants while performing the Rube Goldberg machine. Next, Table 6 shows examples of the expected behaviors we have defined.

Table 6. Examples of expected behaviors.

Role	Phase	Expected behavior
Team leader	Launch	He/She maintains a constant initiative throughout different activities among others participants.
Planning manager	Strategy	He/She has the capacity to identify the time necessary to build the Rube Goldberg machine, as well as, to estimate the resources need in each scenery.
Quality/process manager	Planning	He/She performs changes in the design or final building of the machine to achieve with the rules or conditions in the machine design.

5 Discussion, Conclusions and Future Work

Nowadays Teamwork is becoming a critical factor for the development of high quality software, because most of the software is developed by teams. Then, it is important to integrate teams with a mix of members that can easily work along.

This is the reason why this research work is focused on developing a model to establish effective software development teams focusing on three factors: skills, interactive styles and knowledge. Moreover, the model was developed to focus on the human factor; therefore, it can be used in both environments academy and industry (without restrictions of organization type or work culture).

The proposed model covers building environments based on interactive styles and gamification elements that will allow selecting the right people of a team according to the context and specific needs of an organization. The innovative way offered by our model is that it builds different situations that each role of a team must face trough the software development stages, so that, it avoids getting information influenced by the individual's social desires, memories and/or motivations; allowing diagnosis of human and task factors in similar situations that those presented in the real work environment but performing activities not directly related to software development.

To develop the environments for implementing our model, the Rube Goldberg machine was selected because it will allow both: in one way, it will be possible to introduce participants in a game environment in which they perform a set of activities to show their skills, knowledge and interactive styles in a more attractive and efficient way than with questionnaires; and in the other way, it will be possible to collet data related to skills, knowledge and interactive styles so that the members of a team can be identified and assigned.

As future work, once we finish our proposal of an environment to implement the model, we will perform a case study in at least two different environments to evaluate the viability of our model.

Acknowledgements. CIMAT- Unidad Zacatecas, CUCEI and the Centro de Estudios e Investigaciones en Comportamiento de la Universidad de Guadalajara for the facilities to perform this research.

References

1. Cuevas, G., De Amescua, A., San Feliu, T., Arcilla, M., Cerrada, J.A., Calvo-Manzano, J.A., Garcia, M.: Teamwork and its techniques. In: Software Process Management. Centro de Estudios Ramón Areces, S.A. (ed.) pp. 1–29 (2002). ISBN:84-8004-546-9
2. Project Management Institute PMI: A Guide to the Project Management Body of Knowledge, 5th edn. Project Management Institute Inc, Pennsylvania (2013)
3. Guinan, P.J., Cooprider, J.G., Faraj, S.: Enabling software development team performance during requirements. definition: a behavioral versus technical approach. Inf. Syst. Res. **9**(2), 101–125 (1998)
4. Gorla, N., Lam, Y.W.: Who should work with whom? Building effective software project teams. Commun. ACM **47**(6), 79–82 (2004)

5. Chen, J., Qiu, G., Yuan, L., Zhang, L., Lu, G.: Assessing teamwork performance in software engineering education: a case in a software engineering undergraduate course. In: 2011 18th Asia-Pacific Software Engineering Conference, pp. 17–24 (2011). https://doi.org/10.1109/APSEC.2011.50
6. Muñoz, M., Mejia, J., Peña, A., Rangel, N.: Establishing effective software development teams: an exploratory model. In: Kreiner, C., O'Connor, R.V., Poth, A., Messnarz, R. (eds.) EuroSPI 2016. CCIS, vol. 633, pp. 70–80. Springer, Cham (2016). doi:10.1007/978-3-319-44817-6_6
7. Matturro, G., Raschetti, F., Fontán, C.: Soft skills in software development teams: A survey of the points of view of team leaders and team members. In: Proceeding 8th International Work. Cooperation Human Aspects Software Engineering, CHASE 2015, pp. 101–104, (2015). http://dl.acm.org/citation.cfm?id=2819341
8. Dorling, A., McCaffery, F.: The gamification of SPICE. In: 12th International Conference, SPICE 2012, vol. 290, pp. 295–301 (2012)
9. Humprey, W.: The Team Software Process, Cargenie Mellon, Software Engineering Institute. Technical report CMU/SEI-2000-TR-023, ESC-TR-2000-023 (2000)
10. Humphrey, W., Chick, T., Nichols, W., Pomeroy-Huff, M.: Team Software Process (TSP^{SM}) Body of knowledge (BOK), Cargenie Mellon, Software Engineering Institute. Technical report CMU/SEI-2010-TR-020, ESC-TR-2010-020 (2010)
11. Humphrey, W.: Introduction to the Team Software Process. Addison-Wesley, Massachusetts, USA (2006)
12. Humphrey, W.: TSP^{SM} Coaching developments teams. Addison-Wesley, Massachusetts, USA (2006)
13. Latulipe, C., Long, N.B., Seminario, C.E.: Structuring flipped classes with lightweight teams and gamification. In: Proceeding 46th ACM Technical Symposium Computer Science Education, pp. 392–397 (2015). http://dx.doi.org/10.1145/2676723.2677240
14. Rozman, T., Stjepanovič, T.K., Raspor, A.: An analysis of web-based document management and communication tools usage among project managers. Int. J. Hum. Capital Inf. Technol. Profess. **8**(1), 1–24 (2017). doi:10.4018/IJHCITP.2017010101
15. Kasse Initiatives.: Process Improvement Means Change. In Change management tool kit. v2.0 (2008)
16. Ribes, E.: Psicología General. Trillas, México (1990)
17. Korn, O., Funk, M., Schmidt, A.: Towards a gamification of industrial production. a comparative study in sheltered work environments. Present at 7th ACM SIGCHI Symposium on Engineering Interactive Computing Systems (2015). http://dx.doi.org/10.1145/2774225.2774834
18. Hernández, L., Muñoz, M., Mejia, J., Peña, A.: Gamification in software engineering teamworks: A systematic literature review. In: 2016 International Conference on Software Process Improvement (CIMPS), pps. 1–8. IEEE Conference Publications (2016)
19. Chou, Y.-K.: Actionable Gamification Beyond Points, Badges, and Leaderboards. Octalysis Media (2015)

Towards Developing a Software Process Improvement Strategy Through the Application of Ethical Concepts

Harjinder Rahanu[1(✉)], Elli Georgiadou[1,2], Kerstin Siakas[3], and Margaret Ross[1,4]

[1] Middlesex University, London, UK
harjinder2@mdx.ac.uk
[2] SEEQMA Ltd., Consultancy, London, UK
[3] Alexander Technological Educational Institute, Thessaloniki, Greece
[4] Southampton Solent University, Southampton, UK

Abstract. Aligning Software Process Improvement with the business and strategic goals of an enterprise is a core factor for process improvement. Achieving success in Software Process Improvement (SPI) has shown to be a problematic challenge for countless organisations. SPI, as a discipline, can be described as a set of use cases, each use case describing the logically related activities that must be undertaken. In addition, each use case is a description of the interactions between itself and the participants, i.e. the Actors. The nature of these interactions more often than not may demand, from the participant, the recognition, and fulfilment, of ethical duties. In this paper we customise a theoretical framework developed by the US Content Subcommittee of the Impact CS Steering Committee that specifies traditional moral and ethical concepts, which can be used to identify the moral issues concerning the Software Process Improvement field. An application of these conventional and generic ethical concepts is made to use cases such as: Determining Business Needs; Conducting Process Improvement Assessment; the Tailoring and Creation of Processes; and Deployment. In doing so a number of ethical issues are highlighted. In the application and utilisation of SPI: business process engineers, software engineering teams, process improvement managers, and so on must be aware of these ethical duties, which have been identified by the application of the moral and ethical concepts, as presented in this paper, in order to become more responsible professionals in general. We propose a set of heuristics for ethical engagement with the SPI discipline proposing that an effective SPI strategy must be underpinned with ethical consideration.

Keywords: Ethics · Social responsibility · SPI

1 Software Process Improvement

1.1 Managing the Software Process

Industry, commerce and government have come to the recognition that the application of new software methodologies and technologies have not realised the anticipated gains in productivity and quality. Organisations encounter problems of developing high quality software for their customers. O'Regan (2011) numerates these difficulties as typically concerning: budget and schedule overruns; late delivery of the software; spiralling costs; problems with the quality of the delivered software; customer complaints with regards to the functioning of the software, and staff morale.

Information systems and IT projects have been failing regularly with dire consequences financial and safety consequences. The CHAOS Reports which have been published every year since 1994 provide a snapshot of the state of the software development industry. The 2015 report studied 50,000 projects around the world, ranging from tiny enhancements to massive systems re-engineering implementations. The 2015 results indicate that there is some improvement but still a lot of work to be done around achieving successful outcomes from software development projects. Table 1 summarises the outcomes of IT projects from 2011 to 2015 using the new definition of success factors (on time, on budget with a satisfactory result). A trend from previous reports that continued in the latest survey is how smaller projects have a much higher likelihood of success than larger ones, as shown in this table.

Table 1. Percentages of IT projects outcomes (extract from The CHAOS Report 2015)

Project outcomes	2011	2012	2013	2014	2015
Successful	29	27	31	28	29
Challenged	49	56	50	55	52
Failed	22	17	19	17	19

Challenged and failed projects together account for between 78 to 83% of waste and in the cases of safety critical systems (Logothetis and Wynn 1989; Barbor and Georgiadou 2002; Dalcher 2017) the loss is not only financial but also harmful and general social loss (examples: Challenger Disaster, Cancer treatment in Bristol – radiotherapy, Taurus System). Additionally, lost opportunities through lack of access to new technologies are immeasurable for companies and society at large. Studies by many researchers such as Hirschheim and Newman (1988); Dalcher (2005); Dwivedi et al. (2015) identified the main reasons for systems and projects failures. Although failures are often attributed to technical faults and errors it has long been recognised that by far the most serious reasons for these failures and deficiencies have invariably been identified as political, social, cultural, legal and organisational settings and behaviours.

For example attitudes and practices to knowledge sharing and maturity of process have profound impact on the performance of an organisation. As described by Georgiadou et al. (2011) at the Innovative/*Improving level* the process is characterised by optimisability and continuous improvement. At this highest level of process maturity, knowledge sharing is institutionalised and quantitative. Improvements are achieved from continuous feedback, across teams, within and across projects and across the whole organisation. It is expected that an innovative process requires that all team members understand, embrace and practice the philosophy of knowledge sharing and processes are continuously improving and innovative ideas of all employees find fertile ground. It is expected that an innovative process requires that all team members understand, embrace and practice the philosophy of knowledge sharing and processes are continuously improving and innovative ideas of all employees find fertile ground.

1.2 The Social Dimension of Process Improvement

The field of Social Responsibility (SR) has grown significantly the last decade, both in diffusion scale and in importance. The publication of the ISO26000:2010 voluntary guide, launched in November 2010, and the ECQA Certified Social Responsibility Manager job-role[1] created by the SOCIRES project and supported by the European Union through the Leonardo da Vinci Programme, are proofs of this. The ISO 26000:2010 standard aims to provide guidance regarding SR issues that any organisation (private and public) needs to address.

Despite the fact that there are divergences in the definitions of SR, all definitions seem to have in common the idea of businesses making a decision to commit to social and environmental issues beyond their legal obligations (Siakas et al. 2012). In practice, organisations select their approach to SR by using their own lenses, being influenced by factors at national, regional, industrial and organisational levels. This lack of a unified definition of SR impedes a cohesive empirical SR viewpoint. As a result, SR cannot be measured effectively nor can conclusive findings be pronounced (Siakas et al. 2012). To diminish these inadequacies numerous reporting and ranking instruments (see for example http://asklib.library.hbs.edu/faq/47472) have been developed aiming to compare SR activities of companies. Web sites can also be used to gain insight on how companies are valorising their SR policies (Zompras and Siakas 2014; Garre-Rubio et al. 2012).

The standard is expected to add value to existing initiatives regarding SR by providing harmonised and globally relevant guidance based on international consensus among expert representatives of main stakeholder groups (Koinig et al. 2011). That guidance can then be implemented through appropriate processes and thus becomes subject to process improvement as any other process improvement (Garre-Rubio et al. 2012). The potential benefits an organisation can gain by applying SR practices are amongst others, increased corporate reputation and minimised conflicts with primary stakeholder groups. The performance of an organisation in relation to the society it operates within and the impact it has on the environment has lately become an important indicator of its overall performance and its sustainability (Koinig et al. 2011). Linking SR and SPI processes requires a consideration of SR as a dimension in every process area in the organisation. This requires critical creation of SR-specific Key Performance Indicators (KPIs) for measuring the results of continuous improvement of the strategic performance and actions. Instead of mixing the KPIs with other business indicators, SR indicators should ideally be associated to ISO 26000 core issues and process areas.

To successfully implement SR in organisations, a synergy between organisational strategy and supporting the social rights of individuals at the same time is required, thus

---

[1] http://www.ecqa.org/index.php?id=227.

supporting SR issues as an integral part of an organisation's mission and objectives. The relation between SPI and SR concerns are apparent in some areas, but a detailed examination of the interaction between SPI and SR is required for a full understanding of these. A mapping between SPI and SR based on the SPI Manifesto and the ISO 26000:2010 standard was made by Messnarz et al. (2013). Interactions in both directions were found, which suggests that SR concerns should be considered an integral part of SPI.

Creativity and innovation are the lifeblood of competitive organisations. Organisations that do not innovate and do not adapt to rapidly changing environments (economic, social, political, environmental, and technical) are less likely to be sustainable. However, some ethical constraints may stifle innovation. A dichotomy between innovation and ethics is likely to arise either when the innovation itself or its use is unethical. Farjoun (2010) and Schumacher and Wasieleski (2013) suggested that ethical control mechanisms enable long-term innovation whilst unethical innovation is exclusively short-term which suspends the ethical dimension. Ethical formalisation helps manage turbulent environments whilst unethical innovation is taken as a unique value to be implemented to the classical moral values.

1.3 Process Improvement Models and Methods

There has been an acknowledgement that the central problem is the inability to manage the software process. There have been a number of software process improvement efforts. Amongst a plethora of proprietary Software Process Improvement (SPI)'s from consulting firms, some notable software process improvement standards and models include:

- The Capability Maturity Model Integration [CMMI], the successor to the older CMM, developed at Carnegie Mellon University (CMMI 2010);
- The International Standards Organisation's 9001 Specification [ISO 9001] (ISO 2016);
- The ISO/IEC 15504 IT Process Assessment, which is also termed Software Process Improvement and Capability Determination [SPICE] (ISO 2012);
- Six Sigma, the data driven leadership approach (Pyzdek 2003);
- The 730-2014 IEEE Standard for Software Quality Assurance Processes, which establishes the requirements for initiating, planning, controlling, and executing the Software Quality Assurance processes of a software development or maintenance project (IEEE 2014).

Core to each of these improvement efforts is the idea of a focused and sustained effort towards building a process infrastructure of effective software engineering and management practices. The software process improvement strategy is to transform the prevailing approach to software development into something that is more focused, more repeatable, and more reliable, with regards to the quality of the product manufactured and the timeliness of delivery.

1.4 Defining Software Process Improvement

A Software Process Improvement method is defined as an integrated collection of procedures, tools, and training for the purpose of increasing product quality or development team productivity, or reducing development time (Paulish 1993). An analysis of the various SPI standards and models, as listed above, can be distilled into a generic model that presents the key activities, role and artefacts that constitute the SPI discipline. These are depicted in Fig. 1, which is a schematic representation of SPI using a use case diagram notation.

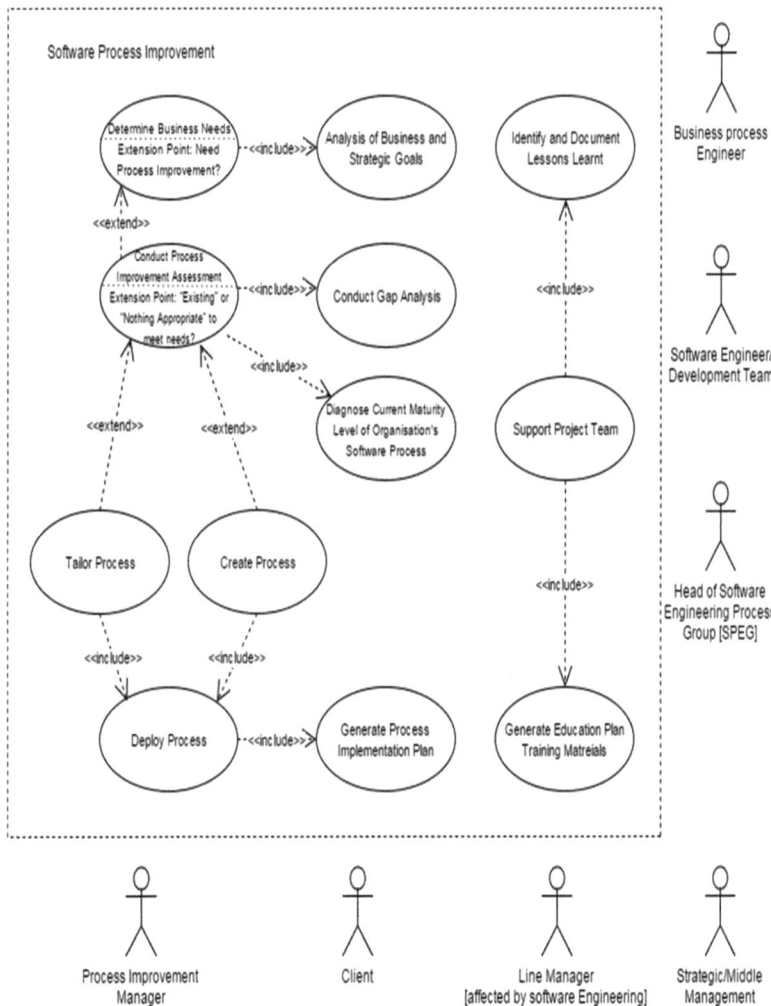

Fig. 1. UML use case representation of the SPI discipline

This graphic depiction will allow for the modelling of the interactions among the elements of the SPI disciple. Using the use case methodology will permit the identification, clarification, and organisation of the SPI discipline requirements. The principal Actors that are concerned in SPI are presented in Fig. 1. In order not to clutter the diagrammatical representation of SPI and attain a degree of clarity it should be noted that the associations between actors respective use cases have not been modelled. Mostly all the identified actors would have, to a larger or lesser degree, associations/interaction with each of the use cases identified in Fig. 1.

This paper argues that ethical issues are potentially raised in each of these interactions between specific actors and respective use cases. For example, in the association between the Head of SPEG (actor) and the Identify and Document Lessons Learnt (use case). This interaction may well demand a Retrospective to be held. An Actor must respect and value alternative viewpoints and, seek, accept and offer honest criticisms of work. Failure to do so implies a neglect of an ethical duty. In Sect. 3 of the paper a number of traditional moral and ethical concepts will be presented, which can be used to identify further moral issues concerning Software Process Improvement field. Via the application of these moral concepts we will list out a number of ethical duties that participants [actors] must fulfil in order that they meet their ethical obligation regarding the SPI.

2 Theoretical Framework and Ethical Concepts

In the development and deployment of computing technology a number of social, legal and ethical issues can be invoked. Legal issues can be resolved via the use of legal doctrine, which is a framework presenting a set of rules, procedural steps, or test, through which rulings can be determined in a given legal case. In the same vein the most important ethical issues surrounding the deployment and development of computer technology can be resolved by making a rational appeal to traditional ethical principles and theories and so extend them to the use of new technologies. The US Content Subcommittee of the Impact CS Steering Committee (Huff et al. 1995) advocated a framework presenting a set of traditional moral and ethical concepts that could be used to flag potential ethical issues in a given case. In terms of personal and professional responsibility, the committee recommended the following six traditional moral and ethical concepts:

1. Quality of life;
2. Use of Power;
3. Risks and reliability;
4. Property Rights;
5. Privacy and
6. Equity and Access.

In order to become a responsible computer professional, the Impact CS Steering Committee argued that one must be able to examine the standards for the rightness and wrongness of actions. For a particular issue, for example, privacy in corporate records or risks in medical technology, it will cover many levels of social analysis (individual: race, class, gender and culture; communities and groups; organisational; institutional; and national and global). In addition, it will cover several different ethical issues and will be spread across differing implementations of the technology.

The theoretical framework developed by the US Content Subcommittee of the ImpactCS Steering Committee has been customised. It specifies the six moral and ethical concepts, listed above, that can help identify ethical issues concerning the Software Process Improvement field. The application of these six conventional and generic ethical concepts is made to SPI activities such as: Determining Business Needs; Conducting Process Improvement Assessment; the Tailoring and Creation of Processes; Deployment; etc., i.e. the use cases identified in Fig. 1, above. We added commentaries, below, which lead to a set of heuristics for ethical application and utilisation of SPI, in Sect. 4.

3 The Ethical Issues Invoked in Software Process Improvement

In order to become more responsible SPI participants in general it is imperative that all are aware of the moral and ethical concepts specified in the framework. It is only through comprehending the issues raised by the framework that business process engineers, software engineering teams, process improvement managers, et al. can achieve a better understanding of the ethical issues concerning the software process and the delivery of quality software.

3.1 Quality of Life

Huff et al. (1995) state although few promoters of new technology would introduce their product with a claim that it reduces the user's quality of life, the concept of quality of life is rarely taken into consideration. Is faster, better, more, always an increase in quality of life for users of technology? Do designers' and decision makers' conceptions of quality of life correspond? More often than not these issues go unconsidered in both development and implementation of technology. These sentiments applied to SPI reveal the following ethical issue.

Software Process Improvement aims at reengineering existing processes. This may well include logistical and motivational (acceptance of change) considerations. Motivational considerations are salient because new processes affect people and data flows and may have unintended consequences. As a result, power and politics, more often than not, come into play, and thus some may offer resistance to the new process. People are inherently resistant to change, and the change facilitated SPI must be taken into consideration. Employee resistance is a crucial factor is a successful SPI, or not (Bayona et al. 2008). An estimate is required to measure how strong a reaction people have toward new reengineered processes. Reengineered processes resulting from SPI influence turnover, transfers, retraining, and changes in employee job status. Therefore, it is understandable that the introduction of reengineered processes requires special effort to educate and train the staff on new ways of conducting business. Thus in order to make the reengineering effective there is an ethical duty to measure whether the SPI project can be put into action or operation in the context of politics, power and motivational considerations (Stair and Reynolds 2011).

3.2 Use of Power

An understanding, of the ethical choices that face both the powerful and the less powerful, is an important step in becoming a responsible professional (Huff et al. 1995). With regards to the efficacy of executing SPI activities it is of vital importance that all participants are empowered with enough knowledge about the Software Process and Software Engineering concepts. This is particularly so in the case where SPI activities were new in an organisation. Thus, there is an ethical duty to encourage and support participants in their professional development. Fulfilling this moral duty would concurrently raise the team capability in Software Engineering concepts in SPI programs, which is viewed as a vital SPI critical success factor (Rocha et al. 2006).

The development and deployment of new technology is not totally constrained by physical or mathematical principles, each design decision for that technology is an exercise of power (Huff et al. 1995). Tayana Conte et al. (2011) observes that the aspect associated with individual decision making of SPI programmes shows that the decisions about SPI judgments should be taken consciously. The reasons need to be analysed, evaluated and discussed with those responsible for the SPI programme. If necessary, these decisions should also be discussed with certain collaborators before they are reported to the entire organisation. Tayana Conte et al. (2011) observes that the aspect associated with individual decision making of SPI programs shows that the decisions about SPI judgments should be taken consciously. The reasons need to be analysed, evaluated and discussed with the responsible(s) for the SPI program. If necessary, these decisions should also be discussed with certain collaborators before they are reported for the entire organisation.

An example of the abuse of power is misrepresentation. It is vitally important that in negotiations between users of the process, the management and stakeholders in the SPI exercise; and the SPI Development Team that the latter do not make claims that are misrepresentations/falsehoods regarding the cost, delivery functionality and quality of the SPI solution. Stair and Reynolds (2011) identify three forms of misrepresentation: fraudulent, negligent and innocent. If the representation has been made fraudulently or recklessly, i.e. not caring whether it is true or not, then at common law the remedy of rescission is available. This sets the contract aside as if it had never been made at all and gives the right to recover any money laid out. In terms of representation made by SPI Development Team and SPI consultants, the approach is to insist that an express term be inserted into the contract to the effect of the representation made. SPI professionals also need to be consciously aware of the fact that most people within the organisation will typically not share their expertise. Thus there is a moral obligation to avoid technical terminology and articulate clearly in terms they may understand.

A further example of the abuse of power and misrepresentation is to undertake work or provide a service that is within your professional competence; or to claim any level of competence that you do not possess. These issues concerning potential abuse of power and misrepresentation are addressed as issue of Professional Competence and Integrity in the British Computer Society [BCS] Code of Conduct and Code of Practice (BCS, Year; BCS 2011).

3.3 Risks and Reliability

Huff, et al. (1995) state that there are inevitable risks associated with technology. Choices among trade-offs in design and implementation for systems will always involve ethical dimensions, and computing professionals should be prepared for them. In order to embark on Software Process Improvement it is important that actors, for example Process Improvement Managers; Heads of Software Engineering Process Groups, and others have an ethical obligation to maintain awareness of technological developments, procedures, and standards that are relevant in the field of SPI. There are notable software process improvement standards and models, as identified above. Therefore a decision as to selection of the most appropriate and applicable model(s) is critical in order that the SPI outcome is successful. Adopting the right Software Process Improvement implementation methodology is a critical success factor (Niazi et al. 2006).

In regards to SPI it's crucial to know that the primary drivers for process improvement are business-oriented. Processing Needs Assessment will help establish whether the scope and applicability of commencing with SPI is present or not. If not then the SPI exercise must be terminated as a result. Implementing a process for its own sake is a bad idea; a process must not be implemented just because someone else does (Ambler 2013) (Niazi et al. 2006). Thus there is an ethical duty to resist any pressure to embark on SPI if the case for doing so is weak/non-existent.

Christiansen and Johansen (2008) identify the lack of involvement amongst users of the process, the management and stakeholders in the SPI exercise as a critical success factor. Dialogue and communication between these groups and the SPI development and deployment team can help, to a degree, redress this issue. There are numerous ways to aid communication, a combination of paper and electronic means, ranging from posters, flyers and brochures; through to Twitter and/or Yammer. Linders (2011) advocates face to face communication, as a richer form of communication, which helps forge stronger bonds of trust. These can, in improvement projects, take the form of Kick-off meetings; all Employee meeting; Training and coaching; open spaces; Team meetings; One on one meeting; and Walking around (walk the talk). Therefore, there is an ethical duty to keep all affected by the SPI in the communication loop. The Right to Know and the Freedom of Expression are important ethical normative principles.

A number of studies have been completed in order that SPI critical success factors are identified (Rothman 2000; Niazi et al. 2006; Bayona et al. 2008). Huff et al. (1995) argue that since error free design is both impossible to achieve and unable to be measured, computer professionals must become familiar with the inevitable risks associated with technology. Thus it follows that, participants in the SPI development and deployment must: research; identify; add to; document; and share, what SPI critical success factors are. By being conscious of these risks the ability to achieve error free SPI implementation may still be impossible the likelihood of successful deployment may be increased.

3.4 Property Rights

Technological advances make it more and more painless for employees to appropriate and misuse their employer's confidential information. In the software process improvement there are many forms of confidential information present. All parties concerned: the client, developers and managers of the SPI need to be aware of and respect confidential information.

In the reengineering of business processes the SPI development have a duty of confidence when they come to the knowledge of confidential information under circumstances in which it would be unfair if it were disclosed to others (Fishman 2007). In the UK, The Human Rights Act has developed the law on breach of confidence so that it now applies to private bodies as well as public ones. In the SPI, breach of confidence is a matter that should also be considered by both the SPI Development Team and the client. The client should be fully aware of the confidential nature in any of the elements of the software. Client maybe provided with source code and the specifications, including systems models, for example, schematic models for the software. The agreement should spell out the duty of confidentiality in respect of these materials, reinforcing the common law duty. If the SPI Development Team has access to the client's information, for example, sales and marketing techniques, and other commercially sensitive information, a reciprocal duty can be placed on the them (Bainbridge 2004).

3.5 Privacy

Huff et al. (1995) state that computing professionals often design systems, which store and transmit data about individuals. Privacy expectations and demands need to be taken into account in the design of systems.

The Software Improvement Group (SIG) (2017) reports three quarters of cyber-attacks and data leaks are caused by errors during software development. Discovery and thus prevention of these mistakes lead to important effects, for example: protection against incidents and fines, visible control over security and privacy, reduced development costs, reduced test costs, and peace of mind. Therefore, in order to control software security and privacy, software must be looked at. This requires systematic reviews and the use of international standards, e.g. ISO25010/ISO29100 for measuring source code qualities and assessment of the development process.

3.6 Equity and Access

By allowing any form of bias, it can be harmful to an organisation by restricting the range of views and experiences of available. Bias, conscious or unconscious, could relate to many issues such as gender, disability whether physical or otherwise, ethnic background, religion, sexual discrimination, or age whether too young or too old. For example, there has been a considerable research comparing the approach to management, negotiation and innovation of males and females at the senior level. By utilising these possible differences and gender traits, an organisation could gain (Bauer and Tremblay 2011). Thus it is vitally important that the actors identified in Fig. 1, who are participants/stakeholders in the SPI, are of a diverse representation.

Figure 1 presents, amongst many use cases, the Support Project Team use case. One salient activity defined in this use case is conducting Retrospectives. This is a fundamental vehicle to discover, share, and pass along the learning from the SPI experience (Ambler 2013). Pivotal to holding ethical Retrospectives are certain ground rules, including:

- Participants must respect and value alternative viewpoints and, seek, accept and offer honest criticisms of work
- Participants must be able to exercise freedom of expression. This will include the **freedom** to hold opinions and to receive and impart information and ideas without judgment and/or reprisal from others.
- Exercise the right to anonymity
- Invited participants to engage in Retrospectives reflect a diverse representation.

Failure to hold to these ground rules implies a neglect of an ethical duty.

4 Heuristics for Ethical Use of Software Process Improvement

A set of heuristics for ethical engagement with the SPI discipline proposing that an effective SPI strategy that is underpinned with ethical consideration:

1. Conduct a Behavioural Feasibility Study in order to measure whether the SPI can be put into action or operation with regards to employee resistance, and politics, power and motivational considerations. Failure to conduct this is an abdication of an ethical duty demanded by the principle of **Quality of Life**.
2. Provide Educational Plans and Training Materials in order to *empower* SPI participants with enough knowledge about the Software Process and Software Engineering concepts. Failure to provide this is an abandonment of an ethical duty demanded by the principle of **Use of Power**.
3. Ensure that SPI professionals have a clear understanding of the professional duties concerning professional integrity and competence as spelt out in the BCS Code of Conduct and BCS Code of Practice. This is a duty spelt out by the principle of **Use of Power**.
4. Ensure that managers of the SPI project maintain knowledge of SPI at the highest level by in order to minimise the probability of failed SPI exercise. This can be achieved by, for example:

a. Access relevant literature
b. Attending conferences and seminars
c. Contact with other leading practitioners
d. Participation in appropriate learned, professional and trade bodies.

This ethical obligation to maintain awareness of technological developments, procedures, and standards that are relevant in the field of SPI is demanded from the principle of Risks and Reliability.

5. Conduct technical reviews or walkthroughs with the technical staff in order to verify that the requirements meet the desired business results. This obligation is required from the principle of **Risks and Reliability**.
6. Use face to face, paper and online communication to disseminate and share recognised and identified SPI critical success factors. This ethical responsibility is mandatory in accordance with the principle of **Risks and Reliability**.
7. Conduct legal audits related to the planning and control of the SPI. Failure to conduct this is an abandonment of an ethical duty demanded by the principles of **Property Rights** and **Privacy**.
8. Draft Contracts and Terms of Agreement: A particular focus on the Confidentiality of Information must be addressed in the formulation and drafting of Employee Contracts and in any Terms of Agreements for services rendered in the SPI between client and SPI Development Team. This duty to the protection and respect of assets is claimed by the principle of **Property Rights**.
9. Deploy international standards, e.g. ISO25010/ISO29100 for measuring source code qualities and assessment of the development process. This duty to consider software security and privacy is necessitated by the principle of **Privacy Rights**.
10. Conduct Ethical retrospectives: Managers of the SPI project to conduct ethical retrospectives. This ethical obligation to conduct retrospectives in accordance with fair representation and exercising freedom to expression and anonymity is demanded from the principle of **Equity and Access**.

5 Conclusion

There has been recognition that Process Improvement is an imperative for the survival of organisations especially in today's competitive world. There is often emphasis on the legality of actions but not enough attention is given to ethical considerations. In fact some believe that ethical constraints are likely to stifle creativity and innovation.

The rationale of adopting and applying the theoretical framework developed by the US Content Subcommittee of the Impact CS Steering Committee was to identify the ethical issues that can be invoked in Software Process Improvement. In doing so the authors conclude that the importance of ethical considerations in processes reengineering can be brought to the attention of the SPI community and thus help raise the visibility of ethical SPI development and deployment.

The paper contributes to the current discourse relating to the continued sharing of SPI experience in the public and private sectors. In particular, a set of heuristics for the development and deployment of SPI has been proposed which will raise awareness of the issues and help guide SPI developers and users of the process, the management and stakeholders in the SPI.

Future work will seek to apply legal principles to the development and deployment of SPI. In addition, professional principles, as explicitly stated in professional codes of conduct and practice can also be applied to the actions of participants in the SPI.

A comparison between the ethical, professional and legal considerations may permit bad laws, and poorly drafted codes of conduct and practice, to be flagged, i.e. those legal and professional regulations that provide little or no moral guidance.

References

Bainbridge, D.: Introduction to Computer Law, 5th edn. Longman (2004)

Barbor, N., Georgiadou, E.: Investigating the applicability of the Taguchi Method to Software Development. In: Proceedings of Quality Week, San Francisco, USA, July 2002

Bauer, G., Tremblay, M.: Women in Executive Power: A Global Overview. Routledge, New York (2011)

Sussy, B.L., Antonio, C.M.J., Gonzalo, C., Tomás, S.F., Angel, S.: Process deployment in a multi-site CMMI level 3 organization: a case study. In: Lee, R., Kim, H.K. (eds.) Computer and Information Science. SCI, vol. 131, pp. 147–156. Springer, Heidelberg (2008). doi:10.1007/978-3-540-79187-4_13

BCS. The British Computer Society BCS Code of Conduct (2015). http://www.bcs.org/category/6030. Accessed 27 April 2017

BCS. The British Computer Society Code of Good Practice (2011). http://www.bcs.org/upload/pdf/cop.pdf. Accessed 27 April 2017

Burr, A., Georgiadou, E.: Software development maturity - a comparison with other industries. In: 5th World Congress on Total Quality, India, New Delhi, February 1995

Christiansen, M., Johansen, J.: ImprovAbilityTK: guidelines for low-maturity organizations. Softw. Process: Improv. Pract. **13**, 319–325 (2008)

CMMI. CMMI for Development, Version 1.3, Technical report. Software Engineering Institute, Carnegie Mellon University, Pittsburgh, PA (2010). http://resources.sei.cmu.edu/library/asset-view.cfm?assetID=9661. Accessed 24 April 2017

Dalcher, D.: Software processes: lessons and reflections. Softw. Process Improv. Pract. **10**(2), 99–100 (2005)

Dalcher, D.: Is it time to rethink project success? (keynote). In: 25th Software Quality International Conference, Southampton, 10 April 2017. (Proceedings in Print)

Dwivedi, Y.K., et al.: Research on information systems failures and successes: status update and future directions. Inf. Syst. Frontiers **17**(1), 143–157 (2015)

Farjoun, M.: Beyond dualism: Stability and change as a duality. Acad. Manag. Rev. **35**(2), 202–225 (2010)

Fishman, S.: Legal Guide to Web & Software Development, 5th edn. Nolo Publishing (2007)

Garre-Rubio, M., García-Barriocanal, E., Siakas, K., Sicilia, M.-A., Koinig, S., Messnarz, R., Clarke, A.: Analysing the corporate responsibility Web pages of consumer electronics companies: implications for process improvement. IET Softw. **6**(5), 451–460 (2012). http://dx.doi.org/10.1049/iet-sen.2011.0207. Accessed 27 April 2017]

Georgiadou, E., Siakas, K.V., Balstrup, B.: The I5P visualisation framework for performance estimation through the alignment of process maturity and knowledge sharing. Int. J. Hum. Capital Inf. Technol. Prof. **2**(2), 37–47 (2011). ISSN 1947-3478

Hirschheim, R., Newman, M.: Information systems and user resistance: theory and practice. Comput. J. **31**(5), 398–408 (1988)

Huff, C., Anderson, R.E., Little, J.C., et al.: Integrating the ethical and social context of computing into the CS curriculum: An Interim Report from the Content Subcommittee of the Impact CS Steering Committee. In: Proceedings of ETHICOMP 1995: An International Conference on the Ethical Issues of Using IT, Leicester UK, 28–30 March, vol. 2, pp. 1–19 (1995)

IEEE. 730-2014 - IEEE Standard for Software Quality Assurance Processes. IEEE (2014). http://ieeexplore.ieee.org/document/6835311/. Accessed 24 April 2017

ISO. ISO/IEC 15504-5:2012, International Organization for Standardization. https://www.iso.org/standard/60555.html. Accessed 25 April 2017

ISO. Selection and use of the ISO 9000 Family of Standards, International Organization for Standardization (2016). ISBN 978-92-67-10656-4

Johnson, J., Gesmer, L., Poort, J., Mulder, H.: CHAOS Report 2015, The Standish Group International, Inc. (2016)

Koinig, S., Sicilia, M.-A., Messnarz, R., Barriocanal, E.G., Garre-Rubio, M., Siakas, K., Clarke, A.: Understanding the relation of SPI and SR: a proposed mapping of the SPI Manifesto to ISO 26000:2010. In: 18th European Software Process Improvement (EuroSPI 2011) Conference, 27–29 June, pp. 7.27–7.37. Roskilde University, Denmark (2011)

Linders, B.: Communication: Making Quality & Process Improvement Visible, Agile Risk Management Open Space (2011). https://www.benlinders.com/2011/communication-making-quality-process-improvement-visible/. Accessed 26 April 2017

Messnarz, R., Sicilia, M.-A., Biro, M., García-Barriocanal, E., Garre-Rubio, M., Siakas, K., Clarke, A.: Social responsibility aspects supporting the success of SPI. Softw. Evol. Process J. (2013). doi:10.1002/smr.1586. Published online in Wiley Online Library (wileyonlinelibrary.com)

Niazi, M., Wilson, D., Zowghi, D.: Critical success factors for software process improvement implementation: an empirical study. Softw. Process: Improv. Pract. **11**, 193–211 (2006). doi:10.1002/spip.261

O'Regan, G.: Introduction to Software Process Improvement. Springer-Verlag Ltd., London (2011)

Paulish, D.: Case Studies of Software Process Improvement Methods. Technical report. Software Engineering Institute, Carnegie Mellon University, Pittsburgh (1993). https://resources.sei.cmu.edu/asset_files/TechnicalReport/1993_005_001_16217.pdf. Accessed 25 April 2017

Pyzdek, T.: The Six Sigma Handbook: A Complete Guide for Green Belts, Black Belts, and Managers at All Levels. McGraw-Hill, New York (2003)

Rocha, A.R., Montoni, M., Santos, G., Oliveira, K., Natali, C., Mian, P.: Success Factors and Difficulties in Software Process Deployment Experiences based on CMMI and MR-MPS.BR. In: 8th Workshop on Learning Software Organizations (LSO), Rio de Janeiro, pp. 77–87 (2006)

Rothman, J.: Four R's of Software Process Improvement: Requirements, Reviews, Retrospectives, and Results (2000). http://www.jrothman.com/articles/2000/01/four-rs-of-software-process-improvement-requirements-reviews-retrospectives-and-results/. Accessed 27 April 2017

Schumacher, E.G., Wasieleski, D.M.: Institutionalizing ethical innovation in organizations: an integrated causal model of moral innovation decision processes. J. Bus. Ethics **113**, 15–37 (2013)

Siakas, K., Sicilia, M.-A., Biro, M., Triantafillou, K.: Social responsibility management: a preparatory study in higher education with suggestions for process reference models. In: 19th European Software Process Improvement (EuroSPI 2012) Conference, Industrial track, Vienna, Austria, 25–27 June, pp. 7.17–7.31 (2012)

SIG. Software Security and Privacy (2017). https://www.sig.eu/what-we-do/software-security-privacy/. Accessed 26 April 2017

Stair, R.M., Reynolds, G.W.: Fundamentals of Information Systems, 6th edn. Cengage Learning, Inc. (2011)

Tayana Conte, D.V., de Souza, C.R.B., Santos, G., Prikladnicki, R.: The Influence of Human Aspects on Software Process Improvement: Qualitative Research Findings and Comparison to Previous Studies. In: Proceedings of the EASE 2012. IET (2011). http://ieeexplore.ieee.org/stamp/stamp.jsp?tp=&arnumber=6272504. Accessed 25 April 2017. ISBN 978-1-84919-541-6

Zompras, A., Siakas, K.: Social responsibility and ISO 26000: how IT companies can contribute. In: Georgiadou, E., Linecar, P., Ross, M., Staples, G. (eds.) Software Quality in Flexible Development Environments, The BCS Quality Specialist Group's Annual International 22nd Software Quality Management (SQM) Conference, 14 April, pp. 131–148. British Computer Society, Southampton (2014)

Diversity and PERMA-nent Positive Leadership to Benefit from Industry 4.0 and Kondratieff 6.0

Gabriele Sauberer[1(✉)], Andreas Riel[2], and Richard Messnarz[3]

[1] Forum European Diversity Management, 1190 Vienna, Austria
gabriele@fedm.eu
[2] Institute of Engineering, Grenoble Alps University, Grenoble, France
[3] ISCN GmbH, Graz, Austria
http://www.fedm.eu, http://www.grenoble-inp.fr,
http://www.iscn.com/

Abstract. This paper introduces the PERMA model of Martin Seligman and the Positive Leadership model of Kim Cameron. The authors discuss the need to apply these models in software development teams, together with managing the diversity of people, languages and systems, as prerequisites of benefiting from Industry 4.0 and the 6th Kondratieff wave.

The Global Trends 2030 and current mega-trends, such as Industry 4.0 require strategies on how to cope with and benefit from diversity of systems, as well as from the linguistic and human diversity in teams and societies.

Keywords: Diversity · PERMA model · 6th Kondratieff wave · Industry 4.0 · Positive Leadership

1 The PERMA Model of Martin Seligman

1.1 5 Measurable Elements of Well-Being

According to Martin Seligman and his well-being theory [1], well-being is a construct; and well-being, not happiness, is the topic of positive psychology.

Well-being has five measurable elements (PERMA) that count toward it:

- <u>P</u>ositive emotion (of which happiness and life satisfaction are all aspects)
- <u>E</u>ngagement
- <u>R</u>elationships
- <u>M</u>eaning and purpose
- <u>A</u>ccomplishment

No one element defines well-being, but each contributes to it. Some aspects of these five elements are measured subjectively by self-report, but other aspects are measured objectively [2]. With PERMA, people and organizations can flourish and excel.

1.2 The Positive Leadership Model

Kim Cameron's Leadership Model [3] is based on four principles and prescriptions:

(1) Capitalize on the heliotropic effect [4]. We have learned to ignore it. Unlearn to ignore it, and positively embarrass someone.
(2) Foster positive energy. Energy is 4 times more powerful than information & influence.
(3) Focus on abundance gaps. People get consumed by problems and obstacles.
(4) Celebrate what goes right. Problems usually dominate our attention.

In organizations, these Positive Leadership principles are introduced and implemented with a set of basic Positive Psychology Tools, see Sect. 1.3. To focus on the "abundance gaps" between the "normal state" and the "positive deviance" is a powerful and proven business and health strategy to excel and achieve "the impossible" (Table 1).

Table 1. Kim Cameron's Deviance Continuum

A Deviance Continuum

	Negative Deviance	Normal	Positive Deviance
Individual:			
Physiological	Illness	Health	Vitality
Psychological	Illness	Health	Flow
Organizational:			
Economics	Unprofitable	Profitable	Generous
Effectiveness	Ineffective	Effective	Excellent
Efficiency	Inefficient	Efficient	Extraordinary
Quality	Error-prone	Reliable	Perfect
Ethics	Unethical	Ethical	Benevolent
Relationships	Harmful	Helpful	Honoring
Adaptation	Threat-rigidity	Coping	Flourishing
	Deficit gaps		Abundance gaps

SOURCE: Cameron, 2003

MICHIGAN ROSS SCHOOL OF BUSINESS © Kim Cameron, University of Michigan

1.3 The Need to Apply the PERMA and Positive Leadership Models in Software Development Teams

Why is well-being important for software development teams? How we can leverage positive emotions, engagement, relationships, meaning and accomplishment to improve team work and the results of software development?

Applied research shows that the methods, tools and techniques of positive psychology make a considerable difference in team performance and the success of individuals, teams and organizations [5].

To focus on the negative deviance results in "business as usual" and frustration. Dealing with the "abundance gaps" leverages the energies to excel and reach most ambitious goals, as the impressing case studies of Kim Cameron show [6].

Professor Kim Cameron, co-founder of the Center for Positive Organizations at the University of Michigan, published his research on organizational virtuousness, downsizing, effectiveness, quality culture, and the development of leadership excellence in more than 130 academic articles and 15 scholarly books.

He was recently recognized as being among the top 10 scholars in the organizational sciences whose work has been most frequently downloaded from Google. His current research focuses on the virtuousness of and in organizations, and their relationships to organizational success [7].

Kim Cameron is applying all his research in practice and in various organizations and organizational settings, mainly in times when the organization faces sincere crisis. His work is based on empirical foundation, theoretical grounding and successful application. In his talks on the occasion of the "Seligman's Europe Tour 2016", he is recommending three basic Positive Psychology Tools and gives advice for its application [8]:

(1) Using Gratitude in Organizations:
   - Start team meetings with the question "What has inspired you this week?"
   - Celebrate successes with your team.
   - Design a wall for positive milestones and provide an ideas box so that leaders and staff alike can use it to pin anything they are grateful for or proud of.
   - Hand a booklet to each of your staff and invite them to keep a gratitude journal.
   - At the end of the year, send a gratitude letter to your employees' families and praise the employee. Tell the family how much you appreciate the effort their family member puts in at work and thank them.
(2) Applying Contribution Principles in the Workplace:
   - An airline handed out reward certificates to their frequent flyer guests in order to recognize their loyalty. The certificates could be handed out to airline staff who stood out in their behavior or performance, either on the ground or during the flight. This way, guests were able to recognize their exceptional behavior.
   - For guests, this had a positive effect due to the benefit experienced through contribution discussed above. For the airline, the impact was twofold. Staff received more praise and recognition, and guests would search for employee excellence, which had a similar effect to writing a gratitude diary.
(3) Applying Strengths-Based Behavior in the Workplace:

- Instead of asking your unhappy customers what went wrong, ask your satisfied customers what went right and do more of that.
- Ask your staff to select 20 people who know them well (co-workers, friends) and get them to write a short paragraph answering questions such as "when have you seen me at my best?" Ask them to use the answers to create their own "best self-portrait" and think about how they can use their strengths even more.
- When giving your staff feedback on their strengths, make use of the following two ideas: "Here is what I noticed in your leadership skills…" and "Here is what lead me to this conclusion…" The second is particularly important.

These three Positive Psychology Tools are an example of how to apply the PERMA model [9]:

- P – Positive Emotions, such as gratitude, joy, playfulness, pride, interest, inspiration, strengthen organizations and motivate teams to excel. When teams enjoy the tasks in their work and lives they are more likely to persevere and battle challenges through creative and alternative solutions.
- E – Engagement and Contribution Principles make a difference: Activities that need our full engagement are important. Tasks that entirely absorb us are creating a 'flow' of engagement that stretches our intelligence, skills, and emotional capabilities in teams.
- R – Relationships and social connections are one of the most important aspects of life. Humans are social animals that thrive on connection, love, and a strong emotional and physical interaction with other humans. Building positive relationships with our peers is important to spread joy and positive emotions at the workplace. Having strong relationships gives us support in difficult times.
- M – Meaning gives people a reason for their life and their work. To understand the greater impact of our work and why we chose to the pursuit that work will help us enjoy the tasks more and become more satisfied, efficient and effective.
- A – Accomplishments are important to push teams to thrive and flourish. Having goals and ambition in life and work can help us to achieve things that can give us this sense of accomplishment.

2 Bad is Bigger than Good: Why We Need to Learn and Train PERMA-nent Positive Leadership

Humans have a bias toward the negative. A systematic bias exists in people that shows that the occurrence of negative factors are more powerful than positive factors—"Bad is stronger than good." [10].

People are more affected by one traumatic or negative event than by one positive or happy event. Particularly important for teams and organizations: People are more affected emotionally and do more mental work from a single negative piece of feedback than from a single positive piece of feedback. Evolutionary theory suggests why: If people ignore negative information, it could cost them their lives. If they ignore positive feedback, it only causes regret.

Therefore, it is not surprising that negative phenomena get more attention than positive phenomena. It takes conscious effort to focus on abundance [6].

Understanding the bias toward the negative means understanding the need for training in Positive Leadership and PERMA. To overcome this bias means to "unlearn" the negative focus and learn to apply the tools of positive psychology and positive leadership.

Kim Cameron gives a large amount of examples of Abundance Tools [6], we will name only a few. All of the tools are highly efficient and effective when it comes to helping people and organizations to not only overcome crisis, but to excel and to flourish:

- Reflected best-self feedback process: A personal feedback tool that provides descriptive stories of individuals' best-selves – when they created extraordinary value. This results in a best-self portrait and action plans designed to capitalize on personal strengths.
- Positive energy networks: A tool to identify positive energizers and the positive energy network that exists in an organization, along with hints for capitalizing on the energy network.
- PMI program: A tool based on one-on-one meetings between managers and their direct reports designed to foster continuous improvement, accountability for performance, and developing employees into extraordinary performers.
- Supportive communication in difficult circumstances: A technique for delivering negative feedback in ways that foster stronger, more collaborative relationships.
- Engagement of employees: Techniques for fostering high levels of engagement among employees by managing ideological capital, social capital, intellectual capital, and financial capital.
- Empowerment of employees: A set of techniques for enhancing the empowerment of employees through self-efficacy, self-determination, personal consequence, personal meaning, and trust.
- Everest goals: A tool for identifying organizational and individual goals which extend beyond normal SMART goal setting and lead to extraordinary levels of achievement.
- Positive practices assessment: A diagnostic survey instrument identifies 38 dimensions of positive practices that are highly predictive of financial performance in organizations.
- Gratitude journals and gratitude visits: A tool used to help individuals experience a gratitude condition daily as well as to experience the impact of a profound interaction based on thanksgiving.
- Positive culture change: A technique for helping organizations transform their cultures toward abundance and positive deviance.
- Fundamental state of leadership: A set of techniques that lead individuals from a normal state of functioning to a state in which leaders are internally-directed, externally-open, others-focused, and purpose-centered.

3 Managing the Diversity of People, Languages and Systems

3.1 Industry 4.0 and Diversity

Digitalization and automation are meant to help people and to take organizations and society to the next level: less routine, but more quality time available for creative thinking and innovation; less heavy and stressful work, but more using our brains and imagination; less manual systems prone to error, but more smart and interconnected systems, learning with Artificial Intelligence, etc.

In reality, there is fear and resistance to change [11]. The reaction to change is as "human" and as old as the bias toward the negative (see Sect. 2), coming from our oldest part of the brain, the limbic system. Prognoses about 50% of jobs killed by Industry 4.0

could easily provoke fight-or-flight response or a "rage against the machine" like in the beginning of industrialization.

How to overcome this fear and resistance to change? How to benefit from Industry 4.0 and the fundamental changes it will bring to our societies?

Embracing change is embracing diversity. Embracing and managing diversity of people, of languages and of systems, is a basic requirement of the presence and the future of a globalized world [12].

Let us start with the diversity of systems. Digitalization intrinsically leads to the integration of several different technologies in products and systems. As software and electronics become ubiquitous and part of almost every system that is part of our daily lives, software and electronics need to be integrated in mechanical, hydraulic, electrical, systems, etc. Even our clothes will become smart thanks to software and electronics woven into future tissues. This ever increasing diverse technology density in modern products and systems necessitates the close collaboration of experts from several different engineering disciplines. To enable this, industrial organizations are moving from concurrent engineering dominated organizations towards integrated engineering organizations that are mainly characterized by multi-disciplinary teams making decisions together rather than sequentially. This close collaboration of interdisciplinary experts needs a strong common terminology basis as a prerequisite for mutual understanding.

Diversity of languages
Global, accessible English for non-native speakers as "lingua franca" is not enough to understand and to shape the future. International markets as well as international software development teams with a variety of languages will keep communicating in their local languages, business and research will be done in local languages together with global English, global Chinese, global Arabic, global Hindi, global Swahili, etc.

Natural languages will mingle and merge with computer languages, speech recognition will reach the next level and the "Universal Translater" from StarTrek will spread.

Language skills and computational thinking are key skills in Industry 4.0. As foreign languages, coding and computational thinking should be a taught already in Kindergarden, as Austrian Computer Society is stressing.

If the use of language(s) is not managed well, we are suffering from linguistic (Babylonian) confusion, causing a lot of inefficient processes prone to error. This applies to societies, countries and organizations alike.

In business and research, managing language mainly means managing corporate language and managing the concepts and terms of a subject field. The importance and value of professional terminology management increasingly is understood and discussed in the software process improvement community [13]. Computer linguists often are the "missing links" between representatives of industries with their domain experts, such as software developers, and language management experts. Professional terminology and translation management has a long history, an old Technical Committee within ISO (ISO/TC37) and a mature, wide-spread and international system of qualification and certification [14].

Diversity of people

In the first standard about Diversity Management, the Austrian standard ÖNORM S 2501:2008, diversity management (DiM) is defined as "a strategic management approach aimed at the targeted consideration and deliberate utilization of the diversity of persons and relevant organizational environments or stakeholders in order to create structural and social conditions under which all employees can develop their abilities and reach their full performance to the benefit of all parties involved and for raising the organization's success" [15].

Translated into accessible English, Diversity Management is a strategic management approach, using the potential of a diverse workforce for the benefits of all parties involved. When SAP hires autistic people for specific task they are very good at (controlling pieces of software and detecting errors), both parties benefit: SAP finds the right people for important tasks, and the autistic people get the opportunity to have a job and live a self-determined life.

When technical universities are desperately looking for female students, and economies suffer from skilled worker shortage in technical and other subject fields, diversity management can help to attract high potentials and high performers, independent from their gender, age, or ethnical background.

In the aging societies of the present and the future, diversity management is essential to overcome skilled worker shortage. And in liberal, open societies, diversity management is a powerful tool to foster equal treatment and social justice.

International software development teams would benefit a lot from professional diversity management, saving a lot of time and resources to cope with low performance or failure of mainly male teams who just lack of the benefits of diversity leading to innovation and excellent results, if they are managed well.

The European Certification and Qualification Association ECQA® developed certificates and training courses for Diversity Manager, taking into account the connection between diversity and innovation [15, 16], as well as the correlation and role of linguistic diversity and human diversity [17]. Diversity management is also important for and included in the job role and certificate for ECQA® Certified Applied Sustainability and CSR Professionals.

Diversity of expertise and educational backgrounds

Industry 4.0 is driven by the establishment of a seamless digital thread of end-to-end information about the products and their related process manufacturing and service provision services. In fact, the digital thread covers the entire life cycle thereby enabling the transversal, inter-disciplinary use of data becoming available in different stages of the life cycle. Such Big Data, however, need people's expertise and experience. Therefore, Industry 4.0 fosters the inter-disciplinary and diverse collaboration between experts from several different domains and life cycle phases. Data become the basic intermediary object for this kind of communication and collaboration, in which linked data sources and sinks create awareness for the complex inter-relationships of diverse disciplines over the life cycle.

3.2 The 6th Kondratieff Wave

We are currently in the middle of the so-called 6th wave of Kondratieff.

The Soviet economist Nikolai Kondratiev (mainly written Kondratieff) was the first to propose and describe cycle-like phenomena in the modern world economy in his book The Major Economic Cycles (1925). In 1939, Joseph Schumpeter suggested naming the cycles "Kondratieff waves" in his honor [18].

Two Dutch economists, Jacob van Gelderen and Salomon de Wolff, had previously argued for the existence of 50- to 60-year cycles in 1913 and 1924, respectively. Since the inception of the theory, various studies have expanded the range of possible cycles, finding longer or shorter cycles in the data [18].

Kondratieff identified three phases in the cycle: expansion, stagnation, and recession, and proposed to apply the theory to the 19th century. He focused on prices and interest rates, seeing the ascendant phase as characterized by an increase in prices and low interest rates, while the other phase consists of a decrease in prices and high interest rates. Subsequent analysis concentrated on output [18].

Why Kondratieff waves are so important? They could explain and predict trends and developments, and who is able to do that would benefit from the future and would be able to shape the future. To surf the waves of Kondratieff is a highly promising imagination. In reality, there is a lack of agreement over the cause of the Kondratieff cycles. Health economist and biostatistician Andreas J.W. Goldschmidt searched for patterns and proposed that there is a phase shift and overlap of the 6th Kondratieff wave of IT and health (shown in Fig. 1).

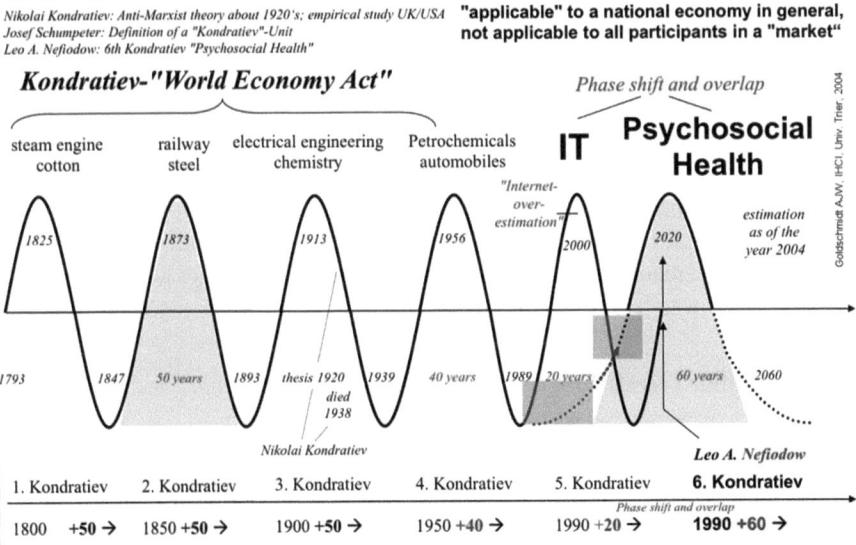

Fig. 1. Kondratieff waves associated with gains in IT and health with phase shift and overlap, Andreas J.W. Goldschmidt, 2004 [18]

According to Nefiodow [19, 20], who associates the sixth Kondratieff wave with holistic health (see below, Fig. 2), we are currently in its second decade and therefore this wave does not have the strength yet to lead the global economy into a steady upswing.

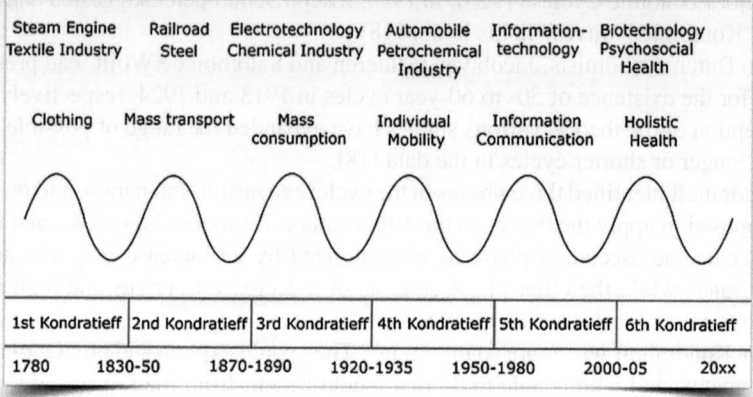

Fig. 2. Nefiodow, L.: The sixth Kondratieff. https://www.kondratieff.net/the-sixth-kondratieff

For this to succeed, health expenditures would need to be more consistently treated as investments than in the past. Outside of the health care sector, there are currently no other candidates through which the industrial nations are able to achieve full employment, real and sustainable growth as well as a forward-thinking social order. The present obstacles to growth can be overcome if health promotion is aimed at the whole person and his/her natural environment. Those countries, markets, organizations and people who consequently tap into and unlock the sixth Kondratieff will be among the winners in the 21st century [19, 20].

Both interpretations would predict a tremendous boost of software development. If Holistic Health is the next "big thing" at global level, IT and software industry will enter into a highly diverse universe of business opportunities and growth. We will need even more professional management of the diversity of people, languages and systems in this universe.

3.3 The Global Trends 2030

In 2012, the National Intelligence Council of the US predicted in its publication "Global Trends 2030: Alternative Worlds" that "The world of 2030 will be radically transformed from our world today. By 2030, no country—whether the US, China, or any other large country—will be a hegemonic power. The empowerment of individuals and diffusion of power among states and from states to informal networks will have a dramatic impact, largely reversing the historic rise of the West since 1750, restoring Asia's weight in the global economy, and ushering in a new era of "democratization" at the international and domestic level. In addition to individual empowerment and the diffusion of state power, we believe that two other megatrends will shape our world out to 2030: demographic patterns, especially rapid aging; and growing resource demands which, in the cases of food and water, might lead to scarcities. These trends, which are virtually certain, exist today, but during the next 15-20 years they will gain much greater momentum" [21, 22].

The mega-trends and game changers described in this publication confirm the need for strategies to cope with diversity and to apply PERMA-nent Positive Leadership, as discussed in this paper.

References

1. Seligman, M.: Flourish: A Visionary New Understanding of Happiness and Well-being. William Heinemann, Random House Australia Pty Ltd., North Sydney (2011)
2. Authentic Happiness Homepage. https://www.authentichappiness.sas.upenn.edu/learn/wellbeing. Last accessed 31 Mar 2017
3. Cameron, K: Positive Leadership and Extraordinary Organizational Performance. Dean's Lecture Series, Melbourne Graduate School of Education, 26 March 2012. http://education.unimelb.edu.au/__data/assets/pdf_file/0003/628491/Kim_Cameron_pp.pdf
4. Spacey, J.: What is the Heliotropic Effect?, 19 January 2017. http://simplicable.com/new/heliotropic-effect. Last accessed 02 April 2017
5. Cameron, K.S.: Practicing Positive Leadership: Tools and Techniques That Create Extraordinary Results. Berrett-Koehler Publishers, San Francisco (2013)
6. Cameron, K.: Positive Leadership and Extraordinary Organizational Performance. Dean's Lecture Series, Melbourne Graduate School of Education, 26 March 2012. http://education.unimelb.edu.au/__data/assets/pdf_file/0003/628491/Kim_Cameron_pp.pdf
7. Kim Cameron's Homepage. https://sites.google.com/a/umich.edu/kimcameron/home. Last accessed 03 Mar 2017
8. Positive Psychology Program Homepage. https://positivepsychologyprogram.com/positive-organisational-development-kim-cameron/. Last accessed 02 April 2017
9. Positive Psychology Program Homepage. https://positivepsychologyprogram.com/perma-model/#apply-perma-model. Last accessed 03 Mar 2017
10. Baumeister, R., et al. (2001), quoted in [6]
11. Lipkin, N.: 5 Reasons Why Change is So Hard: The Science of Change Resistance, Webinar (2017). https://vimeo.com/207658162. Last accessed 02 April 2017
12. Clarke, P.M., et al.: Refactoring software development process terminology through the use of ontology. In: Kreiner, C., O'Connor, R.V., Poth, A., Messnarz, R. (eds.) EuroSPI 2016. CCIS, vol. 633, pp. 47–57. Springer, Cham (2016). doi:10.1007/978-3-319-44817-6_4
13. Riel, A., Messnarz, R., Sauberer, G.: Towards an integrated learning and certification strategy for global innovation. In: Proceedings of the 23rd EuroAsiaSPI^2 Conference, Ankara, pp. 8.15–8.20 (2015)
14. ÖNORM S 2501:2008 Diversity management – General guidelines on principles, systems and supporting techniques. Austrian Standards, Vienna (2008)
15. Sauberer, G.: Der Europäische Diversity Führerschein: Neue Fähigkeiten und Strategien für Diversitäts- und Innovationsmanagement in Europa und weltweit, Masterarbeit zur Erlangung des akademischen Grades Master of Business Administration an der Fachhochschule Burgenland. Austrian Institute of Management, Eisenstadt (2014)
16. Sauberer, G.: An EU-wide methodology and strategy for diversity management. In: Diversity is Reality. Effective Leadership of Diverse Teams in a Global Environment, Brno, pp. 46–58 (2011)

17. Sauberer, G.: Linguistic and cultural diversity within the concept of managing diversity. In: Proceedings of the Conference "Everyday Multilingualism – Lebensweltliche Mehrsprachigkeit", Organized by the Austrian Federal Ministry for Education, The Arts and Culture and the Austrian Commission for UNESCO, Eisenstadt, pp. 94–96 (2008)
18. Wikipedia Homepage. https://en.wikipedia.org/wiki/Kondratiev_wave. Last accessed 31 Mar 2017. Figure 1: https://upload.wikimedia.org/wikipedia/commons/e/e4/Kondratiev-waves_IT_and_Health_with_phase_shift_acc_to_Goldschmidt-AJW_2004.jpg
19. Homepage of Leo A. Nefiodow. https://www.kondratieff.net/the-sixth-kondratieff. Last accessed 31 Mar 2017
20. Nefiodow, L.: The Sixth Kondratieff: A New Long Wave in the Global Economy, 2nd edn. CreateSpace Independent Publishing Platform, Sankt Augustin (2017)
21. Global Trends. https://info.publicintelligence.net/GlobalTrends2030.pdf
22. Homepage of the National Intelligence Council. https://www.facebook.com/odni.nic. Last accessed 31 Mar 2017

Do We Speak the Same Language? Terminology Strategies for (Software) Engineering Environments Based on the Elcat Model - Innovative Terminology e-Learning for the Automotive Industry

Gabriele Sauberer[1(✉)], Blanca Nájera Villar[1], Jens R. Dreßler[2], Klaus-Dirk Schmitz[3], Paul M. Clarke[4,5], and Rory V. O'Connor[4,5]

[1] TermNet, The International Network for Terminology, Vienna, Austria
{gsauberer,bnajera}@termnet.org
[2] DieEinheit, Cologne, Germany
Jens.Dreszler@DieEinheit.de
[3] Technical University of Cologne, Cologne, Germany
klaus.schmitz@th-koeln.de
[4] Dublin City University, Dublin, Ireland
{paul.m.clarke,rory.oconnor}@dcu.ie
[5] Lero, The Irish Software Engineering Research Centre, Limerick, Ireland

Abstract. This paper addresses the need for correct and consistent use of concepts and terms in engineering environments. It provides guidance on how to formulate a corporate terminology policy as a pre-requisite for managing corporate language, designing and implementing a terminology process, and eventually writing definitions and creating new terms. The strategy presented in this paper follows the elcat model, an innovative e-learning initiative that focusses on content development of terminology management modules for the automotive industries. The authors suggest that the role of terminology management is to bring some order to support consistent and more precise language adoption for a period of time. Effective medium to long term terminology management is thereafter enabled through the introduction of a terminology change management procedure.

Keywords: Communication strategies · Terminology policy · Terminology processes · Terminology management

1 Terminology in Engineering Environments

Engineering constantly faces very complex processes as the industry is continually developing new products, whose terminology has to be adapted to very different target groups. These products have to be marketed on various global markets under fierce competitive pressure.

Therefore it is necessary that the decision-makers in the company attach due importance to it. This is important because sufficient resources, i.e. technical equipment and workforce, are required for a systematic planning and effective development of terminology processes.

In engineering environments terminology already exists and needs to be collected, documented, standardized or made accessible in a structured way. This is often the case in large international companies, especially in the wake of mergers, acquisition of other companies, or the development of new products. Other contexts may require the coining of new terms, writing definitions and translation of terms from one language into another is necessary [1].

Terminology is embedded in one way or the other in company's specialised language, i.e. in creating and using technical or special terms and expressions. Therefore terminology needs to be developed, or existing terminology needs to be used:

- tailored according to your individual requirements
- in an efficient way
- taking the specific target groups into account [2].

1.1 What Exactly Does Terminology Mean?

According to ISO 1087-1 [3], terminology is the specialised vocabulary of a subject field, i.e. a set of terms representing the system of concepts of a particular subject field. The work concerned with the systematic capture, description, processing and presentation of concepts and their designations in terminological databases or terminological dictionaries is called terminology work.

Terminology management involves:

- creating new terms
- collecting and documenting existing terms
- formulating definitions for new concepts
- compiling a database for terminology that includes relevant information about grammar, context, usage, style, etc., and administrative information, such as alteration date, etc.

It is important to ensure that target groups both within and outside the company have access to this carefully prepared terminology. To achieve this aim, primary importance is on:

- providing specific target groups with access to relevant terminology
- training all those involved according to their specific needs.

This first topic will be discussed in the next chapter of this paper based on the findings and guidelines elaborated in the elcat project, innovative terminology e-learning for the automotive industry [4]. Following this framework and in the chapter 3, the vast array of dynamic processes, behind these central tasks will be studied in connection with the large number of people with very different skills and interests that are involved.

2 Formulating a Company Policy for the Corporate Language and Communication

A company's terminology policy must be supported by all parties right from the very beginning. It is extremely important to identify all persons that must be involved in the implementation of a terminology policy or strategy [5].

Include all parties in the process from the very start. Create an internal and external network. People will have different interests in or attitudes towards this project. Therefore they should be addressed and involved in different ways. In this way, opinions can be changed in a positive way, or they stay the same. Nevertheless, all opinions are important in order to develop a terminology policy that can be supported by everybody. It is important to discuss expected difficulties, resistance and negative attitudes and conceive strategies to deal with them specifically (Fig. 1).

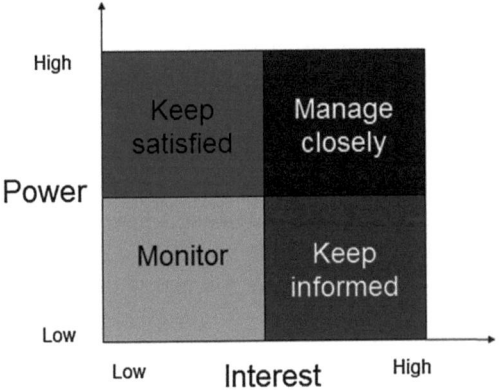

Fig. 1. ISO 29383:2010 Annex A - Tools for stakeholder analysis

This template can be used as a tool for the stakeholder analysis: All persons identified should be assigned to one group, according to their influence and interest in this chart for which different strategies are applied. The group membership is not static and may be constantly changing.

- **Keep Satisfied:** Some effort is required to satisfy this group - but not too much to avoid them feeling bored or annoyed.
- **Manage closely:** These people must be the ones involved the most in the process. They need maximum support and integration in the development process.
- **Monitor:** Observe these people's attitude. Offer information and advice but be careful not to overwhelm them.
- **Inform:** These people should be informed regularly and sufficiently. To avoid dissatisfaction, they should be given the chance to influence key factors.

2.1 Developing and Implementing a Terminology Policy

This section concentrates on the process from the preparation to the implementation of a terminology policy and shall help to anticipate problems, respond proactively and to proceed systematically. The process described here corresponds to ISO 29383 "Terminology policies - development and implementation" [6] (Fig. 2).

Fig. 2. ISO 29383:2010 model for development and implementation of terminology

Preparation
Overview of the current status

When implementing a terminology policy, thorough preparation is the prerequisite for all further steps. Invest time in extensively researching requirements, the purpose and the necessary processes. A terminology policy must perfectly match the conditions if it is to be effectively deployed in the long term.

Possible aspects to take into account are:

- Which languages are spoken?
- Which languages are used in the development department, in marketing, purchase, customer service, etc.?
- Which markets do you serve, where do you export to?
- Are there any guidelines or regulations with regard to terminology, communication, knowledge management or language existing in the company or in individual departments?
- Is it possible or necessary to build on the existing guidelines or regulations or do they have to be integrated into the new strategy?
- Which areas suffer the most serious problems with regard to communication and knowledge management?
- Which people are affected in some way by terminology policy? Do not forget subsidiaries and correspondence with suppliers and contractors!

Comprehensive documentation is useful for collecting information and facts if you are compiling a plan of action, in-house campaigns, press releases and other public announcements. Case studies and concrete figures are helpful for argumentation purposes. Especially, if they come from within the company or industry. Employees from various departments can provide an abundance of material for this purpose.

This first step of preparation is very labour-intensive. But extensive preparation will pay off in subsequent steps. The organisation of a corporate consultation process should be considered when possible, including meetings, questionnaires or interviews with opinion leaders. Involve strategically important employees.

Consulting is carried out to produce a positive attitude and a sense of co-determination and responsibility. It can also serve to animate passive stakeholders to participate.

Formulating and Ratifying Policies

A terminology policy can be documented in various ways, for example in guidelines or strategy documents. The shorter the document, the greater the likelihood that it will be read and used.

However, the basic principles of how to proceed remain the same:

- Compile a corporate terminology policy
- Design a coordination plan with other corporate strategies
- Implementation plan and action plan
- Present strategy
- Decision by executive board

Draft a terminology policy
All necessary preparations have been made during the preparatory phase. Now, the results must be presented in an attractive and appropriate way.

The following points should be observed:

- Specific targets and non-targets
- Extent
- Benefit
- Stakeholders
- Evaluation

When preparing a policy, it is important to remember that those who make the final decision, are not terminology experts, and focus on the concrete benefits for the core business.

Coordination plan
Terminology and terminology management affect all company divisions, from Development, through Finance and the Legal Division, Localisation, Marketing, Corporate Communication, Management, Technical Writing and Purchase [7]. It often happens that these divisions are operating independently of each other. The goal of a corporate terminology policy is to involve all divisions and business areas. Sometimes, you may even find an existing infrastructure for terminology-related issues.

The terminology policy is intended to harmonise these processes and to support the company's overall performance. This can be achieved, e.g. by applying an integration statement illustrating the relationship of terminology policy with the individual business areas. The coordination plan will also help adapt the strategy accordingly under changing circumstances.

Implementation Plan
Successfully implementing a terminology policy is perhaps the most delicate step and requires careful planning and endurance. A terminology policy will be most successful when it is based on existing infrastructures and involves available networks. If it is necessary to create a new infrastructure, make sure to plan and reserve time and financial resources well.

Necessary infrastructure may include:

- Further education and training of employees
- Allocation of staff, hiring new staff if necessary
- Provision of premises, hardware, software and literature
- Support for cleansing and maintaining databases and systems
- Access to corporate documentation

An action plan with a timeframe schedule is an important aid when implementing a terminology policy. It should include the priorities set. Be modest and set moderate, easily achievable goals. Do not underestimate the psychological effect of fast results. They encourage motivation and endurance and also have a positive impact on evaluation results [8].

Presentation/Template

The arguments and the proposed strategy must attract the attention of decision-makers and arouse their interest by addressing issues that concern them. Remember that, from a controller's perspective, your draft is simply one among many budget items competing with each other for resources.

The presentation should therefore be

- Convincing
- clearly written or presented,
- well motivated,
- reinforced by accurate and up-to-date facts and
- be relatively short.

Emphasise in your presentation the strengths and weaknesses of the current situation in the company concerning terminology and explain the consequences of a terminology policy for the overall situation.

Decision

It is important that the terminology policy is not only formally approved, but that it attracts ongoing interest and receives long-term support. Make sure that the topic of terminology remains on the agenda and is remembered through regular communication.

Implementation

Operational planning, organisation and communication is required for implementing a terminology policy. In this step, it is important to win the support and obtain the cooperation of the key stakeholders. Be aware that the terminology policy means change for most employees. Change is often perceived as negative as it creates uncertainty and causes extra work [9].

Creating Sustainability

The aim of a terminology policy is to integrate automatic terminology work into everyday business work flows.

Automation can be established by:

- Qualification of terminology experts, memberships in industry associations
- Regular further training and education of internal and external staff within all departments and areas
- Ensure that the terminology issue is on the agenda at meetings in all departments, so that terminology policy is addressed regularly
- Informal internal networks (which in many companies is explicitly welcome - the terminologist should be known in and be familiar with all areas)
- Software upgrades and network administration
- Communication within the company and externally
- Regular evaluation by an internal or external department in order to be able to respond quickly to changes
- Create flexible infrastructures that allow continued working even in times of financial cuttings.

3 Designing a Terminology Process

The way terminology processes are designed depends on many factors. A central question is whether new terms are created in the company (prescriptive terminology work) or if existing terms are primarily documented (descriptive terminology work). An innovative industrial company creates new products which must be designated in one or more languages. Industrial companies place - or at least should place - great emphasis on creating terms and formulating definitions [10].

Drafting a terminology process is very complex and involves many individual factors that have to be taken into account when planning processes, it would not make sense to design a sample work flow for terminology work in a car company. We'd rather give you inspiration for thought and develop planning aids so that you can design your individual processes efficiently and systematically.

The design of terminology processes depends on the objective factors in the company. Another crucial factor is the importance attached to the various aspects of terminology work. The first priority should be to get an idea of the basic conditions of terminology work and to set priorities.

These important aspects should be clarified in advance:

- whether terminology work in the company is to be approached monolingually, bilingually or multilingually,
- which tasks are to be fulfilled internally and which are to be outsourced,
- how communication is organised within the company and with external service providers (terminologists, translators, technical writers, etc.),
- which employees/divisions/external service providers should have access to the terminology,
- with which suppliers your company co-operates and how you exchange terminology for the parts supplied by them,
- which existing objectives concerning terminology design need to be fulfilled (corporate language),
- and which sources for terminology are being used.

In addition, it is important to provide employees and, as required, external suppliers, who may use tools for terminology work, computer-assisted translation or machine-assisted editing to ensure consistency in the company's language, with the terminology. [11]

Therefore, the systems that are already or will be in use in the company must be included in process planning, i.e.

- terminology management systems
- databases
- editing tools
- terminology extraction tools
- tools for computer-aided translation
- machine translation systems
- knowledge management systems
- knowledge repositories.

Quality should always be in the foreground. However, it is sometimes inevitable to make compromises here for pragmatic reasons such as very tight deadlines set by the client. In these cases, real-time availability of terminology has priority. With regard to other objectives, harmonising existing terminology may be a priority, for others exchangeability of terminological data may be the most important criterion [12].

Possible Priorities in Terminology Work could be quality, harmonisation, quick availability and exchangeability of terminological data.

3.1 Standard Processes and Unique Processes

Examples of Standard Processes in Terminology Work

- New terms and designations are created for new developments.
- Definitions are formulated to describe and differentiate new concepts.
- New terms are assigned their equivalents in other languages.
- The terminology for product X will be made available to external translators.

However, precise planning and assignment of responsibilities should also be considered when deploying special, unique processes as they may sometimes be extensive and far-reaching.

Examples of Unique Terminology Processes

- A terminology database is currently being integrated into the company.
- The company acquires a competitor. The brands are to be continued, but eventually a common corporate identity and a consistent corporate language shall be established. The terminology of the two companies must be harmonised.
- The company acquires a competitor. Differences in terminology shall be maintained. Terminology for both companies is collected centrally, documented and communicated accordingly, so that the technical documentation and translation departments are able to use a clear brand- or company-specific terminology.

3.2 Defining and Modelling Process

Defining terminology processes involves specifying **who** does **what when**.

It is therefore necessary to define the actual processes, to designate the competent persons, to assign responsibilities to them and to set deadlines for performing these tasks [13] (Fig. 3).

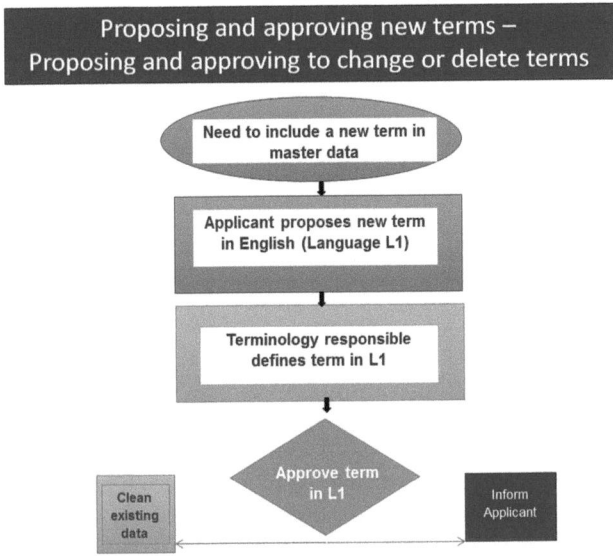

Fig. 3. Example of terminology Process for Approval of terms [13].

4 Terminology Management – Philosophical and Economic Considerations

The challenge associated with terminology is not static as all organisations are in effect evolving their own use of language as time passes – just as is the case for natural language drift in the wider population. The authors suggest that the role of terminology management is to bring some order to support consistent and more precise language adoption for a period of time. Effective medium to long term terminology management is thereafter enabled through the introduction of a terminology change management procedure (Fig. 4).

Terminology management is not a perfect science, rather a starting objective might be economic in nature. There is a point up to which an investment in terminology makes sound economic sense for an organisation and beyond that point, the over-prescription of broader swathes of language and terminology will introduce business inefficiencies.

We suggest that one of the greatest challenges therefore may be the very determination of "how much terminology is enough?" The costs of lack of precision in terminology in any given company or field of endeavour may be a useful indicator to

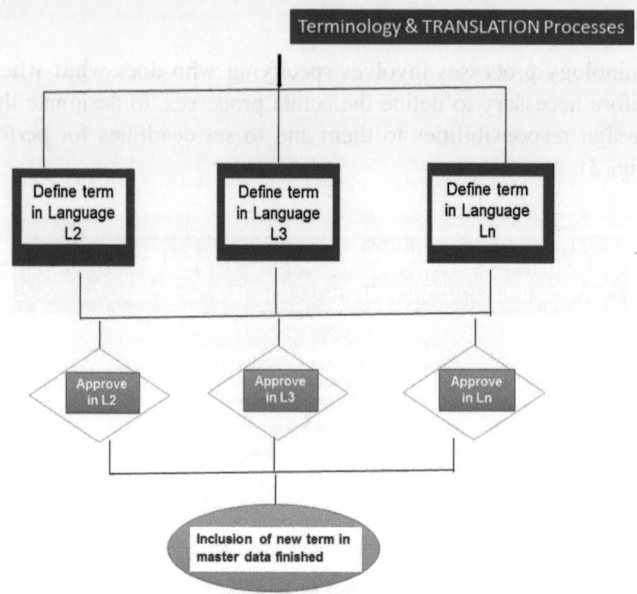

Fig. 4. Example of terminology and translation process [13].

guide a specific response to this question. After all, if a team of medical professionals are undertaking life-threatening surgery, time is not available to clarify specific term meaning and hence a common terminology understanding must pre-exist in the team. Equally, terminological misunderstandings could have very undesirable outcomes for patients undergoing surgical procedures of this nature. We therefore see that terminology influences both efficiency of the job undertaken (how long does it take to complete?) and the quality of the outcomes (how well was the job performed?).

Larger projects involving more people therefore increase the scale of the terminology problem, as does the nature of the work. To put this in some context, if a large team of engineers in involved on a project where poor terminology management is in place, the project will need to cater for two additional risks: (1) that the project may be delayed due to the increased communication required in order to clarify understanding; and (2) the quality of the end product or service may inadvertently be compromised as a result of terminological confusion. The most obvious mitigation strategy for both of these risks is to examine the terminology footprint on the project and determine its areas of weakness, thereafter tightening up on the definition and consistent use of terminology across the project.

The theory we present is reasonably simple and intuitively appealing. However, we must not lose sight of a basic operating constraint: people are involved in the adoption and application of terminology. In the authors' view, the types of concerns introduced by this constraint are varied, some examples of which include:

(1) As humans, our use of language for communication involves a constant interpretation and resulting quasi-understanding of what is intended in language.

(2) As humans, our capacity to assume to have fully understood some point of language is high (perhaps it needs to be in order to operate) but our actual capacity to genuinely and completely understand all points of language is necessarily incomplete. As evidence of this shortcoming, the number of words and their varied meanings in the established mainstream natural language dictionaries considerably exceeds the memory capacity of any individual person – they are sources of reference and guidance, but not sources that are practically suited for rote learning.

These human limitations give rise to a further issue that arise in terminology debates: communications and terminological shortcomings may be intuitively underappreciated by individuals. We assume an understanding to be correct - our biological mechanisms seem to some extent tuned for this type of behaviour – yet it may only be an approximation to the intended meaning. After all, Georg Hegel is reputed to have observed that *truth is found neither in the thesis nor the antithesis, but in an emergent synthesis which reconciles the two.* Truthful meaning in respect of terms is therefore an emergent synthesis of possible/ competing term definitions.

To contextualise this philosophical debate in the context of practical Engineering Terminology, we can extrapolate that certain situations arise, to which we should give careful consideration (refer to Table 1 below)

Table 1. Examples of terminology debates.

Potential situation	Impact & Discussion
Large or complicated projects which seem to require relatively large descriptions may amplify the basic terminology problem	Where complication exists, increased communication, language and terminology are mechanisms for managing our affairs. However, increased communication, language and terminology serve to increase the potential for mis-understanding. In these cases, more robust and formal terminology management may be desirable
Engineers and individuals working on complicated projects may have a natural propensity for underappreciating the terminology challenge (in effect, the terminology issue is therefore latent in nature)	A terminology problem necessarily exists – it is a case of how we choose to deal with it. However, if we choose to deal with it purely through informal human communication mechanisms, the issues arising from interpretation and quasi-communication will invariably lead to gaps in understanding which may manifest as undesirable outcomes
Gaps in terminology usage may ultimately manifest themselves in poor product quality or service delivery or general project issues	Terminology represents the building blocks for effective communication. Terminology is central to work and process management. Where terminology management is sub-standard, we risk introducing product, project and service delivery issues. Consistency and predictability in terms of meeting product and project quality targets is negatively affected

Earlier work from the authors has examined the potential for a latent terminology problem to exist in the software engineering field [14] We found that within software engineering, there is strong evidence to suggest that a terminology problem has arisen, and we have advocated that this problem could be tackled through the use of ontology [15]. We have also seen that this terminology concerns extends to role definition [16]. Indeed and although unintended at the time, some of our earlier work has also demonstrated the complexity that arises in term usage in software engineering, where the very term *success* has been should to be layered in possible interpretation (even though many individuals adopting the term will intuitively assume that they have understood it instantly) [17]. It is perhaps the case the more established engineering fields have a smaller terminology problem than software engineering, but even in these domains the potential for terminology costs and issues to arise remains as where there is a complicated endeavour there is also a need for effective and efficient communication.

5 Conclusions

The purpose of a terminology policy or strategy is to bring "order to chaos" and to a systematic and appropriate use of terminology throughout all company divisions. Company divisions use and are affected by terminology in varying extents and in different ways. In this respect, divisions must apply an individual approach to terminology. Terminology experts often have difficulties to justify their positions and to promote a cooperative environment. One of their key activities involves convincing others. Innovations such as the launch of a terminology database frequently meet with resistance or refusal as many colleagues see it as an added addition to their workload.

A systematic terminology management can only be successfully introduced into the company if employees are convinced that it will make work easier and if all departments are integrated into the corporate strategy from the very beginning. The requirements will be explained in detail in this unit.

Whether terminology management has been successfully introduced in a company is primarily evaluated by controlling and represented in figures. And although the real success can often only be noticed in the long term, early signs of tangible milestones achieved play an important role. The development and implementation of a corporate terminology policy is therefore primarily dependent on the management and communication process. Coherent and convincing arguments are particularly important in this respect.

6 Innovative e-Learning - Content Development of Terminology Management Modules for the Automotive Industries: The ELCAT Model

Goal of this project is the development of an e-learning course which offers a user-friendly and sound introduction to basic principles and methods of terminology management. The target group is the automotive industry and includes management, sales and marketing, standardization, product development, technical documentation, terminologists, translators, language service providers and corporate communications. All these areas are important to involve in the terminology project cycle. The challenge is the lacking linguistic or terminological basis of the users who thus have to be introduced to the topic with care. It is the aim to expand the model later to other industries and as an introductory course for students at universities. The course is prepared in cooperation with members from the automotive and IT industry and is offered in German and English.

The project was originally funded by the Federal Ministry of Education and Research and carried out by the Institute for Information Management (IIM) at the Technische Hochschule Köln. Project partners included TermNet, Audi Academy, Volkswagen AG, 2 W Technische Informations GmbH, SDL Trados, acrolinx, IAI (Institute of the Society for the Promotion of Applied Information Sciences at the Saarland University), University of Vienna, University of Florida, Macquarie University (Sydney).

Elcat is an online training with the most important topics in terminology management. In 2016, cooperation between elcat and the European Certification and Qualification Association (ECQA) was started and the appropriate certificate meeting these needs was created: The ECQA Certified Terminology Manager (CTM) – Automotive [18].

Acknowledgements. This work was supported, in part, by Science Foundation Ireland grant 13/RC/2094. The elcat project was originally funded by the German Federal Ministry of Education and Research and carried out by the Institute for Information Management (IIM) at the Technische Hochschule Köln.

References

1. Steurs, F., Kockaert, H., Sauberer, G., Nájera Villar, B.: Terminology, technical documentation and standards: safety and security for industry, and engineering environments. In: 23rd EuroAsiaSPI2 Conference, Graz University, Austria, 14–16 September 2016. Industrial Proceedings. Whitebox, Denmark (2016)
2. Kockaert, H.J., Steurs, F. (eds.): Handbook of Terminology. John Benjamins, Amsterdam/Philadelphia (2015)
3. ISO 1087-1:2000 Terminology work – Vocabulary – Part 1: Theory and application
4. elcat Homepage. elcat - innovative terminology e-learning for the automotive industry. http://en.my-elcat.com/
5. UNESCO Guidelines for Terminology Policies, 2004 by Infoterm. Terminology-policy portal online: http://www.infoterm.info/activities/terminology_policies.php
6. ISO 29383:2010. Terminology policies - development and implementation
7. Rat für Deutschsprachige Terminologie (RaDT): Knowledge, Brands and Customer Loyalty - Terminology as a Critical Success Factor, ©RaDT 2010 (2010)
8. Rat für Deutschsprachige Terminologie (RaDT): The Basics of Terminology: A Guide for Subject Experts. Köln: Deutscher Terminologie-Tag e.V. 2014

9. Links and information for terminologists: "Deutscher Terminologie-Tag e.V. (DTT)". http://www.iim.fh-koeln.de/dtt; International Network for Terminology (TermNet). http://www.termnet.org/english/products_service/how_to_sell_terminology.php
10. The Wüster Archive - a special node in a European digital archive network. In: Oeser, E., Galinski, C. (eds.) Eugen Wüster. Leben und Werk. Ein österreichischer Pionier der Informationsgesellschaft, pp. 169–174 [2] S.E. TermNet, Vienna (1998)
11. Sager, J.C.: A Practical Course in Terminology Processing. John Benjamins Publishing Company (1990)
12. Nájera Villar, B., Brändle, D.: There is no knowledge without terminology: key factors for organisational learning. In: Winkler, D., O'Connor, R.V., Messnarz, R. (eds.) EuroSPI 2012. CCIS, vol. 301, pp. 300–309. Springer, Heidelberg (2012). doi:10.1007/978-3-642-31199-4_26
13. Weilandt, A.: Terminologiemanagement - Ein prozessorientierter Ansatz am Beispiel der Automobilindustrie, Frankfurt am Main (2015)
14. Clarke, P.M., et al.: An investigation of software development process terminology. In: Clarke, P.M., O'Connor, R.V., Rout, T., Dorling, A. (eds.) SPICE 2016. CCIS, vol. 609, pp. 351–361. Springer, Cham (2016). doi:10.1007/978-3-319-38980-6_25
15. Clarke, P.M., et al.: Refactoring software development process terminology through the use of ontology. In: Kreiner, C., O'Connor, R.V., Poth, A., Messnarz, R. (eds.) EuroSPI 2016. CCIS, vol. 633, pp. 47–57. Springer, Cham (2016). doi:10.1007/978-3-319-44817-6_4
16. Yilmaz, M., O'Connor, R.V., Clarke, P.: Software development roles: a multi-project empirical investigation. ACM SIGSOFT Softw. Eng. Not. **40**(1), 1–5 (2015)
17. Clarke, P., O'Connor, R.V.: The meaning of success for software SMEs: an holistic scorecard based approach. In: O'Connor, R.V., Pries-Heje, J., Messnarz, R. (eds.) EuroSPI 2011. CCIS, vol. 172, pp. 72–83. Springer, Heidelberg (2011). doi:10.1007/978-3-642-22206-1_7
18. ECQA Certified Terminology Manager – Engineering Skill Card. http://www.termnet.org/english/products_service/ecqa_ctm-engineering/2015_online/programme.php

Accessible Information and Accessibility Through ICT: A Mega Trend Creates the Need for Quality Certificates for Web Accessibility Professionals in Europe and Beyond

Ronald Bieber[1], Klaus Höckner[2], and Gabriele Sauberer[3(✉)]

[1] Austrian Computer Society (OCG), 1010 Vienna, Austria
[2] Hilfsgemeinschaft der Blinden und Sehschwachen Österreichs, 1200 Vienna, Austria
[3] Forum European Diversity Management, 1190 Vienna, Austria
gabr.iete@fedm.eu
www.ocg.at, www.fedm.eu

Abstract. This paper gives an overview of the global mega trend accessibility, and about the skills and competences needed for the new profession or job role "Web Accessibility Professional" in Europe and world-wide. The authors discuss accessibility, present good practice from Austria (Accessibility through ICT, IT4Blind, OCG cares) and from EU projects (ACT: Accessible Culture and Training), and propose a draft "skills card" for a new European certificate for Web Accessibility Professionals, based on the standardized procedures and quality standards of ECQA®, the European Certification and Qualification Association.

Keywords: Web accessibility · Accessibility through ICT · Diversity and inclusion · Web accessibility guidelines · Mega trend

1 Accessibility – Why Bother?

1.1 A Short Definition and Explanation of the Term "Accessibility"

Accessibility refers to the design of products and environments for people with disabilities [1].

In other word, the term "accessibility" refers to the fact, that a Person with Disabilities (PwD) can not access to information, goods and services, transport, etc. because of the design of these articles or items makes it impossible for them to get access with their Assistive Technologies (AT).

A simple example: A blind person has no access to pictures and the meaning of the pictures or statistics, if this information is not provided in a textual alternative way. Why? Because in this case, without a textual alternative way, the information in the pictures or statistics can not be read out loud or translated to braille, if the blind person uses a braille output.

Therefore, Accessibility can be seen as the "ability to access", either to information or to places. Accessibility as a build-in-process should ensure, that every person, regardless of his/her disability, can enter to a place/get the information in the same way than a person without disability.

1.2 ICT and Accessibility

Especially for PwDs, ICT and the internet revolution is creating a new world of opportunities and a milestone toward a more flexible, self-determined and independent life. But not only PwDs do have advantages: with a view to an aging society (statistics of Eurostat tells us, that in 2030, a share of more than 30% of the population in Europe will be elder than 65) Computers and software or ICT in general has to be accessible for that growing part of the society.

Web accessibility [2] means that people with disabilities can use the Web and that information is available for them in the same way like for persons without disabilities. More specifically, Web accessibility means that people with disabilities can perceive, understand, navigate, and interact with the Web, and that they can contribute to digital life. Web accessibility also benefits others, including older people with changing abilities due to aging.

Web accessibility encompasses all disabilities that affect access to the Web, including visual, auditory, physical, speech, cognitive, and neurological disabilities.

The Web is an increasingly important resource in many aspects of life: education, employment, government, commerce, health care, recreation, and more. It is essential that the Web be accessible in order to provide equal access and equal opportunity to people with disabilities. An accessible Web can also help people with disabilities more actively participate in society and contribute in the goal of closing the digital gap.

The Web offers the possibility of unprecedented access to information and interaction for many people with disabilities. That is, the accessibility barriers to print, audio, and visual media can be much more easily overcome through Web technologies.

Accessibility is a mega trend and a billion Euro market world-wide, given the demographic changes and needs for new products and services of aging societies.

1.3 Legislation [3]

Some examples: In the US, under the Americans with Disabilities Act of 1990, new public and private business construction generally must be accessible. In Australia, the Disability Discrimination Act 1992 has numerous provisions for accessibility.

In South Africa the Promotion of Equality and Prevention of Unfair Discrimination Act 2000 has numerous provisions for accessibility. In the UK, the Equality Act 2010 has numerous provisions for accessibility. In Norway, the Discrimination and Accessibility Act Diskriminerings og tilgjenglighetsloven defines lack of accessibility as discrimination and obliges public authorities to implement universal design in their areas. The Act refers to issue-specific legislation regarding accessibility in e.g. ICT, the built environment, transport and education. In Canada, relevant federal legislation includes the Canadian Human Rights Act, the Employment Equity Act, and the Canadian Labour Code.

Legislation may also be enacted on a state, provincial or local level. In Ontario, Canada, the Ontarians with Disabilities Act of 2001 is meant to "improve the identification, removal and prevention of barriers faced by persons with disabilities…".

The European Union (EU), which has signed the United Nations' Convention on the Rights of Persons with Disabilities in 2007, also has adopted a European Disability Strategy for 2010–2020 and created a Directive for Accessibility of Public sector Websites and Apps in 2014 as well a Directive for the implementation of EN 301549 for Accessibility in Public Procurement.

In Austria, there are several laws like the Bundesbehindertengleichstellungsgesetz and the e-government law that obliges the public and the official authorities to make Websites accessible in compliance with the Web Content Accessibility Guidelines of the Web Accessibility Initiative (WAI).

2 Good Practice from Austria

Austria is a small country with a population of 8.8 million people. According to preliminary results released by Statistics Austria, 8 773 686 million people were living in Austria on 1 January 2017 [4].

However, Austria is a leading country when it comes to e-government services and good practice in the field of Accessibility: In December 2010, Austria was declared the European champion in e-government for the fourth time in a row [5].

In 2014, Austria receives the United Nations Public Service Award 2014 for the Open Government Data Portal (data.gv.at). In the category "Improving the delivery of Public Services", Austria was awarded 1st place for the nationwide Open Government Data Portal (data.gv.at) by the Federal Chancellery of the Republic of Austria. The portal is a unique platform for providing a comprehensive database of freely accessible national government data. The awarding jury pointed out that Austria was an inspiration and a model for other countries [6].

Accessibility initiatives in Austria are bundled and driven by the Working group "Accessibility through ICT (Accessibility and Assistive Technologies)" of the Austrian Computer Society [7]. One of the most important results of this working group is the syllabus and certification program "IT4Blind" [8] for IT trainers. This program covers all the skills and competences needed to conduct quality trainings for blind people. It serves as a basis and as a model for other certification programs in the field of Diversity and Inclusion initiatives to improve the quality of trainings for people with disabilities.

The Austrian Computer Society (OCG) and its members not only care for Accessibility through ICT, but also for other Diversity & Inclusion topics, such as the project OCG cares [9], helping refugees to learn German, to improve their IT skills and to get internationally recognised certificates (such as the European Computer Driving Licence), or the working group gender#it [10], a Central European Platform for IT Careers for Women.

Good practice in web accessibility comes from the Austrian Association supporting the blind and visually impaired (Hilfsgemeinschaft der Blinden und Sehschwachen Österreichs) and the Austrian Federal Economic Chamber with its academy incite: These partners developed an Austrian Certificate (CWAE - Certified Web Accessibility Expert) [11] and training for Web accessibility Experts, focused on accessible web design [12] in compliance with the Web Content Accessibility Guidelines and Austrian legal regulations: Since 1st January 2006, web accessibility is mandatory for Austrian companies, which triggered the need for IT and Web experts with the respective proven skills and competences.

3 EU Project "ACT: Accessible Culture and Training"

The ACT project [13] addresses the fact accessibility plays a major role in modern knowledge-based Information societies that at EU, international and global level. The potential of Accessibility through ICT and Assistive Technologies (AT) for inclusion and participation of all citizens is increasingly growing allowing for a full integration in everyday life. The percentage of people depending on Accessibility increases and EU demography shows the growing tendency to eAccessiblity dependency for its ageing population. National as well as European legislation supporting eAccessibility is in place and the UN-Convention on the Rights of Persons with Disabilities, the most powerful, global expression in support of Inclusion and Equality, has a clear focus on eAccessibility, AT and Design for All.

Full participation of all citizens in cultural events - as end users or participants - should become part of their daily life as for people without disabilities, restoring the concept of equal opportunity and Human Right of access to culture. Thus, the ACT consortium is convinced that he time has come to establish the new professional profile of a "Media Accessibility Expert/Manager", and its training.

ECQA, the European Certification and Qualification Association, is a consortium member of ACT, responsible for preparing certification after the end of the project. ECQA is monitoring the following 3 processes:

(1) Explain the ECQA® certification process to the ACT consortium and adapt the process to the specific needs and requirements of ACT.
(2) Establish an ACT Job Role Committee (JRC), composed of representatives from industry, academia and other stakeholders, to assure quality and sustainability of the ACT Skills Card, training material and test questions used for certification after the end of the ACT project.
(3) Provide ECQA® certification schemes and guidelines for the ACT skill card, trainers, training materials, test questions, according to ECQA® rules and procedures.

The ACT project will also develop a curriculum design and a Massive Open Online Course (MOOC). Based on the skills and competences portfolio of the ACT project, interested parties can easily build or join the JRC of a future "ECQA® Certified Media Accessibility Manager". Since the European Computer Driving Licence (ECDL), European

Union is aware of the value and benefits of a joint and unified European certification scheme for skills required on the joint European markets.

4 ECQA® Certified Web Accessibility Professional

In order to ensure that Websites and Apps are programmed properly with regards to Web Accessibility, meaning in compliance with ISO 45001 [14] and the Web Content Accessibility Guidelines [15] (WCAG 2.0), a new harmonized set of skills and competences for the new job role "Web Accessibility Professional" is needed at EU and international level.

Based on existing good practice (see Sects. 2 and 3 above) in Europe, and following the standardized procedures and quality standards of ECQA®, the European Certification and Qualification Association, a "skills card" and international certificate "ECQA® Certified Web Accessibility Professional" will be developed with a new Job Role Committee within ECQA®.

The draft skills card and certificate could contain the following four basic Skill Units (U) and Learning Outcomes (LO) of Learning Elements (E):

- WAP.U1: UNDERSTANDING ACCESSIBILITY, DIVERSITY & INCLUSION

In the first learning element of this unit, the basic concepts and terms will be introduced, defined and explained in an EU relevant context of the joint legal regulations and requirements of EU member states. After Element 1 of Unit 1, learners are able to understand the basic concepts and terms accessibility, diversity and inclusion.

- WAP.U1.E1: Concepts and terms of accessibility, diversity and inclusion
- WAP.U1.E1.LO1: S/he understands the basic concepts and terms of accessibility
- WAP.U1.E1.LO2: S/he understands the basic concepts and terms of diversity
- WAP.U1.E1.LO3: S/he understands the basic concepts and terms of inclusion

The second element of Unit 1 is about understanding the types and degrees of disability, and their impact on web design, content creation and the provision of information:

- WAP.U1.E2: Types and degrees of disability
- WAP.U1.E2.LO1: S/he knows the basic types of disability
- WAP.U1.E2.LO2: S/he knows the basic degrees of disability
- WAP.U1.E2.LO3: S/he understands the impact of the basic types and degrees of disability on web design, content creation and the provision of information

Skill Unit 2 deals with accessibility services. The first learning element gives a broad overview on the "what and why" of accessibility services, including relevant standards and legal frameworks at national, EU and international level:

- WAP.U2: WEB ACCESSIBILITY AND ACCESSIBILITY SERVICES
- WAP.U2.E1: Background and rationale of Web Accessibility
- WAP.U2.E1.LO1: S/he understands how PwDs work with websites and accessibility services, and can argue the benefit of accessible web systems, such as Universal Design, Design for All, Responsive Design, etc.

- WAP.U2.E1.LO2: S/he can explain the demographic, social and economic impact and opportunities of web accessibility and accessibility services
- WAP.U2.E1.LO3: S/he is familiar with relevant standards and legal frameworks at national, EU and international level (e.g. e-government, EU directives, UN Convention, etc.)

The second element of Unit 2 focusses on the different accessibility services for various types of disability, and how to use them in practice:

- WAP.U2.E2: Accessibility services
- WAP.U2.E2: LO1: S/he knows the types of audio description and applicable scenarios
- WAP.U2.E2: LO2: S/he knows what Subtitling for the Deaf and the Hard-of-hearing (SDH) is and applicable scenarios of SDH
- WAP.U2.E2: LO3: S/he knows what sign language interpreting is and its applicable scenarios
- WAP.U2.E2: LO4: S/he knows what braille is and its applicable scenarios
- WAP.U2.E2: LO5: S/he knows how to prepare large print/easy-to-read accessible materials.

Unit 3 of the skills card covers the technical skills needed for the implementation of web accessibility. The first 3 learning elements of Unit 3 tackle the four Principles of Web accessibility (https://www.w3.org/WAI/intro/people-use-web/principles): perceivable, operable, understandable and robust:

- WAP.U3: IMPLEMENTING WEB ACCESSIBILITY: TECHNICAL SKILLS
- WAP.U3.E1: Implementing Principle 1 of Web accessibility: Perceivable
- WAP.U3.E1.LO1: S/he is able to provide text alternatives for any non-text content so that it can be changed into other forms people need, such as large print, braille, speech, symbols or simpler language
- WAP.U3.E1.LO2: S/he is able to provide alternatives for time-based media
- WAP.U3.E1.LO3: S/he is able to create content that can be presented in different ways without losing information or structure.
- WAP.U3.E1.LO4: S/he is able to make it easier for users to see and hear content including separating foreground from background
- WAP.U3.E2: Implementing Principle 2 of Web accessibility: Operable
- WAP.U3.E2.LO1: S/he is able to make all functionality available from a keyboard
- WAP.U3.E2.LO2: S/he is able to provide users enough time to read and use content
- WAP.U3.E2.LO3: S/he is able to avoid designing content in a way that is known to cause seizure
- WAP.U3.E2.LO4: S/he is able to provide ways to help users navigate, find content, and determine where they are
- WAP.U3.E3: Implementing Principle 3 and 4 of Web accessibility: Understandable and Robust
- WAP.U3.E3.LO1: S/he is able to make text content readable and understandable
- WAP.U3.E3.LO2: S/he is able to make web pages appear and operate in predictable ways

- WAP.U3.E3.LO3: S/he is able to help users avoid and correct mistakes
- WAP.U3.E3.LO4: S/he is able to maximize compatibility with current and future user agents, including assistive technologies

Element 4 of Unit 3 expects professionals to be familiar with relevant guidelines and standards, and to be able to implement them:

- WAP.U3.E4: Guidelines and international standards
- WAP.U3.E4.LO1: S/he is familiar with the relevant guidelines, such as WCAG and other W3C/WAI guidelines
- WAP.U3.E4.LO2: S/he is familiar with the relevant international standards, such as ISO/IEC 40500:2012, ISO 9241-171:2008, EN 301 549:2014, ETSI TR 102 612:2009, ETSI/TR 202 116:2009
- WAP.U3.E4.LO3: S/he is able to evaluate existing web sites and make them accessible
- WAP.U3.E4.LO4: S/he is familiar with HTML, CSS, Java, Design, etc., and able to integrate accessibility requirements in default designs, considering usability and "usable accessibility"

The fourth and last Skill Unit is about management skills for the implementation of web accessibility. Element 1 deals with policies, stakeholder management and cost calculations, the second learning element tackles the required project management skills of web accessibility professionals:

- WAP.U4: IMPLEMENTING WEB ACCESSIBILITY: MANAGEMENT SKILLS
- WAP.U4.E1: Strategic Management
- WAP.U4.E1.LO1: S/he knows how to develop a sustainable accessibility policy
- WAP.U4.E1.LO2: S/he knows how to identify relevant stakeholders
- WAP.U4.E1.LO3: S/he is aware of the costs implication of accessibility solutions
- WAP.U4.E2: Project Management
- WAP.U4.E2.LO1: S/he is able to provide accessibility guidance in web projects
- WAP.U4.E2.LO3: S/he is able to successfully manage a web accessibility project.

References

1. Christensson, P.: Accessibility. https://techterms.com/definition/accessibility; TechTerm Homepage. https://techterms.com/help/author. Last accessed 02 April 2017
2. W3 Homepage. https://www.w3.org/WAI/intro/accessibility.php. Last accessed 31 Mar 2017
3. Wikipedia Homepage. https://en.wikipedia.org/wiki/Accessibility. Last accessed 02 April 2017
4. Statistik Austria Homepage. https://www.statistik.at/web_en/statistics/PeopleSociety/population/111435.html, Last accessed 02 April 2017
5. Digital Austria Homepage. http://www.digital.austria.gv.at/site/6573/default.aspx. Last accessed 31 Mar 2017
6. Digital Austria Homepage. http://www.digital.austria.gv.at/site/cob__59843/currentpage__0/6575/default.aspx. Last accessed 31 Mar 2017
7. OCG Homepage. http://www.ocg.at/node/347. Last accessed 31 Mar 2017

8. OCG Homepage. http://www.ocg.at/sites/ocg.at/files/medien/pdfs/IT4Blind_Syllabus_1-0.pdf. Last accessed 12 April 2017
9. OCG Homepage. http://www.ocg.at/en/ocg-cares. Last accessed 12 April 2017
10. OCG Homepage. http://www.ocg.at/node/350. Last accessed 12 April 2017
11. incite Homepage. http://www.incite.at/ausbildung/de/zertifizierungen/certified-webaccessibility-expert/ and http://www.incite.at/ausbildung/upload/pdf/folder_zertifizierungen/CWAE/incite_zert_webaccessibility.pdf. Last accessed 12 April 2017
12. Hilfsgemeinschaft Homepage. https://www.hilfsgemeinschaft.at/lehrgang-webaccessibility-barrierefreies-webdesign. Last accessed 12 April 2017
13. ACT Homepage. http://www.actproject.eu/. Last accessed 31 Mar 2017
14. ISO Homepage. https://www.iso.org/iso-45001-occupational-health-and-safety.html. Last accessed 31 Mar 2017
15. W3 Homepage. https://www.w3.org/WAI/intro/wcag. Last accessed 31 Mar 2017

Team Members' Interactive Styles Involved in the Software Development Process

Nora Rangel[1], Carlos Torres[1], Adriana Peña[2(✉)], Mirna Muñoz[3], Jezreel Mejia[3], and Luis Hernández[3]

[1] Centro de Estudios e Investigaciones en Comportamiento de la Universidad de Guadalajara, Calle Francisco de Quevedo # 180, Col. Arcos Vallarta, 44130 Guadalajara, Jalisco, Mexico
nora.rangel@academicos.udg.mx, jtorres@cencar.udg.mx
[2] CUCEI Universidad de Guadalajara, Blvrd. Marcelino García Barragán #1421, esq. Calzada Olímpica, 44430 Guadalajara, Jalisco, Mexico
adriana.pena@cucei.udg.mx
[3] Centro de Investigación en Matemáticas, Av. Universidad no 222, 98068 Zacatecas, Mexico
{mirna.munoz,jmejia,luis.hernandez}@cimat.mx

Abstract. In the process of software development, the importance of a team is unquestionable. Beside the team members' technical knowledge and their skills, the interaction among them is a relevant factor that could affect their efficiency. According to the Team Software Process^{SM} methodology, the phases of the software process and the activities of each team member, involve a multiplicity of situations with different interaction requirements. The objective of this work is to identify the interactive styles relevant to the phases and roles of the team members, through gamification techniques. After that, we would explore how the integration of these individuals with particular interactive styles, will conjointly face the software development process.

Keywords: Interactive styles · Effective teams · Software development teams · Human factor

1 Introduction

The modern world is highly operated by software; individuals generate software in spreadsheets, they process data to get information or they do it just for fun. However, professional software development is a task typically accomplished by teams [1]. A team is a group of people working together, performing a work that involves a common project, where each member must have specific knowledge in specific subjects and specific skills to carry out that project [2].

For the software development, there are a number of methodologies that provide the steps or activities to be followed, in order to elaborate the information systems; a framework for its structure. With the aim to provide a set of engineering best practices to develop software through teams, one of the most known methodologies is the Team Software Process^{SM} (TSP^{SM}), from the Software Engineering Institute [3], which will be here used as reference.

For the software development life cycle, the TSP methodology considers seven phases: launch, strategy, planning, requirement, design, implementation, test and post-mortem. Within the team, its members will have different responsibilities in order to facilitate the team organization. According to the TSP, the selection of team members for a new, or an existing team, needs to take into account the members' skills, aptitudes, interests, and working abilities, which leads to their software engineering roles. The set of roles provided by the TSP methodology are: team leader, planning leader, quality leader, support manager, design manager, implementation manager, and test manager [4].

Each of these roles represents a software engineering that develops software and also carries out an administrative activity related to his/her role and the phase of the process. The administrative tasks have a major or minor responsibility according to each phase, which in turn will generate specific types of interaction with the others and the situation.

The TSP methodology does not deeply evaluate a very important aspect in the building of a team, the human factor. According to Cuevas et al. [5], failures in software projects seem to be the result of teamwork factors rather than technical factors. They also pointed out that the required steps to integrate teams are not as obvious as can be expected; frequently, new teams spend a lot of time working in teamwork techniques. In order to carry on the structure presented in [6], where we proposed to involve individuals interactive styles to build teams for software development, in this paper we connect the role activities in the phases of software engineering, to their specific interactive styles, proper for the type of interactive situation derived.

1.1 Related Work

Yilmaz, Al-Taei & O'Connor [7], stated the importance to build a team taking into account the team members' personality, in order to improve its effectiveness. The way people interact with each other and with the environment have consequences in their performance, particularly when the task requires collaboration, just as in teams for the devolvement of software. In this context, for the Information and Communication Technology (ICT) competences, Ribaud & Saliou [8] pointed out the importance of considering the team members' personality types.

Two of the most used instruments related to personality and team's performance are the Tuckman's model [9] and Belbin's team roles [10]. For the Tuckman's model all groups have a set of developmental stages related to interpersonal and task-activity realms aspects; the team tasks are completed while the members relate to each other. This model for small-group development is aimed for the organizations, contemplating three main aspects: (1) setting the current stage of the group; (2) identifying the realm in which the group behavior falls, considering the task and the interpersonal realms; and (3) the next position of the group regarding the developmental sequence [11]. This model does not cover the selection of the right members for a high performance team.

Belbin [10] argued that at work people tend to behave, contribute, and interrelate with others in certain distinctive ways, they assume a team role. A balanced combination on Belbin's team roles is expected to result in a more successful team than those with an unbalanced composition. Designed questionnaires are the method used to identify the role a person will take in a team. This approach has been related to software development activities [12].

The usage of self-reports, mainly questionnaires and scales, has been broadly employed in the study of personality or in the task of identification of competences. Santacreu, Rubio & Hernández [13] stated that this practice might obey to the consideration that the aspects related to personality is knowledge only accessible to the own individual, although they disagree with this consideration. In any case, a self-report is a relatively easy and non-invasive method for the behavior and personality research, which can provide a great amount of information in a short time. However, this information can be influenced by the individual's social desires, memory and/or motivations [14]. Furthermore, a lack of correspondence between the objective measures of behavior and self-reports, as an evaluation instrument, has been found [15].

The interactive styles, initially proposed by Ribes in [16], suggest that when a person faces options of interaction with similar consequences, signs, and similar dispositional conditions, that person will show consistent behavior or a consistent way of interaction. In such a way that if the conditions are set in a videogame (in this case the role activities for each phase in the software development process), the interaction style of a person can be somehow anticipated.

2 Interactive Styles

As aforementioned, the TSP methodology assigns to team members the achievement of certain tasks within certain situations, each of which has particular requirements related to his/her skills. In our previously proposed model in [6], see Fig. 1, a first step is to identify the role for each member, accordingly to his/her technical skills, the knowledge, abilities and competences proper for the tasks.

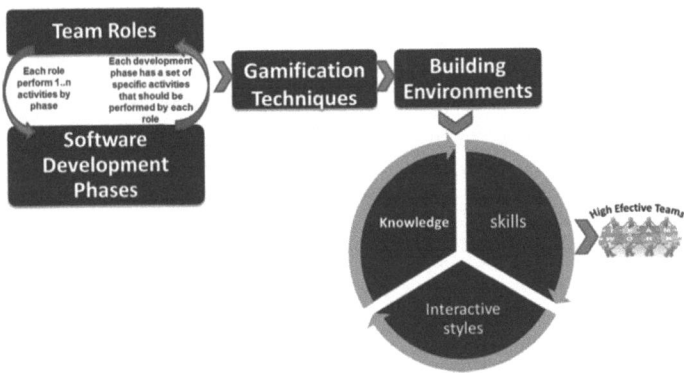

Fig. 1. Model to establish effective software development teams [6].

However, as mentioned, knowledge and skills are not always enough to get effective team executions, which leads to the acknowledgment in this process of the influence of the team members' interactions, as well as the way they face the involved situations in the software development process [6].

Consequently, the proposal of the interactive styles by Ribes [16] is adopted. This proposal recognizes that the effective performance, during the resolution of a task, can be affected by the consistent way in which individuals face different situations. A derivation for the software development process can assume that the team performance has a dependency on the particular way that each member contacts the requirements and circumstances. While these requirements and circumstances will vary at the different moments that constitute the process of software development.

Interactive styles affirm that, although individuals apparently face different situations (i.e. situations with different morphology), these situations can share the same contingency arrangement. In these cases, situations prescribe the same interaction options with consequences, signs and dispositional factors. In this sense, the proposal assumes that

Table 1. Interactive styles and description.

Interactive styles	Situation description
Making decisions	The possibility of only one response to stimulus that are competitive or uncertain in time
Ambiguity tolerance	Responses under functional antagonist proprieties, and/or differences between the signal and the supplementation
Frustration tolerance	Keeping the performance under conditions with no signals of interference, diminishing, loss or delay of the consequences
Achievement or persistency	Keeping the performance under conditions of growing or higher requirements
Flexibility to the change	Changes in responses when facing signaled, not signaled, or unspecified contingencies
Tendency to transgression	Giving a response to a not response signal
Curiosity	Presenting diverse responses to contingencies that not require them, or a preference to variable contingencies
Tendency to risk	Opting for contingencies signaled as with the possibility of biggest gain and/or loss in contrast with constant alternatives
Dependence to signs	Adjusting responses to redundant signs in the contingency
Responsively to new contingencies and signs	Affecting the response when facing new signs of the same contingency, or new contingencies with the same sign
Impulsivity	Corresponding the responses in situations where the components of the contingencies are not homogenous
Conflict reduction	Responding to concurrent opposite or competitive signs

an individual will show a consistent way of behavior, displaying his/her interactive style [16]. Following Ribes [16], twelve provisional arrangements of contingencies or situations allow exploring the individual interactive styles (p. 243); these situations and a brief explanation for each one are presented in Table 1.

It is worth to mention that the temporal and situational consistency behavior have been empirical proved in several studies [17–20]. Furthermore, the interactive styles had been extended to the application environment with the interest of developing objective tests of behavioral type that measure the interactive styles [21–23]; these proposals are seen as an alternative to the classic questionnaires or personality tests.

In this project, gamification techniques are proposed as tools towards an approximation to the software development process situations. A number of gaming tasks will be used or developed to manipulate parameters that generate different contingencies arrangements that should permit the identification of each team member interactive styles. The team members then will be exposed to those related to similar situations according to their team role for the software development.

Some of the gamification techniques for the analysis of interactive styles that proved temporal and situational consistency are next briefly described:

Taking risks. For analyzing the interaction style of taking risks a racehorse game was used in [18, 20, 24]. The participants were offered two different betting options shown in Fig. 2. The left one shows the option with higher winning probabilities but lower profit (payout/winnings) while the right one depictures the second option with lower winning probabilities correlated to higher profit. The profit amount and winning probabilities were manipulated in different trials. The same participants did the same task two months later, presenting consistency over time in their type of choices [18].

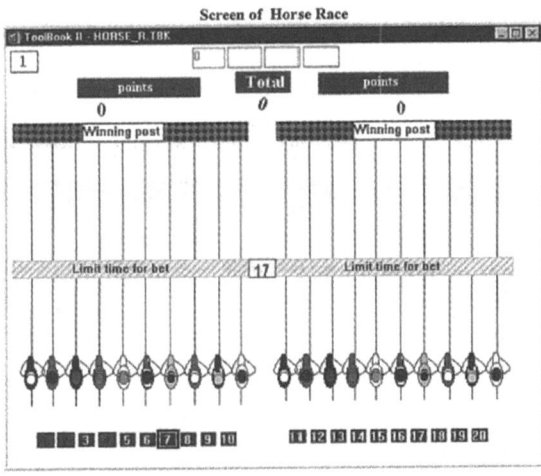

Fig. 2. Horseraces task to evaluate interactive styles in a taking risk situation [19].

In order to evaluate consistency in situations, a morphology different task, but equivalent in functionality was used. In this case, the participants were asked to invest in the stock market. This task was also manipulated with the same profit and winning probability conditions used in the racehorse game, see Fig. 3. Results showed participants' consistency in their choices.

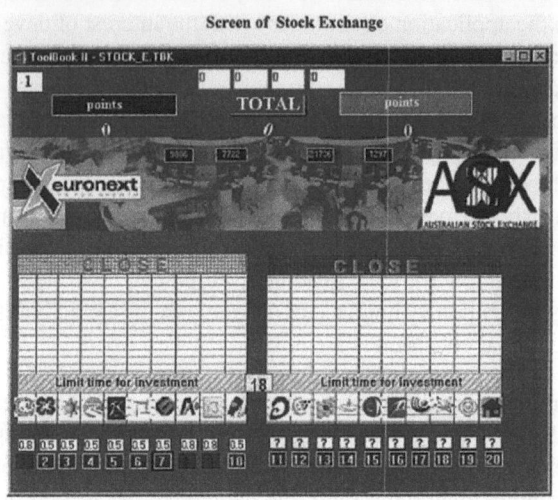

Fig. 3. Stock exchange task evaluate interactive styles in a taking risk situation [19].

Achievement or persistence. In [18, 24] an organizing game (accordingly to shape and format figures) with restricted time, was used. What was analyzed in these trials was the participants' choice for bigger requirements and major supplementation. Two options were presented for the participants in the screen, see Fig. 4: (1) on the left, the restricted time for the task was diminished while presented higher winning points; and (2) on the

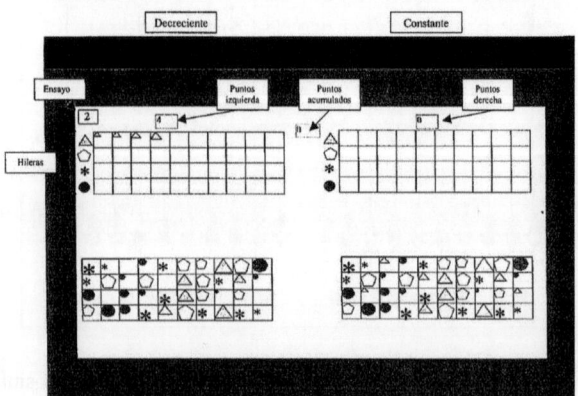

Fig. 4. Figures arrangement task to evaluate interactive style in achievement or persistence situations [24].

right, the time was constant with less winning points. Results showed individual consistencies in two different applications of the same task.

Ambiguity tolerance. In Fuentes [17] approach, a task based on the code-breaking Mastermind™ game was used, see Fig. 5. Participants were asked to break the code, where the feedback was manipulated for the consequence signal correspondence. For a complete ambiguous situation, participants did not receive any feedback. Afterwards, ambiguity was diminishing in time by giving feedback to participants, first for the position and then for the color, or there was a higher probability of receiving feedback. Results showed participants' interactive style consistencies in both types of feedback: less precise or less probable.

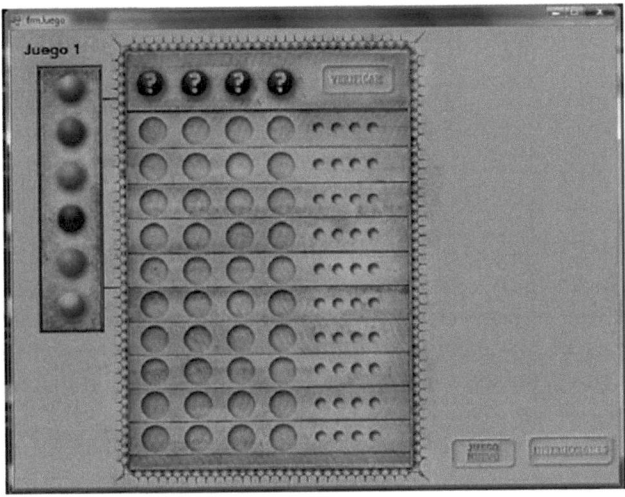

Fig. 5. Code-breaking task to evaluate interactive style in an ambiguity tolerance situation [17].

The participants' behaviors in these different tasks, choices, alternative changes, winning points, number of answers, session time remaining, number of session attempts, etc. were represented in polynomial regressions (with at least 7 degrees of freedom). This statistical analysis was used to understand different functions with consistencies. That means that a person's functional profile shows similarities in different situations at different times. By that, a particular and consistent temporal and situational behavior in equivalent functional situations is shown, which represents their individual interactive style.

2.1 Interactive Styles and TSP Methodology Integration

Based on previous empirical studies [17, 18, 20], each team member will be exposed to situations where their interactive styles can be observed; from this profile and their knowledge and skills (see Fig. 1), the team roles will then be assigned.

As mentioned, each role has several designated tasks. The task performance can be affected by certain interactive styles. From the TSP methodology were extracted the different activities for each role in each phase, and ordered using colors in a spreadsheet to facilitate its visualization (see [25] for details). Two behavior researchers closely familiarized with the interactive styles proposal, analyzed the activities for each role in each phase. In Table 2 the team role are summarized.

Table 2. Interactive styles evaluation in three stages.

1st evaluation stage (After the evaluation of knowledge and skills)	2nd evaluation stage (As responsible of each phase)	3rd evaluation stage (By role)
For all team members	*For all team members*	*For the team leader*
Achievement or persistence interactive style	Making decisions/taking risk Signal dependency Flexibility to change	Ambiguity tolerance Conflict reduction
		For the person in charge of the Implementation and the Test phases
		Frustration tolerance

In a first stage, we propose to evaluate all the team members for the *achievement or persistency* interactive style. This test will provide information about how each team member could face probable changes in the software requirements. In these situations, the requirements are always explicit. Results should allow understanding the point to which the changes in the software requirements will or will not be assumed by the team members.

In a second stage, since each team member, at some point, will function as responsible (leader) in some phases, all the team members can be evaluated for common requirements for this position:

Making decisions/taking risk, individuals in this type of situations will get the possibility of responding to one or more possible alternatives. These alternatives might contend among them in an uncertain or winning/losing situation. Being responsible of the team involves risks, therefore it is important to know under which parameters each team member (as responsible for the team in a particular phase) will or will not make decisions, or take risks.

Signal dependency, in this type of situations is evaluated the response adjustment to repetitive or redundant signals. It is important to understand if the performance of the team members reflects the received redundant signals from the environment. This will evidence if the teamwork can be altered in the fortuitous events occurrence, not relevant for the accomplishment of the phase criteria that they are working on.

Flexibility to change, in this situation it is evaluated how individuals face the contingencies and their multiple independent responses. The TSP methodology generates different situations in each phase; also, the continuous reviews in the development software process will generate changes. Therefore, the requirements in the performance of the team are changing and that is why it is pertinent to evaluate this interactive style that will show the team members adjustment to the mentioned changes.

In a third stage, the interactive styles will be evaluated by role. Once the team members have a designated role according to the first interactive style evaluation, we propose a further evaluation as follows.

To evaluate the *team leader* in situations with parameters related to ambiguity to tolerance and conflict reduction situations.

Ambiguity tolerance, this type of situation presents the impossibility of discrimination among signals and pertinent responses. Even more, sometimes it is impossible to discriminate the relevance, or the signals, with respect to the responses and their consequences. In this sense, it is pertinent to evaluate the team leader because of the decision-making required as responsible or collaborator in a task assignment. Bear in mind that decision-making sometimes involves the lack of information or the lack of knowledge about the consequences of making that decision.

Likewise, the leader team should be expose to *conflict reduction situations* because they involve the response to signals that might be present at the same time, and opposite to each other, with also contrary or competitive consequences. We might want to know how this leader would face these situations, and if he/she is capable of solving that kind of situation, or in what conditions he/she simply cannot. Also, it can be evaluated if the time he/she might spend to solve the problem is or is not adequate.

On the other hand, we propose to evaluate the persons in charge of the *implementation* and *test phases* for the next situations:

Frustration tolerance, in this type of situation individuals face conditions of interference that have not being signaled, as well as the loss or retardation of the consequences during the execution. The implementation and test phases can present not expected results, and the person in charge has to keep a proper personal and team performance in order to achieve the task goals on time.

It is worth to mention that not all the cases can be overseen in this proposal. The different software requirements as well as the available elements for its development should be incorporated. What we are exposing here is what interactive styles can bring to a software development methodology such as TSP aimed for teams. Teamwork implies individuals' interactions, among them and with the situations. In this context, it is convenient the identification of individuals' interactive consistencies in equivalent situations regarding functionality.

3 Discussion and Conclusions

The incorporation of the interactive styles to the TSP methodology provides relevant information to build teams accordingly to the role assignment of each team member for software development; the analysis of interactive styles brings new information regarding different key situations in this process. In addition, once the roles are assigned, the interactive styles provide a way to understand the way in which the team members face certain present situations to get a successful outcome. The way each member faces situations equivalents in functionality to those existing in the software development, have incidence over the effectiveness and the goal achievement of the team as a whole.

This proposal development will be a step forward in the study of the interactive styles; it will also allow a systematic analysis of the interaction among people, always with different ways to face each situation. Individual evaluations for interactive style are the background that will be studied in collaborative situations, to understand their interwoven influence in the teamwork.

Working within a team is becoming a critical factor for the development of high quality software due to the fact that nowadays, teams develop most of the software. Then, it is important that teams can be integrated with members that can easily work along.

Acknowledgements. CIMAT- Unidad Zacatecas, the CUCEI and the Centro de Estudios e Investigaciones en Comportamiento of the Universidad de Guadalajara for the facilities to perform this research.

References

1. Sommerville, I.: Ingeniería del Software. Pearson, México (2011)
2. Chrissis, M.B., Konrad, M., Shrum, S.: CMMI for Development: Guidelines for Process Integration and Product Improvement. Pearson Education Inc., Massachusetts (2011)
3. Humphrey, W., Chick, T., Nichols, W., Pomeroy-Huff, M.: Team software process ProcessSM (TSP) body of knowledge (BOK). CMU/SEI-2010-TR-020, ESC-TR-2010-020 (2010)
4. Humprey, W.: The Team Software Process. CMU/SEI-2000-TR-023, ESC-TR-2000-023 (2000)
5. Cuevas, G., DeAmescua, A., SanFeliu, T., Arcilla, M., Cerrada, J.A., Calvo-Manzano, J.A., Garcia, M.: Teamwork and its techniques. Editorial Universitaria Ramón Areces (2002)
6. Muñoz, M., Mejia, J., Peña, A., Rangel, N.: Establishing effective software development teams: an exploratory model. In: Kreiner, C., O'Connor, R.V., Poth, A., Messnarz, R. (eds.) EuroSPI 2016. CCIS, vol. 633, pp. 70–80. Springer, Cham (2016). doi: 10.1007/978-3-319-44817-6_6
7. Yilmaz, M., Al-Taei, A., O'Connor, R.V.: A machine-based personality oriented team recommender for software development organizations. In: O'Connor, R.V., Umay Akkaya, M., Kemaneci, K., Yilmaz, M., Poth, A., Messnarz, R. (eds.) Systems, Software and Services Process Improvement. CCIS, vol. 543, pp. 75–86. Springer, Cham (2015). doi: 10.1007/978-3-319-24647-5_7
8. Ribaud, V., Saliou, P.: Relating ICT competencies with personality types. In: O'Connor, R.V., Umay Akkaya, M., Kemaneci, K., Yilmaz, M., Poth, A., Messnarz, R. (eds.) Systems, Software and Services Process Improvement. CCIS, vol. 543, pp. 295–302. Springer, Cham (2015). doi:10.1007/978-3-319-24647-5_24
9. Tuckman, B.W.: Developmental sequence in small groups. Physiol. Bull. **63**, 384–399 (1965)
10. Belbin, M.: Team Roles at Work. Elsevier Butterworth Heinemann, Oxford (1993)
11. Tuckman, W., Jensen, M.: Stages of small group development revisited. Group and Organization management, pp. 419–427 (1977)
12. Estrada, E., Peña, A.: Influencia de los roles de equipo en las actividades del desarrollador de software. RECIBE, vol. 2:1, II (2013)
13. Santacreu, J., Rubio, V., Hernández, J.M.: Evaluación objetiva de la personalidad: Una alternativa a los cuestionarios. Análisis y Modificación de Conducta **30**, 803–825 (2004)

14. Arce, R., Velasco, J., Novo, M., Fariña, F.: Elaboración y validación de una escala para la evaluación del acoso escolar. Revista Iberoamericana de Psicología y Salud **5**, 71–104 (2014)
15. Hernández, J.M., Lozano, J.H., Shih, P.C., Santacreu, J.: Validez convergente de dos pruebas de evaluación de la minuciosidad. Psicothema **21**, 133–140 (2009)
16. Ribes, E.: Psicología General. Trillas, México (1990)
17. Fuentes, N.: Una propuesta experimental para el estudio del estilo interactivo de tolerancia a la ambigüedad. Tesis de maestría no publicada. Universidad de Guadalajara (2011)
18. Ribes, E., Contreras, S.: Individual consistencies in behavior: achievemient persistence interactions as personality styles. Psychol. Rep. **101**, 365–377 (2007)
19. Ribes, E., Contreras, S., Martínez, C., Doval, E., Viladrich, C.: Individual consistencies across time and tasks: a replication of interactive styles. Psychol. Rec. **55**, 619–631 (2005)
20. Ribes, E., Sánchez, S.: Individual behavior consistencies as interactive styles: their relation to personality. Psychol. Rec. **42**, 369–387 (1992)
21. Moreno, A., Hernández, J.M., García-Leal, O., Santacreu, J.: Un test informatizado para la evaluación de la tolerancia a la frustración. Anales de Psicología **16**, 143–155 (2000)
22. Rubio, V., Hernandez, J.M., Santacreu, J.: Consistencia y evaluación de la tendencia al riesgo. Universidad de Málaga, Málaga (2005)
23. Santacreu, J., García-Leal, O.: La utilización de tests comportamentales informatizados en el estudio de la personalidad: la evaluación de la persistencia. Psicothema **12**, 93–98 (2000)
24. Contreras, S.: Estudio del estilo interactivo de perseverancia. Tesis de Maestría, Universidad de Guadalajara, México (2005)
25. Muñoz, M., Hernández, L.A., Mejía, J., Peña, A., Rangel, N., Torres, C.: A Model to Integrate Highly Effective Teams for Software Development. Communications in Computer and Information Science, Springer (in press)

Author Index

Al-Barakati, Abdullah 231
Aldahmash, Abdullah 504
Armengaud, Eric 205, 334

Back, Karsten Kristensen 411
Barafort, Béatrix 43
Bieber, Ronald 667
Biffl, Stefan 125
Biró, Miklós 381, 439
Blaschke, Monique 589
Brenner, Eugen 205
Breske, Eva 401

Calderón, Alejandro 111, 241
Cameron, Frank 83
Carneiro, Gisele 125
Castellanos Ardila, Julieth Patricia 162
Clarke, Paul M. 29, 191, 259, 653
Colomo-Palacios, Ricardo 3, 231

de Amescua Seco, Antonio 3
Dias, Daniel 216
Dixon, Mark 72
Doss, Osama 72
Dreßler, Jens R. 653
Drobietz, Mirko 486
Dussa-Zieger, Klaudia 589

Eito-Brun, Ricardo 15
Ekert, Damjan 294, 421
Ekssir-Monfared, Mohsen 589
Elger, Peter 29
Ennis, Adam 29

Ferreira, André L. 216
Fischer, Tobias Christian 310
Flatscher, Martina 323

Gallina, Barbara 83, 162
Gasca-Hurtado, Gloria Piedad 249, 281
Gebler, Tobias 269

Georgiadou, Elli 627
Gerrity, Mark 29
Gómez-Alvarez, María Clara 249, 281
Gorner, Jenny 439
Gozcu, Mert Ali 191
Gravell, Andy M. 504
Griessnig, Gerhard 535
Gulec, Ulas 191

Hammerschmid, Sonja 352, 372
Hartyanyi, Maria 294
Haugset, Børge 72
Hernández, Luis 249, 613, 675
Herranz, Eduardo 231
Höckner, Klaus 667
Howard, Yvonne 504
Humpohl, Joachim 421
Hussain, Shahid 177

Iber, Johannes 138, 150, 360
Indefrey, Adrian 269
Ito, Masao 61

Jakobsen, Peter Møller 99
Johansen, Jørn 99, 411
Jovanović, Miloš 302

Kalinowski, Marcos 125
Kapfhammer, Peter 269
Karać, Jovana 302
Karaomer, Rabia Burcu 567
Kaynak, Onur 567
Kelly, Tim 72
Keung, Jacky 177
Khan, Arif Ali 177
Kiechle, Teresa 269
Klespitz, József 381
Kormann, Gerhard 372
Korsaa, Morten 99, 411
Kösling, Marc 495
Kossak, Felix 381

Kovács, Levente 381
Kreiner, Christian 138, 150, 205, 334, 360, 439, 453
Krisper, Michael 138, 150, 360

Larrucea, Xabier 3, 599
Likar, Borut 294
List, Georg 334

Machado, Ricardo J. 216
Macher, Georg 205
Mack, Jürgen 294
Mäkinen, Timo 83
Malucelli, Andreia 523, 557
Mas, Antònia 43, 302, 471
McCaffery, Fergal 578
McGrath, Sean 29
Mejía, Jezreel 249, 281, 613, 675
Mesquida, Antoni-Lluís 43, 302
Messnarz, Richard 294, 421, 439, 453, 642
Monteiro, Paula 216
Moser, Thomas 372
Mrgole, Urska 294
Much, Alexander 439
Muñoz, Mirna 249, 281, 613, 675

Nazligul, Merve Denizci 191
Nevalainen, Risto 83
Niazi, Mahmood 177

O'Connor, Rory V. 29, 111, 191, 241, 259, 653
Oliveira, Pedro 216
Özcan-Top, Özden 578

Peña, Adriana 613, 675
Pereira, Tiago 216
Petrovic, Sanja 125
Philipp, Michael 589
Poth, Alexander 471, 486, 495, 513
Pries-Heje, Jan 99, 411

Quaritsch, Markus 138

Rahanu, Harjinder 627
Rangel, Nora 613, 675
Rauter, Tobias 150, 360
Reinehr, Sheila 523, 557
Reiner, Michael 372

Riel, Andreas 323, 334, 642
Rodic, Miran 453
Ross, Margaret 627
Ruiz, Mercedes 111, 241

Sabou, Marta 125
Sams, Christoph 334
Sánchez, Alex 3
Sánchez-Gordón, Mary-Luz 3
Santamaria, Izaskun 599
Sasabe, Susumu 471
Sauberer, Gabriele 613, 642, 653, 667
Schmitz, Klaus-Dirk 653
Schneider, Daniel 205
Schnellbach, Adam 535
Schröttner, Evelyn 294
Schweigert, Tomas 401, 411, 589
Sehr, Maik 421
Siakas, Kerstin 627
Siqueira, Alexssander A. 523, 557
Solan, David 29
Stålhane, Tor 72
Stolfa, Jakub 453
Stolfa, Svatopluk 453
Szabo, Janos 294

Torres, Carlos 613, 675
Treanor, Ryan 29
Trenz, Eva-Maria 269
Truntic, Mitja 453
Tuzun, Eray 259

Ünal, Ayşegül 567
Üsfekes, Çağdaş 259

Varkoi, Timo 83
Villar, Blanca Nájera 653
von Falck, Georg 334

Walker, Alastair 547
Winkler, Dietmar 125
Witzgall, Peter 269
Wolf, Fabian 513
Wüstemann, Ingrid 421

Yilmaz, Murat 29, 191, 259
Young, Alison 547

Zhang, He 177

MIX
Papier aus verantwortungsvollen Quellen
Paper from responsible sources
FSC® C105338

If you have any concerns about our products,
you can contact us on
ProductSafety@springernature.com

In case Publisher is established outside the EU,
the EU authorized representative is:
**Springer Nature Customer Service Center GmbH
Europaplatz 3, 69115 Heidelberg, Germany**

Printed by Libri Plureos GmbH
in Hamburg, Germany